SECOND LANGUAGE ACQUISITION

An introductory course

Third edition

Susan M. Gass and Larry Selinker

Routledge
Taylor & Francis Group

NEW YORK AND LONDON

First edition published 1994
by Lawrence Erlbaum Associates, Inc.

This edition first published 2008
by Routledge
270 Madison Ave, New York, NY 10016

Simultaneously published in the UK
by Routledge
2 Park Square, Milton Park, Abingdon, Oxon OX14 4RN

Routledge is an imprint of the Taylor & Francis Group, an informa business

First edition © 1994 Lawrence Erlbaum Associates, Inc.
Second edition © 2001 Lawrence Erlbaum Associates, Inc.
Third edition © 2008 Taylor & Francis

Typeset in Goudy by RefineCatch Limited, Bungay, Suffolk
Printed and bound in the United States of America
on acid-free paper by Sheridan Books, Inc.

Library of Congress Cataloging in Publication Data
Second language acquisition : an introductory course / edited by
Susan M. Gass and Larry Selinker.—3rd ed.
p. cm.
Includes bibliographical references.
ISBN 978–0–8058–5497–8—ISBN 978–0–8058–5498–5—
ISBN 978–0–203–93284–1
1. Second language acquisition.   I. Gass, Susan M.
II. Selinker, Larry, 1937–
P118.2.S424 2008
418—dc22
2007028663

ISBN10: 0–805–85497–5 (hbk)
ISBN10: 0–805–85498–3 (pbk)
ISBN10: 0–203–93284–6 (ebk)

ISBN13: 978–0–805–85497–8 (hbk)
ISBN13: 978–0–805–85498–5 (pbk)
ISBN13: 978–0–203–93284–1 (ebk)

05/07

UNIVERSITY OF
WOLVERHAMPTON

SECOND LANGUAGE ACQUISITION

Praise for the Third Edition
"A tour de force. The authors have taken an already successful introductory course in second language acquisition (SLA) and made it even stronger. The improvements begin in the first chapter at the very beginning of the text. . . . This book should be used by anyone teaching any introduction to SLA, at either the graduate or undergraduate level."
—Fred Eckman, Center for the Advanced Study of Language,
University of Maryland

"This text presents a comprehensive overview of SLA in an accessible, highly readable manner for readers new to this discipline. . . . The new edition includes even more examples than the previous ones, with integrated into the main text an additional question and problem at each chapter."
—Cristina Sanz, Gallaudet University

"Second Language Acquisition: An Introductory Course presents the most balanced, grounded, and clear introduction to a field that has grown rapidly since publication of the second edition is most welcome. [T]he third edition . . . make[s] this breadth of knowledge accessible to students with little background in the feeder disciplines . . . Second Language Acquisition has now become a living standard in our field."
—Richard Young, Professor of English Linguistics,
University of Wisconsin-Madison

About the Authors
Susan M. Gass is University Distinguished Professor in the Department of Linguistics and Germanic, Slavic, Asian and African Languages at Michigan State University. She has conducted research in numerous areas of second language acquisition, including language transfer, language universals, second language research methods, and input and interaction. She is the author/editor of numerous books, has served as the President of the American Association for Applied Linguistics and is the current president of the International Association of Applied Linguistics (AILA).

Larry Selinker is one of the original contributors to the research field of second language acquisition, having introduced the concepts "interlanguage" and "fossilization," and having conducted one of the first empirical studies in "language transfer" research in 1969. He is now preparing a 40-plus year fossilization study on participants first looked at in 1964. He has held professorships at the Universities of Michigan and London and visiting professorships at various universities around the world. Currently, he is Visiting Professor at New York University and is helping to organize Research Production Associates.

To Gertrude Zemon-Gass and H. Harvey Gass, who instilled
in me the love of inquiry

To my parents, Sol and Miriam Selinker, who inspired me
deeply and whom I miss very much

CONTENTS

PREFACE

This is a book about second language acquisition. As such, it deals with the ways in which second languages are learned. We take a multidisciplinary approach in that what we have selected to present in this book represents research emanating from other well-established disciplines. The content of the book is limited, for the most part, to a discussion of adult second language acquisition, although we have included in this third edition information about child language acquisition, both first and second. This is intended to serve as background information.

This book is the third edition of a book originally published in 1994. The field has shown considerable growth, which is reflected in this edition. This book has been updated, and rearranged; new sections have been added and in some cases rewritten, and new chapters have been added as well.

The book is designed to be used in an introductory course for undergraduate or graduate students. The goal is to make the information contained herein available to students with a wide variety of background knowledge. The book can be used with those with a background in languages and/or linguistics and those with little or no background in these areas. The book developed out of our belief that the complexities of the field can and should be brought to the attention of many students, both those who are intending to delve further into the field and those who are only curious about the pervasive phenomenon of learning a second language.

The field of second language acquisition is one about which everyone seems to have an opinion. Even a casual airplane conversation with a seatmate, during which we are asked what we do, always elicits opinions about second language acquisition, some of which are accurate, some of which are not. It is our intent to help set the record straight on this complex research area.

The field of second language learning is old and new at the same time. It is old in the sense that scholars for centuries have been fascinated by the questions posed by the nature of foreign language learning and language teaching. It is new in the sense that the field, as it is now represented, only goes back about 40 years. In the earlier part of the modern phase, most scholarly articles emphasized language teaching and only had a secondary interest in language learning. In other words, the impetus for studying second language learning was derived from pedagogical concerns.

In the past 30–40 years, the field of second language acquisition has developed into an independent and autonomous discipline, complete with its own research agenda. In addition, we have witnessed an increase in the number of conferences (of both a general and a topical nature) dealing exclusively with second language acquisition as well as special sessions on second language acquisition as part of larger conferences. Furthermore, the field now has journals devoted exclusively to research in the field (*Studies in Second Language Acquisition, Language Learning, Second Language Research*) as well as others in which reports of second language studies comprise a major part (e.g., *Applied Linguistics, Applied Psycholinguistics, The Modern Language Journal*). Finally, there are now numerous edited volumes dealing with subareas of the field (e.g., language transfer, language input, language variation, Universal Grammar, Critical Period) and in recent years entire books concerned with subareas of the field as well as numerous texts dealing with research methodologies. In this book we present the old and the new as a way of helping the reader understand some of the history of the field and how we got to where we are today.

What is particularly noteworthy about the field of second language acquisition is its interdisciplinary character. Second language research is concerned with the general question: How are second languages learned? Scholars approach the field from a wide range of backgrounds: sociology, psychology, education, and linguistics, to name a few. This has both positive and negative effects on the field. The advantage is that through the multiplicity of perspectives, we are able to see a richer picture of acquisition, a picture that appears to be more representative of the phenomenon of acquisition in that learning a second language undoubtedly involves factors relating to sociology, psychology, education, and linguistics. On the other hand, multiple perspectives on what purports to be a single discipline bring confusion, because it is frequently the case that scholars approaching second language acquisition from different (often opposing and seemingly incompatible) frameworks are not able to talk to one another. This is so because each perspective brings with it its own way of approaching data and its own research methodology. This book attempts to bring together these disparate threads, to place them within a coherent framework, and importantly, to make the field accessible to large numbers of students.

There are many people to whom we owe a debt of gratitude. Primary among them is Josh Ard, who has been instrumental in many areas of the book. Josh provided detailed information on some of the original chapters. Through discussions with him, we were able to better determine what was relevant and what was not. Furthermore, he provided valuable clues as to what was involved in writing an introductory textbook whose goal was in part to "normalize" the field and make it informative and interesting to novices. His reading of the text many times over led to minor and major changes throughout. Robin Roots also read the entire third edition for content and for style. Jennifer Behney read and commented on all aspects of this edition. She provided insightful comments and prevented us from making some embarrassing mistakes.

Specific colleagues in the field provided detailed comments on earlier editions and completed surveys which helped us figure out where we could be clearer, where we needed to add parts, and where we needed to delete sections from earlier editions. We are grateful to all of them for their feedback. Bill VanPatten read this manuscript and made us see more clearly how we could organize and portray some of the research presented. Alison Mackey read the entire manuscript and many times made us rethink our conclusions and suggested more research for us to look at. Her comments were detailed and insightful. In expressing our gratitude to these individuals, we wish that we could also blame them for any errors (factual or interpretive) in this book. Alas, scholarly ethics do not allow us this luxury and we accept all errors as our own.

Our colleagues and friends in the field deserve special mention. Although they have not all read the manuscript and may not all approve of the conclusions drawn from their writings, they have all been influential in our thinking and our development as researchers in the field. They are too numerous to mention, but they know who they are and we thank them. Colleagues at Michigan State University have taught from this book and have helped us see where we could improve areas. A hearty thank you to them. In preparing for this third edition, Cathleen Petree, our editor from Lawrence Erlbaum Associates and now with Taylor and Francis, solicited opinions and feedback from prior users. In most cases we do not know who these individuals are, but we hope that you will see your excellent suggestions reflected in these new pages. Even though you are anonymous to us, we hope you accept this expression of gratitude. And many thanks to Cathleen for urging us to do this third edition. We know that she had expected this manuscript earlier and we are fortunate that she has been so patient.

A final group to be thanked consists of our students over the years. In our own introductory courses we have tried and tested this material numerous times. Our students have not hesitated to let us know when material was unclear and when some revision was necessary. Again, there are too many to thank personally, but they are out there somewhere, possibly teaching courses in second language acquisition. We hope that they have benefited from the material contained in those courses as much as we benefited from their feedback.

To you, the student, who will make use of the book, we have provided you with a summary of what is known today in the field of second language acquisition. We hope that this book is but the beginning of a deeper quest into the nature of the learning process. We hope that your interest will be piqued by the text itself, but equally important is the emphasis we have placed on the follow-up activities for each chapter. It is our belief that working with structured data is as valuable as reading summaries of what is known. These problems allow students to gain firsthand knowledge of what learners do and do not produce. We have found that hands-on experience is integral to the entire learning process. We have indicated in the text where we feel the accompanying workbook (*Second Language Learning: Data Analysis*—see Gass, Sorace, and Selinker, 1999) will be useful. The data sets contained in this workbook help guide students into seeing the data from the perspective of the learner, rather than from the perspective of the analyst.

The subtitle of this book is *An Introductory Course*. It is well-known in second language acquisition circles that a truly introductory treatment of our field is difficult to achieve. We have tried hard and hope that we have been successful in our endeavor and that we have succeeded in making the subject matter relevant to a wide range of students.

Susan Gass   Larry Selinker
Williamston, Michigan   New York, New York
June 19, 2007

1

INTRODUCTION

1.1 The study of second language acquisition

Second language acquisition (SLA) is a relatively young field. We would be hard-pressed to state a "beginning" date, but it is probably fair to say that the study of SLA has expanded and developed significantly in the past 40–45 years. This is not to say that there wasn't interest in the fields of language teaching and learning before then, for surely there was. It is to say, however, that since that time the body of knowledge of the field has seen increased sophistication.

We are far from a complete theory of SLA, but there is progress. By approaching SLA from a variety of disciplinary perspectives, as we will see in this chapter and in the remainder of this book, we have come a long way from pure descriptive studies to research that connects with other disciplines.

What is the scope of SLA? What does the study of SLA consist of? It is the study of how second languages are learned. In other words, it is the study of the acquisition of a non-primary language; that is, the acquisition of a language beyond the native language. It is the study of how learners create a new language system with only limited exposure to a second language. It is the study of what is learned of a second language and what is not learned; it is the study of why most second language learners do not achieve the same degree of knowledge and proficiency in a second language as they do in their native language; it is also the study of why only some learners appear to achieve native-like proficiency in more than one language. Additionally, second language acquisition is concerned with the nature of the hypotheses (whether conscious or unconscious) that learners come up with regarding the rules of the second language. Are the rules like those of the native language? Are they like the rules of the language being learned? Are there new rules, like neither language, being formed? Are there patterns that are common to all learners regardless of the native language and regardless of the language being learned? Do the rules created by second language learners vary

1

according to the context of use? Do these rules and patterns vary more in individuals in a second language than they vary in the native language? Given these varied questions, the study of second language acquisition draws from and impacts many other areas of study, among them linguistics, psychology, psycholinguistics, sociology, sociolinguistics, discourse analysis, conversational analysis, and education, to name a few.

Given the close relationship between second language acquisition and other areas of inquiry, there are numerous approaches from which to examine second language data, each one of which brings to the study of second language acquisition its own goals, its own data-collection methods, and its own analytic tools. Thus, second language acquisition is truly an interdisciplinary field. This introductory text attempts to shed light on the nature of second language acquisition from multiple perspectives.

One way to define second language acquisition is to state what it is not. Over the years, the study of second language acquisition has become inextricably intertwined with language pedagogy; in the current text, one goal is to disentangle the two fields. Second language acquisition is not about pedagogy unless the pedagogy affects the course of acquisition (this topic will be explored in chapter 11). Although it may be the case that those who are interested in learning about how second languages are learned are ultimately interested in doing so for the light this knowledge sheds on the field of language teaching, this is not the only reason second language acquisition is of interest, nor is it the major reason scholars in the field of second language acquisition conduct their research.

Let us briefly consider some of the reasons why it might be important for us to understand how second languages are learned and what is not learned.

Linguistics

> When we study human language, we are approaching what some might call the human essence, the distinctive qualities of mind that are, so far as we know, unique to [humans].
>
> (Chomsky, 1968, p. 100)

The study of how second languages are learned is part of the broader study of language and language behavior. It is not more central or peripheral than any other part of linguistic study, which in turn has as its larger goal the study of the nature of the human mind. In fact, a major goal of second language acquisition research is the determination of linguistic constraints on the formation of second language grammars. Because theories of language are concerned with human language knowledge, one can reasonably assume that this knowledge is not limited to first language knowledge, and that linguistic principles reflect the possibilities of human language creation and the limits of human language variation. This scope of inquiry includes second languages.

Language pedagogy

Most graduate programs whose goal is to train students in language teaching now have required course work in second language acquisition, unlike a generation ago. Why should this be the case? People have come to realize that if one is to develop language-teaching methodologies, there has to be a firm basis for those methodologies in language learning. It would be counterproductive to base language-teaching methodologies on something other than an understanding of how language learning does and does not take place. To give an example, some language-teaching methodologies are based exclusively on rule memorization and translation exercises. That is, a student in a language class is expected to memorize rules and then translate sentences from the native language to the language being learned and vice versa. However, studies in second language acquisition have made language teachers and curriculum designers aware that language learning consists of more than rule memorization. More important, perhaps, it involves learning to express communicative needs. The details of this new conceptualization of language learning have resulted in methodologies that emphasize communication. In other words, pedagogical decision-making must reflect what is known about the process of learning, which is the domain of second language acquisition.

A second, perhaps equally important but less assuming, rationale related to language pedagogy has to do with the expectations that teachers have of their students. Let's assume that a teacher spends a class hour drilling students on a particular grammatical structure. Let's further assume that the students are all producing the structure correctly and even in an appropriate context. If, after the class is over and the drill is finished, a student comes up to the teacher and uses the incorrect form in spontaneous speech, what should the teacher think? Has the lesson been a waste of time? Or is this type of linguistic behavior to be expected? If a student produces a correct form, does that necessarily mean that the student has learned the correct rule? These sorts of issues are part of what teachers need to be aware of when assessing the success or failure of their teaching. Or, to take an example from a mystery novel, *Speaker of Mandarin* by Ruth Rendell, Inspector Wexford is in a museum and accompanied by Mr. Sung who is showing him the well-preserved body of a woman who had lived 2000 years earlier. Mr. Sung says "Let's go" and Inspector Wexford takes the opportunity to provide an English lesson (p. 4).

Wexford: I wish you wouldn't keep saying that. If I may suggest it, you should say, "Shall we go? Or "Are you ready?"

Sung: You may suggest. Thank you. I am anxious to speak good. Shall we go? Are you leady?

Wexford: Oh, yes, certainly.

Sung: Don't reply, please. I practice. Shall we go? Are you leady? Good, I have got it. Come, let's go. Are you leady to go to the site? Reply now, please.

Thus, after practicing "Shall we go?", Sung, when it is time to make a spontaneous utterance, reverts back to "Let's go." Further, when Sung believes that he is repeating, and therefore, practicing, his repetition of "Are you ready?", his utterance is no different than his original faulty utterance.

Cross-cultural communication and language use

We have noted some expectations that teachers have about students. Similarly, in interactions with speakers of another language/culture, we have certain expectations and we often produce stereotyped reactions. For example, we may find ourselves making judgments about other people based on their language. It turns out that many stereotypes of people from other cultures (e.g., rudeness, unassertiveness) are based on patterns of nonnative speech. These judgments in many instances are not justified, because many of the speech patterns that nonnative speakers use reflect their nonnativeness rather than characteristics of their personality. As an example, consider the following exchange between a teacher and a former student (NNS = nonnative speaker; NS = native speaker):

(1-1) From Goldschmidt (1996, p. 255)
      NNS: I have a favor to ask you.
      NS: Sure, what can I do for you?
      NNS: You need to write a recommendation for me.

Many teachers would, of course, react negatively to the seeming gall of this "request," perhaps initially thinking to themselves, "What do you mean I *need* to write a letter?" when most likely the only problem is this nonnative speaker's lack of understanding of the forceful meaning of *need*. A second example occurred in the life of one of the authors. An international student whom the professor did not know emailed to ask the professor for an appointment, stating that she was interested in the discipline of SLA. The professor wrote back with a suggestion of a time that they finally agreed on. The student arrived at the appointed time and said:

(1-2) NNS: You wanted to see me?

Many would, of course, also react negatively to the seeming strangeness of the introduction, probably initially thinking, "What do you mean I *wanted* to see you; it's you who wanted to see me." So, understanding second language acquisition and, in this case, how nonnative speakers use language, allows us to separate issues of cross-cultural communication from issues of stereotyped behavior or personal idiosyncrasies.

But it is not only cross-cultural questions that are at issue. In the following example, understanding L2 phonology could have helped in the recent but brief horse-racing scandal when a Chilean jockey, after winning the Kentucky Derby, was accused of carrying something in his hand other than his whip. Apparently, he had told a reporter that he wore a Q-Ray, which is a therapeutic bracelet used for arthritic conditions. What had been understood was a "Q-ring," which apparently the reporter had never heard of, probably because it doesn't exist. So, despite the fact that he didn't know what it was, the reporter assumed it to be something illegal. Had the reporter minimally recognized that perception of nonnative speech often occurs through the filter of our native language phonological system and that that perception is not always accurate, the problem might have been avoided. That coupled with the fact that he had never heard of a Q-ring might have suggested the need to seek greater clarification and the two or three day scandal could have been avoided.

Language policy and language planning
Many issues of language policy are dependent on a knowledge of how second languages are learned. For example, issues surrounding bilingualism, such as the English Only Movement in the United States, or the many different types of bilingual education (including immersion programs) can only be debated if one is properly informed about the realities and constraints of learning a second language. National language programs often involve decision making that is dependent on (a) information about second language learning, (b) the kinds of instruction that can be brought to bear on issues of acquisition, and (c) the realities and expectations one can have of such programs. All too often, these issues are debated without a clear understanding of the object of debate; that is, the nature of how second languages are learned.

In sum, second language acquisition is a complex field whose focus is the attempt to understand the processes underlying the learning of a second language. It is important to reemphasize that the study of second language acquisition is separate from the study of language pedagogy, although this does not imply that there are not implications that can be drawn from second language acquisition to the related discipline of language teaching.

Many disciplines quite clearly find themselves as part of the humanities (e.g., literature) or part of the sciences (e.g., biology). Second language acquisition, because of its complexity and its reliance on and import for other disciplines, is not placed so easily. SLA is part of the humanities, in the sense that it is part of the branch of "learning (as philosophy, arts, or languages) that investigate[s] human constructs and concerns as opposed to natural processes (as in physics or chemistry) and social relations (as in anthropology or economics)" (from Merriam-Webster online dictionary), although clearly there are areas of the field that do consider social relations as an integral part of learning. Given that the humanities are concerned with human constructs and concerns, language acquisition is relevant, for one way of understanding the human condition is through an understanding of language. While this is probably uncontroversial, unfortunately this central area of humanistic study is often confined to general issues of language and the human capacity for language as referring to studies of primary language knowledge and the acquisition of primary language. But this book assumes that we cannot adequately examine the nature of language knowledge if we confine ourselves to only a small portion of the world's population; that is, monolingual native speakers.

Second language acquisition, while rightfully part of the humanities, is also part of the social sciences, defined (Merriam-Webster online) as "a branch of science that deals with the institutions and functioning of human society and with the interpersonal relationships of individuals as members of society." Given that second language acquisition deals with interpersonal relations as it does when studying many issues of language use, it is definitely part of the social sciences. Interactions involving nonnative speakers of a language are undoubtedly highly frequent in the broader context of the world's interactions, and, thus, the study of these interactions has a central place in the social sciences and cognitive science. Finally, since some SLA research focuses on the biology of the brain, and what SLA neurophysiology can show about neural workings, SLA itself can be considered a part of the developing cognitive neurosciences.

1.2 Definitions

The study of any new discipline involves familiarizing oneself with the specific terminology of that field. In this section, we present some basic terminology common to the field of second language acquisition, accompanied by brief definitions. Other terms are introduced and defined as the text progresses.

Native Language (NL): This refers to the first language that a child learns. It is also known as the primary language, the mother tongue, or the L1 (first language). In this book, we use the common abbreviation NL.

Target Language (TL): This refers to the language being learned.

Second Language Acquisition (SLA): This is the common term used for the name of the discipline. In general, SLA refers to the process of learning another language after the native language has been learned. Sometimes the term refers to the learning of a third or fourth language. The important aspect is that SLA refers to the learning of a nonnative language *after* the learning of the native language. The second language is commonly referred to as the L2. As with the phrase "second language," L2 can refer to any language learned *after* learning the L1, regardless of whether it is the second, third, fourth, or fifth language. By this term, we mean both the acquisition of a second language in a classroom situation, as well as in more "natural" exposure situations. The word *acquisition* in this book is used broadly in the sense that we talk about language use (sometimes independently from actual acquisition). Some might prefer the term *Second Language Studies* (SLS) as it is a term that refers to anything dealing with using or acquiring a second/foreign language. However, in this book, we continue to use the term *SLA* as a cover term for a wide variety of phenomena, not because the term is necessarily the most descriptively accurate, but because the field has come to be known by that acronym.

Foreign Language Learning: Foreign language learning is generally differentiated[1] from second language acquisition in that the former refers to the learning of a nonnative language in the environment of one's native language (e.g., French speakers learning English in France or Spanish speakers learning French in Spain, Argentina, or Mexico). This is most commonly done within the context of the classroom.

Second language acquisition, on the other hand, generally refers to the learning of a nonnative language in the environment in which that language is spoken (e.g., German speakers learning Japanese in Japan or Punjabi speakers learning English in the United Kingdom). This may or may not take place in a classroom setting. The important point is that learning in a second language environment takes place with considerable access to speakers of the language being learned, whereas learning in a foreign language environment usually does not.[2]

1.3 The nature of language

Fundamental to the understanding of the nature of SLA is an understanding of what it is that needs to be learned. A facile answer is that a second language learner needs to learn the "grammar" of the TL. But what is meant by this? What is language? How can we characterize the knowledge that humans have of language?

All normal humans acquire a language in the first few years of life. The knowledge acquired is largely of an unconscious sort. That is, very young children learn how to form particular grammatical structures, such as relative clauses. They also learn that relative clauses often have a modifying function, but in a conscious sense they do not know that it is a relative clause and could presumably not state what relative clauses are used for. Take as an example the following sentence:

(1-3) I want that toy that that boy is playing with.

A child could utter this fully formed sentence, which includes a relative clause ("that that boy is playing with"), without being able to articulate the function of relative clauses (either this one, or relative clauses in general) and without being able to easily divide this sentence into its component parts. It is in this sense that the complex knowledge we have about our native language is largely unconscious.

There are a number of aspects of language that can be described systematically. In the next few sections we deal with the phonology, syntax, morphology, semantics, and pragmatics of language.

1.3.1 Sound systems

Knowledge of the sound system (phonology) of our native language is complex. Minimally, it entails knowing what sounds are possible and what sounds are not possible in the language. For example, a native speaker of English knows that the first vowel sound in the name *Goethe* [œ] is not a sound in English. This knowledge is reflected in recognition as well as in production, as generally a close English sound is substituted when one attempts to utter that word in English.

Phonological knowledge also involves knowing what happens to words in fast speech as opposed to more carefully articulated speech. For example, if someone wanted to express the following idea:

(1-4) I am going to write a letter.

That person, assuming a U.S. English speaker, would undoubtedly say something like the following.

8

(1-5) I'm gonna wriDa leDer.

Consider the following exchange:

(1-6) Tom: What are you gonna do?
Sally: I'm gonna wriDa leDer.
Tom: You're gonna do what?
Sally: I'm gonna wriDa leDer.
Tom: What? I can't hear you.
Sally: I'm going to write a letter [articulated slowly and clearly].

We can see that speakers know when to combine sounds and when not to. We know that in "normal, fast" speech we combine words, but that in clearer, more articulated speech we do not.

A final point to make is that, as native speakers of a language, we know not only what are possible sounds and what are not possible sounds, but we also know what are possible combinations of sounds and what sounds are found in what parts of words. We know, for example, that in English, while [b] and [n] are both sounds of English, they cannot form a "blend" in the way that [b] and [r] can: *bnick[3] versus brain. Or to take another example, consider the sound at the end of the word ping [ŋ], which is frequent in English. However, it cannot appear in the beginning of words in English, although it can in other languages.

1.3.2 Syntax

In this section, we briefly describe what speakers know about the syntax of their language. This is what is frequently known as grammar, referring primarily to the knowledge we have of the order of elements in a sentence. We point out briefly that there are two kinds of grammar that are generally referred to: (a) prescriptive grammar and (b) descriptive grammar. By prescriptive grammar, we mean such rules as are generally taught in school, often without regard to the way native speakers of a language actually use language. We have in mind such rules as "Don't end a sentence with a preposition," "Don't split infinitives," "Don't begin a sentence with a conjunction," "Don't use contractions in writing," and "Use between with two items and among with more than two" (Associated Press rule; as cited in Safire, 1999, p. 24). To illustrate that these so-called rules are something other than appropriate, McCawley (also cited in Safire) gives the following example: He held four golf balls between his fingers. Even though there are more than two fingers involved, one cannot say: *He held four golf balls among his fingers.

On the other hand, linguists are concerned with descriptive grammars:

9

They attempt to describe languages as they are actually used. Thus, when talking about knowledge of syntax, we are referring to descriptive grammars. The rules just stated are not true of descriptive grammars because native speakers of English frequently violate the prescriptive rules.

As with phonological knowledge discussed in section 1.3.1, native speakers of a language know which are possible sentences of their language and which are not. For example, below, we know that sentences 1-7 and 1-8 are possible English sentences, whereas 1-9 and 1-10 are not possible or are ungrammatical:

(1-7) The big book is on the brown table.
(1-8) The woman whom I met yesterday is reading the same book that I read last night.
(1-9) *The book big brown table the on is.
(1-10) *Woman the met I yesterday whom book same the is reading read I last night that.

So part of what we know about language is the order in which elements can and cannot occur. This is of course not as simple as the preceding examples suggest. Are sentences 1-11 and 1-12 possible English sentences?

(1-11) Have him to call me back.
(1-12) That's the man that I am taller than.

For many speakers of English these are strange sounding, for others they are perfectly acceptable.

Not only do we know which sentences are acceptable in our language, we also know which sentences are grossly equivalent in terms of meaning. For example, sentences 1-13 and 1-14 have the same general meaning in the sense that they refer to the same event:

(1-13) Tom was hit by a car.
(1-14) A car hit Tom.

While we know that both sentences above can be assumed to be paraphrases of one another, we also know that they have slightly different functions in English. If someone asks, *What did that car hit?*, the most likely answer would be *It hit Tom* rather than *Tom was hit by it*. Thus, we as native speakers know not only what is equivalent to what, but also when to use different grammatical patterns.

Another aspect of language that we know is how meaning is affected by moving elements within a sentence. For example, adverbs can be moved in a sentence without affecting the meaning, whereas nouns cannot. Sentences 1-15 and 1-16 are roughly equivalent in meaning:

(1-15) Yesterday Sally saw Jane.
(1-16) Sally saw Jane yesterday.

but 1-17 and 1-18 do not share a common meaning.

(1-17) Yesterday Sally saw Jane.
(1-18) Yesterday Jane saw Sally.

Thus, knowing a language entails knowing a set of rules with which we can produce an infinite set of sentences. In order to see that language is rule-governed and that we can comprehend novel sentences, consider sentence 1-19:

(1-19) The woman wearing the green scarf ran across the street to
see the gorilla that had just escaped from the zoo.

Even though this sentence is probably one you have never encountered before, you have little difficulty in understanding what it means.

But it is important to note that syntax is complex, often abstract and in many instances difficult to describe. For example, we typically think that the subject of a sentence is the performer of some action, as in 1-18 above where Jane is doing the action of seeing, but what about *Josh seems happy*? We know that Josh is the subject, but he isn't performing any action, nor is *it* performing an action in the sentence *it's raining cats and dogs*.

1.3.3 *Morphology and the lexicon*

The study of morphology is the study of word formation. In many cases, words are made up of more than one part. For example, the word *unforeseen* is made up of three parts: *un*, which has a negative function; *fore*, which means earlier in time; and *seen*, which means visualized. Each part is referred to as a morpheme, which can be defined as the minimal unit of meaning.

There are two classes of morphemes that we can identify: bound and free. A bound morpheme is one that can never be a word by itself, such as the *un* of *unlikely*. A free morpheme is one that is a word in and of itself, such as *man, woman, book*, or *table*. Words can be created by adding morphemes, as in the following children's favorite:

establish
establish + ment
dis + establish + ment
dis + establish + ment + ari + an + ism

11

Not only do we know how to form words using affixes (prefixes, suffixes, infixes), but we also know what words can go with other words, as in Mt. *Everest is a high mountain*, but not *The Empire State Building is a high building.*

1.3.4 Semantics

The study of semantics refers to the study of meaning. This, of course, does not necessarily correspond to grammaticality because many ungrammatical sentences are meaningful, or at least interpretable, as can be seen in the following sentences.

(1-20) *That woman beautiful is my mother.
(1-21) *I'll happy if I can get your paper.

These and many other sentences that are uttered by nonnative speakers of a language are perfectly comprehensible, despite the fact that they do not follow the "rules" of English. The reverse side of the picture is the sentence that is grammatically formed but that, because of the content, is meaningless (at least without additional contextualization), as in 1-22:

(1-22) That bachelor is married.

Knowledge of the semantics of a language entails knowledge of the reference of words. For example, in English we know that a *table* refers to an object with a flat top and either three or four legs and that a *leaf* most often refers to part of a tree. But as native speakers we also have to be able to distinguish between the meaning of the *leaf* of a tree and the *leaf* of a table. When we hear an advertisement on television for a table with extra *leafs*, it is this knowledge of homonyms that comes into play to help us interpret the advertisement in the manner intended. For a learner, of course, it is not so easy, as he or she might struggle to imagine a table with tree leaves.

Additionally, it is important to note that the limits of a word are not always clear. What is the difference between a *cup* and a *glass*? For many objects it is obvious; for others it is less so.

Referential meanings are clearly not the only way of expressing meaning. As native speakers of a language, we know that the way we combine elements in sentences affects their meaning. Sentences 1-23 and 1-24 are different in meaning. Thus, we understand that syntax and meaning interrelate.

(1-23) The man bit the dog.
(1-24) The dog bit the man.

In some languages the translation equivalents of those sentences (with possibly different intonation contours) can be interpreted as referring to the same event.

1.3.5 *Pragmatics*

Yet another area of language that we consider and that is part of what second language learners need to learn has to do with pragmatics, or the way in which we use language in context. For example, when we answer the telephone and someone says *Is John there?*, we understand that this is a request to speak with John. It would be strange to respond *yes* with the caller saying *thank you* and then hanging up unless the caller did not want to carry on the conversation with John present or only wanted to know whether or not John was present. Clearly, the phrase *Is X there?* in the context of telephone usage is a request to speak with someone and not an information question. When the intent is the latter—as for example, a parent checking on the whereabouts of a child—the conversation might be slightly modified.

(1-25) Father 1: This is John's father. Is John there?
        Father 2: Yes.
        Father 1: Thanks, I just wanted to know where he was.

Similarly, word order, as discussed earlier, may have an effect on meaning (see sentences 1-23 and 1-24) in some grammatical contexts, but in others it does not.

The following conversation exemplifies this:

(1-26) (Setting: Ice cream store; child, age 4)
        Child: I want a raspberry and vanilla cone.
        Shopkeeper: OK, one vanilla and raspberry cone coming
                 up.
        Child: No, I want a raspberry and vanilla cone.
        Shopkeeper: That's what I'm getting you.

In this instance, the child is using word order to reflect the ordering of scoops of ice cream; the shopkeeper is not. Thus, what we have learned as adult native speakers of a language is the function of word order in our language. In English, it does not necessarily refer to the ordering of physical objects.

1.4 The nature of nonnative speaker knowledge

We have briefly characterized some areas of language knowledge that a native speaker has of a language. Knowing a second language well means knowing information similar to that of a native speaker of a language. Given the complexity of the knowledge that must be learned, it should be clear that the study of the acquisition of that knowledge is a highly complex field.

The basic assumption in SLA research is that learners create a language system, known as an interlanguage (IL). This concept validates learners' speech, not as a deficit system, that is, a language filled with random errors, but as a system of its own with its own structure. This system is composed of numerous elements, not the least of which are elements from the NL and the TL. There are also elements in the IL that do not have their origin in either the NL or the TL. These latter are called new forms and are the empirical essence of interlanguage. What is important is that the learners themselves impose structure on the available linguistic data and formulate an internalized system (IL).[4] Central to the concept of interlanguage is the concept of fossilization, which generally refers to the cessation of learning. The *Random House Dictionary of the English Language* (Flexner and Hanck, 1988, p. 755) defines fossilization of a linguistic form, feature, rule, and so forth in the following way: "to become permanently established in the interlanguage of a second language learner in a form that is deviant from the target-language norm and that continues to appear in performance regardless of further exposure to the target language."

Because of the difficulty in determining when learning has ceased, some hold (e.g., Long, 2003) that it is more appropriate to refer to stabilization of linguistic forms, rather than to fossilization or permanent cessation of learning. In SLA, one often notes that learners reach plateaus that are far from the TL norms. Furthermore, it appears to be the case that fossilized or stabilized interlanguages exist no matter what learners do in terms of further exposure to the TL. Unfortunately, a solid explanation of permanent or temporary learning plateaus is lacking at present due, in part, to the lack of longitudinal studies that would be necessary to create databases necessary to come to conclusions regarding "getting stuck" in another language.

1.5 Conclusion

In this chapter we have presented a series of basic definitions to help the reader begin the journey of the study of second language acquisition. As has been seen, inherent in an analysis of interlanguage data is a focus on the learner and on the processes involved in learning. In the following chapters we present additional information about interlanguages, beginning with a discussion of ways of analyzing second language data.

Suggestions for additional reading

Inside Language. Vivian Cook. Edward Arnold (1997).
Language: Its Structure and Use, 5th ed. Edward Finegan. Heinle (2008).
An Introduction to Language, 8th ed. Victoria Fromkin, Robert Rodman and Nina Hyams. Heinle (2007).
Essential Introductory Linguistics. Grover Hudson. Blackwell (2000).
Linguistics: A Very Short Introduction. P. H. Matthews. Oxford University Press (2003).
Contemporary Linguistics: An Introduction. William O'Grady, John Archibald, Mark Aronoff, and Janie Rees-Miller. Bedford/St. Martin's Press (2005).
The Language Instinct: How the Mind Creates Language. Steven Pinker. Morrow (1994).
Linguistics: An Introduction. Andrew Radford, Martin Atkinson, David Britain, Harald Clahsen, and Andrew Spencer. Cambridge University Press (1999).

Points for discussion

1 A teacher has drilled students in the structure known as indirect questions:

> Do you know where my book is?
> Do you know what time it is?
> Did he tell you what time it is?

As a direct result of the drills, all students in the class were able to produce the structure correctly in class. After class, a student came up to the teacher and asked, "Do you know where is Mrs. Irving?" In other words, only minutes after the class, in spontaneous speech, the student used the structure practiced in class incorrectly. Describe what you think the reason is for this misuse. Had the lesson been a waste of time? How might you go about finding answers to these questions?

2 Consider the distinction between *second language acquisition* and *foreign language learning* as discussed in this chapter. Take the position that they are fundamentally different. How would you defend this position? Now take the opposite position. Consider how the position you take might is affected by the linguistic areas of phonology, syntax, morphology, semantics, and pragmatics.

Next, look at the distinction from a social point of view. Discuss your answers in terms of specific examples from your experience, such as the learning of Spanish in Spain versus the learning of

Spanish in the United States, or the teaching of English in the United States versus the teaching of English in Asia.

3   Consider the differences between child language acquisition and adult second language acquisition. Specifically, consider the example provided in 1-3.

> (1-3) I want that toy that that boy is playing with.

With regard to this sentence, we state in this chapter that "A child could utter this fully formed sentence, which includes a relative clause ('that that boy is playing with'), without being able to articulate the function of relative clauses (either this one, or relative clauses in general) and without being able to easily divide this sentence into its component parts. It is in this sense that the complex knowledge we have about our native language is largely unconscious."

Do you think that this comment is also valid for adults learning a second language? Specifically, do you think that an adult needs to consciously learn the grammar of relative clauses *before* being able to use them spontaneously in interlanguage? Take an example from your own language-learning or language-teaching experience, or one that you know of, and relate it to these child versus adult distinctions. In thinking about this question, take into account the concept of fossilization (as defined in this chapter) versus the concept of stabilization.

4   We state in this chapter that, with regard to fossilization, a solid theoretical explanation of permanent plateaus is lacking at present. In pairs, create a list of some of the main reasons for the well-attested existence of fossilization in interlanguage. Share your list with that of another pair and come up with a common list.

5   In section 1.3.2, we describe the types of knowledge that individuals have about sentences in their native language. We note that there is variation in native speakers' acceptance of sentences, as in sentences 1-11 and 1-12.

> (1-11) Have him to call me back.
> (1-12) That's the man that I am taller than.

Are these sentences acceptable to you? If not, what would you say instead? In what situations, if any, would you say these sentences? Consider how and when such variation might occur in terms of second language syntactic knowledge. For example, a student ended an academic note to a teacher with this spontaneous interlanguage blessing:

> Wish peace be with you.

16

Other students (of the same NL) who were then asked to produce a blessing in a (nonspontaneous) task produced many variations, including this one:

Wish peace be to you.

Is this the same sort of variation as described earlier? Why or why not? How does it affect your answer to know that the original sentence occurred spontaneously and the others did not?

6   Consider in general the nature of nonnative speaker knowledge. In what ways is it similar to or different from native speaker knowledge? We stated in this chapter that nonnative speakers form interlanguages that consist not only of elements from their native language and the target language, but also "autonomous" elements. In this light, consider the following sentences, produced by an Arabic speaker of English:

I bought a couple of towel.
There is many kind of way you make baklawa.
There are about one and half-million inhabitant in Jeddah.

In these examples, which linguistic items (and arrangements of items) do you hypothesize come from the target language, which come from the native language, and which are autonomous? As a way to begin, think about whether learners of English with first languages other than Arabic are likely to utter similar sentences.

7   In this chapter, we discussed possible motivating factors for the study of second language acquisition. What other reasons might there be for investigating how second languages are learned?

8   Following are English translations of compositions written by two schoolchildren in their native language (Tatar) and compositions written by the same children in Russian, their L2. In all instances, the children were describing a picture.

Child 1: Written in Tatar (L1)
The long awaited spring has come. The days are getting warmer and warmer. The blue sky is covered by white fluffy clouds. They skim like sailboats through the sky. The ice is breaking away on the river to the north. The birds have returned after having flown from us to a warm region. The apples have bloomed. Children are planting tomatoes, cucumbers, onions, and other vegetables. They are watering the trees. Azat is planting flowers. Rustam is watering the apples. The children are happily working in the garden. They are very happy.

17

Child 1: Written in Russian (L2)
In the schoolyard there is a large garden. Children are digging in the earth. Children are working in the garden. In the garden there is a pine tree, an oak, and tomatoes. An apple tree is growing there. They are planting flower beds.

Child 2: Written in Tatar (L1)
It was a beautiful spring day. The sun was shining. The birds who had returned from distant lands were singing. The trees were swallowed up by the greenery of the luxuriant spring foliage. The children have come into their garden. There the apple trees have already blossomed. Rustam is watering the flowers. The remaining children are planting vegetables. The teacher is watching the work of her pupils. She's pleased with their work, she smiles.

Child 2: Written in Russian (L2)
In the schoolyard there is a large garden. Children are working there. The garden is big. In the garden there are trees. A child is planting a tree. A child is pouring water from a watering pot. In the garden a poplar is growing.

What kind of information (e.g., descriptive, evaluative) do these children include in their NL descriptions of these pictures? In their TL descriptions of the pictures? What similarities/differences are there between the NL and TL versions of these pictures?

9 In pairs, answer "True" or "False" to the following statements. Justify your responses. Once you come to a consensus, compare your answers to those of another pair.

a   Any child without cognitive disabilities can learn any language with equal ease.
b   Learning a second language is a matter of learning a new set of habits.
c   The only reason that some people cannot learn a second or foreign language is that they are insufficiently motivated.
d   All children can learn a second language accent-free.
e   No adult can learn a second language accent-free.
f   All human beings have an innate capacity to learn language.
g   Vocabulary is the most important part of learning a second language.
h   Vocabulary is the most difficult part of learning a second language.
i   Language instruction is a waste of time.

j   Learning a second language takes no more time than learning a first language.

10 We mentioned that it is difficult to know when learning is ceased. This is the case for our first language as well. To understand this better, think of areas of your first language that you sometimes "stumble" over (e.g., *She laid the book on the table*). List two or three other such areas. Then, think about vocabulary. Are there words in your native language that you are not sure of the meaning of? Pick an arbitrary page of a monolingual dictionary. How many words do you not know?

2

RELATED DISCIPLINES

2.1 SLA and related disciplines

There are many research areas that are related to the field of second language acquisition, some of which were mentioned in chapter 1. This chapter briefly touches on some of these "neighboring" disciplines as a way of introducing the reader to these areas, showing similarities and dissimilarities. While SLA is now an autonomous area of research, it had its roots and initial justification in other areas—for example, language teaching—and it has been strongly influenced by other disciplines, such as linguistics and psychology. However, it had a special relationship with child language acquisition in that child language acquisition formed the basis of research in second language acquisition, with many of the original second language research questions stemming from the same questions in child language acquisition. Other areas, such as third language acquisition or heritage language acquisition, are special instances of second language acquisition and, particularly in the case of heritage language learning, have developed in recent years. Finally, bilingual acquisition blends issues related to second language acquisition and those related to first language acquisition.

We begin this chapter with a brief overview of some of the issues addressed in these related fields. We only give cursory coverage because to do otherwise would take us away from the main focus of this book, second language acquisition. We feel that it is important to give some information on these related areas, however, because they shed light on some of the complexities of SLA. They each have a well-developed history of their own and in most cases even have journals devoted to their issues. In this chapter, we are able to do little more than summarize the scope of work in these areas.

The relationship of each to second language acquisition is different. Some, namely third language acquisition and heritage language acquisition, have a derivative relationship, developing out of related but more specific concerns. Bilingual research has a parallel development with concerns that diverge to some extent from those of second language acquisition, considering, for example, the onset of learning for both languages. To make divisions of types of acquisition, as we have done in this chapter, is somewhat artificial, but necessary for expository purposes. We treat each of these areas below.

2.2 Third language acquisition/multilingualism

As mentioned in chapter 1, second language acquisition has become a cover term for acquisition after a first language has been learned. It often incorporates many different types of acquisition, including third, fourth, and so on, and includes heritage language learning (to be discussed in the subsequent section). This notwithstanding, there is a research area that is becoming more prominent, that of third language acquisition. Since there are multiple languages involved, the questions addressed are quite interesting and inherently more complex than those involved in true second language acquisition. And, individual histories become import-ant. As noted by Cenoz and Genesee (1998, p. 16),

> Multilingual acquisition and multilingualism are complex phenomena. They implicate all the factors and processes associ-ated with second language acquisition and bilingualism as well as unique and potentially more complex factors and effects associ-ated with the interactions that are possible among the multiple languages being learned and the processes of learning them.

As we will see throughout this book, there a number of variables that can impact the extent to which one of the languages involved (the L2 or the L1) will influence the acquisition of the L3. Among these are the age at which L3 learning begins, the context of acquisition, individual characteristics, and language distances among the three (or more) languages.

Examples of language influence can be seen in a number of areas. In 2-1, from Selinker and Baumgartner-Cohen (1995), an English speaker who has just come from France is attempting to speak German.

(2-1) Tu   as   mein Fax   bekommen?
      you   have   my Fax   gotten
      French   French   German   German
      "Did you get my fax?"

The sentence is built on German grammar with split verbs, *as . . . bekom-men* ("have . . . gotten"), but with the French subject pronoun (*tu*) and auxiliary *avoir* ("as"). Other examples come from Dewaele (1998), who gives examples from native speakers of Dutch with English as an L2 producing French as L3 utterances, as in 2-2 and 2-3:

(2-2) Ils veulent gagner more, euh, plus . . .
They want to earn more, uh, more . . .
(2-3) Les gens sont involvés
The people are involved

In 2-3, the correct word is *impliqués* rather than *involvés*. Another lexical mixture is cited by Herwig (2001). A native speaker of English who has French as an L2 and German Swedish as an L3 says *föreslägger* for the Swedish word *föreslär* (the German word is *vorschlagen*—propose).

The difficulty of keeping foreign languages apart was noted by Schmidt and Frota (1986). Their study described an English-speaking learner of Portuguese with Arabic as a prior second language who wondered why he couldn't keep the two languages (Portuguese and Arabic) apart. A well-known quote from King Charles V of Spain (1500–1558) suggests that some individuals have no difficulty keeping languages apart and even assign different functions to each:

I speak Spanish to G-d, Italian to women, French to men, and German to my horse.

But most individuals do not have such control and are not so compartmentalized. Why one cannot keep languages and interlanguages apart and why the mixing and merging of various languages known and being learned occurs are issues at the heart of research on multilingualism. Many learners have described the experience of influence from even unrelated languages ("talk foreign," as described by Selinker and Baumgartner-Cohen, 1995) as in the case involving Portuguese and Arabic. Another example (personal communication) comes from a native speaker of English who had been in Turkey for quite some time. He was traveling in Germany, where he had been before, when he reported on his attempt to speak German: "To my horror, out came Turkish."

There are many areas that impact third language acquisition, including sociolinguistic, psycholinguistic, and cross-linguistic influences. With regard to sociolinguistic issues, there are a number of issues to consider, such as the purpose for learning a second or third language. For example, in many parts of the world, or in many industries or professions, English has become the virtual *lingua franca*, or language used for basic communication, as is the case for Spanish in some areas of the United States. This is quite different from a bilingual home situation. From a psycholinguistic perspective, there are differences for multilingual speakers in how the lexicon is organized. With regard to cross-linguistic influences, we presented examples above that demonstrate how learners of a third language have multiple resources to draw on. Some of the determining variables might be proficiency in the languages known, as well as in the target language, age of user, and linguistic closeness of the languages in question, among others.

2.3 Heritage language acquisition

Heritage language speaker is a relatively recent term, having its origins in the education literature.[1] Heritage language speakers are, broadly speaking, those who have been exposed to a language of personal connection (Fishman, 2001). Valdés (2001b) notes that "it is the historical and personal connection to the language that is salient and not the actual proficiency of individual speakers. Armenian, for example, would be considered a heritage language for American students of Armenian ancestry even if the students were English-speaking monolinguals" (p. 38) and she characterizes a heritage language learner (living in an English-speaking environment) as someone who is "raised in a home where a non-English language is spoken, who speaks or at least understands the language, and who is to some degree bilingual in that language and in English" (2001b, p. 38).

For research into this type of second or foreign language acquisition, an important issue is the exposure and use of the language in childhood. And here, as can be easily imagined, there are numerous problems because exposure and use can vary from individual to individual. Unlike much of the literature on heritage language learners, which considers the language of the ancestral family with or without exposure and use, Polinsky (in press) defines heritage language as the language "which was first for an individual with respect to the order of acquisition but has not been completely acquired because of the switch to another dominant language. An individual may use the heritage language under certain conditions and understand it, but his/her primary language is a different one" (p. 1).

The recognition of heritage language learners as a variable in second language research is recent. Often the concept of heritage language speaker is (unknowingly) ignored, and these individuals are consequently included in studies. Sorace (1993a) is an exception in that she explicitly controlled for heritage language speakers in her study on the acquisition of Italian by eliminating them from her database; "none had Italian origins" (p. 35).

Heritage language acquisition is a form of second language acquisition and a form of bilingualism. Heritage language learners have knowledge of two languages (the home language and the language of the environment/ school), and they are usually dominant in the second language. There is a wide range of linguistic knowledge that heritage speakers have, including those who were born in the second language environment and those who came to the second language environment during their school years. Another consideration is the amount of input in the home, ranging from only the heritage language spoken in the home (with perhaps parents only speaking the heritage language) to those situations in which the heritage language is spoken only sporadically.

Heritage learners often do not become bilingual speakers because they do not continue to speak the heritage language as much as they speak the language of the non-home environment. In some cases, they may not have heard or spoken the heritage language since they were very young because their families switched to the language of the environment. Heritage language learners form a heterogeneous group, since their experiences of the language may be very different. Some learners may have been raised by parents who only spoke the heritage language. However, when they went to school, English may have become their dominant language. Other learners may have only received very limited input of the heritage language in the home while they were very young. Nonetheless, it is generally accepted that the nature of language learning for heritage language learners differs from language learning involving non-heritage language learners (Campbell and Rosenthal, 2000; Valdés, 1995, 2001b). Heritage speakers often possess a subtly different knowledge base of the heritage language than L2 learners of that language with no prior background. In addition, they often differ from monolingual speakers of their heritage language. Sometimes these differences may be subtle and sometimes they may be quite fundamental. Some recent studies have investigated the linguistic differences between heritage language and non-heritage language learners (e.g., Carreira, 2002; Ke, 1998; Nagasawa, 1995; Montrul, 2002, 2004; Polinsky, 1995, 2000, in press; Gass and Lewis, 2007).

2.4 Bilingual acquisition

Bilingualism is a broad term and, like heritage language acquisition, has many forms and configurations. Often the term *bilingual* is used loosely to incorporate multilingualism, as is clear from the introduction to a section of a book by Bhatia and Ritchie (2006). Bhatia (2006) states that "the investigation of bilingualism is a broad and complex field, including the study of the nature of the individual bilingual's knowledge and use of two (*or more*) languages" (emphasis ours) (p. 5). Cenoz, in her review (2005) of Bhatia and Ritchie's book, states "the editors make a remark in the introduction about the use of the word 'bilingualism' in the title of the book and say that they do not exclude additional languages and that the chapters in the book include the 'full range of multilingualism'.

24

However, the use of the term 'bilingualism' is problematic because the Latin prefix 'bi' means 'two' . . ." (p. 638).

The concept of *bilingualism* is interpreted differently in the field of SLA versus fields such as psychology and education. That is, SL researchers reserve use of the term for only those that are truly, as shown through some linguistic measure, the equivalent of native speakers of two languages. Thus, from the perspective of second language researchers, *bilingual* is a difficult term. In its strict meaning, it refers to someone whose language is in a steady state and who has learned and now knows two languages. That is, *bilingual* refers to an end point; "someone is bilingual." Within a second language research context, the end-point interpretation of the term is generally not a focus of inquiry. Rather, second language researchers, because of their interest in discovering the second language acquisition process, might focus instead on near-native speakers or advanced language learners. In general, SLA researchers are most interested in individuals who are in the process of learning, not those who have learned two languages earlier.

This use of the term does not appear to be the case in some of the psychological and educational literature on bilingualism.[2] For example, Edwards (2006) starts off his article on the foundations of bilingualism by saying "Everyone is bilingual. That is, there is no one in the world (no adult, anyway) who does not know at least a few words in languages other than the maternal variety. If, as an English speaker, you can say *c'est la vie* or *gracias* or *guten Tag* or *tovarisch*—or even if you only understand them—you clearly have some command of a foreign tongue . . . The question, of course, is one of degree . . ." (p. 7). He goes on to say, "it is easy to find definitions of bilingualism that reflect widely divergent responses to the question of *degree*" (p. 8). Bhatia (2006) states this in an interesting way when he says "the process of second language acquisition—of becoming a bilingual" (p. 5). In other words, the end result of second language acquisition is a bilingual speaker. Given that bilingualism is seen as the end result and given that we know that native-like competence in a second language is rare, there is some difficulty in discussing bilingualism in this way. Thus, Bhatia and Edwards are referring to two different phenomena. Edwards is saying that one is bilingual at any point in the SL learning process, whereas Bhatia is referring only to the end point and does not deal with whether or not that end point has to be "native" or not. In other words, the issues seem to be of degree—whether or not one is *bilingual* even if not a native speaker of the L2—and of end point—whether or not one is *bilingual* if still in the process of acquisition. SL researchers are more likely to require native competence and also to reserve use of the term for the end state. The bilingualism literature, it seems, allows more latitude in both of these factors.

Valdés (2001a) also discusses the issue of degree when she says "the term *bilingual* implies not only the ability to use two languages to some degree in everyday life, but also the skilled superior use of both languages at the level of the educated native speaker" (p. 40). She acknowledges that this is a narrow definition, for it considers the bilingual as someone who can "do everything perfectly in two languages and who can pass undetected among monolingual speakers of each of these two languages" (p. 40). This she refers to as the "mythical bilingual." She argues that there are, in fact, different types of bilinguals and that it is, therefore, more appropriate to think of bilingualism as a continuum with different amounts of knowledge of the L1 and L2 being represented. In this view, the term *bilingualism* can refer to the process of learning as well as the end result, the product of learning.

Some researchers make a distinction between second language learners and bilinguals, as is clear from the title of an article by Kroll and Sunderman (2003): "Cognitive processes in second language learners and bilinguals: the development of lexical and conceptual representations." In this article, the authors refer to "skilled adult bilinguals," presumably the rough equivalent of *advanced language learners*.

Finally, Deuchar and Quay (2000) define bilingual acquisition as "the acquisition of two languages in childhood" (p. 1), although they point to the difficulties involved in this definition given the many situations that can be in place. They point to De Houwer (1995), who talks about *bilingual first language acquisition*, referring to situations when there is regular exposure to two languages within the first month of birth and *bilingual second language acquisition*, referring to situations where exposure begins later than one month after birth but before age two. Wei (2000, pp. 6–7) presents a useful table of various definitions/types of bilinguals.

As can be seen from Table 2.1, the terminology used in bilingualism is far-reaching and overlaps to some extent with second language acquisition. For example, *successive bilingual* describes the scope of second language acquisition research. Importantly, however, it is difficult to pigeonhole all types of bilingualism because there are numerous situations in which individuals use two languages, from growing up with two languages, to achieving bilingual status as adults, to having the second language as virtually their only language (e.g., displaced refugees). Further, there are different combinations of ability. For example, there are those who function well in some contexts (talking with one's family), but who are not literate in that language, versus those who function well academically in both languages. Valdés (2001a, p. 41) illustrates what she calls a bilingual continuum in Figure 2.1. The two letters represent two languages; the size and the case of the font reflect different proficiencies.

Table 2.1 Definitions of bilingualism

achieved bilingual	same as *late bilingual*
additive bilingual	someone whose two languages combine in a complementary and enriching fashion
ambilingual	same as *balanced bilingual*
ascendant bilingual	someone whose ability to function in a second language is developing due to increased use
ascribed bilingual	same as *early bilingual*
asymmetrical bilingual	see *receptive bilingual*
balanced bilingual	someone whose mastery of two languages is roughly equivalent
compound bilingual	someone whose two languages are learned at the same time, often in the same context
consecutive bilingual	same as *successive bilingual*
coordinate bilingual	someone whose two languages are learned in distinctively separate contexts
covert bilingual	someone who conceals his or her knowledge of a given language due to an attitudinal disposition
diagonal bilingual	someone who is bilingual in a nonstandard language or a dialect and an unrelated standard language
dominant bilingual	someone with greater proficiency in one of his or her languages and uses it significantly more than the other language(s)
dormant bilingual	someone who has emigrated to a foreign country for a considerable period of time and has little opportunity to keep the first language actively in use
early bilingual	someone who has acquired two languages early in childhood
equilingual	same as *balanced bilingual*
functional bilingual	someone who can operate in two languages with or without full fluency for the task in hand
horizontal bilingual	someone who is bilingual in two distinct languages which have a similar or equal status
incipient bilingual	someone at the early stages of bilingualism where one language is not fully developed
late bilingual	someone who has become a bilingual later than childhood
maximal bilingual	someone with near-native control of two or more languages
minimal bilingual	someone with only a few words and phrases in a second language
natural bilingual	someone who has not undergone any specific training and who is often not in a position to translate or interpret with facility between two languages
passive bilingual	same as *receptive bilingual*
primary bilingual	same as *natural bilingual*
productive bilingual	someone who not only understands but also speaks and possibly writes in two or more languages
receptive bilingual	someone who understands a second language, in either its spoken or written form, or both, but does not necessarily speak or write it *continued*

Table 2.1—continued

recessive bilingual	someone who begins to feel some difficulty in either understanding or expressing him or herself with ease, due to lack of use
secondary bilingual	someone whose second language has been added to a first language via instruction
semibilingual	same as *receptive bilingual*
semilingual	someone with insufficient knowledge of either language
simultaneous bilingual	someone whose two languages are present from the onset of speech
subordinate bilingual	someone who exhibits interference in his or her language usage by reducing the patterns of the second language to those of the first
subtractive bilingual	someone whose second language is acquired at the expense of the aptitudes already acquired in the first language
successive bilingual	someone whose second language is added at some stage after the first has begun to develop
symmetrical bilingual	same as *balanced bilingual*
vertical bilingual	someone who is bilingual in a standard language and a distinct but related language or dialect

---

	A	Ab Ab Ab Ab Ab aB Ba Ba Ba Ba Ba	B	
Monolingual				Monolingual

Figure 2.1 Bilingual continuum.

Source: Adapted from Valdés, G. (2001). Heritage language students: Profiles and possibilities. In J. K. Peyton, D. A. Ranard, & S. McGinnis (Eds.), *Heritage languages in America: Preserving a national resource*. Washington, DC: Center for Applied Linguistics. Used with permission.

Despite this range, there have been and continue to be misunderstandings regarding the advantages of being bilingual. One can think of advantages in a number of domains. Baker and Prys Jones (1998) discuss communicative advantages, cultural/economic advantages, and cognitive advantages. With regard to the first of these, some are fairly obvious, including talking to immediate and extended family members. One can imagine a situation in which families emigrate to a country where another language is spoken; the children learn the new language and only barely understand the language of the parents, having become fluent in the language of the new country, whereas the parents do not learn the language of the environment. The communication gap widens with the unfortunate result of noncommunication between parents and children. Beyond these instances of family communication, bilinguals, living in a

28

world of regular language monitoring, often show greater sensitivity to the communicative needs of others. Similarly, having experience in more than one culture provides an understanding to cultural differences among peoples. Further, it is obvious that economic advantages abound in all areas of work—from business to sales.

Finally, there are cognitive advantages, including divergent thinking, creative thinking, and metalinguistic awareness. Metalinguistic awareness is the ability to think about (and manipulate) language. In other words, metalinguistic ability allows one to think about language as an object of inquiry rather than as something we use to speak and understand language. Bialystok (2001a, 2001b) has found bilingual children to have superior abilities in judging grammatical accuracy than monolingual children. Bialystok (1987) investigated bilingual and monolingual children's abilities to count words, which reflects knowledge of what a word is and knowledge of the relationship between word and sentence meanings. She found that bilinguals were advantaged over monolinguals in both of these domains: "Bilingual children were most notably advanced when required to separate out individual words from meaningful sentences, focus on only the form of or meaning of a word under highly distracting conditions, and re-assign a familiar name to a different object" (Bialystok, 1987, p. 138). In general, bilinguals tend to have better abilities in those areas that demand selective attention because that is what one has to do when there is competing information (e.g., two languages). Thus, bilinguals' awareness of language comes at an early age. Knowing two languages provides them with the skills to separate form from meaning, which in turn facilitates reading readiness.

One of the phenomena of early language development (see following section on first language acquisition) is babbling. This occurs toward the end of the first year of life. Maneva and Genesee (2002) noted that children exposed to two languages from birth show language-specific patterns in their babbling and, hence, can already differentiate between the two languages before their first birthday. Matching the appropriate language to speakers and/or context is found in children often as young as 2 (e.g., Genesee, Boivin, and Nicoladis, 1996).

A common phenomenon among bilingual speakers is code-switching, which essentially refers to the use of more than one language in the course of a conversation. Sometimes this might happen because of the lack of a concept in one language and its presence in the other; sometimes it might be for humor; and sometimes it might happen simply because of the social context. For example, Grosjean (2001, p. 3) presents the following diagram (Figure 2.2) to illustrate the issue of language mode, which is "the state of activation of the bilingual's languages and language processing mechanisms at a given point in time" (p. 2). The native language (here called the base language) is always totally activated; it is

Figure 2.2 The language mode continuum.

Source: Grosjean, F. (2001). The bilingual's language modes. In J. Nicol (Ed.), *One mind, two languages: Bilingual language processing*. Malden, MA: Blackwell.

the language that controls linguistic activities. The guest language, on the other hand, can be in low to high activation depending on the context. Only in bilingual language mode (the right side of the diagram) is there almost equal activation, and it is in these contexts when code-switching occurs.

Bilingualism, or at least some form of knowledge of more than one language, is so common throughout the world that Cook has proposed that the "normal" propensity is for humans to know more than one language rather than taking monolingualism as the default position. He refers to this as *multicompetence*, which he defines as the "knowledge of two or more languages in one mind" (Cook, 2003, p. 2; cf. Cook, 1991, 1992). If multicompetence is the "norm," then there needs to be a re-evaluation of what it means to be a native speaker of a language. Cook (2005) argued that there are effects of multilingualism on how individuals process their native language, even individuals with a minimal knowledge of a second language. Cook further argues that the monolingual orientation of second language acquisition belies the reality of the context of language learning in much of the world where knowledge of more than one language is the norm.

2.5 First language acquisition

We conclude this chapter with a brief discussion of child language acquisition. We do so because this field has been important in the development of SLA, particularly in the 1960s and 1970s, as SLA was beginning to establish itself as a viable research discipline. As we will see in later chapters, much SLA research parallels developments in child language acquisition research and over the years has drawn on concepts from this research area to understand second language phenomena. Many of the same questions have been and continue to be addressed and some of the same theoretical explanations form the foundation of both fields.

Learning a first language is an amazing accomplishment. It is a learning task perhaps like no other. At the onset of the language-learning odyssey, a child has much to determine about the language that she or he hears.[3] At the end of the journey, every child who is not cognitively impaired has an intact linguistic system that allows him or her to interact with others and to express his or her needs.

To give an example of the complexity that children face, consider the following example:

> How do children figure out the concept of plurality and the language needed to express plurality. Let's think about the input that children receive. A parent might have one potato chip in his/her hand and say "Do you like potato chips?" Or, at another time the parent might say "Do you want a potato chip?" How does the child distinguish between the generic meaning expressed in the first one and the singular meaning of the second? This is further complicated by the fact that in response to the second question, when the child says "yes," he or she probably receives more than one potato chip.

Language is a form of communication, but children communicate long before they have language—at least in the way we normally think of language. Anyone who has lived in a household with an infant is aware of the various means that infants have at their disposal to communicate their needs. The most efficient of these is crying, but there are other more pleasant means as well. Some of these include smiling[4] and cooing. Coos are not precisely like the regular speech sounds of language, but they do suggest that infants are aware of sounds and their potential significance. For example, from approximately four to seven months, infants use these cooing sounds to play with such language-related phenomena as loudness and pitch (Foster-Cohen, 1999).

2.5.1 Babbling

At approximately six months of age, infants turn to more language-like sounds in what is called babbling. Babbling most commonly consists of consonant–vowel sequences (e.g., *bababa*, *dadada*, and later *bada*). It is frequently the case that some of these early babbling sounds are taken to be "words" by parents or caregivers. For example, *mamama* is frequently and perhaps wishfully interpreted as referring to the child's mother, when in fact the sounds may be nothing more than sounds with no meaning attached. The line between babbling and true words is often a fine one.

31

One device that children use fairly early to express meaning is intonation. Even before they have grammatical knowledge, they can use the appropriate stress and intonation contours of their language to distinguish among such things as statements, questions, and commands. A child can, for example, say *dada* with the stress on the second syllable. One can imagine the child doing so with her arms outstretched with the intention of a command, something like *Pick me up, daddy!* Or, one can imagine a child hearing what appears to be a door opening and saying

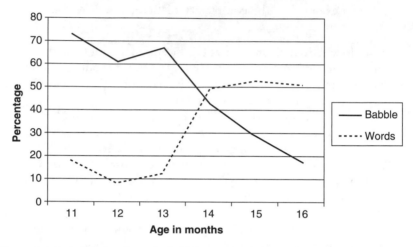

Figure 2.3 Relationship between babbling and words: Child 1 (data from Vihman, 1996, cited in Foster-Cohen, 1999).

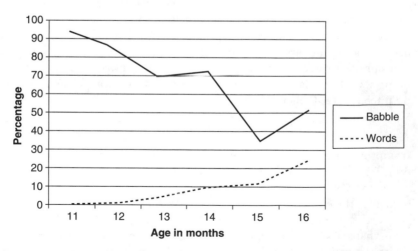

Figure 2.4 Relationship between babbling and words: Child 2 (data from Vihman, 1996, cited in Foster-Cohen, 1999).

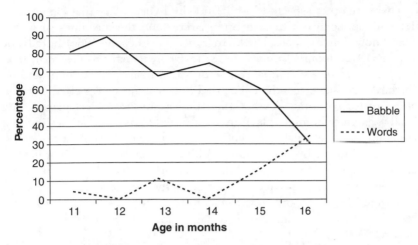

Figure 2.5 Relationship between babbling and words: Child 3 (data from Vihman, 1996, cited in Foster-Cohen, 1999).

dada with rising intonation. This might have the force of a question such as *Is that daddy?*

How does babbling turn into word usage? Does this happen abruptly, or is the change a gradual one? Figures 2.3–2.5 show the relationship between babbling and actual word usage for three children between the ages of 11 months and 16 months.

There are a number of interesting points to be made about these data. First, for all three children, during the five-month period there is a decrease in babbling and an increase in words, although the increase and decrease are not always linear. Second, there appears to be a point where each child "gets" the concept of words as referring to something. Once this occurs (month 14 for Child 1 and Child 2; month 15 for Child 3), there seems to be a drop-off in the amount of babbling that occurs.

2.5.2 Words

What function do words have for children? Words in early child language fulfill a number of functions. They can refer to objects, such as *ba* for bottle; they can indicate a wide range of grammatical functions, such as commands (*I want my bottle*); they can serve social functions, such as *bye* and *hi*. Children have to learn that words can serve each of these functions.

Another point to bear in mind is that words in an adult's language do not always correspond to words in a child's language. "Words" for children might reflect more than one word in the adult language. For example, *allgone* is typically produced at the one-word stage in child language, even though it comprises two words in the adult language.

There are other aspects of adult and child vocabulary that are not in a 1:1 correspondence. Children often overextend the meanings of words they know. For example, Hoek, Ingram, and Gibson (1986) noted one child's (19–20 months) use of the word *bunny* to refer to *doll, hen, shoe, car, picture of people, giraffe, cow, bear, chair, lamp, puzzle, train,* and so forth. At the same age, the child used *bear* to refer to a stuffed toy lion and a picture of a pig. At the same time, a physical object placed on a head (e.g., a book) might playfully be referred to as a *hat*, suggesting that the child can distinguish between objects and their functional uses.

In addition to overextension, children often underuse words. For example, one could imagine a child associating the word *tree* (in the dead of winter) with a leafless tree, but not using the word *tree* to refer to a tree with green leaves. In other words, children often use words with more restricted meanings than the word has in adult usage. This is known as underextension.

2.5.3 Sounds and pronunciation

In these early stages, it is clear that the pronunciation of children's words is not exactly identical to that of adult speech. Among the earliest tasks that children face is figuring out the nature of the sounds they are hearing. Some sounds are distinguished quite early (e.g., the difference between the consonants in [ta] and [da]); others are of course learned later (*wabbit* for *rabbit*). Even when children start using words that more or less resemble adult words, at least in meaning, there are pronunciation differences. Common examples are substitutions, as in the *rabbit* example just given; deletion of syllables, as in *dedo* for *potato* (cf. Ingram, 1986); deletion of sounds, such as *tein* for *train* (cf. Ingram, 1986); and simplification, such as *fis* for *fish*. It is not always clear how to explain these phenomena. Are they a matter of motor control or of perception? The answer is: it depends. Foster-Cohen (1999) provided an interesting example from Smith (1973), whose child couldn't say the word *puddle*. He pronounced it as *puggle*. One could argue that this is a matter of pronunciation abilities, but a further look at this child's pronunciation showed that he used *puddle* for *puzzle*. Hence, this child was making a regular substitution (*g* for *d* and *d* for *z*) but was perfectly capable of making the appropriate sounds, just not in the appropriate place. We also know that children often get angry when adults "imitate" them using their own (children's) pronunciation. For example, when an adult says, "Oh, you want ice cweam [ice cream]," a child is likely to get angry and reply, "No, I want ice cweam, not ice cweam." This shows that children clearly can perceive a difference, although they do not make the difference in their own speech.

2.5.4 Syntax

Earlier we talked about babbling and the move from babbling to words. This initial stage is often referred to as the one-word stage because there is no word combination as of yet. The fact that children at this stage may use words like *allgone* does not contradict this, for this word is likely to be only one word in the child's lexicon. After several months in the one-word stage, children start to combine words (usually at around two years of age). They might say something like *Mommy cry*. What is typical of this phase is that the words that are used are content words (i.e., nouns and verbs). Function words, such as articles, prepositions, and grammatical endings, are notably lacking. As children move beyond the two-word stage, speech becomes telegraphic. The utterances used are much like the ones commonly used when sending a telegram—only the bare minimum so as not to have to "pay" for any more than is necessary. For example, children's utterances might include *Aaron go home, Seth play toy, Ethan no go*. As children's utterances become longer, it is appropriate for researchers to have a measure to determine complexity. Mean length of utterance (MLU) is the standard measure used; it averages number of morphemes over 100 utterances and is a more realistic measure of development than is chronological age.

There are some typical stages that are found in further syntactic development. Lightbown and Spada (2006, pp. 6–7) provide the examples of the acquisition of question formation listed in Table 2.2. Important is the fact that there is a predictable development for all children.

When we return to a discussion of second language acquisition in later chapters, we will see that adults learning a second language also have

Table 2.2 Question formation

Stage 1. Intonation. *Cookie? Mommy book?*
Stage 2. Intonation with sentence complexity. *Yes/no* questions. Children use declarative sentence order with rising intonation: *You like this? I have some?* *Wh-* questions. Question word with declarative order: *Why you catch it?*
Stage 3. Beginning of inversion. *Wh-* questions maintain declarative order. *Can I go? Is that mine? Why you don't have one?*
Stage 4. Inversion. *Do you like ice cream? Where I can draw them?* Use of *do* in *yes/no* questions (but not in *wh-* questions).
Stage 5. Inversion with *wh-* questions. When negation needs to be included, the declarative form is maintained. *Why can he go out? Why he can't go out?*
Stage 6. Overgeneralization of inversion. *I don't know why can't he go out.*

predictable sequences in terms of the acquisition of certain structures. However, the situation with second language learners is more complex because factors involving the native language may assume importance.

2.5.5 Morphology

Much of the impetus for initial work in second language acquisition stemmed from work by Brown (1973) and his astute observation that there was a predictable order of acquisition of certain inflectional morphemes in English. The three children he studied, Adam, Sarah, and Eve, learned English morphemes in roughly the same order despite the fact that this did not always occur at precisely the same age. Brown's research revealed that the emergence of grammatical morphemes was consistent across these children and that this emergence could be related to their overall development, measured in MLUs. Table 2.3 shows the order of acquisition for these three children. What is interesting is that the order does not reflect the frequency of these morphemes in the speech of the children's parents.

There may be a number of reasons as to why this order versus some other order exists. Among them are such notions as salience (e.g., the morpheme -ing, as in *walking*, can receive stress and is salient, whereas the morpheme -ed, as in *walked*, cannot), syllabicity (are they syllables?), and a lack of exception (the *possessive* ending -'s is used without exception, whereas the past tense -ed has exceptions in irregular verbs. We return to the order of morpheme acquisition in chapter 5 (section 5.3) in our discussion of second language acquisition.

Another well-known study comes from Berko (1958), who devised a famous "wug" test to determine knowledge of grammatical morphemes. In this test children were shown a picture of a novel animal and were told

Table 2.3 Mean order of acquisition of morphemes

1. Present progressive (-ing)
2/3. *in, on*
4. plural (-s)
5. Past irregular
6. Possessive (-'s)
7. Uncontractible copula (*is, am, are*)
8. Articles (*a, the*)
9. Past regular (-ed)
10. Third person regular (-s)
11. Third person irregular

Source: Reprinted and adapted by permission of the publisher from *A First Language: the early stages* by Roger Brown, p. 274, Cambridge, Mass: Harvard University Press, Copyright © 1973 by the President and Fellows of Harvard College.

that this was a *wug*. Then they were shown a picture of two of the animals and were led into saying *there are two xxx*. Even preschool children were able to correctly form plurals which showed that they had understood the concept of plurality and the grammatical form to express plurality and were able to apply this knowledge to new contexts. At times, there is regularization of irregular forms (called overgeneralization) and children might say something like *mices*, not recognizing that the word *mice* is already plural. At a later stage, children learn that there are exceptions to regular patterns.

One final point to make is that there are often prerequisites for learning certain forms and that there are often interrelationships among forms. An example can be seen in the acquisition of negatives and questions and the necessary prerequisite of knowledge of auxiliaries (e.g., forms of the verb *to be*, and forms of the verb *to do*). A very early stage involves only rising intonation, but once children are able to put words together, utterances with a *wh-* word (e.g., *where*, *what*, *who*) appear at the beginning of an utterance, such as *Where Ann pencil?*, *Who that?*, *What book name?* (examples from Foster-Cohen, 1999). As children become more sophisticated, other components begin to appear, such as modals, but there are examples without inversion, such as *What he can ride in?* (example from Klima and Bellugi, 1966). At a later stage, children begin to use auxiliaries and also correct order. As Foster-Cohen (1999) points out, as these question forms are developing for *wh-* questions, there is a similar development for *yes/no* questions. Akmajian, Demers, Farmer, and Harnish (1995), referring to work by Foss and Hakes (1978) and Clark and Clark (1977), also note that negatives show a similar pattern with single words such as *no* appearing first, followed by a negative word at the beginning of an utterance, such as *no eat*, followed by negative modals or negative words in sentence internal position, such as, *He not big, I can't do that*. As with questions, this is followed by a wider range of auxiliaries. Thus, the emergence of a number of different forms and structures is noted.

There are certain conclusions that we can draw about children learning their first language. Throughout this book, we will return to these, as most are applicable in a second language context as well.

- Children go through the same developmental stages, although not necessarily at the same rate.
- Children create systematicity in their language and develop rules to govern their language knowledge and language use.
- The rules that are developed do not necessarily correspond to the rules of the adult language.
- There is overgeneralization of grammatical morphemes.
- There are processing constraints that govern acquisition and use.

- Correction does not always work.
- Language acquisition is not determined by intelligence.

2.6 Conclusion

This chapter has focused on different types of acquisition. They are related to the main topic of this book, second language acquisition, in different ways. Child language acquisition has had the most profound influence in terms of the development of the field, but in more recent years, ties have been strengthened between heritage language learning and second language acquisition and between bilingual/multilingual research and second language acquisition. We have also presented some preliminary discussion of theoretical concepts that have been important in the development of the field of SLA. In the remainder of this book, we focus almost exclusively on second language acquisition and in the next chapter we deal with the important concepts of data elicitation and data analysis.

Suggestions for additional reading

Foundations of Bilingual Education and Bilingualism, 4th ed. Colin Baker. Multilingual Matters (2006).

The Handbook of Bilingualism. Taj Bhatia and W. Ritchie (Eds.). Blackwell Publishers (2006).

Trends in Bilingual Acquisition. Jasone Cenoz and Fred Genesee (Eds.). John Benjamins (2001).

Cross-Linguistic Influence in Third Language Acquisition: Psycholinguistic Perspectives. by Jasone Cenoz, Britta Hufeisen, and Ulrike Jessner (Eds.). Multilingual Matters (2001).

English in Europe: The Acquisition of a Third Language. Jasone Cenoz and Ulrike Jessner (Eds.). Multilingual Matters (2000).

Understanding Child Language Acquisition. Paul Fletcher. Hodder Arnold (2005).

An Introduction to Child Language Development. Susan Foster-Cohen. Longman (1999).

Language Acquisition: The Growth of Grammar. Maria Teresa Guasti. Bradford Books MIT Press (2004).

The Bilingual Edge. Kendall King and Alison Mackey. Harper Collins (2007).

Handbook of Bilingualism: Psycholinguistic Approaches. Judith F. Kroll and Annette M. B. De Groot (Eds.). Oxford University Press (2005).

Child Language: Acquisition and Growth. Barbara Lust. Cambridge Textbooks in Linguistics (2006).

First Language Acquisition: The Essential Readings (Linguistics: the Essential Readings). Barbara Lust and Claire Foley (Eds.). Blackwell (2004).

Childhood Bilingualism: Research on Infancy Through School Age (Child Language and Child Development). Peggy D. McCardle and Erika Hoff (Eds.). Multilingual Matters (2006).

Multiple Voices: An Introduction to Bilingualism. Carol Myers-Scotton. Blackwell (2006).
How Children Learn Language. William O'Grady. Cambridge University Press (2005).
The Bilingual Reader. Li Wei (Ed.). Routledge (2000). Revised edition 2006.

Points for discussion

1   If a researcher doesn't get enough information from his or her subjects before carrying out a study, heritage language learners may be included in the sample without the researcher's knowledge. How could this oversight affect the results of the study? Why would it be important for a researcher to control for this variable?

2   Using Table 2.1, decide which type of bilingual each of the following individuals would be (more than one term may be appropriate).

    a   A native speaker of Vietnamese who has been living in the United States for 35 years; speaks English with his American family, friends, and colleagues; and has little or no opportunity to use Vietnamese.

    b   A four-year-old child who speaks English with his Canadian father and Japanese with his Japanese mother and lives in Canada.

    c   An Italian university student who speaks Sicilian at home and with friends, but watches television and films in Standard Italian and uses the standard at the university.

    d   A Ph.D. student who can read Latin texts for her research but doesn't actually speak Latin.

    e   You.

3   Consider a situation in which a native speaker of English is in a restaurant in an English-speaking country speaking to some friends in Italian. At a certain point the English speaker asks the waitress (a monolingual English speaker), "Could we have another carafe of *vino?*" What has happened here?

4   What are the stages of child first language acquisition? Give some examples of each stage.

5   Give evidence that children's receptive skills precede their productive skills in first language acquisition.

6   Which stage in the acquisition order of question formation on Table 2.2 do the following child question forms represent?

    a   "Where we are going? Do you remember last time?"

    b   "Daddy car?"

    c   "I don't know where is the doggie."

    d   "I have some?"

7   What can you hypothesize about a child's morphological acquisition based on the following statements?

a   "Grandma, I seed a lion at the zoo!"
b   "Gigi run fast!"
c   "Two cookie."

8   For the instructor: Prepare a tape of a language that the students do not know and which is related to a second language that the students may have studied (for example, Portuguese in an English-speaking environment, because many will have studied Spanish). Play the tape once or twice. Ask students how much they understand. Then give them the written version of what they heard. Again, ask what they understood. Then ask what information they used to try to understand this L3—for example, their L1, their L2 (Spanish), real-world knowledge. (We thank Amy Thompson for this suggestion.)

In this and subsequent chapters, the reader is directed to relevant data analysis problems in Gass, Sorace, and Selinker (1999), henceforth (GSS). For this chapter, the relevant problems are 3.5 and 3.6.

3

SECOND AND FOREIGN
LANGUAGE DATA

3.1 Data analysis

A central part of understanding the field of SLA is gained by hands-on experience in data analysis and data interpretation. In this chapter, we first present data from second language learners to see how the data can be analyzed and interpreted. We then turn to a discussion of different kinds of data and ways of elicitation.

A given about SLA data is that there is often ambiguity with regard to interpretation. Thus, it is frequently the case that there are no "correct" answers in analyzing interlanguage data, as there might be in doing arithmetic or calculus problems. At best, there are better and worse answers, bolstered by better and worse argumentation. Importantly, the function of good argumentation is to lessen the ambiguity of analysis.

In this section we present several data sets and provide a map through interlanguage analysis in a step-by-step fashion. We hope that this will lead to the reader's being able to understand and possibly challenge the logic and argumentation of each step.[1]

3.1.1 Data set I: plurals

The data presented here were collected from three adult native speakers of Cairene Arabic, intermediate to advanced speakers of English, shortly after they had arrived in the United States. The data source was compositions and conversations. In 3-1 to 3-19 are the utterances produced by these learners:

(3-1)   There are also **two deserts**.
(3-2)   I bought **a couple of towel**.
(3-3)   So, when I like to park my car, there is no place to put it, and **how many ticket** I took.
(3-4)   There is **many kind of way** you make baklawa.

41

(3-5) **The streets** run from east to west, **the avenues** from north to south.

(3-6) I go to university **four days** a week.

(3-7) Just **a few month** he will finish from his studies.

(3-8) Egypt shares **its boundaries** with the Mediterranean.

(3-9) There is **a lot of mosquito**.

(3-10) **Many people** have **ideas** about Jeddah and other cities located in Saudi Arabia.

(3-11) When he complete **nine month** . . .

(3-12) He can spend **100 years** here in America.

(3-13) There are about **one and half-million inhabitant** in Jeddah.

(3-14) **How many month or years** have been in his mind?

(3-15) There are **many tents—and goats** running around.

(3-16) There are **two mountains**.

(3-17) **How many hour?**

(3-18) There are more than **200,000 telephone lines**.

(3-19) Every country had **three or four kind of bread**.

We want the reader to describe the IL patterns of plural usage in these utterances. The first thing to focus on is the phrases set in **boldface** type. Categorize them according to English-like and non-English-like patterns of plural usage, as in Table 3.1. Decide if the choice is clear or not, remembering that data are often ambiguous.

Thus, the first step is to make a list of the sentences according to the criteria of English-like or non-English-like.

In sentences 3-1, 3-5, 3-6, 3-8, 3-10, 3-12, 3-15, 3-16, and 3-18 the analysis of the phrase in boldface is clear: these sentences are English-like because they have an *s* plural marker on the noun.

In sentences 3-2, 3-3, 3-4, 3-7, 3-9, 3-11, 3-13, 3-17, and 3-19 the analysis is also clear, but unlike the previous sentences, they are non-English-like because there is no plural marker on the noun.

The analysis of sentence 3-14 is not clear; the phrase in boldface contains both a plural and a singular noun, so there is a choice in terms of analysis. What one notices is that the form *month*, as a conceptual plural, is non-English-like, whereas the form *years* is English-like. That is, there is interlanguage variation within the same sentence. One analytical option is

Table 3.1 Sample categorization of plurals in Arabic–English IL

English-like	Non-English-like
3-1. two deserts	3-2. a couple of towel

to say that when any element of the plural phrase is non-English-like, then the whole phrase is non-English like. Another option is to create a third category, "ambiguous." We prefer this latter solution because placing target language categories on interlanguage data is potentially misleading in terms of creating general interlanguage rules for interlanguage data (a point we return to later in this chapter). In this case, we see that there is interlanguage variation in the same sentence; this presents a case that is fundamentally different from the others in this data set.

So, at this stage, the chart should either look like the body of Table 3.2 or Table 3.3.

What are some possible interlanguage generalizations that might account for this particular pattern of IL plural marking? First, we determine to what extent there is regularity in the data. We can easily see that

Table 3.2 Possible categorization of plurals in Arabic–English IL

English-like	Non-English-like
3-1. two deserts	3-2. a couple of towel
3-5. the streets, the avenues	3-3. how many ticket
3-6. four days	3-4. many kind of way
3-8. its boundaries	3-7. a few month
3-10. many people, ideas	3-9. a lot of mosquito
3-12. 100 years	3-11. nine month
3-15. many tents—and goats	3-13. one and half-million inhabitant
3-16. two mountains	3-14. how many month or years
3-18. 200,000 telephone lines	3-17. how many hour
	3-19. three or four kind of bread

Table 3.3 Possible categorization of plurals in Arabic–English IL

English-like	Non-English-like	Ambiguous
3-1. two deserts	3-2. a couple of towel	3-14. how many month or years
3-5. the streets, the avenues	3-3. how many ticket	
3-6. four days	3-4. many kind of way	
3-8. its boundaries	3-7. a few month	
3-10. many people, ideas	3-9. a lot of mosquito	
3-12. 100 years	3-11. nine month	
3-15. many tents—and goats	3-13. one and half-million inhabitant	
3-16. two mountains	3-17. how many hour	
3-18. 200,000 telephone lines	3-19. three or four kind of bread	

there are frequent quantifying phrases (*kind of, how many*) in the non-English-like data. One initial hypothesis we might set up is:

> Whenever there is a quantifying phrase or a nonnumerical quantifying word before the noun, there is no overt marking on the plural of that noun.

What we wish to do now is test the suggested generalization. In so doing, there are three possible answers one can arrive at: the sentence in question *supports* the hypothesis, *does not support* it, or *is irrelevant* to the hypothesis. Our analysis is given in Table 3.4.

Sentence 3-13 can be analyzed in one of two ways. Is it a numeral or is it a phrase? In other words, does it represent an actual number or is it a phrase denoting "a large number"? Depending on the conclusion one comes to, it will either support this hypothesis or it is irrelevant to it. One also notes that it is written differently from the TL form (*one and a half-million*). One must ask if this will affect the analysis. We think not, but it does point out the ambiguity possibly generated by combining composition and conversation data. Sentence 3-14 is ambiguous, as pointed out earlier.

Therefore, the hypothesis stated earlier appears to be supported by these data. However, we have still not accounted for all of the data. We now have an IL hypothesis that is something like the following:

> Mark all plural nouns with /s/ except those that are preceded by a quantifying phrase or a nonnumerical quantifying word.

There are still possible exceptions to deal with:

1   *Sentence 3-11*: According to our rule, this should be *months*. However, one could account for this apparent exception by the pronunciation difficulty involved, notably the *nths* cluster at the end of the word. In fact, many native speakers of English simplify this cluster by

Table 3.4 Data support for Arabic–English IL pluralization hypothesis

Support	Does not support	Irrelevant
3-2. *a couple* of towel		
3-3. *how many* ticket		
3-4. *many kind* of way		
3-7. *a few* month		
3-9. *a lot of* mosquito		
3-13. *one and half-million* inhabitant		3-13. Is it a phrase?
3-17. *how many* hour		
3-19. *three or four kind* of bread		

pronouncing the end of the word *ns* rather than *nths*. Thus, simplification is common; the Arabic speakers simplify in one way, native speakers simplify in another.

2 *Sentence 3-14*: We noted that this was a problem in initial categorization. Might it be the case that these learners have created an interlanguage-particular rule that relates plural marking to type of conjunction? We do not know, of course, because one example of each cannot safely lead us to any general conclusion.

3 *Sentence 3-10*: This is possibly ambiguous. In one sense, it could be in our "Irrelevant" category in Table 3.4, in that we could view this as an unanalyzed chunk. On the other hand, it could also be listed under "Support" if we believe that the learner categorizes it as a nonplural form. Finally, it could be in our "Does not support" category if we believe the learner conceptualizes it as a plural and has appropriately given the plural modifier *many*.

Knowing how to deal with apparent exceptions is just as important as knowing how to deal with the bulk of the data. Exceptions can be real and, if in sufficient quantity, may suggest an incorrect initial hypothesis, or they may be reflections of another rule/constraint at play. In the examples presented here, we have attempted to explain away the apparent exception, and, in the case of one of them (*nine month*) have brought in additional data to show the reasonableness of using phonological simplification as an explanation.

Now we wish to go over what might be one of the most important questions of all. When you have reached the best possible analysis with the limited data at your disposal, and when there is still some uncertainty, what *further data* would you like from these learners to test your hypotheses? One type has already been mentioned with regard to sentence 3-13: more data that clearly differentiate oral from written production, because the interlanguage rules generated might vary along this dimension. Another has also been hinted at. If one is trying to understand an individual's IL generalization, then one must only consider that individual's utterances. On the other hand, if one is using pooled data, as we have in this case, then it is to be expected that counterexamples will show up. Thus, for some purposes, we need to gather data where plural phrases are marked individual by individual, as SLA is characterized by sometimes rather large individual differences.

Additional data are needed to determine if the alternative explanations given for the apparent exceptions are correct or not; that is, there is a need to elicit (a) other words ending with difficult consonant clusters and (b) noun phrases with *or*. Yet another type of data we may wish to gather here might involve the various contexts in which these sentences were produced, which might bear on these IL performance data.

We now turn to a data analysis problem that deals with *-ing* marking on English verbs.

3.1.2 *Data set II: verb + -ing* markers

The following utterances were produced by a native speaker of Arabic at the early stages of learning English. At the time of data collection, the learner had had no formal English instruction. All of the sentences were gathered from spontaneous utterances.[2] In parentheses we have provided the most likely intention (given the context) of these utterances when the intention is not obvious from the forms produced.

(3-20) He's sleeping.
(3-21) She's sleeping.
(3-22) It's raining.
(3-23) He's eating.
(3-24) Hani's sleeping.
(3-25) The dog eating. (The dog is eating.)
(3-26) Hani watch TV. (Hani is watching TV.)
(3-27) Watch TV. (He is watching TV.)
(3-28) Read the paper. (He is reading the paper.)
(3-29) Drink the coffee. (He is drinking coffee.)

We have said that the learner is producing what in English would be represented by Verb + *-ing* structures. We have also noted that, in each case, her intention involves progressive meaning. Thus, an initial observation is that she has two forms she can use to express progressive meaning (*eating* versus *watch*).

One hypothesis we can make about these data is that the learner is using an IL rule that restricts the occurrence of Verb + *-ing* to sentence-final position. This is true 100 percent of the time, but such a purely structural hypothesis may ignore important semantic facts. A more complex hypothesis that takes into consideration semantic aspects could be the following:

> Whenever there is an intended progressive, put the Verb + *-ing* form in final position.

This hypothesis can be easily rejected by sentences 3-26 to 3-29. We can attempt a second hypothesis about the use of the simple form of the verb.

> Whenever there is no overt subject, the simple form of the verb is used.

46

This hypothesis is supported by sentences 3-27 to 3-29, but it, too, seems to tell us little about the use (or nonuse) of Verb + -ing.

We now turn to the distinction between transitive versus intransitive sentences;[3] that is, those sentences that have a verb and an overt object (*read the paper*) and those that do not (*sleep*). A third hypothesis can be formulated as follows:

> The Verb + -ing form is used in sentences without overt objects.
> The simple form of the verb is used with transitive verbs with overt objects.

In this light, we notice that sentences 3-20 to 3-24 consist of a subject plus an intransitive verb; when this occurs, we see a form of the verb *to be* plus the Verb + -ing form. In sentence 3-25, however, we see a subject that consists of a determiner (article) plus a noun (*the dog*); in this case, only the Verb + -ing element appears. This sentence is important for the ultimate explanation. In sentences 3-26 to 3-29 there is a transitive verb with an object, and the simple form of the verb is used. Here we see the full force of the principle that the acquisition of a grammatical form is variable, with the Verb + -ing form occurring in intransitive sentences and the simple form in transitive sentences.

How can we account for sentence 3-25? One explanation relates to processing limitations. This learner is able to deal with no more than two- and three-word utterances. It is for this reason that sentence 3-25 is central, since if it were simply a matter of object presence/absence, we would have no way of explaining the lack of the verb *to be*. The presence of *the* and *dog* sufficiently complexifies the sentence to disallow any further elements.

There is yet another possible explanation having to do with this learner's analysis of the progressive. It is likely that the units *he's*, *she's*, *it's*, and *Hani's* (her husband) are stored as single lexical items. If these are stored as single words, then sentence 3-25 is not a problem because, for this learner, the *s* is not part of the verb form.

3.1.3 Data set III: prepositions

The last data analysis set we present concerns prepositions, which are known to be among the most difficult items to master in a second language. Examples of Arabic–English sentences with prepositions follow:

(3-30) You can find it **from Morocco til Saudi Arabia**.
(3-31) There is many kind **of way** you make baklawa.
(3-32) It's some kind **of different**.
(3-33) I don't like to buy a car **from Ann Arbor**.

(3-34) **Since long time**, I'm buying B. F. Goodrich.
(3-35) He finished his studies **before one month**.
(3-36) He will finish **from his studies**.
(3-37) They are many kinds of reptiles which live **at this planet**.
(3-38) I never help my mom **in the housework**.
(3-39) Egypt shares its boundaries with the Mediterranean Sea **on the north, the Red Sea from the east**.

The intended English meanings for the words in boldface are given as follows, with number referring back to the original sentences.

(3-30) from Morocco to Saudi Arabia
(3-31) There are many ways . . .
(3-32) It is quite different . . .
(3-33) in Ann Arbor
(3-34) for a long time
(3-35) a month ago
(3-36) He will finish his studies.
(3-37) on this planet
(3-38) with the housework
(3-39) on the north, the Red Sea on the east

One noticeable factor in the use of prepositions by these learners is the different semantic areas involved: geographical versus temporal. We may wish to put forth the hypothesis that in this interlanguage there is a rule that states:[4]

Use *from* for geographical locations.

This simple IL rule will work for most of the data, but not all. In sentence 3-39 we would predict *from the north* and in sentence 3-36 there is no explanation for *from his studies*. If this rule were borne out through the collection of further data, sentence 3-30 would provide a case of target language behavior by chance (Corder, 1981).

The next set of data from these learners involves phrases in which the TL requires a preposition.

(3-40) We used to pronounce everything **British English**.
(3-41) It doesn't give me problems **future**.
(3-42) He's working **his thesis** now.
(3-43) If I come early, I will register **fall**.
(3-44) The people are outside **this time**.
(3-45) About 20 kilometer out **Jeddah**.
(3-46) I'll wait **you**.

We might describe these learners' behavior as involving a simplification strategy, although in this case that may be a dangerous generalization, for as Corder (1983, 1992) pointed out, learners cannot *simplify* what they do not know. However, learners can clearly realize that they do not know how to use prepositions appropriately in English and adopt the following strategy:

Use no preposition except in specifically constrained instances.

A constrained instance was seen in the first set of sentences in which *from* was used in geographical phrases.

Now compare the third set of sentences gathered from the same learners with those of the first and second sets.

(3-47) Since I came **to the United States**.
(3-48) I have lived **in downtown Ann Arbor**.
(3-49) There are 25 counties **in Egypt**.
(3-50) You might think you are **in Dallas**.
(3-51) I have noticed there are many **of them**.
(3-52) They are genius **in this area**.
(3-53) I will go speak nice **to him**.
(3-54) Beginning **from 1:30 a.m. until 2:00 a.m**.

The third set of data presents correct TL forms, although given what we know about covert errors,[5] some of them at least may only appear to be target-like.

The place expressions *in Egypt*, *in Dallas*, and *in this area* clearly negate the simple hypothesis stated earlier of using *from* for geographical locations. But we should be aware of the possibility that the learners may make a distinction between direction and location. Another possibility is that learners may produce more TL-like preposition usage when other than "obligatory" prepositions are required in the TL. In other words, when there are options, learners are more likely to get things right from sheer luck, even if they do not understand the full range of the language they hear (input). This possibility appears to hold for these data despite the fact that the various options may result in a meaning change. One question that arises with all data collection is the appropriateness of ascribing meaning to learner utterances. It is our point of view that, with most learners, this is best done through the NL, although clearly this is not always possible.

3.2 What data analysis does not reveal

In the previous section, we provided hands-on experience in data analysis and its interpretation. Our goal was to show that good argumentation can lessen the ambiguity inherent in most learner-language data. The analyses leave us with questions that can lead to further study with the collection of new data. The point here is that data should always be collected for a particular purpose, which often arises from the unanswered questions of previous analyses. In this section, we again produce a step-by-step discussion that could lead to further empirical research. Thus, research is often produced by the question, "What else is there that we want to know?" In what follows, we consider some of the data from the previous section, focusing on questions that cannot be answered from the data alone.

Data set I in section 3.1 represents a mixture of data sources. An initial problem is that the data source consists of compositions and conversations. For a thorough and meaningful analysis, one would want to know which sentences in that list are derived from compositions and which from conversations. Thus, if one is interested in finding out more about plurals in Arabic–English learner-language, it would be important to collect new data that separated these data sources from one another. This is particularly important when considering sentence 3-14, where the explanation may be one of pronunciation. If that particular sentence came from a composition, we could essentially eliminate that explanation. Combining oral and written data in one data set is usually not based on sound principles other than the pedagogical purpose of the previous section.

Another difficulty with data set I is that the data are pooled across subjects, and thus the data of individual learners are not isolated. This has led to much discussion over the years in second language acquisition research, because pooled data are regularly presented in the literature. As learning is an individual task, one can question the reasonableness of not being able to identify individual learners. There are certainly good arguments for generalization beyond one individual, but if a research goal includes being able to detail individual interlanguage development (or nondevelopment), then one must either code for such individual differences or create a new study that focuses on such variation.

There are other factors of interest regarding particular sentences that one may wish to sort out through further data collection. As an example, consider sentence 3-55, presented as 3-14 in the previous section:

(3-55) **How many month or years** have been in his mind?

The interlanguage phrase *month or years* is puzzling. How could it possibly be that after the quantifier *How many* one gets the plural without the *s* in *month* but with the *s* in *years* in the same phrase? The discussion in section 3.1 deals only with the fact that the researcher has the choice of analyzing that phrase as non-English-like or creating a third category called "ambiguous;" that is, where the phrase is both English-like and non-English-like.

We stated that we prefer the second solution because it does not place target language categories on second language data. This has been called the "comparative fallacy" (Bley-Vroman, 1983). A goal of SLA research is to discover the system underlying a second language. Comparing second language forms to TL standards may lead analysts down a path that precludes an understanding of the systematic nature of the learner system in question.[6] Sentence 3-14 presents a case that is indeed fundamentally different from the other sentences in data set I. Before speculating further, a researcher might like to see new data gathered concerning the specific question of whether, in *or* phrases in Arabic–English, plurality is expressed as in this example, with a mixture of overtly marked plurals and non-marked plurals, or whether one is dealing with a one-time anomaly that can be safely ignored.

In the previous discussion of Verb + *-ing* markers (data set II), it was pointed out that the Arabic–English speaker appears to have "two forms she can use to express progressive meaning (*eating* versus *watch*)." This is one area where an anomaly exists. We can attempt to resolve the anomaly with further data collection, possibly involving types of verbs. Does transitivity play a role in expressing progressive meaning? Does the existence of overt subjects play a role? Could it be that the *s* representing the verb *to be* is stored with the subject as one unit? Knowledge of the literature can be very helpful here, for there are attested cases where what are considered two words in the target language are stored as one word in the interlanguage. For example, Harley and Swain (1984) note that in French the first person singular of the verb *avoir* (to have) which should be *j'ai* is often expressed in learner French as *j'ai as* (I have have) as in *j'ai as oublié* (I have forgotten), which is the combination of *j'ai* (je + ai [I + first person singular of *avoir*]) + *as* ([second person singular form of *avoir*]). In other words, learners have probably not decomposed *j'ai* as being composed of "I" plus "have." Each of these examples lends itself to further data collection to test a particular hypothesis.

Another point mentioned in section 3.1 concerns the various contexts in which the interlanguage sentences were produced and whether interlanguage forms may be used only in particular contexts. That is, are certain forms produced in some contexts, but not in others?

Finally, from the preceding analyses, one could raise the question of how to formulate descriptive interlanguage rules or principles and whether, with more relevant data, additional rules would be discovered. In general then, when we analyze data, either our own or data from the published literature, we want to always ask this question: What else do we want to find out that is not shown by the data presented? We now turn to ways in which data can be collected.

3.3 Data collection

In recent years there has been increased attention paid to data collection and analysis. This is the case since there has been increasing awareness that it is most difficult to perfectly align the various elicitation tasks that are available and the various ways one can analyze data with the underlying constructs one might wish to study. In terms of data analysis, R. Ellis and Barkhuizen (2005) devote most of an entire book to the various ways one can proceed, including a chapter on data collection. Gass and Mackey (2007) is devoted solely to methods of data collection. In addition, numerous books have appeared that deal with specific data-collection methods (e.g., Dörnyei, 2003, on questionnaires; Duff, 2008, on case studies; Gass and Mackey, 2000, on stimulated recall; Markee, 2000, on conversation analysis).

There are numerous ways of eliciting second language data. As we mentioned earlier, many, but not all, have their origins in other disciplines. This section is not intended to be inclusive. Rather, it is suggestive of the kinds of data and data-elicitation methods that have been used in second language studies.

Second language research findings are often dependent on the way data are collected, that is, on the elicitation technique used. As we shall see in this book, there are many ways of approaching the study of second language acquisition. Each approach often has typical ways of gathering data. While there are typical data-collection approaches, there is flexibility so that there is crossover between approaches and data-elicitation techniques. As Gass and Mackey (2007) note, "The choice of one method over another is highly dependent on the research question being asked" (p. 4).

As mentioned above, many second language research methods have their origins in research methods from other disciplines, notably linguistics, child language acquisition, sociology, and psychology. What we discuss in this section is only a small number of data-collection techniques.

There are a number of ways that one can categorize second language data. First, one can think about the context in which data are collected (e.g., classroom data versus naturalistic data). Second, one can think about two types of performance: (a) actual speech samples and (b) reactions to target-language data. The first are actual learner production data, represented by the data sets in section 3.1.1 and 3.1.2 of this chapter. The second can be thought of as reactions to some target language stimulus (e.g., learners might sit at a computer and respond whether a series of letters on the computer screen represent a word in the second language). Third, there are "thinking" data, that is, what learners say about their learning.

Within these categories, there is another dimension that is relevant, and that is the distinction between longitudinal data and cross-sectional data.

With regard to longitudinal studies, there are four characteristics to be discussed: (a) number of subjects and time frame of data collection, (b) amount of descriptive detail, (c) type of data, and (d) type of analysis.

Longitudinal studies are generally case studies (although not always, as we will see later), with data being collected from a single participant (or at least a small number of subjects) over a prolonged period of time. The frequency of data collection varies. However, samples of a learner's language are likely to be collected weekly, biweekly, or monthly.

Typical of longitudinal studies is the detail provided on a learner's speech, on the setting in which the speech event occurred, and on other details relevant to the analysis of the data (e.g., other conversational participants and their relationship with the participant). The following is a description of one longitudinal study, reported in Lardiere (1998, pp. 12–13) (see also Lardiere, 2007, pp. 21–31 for more detail and specific examples of her description of her background).

> The subject of this investigation, Patty, was born in Indonesia; however, her parents were Chinese and spoke two Chinese languages (Hokkien and Mandarin) both at home and within the local Chinese community. Patty acquired Indonesian (and literacy in Indonesian) in school, but continued using Chinese as her primary language at home, in the local community and with her friends. She was taught rudimentary reading and writing in Chinese after school by her mother, who was a Chinese language teacher, and studied reading and writing in Chinese much more intensively with a tutor from the ages of 12 to 14. At 14, she emigrated to Shanghai, China (and did not set foot again in Indonesia until approximately 25 years later, when she returned for a visit with her family there). She estimates that her Indonesian has undergone considerable attrition, and considers Hokkien and Mandarin Chinese her native languages.
>
> After living in mainland China for two years, Patty emigrated again to Hong Kong. She completed her secondary schooling in Hong Kong, in the meantime acquiring Cantonese and receiving some classroom instruction in English. At the age of 22, she moved to the United States, where she initially attended junior college and received ESL instruction, then transferred to a local university and completed her bachelor's degree, and eventually a master's degree in accounting.

At the time of the first recording reported on here, Patty was 32 and had been living continuously in the United States for about 10 years. During this time, her language environment had been quite mixed—she primarily spoke Cantonese in her urban Chinatown neighbourhood, English at work and at school and with most of her friends, and both Cantonese and English as lingua francas at home with her husband and his family (who were Vietnamese and generally spoke Vietnamese to each other). Within the year prior to the first recording, however, Patty had divorced and moved to a more suburban (and English-speaking) area.

By the time of the second and third recordings, approximately eight-and-a-half years later, Patty had been married to an American native-English speaker for about six years and had spent the intervening years since the first recording totally immersed in a nearly exclusively English-speaking environment. She was promoted to a senior management position in her company, was fairly active in her community and extremely well-acculturated. She was speaking English exclusively at home and at work, with her neighbours and almost all of her friends. In addition, all daily TV, newspapers, magazines, books, videos, etc., were in English; she estimates her proportion of usage of English (vs Chinese) as 'ninety-five to ninety-eight percent'. Her primary Chinese-speaking contact during this time was with a cousin living in another part of the state (who is similarly married to an American, has an English-speaking child, and also lives and works in a nearly exclusively English-speaking environment). Patty was keeping in touch with her cousin approximately once a week by telephone and visiting with her approximately once a month; she observed that they tended to speak Hokkien with each other in private conversation, and English when together with their families and friends.

As can be seen, this is a relatively detailed account of the background information on the object of investigation.

In most longitudinal studies (particularly those that are case studies), data come from spontaneous speech. This does not mean that the researcher does not set up a conversation to generate a particular type of data. It simply means that longitudinal studies do not fit into the experimental paradigm (to be discussed) of control group, experimental group, counterbalancing, and so forth. An important methodological question that arises in connection with spontaneous speech data collection is: How can a particular type of data be generated through spontaneous speech? While there cannot be a 100% guarantee that certain designated interlanguage forms will appear, the researcher can ask certain types of questions in the course of data collection that will likely lead to specific structures. For example, if someone were interested in the interlanguage development of the past tense, learners could be asked during each recording session to tell about something that happened to them the previous day.

Analyses of data obtained through longitudinal studies (and particularly in case studies) are often in the form of descriptive qualitative comments or narrative expositions. While quantification of data may not be the goal of such studies, the researcher may report the frequency of occurrence of some form. In the reporting of results from longitudinally collected data, there are likely to be specific examples of what a learner said and how his or her utterances are to be interpreted.

This type of data is highly useful in determining developmental trends as well as in interpreting various social constraints and input influences (see chapter 10) on the learner's speech. On the other hand, a major drawback concerns the time involved. Conducting this type of longitudinal study/case study requires time in collecting data at regular intervals, as well as in transcription of the speech, which is ideally accompanied by extensive detail on the social, personal, and physical setting in which the speech event took place. A second drawback is related to the lack of generalizability. Given that longitudinal studies are often limited in the number of subjects investigated, it is difficult to generalize the results. It is difficult to know with any degree of certainty whether the results obtained are applicable only to the one or two subjects studied, or whether they are indeed characteristic of a wide range of subjects. Another difficulty with spontaneously produced longitudinal data, and perhaps the most serious one, is that when learners produce a form, there is no way of probing their knowledge any further than what they have produced spontaneously (see data sets in section 3.1). This is particularly the case if the researchers themselves have not collected the data or if the researchers have not generated specific hypotheses and are not predisposed to gathering information about specific forms of speech. For example, if in a particular set of spontaneously elicited data, a learner only produces the present tense of verbs, does that mean that that is all that learner knows? We cannot interpret data only on the basis of what is actually present, because we do not know if absence of forms means lack of knowledge of forms.

A second type of data-collection method involves cross-sectional studies. Here, too, there are four identifiable characteristics that are generally associated with such studies: (a) number of subjects and time frame of data collection, (b) type of data, (c) descriptive detail, and (d) analysis of data.

A cross-sectional study generally consists of data gathered from a large number of subjects at a single point in time, the idea being that we are able to see a slice of development, which is used to piece together actual development.

Unlike case studies, which are based primarily on spontaneous speech, cross-sectional data are often (but not always) based on controlled output. That is, the format is one in which a researcher is attempting to gather data based on a particular research hypothesis. The data, then, come from learners' performance on some pre-specified task.

The type of background information differs from what we have seen with longitudinal studies. Participants are not identified individually, nor is detailed descriptive information provided. A certain amount of background data is likely to be presented in tabular form, as in Table 3.5.

Because cross-sectional data generally involve large numbers of participants, there is typically an experimental format to the research, both in design and in analysis. Results tend to be more quantitative and less descriptive than in longitudinal studies, with statistical analyses and their interpretation being integral parts of the research report.

One can use a cross-sectional design to create a pseudolongitudinal study. In such a study, the emphasis, like that of a longitudinal study, is on language change (i.e., acquisition), with data being collected at a single point in time, but with different proficiency levels represented. For example, if one is investigating the acquisition of the progressive, one would want to know not just what learners can do at a particular point in time (because the question involves acquisition and not static knowledge), but also what happens over a period of time. One way of gathering such data is through a longitudinal study, carefully noting every instance in which the progressive is and is not used (see data set II). Another way of gathering information about linguistic development would be to take a large group of subjects at three specified proficiency levels—let's say, beginner, intermediate, and advanced—and give each group the same test. The assumption underlying this method is that comparing these three groups would yield results similar to what would be found if we looked at a single individual over time. The extent to which this assumption is warranted is controversial.

Table 3.5 Typical data presentation in a cross-sectional design

Language background	No. of participants	Gender	Age	Proficiency
Arabic	24	13F;11M	23–26	8Beg/8Int/8Adv
Spanish	24	12F;12M	23–28	12Beg/12Adv
Japanese	24	11F;13M	21–23	20Beg/4Adv

One advantage to a cross-sectional approach is the disadvantage of longitudinal data: given that there are large numbers of subjects in the former, it is more likely that the results can be generalized to a wider group. The disadvantage is that, at least in the second language acquisition literature, there is often no detailed information about the subjects themselves and the linguistic environment in which production was elicited. Both types of information may be central to an appropriate interpretation of the data. This criticism, of course, is not so much a problem with the research approach as it is with the way results have been reported in the literature.

As noted earlier, longitudinal data are often associated with descriptive (or qualitative) data. Cross-sectional and pseudolongitudinal data, on the other hand, are often associated with quantitative or statistical measures. However, one can easily conduct statistical analyses on longitudinal data and one can easily provide descriptive analyses of cross-sectional data. It is furthermore a mistake to assume that longitudinal data cannot be generalized. One may be able to put together a profile of learners based on many longitudinal studies.

Why would a researcher select one type of data-collection procedure over another? What is most important in understanding this choice is understanding the relationship between a research question and research methodology. While there may not always be a 1:1 relationship, there are certain kinds of questions and certain kinds of external pressures that would lead one into selecting one type of approach to research over another. If, for example, one wanted to gather information about how nonnative speakers learn to apologize in a second language, one could observe learners over a period of time, noting instances of apologizing (either in a controlled experiment or in a naturalistic setting). On the other hand, one could use a cross-sectional approach by setting up a situation and asking large groups of second language speakers what they would say. The latter forces production, the former waits until it happens. While many would argue that the former is "better" in that it more accurately reflects reality, it is also clear that one might have to wait for a considerable amount of time before getting any information that would be useful in answering the original research question. Thus, the exigencies of the situation lead a researcher to a particular approach.

It would be a mistake to think of any of these paradigmatic boundaries as rigid; it would also be a mistake to associate longitudinal studies with naturalistic data collection. One can conduct a longitudinal study with large numbers of speakers; one can also collect data longitudinally using an experimental format. In a study on relative clauses, Gass (1979a, 1979b) gathered data from 17 subjects at six points in time (at monthly intervals). Thus the study itself satisfied the typical definition of longitudinal. However, it did not satisfy the definition of a case study, as it did not involve detailed descriptions of spontaneous speech. On the other hand, given the experimental nature of the study, which involved forced production of relative clauses, it more appropriately belongs in the category of cross-sectional. In other words, the categories we have described are only intended to be suggestive. They do not constitute rigid categories; there is much flexibility in categorizing research as being of one type or another.

We next take a look at two studies to give an idea of the range of data that has been looked at in second language acquisition, one qualitative and one quantitative.

First is a study by Kumpf (1984), who was interested in understanding how nonnative speakers expressed temporality in English (see also chapter 7). One way to gather such information is to present learners with sentences (perhaps with the verb form deleted) and ask them to fill in the blank with the right tense. This, however, would not give information about how that speaker uses tense in a naturalistic environment. Only a long narrative or a detailed picture description is likely to provide that information. Following is the text produced by the native speaker of Japanese in Kumpf's study. The participant is a woman who had lived in the United States for 28 years at the time of taping. For the purposes of data collection, she was asked to produce a narrative account.

> First time Tampa have a tornado come to.
> Was about seven forty-five
> Bob go to work, n I was inna bathroom.
> And . . . a . . . tornado come shake everything.
> Door was flyin open, I was scared.
> Hanna was sittin in window . . .
> Hanna is a little dog.
> French poodle.
> I call Baby.
> Anyway, she never wet bed, she never wet anywhere.
> But she was so scared an cryin run to the bathroom, come to me, an
>   she tinkle, tinkle, tinkle all over me.
> She was so scared.
> I see somebody throwin a brick onna trailer
> wind was blowin so hard
> ana light . . . outside street light was on
> oh I was really scared.
> An den second stop
> So I try to open door
> I could not open
> I say, "Oh, my God. What's happen?"
> I look window. Awning was gone.

(pp. 135–136)

With regard to temporality, there are a few conclusions that Kumpf draws from these data. One is that there is a difference between scene-setting information (i.e., that which provides background information to the story) and information about the action-line. These two functions are reflected in the use or lack of use of the verb *to be* with the progressive. In the scene-setting descriptions, descriptive phrases (*wind was blowin, door was flyin open, Hanna was sittin in window*), the past form of *to be* is apparent. However, when this speaker refers to specific events, no form of the verb *to be* was used (*somebody throwin a brick onna trailer*).

A second finding from this study is the frequency with which certain types of verbs are marked with tense. The copula (*to be*) is tensed 100% of the time; verbs expressing the habitual past (*used to*) are tensed 63% of the time, and continuous action verbs (e.g., *try*) 60% of the time.

Could this information have been elicited through a controlled observation procedure? The first set of results (determining the differences between scene-setting and action-based information), probably not; the second set (frequency of verb tenses), probably yes. In the first instance, it is difficult to imagine an experimental paradigm that would have elicited such information. In the second, one could more easily imagine setting up a situation (even using isolated sentences) in which the same results would have been obtained.

Because these data are limited to one speaker, it is difficult to know whether this is a general phenomenon or not. Results from studies such as this can be verified by attempting to force production from larger numbers of subjects. However, the fact that even one speaker made a distinction between the use of the verb *to be* and its nonuse suggests that this is a possible IL generalization. One question at the forefront of much second language acquisition research is: Are the language systems that learners create consistent with what is found in natural language systems? That is, what are the boundaries of human languages? Given the primacy of questions such as these, the fact of a single individual creating a particular IL generalization (in this case using or not using the verb *to be* to differentiate between two discourse functions) is enough to provide initial answers.

Let's consider a study, also looking at verb tenses, that gathers data within an experimental paradigm. This is one by Gass and Ard (1984), who were concerned with the knowledge that learners have of the various meanings of the progressive and other verb forms (e.g., present, future). Their database came from responses by 139 participants to four different tasks. In the first task, participants were asked to judge the acceptability of sentences in various verb forms in isolation and without context:

(3-56) John is traveling to New York tomorrow.
(3-57) John is seeing better now.

In the second task, the sentences were embedded in short conversations.

(3-58) Mary: I need to send a package to my mother in a hurry.
   Jane: Where does she live?
   Mary: In New York.
   Jane: Oh, in that case John can take it. John is traveling to
      New York tomorrow.

In the third task, there were again isolated sentences, although these were in groups of five, so that they were comparing sentences with each other. Again, acceptability judgments were asked for.

(3-59) The ship sailed to Miami tomorrow.
(3-60) The ship is sailing to Miami tomorrow.
(3-61) The ship will sail to Miami tomorrow.
(3-62) The ship sails to Miami tomorrow.
(3-63) The ship has sailed to Miami tomorrow.

In the fourth task, the subjects were given a verb form and asked to write as long a sentence as possible including the progressive.

What was found was that there was an order of preference of different meanings for the progressive. For example, most subjects ordered the various meanings of the progressive so that the most common was the progressive to express the present (*John is smoking American cigarettes now*); the next was the progressive to express futurity (*John is traveling to New York tomorrow*); the next to express present time with verbs of perception (*Dan is seeing better now*); the next with verbs such as *connect* (*The new bridge is connecting Detroit and Windsor*); and finally, with the copula (**Mary is being in Chicago now*). The authors used this information to gain information about the development of meaning, including both prototypical meanings and more extended meanings. Through spontaneous speech alone (whether a case study or not), this would not have been possible. Only a forced-choice data task would elicit the relevant information. One should also note that controlled observations of spontaneous speech may underestimate the linguistic knowledge of a learner, particularly in those cases where the task is insensitive to the linguistic structure being elicited or is too demanding.

3.3.1 Eliciting speech samples

In this section we discuss elicitation measures used for collecting information about learners' linguistic knowledge. In particular we consider ways of eliciting actual speech samples (see also Chaudron, 2003).

Often one wants actual speech samples within a specific context. For example, Bardovi-Harlig and Hartford (1996) tape-recorded advising sessions. This may not always be feasible; other ways of gathering naturalistic data must be employed. One way is through narratives (as in the Kumpf, 1984, example above). This can often be more complicated than one would think. For example, what does one say to make learners talk? This may depend on the particular focus of investigation. For example, if one wanted to determine a learner's ability to use past tense, a question such as the following could be used: Tell me/write about what you did last weekend. However, if one wanted to learn about a learner's ability to express futurity, one could say: Tell me/write about your plans for next week/summer/year.

Other ways of eliciting narratives are to have learners describe pictures, retell a story, or watch a silent film/film with minimum sound (so that they are not influenced by the language used) and either retell it or give a "play-by-play" account. All but the play-by-play account can easily be done orally or in writing.

Another common way to collect data is elicited imitation which allows a precise experimental design, usually including similar structures that vary along only one linguistic dimension. Thus, this technique can be used to target a specific linguistic area. As the term implies, this is a technique whereby a subject hears a sentence (often tape-recorded) and then is asked to repeat it exactly. If the sentence is long enough, the subject will not be able to remember the sound and repeat it. It is therefore stored as a semantic unit and the learner has to recreate the sentence using his/her knowledge of the second language. This then gives the researcher an indication of the structure of the learner's grammar. An example is given in 3-64 (Flynn, 1987):

(3-64) Stimulus: The doctor called the professor when he prepared the breakfast.
Response: The doctor called the professor and the doctor prepared the breakfast.

Data can be analyzed quantitatively and qualitatively. In the case of a quantitative analysis, one can calculate the percentage of responses that match the target input and therefore obtain information about the extent to which learners perceive the structure in question. A qualitative analysis provides an indication of a learner's developing grammar.

These data are tightly controlled with regard to the type of structure one is attempting to gain information about. For further information, including advantages and disadvantages, see Chaudron (2003, pp. 793–794) and Gass and Mackey (2007). For additional historical context from the child language literature, see Lust, Chien, and Flynn (1987) and Lust, Flynn, and Foley (1996).

Another broad category of data-elicitation techniques is what can be called language tasks. Because there are many variations on this theme, we limit ourselves to some of the most common. These are common when looking at conversational structure and what happens when learners are in an interactive situation (see chapter 10 for more detail). A common characteristic is that participants are paired (either a native speaker and a nonnative speaker or two nonnative speakers) and given a specific task. Some of the common tasks are provided below (cf. Gass and Mackey, 2007, and Mackey and Gass, 2005, for more examples and greater detail).

One task that is common is a picture-description task. One participant is given a picture with instructions to describe it to his or her partner so that the partner can draw it. Or, one participant can be given an object and the other has to guess what it is. Another variation is to give two almost identical pictures and instruct participants to find differences without looking at each other's picture (cf. Polio, Gass, and Chapin, 2006, for an example using this technique). In a variation of the second task, participants can have two almost identical maps and have to describe to each other how to move an object (or an imaginary person) from one place to another (cf. Gass, Mackey, and Ross-Feldman, 2005, for an example using this map task). Another variation is to have one participant describe a picture to another, instructing his or her partner where to place stick-on objects on a board. Finally, a pair (or group) of learners can be given a situation and told to come to a consensus. (Ten individuals are on an island and need to get off, but the only means of escape is a boat, but the boat only holds five people. The task for the group is to decide which five should be saved [e.g., a doctor/nurse, a member of the clergy, a high-school student].) These techniques can be used to elicit specific grammatical information. For example, describing an object in a picture will require the use of prepositions to locate those objects. However, whenever a task is used to elicit certain types of information, it is essential to do a pilot test to make sure that the grammatical information that the researcher suspects will be present is actually present.

Tasks can also be implemented via computer. In fact, researchers have begun to examine computer–mediated communication. Given that computers are frequently used in pedagogical contexts, researchers are beginning to examine the language used in those contexts. The same tasks that are used in face-to-face communication (as described above) can be used in chat-based environments or even in asynchronous communication. The data that are typed can be stored and available for numerous types of analyses, such as self-corrections, pause time (possibly reflecting thinking time), and dictionary look-up use.

Studies using data of this sort can manipulate various social variables. For example, if one wanted to consider the role of age differences, pairs of different age levels could be involved; if one wanted to consider the role of gender differences, pairs could be constructed with this in mind.

Forced production data are often used when studying second language pragmatic behavior. The most common measure is the discourse completion questionnaire. This can be used to gather data concerning particular speech acts (apologies, compliments, refusals, requests, etc.).

Participants are given a (generally written) description of a situation in which the speech act under investigation is required. This is then followed by blank space in which the subject is to write down what he or she would say in the given situation. An example of a situation in which the research focus was status differences in "giving embarrassing information" follows:

(3-65) Giving embarrassing information
        You are a corporate executive talking to your assistant.
        Your assistant, who will be greeting some important guests
        arriving soon, has some spinach in his/her teeth.
                            (Beebe and Takahashi, 1989, p. 109)

The learners are then to write down what they would say in response to this situation.

To ensure that the intended speech act is given in their response, the printed page may have a minidialogue (Beebe, Takahashi, and Uliss-Weltz, 1990, p. 69), as in 3-66, which is intended to elicit refusals:

(3-66) Worker: As you know, I've been here just a little over a
                 year now, and I know you've been pleased with
                 my work. I really enjoy working here, but to be
                 quite honest, I really need an increase in pay.
        You: _____
        Worker: Then I guess I'll have to look for another job.

Clearly, this is a forced situation and one limitation is that another type of response might actually occur. For example, it is possible that the typical response would be one in which the employer refrains from comment.

3.3.2 Eliciting reactions to data

Some data do not require learners to produce data but to react in some way to data. Often these responses are timed, with the idea that speed of response is an indication of processing load. For example, one measure frequently used is sentence matching. One sentence will appear on a computer screen followed by a second sentence. The task is to identify if the sentences are the same or not. It has been found that identical grammatical sentences are responded to faster than identical ungrammatical sentences. By examining reaction times, one can determine whether a learner thinks a particular sentence is grammatical or not. Another type of reaction data is a decision task, whereby a learner might be presented with a word and has to respond as to whether that string of letters or string of sounds is a word in the target language.

Comprehension studies use data reactions to some stimulus or stimuli. For example, learners might be presented with a stimulus sentence and asked to determine which in a series of pictures corresponds to the stimulus.

Perhaps one of the most controversial methods of doing second language research is through the use of intuitional data. Broadly speaking, the term *intuitional data* refers to a type of metalinguistic performance. Learners are asked about their intuitions (or judgments) as to whether or not a given sentence is acceptable (either linguistically or in a particular context). For example, learners of English might be given sentences like the following and asked whether they are good English sentences:

(3-67) He remembers the man who his brother is a doctor.
(3-68) We respect the man with whom you danced with him.
(3-69) He laughed at the boy whom he is taller than him.
(3-70) John admires the woman for whom you wrote the letter.
(3-71) He met the man whom you recommended.

Intuitional data have been widely used in SLA research, yet, more than other research methods, they have been the subject of controversy (see R. Ellis, 2004, 2005; Loewen, 2003). Historically, a considerable amount of SLA research has been (and continues to be) motivated by theoretical principles drawn from the field of linguistics. Along with this theoretical background have come methodologies typically used in linguistics. Primary among these methodologies for collecting linguistic data from native languages is that of grammaticality or acceptability judgment tasks.[7]

It is now commonplace for scholars to think about language not only in terms of language use in everyday communicative situations, but also to examine language "as an object of analysis . . . in its own right" (Cazden, 1976, p. 603). Grammaticality judgments are one (but certainly not the only) form of metalinguistic performance, or language objectification.

In other words, one way of objectifying language is to state whether a given sentence is acceptable or not. What information can that give us? Native speakers' responses are used to infer grammatical properties of a given language. That is, they are used to determine which sentences are part of a language and which are not. While this could conceivably be done by simply observing spontaneous speech, judgment data can reveal more about a language than production data alone. For example, if a native speaker of Italian utters sentence 3-72,

(3-72) La bambina guarda il   giocattolo.
      the baby   looks at the toy

one can infer that that language has the word order of Subject–Verb–Object (SVO). However, with production data alone, one knows little more. One does not know what other kinds of word order that language may or may not have. One does not know if the following sentence is also possible.

(3-73) Mangio io la   pasta.
      eat   I the pasta
      "I eat pasta."

In fact, this order, Verb–Subject–Object, is also possible in Italian,[8] a fact that may or may not be revealed by production data alone (at least not by spontaneous production data). A judgment task, on the other hand, will not miss this fact. In addition, judgment data can provide information about what is not possible in the given language—something production data cannot do.

The question is, how valid are judgment data as measures of what a learner's grammar at a given point in time is capable of generating? There is clearly a difference between judgment data provided by native speakers of a language and second language judgment data. In the former, one is asking native speakers to judge sentences of their own language system in order to gain information about that same system. That is to say, the two systems are isomorphic. In the case of second language learners, one is asking the learners to make judgments about the language being learned at a stage in which their knowledge of that system is incomplete. But here inferences are made not about the system they are being asked about, but about some internalized system of the learners (i.e., there may be a mismatch between the two systems in question).

An issue of importance here is that of indeterminacy, which refers to the incomplete (or lack of) knowledge a learner has of parts of the second language grammar. As Schachter, Tyson, and Diffley (1976) pointed out, there are many sentences about which second language learners have indeterminate knowledge. This is not to say that NSs of a language, either individually or collectively, do not have indeterminate knowledge, for surely they do. But the proportion of indeterminate knowledge in NS grammar is likely to be significantly different from that in learner grammars. For L2 learners it is clear that indeterminacy exists, and it is likely that it embraces an even greater range of data than for native speakers of a language.

Obtaining information about nonindeterminate knowledge is less problematic when using production data because, barring some sort of slip, the language produced is presumably generated by the learner's grammar. However, it is well accepted that production data are often inadequate for specific grammatical studies because the examples of a given grammatical structure are often lacking. But with grammaticality judgments, what we are asking learners to do is evaluate sentences of a language that they do not have total control over; many of the sentences being asked about are beyond the domain of their current knowledge base. Thus, responses to such sentences represent little more than guesses. What is important to note is that grammaticality judgments are complex behavioral activities that must be used with caution and with full understanding of their limitations (Chaudron, 1983; Cowan and Hatasa, 1994; R. Ellis, 1990c, 1991, 2004, 2005; Gass, 1994; Goss, Ying-Hua, and Lantolf, 1994; Loewen, 2003; Mandell, 1999).

Despite these difficulties, a significant amount of work has been done within the field of second language acquisition using grammaticality judgments. Data are collected in a variety of ways. In the simplest form, learners are asked to state whether a given sentence is acceptable in the TL or not. If, for example, a researcher wanted to know whether learners know that English does not allow resumptive pronouns in relative clauses (*I saw the woman who she is your son's teacher*), one might give a list of sentences as was given in the beginning of this section and ask for judgments. However, it is difficult to confidently interpret these results because one cannot be sure that a learner marked a sentence ungrammatical for the same reason that the researcher believes it to be ungrammatical. For this reason, the common technique is to ask learners to correct those sentences they have marked ungrammatical.

Another method is to ask not for dichotomous judgments (correct/incorrect), but to ask for judgments based on degree of certainty. Response sheets might look something like 3-74:

(3-74) He remembers the man who his brother is a doctor.

−3	−2	−1	0	+1	+2	+3
definitely incorrect			unsure			definitely correct

Intuitional data are not limited to judgments of grammaticality. Other means of getting judgments that reflect learners' intuitions are preference judgments, and rankings. In the former, subjects are given sentences and are asked to judge whether the sentences (generally two) are equally grammatical, or whether one is more grammatical than the other. Example:

(3-75) That Mary had climbed a hill was orange.
(3-76) That Mary had climbed a hill was clear.

Or

(3-77) Bill had built a boat.
(3-78) John had climbed a hill.

Ranking is a variation of the preference type task just exemplified. The difference lies primarily in the number of sentences used and the lack of "same degree of grammaticality" as an option.

As mentioned earlier, the use of acceptability judgments in SLA research is not without controversy. However, what is not controversial is the need to get valid information about what individual learners know about the second language. That is, what is the nature of their grammatical system? Two additional methods have been used to determine this: truth-value judgments and sentence matching.

Truth-value judgments have been used primarily for the investigation of learners' knowledge of reflexives. The issue with reflexives has to do with the interpretation of the reflexive; that is, whom it refers to. Given the sentence (from Lakshmanan and Teranishi, 1994),

(3-79) John said that Bill saw himself in the mirror.

what are the possibilities for interpretation? In English, *himself* can refer to Bill, but not to John. However, in other languages, the equivalent of *himself* can refer to either John or Bill. The context is used to disambiguate these two possibilities. A research question might involve determining what knowledge learners have if they are learning a language that allows both possibilities even though their native language only allows one. The methodology involved in determining such knowledge has been the subject of numerous articles (e.g., Eckman, 1994a; Lakshmanan and Teranishi, 1994; Thomas, 1989, 1991, 1993, 1994, 1995; Wakabayashi, 1996; White, Bruhn-Garavito, Kawasaki, Pater, and Prevost, 1997; see Glew, 1998 for a review). An example of a truth-value task can be seen in 3-80 (Glew, 1998).

(3-80) A boy and his father went on a bike ride together. The boy went down a hill very fast. "Don't go so fast!" shouted the father. It was too late, the boy fell off his bike and started crying. The father gave the boy a hug. Then the boy was happy again.

The boy was happy that the father hugged himself.

True _____   False _____

Truth-value judgment tasks are, of course, not without choices. For example, one could just ask a true/false question. Or, one could ask about all possibilities: (a) Can *himself* refer to *the boy*? (b) Can *himself* refer to *the father*?

Intuitional data, while most commonly used at the sentence level, can also be used for judgments of appropriateness, as in the following:

(3-81) You are a member of a research group. Many people are missing from a meeting and it is necessary for someone to notify them about the next meeting. Your boss turns to you and says:

_____a Notify those who are missing, OK?

_____b Perhaps you could notify those who didn't come?

_____c Could you please notify the others about our next meeting?

_____d How about getting in touch with the people who were absent?

_____e I'd appreciate it if you could notify the people who were absent.

_____f You will notify the people who were absent.

Respondents are asked to select the response that, given the constraints of the situation, they feel is the most appropriate.

Other research involving intuitional data requires learners to order utterances in terms of most polite to least polite. The arguments for using intuitional data (or other means of forced data) as opposed to naturally occurring data are much the same as those presented earlier. One cannot obtain a sufficiently rich corpus of data unless one forces the issue. The disadvantages lie in the fact that one cannot automatically equate actual production data with data from questionnaires or other intuitional tasks. What we think we would say in a given situation is not necessarily the same as what we would actually say. Furthermore, it is likely that the contrived situations that researchers create would not actually occur, or—if they do occur—that the given choices are the appropriate way of dealing with the situation.

3.3.3 *Verbal report data*

Verbal reports represent a type of introspective data. They are protocols or reports that come about from asking individuals to say what is going through their minds as they are performing some task. As Mackey and Gass (2005, p. 77) note, "One can often gain access to processes that are unavailable by other means." (For a critique, see Gass and Mackey, 2000; Mackey and Gass, 2005, chapter 3.) There are essentially two types of verbal reports that are used: recalls and think-alouds. Think-alouds are conducted during the activity and recalls are conducted following an activity.

Recalls can be done with some stimulus (e.g., a video or audio of the event that the participant is reporting on, a written paper that a learner has written) or without. In the latter case, there is no stimulus to rely on, only the individual's recollection of the event. In both instances, the crucial information that the researcher wants to obtain are the thought processes at the time of the original event.

Another type of verbal report is what is known as "think-aloud." This involves reporting on the event as it is occurring. As such it involves somewhat of a stream of consciousness. The intent is to understand the thought processes of a learner as he or she is doing a task. Below is an example of data from a verbal report in which the students (learners of Spanish) are working on a crossword puzzle and reporting on a grammar problem. The boldface print indicates words in Spanish.

> Vertical now . . . 2 down, OK I have an *o* here but I don't know why because in 1 across I have *se morio* but I guess it has to be **murio** because 2 down has to be *un* [changes o to *u*] . . . OK I have to but it must be *tu* so it means that 7 across for the past tense of *dormirse* must be **durmio** instead of *dormio* [changes o to u] . . . OK third person plural form of the verb *pedir* they asked for, 5 down . . . *pedieron* [pause] OK I am wondering whether because I have **pidieron** [spells out] and I am thinking it should be *pe-* but that would make it *dormeo* with an *e* instead of *i*, . . . I guess I will see how the other ones go and take a look at that one again . . . OK, the opposite of *no* is *si* which means that for 11 across I have *mentieron* but it should be **mintieron** for the third person plural past tense of *mentir, mintieron* [changes *e* to *i*] <u>which makes me now realize that</u> **pidieron** <u>with an *i* is probably right since the *e* in</u> <u>*mentir* changes to an *i* so the *e* in *pedir* is also going to change to an</u> <u>*i* as well . . .</u> OK 12 down, the opposite of *no* is si, which means that where I have *corregio* it becomes **corrigio corrigio** so the third person singular of past tense *corregir* is **corrigio** [changes *e* to an i] . . . <u>looks like all the *e*'s are becoming *i*'s in the stems</u> . . .

OK, third person singular form of *descubrir* discovered OK it is *descubrio*, OK 17 down possessive adjective in Spanish OK now here yet again I have *to* because I have *se dormieron* and that must become *tu* so it becomes *se **durmieron*** [changes o to u] OK third person singular form of *preferir* preferred, OK now here yet again *prefe-* [spells out] is going to change to **prefi-** [spells out] *prefirio* [changes e to i] . . . OK 25 down, the verb to go in Spanish which is *ir* and I have *er* [spells out] because with 24 across I have *repetieron* but I guess now that e becomes an i becomes **repitieron** . . . [changes e to i] . . . and 25 down is *ir*, <u>so now I am going to go back and change any other ones where I have e in the stem that should become an i,</u> like 1 down, I believe would become *se **divirtieron***, it becomes an i and—everything else looks OK so I guess that's it [9 Minutes].

(Leow, 1998, p. 146)

Source: R. Leow (1998). Toward operationalizing the process of attention in SLA: evidence for Tomlin and Villa's (1994) fine-grained analysis of attention. *Applied Psycholinguistics*, 19. Reprinted with the permission of Cambridge University Press.

3.3.4 Measuring non-linguistic information

Studies investigating attitude, motivation, learning styles, and personality characteristics frequently use instruments borrowed directly or with some modification from the field of psychology.

3.3.4.1 Questionnaires

Questionnaires are commonly used to gain information about attitudes a learner may have toward language learning, either generally or toward the learning of a specific language (see Dörnyei, 2003). As Dörnyei notes, there are a number of question types that can be asked. A sampling of the types of questions follows (from Gardner and Lambert, 1972):

I am studying French because:

_____a I think it will someday be useful in getting a good job.
_____b I think it will help me to better understand French people and their way of life.
_____c It will allow me to meet and converse with more and varied people.
_____d A knowledge of two languages will make me a better educated person.
_____e Any other personal reason.

Another type of question involves completing a sentence (from Dörnyei, 2003, p. 49).

    a   One thing I liked about this activity is . . . .
    b   I found this activity . . . .

Attitudinal ratings are also used in research on motivation and attitudes. Respondents are given polar opposites and asked to judge their impressions of a group of people (e.g., French people from France) on an evaluation scale.

a   Interesting ___ : ___ : ___ : ___ : ___ : ___ : ___ Boring
b   Prejudiced ___ : ___ : ___ : ___ : ___ : ___ : ___ Unprejudiced
c   Happy ___ : ___ : ___ : ___ : ___ : ___ : ___ Sad
d   Hardworking ___ : ___ : ___ : ___ : ___ : ___ : ___ Lazy

Questionnaires are useful when large amounts of data are desired.

3.3.4.2 Interviews

Interviews are generally conducted orally and one-on-one. They can either have fixed questions or they can be less structured, allowing the interviewer to tailor the questions according to the responses of the interviewee.

In studies of the sort mentioned in this section, researchers often use a standardized test of language proficiency against which to measure the attribute under investigation.

3.3.4.3 Diaries

Diaries are journals that a learner keeps (either on his or her own initiative or following a request/assignment given by a teacher). Diaries are often a good source of information about attitudes and motivation and provide a more open-ended forum for such information without the constraints of specific questions (see Schumann and Schumann, 1977, who reported on their attempts to learn Arabic in North Africa and Persian [Farsi] in a U.S. university and in Iran).

3.3.5 Measuring general proficiency: standardized language tests

Standardized language tests are not often used as a source for second language data primarily because the most common type of standardized test is objective and does not yield productive data that can be easily analyzed. (An exception is the work of Ard and Homburg, 1983, 1992, discussed in chapter 5.) Rather, standardized language tests are often used as gauges for measuring proficiency levels. For example, in a given research study, advanced learners may be those who have a TOEFL (Test of English as a Foreign Language) score above a certain level. For those conducting research in languages other than English, there are commercial or institutionally constructed tests available that could be used to measure proficiency. Even with standardized tests, however, there is no absolute accepted cutoff point for advanced, intermediate, beginner, and so forth. In fact, one difficulty in comparing SLA studies is that, because there is no accepted cutoff point, one researcher's advanced category may correspond to another's intermediate category. Thomas (1994), based on a survey of the literature, has identified four common ways of assessing proficiency: (a) impressionistic judgments, (b) institutional status (e.g., first semester of second-year French), (c) specific research-designed test, (d) standardized tests. Because there are so many ways to measure proficiency, the field of SLA is left with considerable difficulty in comparing studies. This is unlike the field of child language acquisition, in which there is a well-accepted means of judging where a child is on the developmental scale.

3.4 Replication

"The essence of the scientific method involves observations that can be repeated and verified by others" (American Psychological Association, 1994, p. 2). Much of SLA research is empirical and such research is in need of replication. SLA research deals with human behavior and thus is often inconsistent. This is complicated by two additional factors: (a) the paucity of participants in many studies and (b) the nature of second language knowledge. Many studies reported in the literature have 10 participants or fewer. This makes it difficult to draw generalizable conclusions about acquisition (either the process or the product). The second point to consider is the nature of second language knowledge. Learners are just that—*learners*. Often their knowledge is indeterminate (Schachter, Tyson, and Diffley, 1976). As mentioned earlier, this refers to the fact that there are certain aspects of the second language that learners are uncertain of. This may be because these are areas of language that they are "working on" and about which they do not have definite knowledge. Their linguistic behavior, then, will be inconsistent, with utterances such as the following, virtually co-occurring.

(3-82) 1 am here since yesterday.
(3-83) I have been here since yesterday.

Polio and Gass (1997) have argued for the importance of replication while at the same time acknowledging that "exact replication" is impossible given that a replication study includes different individuals. Replication studies are an ideal way for those who are new to the field to get their hands dirty with actual data.[9]

3.5 Issues in data analysis

In this section, we focus on issues of analysis. The focus is not on statistical analyses, but rather on the type of information that is relevant to analyses of second language data. Issues of analysis will be found throughout this book, as analysis covers a wide spectrum of issues and is generally situated within the particular approach taken to SLA.

The first issue we consider relates to the determination of development. The field of second language acquisition has not yet come up with an index of development. That is, unlike in child language acquisition research—which is heavily reliant on MLU (mean length of utterance), a measure that averages the number of morphemes per utterance—there is no easy way of determining whether a given learner is more or less proficient than another. Thus, one cannot determine where on a developmental scale a given individual can be placed. This is partly so because of the nature of second language learning. Learners do not have a uniform starting point. From the beginning, their utterances vary in the degree of syntactic sophistication. Furthermore, interlanguages are unique creations. While there may be similarities among speakers of a given NL learning the same TL, and while there may be similarities across TLs, each individual creates his or her own language system. Similarities may be found for a given grammatical structure (e.g., there are commonalities in relative clause formation regardless of language background). However, if we looked at an entire linguistic system, we would be less likely to find broad-sweeping similarities.

As mentioned in section 3.3.5, one way of determining a learner's place along a scale from lesser proficiency to greater proficiency is through the use of standardized tests. This is undoubtedly the most common way, as a quick perusal of research articles suggests. Another way of determining development is through categorization of individuals according to their placement scores for specific language programs (e.g., a beginning class, an advanced class, satisfaction of a university language requirement). However, these are only very rough measures at best.

A more exact means for measuring syntactic development, generally reserved for written as opposed to oral data, is what is known as the T-unit. A T-unit is an independent clause and any associated dependent clauses, that is, clauses that are attached to or embedded within it (Hunt, 1965). Thus, both 3-84 and 3-85 are T-units, but 3-86 is not:

(3-84) John woke up.

(3-85) John woke up, although he was tired.

(3-86) although he was tired.

This was originally a measure used for determining syntactic develop-ment for native speakers, but it has been adapted for use with nonnative speakers, by modifying the definition to incorporate error-free T-units rather than just T-units. While this is a more precise measure than standardized tests, teacher evaluations, or class placement, it is most reliable with written data as opposed to oral data.

In determining oral proficiency, the situation is more complex because there appear to be different measures depending on whether one is con-sidering monologue or dialogue data. Some of the measures that can be considered are pauses, speech rate, and self-corrections after a mistake has been made. For conversational data, additional factors come into play. For example, to what extent can a learner appropriately initiate topic changes? To what extent can nonnative speakers demonstrate appropriate conversational strategies (i.e., holding their own in a conversation)? This might include: (a) providing verbal cues to show that they are listening and/or following a conversation (e.g., *uh huh, yeah*) and (b) responding appropriately given the linguistic, social, and cultural context. To what extent do learners know when it is their turn to take the floor (a factor that may differ cross-culturally)? While all of these are clearly important measures in determining oral proficiency, we do not as yet know how each of these should be "weighted." Nor do we know what can be expected in terms of acquisition, a prerequisite to being able to place learners along a developmental continuum.

A second issue to be noted and one that was discussed earlier in this chapter is that data do not yield unique results. A researcher must inter-pret the results. In order to interpret the results, the researcher must first decide what data to include. That is, what are the relevant data for analysis? Another important consideration is the point of reference for comparison. Early research focused on comparisons between learner output and the NL, on the one hand, and on learner output and the TL, on the other. However, this type of comparison causes researchers to miss the generalizations that learners have constructed for themselves. This fact is often cited as a difference between longitudinal data (specifically, case studies) and cross-sectional experimental studies. The latter often do not provide the richness necessary to understand a learner's system; the former often do not provide specific information about what a learner's grammar includes and excludes.

To see the differences between these two types of studies with regard to the analysis of data, let's consider data presented by Huebner (1979, 1983). These data come from the spontaneous speech of a Hmong refugee from Laos, named Ge, who lived in Honolulu. In his home country, Ge

Figure 3.1 Percentages of occurrences of articles in obligatory Standard English environments.

Source: From "Order-of-acquisition vs. dynamic paradigm: a comparison of method in interlanguage research" by T. Huebner, 1979, *TESOL Quarterly*, 13, 21–28. Reprinted by permission.

had had no training in English, nor did he receive formal instruction while in Hawaii. Data collection began about one month after his arrival in Honolulu and continued every three weeks for approximately one year.

In the morpheme order studies, which we examine in chapter 5, most data come from cross-sectional studies. Furthermore, the data are analyzed as to the suppliance or non-suppliance of a particular morpheme in obligatory contexts. An initial analysis of the data from Ge's use of English articles was conducted using this particular methodology. Results are given in Figure 3.1.

What does Figure 3.1 tell us? First, it shows little development in terms of Ge's knowledge of the article system. Second, it does not show what it is about the article system Ge does and does not know. We have little information about the systematicity that underlies Ge's production and nonproduction of the English article. Further, comparing Ge's data with the English article system suggests that Ge brings nothing more to the learning task than what he can figure out of that system. In other words, if one only compares what the learner is producing with the TL system, one misses the picture of what the learner's system is like. Making a 1:1 comparison between the IL and the TL may prevent the researcher from understanding the full system that the learner has created.

In analyzing second language data there can be considerable difficulty in determining what the targeted structure is, there can be differences in results depending on the methodology used for analysis, and there can also be differences in the results when using a similar methodology.

Another way of analyzing the data is by bringing into the analysis different possible meanings of articles. For our purposes, let's assume the correctness of Huebner's analysis. He claims two binary categories relevant to article use: (a) specific referent and (b) hearer's assumed knowledge. Noun phrase reference can thus be categorized into four types:

Category 1
+specific reference
+hearer's knowledge
Category 2
−specific reference
+hearer's knowledge
Category 3
−specific reference
−hearer's knowledge
Category 4
+specific reference
−hearer's knowledge

In English, Category 1 nouns use the definite article *the*; Category 2 is for generics and can use *the*, *a*, or *ø*; Categories 3 and 4 function similarly, using either *a* or *ø*. (In other languages, it is possible that only two forms exist, one used for Categories 1 and 2 and the other for 3 and 4; or another language still might have one form for Categories 1 and 2 and two separate forms for 3 and 4.)

Category 1
The President met with the Pope yesterday.
The teacher told me to do my homework.
Category 2
I am going to a movie tomorrow.
I am going to the movies tomorrow.
Movies are my favorite form of entertainment.
Category 3
A good person is hard to find.
It's hard to find good employees.
Category 4
I have a good idea.
I always have good ideas.

Using this type of scheme, the results in Table 3.6 obtain. This table shows number of occurrences of each form (*the*, *a*, or *ø*) according to the binary categories of specific referent and hearer's knowledge. The same four points in time are given.

As can be seen, these data differ from those in Figure 3.1 in that in Table 3.6 clear differences exist between Time 1 and Time 4, whereas such differences were not apparent when only correct and incorrect examples were examined.

In Ge's native language, one of the most important concepts for a

Table 3.6 Number of occurrences of article types based on four-part categorization scheme

	Category 1			Category 2			Category 3			Category 4		
	da	*a*	*0*	*da*	*a*	*0*	*da*	*a*	*0*	*da*	*a*	*0*
Time 1	67	1	47	2	0	4	4	2	35	2	12	18
Time 2	133	0	40	1	0	4	3	5	56	33	0	2
Time 3	199	2	13	0	0	7	3	12	27	32	8	8
Time 4	154	2	22	1	0	10	3	9	40	13	8	23

Source: From "Order-of-acquisition vs. dynamic paradigm: a comparison of method in interlanguage research" by T. Huebner, 1979, *TESOL Quarterly, 13*, 21–28. Reprinted by permission.

sentence is what is known as "topic–comment." The first part of the sentence is the topic followed by a comment about that topic. Topics provide old information; thus, information that is by definition within the hearer's knowledge domain. Examples of topic–comment structures produced by Ge are given in 3-87 and 3-88 (Huebner, 1979, p. 27).

(3-87) en beibii, isa in da moder, en da owder broder.
     "And the babies were placed between the adults."
(3-88) Researcher: How did you cross the river?
     Ge: river, isa bowt
          "As for the river, it was a boat."

At Time 1, there is less overt marking for Categories 1 and 2 than at any of the other time periods. At Time 2 there is a major increase in the marking of specific nouns (Categories 1 and 4) regardless of the status of the hearer's knowledge. By Time 4, *the* [da] is almost limited to Category 1 nouns, as it is in English. Huebner concluded that what this type of analysis provides is not a static indication of whether Ge is right or wrong when compared to standard English. Rather, what we see is the dynamic movement toward English, guided by a movement from the underlying topic–comment structure of his NL to the underlying subject–verb structure of his TL. The first table of results shows minimal change; this latter analysis shows considerable change.

Pica (1983) demonstrated this discrepancy in an analysis of the acquisition of morphemes. She discussed two common methods for determining whether someone has acquired morphemes: "suppliance in obligatory context" and "target-like use." She concentrated on the following questions: What is the difference between these two methods? In the first method, suppliance in obligatory context, one determines whether or not standard English requires a particular morpheme. For example, in sentence 3-89,

(3-89) He is dancing

it is obligatory to put an -*ing* on the word *dance* because it is in a context in which a progressive is required. One then looks at the second language data and scores this in the following way: 2 points for correct form; 1 point for a morpheme misformation (e.g., *he's dances*) and 0 points for no morpheme (*he dance*). The following formula then applies:

$$\frac{\text{number of correct suppliance} \times 2 + \text{number of misformations}}{\text{total obligatory contexts} \times 2}$$

The second quantificational method, known as target-like use, incorporates the notion of distributional patterns. While the suppliance in obligatory contexts method provides detail on how accurate a learner is in those contexts where a form is required, it does not give information about possible generalizations to inappropriate contexts. In target-like use analysis, the numerator consists of the number of instances of correct suppliance in obligatory contexts and the denominator consists of not only the obligatory contexts, but also the nonobligatory contexts in which it was supplied.

$$\frac{\text{number of correct suppliance in obligatory contexts}}{\text{number of obligatory contexts} + \text{number of suppliance in nonobligatory contexts}}$$

It is clear that these two formulae differ, but just how does this difference affect the interpretation of data? Pica compared three sets of data: one from a group of learners who were learning English in a classroom environment, one from a group of learners in a naturalistic environment (i.e., no instruction), and one from a third group of learners who learned both through informal means and through formal instruction. Table 3.7 gives the percentage scores for all three groups.

Depending on the analysis used, one comes up with different interpretations of the role of instruction versus noninstruction. For example, if we focus on the scores that come from the suppliance-in-obligatory-context method and examine the results for the progressive -*ing*, the conclusion we would come to is that the learning environment (instruction versus naturalistic) has little effect on the acquisition of the progressive. However, if we look at the results from the target-like-use method, we see an entirely different picture. Here, we would be forced to conclude that naturalistic acquisition is far superior to classroom instruction in learning the progressive.

Thus, the same database can yield different results about learners' knowledge of an L2 (in this case, about the knowledge they have about specific morphemes) depending on the way the data are quantified.

Table 3.7 Comparison of Suppliance in Obligatory Context (SOC) and Target Language Utterance (TLU) percentage scores for each group of subjects according to language context

Morpheme	Instruction only			Naturalistic			Mixed		
	SOC	TLU	Diff.	SOC	TLU	Diff.	SOC	TLU	Diff.
Progressive -ing	97	69	−28	94	87	−7	98	74	−24
Plural -s	93	85	−8	74	72	−2	74	71	−3
Singular copular	95	89	−6	92	88	−4	97	94	−3
Progressive auxiliary	85	59	−26	76	71	−5	66	52	−14
Past irregular	75	66	−9	68	65	−3	73	64	−9
Past regular	51	47	−4	58	58	0	44	44	0
Third person singular	63	52	−11	25	22	−3	22	19	−3

Source: From "Methods of morpheme quantification: their effect on the interpretation of second language data" by T. Pica, *Studies in Second Language Acquisition*, 1983, 6, 69–78. Reprinted by permission.

Difficulties in determining what the targeted structure is that a learner has produced have been discussed in this chapter. There is an additional problem, particularly in attempting to deal with the role of the native language. How can we be sure about the facts of the native language? One concern is the role of dialects. For example, in many dialects in the United States there is no difference between the vowel sounds in *cot* and *caught*. For many other American English speakers, the two words are kept distinct. If we were to conduct a study on the role of the native language in learning the phonology of a second language, how would we know whether the TL of a given speaker is one dialect or another? The answer is relatively easy if we are aware that a difference exists (as in the case of English, due to the fact that there are numerous descriptions that exist), but less easy if we are dealing with a language that has not been described as extensively. However, a more serious problem is the determination of the language variety which a learner has been exposed to.

As an example, consider two studies dealing with the acquisition of relative clauses, one published in 1974 by Schachter and the other by Gass (1979a, 1979b). The particular focus is what is known as pronominal reflexes or pronoun retention, a phenomenon—common in many languages (including informal English)—exemplified in 3-90.

(3-90) There's two fellows that *their* dads are millionaires.
       (Sinclair Lewis, *Babbitt*)

In the 1974 study, Table 3.8 was published:

Table 3.8 Pronominal reflexes in five languages

	Subj.	DO	IO	OPrep	Poss.	OCOMP
Persian	(+)	+	+	+	+	+
Arabic	(+)	(+)	+	+	+	+
Chinese	−	−	+	+	+	+
Japanese	−	−	−	(+)	(+)	
English	−	−	−	−	−	−

Source: From "An error in error analysis" by J. Schachter, 1974, *Language Learning*, 24, 205–214, by Research Club in Language Learning. Reprinted by permission.

Table 3.9 Pronominal reflexes in five languages

	Subj.	DO	IO	OPrep	Poss.	OCOMP
Persian	−	(+)	+	+	+	
Arabic	−	+	+	+	+	+
Chinese	−	−	+	+	+	
Japanese	−	−	−	−	(+)	
English	−	−	−	−	−	−

Source: From "Language transfer and universal grammatical relations" by S. Gass, 1979b, *Language Learning*, 29, 327–344, by Research Club in Language Learning. Reprinted by permission.

In the 1979b study, Table 3.9 was published. (For more detail on this study, see chapter 7.)[10]

What differences are there between Tables 3.8 and 3.9? In the 1974 study, Persian and Arabic are shown to have optional pronominal reflexes, whereas in the 1979 study, Persian and Arabic are shown not to have pronominal reflexes. Similar differences appear in direct object (DO) position. The discrepancy, it turns out, is one of dialect differences. Nonetheless, with different "facts" about the native language, it is easy to see how different results concerning the role of the native language will obtain.

One final related point has to do with the entire notion of "target" from the learner's perspective. We have discussed the difficulty in assessing what the NL forms are that the learner brings to the second-language-learning situation. There is an equally complex issue in that we do not always know what target language variety the learner is "aiming" at. When we spoke of pronominal reflexes, we assumed that English does not have these forms. Yet it doesn't take more than a few minutes of listening to native speakers of English before we hear numerous instances of pronominal reflexes in spontaneously produced utterances. Thus, we cannot pretend to know precisely what knowledge base a learner brings to the learning situation, nor can we pretend to understand what target language model the learner has adopted.

3.6 What is acquisition?

The question of what is acquired is not an easy one; it has been operationalized in different ways in the past (for an extended discussion on this issue, see Norris and Ortega, 2003). One can be misled into thinking that a correct utterance or even two or three correct utterances suggest that a particular structure has been acquired. However, as we will see in the remainder of this book, there are many factors that one must consider. For example, learners appear to "backslide;" that is, correct forms appear, but then seem to disappear. The reasons for this are often complex and will be covered at various points throughout the book. The fact of "backsliding," however, underscores the need and difficulty of pinpointing second language knowledge.

How one defines acquisition depends on what one is looking at. This might range from linguistic knowledge to the ability to use that knowledge in speech and the ability to process language in real time. To show that these are not all the same, consider the fact that an English learner of Italian may know that there is agreement, say between noun and adjective, but may not be able to use that information when confronted with needing to use it in a conversation. Thus, if one is asking whether that learner has learned that there is a concept of agreement in Italian, the answer is *yes*; if one is asking whether that learner has learned to use that information in speech, the answer is *no*.

Various definitions of acquisition of a form are possible: (a) the first appearance of a correct form, (b) a certain percentage of accurate forms (e.g., 90%), (c) the "first of three consecutive two-week samples in which the morpheme is supplied in over 90% of obligatory contexts" (Hakuta, 1976a, p. 137), and (d) "the presence of at least two examples of structures in *two* different posttests" (Mackey, 1999, p. 567). Considering language forms is limiting, however. For example, one needs to consider not only the actual forms, but also the context in which the forms occur. In section 3.5, we mention the concept of obligatory contexts; that is, contexts in which a particular form is required in the target language. Consider the following hypothetical conversation:

Rachel: I read three great books last week.
Miriam: Which one did you like best?
Rachel: The book about Mr. Park's ex-wife who killed Nate Hosen.

Here, Rachel uses the definite article *the* before the noun *book*. English requires the use of *the* in this context, and it is in this sense that we can talk about an obligatory context for the use of the definite article.

In sum, researchers use a variety of criteria to determine when acquisition has taken place. However, one should not lose track of the important and perhaps more interesting factor of emergence. It is not just the point at which something is acquired that is of interest (unless one is comparing the point of acquisition of different forms), but it is also important to consider the stages that a learner goes through in acquiring a particular form (see the discussion of the definite article in section 3.5).

3.7 Conclusion

In this chapter we have presented a means for data analysis and have reviewed different methodologies for data elicitation and data analysis. Throughout the remainder of the book, the reader will be able to put this knowledge to use in doing additional problem sets and in determining what the strengths and/or shortcomings are of current research in SLA. We next move to a central factor in the study of second language acquisition: the role of the native language. We approach this topic by first placing it in its historical context in chapter 4.

Suggestions for additional reading

Questionnaires in Second Language Research: Construction, Administration, and Processing. Zoltán Dörnyei. Lawrence Erlbaum Associates (2003).

Analyzing Learner Language. Rod Ellis and Gary Barkhuizen. Oxford University Press (2005).

Stimulated Recall Methodology in Second Language Research. Susan Gass and Alison Mackey. Lawrence Erlbaum Associates (2000).

Data Elicitation for Second and Foreign Language Research. Susan Gass and Alison Mackey. Lawrence Erlbaum Associates (2007).

Evaluating Research Articles: From Start to Finish. Ellen Girden. Sage Publications (1996).

Second Language Research: Methodology and Design. Alison Mackey and Susan Gass. Lawrence Erlbaum Associates (2005).

Conversation Analysis. Numa Markee. Lawrence Erlbaum Associates (2000).

Second Language Classroom Research: Issues and Opportunities. Jacquelyn Schachter and Susan Gass (Eds.). Lawrence Erlbaum Associates (1996).

Points for discussion

1   Consider the distinction between longitudinal and cross-sectional approaches to research methodology. Do you find this to be an important distinction? List several interlanguage structures you have observed (e.g., questions, articles). In pairs, come up with a rough design using one or the other of these approaches. Once you have done that, find another pair of students who has used the other

approach (longitudinal or cross-sectional) and compare the advantages and disadvantages of each.

2 Find a journal article that deals with longitudinal data. What was the time frame of data collection? How often were data collected? How much detail is provided about the participant(s)? About the environment in which learning took place? About data-collection procedures?

3 It is stated in this chapter that one advantage of a cross-sectional design represents a disadvantage of a longitudinal design. The discussion revolves around the generalizability of results. Is it necessary to set up these two approaches in this fashion? In other words, is there always a cross-sectional/longitudinal dichotomy? Does the concept of "pseudolongitudinal" approach resolve some of the difficulties involved in the two opposing methods? Must there always be a cross-sectional/longitudinal dichotomy?

4 Explain the relationship between research questions and research methodology. What is meant by the strong claim that the two are always linked? Can the same research question be addressed using different methodologies? Devise a research question that focuses on the development of third person singular *s* for learners of English. Think of a situation where, due to feasibility constraints, you have access to two adults learning English and you can see them several times a week. Devise a design based on this situation. Then, consider a situation where you teach English classes to adult migrants, but the class you teach changes every six weeks, at which point you have new students. What design might be appropriate for this situation? Can you answer your question with either design? (This question comes from A. Mackey.)

5 Reread the description of the Kumpf (1984) study on tense/aspect (section 3.3). Evaluate the conclusion that her results could not have been obtained by a cross-sectional methodology.

6 Consider the various ways of collecting interlanguage data discussed here. Take each of the following and describe advantages and disadvantages of each: (a) language tests, (b) psychological tests, (c) questionnaires, (d) attitudinal ratings, (e) elicited imitation, (f) spontaneous data, (g) language games, and (h) intuitions. In your answer you will probably see that all of these are in some way controversial, given that there are both advantages and disadvantages. What does that suggest about doing SLA research in general?

7 If you were to design an SLA study to investigate each of the following topics, what would an appropriate methodology be?

a English articles
b The structure of tense/aspect

    c   Text organizational structure
    d   A comparison of the effectiveness of native/nonnative teachers
    e   Fluency

8   In a study by Mazurkewich (1984), the author used a grammaticality judgment task to elicit data. In a critique of her work, Kellerman (1985) noted that the instructions given to Mazurkewich's subjects were problematic: "put an X next to any sentence that you think is not expressed in good English. There are no right or wrong answers" (p. 99).

    What is problematic about these instructions? Think carefully about precisely what these learners were being asked to do and how the researcher was to interpret the responses. For example, suppose that one of the sentences given was the previous sentence: "Think carefully about precisely what these learners were being asked to do and how the researcher was to interpret the responses." Further suppose that the learner put an X next to this sentence to indicate that the sentence was not a good one. What could you conclude?

9   In this chapter, we stated that data do not yield unique results; that is, there might be multiple interpretations to a particular data set. Is it always the case that data are ambiguous? Can you think of a case where unambiguous results are a possibility? Suppose you are told that in Indian English, extremely fluent speakers accurately produce sentences such as *I want to go there* but do not produce sentences like *I want her to go there*. Instead, they produce *I want that he go there*. What explanation is possible? Let's further suppose that the same can be said for speakers from a variety of unrelated native languages. Does this alter your view? Now suppose that you are further told that this is not true of all Indian-English speakers. Does this affect your answer? How can one determine the source of this interlanguage system?

10   Given the situation described in problem 9, do you think that you would need a longitudinal or a cross-sectional study to help you resolve the potential data ambiguity? Consider our comment in the chapter that longitudinal studies "do not provide specific information about what a learner's grammar includes and excludes."

11   The Pica (1983) study is discussed in some detail in this chapter. In light of her study, compare the research methods of "obligatory context" versus "target-like use." How are they fundamentally different? How do they supply different views of a particular learner's interlanguage at a particular point in time? Over time? Bley-Vroman (1983) called the former method the "comparative fallacy." One of Bley-Vroman's main points is that using the target language as a baseline for interlanguage description skews the interlanguage data away from looking at the interlanguage as an internal coherent system in its

own right. Explain what is meant by this. How do these two methods of analysis fare in this regard?

12 Analyze the following nonnative speaker sentences using both the suppliance-in-obligatory-context method and the target-like-use method. Focus on the past irregular and the past regular verb forms and the plural -s.

> Yesterday morning, I seed two movies and writed three report. Then, in the afternoon, I seed one more movies. I enjoyed myself a lot.

13 Consider the following composition:

> Once upon a time there was a man who called "Taro Urashia" in small village in Japan. One day, when he take a walk near his home, he help one turtle on the seaside. Since he helped the turtle, he was able to get a chance to be invited from sea castle which is deep place in the sea.
>
> He had been entertained with music, good board, dance etc. every nights by beautiful girls of sea castle.
>
> Therefore, he forgot worldly presence and he did not notice how long did he stay there.
>
> Nevertheless he missed the new world, so he said that he wanted to go back to true world.

Analyze this learner's use of articles using the two methods of morpheme analysis discussed in section 3.5 (obligatory context versus target-like use). What differences did you find?

14 Let's assume you want to investigate how native speakers react to compliments by a second language speaker. Let's further assume that you believe that it is not so much the words people use that affect different native speaker reactions, but the stereotypes that native speakers have formed about particular groups of nonnative speakers. How would you go about investigating this?

15 Find two studies of SLA in which the categories beginning, or intermediate, or advanced (or some similar attempt at determining proficiency or developmental level) are used. What are the criteria used for each of these? Are they the same for all categories used? Do you agree with the basis on which learners were categorized? What criteria would you use?

16 In discussing Kumpf's (1984) work (section 3.3), we noted that some of the information that Kumpf dealt with (namely the determination of the frequency of verb tenses) could be obtained through an experimental design as opposed to a case study, which is what she

utilized. How would you design an experiment to understand the acquisition of verb tenses?

17 We noted in this chapter that at times it is not always possible to tell what targeted structure a learner has produced. The sentences that follow were produced by adult university students (data from J. Schachter, originally printed as Problem 8.1 in Selinker and Gass, 1984).

a   I am an accountant in Accounting Department of National Iranian Oil Company in Abadan which is one of the south cities of Iran.

b   There is a tire hanging down from the roof served as their playground.

c   Today you can find rural people that they don't have education.

d   My problem was to find a place has at least a yard for my children.

e   I wanted them to practice Chinese conversation what they learned every day.

f   When I return I plan to do accounting and supervising which is my interest and hope.

g   And it's a lovely view which you can see it from the plan.

h   Libya is quite a big country in which my home town is the biggest city.

i   Their philosophy depends on their education which they still working for it, as I am doing right now.

j   You can also go to the restaurant where you can have a good meal at a quiet table near the window.

k   I saw a group of people waiting for us.

l   Next week you give me a list of machine parts required in this contest.

Identify the restrictive and nonrestrictive clauses in the L2 sentences. List the criteria you used for deciding whether a sentence contains a restrictive or a nonrestrictive relative clause.

18 There is often a high level of inference in analyzing interlanguage data. For example, when looking at learners' utterances during conversational interaction, it may be hard to determine what the speaker's intention was and thus difficult to determine the target of the utterance. A consequence is that it may be difficult to classify the error in a sentence. As an example, consider the following example in which a native speaker (NS) and a nonnative speaker (NNS) are attempting to determine the extent to which two similar pictures have differences.

NS: What about dogs?
NNS: I have a dogs, right.
NS: OK, I have dogs too. How about cats?

In this example, the speakers are engaged in a communicative task, working together to spot the differences between two similar pictures. They could not see each other's picture. At first sight, it is difficult to determine whether the learner's use of the indefinite article or the plural is non-target-like. In other words, in English one could say either *I have a dog* or *I have dogs*. In this case, an examination of the task allows us to see that the native speaker's picture has two dogs, and the learner's picture has only one. Thus, the article was correct and the plural incorrect. However, the native speaker interpreted it differently, assuming she meant that she also had more than one dog. Carry out a similar task in pairs, with one onlooker. Make a note of any potential ambiguities that could arise if you were carrying out the task with a learner. How would you go about resolving such difficulties in interpreting meaning? (This problem is from A. Mackey.)

19 There are numerous difficulties in assessing learner knowledge of reflexives. Consider the following sentence with the several options given as to who *himself* could refer to.

Larry said that Joseph hit himself.

a   Larry
b   Joseph
c   Either Larry or Joseph
d   Someone else
e   Don't know

Native speakers of English know that *himself* can refer to Joseph and cannot refer to Larry. Does this format provide us with this information; that is, with information about what is possible and what is not possible? If it does not, how might you design a task that would provide a researcher with this information?

20 (To instructor) Make a recording of a learner narrating *Pancakes for Breakfast* by Tomie dePaola (or some other relatively simple text).

- Have students listen to the recording in order to make overall comments.
- Make a transcript and hand it out and play the recording again (maybe two times). Tell them to take notes about errors of grammar, lexicon, prosody, pronunciation.
- Have students discuss their differences in groups.

- Play tape again and discuss errors.
- Make a table on the board, such as the following:

Grammar	Lexicon	Prosody	Pronunciation

- Have class as a whole fill in the chart and determine which errors are ambiguous and which are not.
- Play tape again with the idea of listening for things that they may have missed before.
- Follow-up: make additional recordings and have students do their own analysis.

In the event that it is not possible to obtain a tape recording, the following is a transcript of an Arabic speaker learning English. Students can do an analysis focusing on grammar and lexicon, although some speculation can be made about pronunciation errors. (Thanks to Amy Thompson for the problem and the transcript.)

It was a small little house in the middle of nowhere. Inside the house this women was snuggling with her little kitten and her dog on the bed. She was washing her hands dreaming of pancakes. She was wondering how to make them. She grabbed his, her book of recipes and she started reading. 2 cups of flour, 2 sp, two teaspoon of baking powder. 3 tablespoons of butter, 3 tablespoons of sugar, and 1 spoon of salt and some eggs and milk. She found the flour but she didn't have any eggs so she went to the chicken house. She collected some eggs, and she went back inside the house, but she didn't find any mil,. She went to the barn and she started melting her cow. And she came back to the house. Her cat was watching her putting everything together. She started steering everything and she added the butter. But she didn't find the maple syrup. She went out. She bought some ma. Maple syrup. And on her way, she was dreaming how to make those delicious pancakes. By the time she came home, she was shocked. The dog ate all the eggs and the cat drank all the milk. Her dream flew away. She was very disappointed so she went to the neighbor's house. And they invited hair over for dinner. They served hair pancakes. She went back home, she was very full, and her dog was full, her cat was full, and they went to sleep.

See GSS, problems 1.1–1.3.

4

THE ROLE OF THE
NATIVE LANGUAGE:
AN HISTORICAL OVERVIEW

4.1 Introduction

The role of the native language has had a rocky history during the course of second language acquisition research. This subfield of SLA has come to be known as language transfer. As we will see in this chapter, much of the history of this central concept has been tied in with the varying theoretical perspectives on SLA. The acceptance and/or rejection of language transfer as a viable concept has been related to the acceptance or rejection of the specific theory with which it has been associated.

It has always been assumed that, in a second language learning situation, learners rely extensively on their native language. Lado, in his early and influential book *Linguistics Across Cultures* (1957), stated this clearly:

> individuals tend to transfer the forms and meanings, and the distribution of forms and meanings of their native language and culture to the foreign language and culture—both productively when attempting to speak the language and to act in the culture, and receptively when attempting to grasp and understand the language and the culture as practiced by natives.
>
> (p. 2)

Lado's work and much of the work of that time was based on the need to produce pedagogically relevant materials. To produce these native language-based materials, it was necessary to do a contrastive analysis of the native language and the target language. This entailed making detailed comparisons between the two languages in order to determine similarities and differences (see section 4.3 for further elaboration).[1]

To understand why language transfer was accepted as the mainstream view of language learning, it is necessary to understand the psychological and linguistic thinking at the time Lado was writing. In this chapter we review that literature briefly and then show how Lado's writings incorporated the theoretical positions of his time. We then deal with error analysis which was a reaction to contrastive analysis, although clearly investigating learner errors has had a long history.

It is important at this juncture to clarify one important aspect of our understanding of the term *transfer*. Although the original term used in the classical literature on transfer did not imply a separation into two processes, negative versus positive transfer, there has been some confusion in the use of the terms in the second language literature. Implicit in the use of these terms is that there are two different underlying learning processes, one of positive transfer and another of negative transfer. But the actual determination of whether or not a learner has positively or negatively transferred is based on the output, as analyzed by the researcher, teacher, native speaker/hearer, when compared and contrasted with target language output. In other words, these terms refer to the product, although their use implies a process. There is a process of transfer; there is not a process of negative or positive transfer. Thus, one must be careful when using terminology of this sort because the terminology suggests a confusion between product and process. Further discussion of this concept appears in section 4.2.2.

4.2 Behaviorism

Early research into language learning (both first and second) was heavily dependent on the dominant linguistic and psychological paradigms. In this chapter we present some of the background as it relates more generally to language learning, in particular first language learning.

4.2.1 Linguistic background

We turn now to a consideration of some of the assumptions about language and language learning prevalent during the same time. Bloomfield's classic work, *Language* (1933), provides the most elaborate description of the behaviorist position with regard to language.

The typical behaviorist position is that language is speech rather than writing. Furthermore, speech is a precondition for writing. The justification for this position came from the facts that (a) children without cognitive impairment learn to speak before they learn to write and (b) many societies have no written language, although all societies have oral language; there are no societies with only written but no spoken language systems.[2]

Within the behaviorist framework speaking consists of mimicking and analogizing. We say or hear something and analogize from it. Basic to this view is the concept of habits. We establish a set of habits as children and continue our linguistic growth by analogizing from what we already know or by mimicking the speech of others. But what makes us talk and carry on conversation?

To understand the answer to this question within the behaviorist framework, consider the following information:

> Suppose that Jack and Jill are walking down a lane. Jill is hungry. She sees an apple in a tree. She makes a sound with her larynx, tongue and lips. Jack vaults the fence, climbs the tree, takes the apple, brings it to Jill and places it in her hand. Jill eats the apple.
>
> (Bloomfield, 1933, pp. 22–23)

Bloomfield divides a situation like this into three parts:

1 Practical events before the act of speech (e.g., hungry feeling, sight of apple).
2 Speech event (making sound with larynx, tongue, and lips).
3 Hearer's response (Jack's leaping over the fence, fetching the apple, placing it in Jill's hand).

Thus, in this view, speech is the practical reaction (response) to some stimulus.

Whereas this describes the interrelationship between speech and action, it does not provide information about how children learn to behave in this way. Again, we turn to the late Bloomfieldian description of how language acquisition takes place.

1 The first step is interestingly babbling generated by a child, although Bloomfield implies that it is somehow the imperfect repetition of something the child has heard. Assume the child produces something similar to *da*. "The sound vibrations strike the child's ear-drums while he keeps repeating the movements. This results in a habit: whenever a similar sound strikes his ear, he is likely to make these same mouth-movements, repeating the sound *da*. This babbling trains him to reproduce vocal sounds which strike his ear" (pp. 29–30).
2 The next step is a pairing of this stimulus with the response of a native speaker. The process depends on somebody, such as the mother, saying something that resembles the babbling. "For instance, she says *doll*. When these sounds strike the child's ear, his habit (1) comes into play and he utters his nearest babbling syllable, *da*. We say that he is beginning to 'imitate.' Grown-ups seem to have observed this everywhere, for every language seems to contain certain nursery-words which resemble a child's babbling—words like *mama, dada*:

doubtless these got their vogue because children easily learn to repeat them" (p. 30).

3   Bloomfield assumes that stimulus and response explain why the mother would say doll in the first place. "She says *doll* when she is actually showing or giving the infant his doll. The sight and handling of the doll and the hearing and saying of the word *doll* (that is, *da*) occur repeatedly together, until the child forms a new habit: the sight and feel of the doll suffice to make him say *da*. He has now the use of a word. To the adults it may not sound like any of their words, but this is due merely to its imperfection" (p. 30).

4   Bloomfield then has to argue that the absence of the stimulus somehow creates another stimulus which generates the same response. "Suppose, for instance, that day after day the child is given his doll (and says *da, da, da*) immediately after his bath. He has now a habit of saying *da, da* after his bath; that is, if one day the mother forgets to give him the doll, he may nevertheless cry *da, da* after his bath. 'He is asking for his doll,' says the mother, and she is right, since doubtless an adult's 'asking for' or 'wanting' things is only a more complicated type of the same situation." (p. 30).

5   In accordance with behaviorist theory, Bloomfield posits that correct performance yields better results: "If he says *da, da* imperfectly—that is, at great variance from the adults' conventional form *doll*—then his elders are not stimulated to give him the doll. In short, his more perfect attempts at speech are likely to be fortified by repetition, and his failures to be wiped out in confusion. This process never stops. At a much later stage, if he says *Daddy bringed it*, he merely gets a disappointing answer such as *No! You must say 'Daddy brought it'*; but if he says *Daddy brought it*, he is likely to hear the form over again: *Yes, Daddy brought it*, and to get a favorable practical response" (pp. 30–31)

To sum up, from a theoretical perspective, the child learns to make the stimulus–response connection. One such connection is the uttering of the word *doll* (response) when the child sees the object (stimulus). Another connection is the reverse: the child gets the doll (response) when he or she hears the word (stimulus). Thus, learning involves the establishment of a habit by means of which these stimulus–response sets become associated.

4.2.2 Psychological background

The terminology used in a language-learning setting and the associated concepts (e.g., interference/facilitation) come from the literature on the psychology of learning. The leading psychological school of thought of the time was behaviorism. One of the key concepts in behaviorist theory (see also section 4.2.1) was the notion of transfer. The main claim with regard to transfer is that the learning of task A will affect the subsequent learning of task B. What is of interest is how fast and how well you learn something after having learned something else. Some examples will help clarify this notion.

From a physical perspective, if someone knows how to play tennis and then picks up a table tennis racket for the first time, she or he will use the knowledge/skills that have been gained from playing tennis in this new, but related, situation. Thus, old knowledge/skills are transferred to a new situation.

In a transfer experiment related to verbal learning, consider a study by Sleight (1911) in which he was concerned with the ability to memorize prose more easily if one has had "prior experience" in memorizing poetry. He compared four groups of 12-year-old children on their ability to memorize prose. Three groups had prior training on the memorization of (a) poetry, (b) tables of measures, or (c) content of prose passages. A fourth group had no prior training in any type of memorization. Following training, the groups were given tests that tested their ability to memorize prose. The question was: "To what extent does poetry memorization, or more precisely, the skills used in poetry memorization, transfer to memorization of prose?" (The results were nonsignificant.)

Let's consider an example from the area of language learning. According to the initial view of language transfer, if speakers of a particular language (in this case, Italian) form questions by saying:

(4-1) Mangia bene il   bambino?
     eats   well the baby
     "Does the baby eat well?"

then those same (Italian) speakers learning English would be expected to say

(4-2) Eats well the baby?

when asking a question in English.

A behaviorist notion underlying this expectation is that of habits and cumulative learning. According to behaviorist learning theory:

> Learning is a cumulative process. The more knowledge and skills an individual acquires, the more likely it becomes that his new learning will be shaped by his past experiences and activities. An adult rarely, if ever, learns anything completely new; however unfamiliar the task that confronts him, the information and

habits he has built up in the past will be his point of departure. Thus transfer of training from old to new situations is part and parcel of most, if not all, learning. In this sense the study of transfer is coextensive with the investigation of learning.

(Postman, 1971, p. 1019)

While this statement is not specifically intended as a description of language learning, we can see how the concepts were applied to second language learning.

A distinction noted above that is commonly made in the literature is between positive transfer (also known as facilitation) and negative transfer (also known as interference). These terms refer respectively to whether transfer results in something correct or something incorrect, and, to repeat a point made earlier, do not imply two distinct cognitive processes. As an example with relation to second language learning, if a Spanish speaker is learning Italian, when asking a question that speaker might correctly produce

(4-3) Mangia bene il bambino?
      eats   well the baby

because in Spanish one uses the same word order to form questions.

(4-4) ¿Come bien el niño?
      eats   well the baby

This is known as positive transfer. But if that same speaker is learning English and produces

(4-5) Eats well the baby?

the incorrect utterance is known as negative transfer.

With regard to interference, there are two types noted in the literature: (a) *retroactive inhibition*—where learning acts back on previously learned material, causing someone to forget (language loss)—and (b) *proactive inhibition*—where a series of responses already learned tends to appear in situations where a new set is required. This is more akin to the phenomenon of second language learning because the first language in this framework influences/inhibits/modifies the learning of the L2.

Most of the literature on transfer of learning dealt with very specific laboratory experiments (for a full discussion see Postman, 1971). The wholesale application of this framework to situations of second language learning is questionable. There is little empirical evidence in support of the assumption that, for example, forgetting outside the laboratory is a function of the same variables and represents the same processes as those observed in formal laboratory situations. So whereas it may be that learning task A affects the subsequent learning of task B in an experimental setting, one must question whether it is the case that this is so outside the lab. For example, when we go into a video game arcade and play a particular kind of simulation game, such as driving, do we carry over what we do in that situation to driving on the road?

These views did not go unchallenged and, in fact, the challenges were part of the early thinking of the field of SLA in the 1960s and 1970s. We return to this discussion in chapter 5.

We turn now to the work on second language learning that was based on these behaviorist positions. As noted earlier, Lado's work made these theoretical underpinnings explicit. Recall also that the major impetus for this work was pedagogical. In his foreword to Lado's book, Fries noted:

> Before any of the questions of how to teach a foreign language must come the much more important preliminary work of finding the special problems arising out of any effort to develop a new set of language habits against a background of different native language habits . . .
>
> Learning a second language, therefore, constitutes a very different task from learning the first language. The basic problems arise not out of any essential difficulty in the features of the new language themselves but primarily out of the special "set" created by the first language habits.
>
> (Fries, 1957)

Thus, underlying much work in the 1950s and 1960s was the notion of language as habit. Second language learning was seen as the development of a new set of habits. The role of the native language, then, took on great significance, because, in this view of language learning, it was the major cause for lack of success in learning the L2. The habits established in childhood interfered with the establishment of a different set of habits.

From this framework emerged contrastive analysis, because if one is to talk about replacing a set of habits (let's say, the habits of English) with another set of habits (let's say, those of Italian), valid descriptions are needed comparing the "rules" of the two languages. It would be misleading, however, to consider contrastive analysis in a monolithic fashion. In fact, there are two distinct traditions of contrastive analysis that emerged. In the North American tradition, the emphasis was on language teaching and, by implication, language learning. Contrastive analyses were conducted with the ultimate goal of improving classroom materials. As

Fisiak (1991) noted, this is more appropriately considered "applied contrastive analysis." In the European tradition, the goal of contrastive analysis was not pedagogical. Rather, the goal of language comparison was to gain a greater understanding of language. In fact, within the European tradition, it is maintained that contrastive analysis is a subdiscipline of linguistics. Its goal, like the goal of linguistics, is to understand the nature of language. In this book, we focus on the North American tradition as it relates more directly to the field of second language acquisition.

4.3 Contrastive Analysis Hypothesis

What are the tenets of contrastive analysis? Contrastive analysis is a way of comparing languages in order to determine potential errors for the ultimate purpose of isolating what needs to be learned and what does not need to be learned in a second-language-learning situation. As Lado detailed, one does a structure-by-structure comparison of the sound system, morphological system, syntactic system, and even the cultural system of two languages for the purpose of discovering similarities and differences. The ultimate goal is to predict areas that will be either easy or difficult for learners.

> Since even languages as closely related as German and English differ significantly in the form, meaning, and distribution of their grammatical structures, and since the learner tends to transfer the habits of his native language structure to the foreign language, we have here the major source of difficulty or ease in learning the structure of a foreign language. Those structures that are similar will be easy to learn because they will be transferred and may function satisfactorily in the foreign language. Those structures that are different will be difficult because when transferred they will not function satisfactorily in the foreign language and will therefore have to be changed.
>
> (Lado, 1957, p. 59)

The pedagogical materials that resulted from contrastive analyses were based on a number of assumptions, some of which have been discussed in detail earlier in this chapter:

1   Contrastive analysis is based on a theory of language that claims that language is habit and that language learning involves the establishment of a new set of habits.
2   The major source of error in the production and/or reception of a second language is the native language.

3 One can account for errors by considering differences between the
   L1 and the L2.
4 A corollary to item 3 is that the greater the differences, the more
   errors will occur.
5 What one has to do in learning a second language is learn the differences. Similarities can be safely ignored as no new learning is
   involved. In other words, what is dissimilar between two languages is
   what must be learned.
6 Difficulty and ease in learning is determined respectively by differences and similarities between the two languages in contrast.

There were two positions that developed with regard to the Contrastive
Analysis Hypothesis (CAH) framework. These were variously known as
the *a priori* versus the *a posteriori* view, the *strong* versus *weak* view and the
predictive versus *explanatory* view. In the strong view, it was maintained
that one could make predictions about learning and hence about the
success of language-teaching materials based on a comparison between
two languages. The weak version starts with an analysis of learners'
recurring errors. In other words, it begins with what learners do and then
attempts to account for those errors on the basis of NL–TL differences.
The weak version, which came to be part of error analysis, gained
credence largely due to the failure of predictive contrastive analysis. The
important contribution of the former approach to learner data (i.e., error
analysis) was the emphasis it placed on learners themselves, the forms
they produced, and the strategies they used to arrive at their IL forms.

Those arguing against the strong version of contrastive analysis were
quick to point out the many areas where the predictions made were not
borne out in actual learner production (see examples 4-7 to 4-9).

But there were other criticisms as well. Perhaps the most serious difficulty and one that ultimately led to the demise of contrastive analysis, a
hypothesis that assumed that the native language was the driving force of
second language learning, was its theoretical underpinnings. In the 1960s,
the behaviorist theory of language and language learning was challenged.
Language came to be seen in terms of structured rules instead of habits.
Learning was seen not as imitation but as active rule formation (see
chapter 5 for details).

The recognition of the inadequacies of a behaviorist theory of language had important implications for second language acquisition, for
if children were not imitators and were not influenced in a significant way
by reinforcement as they learned language, then perhaps second language
learners were not either. This became clear when researchers began to
look at the errors that learners made. Similar to data from child language
acquisition, second language learner data reflected errors that went
beyond those in the surrounding speech and, importantly, beyond those

in the native language. For example, it is not uncommon for beginning second language learners to produce an utterance such as 4-6:

(4-6) He comed yesterday.

in which the learner attempts to impose regularity on an irregular verb. There was no way to account for this fact within a theory based primarily on a learner transferring forms from the NL to the TL.

Not only did errors occur that had not been predicted by the theory, but also there was evidence that predicted errors did not occur. That is, the theory did not accurately predict what was happening in nonnative speech.

Dušková (1984) presents data from Czech speakers learning English and Russian. She found that those learning English did not transfer bound morphemes, whereas the Czech learners of Russian did. Within a theory based on the transference of NL forms, this could not be explained, for why should transfer occur in one instance, but not in another?

Yet another example is given by Zobl (1980). In data from French speakers learning English and English speakers learning French, Zobl found inconsistencies in actual error production. In French, object pronouns precede the verb, as in 4-7.

(4-7) Je les   vois.
      I them see
      "I see them."

In English, object pronouns follow the verb. However, the following facts emerge in learner data:

(4-8) By French learners of English
      I see them. (produced)
      *I them see. (not produced)
(4-9) By English learners of French (Ervin-Tripp, 1974, p. 119; Selinker, Swain, and Dumas, 1975, p. 145). None of these is possible in French.

      a. Je vois elle.
          I see her.
      b. Le chien a mangé les.
          The dog has eaten them.
      c. Il veut les encore.
          He wants them still.

In other words, French learners of English never prepose the object pronoun. Rather, they correctly follow English word order, which in this case is in violation of French word order. With English speakers, the reverse occurs: they follow the native language word order. If the "habits" of one's native language are the driving force, then why should they be operative in one language, but not the other?[3]

Yet another criticism of the role of contrastive analysis had to do with the concept of difficulty. Recall that a fundamental tenet of the CAH was that differences signified difficulty and that similarity signified ease. Difficulty in this view was equated with errors. If a learner produced an error, or errors, this was a signal that the learner was having difficulty with a particular structure or sound.

But what actually constitutes a sign of difficulty? Consider the following example from Kellerman (1987, p. 82), in which a student wrote:

(4-10) But in that moment it was 6:00.

In a conversation with the student, the teacher wanted her to comment on her use of the preposition *in*. The student insisted that the correct form was *in* but questioned whether it should be *it **was** 6:00* or *it **had been** 6:00*.

If we assume the dictionary definition of *difficulty* which is "hard to do, make, or carry out," then it becomes difficult to apply this concept to the common equation of error with difficulty. Clearly, the learner was having difficulty in the sense of struggling with something that was hard for her to do, but in this case the struggle was with tense usage even though there was no error reflecting that difficulty. On the other hand, there was no doubt in her mind about the correctness of the preposition. From her perspective, that was not an area of difficulty despite the overt error. So, difficulty cannot be unilaterally equated with errors, although (within the CAH) it is the predicted result of linguistic differences. Differences are based on formal descriptions of linguistic units—those selected by a linguist, a teacher, or a textbook writer. It is not a *real* measure of difficulty. To equate difference with difficulty attributes a psycholinguistic explanation to a linguistic description. It is a confusion of the product (a linguist's description) with the process (a learner's struggle with the second language).

We have mentioned some of the problems in assuming the validity of the CAH as Lado (1957) stated it. However, this discussion should not be interpreted as suggesting that there is no role for the native language in SLA, for this is clearly not the case. What it does suggest is that there are other factors that affect second language development and that the role of the native language is far more complex than the simple 1:1 correspondence implied by the early version of the CAH.

Language learning cannot be seen as just a matter of "linguistic hiccups" from native to target language (as Sharwood Smith, 1978, noted [cited in Kellerman, 1979]). There are other factors that may influence the process of acquisition, such as innate principles of language, attitude, motivation, aptitude, age, other languages known, and so forth. These topics are treated in subsequent chapters. For the present, suffice it to say that the acquisition of a second language is far too complex a phenomenon to be reduced to a single explanation.

Two final points need to be made with regard to the significance of contrastive analysis and to Lado's pioneering work. First, it is an oversimplification to think that comparing two languages is a straightforward comparison of structures. Lado in his detailed treatment elaborated on ways in which languages might differ. After a discussion of ways in which different languages expressed similar meanings, Lado (1957, pp. 63–64) stated:

> In the above cases we assumed that the meanings signaled in the two languages were in some way equivalent even if not identical. We went so far as to call them "same." The difficulty in such cases depended on differences in the formal devices used in the two languages to signal the "same" meanings. We now turn to cases in which a grammatical meaning in one of the languages cannot be considered the same as any grammatical meaning in the other language.

Recognition of the complexity of comparing languages became apparent quite early, particularly in works such as that of Stockwell, Bowen, and Martin (1965a, 1965b), who, rather than dichotomize the results of language comparison into easy and difficult and therefore dichotomize the needs of learning into a *yes/no* position, established a hierarchy of difficulty and, by implication, a hierarchy of learning. Included in this hierarchy are different ways in which languages can differ.

For example, in their framework the most difficult category is that in which there is differentiation: the native language has one form, whereas the target language has two. According to this view, an English speaker learning Italian (or Spanish or French) would find the translation equivalent of the verb *to know* difficult, because in Italian there are two possibilities: *sapere*, meaning to know a fact, to have knowledge of something, or to know how to do something; and *conoscere*, meaning to be familiar or acquainted with something. A second and third type of difference between languages occurs when there is a category present in language X and absent in language Y. As an example, consider the English article system. Because Japanese does not have articles, for a Japanese learner of English, a new category must be learned. An example of the third type is an English learner of Japanese where there is an absent category (i.e., no articles). A fourth difference is found in situations in

Table 4.1 Hierarchy of difficulty

Category	Example
Differentiation	English L1, Italian L2: *to know* versus *sapere/conoscere*
New category	Japanese L1, English L2: article system
Absent category	English L1, Japanese L2: article system
Coalescing	Italian L1, English L2: the verb *to know*
Correspondence	English L1, Italian L2: plurality

which the opposite of differentiation occurs, i.e. coalescing (e.g., an Italian speaker learning the English words *to know*). Finally, correspondence occurs when two forms are used in roughly the same way (e.g., plurality in English and Italian). The hierarchy of these differences reveals the complexity of doing cross-linguistic comparisons (Table 4.1).

A second point concerning the significance of the Contrastive Analysis Hypothesis has to do with the importance of empirical validation and the limitations that Lado himself attributed to his work. As we discussed earlier, part of the criticism leveled against contrastive analysis was empirical: not all actually occurring errors were predicted; not all predicted errors occurred. The lack of empirical basis was, in fact, noted by Lado (1957, p. 72):

> *Necessity of Validating the Results of the Theoretical Comparative Analysis*
> The list of problems resulting from the comparison of the foreign language with the native language will be a most significant list for teaching, testing, research, and understanding. Yet it must be considered a list of hypothetical problems until final validation is achieved by checking it against the actual speech of students. This final check will show in some instances that a problem was not adequately analyzed and may be more of a problem than predicted. In this kind of validation we must keep in mind of course that not all the speakers of a language will have exactly the same amount of difficulty with each problem. . . . The problem will nevertheless prove quite stable and predictable for each language background.

Historically, Lado's hypothesis inspired a generation of second language researchers to conduct linguistic field work, that is, to check hypothetical contrastive analysis statements against the actual speech of language learners. This much-cited passage presages the current acceptance of the centrality of individual variation, as will be discussed in chapter 12. One way of fulfilling Lado's injunction to check hypothetical problems against actual learner production was to refocus on learner errors from which developed an approach called *error analysis*.

4.4 Error analysis

What is error analysis? As the name suggests, it is a type of linguistic analysis that focuses on the errors learners make. Unlike contrastive analysis (in either its weak or strong form), the comparison made is between the errors a learner makes in producing the TL and the TL form itself. It is similar to the weak version of contrastive analysis in that both start from learner production data; however, in contrastive analysis the comparison is made with the native language, whereas in error analysis it is made with the TL.

Even though the main emphasis in second language studies during the 1950s and 1960s was on pedagogical issues, a shift in interests began to emerge. The conceptualization and significance of errors took on a different role with the publication of an article by Corder (1967) titled "The significance of learners' errors." Unlike the typical view held at the time by teachers, errors, in Corder's view, are not just to be seen as something to be eradicated, but rather can be important in and of themselves.

Errors can be taken as red flags; they provide windows onto a system— that is, evidence of the state of a learner's knowledge of the L2. They are not to be viewed solely as a product of imperfect learning; hence, they are not something for teachers to throw their hands up in the air about. As with research on child language acquisition (see chapter 2), it has been found that second language errors are not a reflection of faulty imitation. Rather, they are to be viewed as indications of a learner's attempt to figure out some system, that is, to impose regularity on the language the learner is exposed to. As such, they are evidence of an underlying rule-governed system. In some sense, the focus on errors is the beginning of the field of second language acquisition, which at this point is beginning to emerge as a field of interest not only for the pedagogical implications that may result from knowing about second language learning, but also because of the theoretical implications for fields such as psychology (in particular learning theory) and linguistics.

In the same article, Corder was careful to distinguish between errors and mistakes. Mistakes are akin to slips of the tongue. That is, they are generally one-time-only events. The speaker who makes a mistake is able to recognize it as a mistake and correct it if necessary. An error, on the other hand, is systematic. That is, it is likely to occur repeatedly and is not recognized by the learner as an error. The learner in this case has incorporated a particular erroneous form (from the perspective of the TL) into his or her system. Viewed in this way, errors are only errors from a teacher's or researcher's perspective, not from the learner's. Taken from the perspective of a learner who has created a grammatical system (an interlanguage), everything that forms part of that interlanguage system by definition belongs there. Hence, there can be no errors in that system. Errors are only errors with reference to some external norm (in this case the TL). For example, if a learner produces the following negative forms:

(4-11) No speak.
(4-12) No understand.

and if we assume that these are consistent deviations and form part of a learner's system, then it is only possible to think of them as errors with regard to English, but not with regard to the learner's system.

Along with the criticisms that were leveled against contrastive analysis and along with the accompanying emphasis on the learner and the learners' errors, there was a concomitant focus on error analysis.

A great deal of the work on error analysis was carried out within the context of the classroom. The goal was clearly one of pedagogical remediation. There are a number of steps taken in conducting an error analysis.

1   *Collect data.* Although this is typically done with written data, oral data can also serve as a base.
2   *Identify errors.* What is the error (e.g., incorrect sequence of tenses, wrong verb form, singular verb form with plural subject)?
3   *Classify errors.* Is it an error of agreement? Is it an error in irregular verbs?
4   *Quantify errors.* How many errors of agreement occur? How many irregular verb form errors occur?
5   *Analyze source.* See later discussion.
6   *Remediate.* Based on the kind and frequency of an error type, pedagogical intervention is carried out.

Error analysis provides a broader range of possible explanations than contrastive analysis for researchers/teachers to use to account for errors, as the latter only attributed errors to the NL. In comparison, there are two main error types within an error analysis framework: interlingual and intralingual. Interlingual errors are those which can be attributed to the NL (i.e., they involve cross-linguistic comparisons). Intralingual errors are those that are due to the language being learned, independent of the NL.[4] One would therefore expect similar intralingual errors to occur from speakers of a wide variety of first languages. Examples are given in Table 4.2.

Table 4.2 Categorization of errors

Type	Source	NL	TL	Example
Interlingual	NL-based	French	English	*We just enjoyed to move and to play*[a]
Intralingual	Regularization	All	English	*He comed yesterday*

[a]In French, verb complements are in the infinitival form. There is no *ing* equivalent in French.

Error analysis was not without its detractors. One of the major criticisms of error analysis was directed at its total reliance on errors to the exclusion of other information. That is, critics argued, one needs to consider nonerrors as well as errors to get the entire picture of a learner's linguistic behavior.

Perhaps the most serious attempt at showing the inadequacies of error analysis comes from a 1974 article by Schachter. She collected 50 compositions from each of four groups of learners of English: native speakers of Persian, Arabic, Chinese, and Japanese. Her research focused on the use of English restrictive relative clauses (RC) by each of these four groups. The findings in terms of errors are given in Table 4.3 (taken from Table 4.4).

Table 4.3 Number of relative clause errors

NL group	Number
Persian	43
Arabic	31
Chinese	9
Japanese	5
American	0

If we were to interpret these findings from an error analysis perspective, we would have to conclude that the Japanese and Chinese speakers have control over the formation of English restrictive relative clauses and that the Persian and Arabic speakers do not. However, Schachter's analysis went beyond the errors to look at the total production of relative clauses, including error-free relative clauses. This analysis is presented in Table 4.4.

Including errors and nonerrors is far more revealing with regard to the control speakers of various language groups have over restrictive relative clauses. Although it is true that the Persian and Arabic speakers had a

Table 4.4 Relative clause production

NL group	Correct	Error	Total	% errors
Persian	131	43	174	25
Arabic	123	31	154	20
Chinese	67	9	76	12
Japanese	58	5	63	8
American	173	0	173	—

Source: From "An error in error analysis" by J. Schachter, 1974, *Language Learning, 24,* 205–214 by Research Club in Language Learning. Reprinted by permission.

greater percentage of errors than did the Chinese and Japanese learners, it is also the case that the Chinese and Japanese produced roughly half as many relative clauses as did the Persian and Arabic groups. What might account for this discrepancy and why is it significant?

If one considers the ways in which the languages of Schachter's study form relative clauses, it becomes apparent why these results occur. Japanese and Chinese form relative clauses by placing the modifier (the relative clause) before the noun it modifies, as in the following examples:

(4-13) Japanese
Watashi-wa Eigo-o   hanasu josei-o   mimashita.
I   subj English obj. talks   woman obj. saw
"I saw the woman who speaks English."

(4-14) Chinese
Wo kandao nei ge shuo   ying yu   de   nuren.
I   saw   the CL speaks English language RM woman
"I saw the woman who speaks English."
CL = classifier; RM = relative marker

Persian and Arabic relative clauses are similar to English in that the relative clause is placed after the noun it modifies, as in the following examples:

(4-15) Arabic
ana raait Al Emraah allety tatakalem Al-Englizy.
I   saw the woman who   speaks   the English
"I saw the woman who speaks English."

(4-16) Persian
an zaenra   ke inglisi haerfmizaene didaem.
that woman that Eng. speaks   I saw
"I saw the woman who speaks English."

It thus seems reasonable to assume that because of the great distance between the way in which the native language forms relative clauses (as in the case with Japanese and Chinese speakers) and the way in which the target language forms relative clauses, learners do not use the construction with great frequency. When they do use it, they use it cautiously and with a high degree of accuracy. The Persian and Arabic learners, on the other hand, use relative clauses more frequently (and are thus likely to produce more errors), because their NL structure is similar to the TL structure. Hence, the NL is a determining factor in accounting for the facts of relative clause production, yet these facts would not be apparent through an error analysis alone.

A second difficulty with error analysis is the determination of what an error is an error of. Schachter and Celce-Murcia (1971) gave the following examples from Chinese learners of English:

(4-17) There are so many Taiwan people live around the lake.

(4-18) There were lots of events happen in my country.

(4-19) . . . and there is a mountain separate two lakes.

(4-20) . . . and there are so many tourist visit there.

At first glance, these look like relative clauses without the relative marker (*that, who, which*). However, another plausible explanation is one that accounts for these not as failed attempts at relative clause productions, but rather as constructions parallel to topic–comment constructions in the native language of these speakers. That is, these learners are following an appropriate native language pattern of establishing a topic (*Taiwan people, lots of events, mountain, tourist*) and then making a comment about it (*they live around the lake, they happen in my country, it separates two lakes, they live there*). This is not unlike the following construction in English: *You see that man? He just ran a red light* as opposed to *Did you see that man who just ran a red light?*

Schachter (1983, 1992) presented another example of an Arabic speaker learning English.

(4-21) But when oil discovered in 1948 and began export it in 1950 . . .

She interpreted this as a passive construction, the problem being the lack of the tensed form of the verb *to be*. However, it is not clear that this is the only interpretation. One could plausibly argue that this is not a passive, but that the verb *discover* could be interpreted in the TL by the learner as a verb that occurs in both transitive and intransitive variants (like the verb *boil* in *I boiled the water* and *The water boiled*). Thus, there can be a discrepancy between what a researcher determines to be the targeted structure and what the learner was actually attempting to produce.

Yet another inadequacy of error analysis is the attempt to ascribe causes to errors. There is an assumption that, if a form is correct, then the underlying rule is also correct. However, consider a learner who produces the following two sentences:

(4-22) I wanted him to come.
(4-23) I persuaded him to come.

A reasonable assumption is that this learner has learned that these verbs require an infinitival complement. Let's further consider the following two hypothetical sentences, which occur at a later stage:

(4-24) I enjoyed talking to my teacher.
(4-25) I stopped sending packages to my friend.

At this point the conclusion would be that this learner has learned that there are verbs that require gerundive complements. However, at a still later stage, the learner produces:

(4-26) I saw him to come.
(4-27) I enjoyed talking to you.

One might assume from looking at the first two stages that the learner knows that there are two possibilities for forming verbal complements in English, and that, furthermore, the learner knows which verbs take which type of complement. However, when one realizes (in Stage 3) that the learner has not correctly sorted out the facts of English, then one is led to a different analysis: the learner applies infinitival complements at Stage 1, gerundive complements at Stage 2; and only later realizes (Stage 3) that some verbs take one type of complement, and other verbs take another type of complement. At this point, the learner has not yet learned which verb is of which type. The error in sentence 4-26 is significant in that it reveals that the learner does not have the correct rule worked out. However, the absence of error in the previous two stages does not mean correct rule formation; it only suggests a limited sampling bias. It is important to note that, despite the fact that the data from Stages 1 and 2 reflect correct English usage, they are further from the correct system than the data in Stage 3, which shows that the learner is aware of the fact that the two complement types depend on the main verb. In sum, error analysis alone cannot provide us with this information, because an assumption of error analysis is that correct usage is equivalent to correct rule formation.

Finally, we deal with another problematic area of error analysis relating to the source of errors. Within the framework of error analysis, the assumption is that errors can be categorized as belonging to one source or another. Dulay and Burt (1974b) recognized the fact that sometimes one cannot determine whether an error is of one type or another. To reflect this, they established a category called ambiguous goofs, which is defined as "those that can be categorized as either Interference-like Goofs or L1 Developmental Goofs" (p. 115). An example of an interference-like goof is *hers pajamas* produced by a Spanish-speaking child. This reflects Spanish noun–adjective agreement and is not found among English-speaking children learning their first language. An L1 developmental goof, as in *He took her teeths off* (produced by a Spanish-speaking child), is not found in Spanish L1, but is a typical overgeneralization error of English L1 children. An ambiguous error, such as *Terina not can go* (produced by a Spanish speaker), can be interpreted as either an interference error because it reflects a Spanish structure or as a developmental error because it is also found in English-speaking children learning their first language.

However, is it reasonable to say that there must always be a single etiology for errors? That is, must errors be of type X or of type Y, but not both? A few examples will suffice to show that learner production may be influenced simultaneously by multiple sources.[5]

Dušková (1983) reports on the acquisition of the English article system by native speakers of Czech, a language that does not have definite or indefinite articles. She pointed out that the difficulty in ultimately getting the facts of the English article system correct is due to the lack of a comparable system in the NL. However, that alone does not account for all of the problems Czech speakers encounter. Compounding the problem for these Czech speakers is the English article system itself. Here are examples from her data:

(4-28) I should like to learn foreign language.
(4-29) It was very interesting journey.
(4-30) We shall use present solution.
(4-31) I visited Institute of Nuclear Energy in Ljublana.
(4-32) As in many other cases the precise rules do not exist.
(4-33) . . . working on the similar problem as I.

In the first four examples, there is a (possibly) straightforward explanation in terms of the native language as no articles are present. However, in the last two examples, the definite article is used where either no article (4-32) or an indefinite article (4-33) would have been appropriate. Thus, whereas the major underlying source of the problem may indeed be the lack of a category in the NL, the TL also contributes in that there are various functions of articles in English that the learner must sort out.

Error analysis yielded a number of studies in which patterns of acquisition were clearly attributable to knowledge of both the TL and the NL. Schumann (1979), in a study of the acquisition of negation, demonstrated the convergence of linguistic information from two systems. Schumann's study focused on the acquisition of English by Spanish speakers, but his data were also compared to similar acquisitional data from speakers of other languages. In general, he found similar patterns of development, but he also found important differences.

Schumann noted that, initially, negative utterances are formed by using the word *no*, which is placed before the verb, as in the following examples (Stage 1):

(4-34) no understand
(4-35) no you told me
(4-36) no swim
(4-37) no correct

A second stage of development is seen with the occurrence of *don't*, as in 4-38 and 4-39.

(4-38) don't like
(4-39) I don't saw him

Next, learners show an increased use of *not* as opposed to *no* as a negator (4-40)

(4-40) not today

as well as the use of *not* following the verb *to be* and the auxiliary (4-41, 4-42).

(4-41) I'm not old enough.
(4-42) I will don't see you tomorrow.

Still later, learners begin to use variants of *don't* (i.e., *doesn't*, *didn't*), as opposed to the previous stage where *don't* was used in all cases (all persons, present/past).

(4-43) I didn't went to Costa Rica.

And finally, most learners sort out the facts of negation and learn that, in negation, *do* is the element that bears tense and person distinctions.

In looking at the source of errors, one notes that Spanish is a language with preverbal negation, the negative element being *no*.

(4-44) No voy.
no I go
"I don't go."
(4-45) El no puede ir.
he no can   go
"He can't go."

What is most germane to this discussion of error analysis is the fact that when these data are compared to the acquisition of English negation by native speakers of languages other than Spanish (or languages similar to Spanish), slightly different facts emerge. For speakers of languages with preverbal negation (e.g., Spanish, Italian, Greek), Stage 1 is more persistent than it is with speakers of languages without preverbal negation (e.g., German, Norwegian, Japanese). In the speech of learners from this latter group, the *no* + verb stage is short or even nonexistent.

Schumann concluded that, in the case of the Spanish speaker, two forces converge: the native language and facts of development (children learning English also exhibit a preverbal *no* stage in the development of negation). However, in the case of speakers of languages such as Japanese, only one factor is at play: development. A single source will have less influence than converging sources and will lead the learner to move much more rapidly in the developmental sequence.

In sum, error analysis, although important in the recognition that learners were more than passive hiccupers of NL forms and functions, falls short in the analysis of second language data in that it only sees a partial picture of what a learner produces of the second language. One cannot hope to appreciate the complexity of the learning situation by studying one limited part of it.

4.5 Conclusion

In this chapter we presented an historical overview of the role of the native language, showing the historical struggle of moving from behaviorist contrastive analysis to a consideration of the actual speech of learners through the prism of errors. In chapter 5, we deal with more recent conceptualizations of the role of the native language.

Suggestions for additional reading

A *Psycholinguistic Study of Phonological Interference*. Eugene Brière. Mouton (1968).

Language Transfer in Language Learning. Susan Gass and Larry Selinker (Eds.). John Benjamins (1992).

Cross-Linguistic Influence in Second Language Acquisition. Eric Kellerman and Michael Sharwood Smith (Eds.). Pergamon (1986).

An Experimental Study of Phonological Interference in the English of Hungarians. William Nemser. Mouton (1971).

Language Transfer. Terence Odlin. Cambridge University Press (1989).

The Role of the First Language in Foreign Language Learning. Håkan Ringbom. Multilingual Matters (1987).

Rediscovering Interlanguage. Larry Selinker. Longman (1992).

Points for discussion

1   In this chapter we have been concerned with the role of the native language in the formation and use of interlanguage. We have chosen to discuss this factor early in the book and in great detail because it is a factor that has been debated for centuries. The earliest known reference is in the book of Judges, where in chapter 12 the famous story is told of "the men of Ephraim" who went out to battle and did not do so well. In order to detect who was a fleeing Ephraimite and who was not, the Gileadites set up a very practical language test for the Ephraimites, who tradition says could not pronounce the sound *sh*. The actual passage reads as follows:

> Jephthah then called together the men of Gilead and fought against Ephraim. The Gileadites struck them down because the Ephraimites had said, "You Gileadites are renegades from Ephraim and Manasseh." The Gileadites captured the fords of the Jordan leading to Ephraim, and whenever a survivor of Ephraim said, "Let me cross over," the men of Gilead asked him, "Are you an Ephraimite?" If he replied, "No," they said, "All right, say 'Shibboleth',", If he said, "Sibboleth," because he could not pronounce the word correctly, they seized him and killed him at the fords of the Jordan. Forty-two thousand Ephraimites were killed at that time.
>
> (Judges 12:4–6. *The Holy Bible*, New International Version, Hodder and Stoughton, London, 1988)

Evaluate this story in light of the information on the effect of native language influence presented in this chapter. Can you think of other important cases where identification of a person by native language accent has played an important role?

2   As described in this chapter, beginning second language learners produce sentences such as *He comed yesterday* where regular rules are extended to irregular cases. What does this suggest about the

formation of early interlanguage? Can you think of cases in your own language learning where you have tried to impose such regularity improperly? Relate your characterization to the strengths and weaknesses of the contrastive analysis hypothesis.

3 Consider the two types of *interference* discussed in this chapter: retroactive and proactive. In terms of the former, under what circumstances might it be possible to lose some of your native language fluency? What parts of the native language might you predict would be most affected?

4 Consider the process of looking at structures across languages. Do you agree that one can easily note similarities of structures and differences of structures? Do you agree that these cannot equal ease and difficulty of learning? In what circumstances might similarities/differences be compatible with ease/difficulty of learning?

5 Describe the two major positions of contrastive analysis: *a priori* and *a posteriori*. In what ways is this a useful dichotomy? Suppose we were to say that in reality we are not dealing with a dichotomy, but with a continuum, where each of the named positions reflects one of the extremes. Does this conceptualization alter your belief in the usefulness of these positions? Can one then say that the former is predictive, whereas the latter is explanatory?

6 As noted in this chapter, there is a lack of bidirectionality in cases such as the French–English word order of pronouns. In light of this, evaluate the following French sentences produced by native speakers of English:

    (i)   Il veut moi de dire français à il.
           He wants me to say French to him.
           Correct form: Il veut que je lui parle français ("He wants that I to him speak French.")

    (ii)   Un chalet où   on va aller à.
           A cottage where one goes to go to.
           Correct form: Un chalet où on va aller.

From context we know that the intention of these sentences is:

    (ia) He wants me to speak French to him.
    (iia) A cottage that we're going to go to.

Weinreich (1953), in discussing similar examples, claimed that examples of interference such as these are plentiful. Do you want to characterize these as interference? Why or why not?

7 Compare the approaches to the analysis of second language data discussed in this chapter, contrastive analysis and error analysis, with regard to the following:

a   There may be covert errors. A classic example from Corder (1981) is the German speaker who says "You must not take off your hat" when the intent is "You don't have to take off your hat." In what sense is this an error? In what sense is it not?

b   It might be more appropriate to talk about TL-like behavior. The fact that a learner has produced a correct form/sentence in a language does not necessarily mean that it is right.

c   It is not always possible to provide a single explanation for inter-language data.

8   A number of problems arise with the incorporation of the concept of "transfer" from psychology into SLA. Primary among them is the emphasis on controlled experimentation in a laboratory setting within the framework of the psychology of learning. To apply this to a second language situation is difficult because many other variables come into play in second language acquisition that are difficult to control. For example, controlled material presented in a laboratory setting differs from a second language learning situation in the complexity of what is being learned. What other differences can you think of between actual second language learning and experimental learning?

9   In the discussion of errors, it was pointed out that errors are only errors from an external perspective (i.e., a teacher's or a researcher's). Is it possible that there are consistently incorrect forms (i.e., errors) that a learner recognizes as errors but that remain as errors because a learner does not know how to correct them? Do you think that these would be forms "ripe" for change? Or are they likely to fossilize?

10 Four compositions follow. First, do an error analysis of each. Describe the difficulties you encounter in doing this. Are there ambiguities? How could you resolve them? Do you know what the NLs are of these writers? What features determine your choice?

Composition 1

"Things are rough all over" for Socs and Greasers

There are many teenagers in *The Outsiders*, and each of them has several characteristics. There are many differences between the Socs and the Greasers, and each character who belongs to these groups has a different background. However, Cherry's saying, "Things are rough all over," applies to all characters in the story, so both the Socs and the Greasers have some "things" and "roughness." However, their "things" are not equally "rough."

Cherry says "Things are rough all over" as Soc. For Cherry and all the Socs, the part of rough is Rat race. Though they can get everything they want, it does not satisfy them. Because of it, the Socs take actions like Cherry said; we're always searching for something to satisfy us, and never finding it (p. 37). It might be suffering that the Greasers can not experience because they were not born in environment like the Socs. In addition, people who can not find something to satisfy them do antisocial behavior, and they are done to catch the hearts of their parents and people surrounded him. In the fact, Bob did so. His parents gave in to him, but he was not given loves from his parents. He came home drunker than anything to grab his parents' hearts, but he could not get his parents' love. In the other words, "things" are parents' love for Bob, and it was so "rough" for him, so "things are rough" to him. In addition, Cherry says to Ponyboy that the Socs also have sufferings, and it is not easy to solve them; that means Cherry's "things are rough all over."

Of course, not only the Socs but also the Greasers also have "things." For example, Johnny is not given love from his parents, Ponyboy's parents have been dead and he thinks his oldest brother hates him, and both his brothers, Sodapop and Darry, have worries about their brothers. Even Dallas, who seems so tough, suffers and wants to die. Thus, All of them have "things," but their "things" are not equally "rough." For example, Ponyboy's parents never return, and Dallas can't talk with anyone about his "things," but it is possible that Johnny's worry is able to be solved if Jonny talks with his parents. It means their things have two types; fist type is that they can not solve immediately, another type is that they can not solve any more. Moreover, each of their "things" has different difficulty to solve them. In the fact, Pony's brothers can resolve one of their "things" in the end of the story, but many characters still have their "things" by the end. Thus, each of the Greasers has different levels of "roughness."

Cherry wants Ponyboy to understand that both the Socs and the Greasers can not have it made. However, it is so difficult to Ponyboy to understand that because there is a big difference between the Socs and the Greasers. That is wealth. Ponyboy and all the Greasers have lived with preposition and poorness. In addition, the Socs also have their "things" and "roughness." However, the Greasers have problems of preposition and poorness besides their own "things," so "things" are also unequally "rough" between these two groups. When Ponyboy heard Cherry's words, he did not know about similarities and differences between the Socs and the Greasers. In the fact, he had some misunderstanding about the Socs; maybe it was money that separated us (p. 38), and I really couldn't see what Socs would have to sweat about. I thought if I had worries like them I'd consider I'm lucky (p. 36). In addition, he did not perceive "things" and "roughness" of the same team members. Therefore, it was so difficult to him to understand Cherry's words at that time. However, he came to understand Cherry's words gradually. He learned about his friends' and his brothers' suffering by talking with them, and he understood the Socs by hearing about Bob from Randy; he could find that all the Greasers have their "things" and "roughness," and even in the Socs who are rich kids also have worries same as the Greasers. Their worries are different, but it is the fact that all of them have some suffering. As Ponyboy noticed it, he was able to understand Cherry's words.

Cherry's words, "Things are rough all over," are true for all the Socs and the Greasers, but all characters in *The Outsiders* have different "things" and "roughness." The Socs have worries because of the wealth, and the Greasers also have worries because of their backgrounds. However, these differences are not important for Ponyboy. It is important for him that all people belonging to the Socs and the Greasers have suffering and worries, and it is significant that he know the other guys are also human.

Composition 2

Family and its power!

In society exists various groups and one of these is family. Family has an important meaning but sometime we misunderstand what really is! Surely, standard family consists of husband and wife and children but his sense is wider. Family are we, family are friends that share emotions, family is my grandfather, family is my class; it exists everywhere where people join together and form a group sharing everything. In this last month I have had a lot of opportunity to read and learn about it. For instance, I read the book *Nightjohn*, as well as seeing the movie, and I spent a lot of time in sharing thoughts with my classmates about this topic. The most cruel, but significant, example that I can use to explain family and its power is the why slave owners commonly broke up slave families. They had to maintain black people mentally weak to continue to live in their white status, and to reach such bad goal they separated its member to prevent rebellions. They had fear to lose power and money.

In fact, they had big cotton plantations and they owned black people; this gave them power in society and power on the slaves. They had this privileged life, for they hadn't to work but they had to scrutinize the slaves' works only. They were completely served and believed that their white status was superior of the black one. All this characteristics make them trust to be powerful, and to have the right to continue in such behavior. In the book there is a passage that I want to quote because it explains why white people had so fear of rebellion. "'Cause to know things, for us to know things, is bad for them. We get to wanting and when we get to wanting it's bad for them. They think we want what they got (39)." What they got was power, and they were so afraid to lose it that didn't hesitate in whipping slaves until death.

Another reason was money. Having a plantation and owning slaves meant to be rich because every slave has money value and all together formed the muster's wealthy. I want to narrate a passage in the *Nightjohn* that impressed me. The scenario developed in church among an argument between muster and slaves; he was furious and menaced to shot them with the gun, and, all of the sudden, *Sarny* stood up and cried out loud to didn't have fear to be shouted, because they were his wealth and he would never shot. Slaves worked in plantation that produced cotton; more over, they were money and could be traded if there was good opportunity. Indeed, *Sarny*'s mother was sold because she was a good breeder and muster did a good trade.

In the reason why master broke up slaves family lay hidden the family's power. Family is the place where the individual can find his own identity and to develop a sense of power. Identity is very important because everyone needs to know own root. This teaches us who we are and what are our values and our rights. In family we are socialized and we learn how to behave and what to aspect from our environment. Furthermore, everyday by sharing emotions, ideals, dream we grow and become stronger and capable to accept sufferance.

I'm positive with family. I met my wife seventeen years ago and we immediately engaged and after seven years we got married. Nine months ago Viola, my sweetie daughter, was born and I feel to have achieved what I had ever dreamed from my life. Power and money are nothing without love and family.

Maybe this can seem a common sentence, but if you are in my condition, you know what I'm talking about. I can't imagine a life without my family, I get lost without it and I need to thank god for such luckiness.

I want to finish this essay remembered *Nightjohn* movie when *Delie* said him, "You have a new family now and every-where you go you'll find a new one." This is a big truth! In life everyone have good and bad moments, but what is really important is to have someone to share with. Remember that family is everywhere! Family are friends, family are parents, strangers and family are my wife and my Viola.

Composition 3

Peer pressure influences teenagers

Peer pressure influences teenagers in many aspects. It may have positive or negative matters. Friends have the biggest influence on each other. Girls and boys in their teenage period like to stick with each other if they share the same interests, or even if they are in the same status. They also feel uncomfortable when they join new group that is different from the group they usually stick with. In the Outsider's novel, there are two groups; Greasers and Socs. Each group influences its members with different kinds of matters.

There are some usual influences among the members in each group. They do many things which might be in their culture, habits, or they follow each other by apery. For example, Greasers influence each other by letting their hair grow up and they do not like any body to tell them to cut it. Furthermore, most of Greasers wear blue jeans, T-shirts, and tennis shoes or boots. On the other hand, Socs wear nice, expensive clothes with leather shoes. I can see most of the Socs are rich and drive expensive cars while the Greasers who were poor, drive cheap cars and use simple things.

Moreover, there were some negative attitudes in both groups with their members. For example, there was a girl whose named was Cherry said to ponyboy, did not take it personally if I did not talk with you in school. She meaned by that she was from Socs and he was from Greasers and if she talked with him, she would lose her friends and they would give her bad treatment because of the race which they had against each other. Another thing, the guys influenced each other in many bad things: I could see most of them smoked cigarettes and some drink alcohol even though others were young people. In addition for that, there was no body would stop them because there was no one telling them that the smoking and drinking caused many health problems in their life.

There were some bad attitudes from the friends who were surrounded ponyboy. I can see Dally was always trying to tell his friend ponyboy to be tough and strong against other people who faced him like Greasers. In addition, Dally most the time made fun of people, showed off and insulted children in front of his friends ponyboy and Johnny. People do not like get directions. For example, Derry the oldest brother of pony boy always gave him directions which ponyboy did not like while ponyboy liked his second oldest brother Soda more than Derry because he understood him more and considered him like adult and did not give him directions so I could see pony-boy influenced more form Soda.

There are also some positive effects to ponyboy from his friends who were around him. He had a good friend whose named was Johnny always helped him, did not like to fight with other people and one time he bought a book and gave it to him and told him keep reading the book, because book would be best friend and stay with you until you die. One time Johnny had telling ponyboy fight was not good and useless. In addition, there was also a good advice from him that he said to ponyboy several time "stay gold, stay gold and nothing good can stay." I can see also ponyboy learned to help people with his friends Dally and Johnny after the church had burned, even caused his life to death but he tried with them to take out people who were in church and to save their life with his brave and his friends encouragements.

In brief, peer pressure might be good and bad on adults and even more on teenagers. We need to get the positive things from good peer pressure and try to be away from people who have bad influence on us by the advice which Johnny said "stay good" and this would be a great full advice we can learn from life.

Composition 4

My sibling's relationship

Not everyone has luck to have brothers or sisters in the family, but I am the lucky one; I have one brother. He is one year old younger than me. He is not a lovely younger brother and I am also not a lovely elder brother. We always call each others full name, never call each other "brother"; however, we still respect and help each other. Of course, sometimes we do argue and fight, but we are still brothers. There are some similar and contracts relationships between the book, *The Outsiders*. I am going to compare with the book; however, let me tell you something about us first.

My brother and I both had learned music since when we were young. We both learned the same instruments: violin and piano in the same music-elementary school. We both are studying in the U.S. right now. Music is important for both of us, because we had learned since we were young. It's pretty useful; the reason is we would have some common things to do for both of us. Sometimes we played in the same orchestra and sometimes we just played duet together. We always had good time when we play duet. Therefore, sometimes we would perform to some people. We used to study in the same high school for one year. We performed it at many places in that year. For instance, we played at the nursing house, many YMCA's and school's parties. We were happy about met lots of people and we hope they were enjoyed. As the book, brothers like to play each other. Darry, Sodapop, and Ponyboy enjoy the time they are together.

Every brother cares very much about their brothers. I can understand why Darry is very mad about Ponyboy being late to home after the movie, and after Darry and Sodapop very worry about Ponyboy when he and Johnny hide in the church. When my brother and I were in – – –, sometimes he went out with his friends until very late, and he did not call back home or my parents. I could not contact with him either. We were getting worried and angry about it. Therefore, I always kept telling him turn his cell phone on and let us know where he was going and when will he be back.

Every brother would protect their brothers. At begging of the book, Ponyboy got beaten by Socs. At that time, Darry and Sodapop saved Ponyboy. Later on in the story, even thought Dally is not Johnny and Ponyboy's brother, he still protects them as his younger brothers. He told them hide to the church, and tried to save them when they were in the fire. I would try to protect or help my brother when he gets troubles. I believe that he would do the same thing to me, too.

There is one thing I have in common with Darry; my brother and I don't really show love to each others just like Darry does not show love to Ponyboy. As I said before, my brother is not a lovely younger brother and I'm not a lovely older brother. We both think it's pretty nasty to be lovely. However, we still get alone pretty well. We still care each other very much.

As others brothers, sometimes we argue and fight. Like Darry argues with Ponyboy and hits him when Ponyboy was late back to the house. However, brothers are still brothers. There is one thing I think it's good to my brother and I. After we fight, we always get back to each other pretty soon. We don't really keep fighting and fighting. I think that's because we understand and we love each others.

11 Consider the hierarchy of difficulty discussed in section 4.3. Provide examples of each of these categories from your own learning experience. Do you agree that the proposed hierarchy represents degrees of difficulty and that the ordering proposed is the correct one? Why or why not?

See GSS, problem 1.2.

5

RECENT PERSPECTIVES ON THE ROLE OF PREVIOUSLY KNOWN LANGUAGES

5.1 Theories of learning

Throughout this book we deal with numerous approaches to second language learning, many of which have their counterparts in child language research. In chapter 4, we discussed a behaviorist theory of language when discussing the role of the native language. Primarily coming from research on child language acquisition, during the 1950s and 1960s there were challenges to the behaviorist theory of language and language learning. Language came to be seen not as a set of automatic habits, but as a set of structured rules. These rules were claimed to be learned not by imitation, but by actively formulating them on the basis of innate principles as well as on the basis of exposure to the language being learned. Three examples from the child language literature are often cited as evidence against the imitation view of language acquisition.

(5-1) From Cazden (1972, p. 92; no age given)
  Child: My teacher holded the baby rabbits and we patted them.
  Adult: Did you say your teacher held the baby rabbits?
  Child: Yes.
  Adult: What did you say she did?
  Child: She holded the baby rabbits and we patted them.
  Adult: Did you say she held them tightly?
  Child: No, she holded them loosely.

Despite the adult's modeling of the correct past tense form, the child continues to regularize the past tense by adding -ed rather than by changing the vowel. Imitation clearly played no role at this point in this child's talk.

(5-2) From McNeill (1966, p. 69; no age given)
  Child: Nobody don't like me.

> Mother: No, say "nobody likes me."
> Child: Nobody don't like me.
> (eight repetitions of this dialogue)
> Mother: No, now listen carefully; say "nobody likes me."
> Child: Oh! Nobody don't likes me.

(5-3) Original data, Age 3;2

> Child: I don't see no trees.
> Mother: I don't see any trees. Not no trees, any trees.
> Child: No any trees. No any trees.
> Mother: I don't see any trees.

In examples 5-2 and 5-3, the mother attempts unsuccessfully to model the correct form or even to overtly instruct the child. This type of example is often mocked in cartoons. One such cartoon shows a small child saying, "Mommy, Dolly hitted me." The mother responds "Dolly HIT me." The little boy's response was "You too?! Boy, she's in trouble!" (*Time Magazine*, November 1, 1999).

Recall Bloomfield's view of language learning (discussed in chapter 4). He clearly stated that when the child produces an incorrect form, the child receives a disappointing response with the admonition, "No, say it like this." The assumption is that the correct modeling (coupled with negative reinforcement) is sufficient to perfect the child's speech. However, as we have seen in the preceding examples, neither imitation nor reinforcement is a sufficient explanation of a child's linguistic behavior.

It became commonplace in the 1960s to see children as actively involved in creating grammars of their language, as opposed to being passive recipients imitating their surroundings. Children do not just soak in what goes on around them but actively try to make sense of the language they are exposed to. They construct grammars. In so doing they make generalizations, they test those generalizations or hypotheses, and they alter or reformulate them when necessary—or abandon them in favor of some other generalization.

During the 1950s and 1960s it became clear that the utterances of children displayed systematicity. Their language could be studied as a system, *not* just as deviations from the language they were exposed to. Thus, early utterances by children such as *no shoe* and *no book* are not best described as faulty imitation but rather as representing the child's attempt to systematically express negation. It is these assumptions that have come to guide work in second language acquisition as well.

We have very briefly described some of the approaches to the study of child language acquisition. In later chapters in this book, we deal with other approaches, namely innatist approaches (chapter 6) and interactionist approaches (chapter 10). Of additional concern to those interested in SLA is research on child second language acquisition, to which we turn next.

5.2 Child second language acquisition

It has long been recognized that child second language acquisition is a central and important part of the field of second language acquisition. In fact, the so-called "modern period" of SLA had much of its impetus from studies on child second language acquisition.

We begin by noting that the boundaries of child second language acquisition are somewhat arbitrary. Child second language acquisition refers to "acquisition by individuals young enough to be within the critical period, but yet with a first language already learned" (Foster-Cohen, 1999, pp. 7–8), or "successive acquisition of two languages in childhood" (McLaughlin, 1978a, p. 99). What is eliminated from this definition is simultaneous acquisition of two (or more) languages in childhood; this generally falls under the cover term of bilingualism. The question of what constitutes simultaneous acquisition versus sequential acquisition is not an easy one to answer. Even though the precise beginning and end points of the period of child SLA are vague, we surely can take as core to the topic the ages between 5 and 9, when the primary language is mostly settled and before the effects from a critical or sensitive period (see chapter 12) begin to manifest themselves.

That much research on adult second language acquisition had its impetus in child second language studies was noted by Selinker, Swain, and Dumas (1975), in which it was argued that the interlanguage hypothesis originally formulated for adult second language acquisition could be extended to nonsimultaneous child second language acquisition. There it was shown that strategies of language transfer, simplification, and overgeneralization of target language rules affected the second language production of the 7- to 8-year-old children in the French immersion program studied. It was hypothesized that what made a crucial difference to the cognitive processes of the children involved were the settings in which the L2 was being learned. Learner systems did not develop (and possibly even fossilized) in settings where there was an *absence* of native-speaking peers of the target language. Thus, the quality of the input to the learner was seen as a central variable in second language outcome.

Within these two overall contexts of the presence and absence of native-speaking peers of the target language, McLaughlin (1978a) claimed that there is no language transfer in child second language acquisition unless the child is isolated from peers of the target language, the latter being the classic immersion setting. The idea is that if the child has target language peers, there is a greater social context where the child learns the

L2 rules as if the L2 were an L1, with no language transfer occurring. There are several interesting hypotheses that McLaughlin (1978a, p. 117) discusses, one being the regression hypothesis, according to which the child uses the language skills used in first language acquisition with L2 data but "at a very primitive and rudimentary level" (see Ervin-Tripp, 1974). A second hypothesis, the recapitulation hypothesis, involves the child recapitulating the learning process of a native speaker of the target language. In other words, when a child learns a second language she or he uses the same processes available to children of the target language. McLaughlin claimed that there were studies that favor this hypothesis (e.g., Milon, 1974; Ravem, 1968, 1974).

However, McLaughlin also noted what could be considered counter-evidence to this. Referring to work by Wode (1976), he pointed out that "children *occasionally* use first-language structures to solve the riddle of second-language structures" (McLaughlin, 1978a, p. 117; emphasis added). In other words, in child second language acquisition, a child is more likely to use first language structures when confronted with difficult L2 structures.

McLaughlin argued that the same processes are involved in all language acquisition; that is, language learning is language learning. What is involved is a unitary process. He concluded that "there is a unity of process that characterizes all language acquisition, whether of a first or second language, at all ages" (McLaughlin, 1978a, p. 202). His claim was that both L1 and child L2 learners use the same strategies in learning a language.

A general issue that is often a matter of discussion in the scholarly and lay literature is whether it is true that younger is better. McLaughlin concluded that it is not. In general, children have better phonology but older learners often achieve better L2 syntax (see also Long, 1990). As to be expected, more recent empirical work has shown that the picture is even more complex. Rocca (2007) presents evidence that, like first language learners and unlike adult second language learners, child language learners display morphological sensitivity. However, like adult second language learners and unlike first language learners, child second language learners are influenced by language transfer, where language transfer can involve grammatical lexical prototypical links. These studies, which are only the tip of the iceberg, show that the view "the earlier, the better" cannot be taken as an absolute. The question of age differences is dealt with in chapter 12.

We now briefly look at two earlier studies in child second language acquisition that have proven influential: Hakuta (1974a, 1974b) and Ravem (1968, 1974). To compare them, we will focus on their study of the development of question formation in English.

Hakuta (1974b) studied a Japanese child learning English in the United

States. Data were collected over an 11-month period beginning when the child was age 5;4 months. The data were mixed, including TL-like and non-TL-like forms. A sample of the data is presented in 5-4.

(5-4) From Hakuta (1974b, pp. 293–294)
        How do you do it?
        Do you have coffee?
        Do you want this one?
        What do you doing, this boy?
        What do you do it, this, froggie?
        What do you doing?
        Do you bought too?
        Do you put it?
        How do you put it?

With regard to question formation, the longitudinal data show gradual progression. As indicated by the first three examples, it appears that this child understands question formation in English. However, as the child progressed in English, she seemed to carry over the phrase *do you* as a chunk or, to use Hakuta's phrase, a "prefabricated routine," producing both grammatical and ungrammatical questions. *Do you* appears to function as a chunk with both present and past tense (irregular) forms as late as eight months into data collection. In about the sixth to eighth month, *did* appeared in the data: *Did you call?* and *Did everybody saw . . .?* In general, this child seemed to follow a progression in which question forms (*why, where, when*) entered her system differentially. The data appear to represent idiosyncratic interlanguage forms, but on closer examination can be argued to represent a gradual progression toward the acquisition of English forms.

Ravem (1968, 1974) studied a Norwegian child learning English in the United Kingdom. Data were collected every three to four weeks over a four-month period beginning when the child was 6;6. As in Hakuta's study, the data included both TL-like and non-TL-like forms. Examples are given in 5-5.

(5-5) From Ravem (1968, 1974)
        What dyou reading to-yesterday?
        What they doing?
        Like you ice cream?
        Like you me not, Reidun?
        What dyou do to-yesterday?
        What dyou did to-yesterday in the hayshed?
        When dyou went there?
        What you did in Rothbury?

Early on, this child seemed to be forming questions using mostly a declarative sentence word order: *you reading, she (is) doing.* Inversion, as would be predicted from both the native language (Norwegian) and target language (English) grammars, was not used. This was not entirely the case, though, as inversion seemed to happen in *yes/no* questions. Eventually, the correct pattern of inversion was acquired.

Comparing the two studies in this area of question formation, we find that even at the earliest stages neither of the two children seemed to be using a direct language-transfer strategy with *wh-* questions; that is, we do not see in the Japanese–English interlanguage questions such forms as *That, what is . . .?, You, how like . . .?,* which would reflect the Japanese pattern, or in Norwegian–English questions such forms as *What reading you?, What doing she now?,* which would reflect the Norwegian pattern. However, in *yes/no* questions, inversion seems to happen early. Hence, there is no uniform pattern of the acquisition of question formation. In the case of the Japanese child, the correct use of the auxiliary appeared with some *wh-* words before others; with the Norwegian child, inversion occurred in some questions (*yes/no*) but not in others (*wh-* questions). Regarding the acquisition of the auxiliary *do,* we see changes with the Japanese child from apparently correct forms to incorrect forms and then to correct forms again. We return to the concept of change from correct to incorrect to correct in chapter 8 in our discussion of U-shaped learning.

5.3 Child second language morpheme order studies

In chapter 2, we discussed the morpheme order studies conducted by Brown (1973) within the context of child language acquisition. These studies in some sense became the cornerstone of early work in second language acquisition.

As noted in chapter 4, work in the area of language transfer traditionally focused on the behavioral aspects of SLA. However, in the early 1970s a series of studies called the morpheme order studies was highly influential in the development of the field of second language acquisition. These studies were strongly based on the idea developed by Dulay and Burt (1974a, 1974b, 1975) that child second language acquisition was similar to child first language acquisition. This came to be known as the L1 = L2 Hypothesis.

Chomsky (1959) attacked Skinner's work on behaviorism bringing to light that a behaviorist position with regard to language learning (whether first or second) was untenable. Viewing the learner as an active participant in the learning process and as a language creator was essential. For second language acquisition, doing so entailed throwing off the shackles of language transfer. That is, because transfer was strongly associated with behaviorist thought, a way of arguing that second language learning was not a behaviorist-based activity was to argue that transfer was not a major, or even an important, factor in attempts to account for second language learning.

In order to challenge the concept of transfer, studies were conducted to show the percentage of errors attributable to the native language (although it should be noted that NL-based errors at this time were conceptualized as translation equivalents), as opposed to some of the more subtle varieties of error sources described in chapter 4. For example, George (1972) claimed that one third of the errors in his corpus were attributable to the NL; Dulay and Burt (1975) claimed that less than 5% were so attributable in their data. However, these quantitative accounts of language transfer seem less interesting than the ones we examine later which attempt to elucidate which aspects of language phenomena are transferable and which are not. As Richards and Sampson (1974, p. 5) recognize:

> It would however be almost impossible to assess the precise contribution of systemic language interference at this time ... A number of factors interact in determining the learner's approximative system. Until the role of some of these other factors is more clearly understood, it is not possible to evaluate the amount of systemic interference due to language transfer alone.

In chapter 4 we dealt with the criticisms of contrastive analysis. Many of these criticisms were empirical (i.e., predictions were not accurate). However, the most serious challenge to the Contrastive Analysis Hypothesis was theoretical. As stated earlier, the morpheme order studies were a reaction to earlier work that advocated a transfer (hence, behaviorist) approach to the study of how second languages are learned. Approaching the question from a mentalist perspective, Dulay and Burt (1974a, p. 37) developed a theory of what they called creative construction, which is

> the process in which children gradually reconstruct rules for speech they hear, guided by universal innate mechanisms which cause them to formulate certain types of hypotheses about the language system being acquired, until the mismatch between what they are exposed to and what they produce is resolved.

Thus, in this view, there are L2 strategies that are common to all children regardless of their NL. Importantly, emphasis is placed on the centrality of mental processes and the innate propensity for language that all humans have. Given that innateness is at the core of acquisition in

127

this view, it is further assumed that children reconstruct second languages in similar ways regardless of their NL or the language being learned. In other words, processes involved in acquisition are assumed to be the same. Because the goal of research within the creative construction tradition was to substantiate these assumptions, research in child language acquisition assumed importance because in first language acquisition the nonbehaviorist position was unquestionable.

In order to empirically verify these hypotheses, the morpheme order studies emerged. As noted earlier, the morpheme order studies were based on work initially done in child language acquisition by Brown (1973). Dulay and Burt's (1974a) study was the first to apply Brown's findings to child SLA. They hypothesized that similar patterns of development would be found in child first language acquisition and child second language acquisition. These results would suggest a similarity in processes between L1 and L2 learning. And, perhaps more importantly, if similar patterns of development were found to occur between two groups of children with different language backgrounds, one could conclude that developmental factors rather than NL factors were at play and that universal mechanisms for second language acquisition had to be considered primary.

Dulay and Burt's data come from the results achieved by 60 Spanish and 55 Chinese children on a standardized test of English L2 known as the Bilingual Syntax Measure (BSM). The BSM consists of seven colored pictures about which children are asked questions designed to elicit responses on the English grammatical morphemes given in Table 5.1. (See Figure 5.1 for an example from the BSM.)

Using the picture in Figure 5.1, the experimenter is asked to "Point to BOTH HOUSES using whole hand to point" while asking "WHAT ARE THESE?" The anticipated response *houses* would show correct usage of the plural /s/. Another question requires the experimenter to point to the doors of both houses at once and say "AND THESE?" with the anticipated response again involving the plural.

Table 5.1 Areas of investigation from the Bilingual Syntax Measure

Pronoun case	*He doesn't like him.*
Article	*In the fat guy's house*
Singular form of *to be* (copula)	*He's fat.*
-ing	*He's mopping.*
Plural	*windows, houses*
Singular auxiliary	*She's dancing.*
Past—regular	*He closed it.*
Past—irregular	*He stole it.*
Possessive	*the king's*
Third person singular	*He eats too much.*

Figure 5.1 Bilingual Syntax Measure (BSM). Copyright © 1973 by Harcourt Assessment, Inc. Reproduced with permission. All rights reserved.

The researchers determined all of the instances in which each of these morphemes is required in English and then determined an accuracy score for each child based on a ratio of number correct/number required in English. In general, their results showed a similar pattern of development between the two groups of children (Spanish and Chinese), as can be seen in Figure 5.2.

Had the results from the two groups differed, there would have been justification for attributing those differences to the NL. Because there were minimal differences, there was justification for attributing the similarity to universal developmental factors and for diminishing the significance of the role of the NL.

In chapter 6 we deal with innatist approaches to second language acquisition. In general terms, the main issue is the extent to which language acquisition (either first or second) is constrained by universal principles of language. Lakshmanan (1995) made the important point that, through research on child second language acquisition (as opposed to adult second language acquisition), we can obtain a better picture of the biological factors involved in second language acquisition. For example, it would be interesting to find, as Lakshmanan claimed, that child second language acquisition is constrained by universal principles

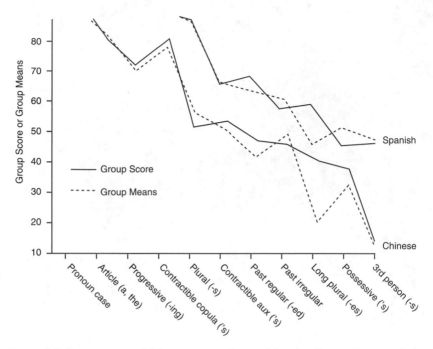

Figure 5.2 Comparison of L2 sequences obtained by the Group Score and the Group Means methods.

Source: From "Natural sequences in child second language acquisition" by H. Dulay and M. Burt, 1974a, *Language Learning, 24*, 37–53 by Research Club in Language Learning. Reprinted by permission.

and that language transfer cannot be ruled out. If nothing else, this would suggest that such principles are available for at least some time after the acquisition of a first language. Despite the centrality of child second language acquisition, there is a lack of detailed theory-driven work, as was noted by Foster-Cohen (1999), who pointed out that child second language acquisition is a severely understudied area in relation to adult SLA and an area wide open for research on many fronts. Recent work in SLA, however, does attempt to extend findings from adult second language research to child language learners (e.g., Mackey and Oliver, 2002; Oliver, 1995, 1998, 2002; Oliver and Mackey, 2003; Philp and Duchesne, in press, Rocca, 2007).

5.4 Adult second language morpheme order studies

In the previous section, we discussed the work of Dulay and Burt (1973, 1974a, 1974b, 1975) on prepubescent children, which was important in its influence on moving the emphasis from a behaviorist view of language

Figure 5.3 Relative accuracy for adult L2 learners of English in eight functors.

Source: Table created from data appearing in "Is there a 'natural sequence' in adult second language learning?" by N. Bailey, C. Madden, and S. Krashen, 1974, *Language Learning,* 24, 235–243 by Research Club in Language Learning. Reprinted with permission.

learning to a view of second language acquisition that relied more on mental processes. It was not clear, however, whether the same findings would apply to the acquisition of a second language by adults. Bailey, Madden, and Krashen (1974) conducted an influential study to investigate precisely this issue. As with the Dulay and Burt study, there were two groups of learners, all learning English. The first group was comprised of 33 native speakers of Spanish and the second group, the non-Spanish group, was comprised of 40 native speakers of a variety of languages (Greek, Persian, Italian, Turkish, Japanese, Chinese, Thai, Afghan, Hebrew, Arabic, and Vietnamese). The BSM was administered to these 73 adults. Results showed consistency with the results of the Dulay and Burt studies (Figure 5.3). Additionally, the two adult groups showed similar results, as is seen in Figure 5.4.

Thus, there appeared to be evidence for the lack of importance of native language influence. This being the case, the mentalist position embodied in Dulay and Burt's Creative Construction Hypothesis gained credence. On the basis of these studies there was justification for positing a "natural order" of the acquisition of English morphemes.

Whereas the morpheme order studies did suggest a more or less invariant order, although far from rigid (see Krashen, 1977, for a review of such studies), there was some evidence even within these studies of the role of the NL. For example, Larsen-Freeman (1975a, 1975b) found that native speakers of Japanese (a language without an article system) learning English had lower accuracy scores on English articles than other groups.

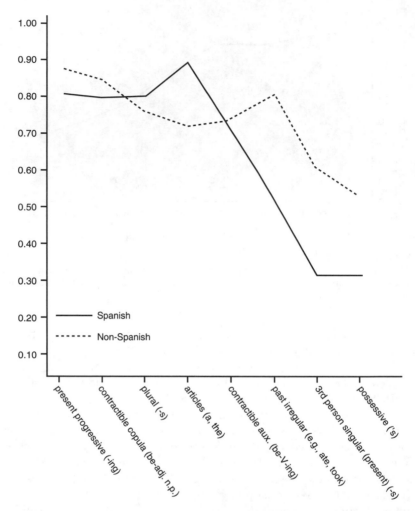

Figure 5.4 Comparison of Spanish and Non-Spanish adults; relative accuracies for eight functions.

Source: From "Is there a 'natural sequence' in adult second language learning?" by N. Bailey, C. Madden, and S. Krashen, 1974, *Language Learning, 24,* 235–243 by Research Club in Language Learning. Reprinted with permission.

Additionally, Hakuta (1974b) found a different order of morpheme acquisition for a Japanese child learning English.

The morpheme order studies were not without problems, some of which are serious, others of which are less so. Below, we list some of the common challenges to this body of research.

First, the results obtained may be an artifact of the Bilingual Syntax Measure. In other words, the test itself may have biased the results; any group of learners given this test would produce similar results. The most detailed study considering this problem came from Porter (1977). Porter administered the Bilingual Syntax Measure to English-speaking children between the ages of 2 and 4, using the same scoring procedure as that found in one of Dulay and Burt's early studies (1973). The order of acquisition was closer to the L2 order than the L1 order, suggesting that the results were an artifact of the test measure rather than a reflection of actual acquisition orders. However, this criticism may be unwarranted: two pieces of evidence are important here.

1   On closer inspection, we see that depending on the method of "counting" accuracy, there is actually little disagreement between the results obtained by Porter and the results of L1 studies (notably that of de Villiers and de Villiers, 1973).

2   Other L2 studies not using the BSM as a data-elicitation measure obtained results similar to those of the BSM (see Andersen, 1976; Krashen, Butler, Birnbaum, and Robertson, 1978; Krashen, Houck, Giunchi, Bode, Birnbaum, and Strei, 1977; Larsen-Freeman, 1975b, 1976; Makino, 1979).

The second criticism concerns the Bailey, Madden, and Krashen (1974) study specifically. The category *non-Spanish* in this study incorporated learners from such a wide variety of language backgrounds that whatever differences may have occurred due to the L1 would be obliterated by such a large disparate group. For example, some of the languages have article systems; some do not. Some of the languages have a rich system of morphology; others do not.

With regard to the morphemes themselves, morphemes with different meanings were categorized together. For example, from an acquisitional point of view, the English article system is more appropriately thought of as having separate morphemes (the indefinite article *a*, the definite article *the*, and nothing). This was discussed in chapter 4 in connection with the data from Dušková (1983). Similarly, Andersen (1977) showed different behaviors of second language learners with regard to the different English articles, suggesting that these morphemes should not have been grouped as a single grammatical structure.

A more serious criticism concerns the methodology itself. Do accuracy orders reflect developmental sequences? As we have pointed out in previous chapters, correct forms may not always signify acquisition of correct rule structures. Furthermore, considering whether or not a learner uses a form in its obligatory context in English misses those contexts in which it is not used in English, but in which the learner uses it. In other words, the total picture of a learner's use of a form is not taken into account. In particular, what is lacking are those instances in which learners have generalized a form to an inappropriate context. An example of this is given by Wagner-Gough and Hatch (1975) in their discussion of both the form and the function of linguistic elements in second language acquisition. Their data come from a 5-year-old Iranian child. As with other children, he learned the -ing form earlier than other grammatical morphemes; in fact, his speech showed pervasive use of this form. However, the mere presence of -ing did not reflect acquisition. He used the progressive -ing not only in appropriate contexts, but also in inappropriate ones. He used -ing when he intended to express:

(5-6) *Immediate intentions*
I my coming. I my go my mother.
(= I'm going to come to you. I'm going to ask my mother.)

(5-7) *Distant future*
I don't know Fred a my going, no go. I don't know coming, go.
(= I don't know if Fred is going or not. I don't know if he's coming or going.)

(5-8) *Past events*
I'm find it.[1] Bobbie found one to me.
(= I found it. Bobbie found it for me.)

(5-9) *Process-state*
Msty, Msty go in there. Hey Judy, Msty going in there.
(Msty is going in there. Hey Judy, Msty is going in there.)

(5-10) *Imperative*
Okay, sit down over here! Sitting down like that!
(= Sit down over here! Sit down like that!)

Thus, given the method of counting correct use in obligatory contexts, the pervasive use of the progressive will yield correct forms in obligatory contexts. However, given the use in inappropriate contexts, it is difficult to maintain the argument that accuracy reflects acquisition.

Another criticism of the morpheme order studies is that there appears to be individual variation in learner data, yet individual data are obscured with grouped data. The evidence for individual data was provided by Hakuta (1974b), whose study of one child suggested other than the natural order, and by Larsen-Freeman (1978), who in analyzing her 1975 study stated: "The results of this study showed individual variability and native language background to exert some influence on the way morphemes were ordered by language groups with a task" (p. 372).

The type of data elicited also appears to be problematic. Rosansky (1976) compared longitudinal and cross-sectional (grouped) data (see chapter 3 for an elaboration of these terms) from six Spanish-speaking learners of English, finding that the two modes of analysis did not coincide (cf. Krashen, 1977, for a criticism of the Rosansky study).

Two final criticisms are noteworthy in that they reflect not the studies themselves, but the conclusions that have been drawn from the studies.

First, the morpheme order studies investigated a limited number of grammatical morphemes (in general, 11 were considered). From these studies, researchers extended the implications to acquisition in general. Whereas it may be the case that there is a predicted order of the acquisition of English morphemes, it is not the case that all of acquisition takes place in a predicted order and that there is justification to minimize the role of the native language.

Second, the major theoretical significance of the studies was to demonstrate that the native language was an insignificant influence and that behaviorism could not be maintained to account for the process of SLA. As a result of diminishing the importance of the NL, researchers believed that it could be argued that a cognitive view of the process of acquisition was the more appropriate theoretical stance to take. However, this line of argument attacks incorrect assumptions when it equates a behaviorist view of learning with the role of the NL. In other words, such an argument "throws the baby out with the bathwater." It is more appropriate to question whether transfer is a habit-based phenomenon or not, because it is not inconceivable that one could adopt a cognitive view of SLA and maintain the significance of the NL. In fact, adopting a cognitive view and incorporating a strong role for the NL is the prevailing view in current SLA research.

In sum, the morpheme order studies have been and continue to be influential in our understanding of the nature of developmental sequences. However, it is not sufficient to posit an order without positing an explanation for that order. Although explanations have been forthcoming, they have unfortunately failed in their completeness. Part of the failure is due, once again, to the attempt to ascribe singular causality. Are morpheme orders due to perceptual saliency (e.g., -ing is easy to hear, -ed is not)? Are morpheme orders due to native language influences? Are they due to semantic factors in that certain concepts may be semantically more complex than others? Are they due to syntactic complexity? Are they due to input frequency? The answer to all of these questions undoubtedly deserves a yes and a no. Long and Sato (1983) claimed that input frequency was the most likely explanatory factor, although they were quick to note that it was doubtful "that input frequency was the only factor likely to be involved" (p. 282). What is more realistic, yet subject to empirical verification, is that these factors all contribute to acquisition order. What is then left to be determined is the relative weighting each factor has. How do all of these factors converge to produce the particular orders obtained? (See Wei, 2000, for a theoretical perspective to the acquisition of morphemes within the context of second language acquisition.)

5.5 Revised perspectives on the role of the native language

As discussed earlier, the question of the native language was historically posed dichotomously. Is language transfer of major importance in forming interlanguages or is it not? This is evident in such statements as:

> language background did not have a significant effect on the way ESL learners order English morphemes.
>
> (Larsen-Freeman, 1978, p. 372)

> Interference, or native to target language transfer, plays such a small role in language learning performance.
>
> (Whitman and Jackson, 1972, p. 40)

> Direct interference from the mother tongue is not a useful assumption.
>
> (George, 1972, p. 45)

But does the role of the NL have to be mechanical and uninteresting? Can there not be "selectivity" by learners in what is transferred and what is not transferred? If the latter question is answered in the affirmative, then transfer can be incorporated into a position consistent with a mentalist view of language. These topics are treated in this chapter. (Chapter 6 treats the role of the native language within the context of a specific formal model of language, namely Universal Grammar.)

Since the late 1970s, research on the role of the native language has taken on a different view, advocating a nonbehaviorist position and questioning the assumption that language transfer has to be part of behaviorism. That is, the assumption is that one can view transfer as a creative process.

That transfer was more appropriately viewed as something more than an involuntary hiccup implied by behaviorism could be seen in the work by Schachter (1974), in which she argued that there was avoidance of use based on facts of the native language. A second study, by Sjoholm (1976), further led to a rethinking and reconceptualization of the role of the NL. Sjoholm found that Finnish-speaking Finns learning English made transfer-induced errors that could be traced to Swedish (their L2) rather than to Finnish. On the other hand, Swedish–Finnish bilinguals (with Swedish as their dominant language) made transfer-induced errors that were traceable to Swedish (their L1), not Finnish (their L2). Thus, it appeared that both groups relied more on Swedish than on Finnish. This is accountable only if we take into account the learner's judgment, or perception as to what is more likely to work in the L2.

A number of studies carried out in Finland involving Finnish speakers learning English and Swedish speakers living in Finland also learning English point to the advantage that the latter group has over the former group. This is attributed to the similarities that exist between Swedish and English and the lack of similarity between Finnish and English. As Ringbom (1987, p. 134) stated:

> What emerges is a consistent difference in test results between groups which are very much the same culturally and education-ally, but which have an entirely different linguistic starting point when they set out to learn English. One conclusion is that the importance of the L1 in L2-learning is absolutely fundamental.

As an explanation, he offered: "Similarities, both cross-linguistic and inter-linguistic, function as pegs on which the learner can hang new information by making use of already existing knowledge, thereby facilitating learning."

During the mid- to late 1970s, the view of transfer that began to pre-dominate can be characterized as qualitative as opposed to quantitative. That is, those interested in second language acquisition were less inter-ested in a wholesale acceptance or rejection of the role of the native language. Rather, the emphasis was on the determination of *how* and *when* learners use their native language and on explanations for the phenomenon.

Most important in this discussion is the broadening and reconceptuali-zation of language transfer and the concomitant examination of the terminology generally employed. Corder (1983, p. 86, 1992, p. 19) recog-nized the difficulty in continuing to use theory-laden terminology:

> I have chosen the title of this paper deliberately, A role for the mother tongue in language learning, because I do not wish to prejudice the nature of my discussion of that role by using the term "transfer" or even less by using the term "interference." I would like to hope that both these terms should be banned from use in our discussions unless carefully redefined. The fact is that they are both technical terms in a particular theory of learning, and unless one is adopting that particular theory in one's discus-sions, it is best to find other terms for any alternative theoretical position one may adopt. The danger of using such technical terms closely associated with particular theories is that they may perhaps quite unconsciously constrain one's freedom of thinking about the particular topic.

It was for precisely these reasons that Kellerman and Sharwood Smith

(1986) suggested the term *cross-linguistic influence*, which is sufficiently broad to include transfer, in the traditional sense, but also avoidance, language loss (whether of the L1 or of another L2), and rate of learning.

5.5.1 Avoidance

In chapter 4 we showed that the native language may influence which structures a learner produces and which structures are not produced (i.e., avoidance). Further evidence comes from work by Kleinmann (1977) in an investigation of Arabic speakers versus a group comprised of Spanish/Portuguese speakers in the use of passives, present progressives, infinitive complements, and direct object pronouns. These four structures were predicted to be of differential difficulty for the learners given the facts of their native languages. In addition to gathering production data, this study differed from Schachter's (1974) in that Kleinmann ascertained that the subjects all "knew" the structures in question, at least from a comprehension perspective. Thus, the differential behavior between his groups could not be attributed to a lack of knowledge, but rather to some choice to use or not to use particular structures to express given concepts. The basis of the choice was related to the NL.

The source of avoidance is in dispute. Whereas there is significant evidence that differences between the L1 and the L2 are the major source of avoidance, as was suggested in the preceding discussion, there is also evidence that the opposite occurs. That is, when great similarities exist between the L1 and the L2, the learner may doubt that these similarities are real. This is discussed in section 5.5.5, with particular reference to the work of Kellerman.

Still another view holds that avoidance has less to do with NL–TL differences, but rather is based on the complexity of the L2 structures in question. For example, in considering the acquisition of phrasal verbs (e.g., *come in, take away, lay aside, shut off, let down, mix up*, etc.), Dagut and Laufer (1985) found that Hebrew-speaking learners of English (Hebrew does not have phrasal verbs) in general preferred the one-word equivalent of the phrasal verbs (*enter, remove, save, stop, disappoint, confuse*). Within the category of phrasal verbs, they preferred those that are semantically more transparent (e.g., *come in, take away*) to those that are less transparent (*let down, mix up*). Thus, Dagut and Laufer concluded that the complexity of the target language structure had a greater impact on the issue of avoidance than did differences between the NL and the TL.

In a study of Dutch learners of English (Dutch, like English, has phrasal verbs), similar results were obtained by Hulstijn and Marchena (1989), who found differences between transparent and nontransparent phrasal verbs but also found that learners did not accept phrasal verbs when there was close similarity between Dutch and English, most likely given their "disbelief" that another language could have a structure so similar to the "unusual" Dutch one.

Finally, in a study by Laufer and Eliasson (1993), there was an attempt to tease apart these variables. In their study of Swedish learners of English, attention was focused on the use or avoidance of English phrasal verbs (*pick up, put down*). Two tests (a multiple-choice test and a translation test) were given to advanced Swedish-speaking learners of English (Swedish is a language with phrasal verbs). The researchers considered whether the responses to (or translations of) Swedish phrasal verbs consisted of single-verb synonyms or English phrasal verbs. The results were compared with results from Hebrew-speaking learners of English (remember that Hebrew does not have phrasal verbs). Different types of phrasal verbs were considered, including figurative ones (e.g., *back up = support, turn up = arrive*) and literal ones (e.g., *come down = descend, put in = insert*). The researchers found that the best predictor of avoidance is the L1–L2 difference. Although L1–L2 similarity and inherent complexity (figurative versus literal phrasal verbs) have a role, the only factor that consistently predicts avoidance is the L1–L2 difference variable.

5.5.2 Differential learning rates

Ard and Homburg (1983, 1992) advocated a return to the original concepts embodied in the terminology of the psychology of learning. In particular, they viewed transfer as a facilitation of learning. They compared the responses of two groups of learners (Spanish and Arabic) to the vocabulary section of a standard test of English. Of major interest were the response patterns to different items. One would expect differences in response patterns to those items in which a Spanish word and an English word were cognates, as in the following example,

(5-11) It was the first time I ever saw her *mute.*
    (a) shocked
    (b) crying
    (c) smiling
    (d) silent

but not to items in which all words were equally distant from the native languages of the learners, as in example 5-12:

(5-12) The door swung slowly on its old _____.
    (a) fringes
    (b) braids
    (c) clips
    (d) hinges

The Spanish learners did consistently better on this latter type of item than did the Arabic speakers. Ard and Homburg discussed this in light of learning time and hence accelerated learning rates. The Spanish speakers, because so many cognates exist between their NL and the TL, can focus more of their "learning time" on other aspects of language (in this case, other vocabulary items). It is the concentration on other vocabulary which results in a facilitation of learning. Thus, knowing a language that is related in some way to the TL can help in many ways, only some of which can be accounted for by the mechanical carryover of items and structures.

There is another perspective to be taken on the concept of differential learning rates. One such view was discussed in chapter 4 with regard to Schumann's (1979) work on negation, when it was pointed out that an NL structure that corresponded to a TL developmental sequence was a factor in preventing learners from moving on to the next sequential stage. In other words, the internal system of the learner's L2 grammar exhibited delayed reorganization.

A similar view is adopted by Zobl (1982), who discussed the concepts of (a) delayed rule reorganization, or in his words "the pace with which a sequence is traversed" (p. 169), and (b) the number of structures in a given developmental sequence. With regard to pace of development, Zobl pointed to data from Henkes (1974) in which three children (French, Arabic, Spanish) were observed in their acquisition of English. A particular concern was the acquisition of the copula (the verb *to be*), a form present in French

(5-13) Sa maison est vieille.
      his house   is   old

and in Spanish

(5-14) Su casa   es vieja.
      his house is old

but absent in Arabic

(5-15) baytuhu   qadimun.
      house his old
      "His house is old."

Consistent with the work of the time, notably a diminution of the importance of the NL, Henkes attempted to show that, for the Arabic child, the lack of use of the copula is not native language-related, as both of the other two children also failed to use the copula consistently.

However, as Zobl pointed out, what is particularly interesting is the fact that, whereas the Arabic child continued to use the copula variably, even at a fairly advanced state of syntactic acquisition, the other two children regularly employed the copula at this stage. Thus, although the same pattern of copula use was observed in all three children, it took the Arabic child longer to get the facts of English straightened out due to the absence of the category in the NL.

5.5.3 Different paths

The previous section dealt with rate of acquisition across a similar path. In many instances, however, paths of acquisition are not identical for speakers of all languages. Zobl (1982) compared the acquisition of the English definite article by a Chinese-speaking child and a Spanish-speaking child. With the Chinese-speaking child, early evidence of a form that appears to serve the function of a definitizer is the use of *this*. What is further noteworthy is that when there is native speaker modeling of *this*, it tends to be retained in the child's speech, whereas when there is a model of the definite article *the*, it is deleted or changed to *this* (see Table 5.2). Thus, the data in Table 5.2 show that the definitizer *this* developmentally precedes the article *the*.[2]

On the other hand, from the beginning of data collection with the Spanish-speaking child, both *this* and *the* were frequent, as can be seen in Table 5.3.

Table 5.2 Data from Chinese-speaking learner of English

NS	NNS
1. Is this airplane your brother's?	*This airplane . . . Brent*
2. Show me the airplane.	*Show me airplane?*
3. Put it on the chair.	*Chair? This one?*
4. Ask Jim "Where's the turtle?"	*Jim, where's turtle?*
5. You want to push the pen.	*I want to push pen.*
	Push, pencil
6. Is the table dirty?	*Yes, this is dirty.*
	Table is dirty.
7. Whose bike is this?	*This . . . Edmond's.*
	Mark, I want this bike.
8. What are you going to do with the paper?	*I want this paper school.*
9. Ask Jim if he can play with the ball.	*Jim, can you play the ball?*
10. Ask Jim if you can have the pencil.	*Jim, you want this pencil?*
11. Is he washing the car? What is he doing?	*Washing car.*

Source: From "A direction for contrastive analysis: the comparative study of developmental sequences" by H. Zobl, 1982, *TESOL Quarterly, 16*, 169–183. Reprinted by permission.

Table 5.3 Data from Spanish-speaking learner of English

1. Hey hey this. Here the toy.
2. The car.
3. Lookit this. Lookit this cowboy.
   Here. This cowboy.
   Indians D'Indians. That d'Indians.
4. This one . . . that truck.
   I gonna open that door.
   Get the car.
   Shut the door.
5. The car.
   Same thing this car.

Source: From "A direction for contrastive analysis: the comparative study of developmental sequences" by H. Zobl, 1982, *TESOL Quarterly, 16,* 169–183. Reprinted by permission.

Furthermore, when modeling of *the* occurred, there was not the same change to *this,* as was seen with the Chinese-speaking child. Additional examples from the native Spanish-speaking child are given in Table 5.4.

Table 5.4 Data from Spanish-speaking learner of English

NS	NNS
1. Look.	*Lookit the little house.*
2. You gonna draw the man?	*The man.*
3. Guero, she wanna know what are you making.	*I make. I make it the blue.*
4. Are you going to get me a cup?	*Where's the cup? Get the cup.*

Source: From "A direction for contrastive analysis: the comparative study of developmental sequences" by H. Zobl, 1982 *TESOL Quarterly, 16,* 169–183. Reprinted by permission.

The differences between these two children suggest that facts of their native languages lead them down two different paths—the Chinese child through a stage in which *this* occurs before the definite article, and the Spanish child to a starting point in which the definite article and the demonstrative *this* co-occur.

A similar perspective comes from Wode (1977), who argued that there is a predictable order of structures and that certain developmental structures must be used by learners before the NL can be expected to have an influence on second language production. He discussed the acquisition of English negation by German L1 children.

The first stage of negation, as we have already seen, is preverbal *no,* in which there is no evidence of NL influence.

(5-16) No cold.
(5-17) No play baseball.

Only at a later stage do the following sentences appear:

(5-18) That's no right.
(5-19) It's no Francisco.

At this stage of development, the child is able to see a similarity between German and English negation, because in German the negative morpheme appears after the verb *to be*.

(5-20) Es is nicht wahr.
　　　 it is not true

It is at this stage that these German-speaking children produce the sentences in 5-21 and 5-22, sentences that are clearly influenced by German, which forms negatives by placing the negative marker after the verb in main clauses:

(5-21) I'm steal not the base.
(5-22) Marylin like no sleepy.

Thus, learners must see some resemblance between the language they are learning and their native language before they are able to recognize that the NL might be "useful" to them. This can also be stated as the Transfer to Somewhere Principle which we deal with in section 5.5.5.

5.5.4 Overproduction

Not only do we find there are different paths of development, but we also find quantitatively different uses of forms depending on the native language. For example, Schachter and Rutherford (1979) examined compositions written in English by Chinese and Japanese speakers. Both of these languages are of the type that relies heavily on the concept of topic. Sentences are organized around a topic–comment structure, as in 5-23:

(5-23) As for meat [topic], we don't eat it anymore [comment].

What Schachter and Rutherford found was an overproduction of sentences like the following:

(5-24) It is very unfortunate that . . .

and sentences with *there is* or *there are*:

(5-25) There is a small restaurant near my house in my country.
　　　 Many things of the restaurant are like those . . .

They claimed that these structures were being used to carry the weight of a particular discourse function, even though the TL makes use of other forms for that same function. They hypothesized that the NL is at play here: there is an influence of NL function (the need to express topic–comment type structures) to L2 form. Han (2000) further investigated this structure supporting earlier research, claiming that this structure, which she refers to as a *pseudo-passive*, becomes more like a target-like passive as learners become more syntactically sophisticated. She examined spontaneous writing of two Chinese learners of English (advanced proficiency) finding both a true passive and a structure that looks more like a topic–comment structure in the same writing, as is shown below.

> (5-26) From Han (2000, p. 88)
> They told me that the attractive offer will be sent to me a bit later since **what I sent to them have not received**.

The first part of this sentence includes a target-like passive, whereas the second part, *what I sent to them* (topic) and *have not received* (comment) is more L1-like. What is noteworthy, however, is that the first part of the sentence may be somewhat formulaic and may have been used as a formulaic chunk from a letter the writer had received. Clearly, this example shows that the L1 exerts a subtle influence even at later stages of proficiency.

5.5.5 Predictability/selectivity

In the late 1970s interest in the role of the NL shed its earlier dichotomous perspective and took on a *when* and *under what conditions* perspective. That is, the question was: Under what conditions does transfer take place?

Andersen (1983) developed the Transfer to Somewhere Principle, which stated that

> A grammatical form or structure will occur consistently and to a significant extent in interlanguage as a result of transfer *if and only if* there already exists within the L2 input the potential for (mis-)generalization from the input to produce the same form or structure.
>
> (p. 178)

This proposal has limitations (for example, this is limited to syntax, and there is little possibility of disproving it because the potential must be in the mind of the learner and it is difficult to show that there was no potential), but it does contribute to the discussion in which the learner and his or her perceptions, rather than merely language, are at the center.

The notion underlying contrastive analysis—that similarities implied learning ease and that differences implied learning difficulty—proved to be invalid. Kleinmann (1977) suggested the opposite: when something in the L2 is very different from the L1, there is a "novelty effect." In his study, this was the case with the progressive, which is absent in Arabic, yet Arabic speakers learned this early and well. It may be that the frequency of the progressive in English, along with its perceptual saliency, leads learners to notice that structure more easily than other structures.

Supporting evidence comes from Bardovi-Harlig (1987). She examined differences in the order of acquisition between sentences like 5-27 and 5-28.

(5-27) Who did John give the book to?
(5-28) To whom did John give the book?

Theoretical considerations based on markedness (forms more common among the languages of the world are unmarked, whereas those less common are marked; see chapter 6 for a detailed discussion of the concept) predict the acquisition of 5-28 before 5-27. However, the data show the reverse pattern: 5-27 is acquired before 5-28. Bardovi-Harlig identified salience as the main contributing factor to the unexpected outcome. In her terms, salience is defined as the availability of input. It is because there is a greater quantity of input for sentences such as 5-27 as opposed to 5-28 to which learners are exposed that the acquisition patterns are what they are.

The role of salience in SLA received greater support from Doughty (1991) in a study of relativization. She compared three groups of subjects engaged in a computer-assisted language-learning project. The groups differed in the format of presentation of the language material. Besides a control group, there were two experimental groups: a meaning-oriented treatment group and a rule-oriented treatment group. As the names suggest, in the latter group there were explicit metalinguistic statements about relative clauses, whereas in the meaning-oriented treatment group there were no such explicit statements. If it is correct that salience can come about through focusing a learner's attention on particular grammatical features, then one would expect that the rule-oriented treatment group would do better on a posttest than the other two groups. This was not the case: the two experimental groups improved more or less equally. However, a closer examination of the experimental materials brings us back to the question of salience and what it is that makes something salient. There are many ways in which increased salience can be brought about. Among these is frequency of input (possibly at both ends—that is, highly frequent and highly infrequent items/structures). Form-focused instruction is yet another (see chapter 11 on instructed SLA). Although, there is a caution—studies cannot in absolute terms determine how externally manipulating salience impacts what happens in a learner's head.

Returning to Doughty's study, we see that both saliency and redundancy (i.e., frequency) were built into the tasks of the meaning-oriented treatment group. In the experimental material, this group saw reading passages with certain features, namely head nouns and relative clause markers, highlighted on the screen. Additionally, there was typographical capitalization of the juxtaposed head noun and relative clause marker, thereby visually making this part of the reading passage salient to the learner. Thus, if salience has an important role in SLA, Doughty's results (given her particular methodology) are what would be predicted, as both forms of pedagogical intervention focused on drawing learners' attention to relative clause formation. (We return to the concept of attention in chapter 8.)

Thus, as Kleinmann (1977) suggested, some L1–L2 differences may prove to be relatively "easy" to learn due to their saliency in the L2 input. In a similar vein, Ringbom (1987) pointed out that similarities may obscure for the learner the fact that there is something to learn. Oller and Ziahosseiny (1970) suggested that learning is "the most difficult where the most subtle distinctions are required either between the target and native language, or within the target language" (p. 186).

Both the Ringbom and the Oller and Ziahosseiny views are consistent with placing the learner (rather than just the learner's language) at the center. How the learner relates the first to the second language is of primary importance in understanding how second language learning is affected by knowledge of the first language.

One of the most interesting proposals in the area of cross-linguistic influences was that made by Kellerman (1979). Basic to his view of the role of the NL is the learner's perception of the distance between the first and second languages. The significance of this work, and other work of the time, is the attempt to place the study of transfer, or cross-linguistic influences, within a cognitive domain, thereby discrediting the implicit assumption of the necessary relationship between transfer and behaviorism. In this view, the learner is seen as "making decisions" about which forms and functions of the NL are appropriate candidates for use in the second language. The constraints on language transfer transcend the linguistic boundaries of similarity/dissimilarity of the native and target languages and encompass as a major variable the learner's decision-making processes relating to the potential transferability of linguistic elements. This is not to say that similarity/dissimilarity dimensions are

146

irrelevant, for clearly this is not the case. Considerations of similarity/dissimilarity are central to a learner's decision-making processes.

If learners use the NL to make predictions about the TL, what is the basis on which these decisions are made? In Kellerman's framework, linguistic information is categorized along a continuum ranging from language-neutral information to language-specific information. What is meant by this?

Language-neutral items are those items a learner believes are common across all languages (or at least the NL and TL). The accuracy of this belief is irrelevant, because what is of concern is how the learner views the situation. Language-neutral parts of language might include writing conventions, certain aspects of semantics, stylistics, and/or certain grammatical structures. It is reasonable to assume that without prior knowledge, a prototypical speaker of English brings to a language-learning situation the belief that all languages use commas, periods, quotation marks, question marks, and so forth, in the same ways as they are used in English. Similarly, our same speaker of English is likely to believe that all languages are able to express the semantic concept embodied in 5-29.

(5-29) The ball rolled down the hill.

Our learner would probably begin with the assumption that learning to express this concept in a second language only involves learning the specific lexical items and appropriate word order of the language being learned.

From the domain of syntax, there are also structures in a second language to which learners most likely expect to find translation equivalents. Simple structures such as

(5-30) The sky is blue.

are not likely to be considered structures that other languages do not have.

On the other extreme of the continuum are language-specific items. These are elements that a learner views as unique to his or her language. Included in this category are a great deal of the syntactic structure of a language, much of the phonology of language, idioms, inflectional morphology, slang expressions, and collocations.

None of these categories are absolute. For example, idioms and collocations can be of different types, with some being more transparent than others. An idiom like *kick the bucket* would most likely be considered language-specific by most people, given that the meaning of the composite cannot be determined from the meanings of the different words.

Learners would not be expected to do a word-for-word translation of the idiom when using a second language. Thus, an English speaker learning Italian would be unlikely to say something like this:

(5-31) *Quel vecchio   ha dato un calcio al   secchio.
that   old [man] gave   a   kick to the bucket
"That old man kicked the bucket."

On the other hand, a collocation like *make a difference* appears to be more transparent in meaning; hence, our speaker might indeed be expected to say this:

(5-32) Quel libro ha   fatto una differenza.
that book has made a   difference
"That book made a difference."

The knowledge reflected in this continuum, representing how one views one's own NL in terms of language-specific versus language-neutral items, is known as a learner's psychotypology.

However, the language-specific/language-neutral continuum is not intended to be absolute. An additional important variable is perceived language distance (presumably closely related to actual language distance). Languages that are closely related may influence learners in their beliefs about what is language-neutral and what is language-specific. For example, whereas we suggested earlier that phonology may be considered language-specific, this may only be the case for learners learning very dissimilar languages (e.g., Japanese speakers learning Polish). Spanish speakers learning Italian may consider all of their NL phonology as being "the same" as that of the TL phonology. Hence, in this learning situation, we would expect to find much more transfer. This is schematized in Figure 5.5.

The Xs indicate the extent to which the NL is expected to influence the L2. What is crucial is that the degree of language closeness is based on a learner's *perception* of both the distance (not necessarily the actual language distance) between the languages and on the learner's perception

	Close								Distant
Neutral	X	X	X	X	X	X	X	X	X
	X	X	X	X	X	X	X		
	X	X	X	X	X				
	X	X	X						
	X	X							
Specific	X								

Figure 5.5 Schematized version of Kellerman's model of language transfer.

of the organization of his or her NL (i.e., the extent to which parts of one's language are considered language-neutral/language-specific, and the extent to which the determination of language specificity is rigid or is susceptible to change, based on the perception of language distance).

In an empirical study, Kellerman (1979) attempted to show how intuitions about NL semantic space are used to predict translatability of items (in this case, various meanings of a single lexical item), from which one can infer transferability.

To determine NL influences, he gave Dutch learners of English a list of Dutch sentences with various meanings of the word *breken* (to break; see problem 1 in "points for discussion"), and asked them which of the translation equivalents they thought could be used in English.

What Kellerman found was that the concept of *coreness* was important. Coreness is determined by a combination of such factors as frequency, literalness, concreteness, and listing in a dictionary. In considering lexical items with multiple meanings, we can differentiate between core meanings and noncore meanings. Core meanings are those that are most frequently used (*He broke his leg, She broke his heart*), have literal meaning (*He broke his leg*), are concrete rather than abstract (*The cup broke*), and are listed first in a dictionary or are the first to come to mind. It is unlikely that any dictionary would give the meaning in *His voice broke when he was 13* as one of the first meanings of the verb *to break*. Similarly, a teacher, when asked to explain the meaning of *break* in class, is unlikely to use the sentence *The news story broke at six o'clock* as the first (or even any) attempt at definition.

Core meanings are likely to be equivalent to language-neutral items, whereas the noncore meanings are likely to be equivalent to language-specific items. What does this say for a theory of transfer? To answer this question, consider Figure 5.6, which is a revised version of Figure 5.5. Again, the Xs indicate those areas where we are likely to find NL influences.

Thus, in probabilistic terms we can predict where transfer will and will not occur. The greatest likelihood of transfer is in core elements, regardless of perceived distance. The second area of probable transfer is

	Close								Distant
Core	X	X	X	X	X	X	X	X	X
	X	X	X	X	X	X	X		
	X	X	X	X	X				
	X	X	X						
	X	X							
Noncore	X								

Figure 5.6 Revised model of language transfer.

between languages perceived as close (e.g., Spanish/Italian, Dutch/German), regardless of the status of core versus noncore elements.

Placing the learner in the center of the determination of transfer also implies that these predictions are not absolute across time. It may be that a learner begins learning a language with the expectation of great similarity, only to find that there are more differences than originally anticipated. This would necessitate a revision in what was considered transferable. Conversely, a learner might begin the study of a second language with the expectations of great differences, only to find that there are more similarities than originally anticipated. So the categories of language-neutral (coreness) and language-specific (noncoreness) are variable, along with the perceived NL–TL distance.

In summary, there are three interacting factors in the determination of language transfer: (a) a learner's psychotypology, that is, how a learner organizes his or her NL; (b) perception of NL–TL distance; and (c) actual knowledge of the TL.

Transfer, then, is only predictable in a probabilistic sense. One can never predict in any given situation whether a learner will be influenced by the facts of the NL or not. In terms of falsifying this view, one must also think in probabilistic terms. What would count as counterevidence? Large numbers of learners going against the predictions of this learner-centered model of transfer would call into question its predictive value. A single occurrence would not. A single instance of a learner transferring a nonpredicted element—let's say, the idiom *kick the bucket*—would not serve to counter the validity of this model.

Recent work on language transfer has added new dimensions to our understanding of the concept with notions such as "conceptual transfer" being introduced. This refers to the transfer of semantic concepts. Odlin, who in 1989 provided the first general summation of language transfer studies, in more recent work (2005, 2008) has considered research on linguistic relativity as well as investigations of the transfer of concepts and meaning. In a study by Odlin and Alonso-Vázquez (2006), the evidence indicates that what is seemingly a present or past perfect verb phrase can have distinct meanings in the interlanguage that vary considerably according to the learner's L1. Thus, while French-speaking learners of English tend to overuse the English perfect by referring to past events (e.g., *I have gone to Rome last year*), Spanish speakers often use the perfect in target-like ways (e.g., *I have gone to Rome a few times*). In contrast to these groups, Turkish speakers often use the past perfect to refer to events that they have no direct knowledge of, as in *My friend had gone to Rome last year* while the same learners use the past simple for events that they do have direct knowledge of, as in *I went to Rome last year*. The differences between the use of the perfect by French speakers and Turkish speakers reflect grammatical and conceptual meanings in their native language. Turkish systematically contrasts past events that a speaker knows of firsthand from past events known only from inference or hearsay. This obligatory contrast in Turkish often finds its way into interlanguage English verb phrases, just as when the French *passée composée* influences Francophones' choices of perfect forms. These studies show that the language-specific semantic and conceptual character of the L1 has important implications for our concept of language transfer that are only beginning to be understood.

5.5.6 Second language processing

As the field of SLA continues to develop, a greater emphasis has been on how learners process language. This area is discussed in greater detail in chapter 8, but we include a brief discussion here because it relates to the role of the L1. For example, Frenck-Mestre (2005) reviews studies that suggest different processing strategies between learners and native speakers where the learners resemble native speakers of the L1 rather than native speakers of the L2. She analyzes the results of learners of French (native speakers of Spanish and of English) processing sentences such as *Jean saw the daughter of the woman who was leaving the shop*. Each group of learners (English and Spanish) was divided into two levels of proficiency depending on their length of residence in France. Spanish and French native speakers each have a tendency to interpret *who was leaving the shop* as referring to the first noun phrase (*the daughter*), whereas English interprets the relative clause as referring to the second noun phrase, *the woman*. Beginning learners rely on their L1 processing strategies as they comprehend these sentences, whereas more advanced learners (the English learners of French) move to an L2 processing strategy and interpret the relative clause as referring to the first noun phrase. This suggests an important role for L1 processing when confronted with the L2.[3]

In a series of three experiments, VanPatten and Keating (2007) investigate the acquisition of tense processing by L2 learners. They found that learners begin with a universal processing principle and not with their L1 processing strategy, although they do abandon their L1 strategies with greater proficiency. VanPatten and Keating were contrasting reliance on adverbs as a way of interpreting tense (e.g., *last night*) and finite verbs. It may be that with more complex syntax, as in the case of the Frenck-Mestre studies, a greater reliance on the L1 may be found.

5.6 Interlanguage transfer

To more completely understand language transfer, it is necessary to go beyond the NL and the TL. In this section we focus on interlanguage transfer and attempt to integrate it into our overall concept of language transfer.

By definition, interlanguage transfer is the influence of one L2 (using the broad sense of this term) over another. Interlanguage transfer raises a number of important theoretical issues. Does the gradually acquired knowledge of a language beyond the second make a difference in the types of transfer seen? How is knowledge of a prior interlanguage used (or not used) in the addition of a third, fourth, or fifth language? When there is evidence of interlanguage transfer, how does this relate to influence from the first language? Just as there exists, under certain conditions, reverse transfer from interlanguage back into the native language, there is a parallel set of influences from interlanguage back into previous interlanguages, from earlier interlanguages into newly developing ones and even from various interlanguages back into the native language (see Cook, 2003, for a series of studies on the latter). Most importantly for current theories of language transfer, based on solely two languages in the multilingual mind, what are the principles that block native language transfer in the domain of multiple language acquisition and that encourage (or discourage) fossilization? What principles (other than those discussed earlier) have been suggested for the facilitation of interlanguage transfer and the often concomitant blocking of native language transfer?

As instance of interlanguage transfer was provided in chapter 2 in the example of a French sentence built on a German syntactic model and produced by a native speaker of English. Also mentioned in chapter 2 was work by Dewaele (1998), who investigated lexical inventions in two versions of oral French interlanguage: one where the French interlanguage was the second language of native speakers of Dutch, and the other where French was the third language with English as a prior second language. One goal was to see if there was interlanguage transfer in the latter group from its L2 English (with the native language Dutch being blocked). The design was set up so that if this group drew more on their previous interlanguage English and not their native Dutch, then interlanguage transfer could be shown because this could not happen with the first group, which had only French as an interlanguage. The results showed that the group that had only one second language (French) drew heavily on the native language (Dutch), whereas the group that had two interlanguages drew on the first foreign language (English) in creating French lemmas.

De Angelis (1999) examined the production of Italian by a French-Canadian L1 speaker with three foreign languages: Spanish, English, and Italian. She identified two types of interlanguage transfer: (a) full lexical interlanguage transfer and (b) partial lexical interlanguage transfer. The first type of transfer grouped instances in which an entire nontarget word from an earlier interlanguage was used in the production of the target language (Italian). The second type of transfer grouped instances in which partial morphological information from a nontarget interlanguage word was used in the Italian target language production. De Angelis found occurrences of both types of interlanguage transfer from Spanish into Italian, which, following one of the key principles in this domain, showed strong patterns of phonological similarity between the two languages. The results were discussed in terms of how phonological similarity between or among languages creates the condition for activation to spread to nontarget words in other languages, and how lexical items come to be in competition for selection. A number of suggestions were outlined as to why native language transfer may have been blocked, with the "talk foreign" mode apparently appearing to be important for inter-language speakers.

In attacking a key question in this research area, Klein (1995, citing a 1994 paper) asked whether knowledge of more than one language facilitates the acquisition of additional languages within a Universal Grammar (UG) model of acquisition (see chapter 6). She tested matched groups of monolinguals (English as an L2) and multilinguals learning English as a third or fourth language on the acquisition of (a) lexical learning and (b) syntactic learning. She found that multilinguals out-performed monolinguals in both types of learning and concluded that multilinguals develop qualities that help trigger UG parameters. The qualities were metalinguistic awareness and enhanced lexical learning, as proposed by Thomas (1988), and a less conservative learning pro-cedure, as proposed by Zobl (1992). For the view that multilinguals are better learners than monolinguals, there is both supporting evidence (e.g., Ramsay, 1980) and nonsupporting evidence (Nayak, Hansen, Krueger, and McLaughlin, 1990). The possibility of transfer as a facilita-tion strategy (cf. Corder, 1967) is not discussed in these references but could be a central variable in answering this question.

Other studies in multiple language acquisition could be reread as supporting the positive versus negative effects of interlanguage transfer in terms of mental structuring and organization of the bilingual lexicon. Abunuwara (1992) measured interference effects among Arabic L1 speakers with Hebrew and English as second languages. Her results suggest (a) a coordinate (independent) relation among the two nonnative languages, (b) a compound (interdependent) relation between the native language and the weakest nonnative language, and (c) an intermediate relation between the native language and the strongest nonnative language.

A study by de Groot and Hoeks (1995) tested the relationship between proficiency and lexico-semantic organization in two sets of "unbalanced" trilinguals (Dutch–English–French). The native language and the weak foreign language were hypothesized to have a "word-association" lexical structure, whereas the native language and the stronger foreign language were hypothesized to have a "concept-mediation" lexical structure. The data suggest that foreign-language proficiency determines lexico-semantic organization in multilingual speakers.

Language similarity and its effects have been discussed by a number of researchers in the area of multiple language acquisition studies (De Angelis, 1999; Dewaele, 1998; Ringbom, 1987; Selinker and Baumgartner-Cohen, 1995; Stedje, 1977; Vildomec, 1963; Williams and Hammarberg, 1998). Vildomec (1963) made the observation, which researchers are still evaluating and testing today, that in early L3 production certain functors, such as prepositions, articles, and conjunctions, tend to come from the second language and not the native language. This may occur even when the two languages are not phonetically similar.

The use of function words from a second language rather than the native language in third language production has also been discussed in Stedje (1977), Ringbom (1987), and Williams and Hammarberg (1998). Stedje (1977), who examined Finnish learners of German as a third language with Swedish as the second, found that function words were predominantly transferred from the second language rather than from the native language. In a study examining the data of essays written in English (L3) by Finnish students with Swedish as a second language, Ringbom (1987) found 187 instances of complete language switches from Swedish L2 and only 8 from Finnish L1; in the instances of transfer from Swedish, 67% of the lexical items were content words and 33% were function words. Williams and Hammarberg (1998, p. 296) examined instances of what they called "non-adapted language switches" (i.e., transfer without modification) in a two-year longitudinal study of a learner of Swedish as a third language whose native language was English and first inter-language was German. An important finding was that, even when no direct similarity could be found, some German L2 lexical or structural features were present in the learner's Swedish L3. The authors proposed that the German second language was activated in parallel to the third language.

Cenoz (2001) discussed a number of factors that might influence cross-linguistic influence in general (e.g., age, context of use, proficiency) and provided empirical evidence on the acquisition of English by Spanish/ Basque bilinguals, with some dominant in one language and others dominant in the other. She found that linguistic distance is one factor. Basque is unrelated to Spanish or English and there was greater evidence of transfer from Spanish to English than from Basque to English. This was the case for all learners regardless of language dominance. Language distance is not the only factor. Age is another, with older learners showing more cross-linguistic influence than younger children. There are language-related factors as well, with more transfer of content words than function words. An interesting finding is that, when words in English are "foreignized," only Spanish words are at the base and not Basque words.

If the results of some of these studies could be shown to exist longitudinally, we would have evidence not only of the existence of interlanguage transfer but also of its persistence. If this were indeed shown, we could return to one crucial conclusion about theories of language transfer: theories of language transfer that purport to be general must include multiple language acquisition where interlanguage transfer is common and should in principle show that transfer effects exist longitudinally. It is clear that language transfer from one interlanguage to another and the principles blocking native language influence must be incorporated into any general theory of transfer.

5.7 Conclusion

In this chapter and in chapter 4, we have traced the history of the concept of transfer from its earlier behaviorist origins to today's mentalist conceptualization. In chapters 6 and 7 we relate the concept of transfer to current issues in linguistically-based models of second language acquisition.

Suggestions for additional reading

Cross-Linguistic Influences in the Second Language Lexicon. Janusz Arabski, Multilingual Matters (2006).

Cross-Linguistic Influence in Third Language Acquisition: Psycholinguistic Perspectives. Jasone Cenoz, Britta Hufeisen, and Ulrike Jessner (Eds.). Multilingual Matters (2001).

Effects of the Second Language on the First. Vivian Cook (Ed.). Multilingual Matters (2003).

Language Transfer in Language Learning. Susan Gass and Larry Selinker (Eds.). John Benjamins (1992).

Foreign Language and Mother Tongue. Istvan Kecskes and Tunde Papp. Lawrence Erlbaum Associates (2000).

Cross-Linguistic Influence in Second Language Acquisition. Eric Kellerman and Michael Sharwood Smith (Eds.). Pergamon Press (1986).

Language Transfer. Terrence Odlin. Cambridge University Press (1989).

The Role of the First Language in Foreign Language Learning. Håkan Ringbom. Multilingual Matters (1987).

Points for discussion

1   The data that follow are from responses of 81 native speakers of Dutch who were learning English (data from Kellerman, 1979; see also problem 2.1 in Gass, Sorace, and Selinker, 1999). Students were given

each of the grammatical Dutch sentences in column 1 (all with the word *breken* "to break") and were asked to indicate if they believed that the English translation equivalents (in column 2) were grammatical in English. The degree to which they thought each sentence would be possible in English is given in column 3 as a percentage of the 81 respondents who said it was grammatical.

Dutch sentence (all are grammatical)	English equivalent	% responses translatable
1. Welk land heeft de wapenstilstand *gebroken*.	Which country has broken the cease-fire?	28
2. Zij *brak* 't wereldrecord.	She broke the world record.	51
3. Zij *brak* zijn hart.	She broke his heart.	79
4. De golven *braken* op de rotsen.	The waves broke on the rock.	35
5. Hij *brak* zijn woord.	He broke his word.	60
6. Hij *brak* zijn been.	He broke his leg.	81
7. Het ondergrondse verzet werd *gebroken*.	The underground resistance was broken.	22
8. Dankzij 'n paar grapjes was 't ijs eindelijk *gebroken*.	Thanks to a few jokes, the ice was finally broken.	33
9. 'n Spelletje zou de middag enigszins *breken*.	A game would break up the afternoon a bit.	11
10. Zijn val werd door 'n boom *gebroken*.	His fall was broken by a tree.	17
11. 't Kopje *brak*.	The cup broke.	64
12. Nood *breekt* wet.	Necessity breaks law (a saying).	34
13. Sommige arbeiders hebben de staking *gebroken*.	Some workers have broken the strike.	9
14. Na 't ongeluk is hij 'n *gebroken* man geworden.	After the accident, he was a broken man.	61
15. Zijn stem *brak* toen hij 13 was.	His voice broke when he was 13.	17
16. De man *brak* zijn eed.	The man broke his oath.	47
17. De lichtstralen *breken* in het water.	The light rays break (refract) in the water.	25

a   Consider the percentage of sentences judged translatable in column 3. Order these sentences in terms of greater to lesser translatability of the Dutch word *breken*.

b   Consider the English translation equivalents in column 2. Given the meanings of the Dutch sentences, what differences are there that might account for the varying degrees of translatability ascribed to them? For example, how do you account for 81% acceptance for item 6, 79% acceptance for item 3, but only 64% acceptance for item 11?

   c   How might your analysis predict the translatability of the equivalent of *break* in your native language or in another language you know?

2   Compare the Contrastive Analysis Hypothesis prediction of transfer with Kellerman's predictions. In what ways do they differ? In what ways are they similar?

3   The following data are from native speakers of Czech learning English and Czech speakers learning Russian (Dušková, 1984). Column 1 (L2 English) represents unattested forms (indicated by *). In other words, Czech learners never produce plurals or past tense forms, as given in column 1.

	L2 English	NS Czech	L2 Russian	NS Russian
Plural forms	*teacher*ele*	ucitelé	ucitele	ucitelja
	*workwoman*ici*	delnice	rabotnice	rabotnicy
Past tense	*arisen*ul*	vznikl	vozniknul	voznik
		vzniknul		
	*he dieel	umrel	on umrel	on umer

As can be noted, there is widespread transfer of endings from Czech to Russian, but not from Czech to English. Why do you think this is so? Why should these facts be troublesome for an NL-based theory of second language acquisition?

4   Tape-record three different second language speakers (with different native languages). Ask native speakers of English to identify the native language of the speakers on the basis of the accent. Is it relatively easy? What made it easy or difficult for them to make the appropriate identification? Now take the compositions given in problem 10 of chapter 4. Can native speakers make the appropriate identification? What made it easy or difficult for them to make the appropriate identification in this instance?

5   Consider the phenomenon of avoidance discussed in this chapter. It has been primarily investigated in the domain of syntax. Why do you think this emphasis has occurred? Can avoidance be as easily studied in phonology? In vocabulary? Why or why not?

     How valid is it to attribute avoidance to lack of use? Could one conceptualize lack of use as not necessarily avoidance, but as *deliberate* choice of another structure? How could one empirically investigate this possibility?

6   Handel, a native speaker of German, wrote the *Messiah* in England with English words taken primarily from the text of the King James version of the Bible as a starting point. Scholars have long noted

(*Programme Notes Good Friday Concert*, Royal Albert Hall, 1998) that there are non-English, as well as non-German, stresses on some of the verses—for example, the famous

For' unto us a child is born.

versus the expected

For unto us' a child is born. (Isaiah 9:6)

In the Italian version of this verse, the first word is stressed, as in the following:

Poiché' un bambino è nato per noi (Isaia 9:6)
for   a   child   is born for us

Handel earlier in his life lived in Italy for three years. Also, opera was commonly written in Italian during this time and Handel himself was proficient in the style of Italian opera.

Can interlanguage transfer be involved in explaining stress patterns in Handel's *Messiah*? Note that the stress in the Italian word *poiché* is on the second syllable. Does this affect your answer? Does intended stress on words affect musical structure or vice versa? If you can come up with an explanation of why the *Messiah* has the stresses it does, can you think of any way of testing whether this is interlanguage transfer? For example, can you predict something that by normal rules of English stress placement should not appear in the *Messiah*?

See GSS, problem 2.1.

6

FORMAL APPROACHES TO SLA

6.1 Introduction

Linguistics has impacted research in second language acquisition since the early days of SLA research, with virtually every theory of linguistics having had some relevance to SLA research. In this chapter, we focus our discussion of that relationship on the area of research that has dominated the theoretical study of second language acquisition over the years, Universal Grammar. This area of research is dealt with in this chapter along with issues of phonology; typological universals are discussed in chapter 7.

As we stated in chapter 1, the field of SLA, a relatively young discipline, has been influenced in its formation by other disciplines. In turn, SLA has also exerted influence on these source disciplines. At present, some would conceptualize SLA as an independent field with its own research agenda and with a multidisciplinary focus, whereas others would conceptualize it as a subdiscipline of one source discipline or another. It is our view that because SLA has a substantial body of research and a strong research tradition, it is best thought of as an independent discipline with strong ties to other disciplines.

In this and the following three chapters, we focus on three areas in which the SLA relationship with other academic disciplines has been most heavily felt: linguistics (chapters 6, 7), psychology (chapter 8), and sociolinguistics broadly construed to include sociocultural orientations (chapter 9). This is not to say that these are the only areas in which SLA has strong ties. Rather, they are selected as representative. We focus generally on the influence on SLA from these disciplines, but in a few places we discuss what influence SLA has, or can have, on these fields. With regard to the influence each of these fields has on SLA, the difference can be found in the general emphasis: linguistics focuses on the products of acquisition (i.e., a description of the linguistic systems of L2 learners), psychology focuses on the process by which those systems are created (e.g., a description of the process of the way in which learners create learner systems), and sociolinguistics focuses on social factors that influence the acquisition of the linguistic system and the use of that system. However, one feature all areas share when considering SLA is a concern with the *learning problem*: how is it that learners acquire, when they do, the complexities of a second language?

This chapter deals with nativist approaches to language, which claim that at least some aspects of language learning involve innateness. Within this general category, two main positions are noted: general nativism and special nativism. The general nativist position (see Eckman, 1996; Hamilton, 1996; O'Grady, 1996, 2005; Wolfe-Quintero, 1996) maintains that there is no specific mechanism designed for language learning. Rather, "there are general principles of learning that are not particular to language learning but may be employed in other types of learning" (Eckman, 1996, p. 398). Special nativism includes theories of language (learning) that posit special principles for language learning, principles that are unique to language (learning) and that are not used in other cognitive endeavors. Both the general nativist and special nativist positions agree that there is something innate involved in language learning; it is the nature of the innate system that is in question. Is it available only for the task of language learning or is it also available for more general learning tasks? This chapter treats only the special nativist approach, known as Universal Grammar (UG). Central to these approaches is an understanding of language as a system with its own rules.

6.2 Universal Grammar

The UG approach to second language acquisition begins from the perspective of learnability. The assumption of innate universal language properties is motivated by the need to explain the uniformly successful and speedy acquisition of language by children in spite of insufficient input. In this section, we deal with UG principles, UG parameters, and lexical and functional categories.

In UG theory, universal principles form part of the mental representation of language, and it is this mental grammar that mediates between the sound and meaning of language. Properties of the human mind are what make language universals the way they are. As Chomsky (1995, p. 167) noted: "The theory of a particular language is its *grammar*. The theory of languages and the expressions they generate is *Universal Grammar* (UG); UG is a theory of the initial state S_o of the relevant component of the language faculty." The assumption that UG is the guiding force of child language acquisition has long been maintained by many, but only in the past two decades has it been applied to second language acquisition. After all, if properties of human language are part of the mental representation of language, it is assumed that they do not cease being properties in just those instances in which a nonnative language system is being employed.

The theory underlying UG assumes that language consists of a set of abstract principles that characterize core grammars of all natural languages. In addition to principles that are invariable (i.e., all languages have them) are parameters that vary across languages. Cook (1997, pp. 250–251) made an interesting analogy between driving a car and principles and parameters:

> Overall there is a principle that drivers have to keep consistently to one side of the road, which is taken for granted by all drivers in all countries.[1] Exceptions to this principle, such as people driving down motorways on the wrong side, rate stories in the media or car chases in action movies. The principle does not, however, say, *which* side of the road people should drive on. A parameter of driving allows the side to be the left in England and Japan, and the right in the USA and France. The parameter has two values or "settings"—left and right. Once a country has opted for one side or the other, it sticks to its choice: a change of setting is a massively complex operation, whether it happens for a whole country, as in Sweden, or for the individual travelling from England to France. So, a universal principle and a variable parameter together sum up the essence of driving. The principle states the universal requirement on driving; the parameter specifies the variation between countries.

How does UG relate to language acquisition? If children have to learn a complex set of abstractions, there must be something other than the language input to which they are exposed that enables them to learn language with relative ease and speed. UG is postulated as an innate language facility that limits the extent to which languages can vary. That is, it specifies the limits of a possible language. The task for learning is greatly reduced if one is equipped with an innate mechanism that constrains possible grammar formation. Before relating the question of UG to SLA, we turn briefly to issues from child language acquisition to explain the basic argumentation of this theory.

The theoretical need for an innate language faculty is based on a negative argument. The claim is that, on the basis of language input alone, children cannot attain the complexities of adult grammars. Innate linguistic properties fill in where the input fails. What does it mean to say that the input is insufficient? It is not merely an antibehaviorist notion that argues against an input/output scheme. Rather, it is based on the fact that children come to know certain properties of grammar that are not obviously learnable from input, as illustrated by the following examples from English discussed by White (1989):

(6-1) I want to go.
(6-2) I wanna go.
(6-3) John wants to go but we don't want to.
(6-4) John wants to go but we don't wanna.
(6-5) Do you want to look at the chickens?
(6-6) Do you wanna look at the chickens?
(6-7) Who do you want to see?
(6-8) Who do you wanna see?

Examples 6-1 to 6-8 show the range of possibilities for changing *want to* to *wanna*. However, there are many times in English where the sequence *want to* cannot be replaced by the informal *wanna*, as in 6-9 to 6-12:

(6-9)   Who do you want to feed the dog?
(6-10) *Who do you wanna feed the dog?
(6-11) Who do you want to win the race?
(6-12) *Who do you wanna win the race?

Without prior information to guide learners, it would be difficult to determine the correct distribution of *want to* versus *wanna* in informal English. The input does not provide sufficiently specific information about where to use *wanna* and where not to use it. White explained that there are principles of UG involving question formation to account for the distribution of these English forms. Briefly, sentence 6-7 can be represented by something like *You want to see* X and 6-9 by something like *You want* X *to feed the dog*. Note the location of X, the element about which a question is being asked. In 6-9, but not in 6-7, the question is about an element (X) that is placed between *want* and *to*. This is what effectively blocks contraction. In 6-7, *want* and *to* are adjacent, thereby allowing contraction; that is, no intervening element blocks it. Importantly, the input alone does not provide this information. This argument is called the poverty of the stimulus.

One could, of course, argue that direct or indirect intervention is indeed forthcoming and that one does not need innateness to explain language acquisition. However, in most instances, the language-learning environment does not provide information to the child concerning the well-formedness of an utterance (Chomsky, 1981, 1986), or even when it does, it provides information only about the ungrammatical (or inappropriate) utterance, not about what needs to be done to modify a current hypothesis. Furthermore, as we saw in chapter 5 (section 5.1),

162

even with explicit correction, children's grammars are often impervious to change.

Theoretically, there are two kinds of evidence available to learners as they make hypotheses about correct and incorrect language forms: positive evidence and negative evidence.[2] Positive evidence comes from the speech learners hear/read and thus is composed of a limited set of well-formed utterances of the language being learned. When a particular sentence type is not heard, one does not know whether it is not heard because of its impossibility in the language or because of mere coincidence. It is in this sense that the sentences of a language that provide the input to the learner are known as positive evidence. It is on the basis of positive evidence that linguistic hypotheses can be made. Negative evidence, on the other hand, is composed of information to a learner that his or her utterance is deviant with regard to the norms of the language being learned. We provide more detail on this in chapter 10. For now, suffice it to say that negative evidence can take many forms, including direct correction, such as *That's not right* or indirect questions, such as *What did you say?*

The child language literature suggests that negative evidence is not frequent (see Brown and Hanlon, 1970, and the theoretical arguments by Baker, 1979), is often ignored, and can therefore not be a necessary condition for acquisition. Because positive evidence alone cannot delineate the range of possible and impossible sentences, and because negative evidence is not frequently forthcoming, there must be innate principles that constrain *a priori* the possibilities of grammar formation.

In sum, Universal Grammar is "the system of principles, conditions, and rules that are elements or properties of all human languages" (Chomsky, 1975, p. 29). It "is taken to be a characterization of the child's prelinguistic state" (Chomsky, 1981, p. 7). Thus, the necessity of positing an innate language faculty is due to the inadequate input, in terms of quantity and quality, to which a learner is exposed. Learning is mediated by UG and by the L1, as we will see below.

How does this relate to second language acquisition? The question is generally posed as an access-to-UG problem. Does the innate language faculty that children use in constructing their native language grammars remain operative in second language acquisition? More recently, this question is formulated as an issue of initial state. What do second language learners start with?

6.2.1 Initial state

The question posed in this section is: What is the nature of the linguistic knowledge with which learners begin the second language acquisition process? That is, what is the unconscious linguistic knowledge that learners have before receiving L2 input, or, to take a variant of the question, what are early L2 grammars like? The two variables influencing this debate are transfer (i.e., the availability of the first language grammar) and access to UG (i.e., the extent to which UG is available).

Two broad views are discussed here: the Fundamental Difference Hypothesis (Bley-Vroman, 1989; Schachter, 1988), which argues that what happens in child language acquisition is not the same as what happens in adult second language acquisition, and the Access to UG Hypothesis, which argues that the innate language facility is alive and well in second language acquisition and constrains the grammars of second language learners as it does the grammars of child first language learners. We take a look at each of these positions, the latter in actuality being made up of several branches.

6.2.1.1 Fundamental Difference Hypothesis

As was seen in chapters 4 and 5, much of the work in second language acquisition was driven by the notion that first and second language acquisition involve the same processes. This is not to say that differences were not noted; rather, proposals to account for these differences were made with an attempt to salvage the major theoretical claim of L1 and L2 similarities.

The Fundamental Difference Hypothesis starts from the belief that, with regard to language learning, children and adults are different in many important ways. For example, the ultimate attainment reached by children and adults differs. In normal situations, children always reach a state of "complete" knowledge of their native language. In second language acquisition (at least, adult second language acquisition), not only is "complete" knowledge not always attained, it is rarely, if ever, attained. Fossilization, representing a non-TL stage, is frequently observed (Han, 2004; Long, 2007).

Another difference concerns the nature of the knowledge that these two groups of learners have at the outset of language learning. Second language learners have at their command knowledge of a full linguistic system. They do not have to learn what language is all about at the same time that they are learning a specific language. For example, at the level of performance, adults know that there are social reasons for using different language varieties.[3] What they have to learn in acquiring a second language system is the specific language forms that may be used in a given social setting. Children, on the other hand, have to learn not only the appropriate language forms, but also that there are different forms to be used in different situations.

Related to the idea that adults have complete knowledge of a language system is the notion of equipotentiality, expressed by Schachter (1988).

She pointed out that children are capable of learning *any* language. Given exposure to the data of a language (i.e., the input), a child will learn that language. No language is easier to learn than another; all languages are equally learnable by all children. This is not the case with second language learners. Spanish speakers have less difficulty learning Italian than they do Japanese. If language relatedness (perceived or actual) were not a determining factor in ultimate success, we would expect all learners to be equally able to learn any second language. This is not borne out by the facts.

One final difference to mention is that of motivation and attitude toward the target language and target language community (see chapter 12 for a fuller discussion). It is clear that, as in any learning situation, not all humans are equally motivated to learn languages, nor are they equally motivated to learn a specific language. Differential motivation does not appear to impact a child's success or lack of success in learning language. All human beings without cognitive impairment learn a first language.

In sum, the basic claim of the Fundamental Difference Hypothesis is that adult second language learners do not have access to UG. Rather, what they know of language universals is constructed through their NL. In addition to the native language, which mediates access to UG, second language learners make use of their general problem-solving abilities. Second language learners come to the language-learning situation knowing that a language contains an infinite number of sentences; that they are capable of understanding sentences they have never heard before; and that a language has rules of syntax, rules of combining morphemes, limits on possible sounds, and so forth. With specific regard to syntax, learners know that languages can form questions and that the syntax of questions is syntactically related to the syntax of statements. They know that languages have a way of modifying nouns, either through adjectives or relative clauses.

This information is gleaned by means of knowing that the NL is this way and by assuming that these facts are a part of the general character of language rather than a part of the specific nature of the native language. Thus, the learner constructs a pseudo-UG, based on what is known of the native language. It is in this sense that the NL mediates knowledge of UG for second language learners.

6.2.1.2 *Access to UG Hypothesis*

The opposing view to the Fundamental Difference Hypothesis is the Access to UG Hypothesis. The common perspective is that "UG is constant (that is, unchanged as a result of L1 acquisition); UG is distinct from the learner's L1 grammar; UG constrains the L2 learner's interlanguage grammars" (White, 2003, p. 60). White (2003) outlines five positions with regard to the initial state of second language learning; the first three take the first language as the basis of the initial state and the second two take UG as the initial state: (1) Full Transfer/Full Access, (2) Minimal Trees, (3) Valueless Features, (4) Initial Hypothesis of Syntax, and (5) Full Access (without transfer).

Before beginning the discussion of access to UG, it is important to make one further distinction and that is between lexical and functional categories. In addition to principles, part of the innate language component consists of lexical and functional categories. Lexical categories are the categories that we learn about in school: nouns, adjectives, verbs, adverbs, and so forth. These can be thought of as content words. Functional categories, on the other hand, are words that serve particular functions (e.g., articles, possessives) or they may be categories consisting of grammatical morphemes (e.g., plurals, tense markers).

Functional categories can be thought of as grammatical elements that in a sense form the glue of a sentence. Examples of functional categories are determiners (e.g., *a, the, our, my, this*), complementizers (e.g., *if, whether, that*), and grammatical markers (past tense endings, case markings, plural endings, and gender marking). These differ from lexical categories in a number of ways. In general, functional categories represent a fixed set of words in a language, whereas lexical categories can be added to as the need arises (consider the recent addition to the English lexicon of the word *dotcom*, as in *dotcom industry* or in the recent *Time* magazine headline "Doom stalks the dotcoms").[4]

However, the most important distinction has to do with whether or not a class of words is associated with lexical properties. Prepositions, for example, though typically having the functional category characteristic of a fixed set of words in a language, are best thought of as a part of the lexical category. This is so because prepositions are often associated with such roles as agent (who does what to whom), patient (who is the recipient of the action), and location. For example, in English the preposition *by* can be associated with an agent in passive sentences (*John was kissed by Mary*), and the preposition *in* can take on the role of location (*John was kissed in the park*).

We now turn to different conceptualizations of the roles of the L1 and UG as possible starting points for L2 acquisition.

L1 AS THE BASE

1   *Full Transfer/Full Access*
This position assumes that the starting point is the L1 grammar, but that there is full access to UG during the process of acquisition (Schwartz, 1998; Schwartz and Sprouse, 1994, 1996, 2000; Whong-Barr, 2005). The learner is assumed to use the L1 grammar as a basis

but to have full access to UG when the L1 is deemed insufficient for the learning task at hand. L1 and L2 learning differ, and there is no prediction that learners will eventually attain complete knowledge of the L2.

2   *Minimal Trees Hypothesis*
Recall that in the previous position, full transfer/full access, learners draw on both the L1 and UG. The first option was to draw on the L1 and, where that was insufficient, to draw on UG. The Minimal Trees Hypothesis also maintains that both L1 and UG are available concurrently (Vainikka and Young-Scholten, 1994, 1996a, 1996b). However, the L1 grammar that is available contains no functional categories, and these categories, initially, are not available from any source. The emergence of functional categories is not dependent on the L1 and hence there is no transfer; rather, they emerge in response to L2 input. The development of functional categories of learners from different languages will be the same. On this view, learners may or may not reach the final state of an L2 grammar, depending on what is available through the L1 and what is available through UG. They should be able to reach the final state of an L2 grammar with regard to functional categories.

3   *Valueless Features*
This is the most technical of the hypotheses and will be dealt with in the least detail. In essence, the claim is that there is weak transfer (Eubank 1993, 1993/1994, 1996). The L1 is the primary starting point. Unlike the Minimal Trees Hypothesis, both functional and lexical categories are available from the L1, but the strength of these features is not available. There are consequences of feature strength in areas such as word order. Acquisition involves acquiring appropriate feature strength of the L2. Learners should be able to fully acquire the L2 grammar.

UG-BASED

4   *The Initial Hypothesis of Syntax* (Platzack, 1996)
This position maintains that, as in child language acquisition, the starting point for acquisition is UG.

5   *Full Access/No Transfer*
This position maintains that, as in child language acquisition, the starting point for acquisition is UG (Epstein, Flynn, and Martohardjono, 1996, 1998; Flynn, 1996; Flynn and Martohardjono, 1994). There is a disconnection between the L1 and the developing L2 grammar. A prediction based on this position is that L1 and L2 acquisition will proceed in a similar fashion, will end up at the same point, and that all L2 acquisition (regardless of L1) would proceed

along the same path. Learners should be able to reach the same level of competence as native speakers. If there are differences, they are performance-related rather than competence-related.

In the following sections, we examine data that bear on these issues of access to UG. There are two types of relevant data: data relating to UG principles that are invariant, and data relating to UG parameters that vary across languages.

6.2.2 UG principles

White (1989) reported on a study by Otsu and Naoi (1986) dealing with the principle of structure dependence. The basic concept behind this principle is that linguistic principles operate on syntactic (or structural) units. That is, most importantly, according to this view, what makes language knowledge different from other types of knowledge is the notion of structure dependency; language is not just a string of unstructured segments. White pointed out that this accounts for the grammatical question in 6-14 and the ungrammaticality of 6-15.

(6-13) The boy who is standing over there is happy.
(6-14) Is the boy who is standing over there_____happy?
(6-15) *Is the boy who_____standing over there is happy?

The rule for question formation makes reference to the subject, which in the case of 6-13 is a complex subject consisting of a determiner phrase (*the boy*) and a relative clause (*who is standing over there*). The rule does not make reference to a nonstructural unit, such as "the first verb." Thus, *yes/no* questions are formed by moving the main verb to the front of the sentence, not by moving the first verb in the sentence to the front (as in 6-15).

Otsu and Naoi tested knowledge of structure dependency among Japanese learners of English. In Japanese, questions are formed by adding a question particle to the end of a sentence. No word-order changes are made. The learners tested knew how to form simple questions and passed a test showing knowledge of relative clauses, but they had no knowledge of question formation involving complex subjects. It was hypothesized that if a UG principle, structure dependence, were operative, it could not have come into the learner language system through the L1 as the L1 does not have a principle of structure dependence relevant to question formation. Thus, the only way the principle of structure dependence could have come into the learners' second language grammar is through direct access to UG. In general, the results of this study support the notion that learners' grammars are constrained by principles of UG, in this case the principle of structure dependence.

Another study relevant to the issue of UG principles is one by Schachter (1989). She tested the principle known as subjacency, which limits the amount of movement that can take place within sentences. Consider the following contrived conversation:

Speaker 1: I agree with the idea that David loves Mary Jo.
Speaker 2: I didn't hear you. *Who do you agree with the idea that David loves?

The ungrammaticality of *Who do you agree with the idea that David loves?* is due to the fact that, in English, movement of the question word from the position of the original noun phrase (*Mary Jo*) to its new sentence-initial position is constrained by the distance and intervening syntactic structures between the two positions.[5] In Speaker 2's sentence, the necessary syntactic relationships cannot hold; that is, the movement rule is violated and, hence, the sentence is ungrammatical.

Schachter (1989) tested knowledge of this principle by eliciting grammaticality judgments by native speakers of Indonesian, Chinese, and Korean learning English. In a separate article, Schachter (1990) added a group of Dutch speakers to her database. The languages in question have different requirements on subjacency. In Korean, there is no evidence of subjacency; in Chinese and Indonesian, there is some evidence of subjacency, although in both of these languages *wh-* movement is more limited than in English; and in Dutch, subjacency restrictions are much the same as in English. The results of Schachter's study suggest that the Dutch speakers recognize that English is constrained by the principle of subjacency; the results for the other groups are not as clear. The Korean-speaking learners, in keeping with the no-access position, were not constrained by subjacency. The Chinese and Indonesian speakers behaved more English-like than the Korean speakers, but their interlanguage grammars could not be said to be constrained by the principle of subjacency.[6]

A third example comes from White's (2003) discussion of the results of studies based on the Empty Category Principle (ECP) (Chomsky, 1981). In essence, the ECP is a way of accounting for asymmetry found in the use or nonuse of case particles. Examples can be seen from Japanese in 6-16, 6-17, and 6-18.

(6-16) John ga   sono hon o   yonda.
       John NOM that book ACC read-PAST
       "John read that book."
(6-17) John ga   sono hon yonda.
       John NOM that book read-PAST
(6-18) *John sono hon o   yonda.
       John that book ACC read-PAST

6-16 is grammatical with both a nominative and an accusative case marker; 6-17 is possible with a nominative case marker and no accusative case marker, but 6-18 is ungrammatical because it has only an accusative case marker, but no nominative case marker. Kanno (1996) investigated whether beginning learners of Japanese were able to recognize this discrepancy, arguing that, if they recognized the asymmetry in the early stages of learning, one could assume that the ECP functions in early second language learning.[7] Both L2 learners and native speakers of Japanese accepted accusative case drop sentences more than nominative case drop. This suggests that ECP does in fact function in the early grammars of L2 learners.

Thus, with regard to UG principles, there is conflicting evidence as to whether learners have direct access to UG, have access through the NL, or have no access at all.

6.2.3 UG parameters

There are certain linguistic features that vary across languages. These are expressed through the concept of linguistic parameters. Parameters have limited values. In learning a first language, the data a child is exposed to will determine which setting of a parameter that child will select. Whereas parameters are not invariable, as we saw with principles, they are limited, thereby easing the burden on the child. In other words, if parameters exist, the child's task is eased, because there is a limited range of options to choose from.

The issue for second language acquisition is the determination of whether and how a given linguistic parameter can be reset. Let's assume a parameter with two values. Let's further assume a native speaker with a NL setting in one way who is learning a second language with a setting in another way. If UG is available to that learner, there should be little difficulty in resetting the parameter because the speaker has access to both settings through UG. If UG is operative only through the L1 (as the Fundamental Difference Hypothesis suggests), then we would expect only those features that are available through the L1 to manifest themselves in the L2. Finally, if UG is not operative at all, we would expect none of the UG features to be available.

One of the most interesting aspects related to the concept of parameters is that they involve the clustering of properties. Once a parameter is set in a particular way, all related properties are affected. In other words, there are consequences for other parts of the grammar. We examine one such parameter, known as the pro-drop parameter. This parameter encompasses a number of properties, namely (a) the omission of subject pronouns, (b) the inversion of subjects and verbs in declarative sentences, and (c) *that*-trace effects—that is, the extraction of a subject (leaving a trace) out of a clause that contains a complementizer. A language will either have all of these properties or none of them. Languages like Italian and Spanish are [+pro-drop] and have all of the associated properties, whereas English and French are [−pro-drop], having none of them. Examples from English and Italian that illustrate the differences follow:

Italian	English
Omit subject pronouns	Obligatory use of subject pronouns
Va al cinema stasera.	She is going to the movies this evening.
goes to the movies this evening	*is going to the movies this evening
Subject–verb inversion	
È arrivata Laura.	Laura has arrived.
is arrived Laura	*has arrived Laura
That-trace	
Chi hai detto che è venuto?	Whom did you say came?
who you said that is come?	*Whom did you say that came?

White (1985) and Lakshmanan (1986) presented data from Spanish and French learners of English (White) and Spanish, Japanese, and Arabic learners of English (Lakshmanan) on precisely these three structures.[8] White found that the learners did not recognize these three structures as related. Although there was a difference in judgments of acceptability between the Spanish and the French speakers on the first type of sentences (i.e., those with and without overt subject pronouns), there was no difference between the two groups on the other two types of sentences. Thus, these learners did not see these three properties as a unified parameter. Lakshmanan's results were similar. Her groups of learners responded similarly to the first two sentence types but differently with regard to the third, again suggesting that these properties were not seen by these learners as unified under the umbrella of a single parameter.

There is evidence, however, that is more compelling with regard to the clustering of properties. Hilles (1986) assumed different properties of the pro-drop parameter in her investigation of the acquisition of English by a native speaker of Spanish named Jorge: (a) obligatory pronoun use; (b) use of nonreferential *it*, as in weather terms (*it's raining, it's pouring*) and use of nonreferential *there*, as in *There is rain in the forecast*; and (c) use of uninflected modals (e.g., *must, could*). Hilles showed that these three features were related in the speech of her learner. Specifically, there was an inverse relationship between Jorge's lack of referential subject use and the appearance of modal verbs. As Jorge began to use subject pronouns in English (i.e., as his null-subject use went down), he also began to use modals as noninflected forms. Hilles hypothesized that the triggering factor for the switch from [+pro-drop] to [–pro-drop] was the use of nonreferential subjects. This was an indication that this learner had truly understood the mandatory nature of subjects in English.

Park (2004) analyzed pronominal subjects and objects. She observed that Spanish speakers learning English frequently drop subject pronouns, whereas Korean speakers learning English frequently drop object pronouns. She attempts to account for this discrepancy through the interpretability of agreement features in the native languages.

The results of research on L2 parameters, like those of the research on principles discussed in section 6.2.2, is mixed. There are data supporting the view that UG constrains the grammars that learners can come up with; there are data arguing against this position. Thus, the answer to the question of whether L2 acquisition is fundamentally the same as L1 acquisition is *no*; the answer to the question of whether L2 acquisition is fundamentally different from L1 acquisition is also *no*. Although it may be the case that universal principles (either typological or formal) guide L2 acquisition, it is also the case that there are areas of conflict between NL and TL grammars yielding grammars that fall beyond the domain of what would be predicted if the only constraining factor were universals. However, White (2003, p. 149), following her discussion of parameters, concludes that "[d]espite conflicting evidence and conflicting theories, results from several studies suggest that interlanguage grammars conform to parameters of UG."

Within the Minimalist framework (Chomsky, 1995, 2000, 2002), the lexicon assumes great importance. Parameterization within the Minimalist Program is no longer in the syntax, but in the lexicon. Most of the constraints on language described earlier in terms of complex principles and parameters now fall out of a handful of general constraints on movement and the specific information stored in the lexicon of individual languages. Furthermore, most of the parametric variation relates to grammatical features such as tense and agreement. When we think of learning vocabulary, what we typically think of is learning the "meanings" of words (e.g., what the word *chair* refers to or what *subterfuge* means). But knowing that, for example, *break* is defined as "to disjoin or reduce to pieces with sudden or violent force" (*American Heritage Dictionary*) is only part of what we know about the word *break*. Knowing a word entails much more than that, and the additional knowledge is as important as any other piece of knowledge we have of language. For example, we also know that the verb *break* is irregular in its past tense formation, whereas *love* is not. We know that a sentence such as

(6-19) Harvey broke the glass jar.

is a good English sentence, but 6-20 is not.

(6-20) Harvey broke.[9]

We know that some words require objects (*hit*), other words allow objects but do not require them (*eat*), and still other words disallow objects (*sleep*). This is part of what we know about a language. Within Minimalism, parameters are part of the lexicon and language learning is largely lexical learning.

An example of how parametric variation is attached to the lexicon comes from the use of reflexives. Given an English sentence such as 6-21:

(6-21) The mother told the girl to wash herself.

speakers of English recognize that the word *herself* must refer to *the girl*. But the same is not true in sentence 6-22, where *her* can refer to the mother or to someone else.

(6-22) The mother told the girl to wash her.

Thus, the word *herself* in English contains information about possible antecedents. Other languages choose different options. For example, in Japanese, one reflexive form, *zibun*, can be ambiguous, as in 6-23 (from Lakshmanan and Teranishi, 1994):

(6-23) John-wa   Bill-ga   kagami-no   naka-de   zibun-o
        John-TOP Bill-NOM mirror-GEN inside-LOC self-ACC
                                                    mita to   itta
                                                    saw   that said
        "John said that Bill saw self in the mirror."
        (Either John or Bill can have seen himself.)

In 6-24, the reflexive *zibun-zisin* removes the ambiguity.

(6-24) John-wa Bill-ga kagami-no naka-de zibun-zisin mita to itta.
        "John said that Bill saw himself in the mirror."
        (John cannot have seen himself.)

Languages thus contain information in the lexicon that signals grammatical relationships.

There are two important questions that are in need of resolution. (a) Are universals the major organizing factor of learner language grammars? (b) If so, are the two types of universals discussed here and in the subsequent chapter only variants of one another, or is one a more appropriate model than the other?

6.2.4 Falsification

In trying to come up with a parsimonious account of how second languages are acquired, it is necessary to have a theory that will explain (and predict) the facts of learner grammars. In order to determine the accuracy of our theories, an important consideration is the issue of falsification. Our theory must predict what will occur and what will not occur. It is only in this way that we can test the accuracy of our hypotheses. In other words, our theories need to be falsifiable based on the data.

Learner languages are highly complex systems and, to some extent, are unique, making it difficult to make absolute predictions. Thus, it is more appropriate to think about probabilistic predictions. Unlike L1 grammars, no two individuals have the same L2 grammar, and hence there is no way of predicting what will happen to a grammar when new information is added, causing changes in the existing system. One might think of this as the kaleidoscope factor. Each kaleidoscope pattern differs. Any change in the system (a shake or twist to the kaleidoscope) will result in a different unpredictable pattern.[10] One can make certain predictions, but given the many factors involved in a kaleidoscope (does one twist the box or shake it, how hard, etc.?), one cannot make absolute predictions. One can only establish guidelines within which all of the images are likely to fall.

The advantage of research within a UG framework is that, because it is based on a well-defined linguistic theory, more accurate predictions can be made, although the arguments made earlier regarding absolute versus probabilistic predictions still hold (see also Pinker, 1987).

When there are counterexamples—that is, when the predictions are not borne out—there are various approaches one can take: (a) assume a no-access to UG position, as we have seen with regard to the Fundamental Difference Hypothesis; (b) attribute the results to methodological problems; (c) attribute the results to an undefined performance component; (d) attribute the results to mapping factors; or (e) assume the theory is false.

Within UG the fifth possibility has been common. Because the predictions are based on theoretical constructs that are abstractions (that thus have to be argued rather than empirically verified), and because the theory is in a state of development, there is little concrete evidence that one can bring to bear to show that the linguistic analysis of a principle or parameter is indeed the correct one. Thus, if one maintains the assumption that second language grammars are natural grammars, then SLA data can be brought into the arguments in the field of linguistics in the determination of linguistic principles and parameters.

Because of the changing nature of the linguistic constructs on which it is based, UG-based research is difficult to falsify. Upon being confronted with data apparently contradicting the predictions of UG access, it is equally possible to argue that the underlying linguistic formulation was the incorrect one.

To illustrate this point, reconsider the discussion of the pro-drop parameter. We noted that there were differing views as to what constituted the appropriate clusters in this parameter. In White's study, the predicted clusterings were not evidenced in the data. A possible conclusion she comes to is:

> It is of interest that some recent proposals suggest that the possibility of VS word order [i.e., subject inversion] is not, in fact, part of the pro-drop parameter, but derives from other principles of grammar (Chao 1981; Safir 1982; Hyams 1983), a position that these results would be consistent with.
>
> (White, 1985, p. 59)

Thus, rather than assuming a no-access position, White suggests the possibility that the parameter has been inaccurately described.

Yet another way of viewing the falsification problem is to allow for violations of universals, as these violations are temporary, given the ever-changing nature of learner languages. UG then serves as a "corrective mechanism" (see Sharwood Smith, 1988). A violation is only to be taken as a serious violation if it can also be shown that the person's interim system (i.e., his or her learner language) has stabilized. This would mean that most cross-sectional studies would have to be eliminated, because it is only with longitudinal data that we can determine whether a grammar has stabilized/fossilized or not. There is an added difficulty here. As we have no independent means of determining whether stabilization/fossilization has taken place, we can never know when we are confronted with a stabilized grammar and when we are not. Thus, if we are to take this view, we cannot determine whether or not universal principles are violated. But if the principles are followed, then we can conclude that second language grammars are constrained by the particular principles. If the principles are not followed, there is little that can be concluded. We have no way of determining with certainty that the principles are permanently not followed.

If we consider the initial-state discussion earlier in this chapter, it is clear that there are difficulties defining what is meant by *initial-state*. For example, how early must data be to be relevant? First day of exposure, first utterance? What about a period of nonproduction before production begins? Is this relevant? Does it exist? If these data are relevant, then is there any way of falsifying certain claims (for example, whether functional categories are in place or not)? Or, to think about the Valueless Feature Hypothesis, if research is conducted with early learners—say, those in their first year or semester of study—and they had acquired feature strength, does that mean that the semester or year of exposure was sufficient to acquire strength or does it mean that they started with specified feature strength, rendering the hypothesis false?

To take a similar example, recall that one of the questions in UG-based research is the extent to which functional categories are available in early stages of learning. For example, it is frequently the case that there is little morphological marking in early L2 production, suggesting the absence of functional categories. However, plural marking is often absent at very late stages of SLA, making it difficult to maintain that omission is solely due to an absence of functional categories. Therefore, on the surface, one might consider a certain type of data as evidence of falsification whereas different explanations might be plausible for the same phenomenon in different contexts.

6.3 Transfer: the UG perspective

In chapters 4 and 5 we discussed historical and current views of transfer respectively. Conducting SLA research within a paradigm such as the one discussed in this chapter necessitates a reconsideration of the concept of transfer. The question arises: What new insights do recent linguistic approaches and, in particular, theoretical paradigms provide regarding the old concept of transfer?

White (1992) provided detail on this issue. She notes four areas that make current views of the phenomenon of transfer truly different from earlier conceptualizations, particularly those embodied in the framework of contrastive analysis. We deal with three of these areas here: levels of representation, clustering, and learnability.

6.3.1 Levels of representation

Within a theory of Universal Grammar, our knowledge of syntax is best represented by positing different levels of grammatical structure. To simplify matters, assume that there is an underlying structure and a surface structure. To understand the difference, consider 6-25:

(6-25) Visiting relatives can be boring.

This sentence can be parsed in one of two ways, each with a different meaning.

(6-26) When I visit relatives, I am bored.
(6-27) Relatives who visit me can be boring.

The two different meanings are a result of two different underlying syntactic structures that can be computed for sentence 6-25.

If sentences have multiple levels of representation, one can imagine that transfer could occur not just on the basis of surface facts, but also on the basis of underlying structures (see Tarone, Frauenfelder, and Selinker, 1976).

6.3.2 Clustering

With regard to clustering, recall that within a UG theory claiming that learning involves setting/resetting of parameters, there are properties that cluster together within a parameter. Within this framework (as with typological universals, discussed in chapter 7), one is concerned with how multiple properties of language do or do not behave in a like fashion. Further, there is evidence that mixed values are adopted for multivalued parameters and continuous linguistic features (for examples, see Broselow and Finer, 1991; Gass, 1984).

Within earlier approaches to transfer (particularly a contrastive analysis approach), there was no way to show how related structures were linked in the minds of second language learners. Nonetheless, a model that involves structural relatedness clearly represents an innovative approach to language transfer.

6.3.3 Learnability

A UG perspective on SLA is heavily dependent on arguments of learnability. In particular, the issue of positive evidence is central because learners construct grammars on the basis of the input (the positive evidence to which the learner is exposed) together with principles of UG. But, there are some language structures that may be in a superset/subset relationship. In fact, a learning principle, the Subset Principle, has been proposed that ensures that language learning can proceed on the basis of input alone. When there are multiple possibilities in a language, child learners adopt the most restrictive grammar possible so that she or he can proceed to learn the appropriate forms on the basis of input alone. If she or he were to assume a superset grammar, there would be no way to retreat from that grammar. Consider adverb placement in French and English. In French, adverbs can be positioned in a greater number of places than in English. In English, sentence 6-28 is ungrammatical, whereas the French counterpart is not.

(6-28) *The man is drinking slowly his coffee.

If an English child were to start with a grammar that allowed all possibilities for adverb placement, it would be difficult to learn on the basis of positive evidence (input) alone that the grammar was actually more restrictive.

Looking at this across languages, we can see that the input necessary for the learner may be different depending on the superset/subset relationship of the two languages in question on a particular feature. For a French learner learning English, she or he has to learn that 6-28 is ungrammatical (and, in fact, this is learned late and is characteristic of a French person speaking English), whereas, an English learner learning French only has to hear the broader range of possibilities to know that French has more possibilities for adverb placement.

Where positive evidence is readily available, allowing a learner to reset a parameter, little transfer (and, when present, of short duration) is predicted (as in the case of the L2 being a superset of the L1). On the other hand, when positive evidence will not suffice to provide learners with adequate information about the L2, possibly necessitating negative evidence, transfer is predicted (as when the L2 is a subset of the L1).

6.4 Phonology

Another area where SLA and linguistics intersect is phonology. The study of L2 phonology is not unlike other areas of L2 acquisition in that it attempts to account for the patterns of knowledge and use of L2 learners, in this case of pronunciation and perception. It is commonly accepted that the native language origin of a second language speaker is often identifiable by his or her accent. In fact, nonnative speaker pronunciation is often the source of humor, as in the case of comedians mimicking particular accent types, or in cartoon characters adopting nonnative accents.

The acquisition of a second language phonology is a complex process. An understanding of how learners learn a new phonological system must take into account linguistic differences between the NL and the TL systems as well as universal facts of phonology. Phonology is both similar to and different from other linguistic domains. It is similar to what we have seen in other parts of language in that some of a learner's pronunciation of the second language is clearly attributable to the NL, whereas some is not. It is different in that not all of the concepts relevant to syntax are applicable to phonology. For example, avoidance is a common L2 strategy used when a syntactic construction is recognizably beyond one's reach. Thus, if a learner wants to avoid passives, it is relatively easy to find an alternative structure to express the same concept. However, if a learner wants to avoid the sound [ð], as in *the* in English, it would be virtually impossible. Phonology differs from syntax in that in the former, but not the latter, most people can detect the linguistic origin of a speaker (although see arguments in Ioup, 1984, relating to "syntactic accent").

Table 6.1 Hierarchy of phonological difficulty

NL	TL	
0	Obligatory	difficult
0	Optional	
Optional	Obligatory	↑
Obligatory	Optional	
Obligatory	0	
Optional	0	
Optional	Optional	↓
Obligatory	Obligatory	easy

Source: Adapted from R. Stockwell and J. Bowen. *The Sounds of English and Spanish.* Chicago: University of Chicago Press. Reprinted by permission.

As discussed in chapter 4, in its simplest form, the Contrastive Analysis Hypothesis did not make accurate predictions. It did not predict why speakers of language X learning language Y would have difficulty on a given structure, whereas speakers of language Y learning language X did not have difficulty on that same structure. These discrepancies were also evident in phonology. As an example, consider Stockwell and Bowen's (1965) proposed hierarchy of difficulty (Table 6.1). The hierarchy (ordered from most difficult to least difficult) attempts to make predictions of difficulty based on whether or not phonological categories are absent or present and, if present, whether they are obligatory or optional. Thus, if a learner comes from a language that has no phonemic contrast between two sounds (e.g., /l/ and /r/) and is learning a language where that contrast is obligatory, she or he will have difficulty. However, if the first language and the target language both have the same contrast, there will be little difficulty in learning.

6.4.1 *Markedness Differential Hypothesis*

Hierarchies of this type are also proposed within other phonological frameworks. In particular, Eckman (1977) proposed what he called the Markedness Differential Hypothesis, which was based on a phonological theory of markedness. One way to think of markedness is that an unmarked form, whether phonological or syntactic, is one that is more common, more usual in the world's languages than a marked one. It is perhaps easier to understand this concept in an area other than phonology. If we consider words denoting professions, avocations, or societal roles, we see that male terms are the basic ones (e.g., *actor, poet, host, hero*), whereas the female counterparts have suffixes added on to the male term (*actress, poetess, hostess, heroine*). The male term is taken to be the basic one (unmarked) and the female term is the marked derivative.

If we apply the same concept to phonology, we can describe cross-linguistically which sounds are common to many languages (the unmarked ones) and which are not (the marked ones). Dinnsen and Eckman (1975) proposed that voicing[11] contrasts in languages are not uniform in all positions in a word. Table 6.2 gives linguistic facts on which the proposed Markedness Differential Hierarchy was based. The linguistic information shows a progression from least marked (most frequent and possibly easiest) language type to most marked.

The hierarchy reflecting this is known as the Voice Contrast Hierarchy, which states that a contrast in initial position is the least marked, and a contrast in final position is the most marked. The interpretation of this is such that we can predict that a language that maintains a marked contrast (i.e., a contrast in word-final position) also maintains a contrast in all positions that are less marked.

How does this apply to a second language learning situation? What is predicted is that a speaker of a language with a more marked NL structure (or in this case, a more marked contrast) than that which occurs in the TL will have an easier time learning the TL structure/contrast than a speaker whose NL is less marked than the TL. This correctly predicts, for example, that a speaker of English (with a voicing contrast in final position [*tab* vs. *tap*]) will have no difficulty in producing German words where there is no contrast in final position. On the other hand, a German speaker learning English has to learn to make a contrast in final position (a more marked structure than the German NL) and will be expected to produce errors.

Table 6.2 Markedness Differential Hierarchy

Description	Languages	
Languages that maintain a superficial voice contrast in initial, medial, and final positions	English, Arabic, Swedish	More frequent
Languages that maintain a superficial voice contrast in initial and medial positions, but fail to maintain this contrast in final position	German, Polish, Greek, Japanese, Catalan	
Languages that maintain a superficial voice contrast in initial position, but fail to maintain this contrast in medial and final positions	Corsican, Sardinian	
Languages that maintain no voice contrast in initial, medial, or final positions	Korean	Less frequent

Source: Slightly modified from "Markedness and the Contrastive Analysis Hypothesis" by F. Eckman, 1977, *Language Learning*, 27, 322. Reprinted with permission.

Thus, within the markedness hypothesis framework, the interest is not in denying the importance of transfer (although most work in which transfer was minimized recognized the inevitability of using the NL in the area of phonology) but in determining the principles that underlie its use. It is for this reason that the Contrastive Analysis Hypothesis was not abandoned in phonology with the same vigor as in syntax. Rather, the attempt was to reconfigure it and incorporate additional principles.

What work in phonology shows, not unlike work in syntax, is that one must consider both the facts of the NL and developmental or universal facts in attempting to understand why learners produce the language they produce and why they create the kinds of IL rules that underlie their production.

However, there is more to the picture than purely linguistic information. Sociolinguistic information is also relevant to an understanding of second language phonology. Beebe (1980) showed that the social values of sounds in the native language affect transfer. Her study dealt with the acquisition of English pronunciation by native speakers of Thai. In Thai the phoneme /r/ is pronounced in many different ways depending on the linguistic and social context. In her English data from Thai native speakers, she found that the formal variety of a Thai /r/ (a trilled *r*) was used in formal English contexts but not in informal ones. Svetics (personal communication) similarly reported that two Greeks, when speaking English, pronounced [dʒ] and [tʃ], as in *bridge*, or *lunch*, as [dz] and [ts], respectively, because the former two sounds are only used in Greek by uneducated individuals.

Most of the studies reported on thus far considered individual sound segments, but recent work has looked at units larger than individual segments; for example, syllables (Broselow, Chen, and Wang, 1998; Carlisle, 1998). Young-Scholten and Archibald (2000), in their review of L2 syllable structure, asked a number of important questions, including: To what extent are L2 syllables constrained by allowable L1 syllable structures and to what extent do universal principles apply or even prevail? As in other areas of SLA, it appears that both forces are operational.

Not only are sounds of a language transferred, but there is also evidence that learners attempt to maintain their NL syllable structure. When the target language permits syllable structures that are not permitted in the native language, learners will make errors that involve altering these structures to those that would be permitted in the native language (Broselow, 1987). For example, in Spanish, the initial English sequence in *snob* is not a permissible sequence in word-initial position. Spanish speakers are known to insert an epenthetic (addition of an additional sound) vowel, producing *esnob*. Similarly, Arabic speakers pronounce the English word *plastic* as [bilastik] (in Arabic there is no contrast between

[p] and [b] in word-initial position, which results in [bilastik] rather than [pilastik]).

As with other areas of phonology, one can order syllable types in terms of markedness so that learners moving from a language with a less marked syllable structure (e.g., consonant/vowel [CV]) to one that has a more marked syllable structure [CVC] tend to produce language closely approximating the NL syllable structure. On the other hand, evidence of conformity to the NL syllable structure by a speaker of a language with a more marked syllable structure is not apparent.

Thus, L2 syllable structure is in part shaped by the NL. It is, however, also affected by universal tendencies. Tarone (1980) showed that L2 learners of English simplified L2 syllables (e.g., through deletion or through epenthesis) even though the syllable type was allowed in the Ll. An example is the addition of a final sound to the English word *sack* by Korean learners, resulting in [sæke], even though the sequence of CVC (consonant-vowel-consonant) is allowable in Korean. Tarone suggested that learners revert to the basic (universal) CV syllable structure regardless of L1.

It is well-known that certain consonant clusters are difficult for L2 learners (e.g., *fifth*, *fists*). Another universal tendency that has been proposed is that clusters of consonants tend to sort themselves out earlier at the beginning of words than at ends of words. This is borne out by L2 data. Anderson (1987) looked at English L2 data from Egyptian-Arabic and Chinese speakers. Egyptian Arabic has no initial clusters, but does have final clusters. Chinese has neither. Yet both groups were found to have more difficulty with final clusters than with initial clusters.

Young-Scholten and Archibald (2000), in their review of L2 syllable structure, pointed to type of exposure as a possible factor involved in acquisition. They noted that L2 learners use epenthesis more than L1 learners as a simplification strategy.

Young-Scholten (1995, 1997) and Young-Scholten, Akita, and Cross (1999) argued that, when exposure comes from a classroom context where there is a reliance on written texts, epenthesis is frequent regardless of the L1. If exposure does not come through written texts, epenthesis as a simplification strategy is less frequent. Young-Scholten's argument is that written information makes it more likely that learners will retain phonological information. This, however, does not obviate the need for simplification when learners' L1 constrains their phonology. Another possible means for simplification is through deletion (e.g., of unstressed syllables—a strategy used in child language acquisition). Young-Scholten and Archibald pointed out that this is rare in adult L2 learners precisely because of their familiarity with the written text. Hence, they are left with the other common simplification strategy of epenthesis.

6.4.2 Similarity/dissimilarity: Speech Learning Model

In addition to considering notions of markedness, there has also been an emphasis on similarity between the L1 and the L2. Flege (1992, 1995) claims that L2 sounds that are similar/equivalent to L1 sounds are difficult to acquire because the learner does not perceive them or classify them as different and hence does not set up a new category of contrast. Flege's Speech Learning Model (1992, 1995) makes the following claims:

> A new phonetic category can be established for an L2 sound that differs phonetically from the closest L1 sound if bilinguals discern at least some of the phonetic differences between the L1 and L2 sounds . . . Category formation for an L2 sound may be blocked by the mechanism of equivalence classification. When this happens, a single phonetic category will be used to process perceptually like L1 and L2 sounds (diaphones). Eventually, the diaphones will resemble one another in production.
>
> (Flege, 1995, p. 239)

More recently, he elaborates on this.

> The SLM [Speech Learning Model] also hypothesizes that the perceived phonetic dissimilarity of an L2 sound from the closest L1 sound is a determinant of whether a new phonetic category will or will not be established for the L2 sound. The more distant from the closest L1 speech sound an L2 speech sound is judged to be, the more likely it is that L2 learners—regardless of age—will establish a new category for the L2 sound.
>
> (Flege, 2007, p. 367)

Flege's claims have been substantiated reasonably well (Flege, 1987a, 1987b, 1990, 1993; Aoyama, Flege, Guion, Yamada, and Akahane-Yamada, 2004), although, as has been discussed elsewhere in this book, constructs are not always clear cut in SLA research. For example, how does one define similar? Does the theory need to be supported in total or is probabilistic approximation appropriate?

Additional work by Flege, Birdsong, Bialystok, Mack, Sung, and Tsukada (2006) relates second language pronunciation not to similarity necessarily, but to length of residence as opposed to age. This conclusion was based on pronunciation judgments of the English speech of Korean children and adults. The researchers found that the greatest predictor of pronunciation was length of residence, which corresponds to amount of input.

Major and Kim (1999) modified the work of Flege by proposing the Similarity Differential Rate Hypothesis, which makes a slightly different claim; that is, that there is a rate difference between the acquisition of similar versus dissimilar sounds, with dissimilar sounds being acquired faster than similar sounds.

In the next sections, we deal with two additional approaches to second language phonology: Optimality Theory and the Ontogeny Phylogeny Model.

6.4.3 Optimality Theory

Optimality Theory is a relative newcomer to the theoretical scene in linguistics (see Prince and Smolensky, 1997) and an even later arrival in SLA. It had its beginnings in phonology but has more recently extended its domain to syntax and semantics, although this extension has yet to be seen in the pages of second language journals. Optimality Theory does not avail itself of the concept of rules *per se*, but rather, the basic concept is one of universal constraints and the rankings of those constraints. Constraints are innate and apply across all languages. There are two types of constraints: faithfulness constraints and markedness constraints. The former match the input with the output and the latter ensure the well-formedness of the output. There are at times conflicts among constraints, but these conflicts are resolved by a language-specific ordering of constraints. Variation across languages is a result of the differential ordering of constraints, and second language learning involves the reranking of native language constraints. Tesar and Smolensky (1996, 1998) claim that "reranking of constraints will stop when learners no longer detect differences between their own output and the language surrounding them" (as cited in Levelt, Schiller, and Levelt, 1999, p. 294).

Hancin-Bhatt and Bhatt (1997) investigated the acquisition of English beginnings and ends of words by Spanish and Japanese learners. The main task in question was to listen to two sentences (one grammatical and one ungrammatical) and repeat the sentence that was grammatically correct. Embedded in these sentences was the target (a pseudo-word) item (in italics). Below are examples of two sentences:

(6-29) Mary hopes they are ready to *frulm* today.
(6-30) Mary hopes them are ready to *frulm* today.

They analyzed the results within the framework of Optimality Theory; some of the errors that their learners made were due to language-specific rankings while others were due to rankings that are universally dominant.

Hancin-Bhatt (2000) investigated the acquisition of syllable codas by Thai learners of English. Thai is more restrictive than English as to what can occur in syllable-final position. Bhatt found that there is an interaction between NL constraint rankings and TL constraint rankings. She makes the argument that the rerankings that occur in the course of acquisition occur in an ordered fashion.

Broselow, Chen, and Wang (1998) also analyzed their results of Mandarin speakers' learning of English and in particular simplification of English words. They argued that this was the result of constraint rankings, bringing in the concept of markedness to talk about constraint rankings. They refer to the emergence of the unmarked, by which they mean that the interlanguage will have constraints that are ranked low in both the L1 and the L2 and hence masked by the effect of higher-ranking constraints. This is the source of novel L2 pronunciations.

Substitutions are a widespread and recognized phenomenon in the pronunciation of a second language. Lombardi (2003, citing Edwards, 1994) illustrates the effect of this in the following anecdote:

> One of my favourite errors occurred in an American war film, subtitled in French. One of the soldiers peers into the distance, and another says, "Tanks?"
> The subtitle reads "Merci."
>
> (Lombardi, 2003, p. 225)

Lombardi (2003) considered the substitutions that Russian and Japanese speakers make when trying to produce English interdental sounds. Russian speakers have a [θ] to [t] pattern and Japanese speakers a [θ] to [s] pattern. Using data from a range of languages, she argues that constraint rankings better account for this phenomenon than do rule-based approaches, given that the latter often require the addition of new rules. Learners begin with a universal substitution (that of using stops). She argues that this is the initial state that comes from UG, but that there are ranking constraints that also influence the phonological output of L2 learners, namely an L1-based reranking.

Eckman, Elreyes, and Iverson (2003) continue work on contrasts that have been common in the phonology literature. They consider three types of contrasts: (1) the TL has two contrasting sounds, neither of which is present in the NL; (2) the TL has two contrasting sounds, one of which is present in the NL; and (3) the TL has two contrasting sounds, both of which are present in the NL, but which do not contrast. Their general hypothesis was that second language phonological rules conform to the general principles of phonological theory available in first language learning. As an example, they considered predicted stages of development for a Korean learner learning English. For example, they predict the following stages for the acquisition of [s] and [š], which in Korean are in allophonic variation, an example of contrast 3 above.

Stage 1: No contrast: *sea* and *she* are pronounced [ši].

Stage 2: Partial contrast: distinction between derived words and nonderived words (*messing* and *meshing* versus *sea* and *she*). The former are distinct, but the latter pair are homophones.

Stage 3: Full contrast: native rules are not applied in any context, derived or basic.

Their investigation of second language learners in a cross-sectional and instructional setting suggested that, indeed, the acquisition of phono-logical contrasts adheres to universal principles of phonology. Their work relies on the concept of rules, whereas Optimality Theory relies on constraints. Eckman and his colleagues argue that their data on contrasts cannot be captured within an approach, such as Optimality Theory, which only allows constraints.

6.4.4 *Ontogeny Phylogeny Model*

This model is intended to capture the basic patterns of interlanguage and captures phonological relationships between L1 and L2 as well as uni-versals. Major (2001) states these relationships as follows: "L2 increases, L1 decreases, and U [universals] increases and then decreases" (p. 82). At the early stage, the learner only has a first language and a "dormant" U (except those parts of U that are operational in the L1). It is important to note that U refers to the "universals of language that are not already part of the L1 or L2 system" (p. 83). This relationship is illustrated by Figures 6.1 to 6.6.

There are four corollaries to the Ontogeny Phylogeny Model; namely, the chronological, stylistic, similarity, and markedness corollaries. The first is intended to capture second language development; the second, contextual variation (e.g., formal, casual speech); the third, similarity/dis-similarity in language; and the fourth, issues of markedness in language. As can be seen below, each corollary specifies the relationship between the three constructs: L1, L2, and U.

Chronological corollary: IL develops chronologically in the following manner: (a) L2 increases, (b) L1 decreases, and (c) U increases and then decreases (p. 85). This is demonstrated in Figures 6.1 to 6.6.

Stylistic corollary: IL varies stylistically in the following manner: as style becomes more formal, (a) L2 increases, (b) L1 decreases, and (c) U increases and then decreases (p. 93).

Similarity corollary: In similar phenomena, IL develops chrono-logically in the following manner: (a) L2

186

Figure 6.1 Stage 1.

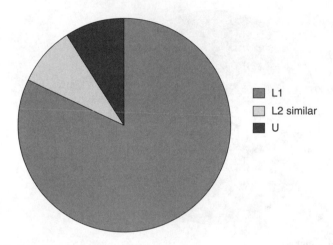

Figure 6.2 Stage 2.

increases slowly, (b) L1 decreases slowly, and (c) U increases slowly and then decreases slowly. Thus the role of L1 is much greater than U, compared to less similar phenomena. By implication, the less similar the phenomena (i.e., the more dissimilar), the more important the role of U is compared to L1 (p. 100).

Markedness corollary: In marked phenomena, IL develops chronologically in the following manner: (a) L2 increases slowly, (b) L1 decreases [at a normal rate] and then decreases slowly, and (c) U

Figure 6.3 Stage 3.

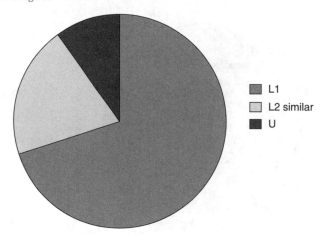

Figure 6.4 Stage 4.

increases rapidly and decreases slowly. Thus, except for the earliest stages, the role of U is much greater than L1, compared to less-marked phenomena (p. 107).

As can be seen, Major is concerned not only with interlanguage development (chronological), but also with issues of variation which is captured through the stylistic corollary, and linguistic relationships, such as similarity and markedness.

Figure 6.5 Stage 5.

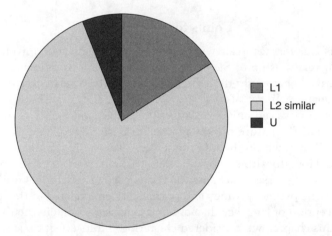

Figure 6.6 Stage 6.

Source (Figures 6.1–6.6): © 2001 from *Foreign Accent* by R. Major. Reproduced by permission of Lawrence Erlbaum Associates, a division of Taylor & Francis Group.

6.5 Conclusion

This chapter has dealt with the acquisition of linguistic phenomena from a formal perspective. In the following chapter, we deal with functional models of language and the impact of these approaches on the study of second language acquisition.

Suggestions for additional reading

Tense and Aspect in Second Language Acquisition: Form, Meaning, and Use. Language Learning Supplement. Kathleen Bardovi-Harlig, Blackwell (2000).

Chomsky's Universal Grammar. Vivian Cook. Basil Blackwell (1988).
Linguistic Perspectives on Second Language Acquisition. Susan Gass and Jacquelyn Schachter (Eds.). Cambridge University Press (1989).
Language Acquisition Studies in Generative Grammar. Teun Hoekstra and Bonnie D. Schwartz (Eds.). John Benjamins (1994).
Foreign Accent: The Ontogeny and Phylogeny of Second Language Phonology. Roy Major, Lawrence Erlbaum Associates (2001).
Syntactic Theory and the Structure of English: A Minimalist Approach. Andrew Radford. Cambridge University Press (1997).
The Development of Past Tense Morphology in L2 Spanish. Rafael Salaberry, John Benjamins (2001).
Tense and Aspect Morphology in L2 Acquisition. Rafael Salaberry and Yasuhiro Shirai (Eds.), John Benjamins (2002).
Inquiries in Linguistic Development: In Honor of Lydia White. Roumyana Slabakova, Silvina A. Montrul, and Philippe Prévost (Eds.), John Benjamins (2006).
Second Language Acquisition and Universal Grammar. Lydia White, Cambridge University Press (2003).

Points for discussion

1   This chapter has dealt with the concept of language universals and their relationship to SLA. Consider the notion of interlanguage universals. What might these be? How would these relate to the concept of language universals?

2   In what ways can universals affect the development of IL grammars in terms of the nature of how grammatical knowledge relates to input? Recall that, within the UG framework, learnability takes on a central role. How does this concept relate to Kellerman's (1979) notion of transfer discussed in chapter 5? Focus particularly on his notion of a learner's psychotypology and of transfer being related to the learner's perception of language distance and language specificity/neutrality.

3   In this chapter, we considered clustering and its effect on second language grammars, particularly in regards to the pro-drop parameter. What might the function of the use or nonuse of pronouns be? That is, why are pronouns obligatory in English and not so in other languages? How can our knowledge of parameter clusterings help language teachers?

    Suppose that linguistic research finds that the clusterings are incorrect—that, in fact, the clusterings involve other linguistic properties. What sort of dilemma would this finding pose to second language researchers? How might the dilemma be turned around to put second language researchers in a position of making valuable contributions to arguments about the nature of language? How would language teachers fit into this debate and what would their contributions to it be?

See GSS, problems 3.1–3.4, 3.7–3.9, and 4.1.

7

TYPOLOGICAL AND FUNCTIONAL APPROACHES

7.1 Introduction

This chapter has as its main focus two different approaches to SLA: typological and functional. Typological approaches stem from the study of the patterns exhibited in languages worldwide, and functional approaches have as their main interest the study of how language functions. Functional approaches generally entail a consideration of multiple areas of language, such as tense/aspect, which combines verb meanings, morphological form, and phonology.

7.2 Typological universals

The study of typological universals stems from work in linguistics by Greenberg (1963). In this approach to the study of universals, linguists attempt to discover similarities/differences in languages throughout the world. That is, the attempt is to determine linguistic typologies or what "types" of languages are possible. One of the most important discoveries of this approach is that one can generalize across unrelated and geographically nonadjacent languages regarding the occurrence and co-occurrence of structures. Many of the typological universals are expressed in terms of implications, such that, if a language has feature X, it will also have feature Y. In Greenberg's original work, many universals (or universal tendencies) were based on word order, as in the following: "In languages with prepositions, the genitive almost always follows the governing noun, while in languages with postpositions it almost always precedes the noun" (Greenberg, 1963, p. 78).

For example, in languages with prepositions, like French, Russian, and Italian, we expect to find the noun representing what is being possessed preceding the possessor. In fact, this is the case. All three languages form genitives in the same way:

French
(7-1) le   chien de mon ami
  the dog of my friend
Russian
(7-2) sobaka moego   druga
  dog   my GEN friend GEN
Italian
(7-3) il   cane di mia madre
  the dog of my mother

In languages with postpositions, such as Turkish, what we call prepositions follow the noun, as can be seen in 7-4 and 7-5, where the morphological markers follow the noun:

Turkish
(7-4) (From Jannedy, Poletto, and Weldon, 1994, p. 153)

  a deniz = an ocean
  b denize = to an ocean
  c denizin = of an ocean

(7-5) Example of genitive (from Comrie, 1981)
  ev-   in   pencere- s-   i
  house possessor window separates vowels possessed
  "the window of the house"

English is somewhat exceptional in that it allows not only the predicted order (*the leg of the table*), but also the unpredicted word order (*my friend's dog*).
 Other language universals can be stated in rigid (or absolute) terms, for example:

Languages with dominant verb–subject–object (VSO) order are always prepositional.

This universal can be exemplified by a language such as Welsh, which has verb-first word order and prepositions (example from Comrie, 1981, p. 81).

(7-6) lladdwyd   y   dyn gan y   ddraig.
  killed-passivethe man by the dragon
  "The man was killed by the dragon."

Assuming that interlanguages are subject to the same constraints, what can we expect? The most important test case would come from speakers whose NL differs from the TL with regard to the specific universal in question, because if the two languages in question were similar, one could claim that it was only a matter of language transfer. That is, to test the hypothesis that universals are at stake, one must eliminate the possibility that the universal in question came from the NL. To take a hypothetical example, if a native speaker of a language with postpositions learns Italian, we would expect that once the learner has learned that Italian has prepositions, she or he would know that the genitive must follow the noun.

Why is an understanding of language universals important to the study of second language acquisition? One of the early questions regarding the nature of second language systems was the extent to which they could be considered a "natural language."

> underlying the IL hypothesis is the unwritten assumption that ILs are linguistic systems in the same way that Natural Languages are. (By "natural language" I mean any human language shared by a community of speakers and developed over time by a general process of evolution.) That is, ILs are natural languages.
>
> (Adjemian, 1976, p. 298)

What does it mean to say that ILs, or learner languages, are natural systems? It does not mean that all ILs are as complex as all natural languages, for clearly they are not. The majority of complex syntax does not develop until late in the process of learning. What it does mean is that if a given linguistic phenomenon appears to be impossible in any of the world's languages, then it will also be an impossible form in a second language system.

As an example, we consider word order phenomena from a selection of languages of the world. In Hindi, French, and Japanese, the following sentences are possible:

Hindi (from Jannedy, Poletto, and Weldon, 1994)
(7-7) Ram-ne   seb   kʰaya.
       Ram   apple   ate
       "Ram ate an apple."
(7-8) Ram Angrezi bol   səkta hɛ.
       Ram English speak able   is
       "Ram can speak English."
(7-9) larke-ne čari-se   kutte-ko mara.
       boy   stick with dog   hit
       "The boy hit the dog with a stick."
(7-10) ǰis   lark-ne kutte-ko mara vo mera bhai   he.
       which boy   dog   hit he my   brother is
       "The boy who hit the dog is my brother."

(7-11) Ram-ki bahin
Ram's sister
"Ram's sister"

(7-12) safed pʰul
white flower

French
(7-13) Jean a mangé une pomme.
Jean has eaten an apple
"Jean ate an apple."

(7-14) Jean peut parler anglais.
Jean can speak English
"Jean can speak English."

(7-15) Le garçon a frappé le chien avec un baton.
the boy has hit the dog with a stick
"The boy hit the dog with a stick."

(7-16) Le garçon qui a frappé le chien est mon frère.
the boy who has hit the dog is my brother
"The boy who hit the dog is my brother."

(7-17) La soeur de Jean
the sister of Jean
"Jean's sister"

(7-18) une fleur blanche
a flower white
"a white flower"

Japanese (from Jannedy, Poletto, and Weldon, 1994)
(7-19) Taroo-ga ringo-o tabeta
Taroo apple ate
"Taroo ate an apple."

(7-20) Taroo-wa Eigo-ga hanaseru
Taroo English speak can
"Taroo can speak English."

(7-21) sono otokonoko-wa boo-de inu-o butta
that boy stick with dog hit
"That boy hit the dog with a stick."

(7-22) inu-o butta otokonoko-wa watashi-no otooto-da
dog hit boy my brother is
"The boy who hit the dog is my brother."

(7-23) Taroo-no imooto
Taroo's sister
"Taroo's sister"

(7-24) shiroi hana
white flower
"white flower"

If we consider the categories of object, verb, auxiliaries, prepositions/postpositions, nouns and relative clauses, possessives, and adjective–noun order, we can see in the following table (Table 7.1) the generalizations that can be seen based on these data and from English.

We can think of languages as being "head-initial" or "head-final," where the "head" is a verb, or a noun, or a preposition in relation to other units within its constituent. Thus, in a head-initial language, the verb will precede the noun, and, in a head-final language, the verb will follow the object. If we consider one of the basic differences in languages, the order of verbs and objects, we can think of the patterns in Table 7.2.

There are some oddities; that is, languages or parts of languages where the predicted patterns do not obtain, as in the following examples.

- *Hindi and Japanese relative clauses*
  - From these data Hindi and Japanese appear to be OV languages; that is, the object precedes the verb.
  - The relative clause precedes the noun in Japanese but follows it in Hindi.

- *English Adjective Noun order*
  - From these data English appears to be a VO language; that is, the verb precedes the object.

Table 7.1 Word orders

	Hindi	French	Japanese	English
Basic order (V + O)	OV	VO	OV	VO
Aux + Verb	V Aux	Aux V	V Aux	Aux V
Preposition + Noun (Postposition)	N Post	Prep N	N Post	Prep N
N + Relative Clause	N + RC	N + RC	RC + N	N + RC
Possessive	Poss + N	N + Poss	Poss + N	Both
Adj + N	Adj + N	N + Adj	Adj + N	Both (Adj + N dominant)

Table 7.2 OV and VO word orders

OV (head-final)	VO (head-initial)
V Aux	Aux V
N Post	Prep N
??	N + RC
Poss N	N + Poss ??
Adj + N	???

○ The adjective precedes the noun rather than following it, as in other VO languages.

○ There are instances where the adjective follows the noun:

She likes all things Japanese/She likes all Japanese things.

The question, then, for second language acquisition is: To what extent do the constraints that govern natural languages also govern learner language systems? Put differently, to what extent is the variability of learner languages limited? Would we be likely to find evidence of interlanguages that violate these generalizations? More specifically, would a Japanese speaker learning English be likely to postpose a preposition (i.e., use postpositions rather than prepositions)? One answer to this question has been formulated as the Interlanguage Structural Conformity Hypothesis:

All universals that are true for primary languages are also true for interlanguages.

(Eckman, Moravcsik, and Wirth, 1989, p. 195)

There are many ways in which universals can be expected to affect the development of second language grammars:

(a) They could absolutely affect the shape of a learner's grammar at any point in time. If this is correct, there would *never* be any instance of a violation of a given universal evident in second language grammars.

(b) They could affect acquisition order, whereby more marked forms would be the last to be acquired, or, in the case of implicational universals, one could expect fewer errors in the less marked forms.

(c) They could be one of many interacting forces in determining the shape of learners' grammars.

Some universals may be thought of as having greater influence than others. For example, if we return to the word order examples given earlier, we saw that English word order with regard to noun–adjective order is not consistent with the prediction made by knowing that English is a verb–object language. What might we expect the implication of this universal to be with regard to learner language? Gass and Ard (1980) reported on data from Spanish learners learning English and English learners learning Spanish. They predicted that, for universals based on diachronic factors, the effect on interlanguages is not as strong as universals based on other motivating factors (e.g., physical factors as in the case of some aspects of phonetics). They argue that the English adjective–noun order is an artifact of historical factors and will not significantly affect interlanguage development. This prediction was borne out in their examination of 29 compositions of Spanish learners of English ranging from beginning to high intermediate. Of the 141 examples of nouns and adjectives, there was only one instance of a noun–adjective sequence. Additionally, as noted by Dvorak and reported in that article, English learners of Spanish initially make errors in the adjective/noun sequence, although the problem is straightened out early. Thus, it appears that the issue is more one of native language influence than of universal influence.

7.2.1 Test case I: the Accessibility Hierarchy

We next examine a few test cases in which typological/implicational universals are investigated from an SLA perspective. Perhaps the most widely discussed implicational universal is one dealing with relative clause formation. The universal itself, known as the Accessibility Hierarchy (AH), was discussed at length by Keenan and Comrie (1977). The basic principle is that one can predict the types of relative clauses that a given language will have based on the following hierarchy:

Accessibility Hierarchy (AH)
SU > DO > IO > OPREP > GEN > OCOMP[1]

Two claims are important here. First, all languages have subject relative clauses; and second, predictions can be made such that if a language has a relative clause of the type X, then it will also have any relative clause type higher on the hierarchy, or to the left of type X. Thus, if we know that a language has object of preposition relatives (*That's the woman about whom I told you*), we know that it also has subject, direct object, and indirect object relatives. There is no *a priori* way to predict the lowest relative clause type. But when the lowest type is known, we are able to make claims about all other relative clause types in that language.[2]

There have been further claims that the hierarchy reflects the ease of relativization and/or certain discourse constraints.[3] If this is the case, ease or difficulty should not differentially affect languages that an individual uses. That is, if it is truly a matter of difficulty that makes OComp relative clauses less frequent (and more difficult) in languages of the world, then OComp relatives should not be more difficult than other relative clause types in only one of the language systems that a learner has available (i.e., the NL vs. the learner language).

To substantiate this claim, Gass (1979a, 1979b) presented data from learners of English with a wide range of native languages (Italian, Arabic, Portuguese, Farsi, French, Thai, Chinese, Korean, and Japanese). In that study, based on data from (a) free compositions, (b) sentence combining, and (c) grammaticality judgments, it was argued that the production of relative clauses by second language learners could be predicted on the basis of the AH. Figure 7.1 is an illustration of the results from the

Figure 7.1 Percentages of sentences correct on combining task (all groups) (N = 188). *These two positions have been combined due to their analogous behavior in English relative clauses.

Source: From "Language transfer and universal grammatical relations" by S. Gass, 1979b, *Language Learning*, 29, 327–344 by Research Club in Language Learning. Reprinted by permission.

sentence combining task of that study. With the exception of the genitive,[4] the predictions of the Accessibility Hierarchy are borne out.

A second important aspect of the hierarchy is the implication regarding the use of resumptive pronouns (pronominal reflexes) in relative clauses. Examples of sentences with resumptive pronouns are given in 7-25 and 7-26:

(7-25) She danced with the man who [*he] flew to Paris yesterday.
(7-26) The woman whom he danced with [her] flew to Paris yesterday.

There is an inverse relationship between the hierarchy and resumptive pronouns, such that it is more likely that resumptive pronouns will be used in the lower hierarchical positions than in the higher ones.

Resumptive Pronoun Hierarchy
OCOMP > GEN > OPREP > IO > DO > SU

Hyltenstam (1984) investigated resumptive pronouns in some detail. His data come from the acquisition of Swedish as a second language by speakers of Spanish, Finnish, Greek, and Farsi. These languages vary in the positions that can be relativized as well as in the optional and obligatory use of resumptive pronouns. Swedish has the full range of relative clauses (SU to OComp), but has no resumptive pronouns in any of the relative clause positions. The task used by Hyltenstam was a picture identification one, in which subjects were asked a question such as, *Who is in picture number 5?* with the target response being a relative clause, *the man who is running*. The results from Hyltenstam's study conform to the predictions of the hierarchy, with more pronominal reflexes occurring in positions lower on the hierarchy than in those positions higher on the hierarchy.[5]

In sum, the results from studies on the universal predictions of the Accessibility Hierarchy support the notion that learner grammars are constrained in a similar way to natural language grammars. There is general support for the universality of the Accessibility Hierarchy, although in recent years work in this area has expanded to cover a wider range of languages. Hamilton (1994) takes this research a step further and questions the extent to which this universal truly is universal. In general, though, the evidence does support this universal principle.

In more recent years, it has become clear that the range of studies on relative clauses has been limited and that a broader consideration of languages is needed. In fact, Comrie (2003) proposes a different typology for some East Asian languages. O'Grady, Lee, and Choo (2003) noted a preference for subject over direct object relative clauses in Korean. Additionally, Cho (1999) presented data from Korean that supported the Accessibility Hierarchy. However, Jeon and Kim (2007) considered two kinds of Korean relative clauses: head-external and head-internal relative clauses. There are a number of syntactic differences between these two relative clause types. In a study of 40 learners of Korean, Jeon and Kim found limited support for the predictions of the Accessibility Hierarchy. In head-external relative clauses, there was a preference for subject over direct object relative clauses, but in head-internal relative structures evidence for that preference did not exist.

In a study of the acquisition of Japanese by Cantonese, English, and Korean speakers, Ozeki and Shirai (2007) introduced another level of complexity—that of animacy. They considered oral data and found that even low-proficiency learners used more direct object and oblique (other than subject and direct object, e.g., object of preposition) relative clauses than subject relatives, contradicting the predictions of the hierarchy. Further, a subset of the learners (Chinese and English native speakers) associated subject relative clauses with animate head nouns and direct object relative clauses with inanimate head nouns. In a follow-up study with Cantonese learners of Japanese, Ozeki and Shirai used a sentence-combining task. They found that subject and direct object relatives were easier than oblique relative clauses, as would be predicted, but that when learners converted direct object and oblique relative clauses into subject relative clauses, it was nearly always done with animates as heads. Thus, the selection of relative clause types is sensitive to animacy.

Kanno (2007), in a study of Chinese, Sinhalese, Vietnamese, Thai, and Indonesian-speaking learners of Japanese, found that having a semantic cue available aids in the processing of relative clauses. Interestingly, when processing becomes difficult (e.g., when a semantic cue is not available), properties of the L1 affect interpretation.

All in all, research on relative clauses suggests that the hierarchy is adhered to, but that the situation shows greater complexity (e.g., semantics, language specifics) than thought in the early years of research. As Eckman (2007, p. 327) states, "If the hierarchy [Noun Phrase Accessibility Hierarchy] is not as strongly supported when other language types are brought into the data pool, then we need to make hypotheses about what kinds of principles could be postulated that would subsume both the SLA data from RC acquisition in European languages as well as the SLA data from typologically distinct languages."

7.2.2 Test case II: the acquisition of questions

A second test case of the relationship between universals and second language acquisition comes from data on the acquisition of questions. Eckman, Moravcsik, and Wirth (1989) return to some of the early Greenbergian universals (1963) to determine whether these universals, developed on the basis of natural language data, could also be said to be valid for second language learner data. Eckman, Moravcsik, and Wirth stated the two universals and their SLA interpretation as follows (pp. 175, 188):

1 Wh- inversion implies wh- fronting: "Inversion of statement order (in Wh- questions) so that verb precedes subject occurs only in language where the question word or phrase is normally initial."
   la. Reinterpreted for learner languages as: "The relative frequency of occurrence of subject–verb inversion in wh-questions is never larger than the relative frequency of occurrence of the fronting of the wh- word."
2 Yes/No inversion implies wh- inversion: "This same inversion (i.e., inversion of statement order so that verb precedes subject) occurs in yes/no questions only if it also occurs in interrogative word questions."
   2a. Reinterpreted for learner languages as: "The relative frequency of occurrence of subject–verb inversion in yes/no questions is never larger than the relative frequency of occurrence of subject–verb inversion in wh- questions."

These universals are interpreted to suggest that the presence of subject–verb inversion in *yes/no* questions (a question that requires a *yes/no* answer) in a language, as in 7-27,

(7-27) Will you see my friend?

implies the presence of verb (auxiliary in English) before subject in *wh-* questions, as in

(7-28) Whom will you see?

which in turn implies the presence of *wh-* fronting (where the *wh-* word is at the beginning of the sentence), as in 7-29:

(7-29) Whom will you see? (vs. You will see whom?)

Thus, if a language has *yes/no* inversion, it will also have verbs before subjects in *wh-* questions and it will also have *wh-* words at the beginning of sentences. In markedness terms, *yes/no* inversion is the most marked and *wh-* fronting the least.

To evaluate these claims as they relate to SLA, Eckman, Moravcsik, and Wirth (1989) gathered data on question formation by 14 learners of English, who were native speakers of Japanese, Korean, or Turkish. In interpreting nonnative speaker data, one must first determine what it means to acquire a form, as discussed in chapter 2. In many studies, 90% accuracy rate has become the standard. This of course is an arbitrary cutoff point, but one that many are satisfied with.

The data presented in this study show that in fact learners are constrained by the implicational universal. Those learners who had acquired the most marked question type (*yes/no* inversion) had also acquired the other two. Interestingly, and herein lies one of the main difficulties of second language acquisition research, of the 14 subjects, data from one did not follow the predictions of the universal. How is this to be interpreted? Does it suggest that the universal is not valid for second language data? If so, the result would be the invalidation of the claim that the range of the domain of language universals is all human languages, including learner languages.

An alternative interpretation lies in the explanation of the one exception. Are there extenuating circumstances that might militate against the strength of this universal? Because there are so many factors that compete in second language acquisition (including NL, TL, pragmatics, processing limitations, attitude, motivation, attentiveness), it is unlikely that predictions can be made in an absolute fashion. It is only when the exceptions seem to outweigh the predictions of universals that we can begin to invalidate claims. In other words, the most we can hope for with second language predictions are tendencies or probabilistic predictions. In fact, with the one exception in the Eckman, Moravcsik, and Wirth study, the researchers provided an explanation related to processing constraints. Thus, for 13 of the subjects, the linguistic universal wins out, but for one, a processing principle relating to less complex versus more complex structures wins out. Why processing principles provide the major constraints for one individual whilst linguistic universals provide the major constraints for the majority remains an unanswered question. This result highlights the importance of individual variation.

7.2.3 Test case III: voiced/voiceless consonants

A third study that we discuss in the context of language universals comes from the domain of phonology. The data presented in Eckman (1981a, 1981b) are from speakers of Spanish and Mandarin Chinese learning English. The area of investigation is word-final voiced and voiceless consonants. Table 7.3 presents the data from the Spanish speakers and Table 7.4 presents the data from the Mandarin Chinese speakers.

From the data in Table 7.3 (the Spanish-speaker data), one can observe the following: word-final obstruents are voiceless.[6] The data from the Mandarin speakers are somewhat different in that we do not see devoicing. Rather, what we see is the following: Add a schwa (ə) following a word-final voiced obstruent (schwas represent reduced sounds as in [dəpartmənt], department). Thus, both groups of speakers begin with the same problem—how to resolve the difficulty of producing words with word-final voiced obstruents which is a marked structure in languages. The Spanish speakers solve the problem by devoicing the obstruents; the Mandarin speakers resolve the problem by adding a schwa to the end of words. There are two questions that need to be addressed. Why should both groups have the same problem? Why should each group attempt to resolve it in a different manner?

The answer to the first question involves a consideration of two facts, one relating to the NL and the other to language universals. With regard to the NL, neither language has a voice contrast in final position. With regard to universal markedness principles, it has been argued (see section 6.4.1) that a voicing contrast in final position is the most marked (and hence presumably the last voicing contrast to be learned). Both of these facts combine to predict the learner language facts that we have seen, namely a difficulty with voicing contrast in final position.

The second question, regarding the differential resolution to the problem, is more difficult to deal with. The solution by the Spanish speakers of devoicing final obstruents is one found in many languages of the world; for example, German, Catalan, Polish, and Russian. The

Table 7.3 Interlanguage data from Spanish speakers

Learner 1		Learner 2	
IL phonetic form	*Gloss*	*IL phonetic form*	*Gloss*
[bɔp]	Bob	[rav]	rob
[bɔbi]	Bobby	[ravər]	robber
[rɛt]	red	[bɔp]	Bob
[rɛðər]	redder	[bɔbi]	Bobby
[bik]	big	[smuθ]	smooth
[bigər/biɣər]	bigger	[smuðər]	smoother
[bref]	brave	[rɛθ/rɛð]	red
[brevər]	braver	[rɛðər]	redder
[prawt]	proud	[du]	do
[prawdəst]	proudest	[riðu]	redo
[wɛt]	wet	[bek]	bake
[wɛtər]	wetter	[priβek]	prebake
[sik]	sick	[wɛt]	wet
[sikəst]	sickest	[wɛtər]	wetter
[ðə]	the	[sef]	safe
[son]	zone	[sefəst]	safest
[fʌsi]	fuzzy	[ðə]	the
[faðər]	father	[ðis]	this
[fris]	freeze	[pig]	pig
[tæg]	tag	[bæd]	bad
[bɛd]	bed	[bɛt]	bed
[pɪg]	pig	[bik/big/biɣ]	big

Source: From "On the naturalness of interlanguage phonological rules" by F. Eckman, 1981, *Language Learning, 31,* 195–216 by Research Club in Language Learning. Reprinted by permission.

solution by the Mandarin speakers, however, is unlike patterns found in other languages of the world. At first glance, this could be taken as evidence that learner languages do not fit within the domain of natural languages, for here we have a learner language rule unlike a rule in any natural language. However, the creation of a nonnatural-language rule, like the one presented here, can be explained on the basis of the language contact system. In natural languages, one does not have the conflict between two language systems, as we have with the formation of second language grammars.

In Mandarin Chinese there are no obstruents (voiced or voiceless) in word-final position. Thus, to devoice the obstruents, as the Spanish speakers do, does not solve the initial problem of violating NL constraints, as another constraint would be violated as a result. Hence, the Chinese speakers opt for a solution that combines the NL phonetic constraints of absence of word-final obstruents with the frequent use in the TL of the vowel schwa.

Table 7.4 Interlanguage data from Mandarin speakers

Learner 1		Learner 2	
IL phonetic form	*Gloss*	*IL phonetic form*	*Gloss*
[tæg/tægə]	tag	[ænd/ændə]	and
[rab/rabə]	rob	[hæd/hædə]	had
[hæd/hæsə]	had	[tɔb/tɔbə]	tub
[hiz/hizə]	he's	[staDɪd/staDɪdə]	started
[smuðə]	smoother	[fɪʊd/fɪʊdə]	filled
[rayt]	right	[bɪg/bɪgə]	big
[dɛk]	deck	[rɛkənayzdə]	recognized
[zɪp]	zip	[ɪz/ɪzə]	is
[mɪs]	miss	[sɛz/sɛzə]	says
[wɛt]	wet	[wɔtə]	water
[dɪfər]	differ	[afə]	offer
[ovər]	over	[lidə]	leader
[bigər]	bigger		
[kɪkɪn]	kicking		
[tægɪn]	tapping		
[lebər]	label		
[lɛtər]	letter		
[blidɪn]	bleeding		
[lidə]	leader		

Source: From "On the naturalness of interlanguage phonological rules" by F. Eckman, 1981, *Language Learning, 31*, 195–216 by Research Club in Language Learning. Reprinted by permission.

7.2.4 Falsifiability

In the history of SLA research, what has the mechanism been for dealing with linguistic counterexamples? Within the domain of typological universals, researchers have weakened their strong claims to probabilistic ones or frequency claims, as we saw with regard to question formation in the case of the Structural Conformity Hypothesis in particular. A second related way is to claim that the interlanguage itself is shown in the variation, compared to what native speakers do (Selinker, 1966). A third common means has been the attempt to explain the exceptions, generally with recourse to the NL or the TL, or to the methodology used in data collection. For example, in discussing the addition of schwa by the Mandarin Chinese learners of English in word-final position (section 7.2.3), the fact that the Chinese learners created a system unlike any system known in the domain of first languages (and, hence, supposedly outside of the domain of language universals), the attempt was made to explain the pattern in terms of the facts of the NL and the TL. Similarly, in the work on relative clauses (section 7.2.1), the predictions made by the Accessibility Hierarchy were not borne out in all cases. Attempts have been made to account for the discrepancies in terms of the data-collection measure.

There has been little attempt to claim that the universal is inaccurately described—a logical possibility, as we will see later. Because the linguistic facts of typological universals, being based on surface facts of languages, are reasonably well established, it is unlikely that this latter possibility would carry much weight. Nevertheless, were there widespread evidence that typological universals did not hold for learner languages, and there were no compelling arguments as to why this should be so, there would be two possible conclusions: (a) the domain of language universals is that of natural languages and not second languages, or (b) the domain of language universals is that of all linguistic systems—any failure to comply with a putative language universal would then be taken as evidence that the description of that universal is incorrect.

7.2.5 Typological universals: conclusions

For implicational universals to have any importance in the study of second language acquisition, two factors must be taken into consideration. First, one must understand why a universal is a universal. It is not sufficient to state that second languages obey natural language constraints because that is the way languages are. This only pushes the problem of explanation back one step. Second language acquisition can contribute to the general study of language by showing whether universal constraints are operative in newly created languages. But it can only contribute to a general understanding of language if it can also explain if and why a particular universal is a universal. Second, there must be an arguable relationship between the features in question. There must be a connection between the feature that is implied and the feature that does the implying. In other words, there must be a relationship between more marked and less marked forms.

The first of these factors relates to the underlying explanation for the implication; the second relates to the plausibility of joining what might appear to be two unrelated grammatical forms. Explanations have generally taken the form of processing constraints, functional considerations, or pragmatics. These explanations have in common the fact that they deal with the way language functions and the ways humans use language. However, the picture may be more complex; current research attempts to determine whether learners relate structures that are said to be related by the theoretical model on which the descriptions are based. In fact, Gass and Ard (1984) and Eckman (1992) argued that not all language universals will equally affect the formation of second language grammars. Gass and Ard argued that one must look at the underlying source of the universal and understand why structures are related to determine whether they will or will not affect SLA, whereas Eckman claimed that universals must involve the "same" structure (e.g., relative clauses, question formation) before they will have an effect on the development of second language grammars.

In chapter 6, we discussed the kind of evidence necessary for language learning to proceed (see section 6.3.3). Typological approaches have had little to say about the type of evidence necessary for learning and hence have had little to say about learnability issues.

Finally, we turn to the role of the L1. We can schematize three approaches to transfer in Table 7.5.

7.3 Functional approaches

In chapter 6 and the early sections of this chapter, we considered inter-languages from the perspective of linguistic structures. The second part of this chapter looks at second language acquisition from the perspective of how language functions; that is, how language is used for communication purposes. The major concern in this section is how different forms are used to express different functions, in other words, how form and function relate to one another. Whereas in the preceding chapters we considered isolated parts of language (e.g., syntax, morphology), functional approaches, because they consider meaning as central, simultaneously take into account many aspects of language, including pragmatics, semantics, syntax, morphology, and the lexicon. In other words, multiple levels of language are considered simultaneously. We first turn to tense and aspect and then to issues of discourse.

7.3.1 Tense and aspect: the Aspect Hypothesis

A major question asked by researchers studying tense and aspect is: How do learners recognize what morphological markers (e.g., past tense, progressive) go with what verbs?

As we showed earlier, the issue of the acquisition of morphological items has long been a feature of second language research.

Earlier work looked at the actual morphemes and tried to figure out the order in which they are acquired. In the 1980s, a more sophisticated

Table 7.5 Differences in three approaches to the study of transfer

	Universal Grammar	Typological	Contrastive Analysis
Levels of analysis	+	−	−
Property clusters	+	+	−
Learnability	+	−	−

approach was taken to the L2 acquisition of tense–aspect morphology. The Aspect Hypothesis claims that "first and second language learners will initially be influenced by the inherent semantic aspect of verbs or predicates in the acquisition of tense and aspect markers associated with or affixed to these verbs" (Andersen and Shirai, 1994, p. 133). This approach is semantic in nature and focuses on the influence of lexical aspect in the second language acquisition of tense–aspect morphology. The original impetus for the hypothesis came from L1 acquisition studies, specifically Antinucci and Miller (1976), who carried out a study of LI acquisition of Italian and English (see critique by Weist, Wysocka, Witkowska-Stadnik, Buczowska, and Konieczna, 1984). Andersen (1986, 1991) formulated the hypothesis in its present form with a specific focus on SLA (see also Andersen and Shirai, 1994; Bardovi-Harlig, 1994).

Andersen (1986, 1991) presented a study of two native speakers of English, one child and one adolescent, learning L2 Spanish. He noticed an interesting distinction in their development of tense–aspect marking: the past tense (preterit) markers emerged with punctual and achievement verbs, whereas the imperfect markers emerged with verbs that indicate states. These verb types are illustrated in the following examples:

(7-30) se partió (punctual)
         it broke
(7-31) enseñó (achievement)
         s/he taught
(7-32) tenía (state)
         s/he had (imperfect form)

Punctual verbs, according to Andersen (1991, p. 311) are "momentary in duration. They may be thought of as being reduced to a point." Bardovi-Harlig (1999b) characterizes aspectual classes as follows:

> States persist over time without change (e.g., *seem*, *know*, *need*, *want*, and *be*, as in *be tall*, *big*, *green*). Activities have inherent duration in that they involve a span of time, like *sleep* and *snow*. They have no specific endpoint as in *I studied all week* and, thus, are atelic (e.g., *rain*, *play*, *walk*, and *talk*). Achievements capture the beginning or the end of an action (Mourelatos, 1981) as in *the race began* or *the game ended* and can be thought of as reduced to a point (Andersen, 1991). Examples of achievement verbs include *arrive*, *leave*, *notice*, *recognize*, and *fall asleep*. Accomplishments (e.g., *build a house* or *paint a painting*) are durative like activities and have an endpoint like achievements.
>
> (p. 358)

Based on his empirical results, Andersen postulated a sequence of developmental stages. The development of the past tense seemed to spread from achievement verbs to accomplishment verbs to activities and finally to states. The situation is different for the imperfect, which appears later than the perfect. It spreads in the reverse order—from states to activities to accomplishments, and then to achievements. Thus, Andersen argued that when tense–aspect morphology emerged in the interlanguage of these two subjects, it was constrained by lexical aspect in terms of the types of verbs described above.

A similar phenomenon has been reported in a variety of L2 naturalistic and classroom settings (e.g., Bardovi-Harlig, 1992a, 1992b; Bardovi-Harlig and Bergström, 1996; Bardovi-Harlig and Reynolds, 1995; Flashner, 1989; Hasbún, 1995; Kaplan, 1987; Kumpf, 1984; Robison, 1990, 1995; Rocca, 2002; Shirai, 1995; Shirai and Kurono, 1998; see also reviews by Andersen and Shirai, 1994, 1996, and Bardovi-Harlig, 1999b, 2000). Findings from research in a number of target languages generally show the following:

1   Past/perfective morphology emerges with punctual verbs and verbs indicating achievements and accomplishments. The morphology then gradually extends to verbs expressing activities and states.
2   Imperfective morphology emerges with durative and/or stative verbs (i.e., activities and states), then gradually spreads to achievement/accomplishment and punctual verbs.
3   Progressive morphology is strongly associated with durative and dynamic verbs (i.e., activities).

Other studies are revealing in this regard. First, in a classroom setting, Housen (1995) observed over a three-year period of time six learners of L2 English whose native languages were French and Dutch. Data from the children, 8 years old at the beginning of the study, were longitudinally collected at six-month intervals. Housen's results were mixed; the influence of telicity on perfective morphology was not as strong as predicted. The strongest support for the Aspect Hypothesis came from the progressive marker, which was initially restricted to activities and then gradually covered all aspectual classes. It even overextended to states. Examples follow in 7-33 to 7-36:

(7-33) She dancing. (activity)
(7-34) And then a man coming . . . (accomplishment)
(7-35) Well, I was knowing that. (state)
(7-36) Other boys were shouting "watch out!" (achievement)

The French learners were overall less proficient than the Dutch learners and never reached the stage where they could use the regular past morphology productively. Transfer factors were also involved, in that learners appeared to be predisposed by the basic distinctions in their L1 tense–aspect system to look for similar distinctions in the L2 input, specifically in the case of the past/nonpast distinction, where Dutch is closer to English. But in the progressive/nonprogressive distinction, where neither of the native languages obligatorily encodes progressive aspect, the learners seemed to resort to universal conceptual proto-types and appeared to interpret the progressive as a marker of inherent durativity.

In another study, Rohde (1996, 2002) analyzed naturalistic L2 data of four L1 German children learning English during a six-month stay in California. An analysis of uninflected and other nontarget-like verb forms showed the following:

Use of progressive with infinitive or first/third person plural function:
(7-37) I can fishing.
(7-38) They going all, all the fishes going round my eggs and they bite.

Use of progressive in past contexts:
(7-39) I think Birgit was kissing.
(7-40) We was going up there.

Omission of past inflections on irregular and unfamiliar verbs:
(7-41) Tiff, I sleep yesterday outside.
(7-42) I just kick him.

Marking of future events with the construction *I'm* + verb:
(7-43) I'm go home.
(7-44) I'm get it for Tiff.

Unsystematic use and nonuse of inflections:
(7-45) What do your foot? [German: Was macht dein Fuss? = What does your foot do?]
(7-46) Hey Johnny is loving me.

As a result of these findings, Rohde maintains that the Aspect Hypoth-esis applies with an important caveat: the influence of lexical aspect is gradient and wanes according to the learner's age, the particular L1/L2s involved, and the length of target language exposure.

The Aspect Hypothesis is a rich hypothesis drawing upon many forms of linguistics. It is important to note that very early forms of temporal expressions appear without any overt linguistic marking. How then do learners express temporality? Bardovi-Harlig (1999b) suggested four ways: (a) build on conversational partner's discourse, (b) infer from context, (c) contrast events, and (d) follow chronological order in narration. These are essentially pragmatic means for accomplishing what cannot be accomplished linguistically.

The next stage is the beginning of the learner's use of language to express temporality. Predominant in this phase is the use of adverbials (e.g., *yesterday*, *then*, *after*, *often*, *twice*). Interesting is the fact that the ready availability and sufficiency of adverbials may delay acquisition of temporality (Giacalone Ramat and Banfi, 1990). In fact, Dietrich, Klein, and Noyau (1995) suggest that some untutored learners may not progress past this stage (see discussion of Kumpf's work in chapter 3).

7.3.2 The Discourse Hypothesis

Another way of looking at the acquisition of tense/aspect is not to consider lexical meaning, as with the Aspect Hypothesis, but to look at the structure of the discourse in which utterances appear. In general, there are two parts to discourse structure: background and foreground. Foreground information is generally new information that moves time forward. Background information is supporting information. Unlike foregrounded material, it does not provide new information but might serve the purpose of elaborating on the information revealed through the foregrounded material. Within the context of the Discourse Hypothesis, it is claimed that "learners use emerging verbal morphology to distinguish foreground from background in narratives" (Bardovi-Harlig, 1994, p. 43). An example of how this might come about was seen in chapter 3 in the discussion of data from Kumpf (1984).

Jarvis (2002) investigated article use in English by second language learners from the perspective of discourse universals. His data from Finnish-speaking and Swedish-speaking learners of English were gathered from written narratives (in two parts) of a silent film. The narratives were analyzed by isolating all referents to the film's female protagonists and categorizing these references as to the contextual category: (a) new topic, (b) new comment, (c) current topic, (d) current comment, (e) known topic, and (f) known comment. These were defined in the following way (p. 395):

New topic	A previously unmentioned NP[7] referent that serves as the subject . . . of the main clause of a T-unit where no other NP referent has been mentioned previously;
New comment	A previously unmentioned NP referent that does not meet the criteria for a new topic;

Current topic	A NP referent that was mentioned in the preceding T-unit or earlier in the current T-unit and is the subject of the main clause of the current T-unit or as the only NP referent in the main clause that was mentioned previously; A NP referent in a subordinate clause—though not in reported speech—if it is coreferential with the topic . . . of the main clause;
Current comment	A NP referent that was mentioned in the preceding T-unit or earlier in the current T-unit but does not meet the criteria for current topic;
Known topic	A NP referent that was mentioned earlier in the text, but not in the preceding T-unit or earlier in the current T-unit, and is the subject of the main clause is the only NP referent in the main clause mentioned previously;
Known comment	A NP referent that was mentioned earlier in the text, but not in the preceding T-unit or earlier in the current T-unit, and does not meet the criteria for known topic.

The results show a complex interplay between the native language and discourse constraints. In particular, the results suggest that learners distinguish between new, current, and known NP referents, although the native language does influence these choices. The distinction between topic and comment is less straightforward and Jarvis suggests that this may cast doubt on the universality of this distinction, although he acknowledges that his learners were not at the very early stages of acquisition. One interesting suggestion made is that learners may simultaneously entertain multiple hypotheses regarding article use.

Bardovi-Harlig (2004a, 2004b, 2005) investigated learners of English, showing that *will* emerges prior to *going to* as an expression of futurity. Bardovi-Harlig (2004a) considers three explanations: (a) formal complexity, (b) *will* as a lexical marker, and (c) the one-to-one principle. The one-to-one principle "is a principle of one *form* to one meaning" (Andersen, 1984, p.79; emphasis in original). With regard to formal complexity (*going to* is more complex than *will*), she argues that this might explain why *will* emerges first, but not why *going to* is infrequently used.[8] The second explanation that she explores is the possibility that learners perceive *will* as a lexical rather than a grammatical marker. This fits in with the general observation that lexical marking often precedes grammatical or morphological marking in SLA. In other words, learners use lexical items (e.g., *tomorrow*) before using grammatical means to express future. This is made easier by the fact that it is a single word and, further,

her data show only few instances of the reduced form (*'ll*). The third explanation relies on the one-to-one principle first articulated by Andersen (1984): "an IL should be constructed in such a way that an intended underlying meaning is expressed with one clear invariant surface form (or construction)" (p. 79). This principle, he claims, is a "first-step" in constructing a second language grammar and guides learners as they construct "a minimal but functional IL system" (p. 79). Bardovi-Harlig argues that *will* is the general future marker at the early stages. If the one-to-one principle is valid, in order for *going to* to enter the system, learners have to assign a new meaning separate from the meaning of *will*. Following Dahl (1985, 2000), Bardovi-Harlig (2004a) makes the argument that *going to* has the meaning of " 'in preparation' or impending use. The concept of 'immediacy' may be built in to the meaning associated with the form" (p. 133).

Bardovi-Harlig (1998), through data from second language learners of English, finds support for both the tense/aspect and discourse hypotheses. She comes to the following conclusions (p. 498):

1 Achievements are the predicates most likely to be inflected for simple past, regardless of grounding.
2 Accomplishments are the next most likely type of predicate to carry the simple past. Foreground accomplishments show higher rates of use than background accomplishments.
3 Activities are the least likely of all the dynamic verbs to carry simple past, but foreground activities show higher rates of simple past inflection than background activities. Activities also show use of progressive, but this is limited to the background.

These findings clearly show that lexical meaning (as seen by the distinction among verb types) is one determinant of verbal morphology; discourse structure (as seen by the differential use of morphology for foreground vs. background material) is another. Thus, both the Aspect Hypothesis and discourse structure work together to account for the way tense/aspect morphology and meaning are acquired.

7.3.3 *Concept-oriented approach*

The concept-oriented approach begins with the assumption that learners begin with the need to express a given concept—for example, an event in the past. Thus, basic to this approach is the need to map certain functions that the learner wants to express to the form that she or he needs to express it. With adult learners, the function (i.e., concept) is already known as the relevant concepts are available through their first language. Earlier in this chapter we discussed Andersen's one-to-one principle, which is essentially an expression of one form/one meaning. Andersen (1990) discusses the possibility of multifunctionality, recognizing that there are times when a learner needs to "search" the input to understand additional meanings expressed in the input. An example might be the present progressive, which can mean an act in the present (*I am writing these words now*) or an act in the future (*I am flying to Shanghai tomorrow*). A great deal of research within this analytical framework has been conducted by Bardovi-Harlig, who has considered the acquisition of tense in numerous venues (e.g., 2004a, 2004b, 2006, 2007), as well as in work by the European Science Foundation (e.g., Dietrich, Klein, and Noyau, 1995).

7.4 Conclusion

In sum, what has emerged from research in the domain of linguistics discussed in this and the previous chapter is that universals (both typological and UG-based) clearly have an important impact on the formation of second language grammars. What is in need of further examination is the extent to which universals operate alone or in consort with NL and TL facts and the discovery of whether or not all universals equally affect second language grammars.

Suggestions for additional reading

Tense and Aspect in Second Language Acquisition: Form, Meaning, and Use. Kathleen Bardovi-Harlig. Blackwell (2000).
Crosscurrents in Second Language Acquisition. Thom Huebner and Charles A. Ferguson (Eds.). John Benjamins (1991).
Foreign Accent: The Ontogeny and Phylogeny of Second Language Phonology. Roy Major. Lawrence Erlbaum Associates (2001).
The L2 Acquisition of Tense–Aspect Morphology. M. Rafael Salaberry and Yasuhiro Shirai (Eds.). John Benjamins (2002).

Points for discussion

1 Take the example of relative clause formation, as discussed in this chapter. It was claimed that there is a universal such that every language that has indirect object relativization also has direct object relativization. What sort of data would you want to gather to substantiate this claim for SLA? This universal is a static claim; that is, it makes a claim about a given language/interlanguage at a given point in time. Consider it from an acquisitional point of view. What would the language learning prediction be? Does this universal predict acquisition order? What sort of experimental design would you use to test this?

2   Consider the notion of resumptive pronouns in relative clauses dis-
    cussed in this chapter. In ILs it is common to find sentences like the
    following:

> That's the man whom I told you about [*him*].

Let's assume that sentences like this are produced by speakers who
have pronominal reflexes in their native language. To what would you
attribute this IL form?

Assume that the sentence below is produced by speakers of a
language with no pronominal reflexes. To what would you attribute
this IL form? Are these analyses in contradiction? How would you
reconcile these differences?

> That's the woman that I'm taller than her.

These IL sentences are common in some dialects of English,
particularly in colloquial speech. How does this affect your analysis?

3   Consider the case where you have a language in which genitive phrases
    follow nouns, as in the following French example:

> le chien de mon ami
> the dog of my   friend

In English, two structures are possible—one in which the possessor
follows the noun and one in which it precedes it.

> the dog of my friend
> my friend's dog

Whereas both of these English sentences are possible, the first one
sounds strange. On the other hand, of the following two groups of
sentences in English:

> the leg of the table
> a leg of lamb

> the table's leg
> a lamb's leg

it is the second group that is less likely to be said. How would you
explain this? What would you predict regarding a learner's IL production? Considering both transfer and input, how would a learner figure
out the facts of English?

A French/Italian/Spanish speaker learning English has to go from one form to two, whereas the other direction requires a learner to go from two forms to one. Which do you think would be more difficult, and why?

4　Considering the previous problem, let's assume that a hypothetical learner has sorted out the correct English facts about possession. Then she encounters *the book of Job* and has also become aware of the ungrammaticality of *Job's book* in this context. Do you think that this might then alter her original analysis? Do you think she might begin to produce phrases like *the table's leg* or might go into a restaurant and order *a lamb's leg*? Why or why not?

5　Consider the following definitions for the basic meanings of the progressive/present/future tenses in English:

a　*Progressive* (*to be* + verb + *-ing*): ongoing witnessed activity that persists for an extended period of time.

b　*Simple present* (base verb): lawlike regular state or expected events characteristic of their subject at the present time.

c　*Future* (*will* + verb): states or events expected in foreseeable future.

The data presented here are from Spanish and Japanese learners of English (data from Gass and Ard, 1984). These learners had been asked to judge the acceptability of the following sentences in English.

	Spanish n = 52 % "acceptable" responses	Japanese n = 37 % "acceptable" responses
1. Dan sees better.	65	43
2. Dan is seeing better now.	81	19
3. Mary is being in Chicago now.	8	5
4. John is travelling to New York tomorrow.	8	32
5. The new bridge connects Detroit and Windsor.	79	73
6. The new bridge is connecting Detroit and Windsor.	46	24
7. John travels to New York tomorrow.	8	19
8. John will travel to New York tomorrow.	86	81
9. John is smoking American cigarettes now.	88	76
10. The new bridge will connect Detroit and Windsor.	67	87
11. Fred smokes American cigarettes now.	56	51
12. Mary will be in Chicago now.	10	14
13. John will smoke American cigarettes now.	10	3
14. Mary is in Chicago now.	88	92

215

Focus on the progressive, simple present, and future tenses. For each, order the sentences from those most frequently judged acceptable to those least frequently judged acceptable. Do this separately for each of the two language groups. Are the two language groups comparable? What explanation can you give for the different percentages of each of the two language groups? What explanation can you give for the differential acceptability of the various uses of each tense by both groups? In your answer you might want to consider the different semantic concepts embodied in each of the verb tenses: completed action, incomplete action, and action in progress.

What do these data suggest about the interaction between syntax and semantics in SLA?

Consider sentences 4 and 7, the translation equivalents of which are possible in Spanish. However, the acceptability of these sentences in English is low in the Spanish speakers' judgments. How can you account for this? What does this suggest about the interaction of the NL and language universals?

What do these data suggest about the acquisition of tense/aspect systems in an L2? Is acquisition gradual or is it an all or nothing phenomenon?

6   The data below are from a native speaker of Arabic enrolled in an intermediate level of an intensive English program. He had seen a movie titled *Little Man, Big City*. The following is his oral account of that movie.

> I saw today a movie about a man in a big city. I want to tell you about a movie, my friend. The movie began with a man about forty years old or forty-five in his apartment in the city and he was disturbed by alarm clock, TV, and noisy outside the house or outside the apartment and he woke up in a bad temper and he wanted a fresh air, he went when he opened the window to get this fresh air, he found a smoke, smoke air, dirty air. The movie also showed that the man not only disturbed in his special apartment or special house, but in everything, in work, in street, in transportation, even in the gardens and seashores. Man in the city has to wake up very early to go to the work and he has to, as the movie shows, he has to use any means of transportation, car, bus, bicycle and all the streets are crowded, and he has no no choice or alternatively to use and he is busy day and night. At day, he has to work hard among the machines, the typewriters and among papers, pencils and offices in the city. And when he wanted to take a rest in his house or outside his house in the garden or the seashore . . . He can't because the seats are crowded with people. When he

216

wanted to take a meal in restaurant, the restaurant is crowded, everything is crowded in the city and very, very—it's not good place or good atmosphere to to live in. The movie showed that. And the man began to feel sick and thus he wanted to consult the doctors to describe a medicine or anything for for health, but the doctors also disagreed about his illness or they couldn't diagnose his illness correctly. This they show at first. Want to make us know about the life in the city. The man began to think about to find a solution or answer for this dilemma. OK dilemma? Dilemma. He thought that why not to go to the open lands and to build houses and gardens and and to live in this new fresh land with fresh air and fresh atmosphere and why don't we stop smoking in the factories by using filters, filters and stop smoking from the cars and all industrial bad survivals or like smoking like dirty airs and so on. The man also wanted to make kids or childrens in the houses not to play or to use sports inside houses, but to go outside the houses in the garden and to play with balls, basket anything. They like to play. And also he wanted to live in a quiet and calm apartment. People inside houses must not use TV in a bad way or a noisy way. Must use it in a calm way or in a quiet way and that, I think, that is a good solution or a good answer for this city dilemma.

Categorize the data by separating this speaker's use of the present tense from his use of the past tense. Focusing on tense shifts, from past to present and vice versa, work out an IL generalization that might account for this shift.

7   Below is a written version of the same movie by the same speaker.

I saw a movie about a man in a city (big city). I want to tell you what I saw and what is my opinion. The movie began with a man about forty years old, in his apartment in a big city. He was disturbed by many things like Alarm O'Clock, T.V., Radio and noisy outside. He want a fresh air, but he could not because the city is not a good place for fresh air. There are many factories which fill the air with smoke. The movie showed the daily life of a man in the city. He is very busy day and night. He had to go to his work early by any means of transportation, car, bus, bicycle. The streets are crowded, everything in the city is crowded with people, the houses, streets, factories, institutions and even the seashores. Man in a big city lives a hard and unhealthy life, noisy, dirt air, crowded houses and smoke are good factors for sickness. The man in the big city tried to find answer to this dilemma. Instead of living in crowded, unhealthy places, he wanted places that must be used for living. People must live in good atmosphere climate and land. Gardens, which are god places for sports, must surround houses. My opinion is that man's solution for the problem is good and acceptable especially for health.

Categorize the data by separating the speaker's use of the present tense from his use of the past tense. Focusing on tense shifts, from past to present and vice versa, work out an IL generalization that might account for this shift.

See GSS, problems 1.2, 3.10, 4.2–4.4, and 5.1.

8

LOOKING AT INTERLANGUAGE PROCESSING

8.1 Introduction

Like the field of linguistics, the field of psychology has significantly influenced the study of SLA. In this chapter, we outline approaches to second language acquisition with a basis in psycholinguistic processing rather than in the structure of linguistic products. We begin the chapter by discussing connectionist/emergentist approaches to second language learning (section 8.2) followed by processing approaches, in particular, processability theory and information processing (section 8.3). We then move to a discussion of knowledge types (acquisition–learning, declarative/procedural, implicit/explicit) (section 8.4) and the interface between knowledge types (section 8.5). Finally, we deal with concepts that are prevalent in the psycholinguistic literature and that relate to second language learning; namely, attention, working memory, monitoring, and U-shaped learning (section 8.6). It is important to note once again that there is an important difference in emphasis between linguistics and psychology in their relationship to SLA. In linguistics the emphasis is on constraints on grammar formation, whereas in psychology the emphasis is on the actual processing mechanisms involved in SLA as well as on issues (e.g. working memory capacity) that affect those mechanisms. This is not to say that there is no overlap, only that each approach has its own particular emphasis.

8.2 Connectionist/emergentist models

In this approach to language learning, also referred to as constructivist approaches, the emphasis is on usage. Learning does not rely on an innate module, but rather it takes place based on the extraction of regularities from the input. As these regularities or patterns are used over and over again, they are strengthened. Frequency accounts (N. Ellis, 2002) are an example. Frequency accounts of second language acquisition rely on the assumption that "[h]umans are sensitive to the frequencies of events in

219

their experience" (p. 145). The approach is exemplar-based in that it is the examples that are present in the input that form the basis of complex patterns and from which regularities emerge. According to N. Ellis (2002, p. 144), "comprehension is determined by the listeners' vast amount of statistical information about the behavior of lexical items in their language." In other words, language is not driven by an innate faculty; rather, the complex linguistic environment provides the information from which learners abstract regularities. Assuming that aspects of language are sensitive to frequency of usage, there are implications for how one conceives of grammar. The representation of language, in this view, relies on the notion of variable strengths that reflect the frequency of the input and the connections between parts of language.

In this approach, learning is seen as simple instance learning (rather than explicit/implicit induction of rules), which proceeds based on input alone; the resultant knowledge is seen as a network of interconnected exemplars and patterns, rather than abstract rules.

Even though connectionist approaches have been around for a number of years, it is only recently that research within a second language context has begun to take place. *Connectionism* is a cover term that includes a number of network architectures. One such approach is parallel distributed processing (PDP). At the heart of PDP is a neural network that is generally biologically inspired in nature. The network consists of nodes that are connected by pathways. Within connectionism, pathways are strengthened or weakened through activation or use.

Learning takes place as the network (i.e., the learner) is able to make associations, and associations come through exposure to repeated patterns. The more often an association is made, the stronger that association becomes. New associations are formed and new links are made between larger and larger units until complexes of networks are formed. Recall the discussion of the morpheme order studies in chapter 5. One of the explanations for the order of acquisition of morphemes comes from Larsen-Freeman (1976), who proposed that frequency of occurrence is a major determinant. To frame this explanation within the framework of connectionism, we would want to say that learners are able to extract regular patterns from the input to create and strengthen associations, although they may not be aware that this is what they are doing. N. Ellis and Schmidt (1997), in an experiment based on a connectionist model, supported Larsen-Freeman's suggestion, finding frequency effects for the acquisition of second language morphology.

Not many second language studies have been conducted within the framework of connectionism.[1] As noted earlier, connectionist systems rely not on rule systems but on pattern associations. Thus, if such a model is to work, we will need to have a clear understanding of how to determine strength of associations. It stands to reason that the strength

of associations will change as a function of interaction with the environment, or, put differently, with the input. It is to be noted that in the case
of second language acquisition the strength of association may already
(right or wrong) be present; that is, a pattern of connectivity may already
have been established. In other words, the L1 is already in place and,
therefore, there is a set of associations with their strengths fixed. These
associations can possibly interfere with the establishment of an L2
network.

Sokolik and Smith (1992) devised a computer-based experiment on the
learning of French noun gender. The program was designed to be trained
on and tested on French nouns without any discourse context (e.g., article
or adjective agreement). Regular nouns were used (including words
ending in -tion or -esse, which are feminine, and words ending in -eur or
-ment, which are masculine) as well as irregular nouns (e.g., peur "fear,"
which is feminine). The program was able to correctly identify noun
gender and to identify the gender of words never before encountered.
When a set of unrelated preexisting weights was added to the model,
learning was slowed. Sokolik (1990) suggested that, as a function of age,
learners are less able to establish connectionist patterns. We turn next to
the Competition Model, which also relies on the establishment of cues
and the strength of cues.

The basis for the Competition Model comes from work by Bates and
MacWhinney (1982), although more recent research (e.g., MacWhinney,
2002, 2004) expands on the underlying concepts. The Competition
Model was developed to account for the ways monolingual speakers
interpret sentences. A fundamental difference between this model and
what we have seen with a UG model (chapter 6) is that, whereas the latter
separates the form of language from its function, the Competition Model
is based on the assumption that form and function cannot be separated.
According to MacWhinney, Bates, and Kliegl (1984, p. 128), "the forms
of natural languages are created, governed, constrained, acquired and
used in the service of communicative functions."

It is important to understand that the Competition Model, similar
to other psycholinguistic approaches to SLA, is concerned with how
language is used (i.e., performance), as opposed to being concerned
with a determination of the underlying structure of language (i.e.,
competence).

We provide a brief description of the main tenets of the Competition
Model before considering its application to a second language context.
A major concept inherent in the model is that speakers must have a way
to determine relationships among elements in a sentence. Language processing involves competition among various cues, each of which contributes to a different resolution in sentence interpretation. Although the
range of cues is universal (i.e., the limits on the kinds of cues one uses

are universally imposed), there is language-specific instantiation of cues and language-specific strength assigned to cues.

Let's consider two languages with different word order possibilities: English and Italian. English word order is rigidly of the form subject–verb–object (SVO). Consider the English sentence in 8-1:

(8-1) The cows eat the grass.

Native speakers of English use various cues to determine that *the cows* is the subject of the sentence and that *the grass* is the object. First, a major determining cue in understanding this relationship is word order. Native speakers of English know that in active declarative sentences, the first noun or noun phrase is typically the subject of the sentence. Second, knowledge of the meaning of lexical items contributes to correct interpretation (cows eat grass rather than grass eats cows). Third, English speakers use animacy criteria (i.e., whether the noun is animate or inanimate) to establish grammatical relationships. Finally, morphology (in this case, subject–verb agreement) contributes to interpretation because the plurality of *the cows* requires a plural verb (*eat*). In sum, all elements converge in coming up with the interpretation of *the cows* as the subject and *the grass* as the object.

There are examples in language where interpretation is not so straightforward. In other words, there are examples where convergence is not the result. In these instances the various cues are in competition. Let's assume a sentence such as 8-2.

(8-2) The grass eats the cows.

Here, English speakers are surprised; there is competition as to which element will fill the subject slot. Using word order as a cue, *the grass* should be the subject; using meaning and animacy as cues, *the cows* is the most likely subject; using morphology as a cue, it is *the grass* because it is the only singular noun in the sentence. Thus, in this unusual sentence, there is a breakdown in our normal use of cues; as a result, there is competition as to which noun phrase will fill the slot of subject. Different languages resolve the conflict in different ways. English uses word order and agreement as primary determinants. Other languages, such as Italian, resolve the problem of interpretation by using different cues.

Following are examples from Italian that illustrate some of the word order possibilities (which vary in intonation as well as syntax) in that language.

		Word order
(8-3)	Giovanna ha comprato il pane. Joan has bought the bread	SVO
(8-4)	Allora, compro io il vino. then buy I the wine "Then, I'll buy the wine."	VSO
(8-5)	Ha comprato il vino Aldo. has bought the wine Aldo "Aldo has bought the wine."	VOS
(8-6)	No, il vino l' ha comprato Antonella. no the wine it (obj.) has bought Antonella "No, it's Antonella who bought the wine."	OVS

Given the large number of word order possibilities, how is interpretation possible in a language like Italian? How does an Italian speaker know which noun is the subject of the sentence? Or, in this conversation, how does an Italian know who is going to do what or who is responsible for what? In Italian, word order assumes a lesser role in interpretation than it does in English and morphological agreement, semantics, and pragmatics assume greater importance.

For second language acquisition, the question is: How does one adjust one's internal speech-processing mechanisms from those appropriate for the native language to those appropriate for the target language? Does one use the same cues as are used in the NL and are those cues weighted in the same way as they are in the NL? Or, do these mechanisms from the native language act to constrain interpretation as one is trying to understand a rapidly fired message in the target language?

One possibility is that, in L2 sentence interpretation, the learner's initial hypothesis is consistent with sentence interpretation in the NL. However, there may be universal tendencies toward the heavy use of particular cues. What methodology is used to gather information of this sort? In general, the methodology used in second language studies based on the Competition Model is the same. Learners whose native language uses cues and cue strengths that differ from those of the target language are presented with sentences designed to present conflicting cues and are asked to determine what the subjects of those sentences are. Thus, native speakers of English learning Italian would be given a sentence such as 8-7.

> (8-7) La matita guarda il   cane.
>   the pencil looks at the dog

and would be asked to determine whether the subject is *la matita* "the pencil" or *il cane* "the dog." Using English cues, it would be *the pencil*, because word order takes precedence over all other cues. Using Italian cues, it would be *the dog*, because semantic and pragmatic cues are the strongest (in the absence of a biasing agreement cue).

A number of studies have been conducted using this paradigm. One of the findings is that, under certain circumstances, a meaning-based comprehension strategy takes precedence over a grammar-based one. For example, English speakers learning Italian (Gass, 1987) and English speakers learning Japanese (a language that relies on the pragmatics of the situation for sentence interpretation, as well as on case-marking and lexico-semantic information; Harrington, 1987; Kilborn and Ito, 1989; Sasaki, 1991, 1994) readily drop their strong use of word order cues and adopt meaning-based cues as a major cue in interpreting Italian and Japanese sentences. On the other hand, Italian speakers learning English and Japanese speakers learning English maintain their native language meaning-based cues as primary, not readily adopting word order as a major interpretation cue.

Although the tendency of learners to adopt a meaning-based strategy as opposed to a grammar-based one is strong, there is also ample evidence that learners first look for those cues that are dominant in their NL as their initial hypothesis. Only when that appears to fail (i.e., when learners become aware of the apparent incongruity between L1 and L2 strategies) do they adopt what might be viewed as a universal prepotency: that of using meaning to interpret sentences.[2]

Particularly relevant to this area of research is the finding (Sasaki, 1994) that English learners of Japanese make use of rigid word order as a cue (in this case the SOV word order of Japanese) even before they figure out how rigid Japanese word order is. In other words, English native speakers assume rigid word order as the first hypothesis, just like in their NL. Their first task is to figure out what that word order is. Once they figure out that Japanese has SOV order, they rigidly apply the new word order. This is supported by data from Japanese learners of English who were asked to differentiate between sentences such as 8-8 and 8-9 in terms of identifying the appropriate subject of the second verb (Gass, 1986).

(8-8) The man told the boy to go.
(8-9) The man promised the boy to go.

The data showed that learners first learned that English is a rigid word order language before learning what the appropriate word order is.

Research conducted within the framework of the Competition Model needs to take context into consideration. For example, Sasaki (1997a, 1997b) showed that individual variation in responses is a significant factor and that the context of presentation of sentences affects the way sentences are interpreted. His 1994 study of Japanese learners of English and English learners of Japanese showed effects of proficiency: there is greater or lesser dependence on case-marking cues depending on proficiency level.

Rounds and Kanagy (1998) investigated English-speaking children in Japanese immersion programs. Their results conflict with some of the previous results, in particular those suggesting an overreliance on semantic strategies. The children in the Rounds and Kanagy study selected a word order strategy, relying on the basic SOV order of Japanese. According to Sasaki's (1991) prediction, they should have soon learned that the word order strategy would fail, because Japanese has OSV as well as SOV order; in other words, the learners should have soon realized that word order is not a sufficient cue to sentence interpretation in Japanese. In the Rounds and Kanagy study, however, the children continued to use word order as their primary strategy. The researchers attributed this result to the environment in which the study took place; that is, the input children received was limited in that it came primarily from their teacher and the limited reading materials that contained mostly SOV sentences. Thus, in trying to understand how learners interpret sentences, there are numerous complex conditions that need to be taken into account.

In sum, the research conducted within the Competition Model suggests that learners are indeed faced with conflicts between native language and target language cues and cue strengths. The resolution of these conflicts is such that learners first resort to their NL interpretation strategies and, upon recognition of the incongruity between TL and NL systems, resort to a universal selection of meaning-based cues as opposed to syntax-based cues before gradually adopting the appropriate TL biases as their L2 proficiency increases. What then is involved in second language processing, at least with regard to comprehension, is a readjustment of which cues will be relevant to interpretation and a determination of the relative strengths of those cues. What is not known is how learners recognize which NL cues lead to the wrong interpretation and which cues lead to the correct interpretation. In fact, Bates and MacWhinney (1981) noted that one second language user, even after 25 years of living in the target language country, still did not respond to sentence interpretation tasks in the same way as native speakers of the target language. This latter result adds another bit of strong evidence to the proposed Fundamental Difference Hypothesis discussed in the previous chapter.

As with the linguistic approaches we have considered, there are certain difficulties inherent in looking at and interpreting data in this way. One such difficulty is what we might call processing uniqueness. Is there only one way of arriving at a particular interpretation? Assume that learners are presented with the following sentence and are asked to respond to that sentence in terms of the grammatical subject:

(8-10) The pencil sees the boys.

Assume also that the learners select *the boys* as the subject. Are they doing this because they have a preference for animate objects as subjects—that is, their strategy is "select the animate noun"—or do they make this selection because they are rejecting inanimate nouns as possible subjects? In this latter case, their strategy is "choose anything but the inanimate noun." The research done to date has not been able to differentiate between these two different strategies.

A second difficulty in the interpretation of the results concerns fundamental differences between syntax-based languages and meaning/pragmatics-based languages. One of these differences is mathematical. In a word order language, such as English, there is one basic word order possibility in declarative sentences (although clearly English can move words around, as in *That movie, I want to see it* [OSVO]). In Italian there are many possibilities, as we have seen. Thus, the difference may not be one of syntax and semantics but one of the kind of evidence one needs to confirm or disconfirm hypotheses. If one starts from an English L1 position, with one basic word order, all that one has to do is hear/read the many Italian possibilities. On the other hand, if one begins with an Italian L1 position, in the absence of negative evidence (see section 6.2), or correction, there is no way of knowing that the many Italian possibilities are not possible in English. In this latter case, learners hear one possibility (SVO order); the absence of other possibilities in the input may mean that they do not exist or that coincidentally they have not been heard. Thus, in the case of the English speaker learning Italian, learning (and adjustment of cue strengths) can take place on the basis of positive evidence alone. In the case of the Italian speaker learning English, negative evidence may be necessary for the learner to realize that word order is a reliable cue in English. This alone would predict that the learning of English in this area would be a more difficult task than the learning of Italian. Which interpretation is the appropriate one is a matter as yet undetermined.

In sum, learners are seen as sorting out the complexities of language through repeated exposure, through the extraction of regularities, and through the demands of use. Form–function mappings are dependent on the reliability of the input. That is, the more reliable a cue (e.g., word order in English), the easier (and faster) it is to learn.

8.3 Processing approaches

Processing approaches are characterized by a concern with the processing mechanisms and capacities of the human brain and how those mechanisms and capacities operate when dealing within the context of second language learning. The first approach we deal with is known as Processability Theory.

8.3.1 Processability Theory

Processability Theory, also discussed in chapter 11, relies on the concept of a linguistic processor. In its simplest form, Processability Theory (cf. Pienemann, 1999, 2007) proposes that production and comprehension of second language forms can only take place to the extent that they can be handled by the linguistic processor. Understanding how the processor works allows predictions to be made about the developmental paths that learners take. As an example of how this works, consider the sequence that learners of English follow when learning questions. In Table 8.1 (based on Pienemann and Johnston, 1987) is the proposed developmental sequence for the acquisition of English questions.

This model makes a strong prediction of word order development such that in Stage 1 a learner will start off (apart from single words and/or chunks) with canonical order, such as SVO. Stage 2 involves some movement, but movement that does not interrupt the canonical order. This is followed by Stage 3, in which canonical order is interrupted. In Stage 4, grammatical categories are recognized. And, finally, in Stages 5 and 6, learners recognize substrings.

The question arises as to why question formation should be subject to the kind of constraints seen in this model. One explanation that has been put forward by Clahsen (1984) includes three processing mechanisms that constrain movement from one stage to the next:

1   *Canonical order strategy*: This predicts that strategies that separate linguistic units require greater processing capacity than strategies that involve a direct mapping onto surface strings. For example, early learners generally use a single basic word order (e.g., in English, SVO). Elements do not interrupt this sequence.

2   *Initialization/finalization strategy*: When movement takes place, elements will be moved into initial and/or final position rather than somewhere in the middle of a sentence. This aids in both processing and memorization, given research findings of the salience of first and last positions.

3   *Subordinate clause strategy*: Movement in subordinate clauses is avoided. In general, subordinate clauses are processed differently because one has to hold material in memory without a complete semantic analysis. When movement is learned, it happens in main clauses before it does in subordinate clauses.

These processing strategies, which deal with movement, are claimed to

Table 8.1 Developmental stages of English question formation

Developmental stage	Example
Stage 1: Single units	
Single words.	What?
Single units.	What is your name?
Stage 2: SVO	
Canonical word order with question intonation.	It's a monster?
	Your cat is black?
	You have a cat?
	I draw a house here?
Stage 3: Fronting (*wh-* word/*do*)	
Direct questions with main verbs and some form of fronting.	Where the cats are?
	What the cat doing in your picture?
	Do you have an animal?
	Does in this picture there is a cat?
Stage 4: Pseudo inversion: *yes/no* questions, verb *to be*	
In *yes/no* questions an auxiliary or modal (e.g., *can/could*) is in sentence-initial position.	Have you got a dog?
	Have you drawn the cat?
In *wh-* questions the verb *to be* and the subject change positions.	Where is the cat in your picture?
Stage 5: *Do*/auxiliary second	
Q-word → auxiliary/modal → subject (main verb, etc.).	Why (Q-word) have (auxiliary) you (subject) left home?
Auxiliary verbs and modals are placed in second position after *wh-* question words and before subjects (applies only in main clauses/direct questions).	What do you have?
	Where does your cat sit?
	What have you got in your picture?
Stage 6: *Can* inversion, negative question, tag question	
Can inversion: *wh-* question inversions are not present in embedded clauses.	Can you see what the time is?
	Can you tell me where the cat is?
Negative question: A negated form of *do*/auxiliary is placed before the subject.	Doesn't your cat look black?
	Haven't you seen a dog?
Tag question: An auxiliary verb and a pronoun are attached to the end of a main clause.	It's on the wall, isn't it?

Source: From Stepping up the pace—input, interaction and interlanguage development: an empirical study of questions in ESL, by A. Mackey, 1995. Unpublished doctoral dissertation, University of Sydney, Australia. Reprinted by permission.

account for the acquisition order of English questions, which of course requires movement.

Within this approach, there is a Processability Hierarchy, which, in short, states that the processor checks on the match between the grammatical information within a sentence. What this means is that within a sentence such as *The girl walks to school*, the processor checks to see if parts of a sentence match; in this case the match involves singularity—singular subject *the girl* and singular verb *walks*. But in order for this "matching" to work, learners need to develop a number of procedures, for example, procedures for putting together parts of the sentence (e.g., *the* and *girl*) and procedures for comparing relevant grammatical information (for example, in a language in which there is no subject–verb agreement, such a matching procedure is not relevant). Lack of agreement would suggest that the learner has not yet developed appropriate procedures for matching grammatical information. Pienemann (1999) established a hierarchy relevant to the ordering of procedures, as follows:

1   no procedure (e.g., single word utterances)
2   category procedure (e.g., adding a plural morpheme to a noun)
3   noun phrase procedure (e.g., matching gender, as in *la casa* [the house], where both determiner and noun are feminine)
4   verb phrase procedure (e.g., movement of elements within a verb phrase)
5   sentence procedure (e.g., subject–verb agreement)
6   subordinate clause procedure (e.g., use of a particular tense based on something in the main clause)

This hierarchy is implicational in that one procedure is a prerequisite for the next. Even though these are universal procedures, there is some leeway for learners to create individual solutions to processing limitations. For example, in Table 8.1 above, we saw the following examples for Stage 3 questions:

(8-11) Where the cats are?
(8-12) What the cat doing in your picture?
(8-13) Do you have an animal?
(8-14) Does in this picture there is a cat?

Learners produced a range of forms to avoid the complexity of movement. As noted, the principles are invariant. What is less understood are the language-specific facts representing a range of languages (for an example of how one determines relevant procedures for a language, see Kawaguchi, 2005).

We turn our attention next to another psycholinguistic approach to second language acquisition, information processing.

8.3.2 Information processing: automaticity, restructuring, and U-shaped learning

McLaughlin (1990a) noted two concepts that are fundamental in second language learning and use: automaticity and restructuring. Automaticity refers to control over one's linguistic knowledge. In language performance, one must bring together a number of skills from perceptual, cognitive, and social domains. The more each of these skills is routinized, the greater the ease with which they can be put to use.

Restructuring refers to the changes made to internalized representations as a result of new learning. Changes that reflect restructuring are discontinuous or qualitatively different from a previous stage. Learning means the inclusion of additional information which must be organized and structured. Integrating new information into one's developing second language system necessitates changes to parts of the existing system, thereby restructuring, or reorganizing, the current system and creating a (slightly) new second language system. Mere addition of new elements does not constitute restructuring.

An underlying assumption in looking at second language acquisition from the perspective of these two concepts is that human beings have a limited capacity for processing. Central to the ability to process information is the ability to attend to, deal with, and organize new information. Because of the limited capacity that humans have available for processing, the more that can be handled routinely—that is, automatically—the more attentional resources are available for new information. Processing resources are limited and must be distributed economically if communication is to be efficient. Put differently, trying to read a difficult scholarly article is done less efficiently if one is watching TV simultaneously. Too much attention is drawn away from the article and to the TV. When there are no other demands on our attention (e.g., reading the article in the quiet of the library), it takes less time to read and understand the article. (See section 8.6.1 for a more detailed discussion of the role of attention in SLA.)

8.3.2.1 Automaticity and restructuring

One way of viewing SLA is to see it as the acquisition of complex skills, much like learning other skills such as playing tennis or playing the violin. From this perspective, the role of automaticity assumes great importance. When learning to play tennis, for example, one cannot be deliberative about every movement of the racket or movement of one's feet. Rather, when one is approaching the net, one automatically moves one's feet in a particular way and gets the racket set without thinking deliberately about each step or position of the racket. We deal in a later section with the concept of attention, which is closely related to the concept of automaticity. At this point, we turn to automaticity.

There are a number of ways that automaticity can be conceptualized, but the most central of these is that there is fast, unconscious, and effortless processing.

When there has been a consistent and regular association between a certain kind of input and some output pattern, automatization may result; that is, an associative connection is activated. This can be seen in the relative automaticity of the following exchange between two people walking down the hall toward each other:

Speaker 1: Hi.
Speaker 2: Hi, how are you?
Speaker 1: Fine, and you?
Speaker 2: Fine.

The conversational routine is so automatic in a language one knows well that most people have had the experience of responding *fine* before the question is even asked and of responding *fine* when it turns out that a different question is being asked, as in the following conversation:

Speaker 1: Hi, Sue.
Speaker 2: Good morning, Julie.
Speaker 1: Fine, and you?

A comparable example took place at a G8 summit in Okinawa, Japan. Prior to the summit, Prime Minister Mori of Japan spent time brushing up on his English. Upon meeting President Clinton, he apparently became flustered and, instead of saying, *How are you?* said instead: *Who are you?* President Clinton responded: *I'm Hillary Clinton's husband.* However, Prime Minister Mori, unaware that he had asked the wrong question, was anticipating a response something like *I'm fine, and you?* and responded *I am too.*[3]

Crookes (1991) discussed the significance of planning and monitoring one's speech. It is at the level of planning (e.g., preplanning an utterance) that a learner makes a "decision" about what to say and what structures to use. That is, a learner has some choice over which structures will be used and hence practiced. Assuming that practice is a way toward ultimate automatization, then it is clear that decisions of what to practice are crucial in the determination of future language use. Thus, as Crookes pointed out, preplanning is important in determining what will and what will not become automatized and, as a result, what parts of one's IL will become more automatic.

Similar arguments have been made by Bialystok (1978), who argued that explicit knowledge can become implicit through the use of practice. Practice can, of course, take place in the classroom and can be determined by the learner through the preplanning of utterances.

There is empirical evidence to support the benefits of planning in affecting the complexity of the discourse (Crookes, 1989; R. Ellis, 1987b; Williams, 1990). In general, planning an utterance leads to the ability to utilize more complex language which, in turn, can lead to the automatization of complex language and ability to plan language with even greater complexity.

The role of monitoring is also important. Here it is important to differentiate between Monitoring as part of a theoretical construct developed by Krashen, and *monitoring*, which refers to the activity of paying attention to one's speech. In the latter use of the term, one can imagine a situation in which learners, in monitoring their speech, note the successful use of a form and are then able to use it in a subsequent conversation. That is, through careful monitoring of one's own speech, one can pick out successful utterances and use them as a basis for future practice (see Crookes, 1991).

Controlled processing is another mechanism of language use. With controlled processing, the associations have not been built up by repeated use. Rather, attentional control is necessary. Thus, one would expect a slower response. Consider the same greeting situation as given earlier, but this time in a language unfamiliar to you. If you were learning Japanese and someone said to you:

Speaker 1: Genkideska ("How are you?")

the response, *Anatawa*, would not come so easily or automatically. It might take some attention for you to dig up the appropriate response to that question. The distinction between controlled and automatic processing is one of routinization and the creation of associations in long-term memory, not one of conscious awareness, as Krashen's acquisition–learning distinction suggests (see section 8.4.1). The distinction is also not one of separateness, because automatic processing presupposes the existence of controlled processing.

Second language acquisition, in this view, takes place by the initial use of controlled processes. With time and with experience in specific linguistic situations, learners begin to use language more automatically, thus leaving more attentional resources for new information that requires more control. Segalowitz (2003) points out that the picture in reality is not so clear cut. Grammatical learning is not simply a matter of moving from the knowledge of examples to automatic use based on rules; nor does it move from the effortful use of rules to automatic retrieval of chunks stored in memory. Segalowitz and DeKeyser (2001) suggest a need to investigate these two modes together (rule-based learning and exemplar-based learning) in order to understand how learners put information together to produce language in a way that native speakers do; that is, fast, effortless, and unconscious.

We mentioned above that the role of attention (see section 8.6.1) is intimately connected to automaticity in that when information use (e.g., in production or in reading, or in going to the net in tennis) is automatic, there is less attention paid to each action along the way. Consider Table 8.2 from McLaughlin, Rossman, and McLeod (1983). Here we have a sketch of different types of processing information depending on two variables: degree of control and degree of attention.

There are various ways in which learners can "attack" the process of learning a second language, depending in large part on where they focus attention. Cell A reflects a learner who focuses attention on formal properties of learning in a controlled way. This would most likely be the type of learner who would come out of a formal classroom learning experience. Cell C reflects a learner in a situation in which the use of the language is not automatic, but in which the use of the language does not necessitate explicit attention. Cells B and D reflect automatic, routinized language use. In Cell B, however, task demands, such as a formal test, might necessitate a learner's attention, whereas Cell D reflects the normal situation of language use by native speakers and by fluent non-native speakers. Segalowitz (2003) describes the interaction as follows:

As various component mental activities become practiced,

Table 8.2 Possible second language performance as a function of information-processing procedures and attention to formal properties of language

Attention to formal properties of language	Information processing	
	Controlled	Automatic
Focal	(Cell A) Performance based on formal rule learning	(Cell B) Performance in a test situation
Peripheral	(Cell C) Performance based on implicit learning or analogic learning	(Cell D) Performance in communication situations

Source: From "Second language learning: an information-processing perspective" by B. McLaughlin, T. Rossman, and B. McLeod, 1983, *Language Learning, 33,* 135–158 by Research Club in Language Learning. Reprinted by permission.

their time of operation will speed up, and less of the total time of performance will be devoted to those particular mental operations. Mechanisms that were formerly rate-determining because they were quite slow may, after training, no longer be so because they operate so quickly that other, slower mechanisms become the rate-determining components by default. The now fast mechanisms may operate so rapidly that the remaining slower processes may not be able to interfere with their operation. The products of these now fast mental operations may no longer be available for verbal report and hence not experienced as being consciously executed, etc. In this sense, they have become automatic.

(pp. 386–387)

The second concept of import within the framework of information processing is that of restructuring, which takes place when *qualitative* changes occur in a learner's internal representation of the second language or in the change in the use of procedures—generally from inefficient to efficient. In terms of child language acquisition, McLaughlin described restructuring in the following way: "Restructuring is characterized by discontinuous, or qualitative change as the child moves from stage to stage in development. Each new stage constitutes a new internal organization and not merely the addition of new structural elements" (1990a, p. 117).

To return to our kaleidoscope analogy, if a new colored element were inserted into the system, with no other changes, restructuring would not have taken place. If, on the other hand, a new element were added, disturbing the existing system and thereby necessitating reorganization, restructuring would have taken place. Table 8.3 presents data from R. Ellis (1985a) to illustrate this.

At Time 1 only one form, *no*, is used. At Time 2, a new form, *don't*, has entered this learner's system. Now *no* and *don't* are being used in

Table 8.3 Evidence of restructuring

Time 1	Time 2	Time 3	Time 4
I am no go.	I am no go.	I am no go.	I am no go.
No look.	No look.	Don't look.	Don't go.
I am no run.	I am don't run.	I am don't run.	I am no run.
No run.	Don't run.	Don't run.	Don't run.

Source: From *Understanding Second Language Acquisition*, by R. Ellis, 1985a. Oxford: Oxford University Press. Reprinted by permission of Oxford University Press.

apparent free variation in both indicative and imperative forms. By Time 3, this learner has created a system in which there are the beginnings of a one-to-one correspondence between form and function. *Don't* is now the only form used for imperatives, whereas for indicatives both forms remain. Thus, restructuring takes place at Time 3, when the learner has begun to sort out the form/function relationship. The learner in this case is reorganizing and reshuffling her L2 knowledge until she has appropriately sorted out form/function relations (if that stage is ever reached).

Lightbown (1985, p. 177) provides the following rationale for restructuring:

> [Restructuring] occurs because language is a complex hierarchical system whose components interact in nonlinear ways. Seen in these terms, an increase in error rate in one area may reflect an increase in complexity or accuracy in another, followed by over-generalization of a newly acquired structure, or simply by a sort of overload of complexity which forces a restructuring, or at least a simplification, in another part of the system.

A final example of restructuring comes from the work of Ard and Gass (1987), who examined the interaction of syntax and the lexicon. They gave two groups of learners, characterized as high and low pro-ficiency, a grammaticality judgment task containing four sentence types. Results showed that there was less differentiation among lexical items in the lower proficiency group than in the higher proficiency group. Dif-ferent lexical items in the same syntactic frame did not have a great effect on the less proficient learners' judgments of English sentences. Thus, sentences such as 8-15 and 8-16 were more likely to be responded to in a like manner by the lower level learners than by the more proficient learners.

(8-15) The judge told the lawyer his decision.
(8-16) *The judge informed the lawyer his decision.

One can interpret these findings to mean that low proficiency learners interpret sentences syntactically, ignoring semantic and lexical aspects of sentences. At higher levels, greater lexical and semantic differentiation was noted. What this research suggests is that learners may begin with a given rule that covers all cases of what they perceive to be a particular structural type. A second step occurs when an additional rule becomes available to them. They now have two choices available. Either they can alternate the rules (as in the early stages of the negative forms *do* and *don't*, discussed earlier) or they can alter the first and possibly the second of these rules until the correct distribution and patterning are established. Thus, when, as a function of proficiency, additional syntactic patterns become available to learners, destabilization occurs. And it is destabilization that is at the base of language change.

McLaughlin and Heredia (1996) relate restructuring, or representational changes, to a novice–expert continuum, whereby researchers study changes that take place when a beginner at some skill gains greater expertise. In their summary, they note that "experts restructure the elements of a learning task into abstract schemata that are not available to novices, who focus principally on surface elements of a task. Thus, experts replace complex subelements with schemata that allow more abstract processing" (p. 217).

In relating this to language learning, one can think of chunk learning whereby learners have fixed phrases, but may not have unpackaged these phrases into anything meaningful. Rather, the string of sounds is a chunk with a holistic meaning. As she or he becomes more proficient, the component parts become clear. In these situations, when this occurs, a learner's speech may on the surface appear simpler, but may in reality represent greater syntactic sophistication. Thus, the learner has moved from formulaic speech to speech that entails an understanding of structure. To put this somewhat differently, the learner is moving from exemplar-based learning to a stage in which representations are more rule-based.

8.3.2.2 U-shaped learning

Destabilization, as discussed above, is a consequence of restructuring and often results in what are known as U-shaped patterns.[4] U-shaped patterns reflect three stages of linguistic use. In the earliest stage, a learner produces some linguistic form that conforms to target-like norms (i.e., is error-free). At Stage 2, a learner appears to lose what he or she knew at Stage 1. The linguistic behavior at Stage 2 deviates from TL norms. Stage 3 looks just like Stage 1 in that there is again correct TL usage. This is illustrated in Figure 8.1.

Lightbown (1983) presented data from French learners of English in a classroom context. She examined the use of the -ing form in English among sixth, seventh, and eighth grade learners. Sentence 8-17 was a typical Grade 6 utterance when describing a picture.

(8-17) He is taking a cake.

By Grade 7, 8-18 was a typical response to the same picture.

(8-18) He take a cake.

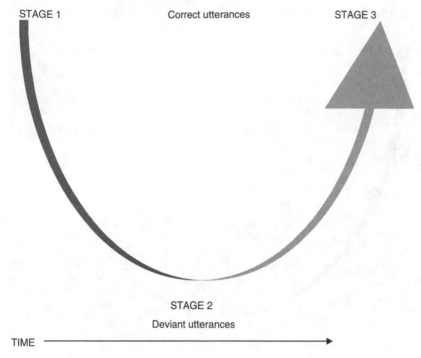

STAGE 1   Correct utterances   STAGE 3

STAGE 2

Deviant utterances

TIME

Figure 8.1 Schema of U-shaped behavior.

How can we account for an apparent decrease in knowledge? Light-bown hypothesized that initially these students were presented only with the progressive form. With nothing else in English to compare it to, they equated it with the simple present of French. That is, in the absence of any other verb form, there was no way of determining what the limits were of the present progressive. In fact, with no other comparable verb form in their system, learners overextended the use of the progressive into contexts in which the simple present would have been appropriate. When the simple present was introduced, learners not only had to learn this new form, but they also had to readjust their information about the present progressive, redefining its limits. Evidence of the confusion and subsequent readjustment and restructuring of the progressive was seen in the decline in both use and accuracy. It will take some time before these learners eventually restructure their L2 knowledge appropriately and are able to use both the progressive and the simple present in target-like ways. Thus, given these data, a U-shaped curve results (assuming eventual target-like knowledge), as in Figure 8.2.

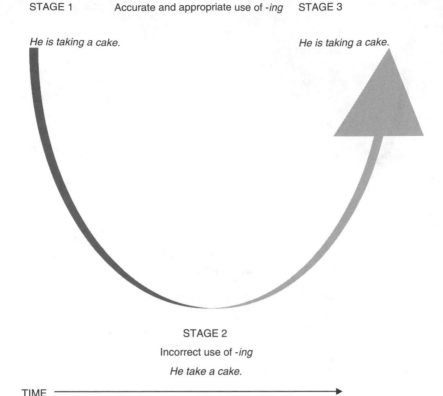

STAGE 1   Accurate and appropriate use of -*ing*   STAGE 3

He is taking a cake.   *He is taking a cake.*

STAGE 2

Incorrect use of -*ing*

He take a cake.

TIME

Figure 8.2 Schema of U-shaped behavior: use of -*ing*.

8.3.3 Input Processing

This area of research deals with how learners comprehend utterances and, particularly, how they assign form–meaning relationships. Different researchers have looked at various aspects of this issue.

VanPatten in work over the past two decades has proposed a model which he labels *Input Processing* (see, for example, VanPatten 2007a, 2007b). There are two main principles and numerous corollaries.

Principles of L2 Input Processing

1   *The Primacy of Meaning Principle*: Learners process input for meaning before they process it for form.

a   The Primacy of Content Words Principle: Learners process content words in the input before anything else.

b   The Lexical Preference Principle: Learners will tend to rely on lexical items as opposed to grammatical form to get meaning when both encode the same semantic information.

c   The Preference for Nonredundancy Principle: Learners are more likely to process nonredundant meaningful grammatical forms before they process redundant meaningful forms.

d   The Meaning Before Nonmeaning Principle: Learners are more likely to process meaningful grammatical forms before non-meaningful forms irrespective of redundancy.

e   The Availability of Resources Principle: For learners to process either redundant meaningful grammatical forms or nonmeaning-ful forms, the processing of overall sentential meaning must not drain available processing resources.

f   The Sentence Location Principle: Learners tend to process items in sentence-initial position before those in final position and those in medial position.

2   *The First Noun Principle*: Learners tend to assign subject or agent status to the first (pro)noun they encounter in a sentence.

a   The Lexical Semantics Principle: Lexical semantics of verbs may attenuate learners' reliance on the first noun principle.

b   The Event Probabilities Principle: Event probabilities may attenuate learners' reliance on the first noun principle.

c   The Contextual Constraint Principle: Learners may rely less on the first noun principle if preceding context constrains the possible interpretation of the following clause or sentence.

(2007b, pp. 268–269)

These principles and their corollaries are an attempt to account for how processing takes place—from meaning (Principle 1) to form (Principle 2). Within each principle are corollaries which attempt to account for why certain parts of an utterance/sentence take center stage rather than others (content words, lexical items before forms, nonredundant information, etc.) and why meaning might override form (e.g., lexical semantics, real-world knowledge/events, and context). VanPatten and Keating (2007) (discussed in chapter 5) found that L2 processing begins with a universal principle (in that study they investigated the Lexical Preference Principle—1b above) with "L2 specific parsing routines kick[ing] in at some point" (p. 36).

There are other approaches to the processing of input as well. For example, O'Grady (2003) suggests that "the computational system may be too underpowered to reliably execute the more demanding tasks involved in natural language processing . . . Whereas children routinely overcome this deficit, its effects in the case of adults may be longer lasting, con-tributing to the pattern of partial attainment that is typical of second language learning" (p. 53). He also suggests (p. 58) that second language learning is a venue for observing "the acquisition device functioning under conditions of duress—either because of extreme limitations on the available input (as in the case of classroom learning) or because one or more of its component modules have been compromised, or both." He proposes that structural complexity is a source of processing difficulty. Research to support this view is seen in work by O'Grady, Lee, and Choo (2003), who found that in comprehending relative clauses, subject relative clauses were easier than direct object relative clauses (73.2% versus 22.7%) for their group of learners of Korean, suggesting structural complexity as a source of the difficulty. Jeon and Kim (2007) find support for the difference in relative clause types, although their study raises additional questions regarding relative clause structures in Korean as well as issues of animacy. The issue of computational complexity is supported by these data, as it is in other data based on relative clause production.

Carroll (2001) proposes the Autonomous Induction theory, which attributes difficulties in learning a second language to parsing problems. Acquisition moves forward when there is a failure in the parsing of utterances. Learning is an inductive process in this view (learning takes place by being presented with examples—input—and making generalizations from those examples) and learning is triggered by a failure to process incoming stimuli. Parsing involves a categorization of the stream of sounds that one hears into some meaningful units (e.g., lexical, functional, syntactic). When one hears an L2 utterance, one has to assign appropriate relationships, that is, one has to parse the elements into something that makes sense. Thus, let's assume a complex sentence such as *That's the cat whom the dog bit*. Let's further assume that a learner hears this and parses it as if it were *That's the cat who bit the dog*, given that the latter is an "easier" relative clause structure. Finally, let's assume that the learner knows from prior events that it was the dog who had done the biting. It is at this juncture that there is a signal to the parser that there needs to be an adjustment. This is not to say that there will always be a positive result and that the parsing mechanism will be adjusted; it is to say that this is the mechanism by which such adjustments may take place. As Carroll (2007, p. 161) puts it, the language acquisition device "is triggered when the parsing system fails."

Clahsen and Felser (2006) consider processing mechanisms of child L1 learners and adult L2 learners (as well as adult native speakers). They found different emphases in terms of parsing. For children learning their L1 and adult native speakers, syntax-based principles dominate. Children do not make use of lexical-semantic or referential information to the same degree as adults. This, they suggest, may be due to different abilities at lexical retrieval and different working memory capacities. Adult L2 learners were found to rely less on syntactic information and more on lexical-semantic and pragmatic information (see discussion earlier in this chapter regarding the Competition Model). They proposed the *Shallow Structure Hypothesis* "according to which the sentential representations adult L2 learners compute for comprehension contain less syntactic detail than those of native speakers" (p. 35).[5]

In sum, all of these approaches deal with the important role that the processing of language input plays, although the emphases are slightly different, with VanPatten's main concern being on establishing form–meaning connections, O'Grady's emphasis on computational complexity, Carroll's on the parser, and Clahsen and Felser on the different parts of grammar used in comprehension/processing.

8.4 Knowledge types

In this section, we approach the topic of knowledge types by assuming that second language acquisition is like other types of cognitive learning, and the emphasis is on describing in terms of general cognition how linguistic knowledge is acquired and organized in the brain.

There are a number of ways in which one can represent second language knowledge. Some have already been mentioned in previous sections but will be dealt with in greater detail here. The first distinction we deal with is the acquisition–learning distinction.

8.4.1 Acquisition–Learning

The Monitor Model, first described by Krashen in the 1970s, has had a long and lingering effect on the field. There are five basic hypotheses in this model: (a) the Acquisition–Learning Hypothesis, (b) the Natural Order Hypothesis (see chapter 11), (c) the Monitor Hypothesis (to be discussed below), (d) the Input Hypothesis (see chapter 10), and (e) the Affective Filter Hypothesis (see chapter 12).

Krashen (1982) assumed that second language learners have two independent means of developing knowledge of a second language—one way is through what he called *acquisition* and the other through *learning*.

> *acquisition* [is] a process similar, if not identical to the way children develop ability in their first language. Language acquisition is a subconscious process; language acquirers are not usually aware of the fact that they are acquiring language, but are only aware of the fact that they are using the language for communication. The result of language acquisition, acquired competence, is also subconscious. We are generally not consciously aware of the rules of the languages we have acquired. Instead, we have a "feel" for correctness. Grammatical sentences "sound" right, or "feel" right, and errors feel wrong, even if we do not consciously

know what rule was violated . . . In nontechnical terms, acquisition is "picking up" a language.

The second way to develop competence in a second language is by language learning. We will use the term "learning" henceforth to refer to conscious knowledge of a second language, knowing the rules, being aware of them, and being able to talk about them. In nontechnical terms, learning is "knowing about" a language, known to most people as "grammar", or "rules". Some synonyms include formal knowledge of a language or explicit learning.

(Krashen, 1982, p. 10)

In Krashen's view, not only does language development take place in two different ways, but learners also use the language developed through these two systems for different purposes. Thus, the knowledge acquired (in the nontechnical use of the term) through these means remains internalized differently. What is more, knowledge learned through one means (e.g., learning) cannot be internalized as knowledge of the other kind (e.g., acquisition).

How are these two knowledge types used differently? The acquired system is used to produce language. The acquisition system generates utterances because, in producing language, learners focus on meaning, *not* on form. The learned system serves as an "inspector" of the acquired system. It checks to ensure the correctness of the utterance against the knowledge in the learned system.

8.4.2 Declarative/procedural

Another distinction frequent in the literature is the difference between declarative and procedural knowledge or sometimes declarative and procedural memory. Declarative knowledge is concerned with knowledge *about* something and declarative memory underlies learning and storage of facts (e.g., Newfoundland dogs are generally black). With regard to language, declarative knowledge relates to such aspects of language as word knowledge (collocation, pronunciation, meaning). In general, this information is relatively accessible to conscious awareness; that is, we can retrieve that information when called upon to do so. Procedural knowledge or procedural memory relates to motor and cognitive skills that involve sequencing information (e.g., playing tennis, producing language). Using language (e.g., stringing words together to form and interpret sentences) is thought to involve procedural knowledge and, unlike declarative knowledge, is relatively inaccessible. The distinction between these two has important consequences for learning because it is thought that, with age, the ability to use procedural knowledge to learn new operations decreases and older second language learners need to rely more on declarative information in learning. O'Grady (2006) uses this to account for the difficulty in learning past tense in English by second language learners. Using data from Goldschneider and DeKeyser (2005, p. 72) that shows the difficulty involved in English past tense, O'Grady suggests that the difficulty has to do not with the relatively transparent phenomenon of adding -ed to a verb that refers to a past event but with the difficulty in computing aspect (see chapter 7) because tense depends on the prior determination of aspect.[6] It is this computation that makes past tense acquisition difficult for learners.

8.4.3 Implicit/explicit

Another distinction frequently made is between implicit and explicit knowledge, a distinction which has its roots in psychology. Explicit and implicit knowledge are not unrelated to the distinction discussed in the previous section. Declarative memory can be seen as forming the basis of explicit knowledge and procedural knowledge underlies implicit knowledge. Where there is a difference, however, is that in the case of explicit versus implicit knowledge, awareness is a key issue (see DeKeyser, 2003; Doughty, 2003; N. Ellis, 2005; R. Ellis, 2005; Isemonger, 2007; R. Ellis and Loewen, 2007). Even though there may be a general relationship between declarative/procedural and explicit/implicit, the relationship cannot be considered rigid since there may be instances when declarative memory contains information that is not explicit.

A related distinction is between implicit and explicit learning. The latter, as Hulstijn (2005) notes, "is input processing with the conscious intention to find out whether the input information contains regularities and, if so, to work out the concepts and rules with which these regularities can be captured" (p. 131). On the other hand, implicit learning "is input processing without such an intention" (p. 131). Ellis defines the concept of implicit learning without reference to input processing. In his words, implicit learning is "acquisition of knowledge about the underlying structure of a complex stimulus environment by a process which takes place naturally, simply and without conscious operations" (N. Ellis, 1994, p. 1). Explicit learning "is a more conscious operation where the individual makes and tests hypotheses in a search for structure" (N. Ellis, 1994, p. 1). Both types of knowledge can be used in generating utterances by native and nonnative speakers, although native speakers presumably rely much less on explicit knowledge than on implicit knowledge. The use of explicit knowledge may be relegated to particular difficulties, such as the lie–lay distinction in English. Viewing knowledge as a continuum, it is easier to conceptualize explicit knowledge becoming implicit (through practice, exposure, drills, etc.) and vice versa.

8.4.4 Representation and control

Bialystok and Sharwood Smith (1985) noted that there are two aspects of importance in describing knowledge of a language: knowledge representation (the level of analysis and mental organization of linguistic information) and control over that knowledge (the speed and efficiency with which that information can be accessed). They made four points about the nature of learners' grammatical knowledge and how that knowledge differs from native speaker knowledge in a number of ways.

1   Extent of analysis in the grammar.
2   Greater analytic sophistication does not necessarily entail greater approximation to the target language.
3   Reanalysis does not necessarily entail greater complexity (depth of analysis).
4   Greater analysis does not necessarily entail greater conscious awareness.

We elaborate on points 2 to 4 below.

With regard to point 2, increasing ability to analyze target language structures does not necessarily entail correctness. What is meant by increased analysis? In many instances, learners use what are referred to as *prefabricated patterns* or language "chunks." Prefabricated patterns are those bits of language for which there has been no internal analysis. "[They] enable learners to express functions which they are yet unable to construct from their linguistic system, simply storing them in a sense like larger lexical items . . . It might be important that the learner be able to express a wide range of functions from the beginning, and this need is met by prefabricated patterns. As the learner's system of linguistic rules develops over time, the externally consistent prefabricated patterns become assimilated into the internal structure" (Hakuta, 1976b, p. 333).

For example, consider the data in 8-19 to 8-22 from a child second language speaker (Wong-Fillmore, 1976):

(8-19) Lookit, like that.
(8-20) Looky, chicken.
(8-21) Lookit gas.
(8-22) Lookit four.

Presumably, this child uses the phrase *lookit* or *looky* to get the attention of another individual and has not understood that *lookit* is made up of the two words *look at*.[7] At a later point in time, however, this child produces the following:

(8-23) Get it, Carlos.

244

(8-24) Get it!
(8-25) Stop it!

One might speculate that the child at this point reanalyzed *lookit* as being comprised of *look* and *it*, thus allowing him to extend his second language use to novel environments, such as those seen in 8-23 to 8-25. There is no evidence from these data that the correct target analysis of *look* and *at* was ever reached by this child, although there were different stages of analysis that the child went through.

Point 3 above addresses the issue of reanalysis. Reanalysis does not necessarily mean that the learner is moving in a target language direction, nor that the analysis has become any more complex. Recall the examples given in chapter 4 in which a learner first produces sentences such as the following:

(8-26) I wanted him to come.
(8-27) I persuaded him to come.

Later, the learner produces:

(8-28) I enjoyed talking to my teacher.
(8-29) I stopped sending packages to my friend.

In Stage 1 the learner only produces infinitival complements; in Stage 2 the learner only produces gerundive complements. There has been a reanalysis of the English complement system, although the second stage is no closer to the English system than the first stage, nor can it be considered any more complex than the first stage. In fact, in terms of sophistication, Stage 2 could be considered less complex than Stage 1 because in Stage 1 the learner has used an object and, in the case of pronouns, has to assign case to it.

Point 4 addresses conscious awareness. The use of a system (correct or incorrect vis-à-vis TL norms) is not dependent on a learner's conscious awareness of the system or on his or her ability to articulate what the system is. What increased analysis does is allow the learner to make greater use of the system and not necessarily increase the learner's conscious awareness of that system. Thus, determining the component parts of a chunked phrase allows the learner to use those component parts in other linguistic contexts. Increased awareness may or may not come as a result.

8.5 Interface of knowledge types

We have discussed various ways of representing knowledge. In this section, we outline three ways to conceptualize the interface between knowledge types.

8.5.1 No interface

This position is best represented by Krashen's acquisition–learning distinction. It is clear that learners have different ways of internalizing information. The question, however, is whether or not learners develop two independent systems. Krashen stated explicitly that what has been learned cannot become part of the acquired system. However, if evidence of an acquired system is fluent, unconscious speech, then it is counterintuitive to hypothesize that nothing learned in a formal situation can ever be a candidate for this kind of use. The counterargument would consist of saying that information about a particular grammatical structure, for example, would be "housed" in two separate linguistic systems; if nothing else, this is clearly an inefficient way for the brain to cope with different kinds of information.

A second objection to the non-interface between acquisition and learning comes from consideration of those learners who learn language only in a formal setting. Let's further specify those learners whose instruction is in the NL as opposed to the target language. By Krashen's definition we would expect that they only have a learned system, as there is no way of "picking up" information for their acquired system. Recall that speaking is initiated through the acquired system. In such instances, how would learners ever generate utterances? Without an acquired system, there would be no initiation of L2 production.

A third objection to the distinction drawn within this framework has to do with falsifiability. Krashen provided no evidence that learning and acquisition are indeed two separate systems, a proposal that, at best, is counterintuitive; nor has he provided a means for determining whether they are or are not separate. Lack of specific criteria leaves one with no means of evaluating the claims. The hypothesis remains an interesting one, but nothing more than that.

8.5.2 Weak interface

N. Ellis (2005, 2007) argues for a relationship between explicit knowledge and implicit knowledge. Essentially he argues that they are "dissociable but cooperative" (2005, p. 305). His argument is more subtle than a view which states that explicit knowledge gets turned into or is converted into implicit knowledge. Both can work cooperatively in any given instance.

246

He provides the example of walking—we only think about walking when something goes awry, as when we stumble. At that point, we can call in a system of explicit knowledge at those moments when implicit knowledge fails us. This is also the case in normal communication. As fluent native speakers, we rarely think about our speaking except when we stumble (e.g., when we can't find the right word). In his view conscious and unconscious processes are involved at all steps of the way in any cognitive task, language being no exception.

8.5.3 Strong interface

DeKeyser (1997) argues that second language learning is like other forms of learning, both cognitive and psychomotor. The basic argument is, that regardless of what one is learning (e.g., language or tennis), learning progresses from knowledge *that* (declarative) relating to some skill or behavior to knowledge *how* (procedural) and finally to automatization of procedural knowledge. The first type of knowledge can be obtained through observation and analysis or through verbal instruction (or both). The next step is to move from the stage of conceptualization (declarative knowledge) to using that knowledge (procedural knowledge); in other words, to some sort of performance (producing language, understanding language, swinging a tennis racket). But this is only the beginning, for procedural knowledge needs to become fast and without deliberation. Practice (whether time spent in training, such as Roger Federer playing tennis, or time spent using an L2 in a foreign country, such as is the case for language learners) is necessary to ensure that particular behaviors are quick, and with diminished attention paid to the particular task (in the case of language learners, producing and/or understanding language).

DeKeyser (1997) presented data from learners of an artificial language. Participants were presented with four rules. One group received comprehension practice for two rules and production practice for the other two. A second group received production practice for the two rules that the first group had received comprehension practice on and comprehension practice for the two rules that the first group had received production practice on. A third group had an equal amount of production and comprehension practice for all rules. Through reduced error rates and faster reaction times for those rules that they had practiced, participants showed movement from declarative knowledge to proceduralization to automaticity (a slower process than proceduralization). This suggests that declarative knowledge (rule presentation, in this case) followed by practice led to greater proceduralization and automaticity; that is, more robust knowledge. What was interesting was that there was a lack of evidence of skill transfer (from production to comprehension and vice versa), suggesting the skill-specificity of second language knowledge. This is further supported in work by de Jong (2005), whose work with learners of Spanish showed that practice in aural comprehension yielded greater speed in comprehension, but not in a reduced number of production errors.

8.6 Psycholinguistic constructs

8.6.1 Attention

According to the *American Heritage Dictionary*, attention refers to "the concentration of the mental powers upon an object." It has come to be one of the most important constructs in second language research. In fact, Schmidt (2001) claims that it "appears necessary for understanding nearly every aspect of second and foreign language learning" (p. 6). There are a number of approaches to attention and particularly to its relationship to awareness. One of the early treatments of attention in the SLA literature came from Tomlin and Villa (1994). They proposed three components to attention: alertness (readiness to receive incoming stimuli), orientation (direction of resources to stimulus), and detection (registration of stimulus). Detection is the major component and is what drives learning. The other two are in a sense support, since they contribute to the likelihood that detection will occur. In this model, detection does not entail awareness and, consequently, learning can take place without awareness.

Schmidt (1990, 1993a, 1994, 1995, 2001) proposed the *noticing hypothesis*. Awareness (through attention) is necessary for noticing which in turn is essential for learning. Underlying this hypothesis is the idea of noticing a gap. Schmidt and Frota (1986) suggested that "a second language learner will begin to acquire the target like form if and only if it is present in comprehended input and 'noticed' in the normal sense of the word, that is consciously" (p. 311). The idea presented here is that learning requires that a learner be actively involved or attending to L2 forms in order for learning to take place. In chapter 10, we return to some of these concepts—in particular, the concept of output, or using the language as a way of recognizing difficulty and subsequently noticing L2 forms.

Robinson (1995, 1996) utilizes both the Tomlin and Villa and Schmidt models in his account of attention. He claims that noticing is just a later stage in the model and that detection is prior to it, thereby combining both approaches into an expanded model.

Yet another approach to the role of attention is detailed in chapter 14 and is based on Gass's (1988a) integrated model of second language acquisition. She adds "apperceived input" into the mix, which is a prior stage to noticing, more akin to Tomlin and Villa's stage of detection, but there is not a level of awareness at this point. This model will be discussed in chapter 14.

There have been a number of studies considering the role of attention and awareness in language learning. Most studies show a connection between awareness and learning. For example, in a series of studies Leow and his colleagues (Leow, 1997, 2000, 2001; Rosa and Leow, 2004; Rosa and O'Neill, 1999) showed, through verbal report data during a task, that there was an association between awareness of a form and the learning of that form. They were also able to show that levels of awareness were an important part in understanding when learning took place. They found that awareness at the level of noticing was less important than awareness at the level of understanding.

Williams (2004), on the other hand, found that there could be learning without awareness. In a carefully designed study of an artificial microlanguage, participants first learned the meanings of nouns and determiners in this language. They then listened to a series of words and then had to repeat the word out loud, state if the referent of the noun was animate or inanimate, and translate the word into English. There were determiners that designated whether the nouns were animate or inanimate. There was a test phase following this treatment phase in which participants were given an English phrase and had to choose between two translations. One phrase had the correct determiner (animate or inanimate) and noun, and the other had the incorrect determiner and noun. The next phase was to determine if the learners were aware of the animacy relationship; if they were, they did not continue with the study. Only those who were not aware of the determiner/noun animacy relationship continued. These learners performed better than chance on a later test, suggesting that they were able to learn even though there had not been an indication of awareness.

In another study, Gass, Svetics, and Lemelin (2003) considered attention from the perspective of its differential role on different parts of the grammar (lexicon, morphosyntax, syntax). Learners were placed into a focused attention group or into a nonfocused attention group. They found that learning occurred in both conditions, suggesting that learning without attention might indeed be possible (although clearly learners in the nonfocused attention group might have figured out the scope of the study and were able to attend to the object of inquiry). Focused attention was most beneficial for syntax and least for the lexicon. In addition, there was a diminished effect for proficiency, with focused attention having a greater effect in early stages of learning.

Attention and memory are closely aligned in many accounts of second language learning. We turn next to this latter area of research.

8.6.2 Working memory

Over the past decade, there has been significant interest in the psychological construct of working memory in SLA research. In brief, working memory refers to the structures and processes that humans use to store and manipulate information. The term that preceded working memory was most often short-term memory. The major difference is that working memory focuses on the manipulation of information rather than just the storage of information, as was the case with short-term memory. Miyake and Shah (1999) provide a useful definition: "working memory is those mechanisms or processes that are involved in the control, regulation, and active maintenance of task-relevant information in the service of complex cognition, including novel as well as familiar, skilled tasks" (p. 450).

There are a number of models of working memory in the psychology literature. For example, a common one is the Baddeley and Hitch model (1974), which proposes two slave systems which are responsible for system maintenance (see also Baddeley, 2003a, 2003b). One system is known as the articulatory loop and the other as the visuo-spatial sketch pad. The articulatory loop contains phonological information which is maintained by articulating the phonological information. For example, when you want to remember a phone number and you do not have pen and paper to write it down, you will repeat the number over and over until you can get to a phone to dial the number or can find pen and paper to write it down. The second slave system is the visuo-spatial sketch pad, which, as its name implies, stores visual and spatial information.

In addition to the two slave systems is the central executive, which is the overall supervisor and coordinator of information. The central executive focuses attention on some things, inhibits others, and is the overall coordinator when more than one task needs to be done at a time. Baddeley (2000) extended this model to include a fourth component, an episodic buffer, which is the holder of information that includes and integrates other information (e.g., visual, semantic, phonological). For example, consider the situation in which someone says something to you but you are only half paying attention. If the speaker prods you to respond, you can probably recall the words uttered, but this memory trace will only last for a short period of time.

A slightly different conceptualization of working memory comes from Conway, Kane, Bunting, Hambrick, Wilhelm, and Engle (2005). They see working memory as "a multicomponent system responsible for active maintenance of information in the face of ongoing processing and/or distraction" (p. 770). One's ability to maintain information is the result of domain-specific storage (with processes of rehearsal) and "domain-general executive attention" (p. 770). They provide the following exemplification of how this might work in novice and experienced chess players:

> [A] novice chess player will rely more on domain-general executive attention to maintain game information (e.g., recent moves or future positions) than on domain-specific skills (e.g., learned strategies and position patterns). In contrast, an expert chess player typically will rely more on domain-specific processes and skills to maintain information. However, even the expert might need to call upon executive attention under some circumstances, such as playing the game in particularly demanding situations or under some sort of cognitive or emotional load.
>
> (pp. 770–771)

One can readily imagine how this might apply to learning a second language, where there are numerous competing demands, some of which are emotional (speaking a second language in front of others) and some of which involve great cognitive effort.

Working memory capacity varies from individual to individual. So, the ability to juggle numerous language tasks also varies from individual to individual. This is generally referred to as working memory capacity. There are numerous ways that researchers have used to determine working memory capacity and, like all elicitation measures, there is difficulty in perfectly aligning the elicitation task with the underlying construct. It is important to note that defining the construct and measuring it are not the same. Most measures use a dual-task format combining some memory measure with a processing memory. Common among these is the reading span task (cf. Daneman and Carpenter, 1980). In these tasks, participants may read a number of sentences and are told to remember the last word of each sentence. At the end of a set of sentences (usually two to six), they are asked to write down (in order) the last word of each sentence. So that rehearsal will not take place, often they are asked to respond to the plausibility of each sentence.

In recent years, there have been a number of studies relating working memory capacity to language learning. The results are not always straightforward. Many of these use some sort of span task (listening or reading) and the question arises as to the language of the working memory task. An interesting study by Miyake and Friedman (1998) found links between L1 and L2 working memory scores, but most important for language learning is the finding that there is a relationship between L2 working memory and comprehension of syntax. Similarly Harrington and Sawyer (1992) and Osaka and Osaka (1992) found correlations between L1 and L2 working memory scores. Mackey, Philp, Egi, Fujii, and Tatsumi (2002), finding a relationship between working memory and noticing, also found a correlation between L1 and L2 working memory scores.

Service, Simola, Metsaenheimo, and Maury (2002) and Gass, Roots, and Lee (2006) found that the correlations between L1 and L2 working memory depended on proficiency. In the Gass et al. study, there was a significantly weaker correlation with lower proficiency learners than with more advanced speakers.

Not only is the language of the working memory task at issue, but also there is a need to consider the closeness of the languages in question. For example, van den Noort, Bosch, and Hugdahl (2006) suggest that the interaction between working memory capacity and language proficiency may be language-specific.

Some studies have used simple verbal working memory measures (such as a digit-span task) and therefore only tap the storage component, whereas other studies use more complex measures that tap both storage and processing, such as a reading or listening span task. Here again, there is not uniformity as to differences in L1 and L2 capacities. For example, Ardilla, Rosselli, Ostrosky-Solis, Marcos, Granda, and Soto (2000) used a digit-span task with bilingual Spanish–English speakers. There were differences between the languages that they were tested in, finding differences between early and late bilingual (Ardilla, 2003).

Other studies have considered phonological short-term memory and the relationship of this measure to L2 learning. These measures relate to the articulatory/phonological loop subsystem of Baddeley's model. Generally, this refers to the ability to hear phonological input and to repeat it. The most common means of eliciting data to reflect this capacity is the nonword pairs recall test, although known words have also been used. In this test, participants hear a nonword stimulus (phonologically possible in the language of administration), and after a pause are asked to repeat the string of sounds.

Phonological short-term memory capacity has been linked to a number of areas of second language learning, most specifically vocabulary and syntax. For example, Papagno and Vallar (1992) compared phonological short-term memory capacity with the ability to repeat known and novel words, and found a relationship between short-term memory capacity and novel words, but not known words, probably due to the fact that semantic representations were presumably already in place for the known words. Service and Craik (1993) showed a relationship between phonological short-term memory and the ease or efficiency with which new vocabulary was learned.

Service and Kohonen (1995) conducted a longitudinal study of L2 English (L1 Finnish), also noting a relationship between phonological short-term memory capacity and the acquisition of L2 vocabulary.

Not only is there an apparent relationship between the learning of vocabulary and an individual's phonological short-term memory capacity but there is also a relationship with the learning of grammar.

An important part of learning a new language is the ability to retain relevant information long enough to figure out what it means or to analyze it syntactically. It therefore stands to reason that those who have the capacity to do this to a greater extent would also be those who are more successful at learning all aspects of language.

Recent studies have supported the relationship between phonological short-term memory and the learning of grammar. For example, N. Ellis and Schmidt (1997), in a laboratory study using an artificial language, found a relationship between the phonological memory task and the learning of the grammar of this new language. (The language had SOV word order and had noun–adjective agreement, singular–plural, agreement, and transitive/intransitive marking.)

In yet another study using an artificial language, Williams and Lovatt (2003) used L1 English speakers with Italian words as an L2 (none of the participants knew Italian) and a semi-artificial language (using Italian as the base). The results showed that phonological short-term memory was related to rule learning and even to abstract aspects of grammar.

Working memory research in SLA is in its infancy. As with other constructs in SLA (e.g., competence), it is not always clear how best to measure it. Many of the differences in second language working memory research need to be understood in the context of data collection. Conway, Kane, Bunting, Hambrick, Wilhelm, and Engle (2005) provide an excellent overview of the methodology involved in reading span tasks.

8.6.3 Monitoring — *preventing the report TBL (focus on form)*

As mentioned earlier, the Monitor is a construct central to Krashen's Monitor Model. The Monitor is related to the distinction discussed above between acquisition and learning. Recall that only the acquired system is responsible for initiating speech. The learned system has a special function—to serve as a Monitor and, hence, to alter the output of the acquired system. Krashen presented a diagram of this event, as shown in Figure 8.3.

Figure 8.3 Acquisition and learning in second language production.

Source: From *Principles and Practice in Second Language Acquisition* by S. Krashen, 1982, Pergamon. Reprinted by permission of the author.

But the Monitor cannot be used at all times. There are three conditions that must be met,[8] although Krashen claimed that, whereas these are *necessary* conditions, they are not necessarily *sufficient* because the Monitor may not be activated even when all three conditions have been satisfied. The three conditions for Monitor use are as follows:

1   *Time*. Learners need time to consciously think about and use the rules available to them in their learned system.
2   *Focus on form*. Although time may be basic, one must also be focused on form. Learners must be paying attention to how they are saying something, not just to what they are saying.
3   *Know the rule*. In order to apply a rule, one has to know it. In other words, one has to have an appropriate learned system in order to apply it.

Thus, the Monitor is intended to link the acquired and learned systems in a situation of language use. The Monitor consists of learned knowledge and the only function of learned knowledge is to edit utterances. Following from this is the idea that the Monitor can only be used in production; it is useless in comprehension. How, then, do learners in a classroom setting in which only the NL is used ever comprehend the L2, as, for all intents and purposes, they have no acquired system? The following is an anecdote that describes how learned knowledge (if by that we mean conscious knowledge of rules) can be used in decoding:

> The other day while listening to the radio, I heard the announcer announce *wagunaa no kageki, kamigami no kasoware*. Knowing that *kageki* = "opera" and that *kami* = either "god" or "hair" or "paper," and knowing that there is a (fairly unproductive) rule in Japanese for pluralizing by reduplication, I concluded that *kamigami* must be the plural of *kami* "god," and that therefore *wagunaa* must be Wagner and *kasoware* must mean "twilight," and that I was in danger of hearing *Die Gotterdammerung*.
> (Gregg, 1984, pp. 82–83)

Gregg went on to report that he was using learned knowledge, not acquired knowledge, because he had never used the reduplication rule productively. As he explained, he used this rule consciously and quickly enough to turn off the radio in time not to have to listen to Wagner.

In addition to anecdotal evidence, which is clearly available to anyone who has used a second language, there are once again difficulties in terms of testability. As there are no absolute criteria for determining when the Monitor is in use and when it is not, any counterexample (such as non-Monitor use when there is a focus on form) can be countered with the argument that "there wasn't sufficient focus on form" or that mere focus on form is not a guarantee of Monitor use. In essence, with no way to determine whether it is in operation or not, there is no way to determine the validity of such strong claims. This is not to say that learners, or native speakers, do not monitor their speech, for clearly this would not be accurate. (Self-correction is the result of monitoring.) The argument is against the theoretical notion of a Monitor and its unique association with *learned* knowledge. We must thus distinguish between claiming anthropomorphic status for terms such as "The Monitor" and "The Linguistic Processor" and the psycholinguistic processes of monitoring and processing linguistic information.

8.7 Conclusion

In this chapter we have reviewed psycholinguistic approaches to the study of SLA (other topics heavily influenced by the field of psychology will be dealt with in chapter 12). We have illustrated the major concerns of such approaches, focusing on the ways in which L2 learners organize their second language knowledge, on how learners use L2 knowledge, and on how subsequent learning affects the restructured organization of L2 knowledge. But how all this obvious processing is integrated in a detailed way into the formation of interlanguage structure is far from clear. There has been little emphasis on contextual factors which add to our understanding of this puzzle. We next move to a consideration of social and contextual variables as they affect the learning and production of a second language.

Suggestions for additional reading

Implicit and Explicit Learning of Languages. Nick Ellis (Ed.). Academic Press (1994).
Rethinking Innateness: A Connectionist Perspective on Development. Jeffrey Elman, Elizabeth Bates, Mark Johnson, Annette Karmiloff-Smith, Domenico Parisi, and Kim Plunkett. MIT Press (1996).
Attention and Awareness in Foreign Language Learning. Richard Schmidt (Ed.). Second Language Teaching and Curriculum Center, University of Hawai'i at Manoa (1995).

Points for discussion

1   Consider the difference between linguistic products (i.e., the IL form) and psycholinguistic processes (the internal mechanisms used to arrive at those forms). The Competition Model claims that learners use particular cues to arrive at appropriate interpretation. How can learners come to know that the NL interpretation strategy may be an inappropriate one for the L2? Do you think that it would be easier to

go from a language like Italian, which allows for a wider range of sentence types, to one like English, which allows for a smaller set of sentence types? Or would the opposite be true?

2   Fries (1945) discussed the sentences *The man killed the bear* and *The bear killed the man*. In that discussion, he said that there is essential meaning not only in the form of words (*man/men* and *bear/bears*), but also in their arrangements. Therefore, the words *kill*, *bear*, and *man* alone do not provide all essential information for understanding the meaning of the sentence *The bear killed the man*. "There must be some method or device for pointing out the performer of the act and distinguishing him from the one upon whom the act is performed" (Fries, 1945, p. 28). How does this view differ from the one expressed by the Competition Model? Relate Fries's discussion to what you would expect Italian learners of English and English-speaking learners of Italian to *produce* in terms of word order in a second language. When would you expect communication breakdowns? What sorts of breakdowns would you expect? Would you expect production to be as much of a problem as perception? Would you expect Italian learners to use free word order in English? Why or why not? Are there other aspects of language that might help disambiguate free word order sentences in Italian?

3   The following are parts of Krashen's various hypotheses. Respond to the following:

- *Hypothesis 1*: Do you agree that because there may be a difference between learning in a classroom and acquisition outside a classroom, learners learn in two very distinct ways? A student once said: "If this is true and you have learned French in a classroom and go to France, then it won't help you." Is this a logical conclusion—that is, one that can be drawn from the distinction between acquisition and learning? Why or why not?

- *Hypothesis 2*: Do you agree that, if a learner tends to monitor his or her own form, doing so gets in the way of acquiring language? Integrate into your answer the concept of speed—that is, the idea that the monitor cannot be used at all times because of the speed of speech.

- *Hypothesis 3*: Do you agree that one acquires all forms in a second language in a particular order regardless of the input? Discuss this in terms of the three conditions of *time*, *focus on form*, and *know the rules*.

4   Consider the following data, from a beginning learner of English with Arabic as an L1 (Hanania, 1974). Data are given from four points in time.

Time 1
No (imperative)
No English ("I can't speak English")

Time 2
No (answer to question)
I can't speak English
My husband not here
Not raining

Time 3
No (answer to question)
I can't speak English
My husband not here
My husband not home
Don't touch
Don't touch it

Time 4
My husband not here
Hani not sleeping
I can't speak English
No, I can't understand
I don't know
Don't eat
No, this is . . . (answer to question)

What is the progression from the first time period to the fourth in terms of this learner's development of English negation? Give specifics about her knowledge at each time period.

There is some evidence that *can't* and *don't* are being used as unanalyzed units. What evidence can you bring to bear to support this conclusion?

Focus on Time 4. Do *can't* and *don't* still seem to be unanalyzed units? Why or why not? Has restructuring taken place?

5 The following sentences were produced by an 11-year-old Spanish-speaking child who had lived in the United States since age 7 (data provided by B. Wald, originally printed as problem 1.5 in Selinker and Gass, 1984). The intended meanings of the child's utterances (gleaned from context) are given in parentheses.

- When I do something they don't hit me. (When I do something wrong they don't hit me).

- The mother doesn't want to take him away. (His mother didn't want to take him away.)
- He doesn't hear 'cause he was already dead. (He didn't hear because he had already died.)
- He don't buy us nothing. (He never buys us anything.)
- She don't help her nothing, muy floja. (She never helps her; she's real lazy.)
- They still doesn't know 'cause they work in another country. (They hadn't found out yet because they were working in another country.)

What systematic distinction does this learner make between her use of *don't* and *doesn't*? What does this suggest about imposing TL interpretation on second language utterances?

6   In this chapter we introduced the concept of U-shaped learning. Can you think of instances in your own learning when you recognize that this is what was going on? Provide specific examples.

9

INTERLANGUAGE IN CONTEXT

9.1 Introduction

This chapter focuses on external social and contextual variables as they affect the learning and production of a second language. The basic premise of sociolinguistic-based SLA research is that second language data do not represent a static phenomenon, even at a single point in time. Many external variables (such as the specific task required of a learner, social status of the interlocutor, the relationship of the interlocutors to one another, gender differences, and so forth) affect learner production and the developing interlanguage system. The resultant effect is that learners in some instances produce different forms dependent on external variables. We begin the discussion of such variables with a consideration of interlanguage variation.

9.2 Variation

Interlanguages seem to exhibit more variability than do native languages. For example, a learner might alternate between forms to express the same language function. Examples are given in 9-1 and 9-2, in which the learner alternates between *no* and *not*.

(9-1) My husband not here.
(9-2) No English.

What is the source of this variability? In chapter 8, we discussed one source of variability with regard to the variable use of the two forms of negation, *no* and *don't*. Initially, the variation in the use of these two forms was nonsystematic. That is, the forms were used interchangeably with no apparent difference in meaning. With increased proficiency, the nonsystematic use of these forms became a source for learners' hypotheses about their use. There was a gradual establishment of a one-to-one form/function relationship. Thus, variation was the initial step in the eventual emergence of target-like usage. A similar example comes from R. Ellis (1984) in his description of an 11-year-old boy, a native speaker of Portuguese learning English. He produced the following two utterances:

(9-3) No look my card.
(9-4) Don't look my card.

During this child's first month in the United Kingdom, he produced 18 negative utterances, 17 using *no* and 1 using *don't* (9-4). In the following month, there was an increase in the number of *don'ts*, although *nos* were still more frequent. In the sixth month, negatives with *not* were most frequent. Thus, the number of *nos* decreased and the number of *don'ts* increased. In the middle of the transition period, there was considerable variation between the two forms.

Similar data are seen in the domain of phonology. Gatbonton (1978), in a cross-sectional study involving three sounds—[θ], as in *thing*; [ð], as in *soothe* or *the*; and [h], as in *behind*—found that learners begin with a single sound that is used in all linguistic environments. At a later point in time, a second sound enters the system. The second sound is then in free variation with the first. Later stages involve sorting the forms out into their appropriate environments.

Variationist perspectives on SLA (e.g., Adamson, 1988; Bayley and Preston, 1996; Preston, 1989; Tarone, 1988) focus "on the correlations of social facts and linguistic forms, the influence of linguistic forms on one another, and the place of variation within the study of language change" (Preston, 2002, p. 141). Preston (2000, 2002) makes the important connection between variationist approaches to SLA and their psycholinguistic underpinnings. In particular, he outlines three areas (levels, in his words) of interest and argues for a psycholinguistic account for each one.

In the first instance, there is a linking between sociocultural information and linguistic forms. This is illustrated in Figure 9.1 (Preston, 2000). Preston (2002) argues that "[s]peakers have two (or more) forms available in their linguistic . . . competences . . ., and another device (some sort of sociocultural) one tells them which to choose" (p. 144). This model incorporates those individuals with more than one grammar (bilinguals) to choose from, as illustrated in Figure 9.1. A choice of one form or another may be based on a set of probabilistic weights that are part of each occurrence.

There is a second area to Preston's model, and that is the variation due to linguistic as opposed to social factors. In fact, Preston points out that linguistic variation is generally stronger than choices made on the basis of sociocultural factors. Figure 9.2 illustrates the inclusion of linguistic information into Preston's model.

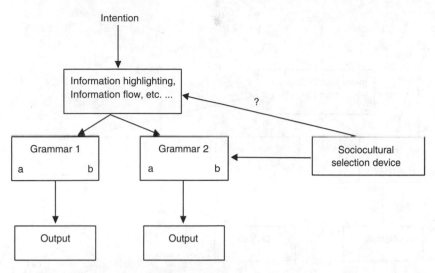

Figure 9.1 A Level I psycholinguistic model of interlanguage variation (Preston, 2000). Reprinted by permission.

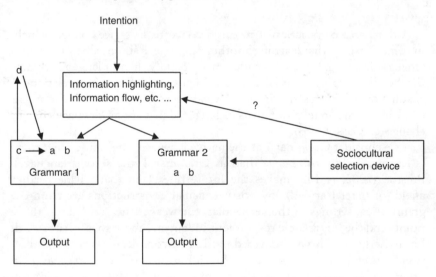

Figure 9.2 A Level II psycholinguistic model (Preston, 2000). Reprinted by permission.

This model incorporates linguistic influence (looking at only one of the grammars of a bilingual speaker). In this instance, there are two modes of influence. One is a "linguistic fact" (c) which influences the selection of a or b. A second possibility is that this "linguistic fact" (c) is influenced by something outside the grammar (d) which could be nonlinguistic (such as information status). Both are presumed to be possible.

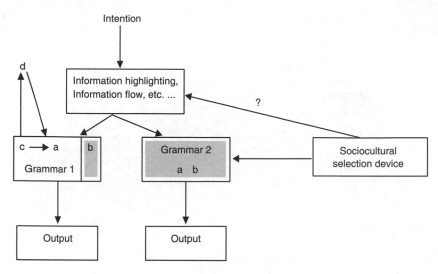

Figure 9.3 A Level III psycholinguistic model (Preston, 2000). Reprinted by permission.

A third area of variationist research concerns language change, which, in some sense, is what learning another language is about, albeit in second language learning, it happens much more rapidly than in language change in the more traditional sense.[1] In Figure 9.3, Preston incorporates shading, which represents areas of "weakness" in a grammar. One might think about this in terms of areas of language that are more susceptible to change (cf. Gass, 1988a).

If we consider Grammar 1 as the native language, one can see that there is less possibility for change than in Grammar 2 (the second language). Preston (2002, p. 150) makes the interesting claim that, "[t]he further afield (or 'later learned') any postvernacular constructions are from the grammatical settings of the vernacular, the weaker the grammar at those points and the less reliable respondent judgments about that territory will be" (exactly as we have discovered in SLA "incompleteness" or "fossilization" studies, e.g., Coppieters, 1987; Johnson and Newport, 1989). In other words, one expects more variability in judgments (which Preston claims to reflect performance) in learner languages than in native languages. In the next sections we refer to studies that deal with these areas of influence on form.

9.3 Systematic variation

There is another type of variation that may occur from the early stages—systematic variation. Systematic variation is evidenced when two or more sounds/grammatical forms vary contextually. Some variation is linguistically based; other is sociolinguistically determined. We deal first with linguistically based variation.

9.3.1 Linguistic context

In a study investigating phonological variation by native speakers of Japanese learning English, Dickerson (1975) found that the target sound [r] was more frequently used before a low vowel (e.g., [a]) than before a mid vowel (e.g., [I], [ɛ], or [ɔ]), and more frequently before a mid vowel than before a high vowel ([i] or [u]). Figure 9.4 is taken from Dickerson and Dickerson (1977). Five pronunciations for English /r/ are exemplified as a function of the phonetic environment in which they occur.

As can be seen, not only are different variants used, but also the patternings differ depending on the following vowel.

Similarly, Sato (1984) considered the reduction of consonant clusters in English by two Vietnamese children. Examples of reductions are given in Table 9.1.

Sato noted a difference in the TL production of consonant clusters depending on whether the cluster was at the beginning of the syllable or at the end. Syllable-initial clusters were more accurately produced than syllable-final clusters (see also chapter 6).

Linguistic context has been found to affect morphology and syntax

Variants of /r/ by Japanese learners of English
[ð]   voiced nonretroflexed flap
[ľ]   voiced lateral flap
[l]   voiced lateral
[ř]   voiced retroflexed flap
[r]   voiced retroflexed semiconsonant

Figure 9.4 Pronunciation of English /r/ in three different linguistic environments.

Source: From "Interlanguage phonology: current research and future directions" by L. Dickerson and W. Dickerson 1977. In S. Corder and E. Roulet (Eds.), *The Notions of Simplification, Interlanguages and Pidgins and Their Relation to Second Language Learning*, Actes du 5ème Colloque de Linguistique Appliquée de Neuchâtel, pp. 18–29, AIMAV/Didier. Reprinted by permission.

Table 9.1 Reduction of English consonant clusters by Vietnamese children

Standard English	Learner production
[groʷ] "grow"	[goʷ]
[pleis] "place"	[pəleis]
[læst] "last"	[læ ʃ]

Source: Data from "Phonological processes in second language acquisition: another look at interlanguage syllable structure" by C. Sato, 1984, *Language Learning, 34,* 43–57. Reprinted by permission.

as well. In morphology, Young (1991) investigated the use of plural markings by second language learners. In a study of Chinese native speakers learning English, Young collected interview data from 12 subjects on two separate occasions, using two different interviewers. The 12 subjects were divided into two proficiency levels (High and Low) on the basis of their results on standardized test scores. Young provided evidence for variation in the use and nonuse of the plural /s/ even on the same lexical item. Examples from his data are given in 9-5 and 9-6.

(9-5) Mary: The store is.a.just sells all the *books*
       Mary: all the *book* is have to ship from Taiwan
(9-6) Jennifer: I think because my brother.a.hate *girls* when he was a
       Interviewer: Really?
       Jennifer: Mm.was terrib-.he she.he's very strange I mean he.you know even he was in the high school he wouldn't talk to *girl* you know

Young established a number of hypotheses, only some of which are relevant to a discussion of the linguistic context in which plural nouns occur. He found that there was variation conditioned by the phonological environment (by both the preceding and following segment). A summary of these results showing the precise conditioning factors is given in Table 9.2.

Interestingly, these results hold only for low proficiency learners. For higher proficiency learners, the most important factor in determining whether or not plural nouns are marked with /s/ is the presence or absence of plural markings elsewhere in the noun phrase. Contrary to what would be expected from data of natural languages (and from pidgins), there is a greater likelihood for plural nouns to be marked in a

Table 9.2 Phonological environment as a constraint on /s/ plural marking

Factor	% of plural usage	Prob. wghts[2]
Preceding segment		
Nonsibilant fricative (/f/, /v/)	78	.67
Vowel	71	.53
Stop (/p/, /t/, /k/, /b/, /d/, /g/)	66	.53
Nasal (/m/, /n/)	58	.46
Sibilant (/s/, /z/, ð, ʒ)	54	.41
Lateral (/l/)	42	.30
Following segment		
Vowel or glide (/w/, /y/)	70	.56
Pause	64	.49
Consonant or liquid (/l/, /r/)	60	.44

Source: Adapted from *Variation in interlanguage morphology* by R. Young, 1991, New York: Peter Lang. Reprinted by permission.

phrase such as *two boys* than in phrases such as *the boys*. This is so in what Young referred to as "measure" nouns (years, days, minutes, kilometers, dollars, etc.) Examples from Young's (1991) study are given in 9-7 through 9-11.

(9-7) I stay Boston only only five da-five days

(9-8) It's a drive it's twenty minutes

(9-9) I come Philadelphia its a. mm. forty years

(9-10) The second day the stock of RCA the market can drop by two dollars. dram- you know drastically

(9-11) So in fact the distance is very long. about. twelve to thirteen kilometers.

In phrases where plurality is not indicated redundantly, there is less likelihood of -s marking on the noun.

In addition to the phonological environment, there are other factors that relate to plural marking. For example, Young found syntactic determinants as well as determinants based on the position of the noun within the NP. In fact, the greatest influence was the position of the noun within the NP (whether a pronominal modifier or head), with a weighting of .86.

In syntax there is similarly variation based on linguistic context. Hyltenstam's (1977) study of the acquisition of Swedish negation by native speakers of 35 different languages serves as an illustration. In Swedish, the placement of the negative word *inte* is dependent on whether the negated verb is in a main clause or a subordinate clause, as seen in 9-12 and 9-13.

(9-12) Kalle kommer inte idag.
      Charlie comes not today
      "Charlie isn't coming today."
(9-13) Det är skönt att Kalle inte kommer idag.
      it's fine that Charlie not comes today
      "It's fine for Charlie not to come today."

The first stage learners follow in the acquisition of Swedish negation is to uniformly put the negator before the verb, not differentiating between main and subordinate clauses. This is consistent with what we have seen earlier, in that learners begin with a simple undifferentiated hypothesis: there is a one-to-one correspondence between form and function. When learners, as a function of greater proficiency, begin to recognize that their own systems do not correspond to the language they are exposed to, there is a need to revise the current hypothesis, in many cases resulting in greater complexity. In the case of Swedish, the change to the TL system has as an intermediate stage the placement of the negative marker after some finite auxiliary verbs. This then spreads to more and more verbs. At this stage, there is then variability between placement before and after verbs. The same pattern is repeated with nonauxiliary finite verbs. At this point, learners are still not in conformity with the target system; they must now begin the process of differentiating between main and subordinate clauses. This takes place in the same gradual way as before, with the learners first placing the negator before main verbs and only later before both main and auxiliary verbs. What is important to note is that all through this process there is considerable variability, depending in large part on whether the context is a main verb or an auxiliary verb.

Thus, systematic variation is found in phonology, morphology, and syntax. It is evidence of learners' need to impose regularity on their own interlanguage system.

9.3.2 Social context relating to the native language

There are sources other than the linguistic environment that govern variation, such as social factors relating to the NL.

One of the earliest studies to consider the role of social factors in second language acquisition was that of Schmidt (1977), in which he investigated the pronunciation of the sounds /θ/ as in *thing* and /ð/ as in *this* by two groups of Cairene Arabic speakers. One group was comprised of university students and the other of working-class men. In colloquial Egyptian Arabic, there are lexical triplets with the sound /θ/ alternating with /s/ and with /t/, as in the three possible pronunciations of the word *third*: [θaːliθ], [saːlis], and [taːlit]. The main difference in Schmidt's two groups of native speakers occurred in the use of the /θ/ variant in Arabic. All of the university students produced the /θ/ variant some of the time, whereas the majority of the working-class group never pronounced words using the /θ/ variant. Thus, the /θ/ variant appears to be a prestige variant, associated with the educated class. What is important to note is that, in terms of Classical Arabic, the /θ/ variety is the correct one.

Schmidt's study was additionally concerned with the pronunciation of /θ/ in English. Because /θ/ is a prestige form in Egyptian Arabic, it could be assumed that the more formal the situation is for elicitation of English, the greater the occurrence of /θ/. Schmidt's database consisted of 34 native speakers of Arabic, from whom three types of data were elicited, ranging in formality from reading a passage (the least formal) to reading a word list to reading pairs of contrasting words (the most formal). The percentage of /θ/ variants for each of these elicitation tasks is given in Table 9.3.

A closer look at a subset of the participants revealed that they could be divided into two groups—those who terminated their studies after secondary school and those who did not. Here, the results parallel those we saw earlier with the data from Arabic: the more educated group used a higher percentage of /θ/s in English than the less educated group, although for both groups there was variation along the formality/informality scale. These results are given in Table 9.4.

Table 9.3 Percentage of /θ/ variants from Cairene Arabic Speakers on three English tasks

Reading a passage	Reading a word list	Reading pairs of contrasting words
54	73	73

Source: Adapted from Schmidt (1977).

Table 9.4 Mean scores for the θ-variable in English and Arabic for two groups of secondary students

		6 learners Less educated	16 learners More educated
Arabic	Reading passage	8.66	45.63
	Word list	43.33	70.62
	Minimal pairs	68.33	78.75
English	Reading passage	19.66	60.25
	Word list	40.00	86.25
	Minimal pairs	53.33	79.38

Source: Adapted from Schmidt (1977).

Thus, social factors in the native culture, in this case a formality/informality distinction as well as NL prestige forms, influence the forms learners use in a second language.

Another study showing the importance of social factors was that of Beebe (1980), who investigated the use of /r/ by Thai learners of English. Beebe's participants were given two tasks; in one, learners were engaged in conversation, and in the other learners read from a word list. Thus, one was an informal situation in which language was not the focus and the other a formal one in which there was a greater focus on language. In Beebe's analysis, she considered instances of initial /r/ and instances of final /r/. In final position, the correct TL variant was used 41.1%[3] of the time in the informal situation, whereas in the formal situation (i.e., reading a word list), the correct TL variant was used 72.2% of the time (although it is to be noted that there were many fewer tokens in the formal situation than in the informal one). In looking at the data from the pronunciation of initial /r/, the pattern is reversed. In the informal situation, the accuracy rate was 38.5%. In the formal situation, the accuracy rate was 8.9% (see Table 9.5).

The situation that we find relating to final /r/ is what would be predicted on the basis of task type, as is discussed later in this chapter. However, the initial /r/ data are puzzling in this regard. Beebe proposed an explanation that relates to the role of the NL. The NL variants used in the formal situation are, in fact, prestige variants of initial /r/ used in Thai. Thus, in the word list, the socially prestigious form is being transferred to a TL context.[4]

Thus, variation in second language use may have a basis in the social norms of the NL. However, there are other sources of variation. We consider conversational partner (or interlocutor), task type, and conversational topics in the next section.

9.3.3 Social context relating to interlocutor, task type, and conversational topic

We often adjust our speech style according to the situation and the speaker with whom we are talking. It is well-known that the way we speak

Table 9.5 Percentage of TL variants of /r/

Informal situation (%)	Formal situation (Reading a word list) (%)
/r/ in final position	
41.1	72.2
/r/ in initial position	
38.5	8.9

Source: Adapted from Leslie M. Beebe (1980).

in a family situation is different from the way we speak in a formal job interview. We turn to similar issues in the understanding of nonnative speaker speech.

One way of accounting for speech effects attributed to interlocutor differences is through Speech Accommodation Theory (Giles and Smith, 1979; Giles and St. Clair, 1979; Thakerar, Giles, and Cheshire, 1982), which begins from the observation that speech patterns tend to converge/ diverge in social interaction. Thakerar, Giles, and Cheshire, (1982, p. 207) defined convergence and divergence as follows:

> Convergence . . . a linguistic strategy whereby individuals adapt to each other's speech by means of a wide range of linguistic features including speech rates, pause and utterance lengths, pro- nunciations, etc. . . . whereas divergence refers to the manner by which speakers accentuate vocal differences between themselves and others.

Why should speakers accommodate their speech to that of others? There are a number of reasons, all social in origin. Speaking like others (not unlike dressing in a manner similar to others) is intended to have the benefit of gaining the approval of others. It also identifies one as a member of the same social group, class, or ethnic background. The studies designed to consider IL variation from this perspective in general find convergence among speakers. For example, in a study by Beebe and Zuengler (1983), data were collected in Thai from Chinese–Thai children in two separate interviews, one with an ethnic Chinese speaker and one with an ethnic Thai speaker. (Chinese was the first language and Thai the second of these children.) Beebe and Zuengler focused on six Thai vowels and two Chinese consonants, given in Tables 9.6 and 9.7.

As can be seen, the interlocutor had an effect on the speech of these nonnative speakers for both vowels (Table 9.6) and consonants (Table 9.7). They accommodated to the speech of their interlocutors by mak- ing speech adjustments that made them sound more "Thai" or more "Chinese" depending on the ethnic background of the interlocutor.

Perhaps one of the most frequently investigated topics within the sociolinguistic/SLA literature concerns the differential results obtained as a function of data-elicitation task. The basis of this work is that of Labov (e.g., 1969, 1970), who noted that different forms are likely to occur depending on the speech situation.

Tarone (1979, 1983) extended Labov's work, which had been based on observations of native speakers, to the second language learning context. She argued that missing from the original interlanguage formulation is the idea that a second language learner's system is a variable one, changing when the linguistic environment changes. (In fact, the title of one of her

Table 9.6 Percentage of Thai variants (Standard Bangkok Thai) used by 61 bilingual Chinese–Thai subjects with Thai and Chinese interviewers (all interviews were conducted in Thai)

	Interviewer	
Variant	*Thai*	*Chinese*
[uu]	47	35
[ɛɛ]	42	31
[əə]	30	23
[o]	61	48
[aa]	65	61
[a]	92	91

Source: From "Accommodation theory: an explanation for style shifting in second language dialects" by L. Beebe and J. Zuengler, 1983. In N. Wolfson and E. Judd (Eds.), *Sociolinguistics and Second Language Acquisition,* pp. 195–213, Newbury House. Reprinted by permission.

Table 9.7 Percentage of Chinese variants used by 61 bilingual Chinese–Thai subjects with Thai and Chinese interviewers

	Interviewer	
Variant	*Thai*	*Chinese*
[ŋ]	9.5	16.1
[k]	5.8	10.7

Source: From "Accommodation theory: an explanation for style shifting in second language dialects" by L. Beebe and J. Zuengler, 1983. In N. Wolfson and E. Judd (Eds.), *Sociolinguistics and Second Language Acquisition,* pp. 195–213, Newbury House. Reprinted by permission.

early articles, from 1979, was "Interlanguage as chameleon.") According to Tarone, the learner's grammatical system exhibits more systematicity or consistency in the *vernacular* style and less so in what she calls the *superordinate* style. These two systems are defined in terms of the amount of attention paid to speech. The vernacular system is that system in which the least attention is paid to the form of one's speech, and the superordinate style is that system in which the most attention is paid to speech form. These two, then, reflect the outer boundaries of a continuum of styles, the use of which is partially determined by attention to form, which in turn is at least partially determined by the social setting of a speech event.

Figure 9.5 Pronunciation of /r/ as a function of task.

Source: From, "Interlanguage phonology: current research and future directions" by L. Dickerson and W. Dickerson, 1977. In S. P. Corder and E. Roulet (Eds.), *The Notions of Simplification, Interlanguages and Pidgins and Their Relation to Second language learning,* Actes du 5ème Colloque de Linguistique Appliquée de Neuchâtel, pp. 18–29, AIMAV/Didier. Reprinted by permission.

An early study in this area is by Dickerson and Dickerson (1977). Earlier, we discussed these data in terms of linguistic context. Here we focus on this research as a function of task type (see Figure 9.5). The data from Japanese speakers of English relate to the production of /r/ in two contexts: following a consonant and preceding either a mid vowel or a high vowel. As can be seen from the data, there are differences in accuracy as a function of the type of task (free speech, dialogue reading, word list reading) the learner is engaged in. It is hypothesized that these three tasks can be ordered along the continuum of "attention to speech": there is less specific focus on form in the free speech situation and more with the word list. Accuracy is observed to the greatest extent in those tasks in which there is the greatest focus on form. However, there is difficulty with this conceptualization of the relationship between task type and accuracy, because there is no independent evidence that these tasks should be ordered in this way. Perhaps, most attention is found in the dialogue reading. Or, perhaps the amount of attention is not uniform among all individuals across task types. If this latter possibility is the case, one would expect individuals to vary as to which task demands the most or least attention.

An important consideration is the relationship between accuracy and systematicity. Recall that the vernacular is believed to be the most systematic, but in the data from Dickerson and Dickerson we saw that it was also the least accurate. Systematicity is intended to mean only that there is the least "invasion" from other systems. Thus, one could expect that the vernacular because it is the most internally consistent is less likely to be influenced by the TL system. Hence, it will also be the least accurate. On the other hand, the superordinate style is one in which the most attention is paid to speech and in which there appears to be the most influence from the TL and, hence, representative of the most accurate, but possibly the least systematic, system.

Attention to speech as the only variable involved in accounting for different forms may be too simplistic an explanation for variation. Gass (1980), in an investigation of the acquisition of relative clauses, compared two task types. She used a grammaticality judgment task and a sentence-combining task. In the former, learners were asked to judge the grammaticality of sentences in their L2. In the latter task, learners were given sentences, such as 9-14, and were told to combine them into a single sentence, with the targeted sentence being something like 9-15:

(9-14) The boy ran home. The boy was crying.
(9-15) The boy who was crying ran home.

The main focus was on the use of the NL by second language learners. In comparing the results of the two tasks (acceptability judgment and sentence combining), Gass found different results, leading her to emphasize that different data-elicitation techniques may yield different conclusions. The point is that the concept of attention to speech may be less important than understanding the processes involved in doing various tasks. For example, the grammaticality judgment task is primarily a decoding task in which two steps are involved in deciding to reject or accept a given sentence. First, learners must interpret the sentence in some way. Second, they must determine if it fits the patterns of English as represented by their interlanguage. In other words, a learner must attempt to match the sentence with an internalized linguistic system. On the other hand, a sentence-combining task is a production task in which a learner must focus on the form of the sentence while simultaneously maintaining the original meaning. Thus, each task that a learner performs will place different demands on the learner, attention to speech being but one.

Even in data that do reflect more clearly a difference in attention to form, the results do not bear out the hypothesized relationship between accuracy and attention to speech, as exemplified by the Dickerson and Dickerson data. In particular, Sato (1985) found the opposite relationship to hold. In her study of word-final consonant production and consonant clusters of a Vietnamese child learning English, the trend observed by Dickerson and Dickerson did not hold. Data were collected from three tasks at four points in time: (a) free conversation, (b) oral reading of continuous text, and (c) elicited imitation of words and short phrases. (At Time 4, Task 2 was replaced by the recitation of a rehearsed text.) Tables 9.8 and 9.9 give the results from the tasks used.

Table 9.8 Target-like production of word-final consonants by task (% correct)

Task	Time 1	Time 2	Time 3	Time 4
Conversation	52.00	72.41	73.55	68.96
Oral reading	61.54	61.65	63.70	70.81
Imitation	78.57	64.52	79.45	72.73

Source: From "Task variation in interlanguage phonology" by C. Sato, 1985. In S. Gass and C. Madden (Eds.), *Input in Second Language Acquisition*, pp. 181–196, Newbury House. Reprinted by permission.

Table 9.9 Target-like production of word-final clusters by task (% correct)

Task	Time 1	Time 2	Time 3	Time 4
Conversation	5.88	5.41	21.69	14.63
Oral reading	19.78	28.89	30.69	6.15
Imitation	12.50	26.92	49.17	31.82

Source: From "Task variation in interlanguage phonology" by C. Sato, 1985. In S. Gass and C. Madden (Eds.), *Input in Second Language Acquisition*, pp. 181–196, Newbury House. Reprinted by permission.

As can be seen, in neither the production of consonants nor in the production of consonant clusters does the predicted relationship hold, although, once again, it is not clear which task would be the one with the most attention paid to speech. Sato clearly pointed out that defining speech styles only in terms of attention to speech is an overly simplistic view of how learner production varies.

Tarone, too, recognized the limitations of a linear, monolithic perspective on variation. In a 1985 study, she looked at morphemes that informal observation had indicated were often omitted even by advanced learners. She found that it was not the case that the vernacular was the least accurate. In this study, there were three tasks: (a) grammaticality judgment (most attention to form), (b) oral interview about the learner's major field of interest, and (c) oral narration (least attention to form).

Tarone's analysis and explanation of these findings incorporated the notion of discourse function. That is, one cannot simply say that the type of task will dictate what forms will be used. One also needs to look at the function of those forms within a discourse context. For example, plural -s did not shift along the predicted continuum; other morphemes—such as third person singular—conformed to the hypothesized attention to form/ accuracy relationship; whereas still others—such as English articles and direct object pronouns—exhibited a trend opposite to what was predicted. Tarone's explanation resides in the contextual roles of these different forms. In context, the third person singular is redundant. That is, there are other cues in the sentence or the preceding context that specify the person and number of the verb. On the other hand, in a narrative context and, perhaps to a lesser extent, in discussing one's field, articles and pronouns are important in maintaining and establishing appropriate relationships. Thus, the demands of the narrative and interview tasks were such that there was greater pressure for accuracy of certain forms but not of others. The morphemes that were needed to convey meaning and which provided a cohesive narration were increasingly provided as the tasks required more focus on meaning. At the same time, the morphemes that were empty in terms of meaning were increasingly deleted as the task required more focus on meaning. That is, attention was a factor as tasks increased or decreased in their focus on form, but not all morphemes were equal in the amount of attention they attracted. Morphemes that carried meaning were attended to and supplied more as tasks required more focus on meaning, while morphemes that carried no meaning were attended to and supplied less.

Whereas attention to form and discourse function may contribute to the internal consistency of learner systems, discourse topic is important as well. Eisenstein and Starbuck (1989) gathered oral data from 10 English as a Second Language learners on two topics: one that an individual had specified as being a topic of great interest and the other that the individual had specified as being of little or neutral interest. They included accuracy measures on a number of grammatical categories, including tense usage, verb formation, verb meaning, and tense meaning. In general, accuracy was lower on those topics in which there was emotional investment; in other words, on those topics that had been designated as having great interest for the subject. One could argue that this is related to the notion of attention to speech, because it is precisely in instances of high investment that one would expect great attention to the meaning and, as a result, less attention to form.

There is additional evidence for the effect of topic on L2 production (Woken and Swales, 1989; Zuengler, 1989), although in both of these studies, it was not linguistic accuracy that was considered, but linguistic behaviors. In Zuengler's study, she paired a native speaker (NS) and a nonnative speaker (NNS) who were majoring in the same field (statistics, dairy science, or electrical engineering). Each pair had two conversations, one on a neutral topic about which each was presumed to have equal knowledge (food) and the other on a topic relating to their major. In some pairs, the NS was further along in his or her studies and in others it was the NNS who had more advanced topic knowledge. The measures that were considered were interruptions, amount of talk, and the number of questions asked. All of this contributed to a determination of conversational dominance. The results suggest that conversational dominance is not conditioned by linguistic knowledge alone, because NSs did not uniformly dominate the conversations. Rather, dominance was better understood in terms of content knowledge.

A similar study was conducted by Woken and Swales (1989), who also varied topic knowledge. Their subjects (native and nonnative pairs) differed in terms of their knowledge of computers. Each NNS had expertise in a particular computer program, whereas none of the NSs were familiar with the program. The task involved the NNS instructing the NS on the use of the program. Woken and Swales' measures consisted of linguistic measures (such as number and length of clauses and number of questions asked) and nonlinguistic measures (such as number of vocabulary explanations and direction-giving). Their results are similar to those of Zuengler, showing that dominance and control in a conversation must be considered complex phenomena. The common view is that NSs control the conversation by virtue of the fact that they have more linguistic resources available to them. However, the effect of topic knowledge (as well as other social variables such as status and familiarity) must be taken into account. Thus, there is a complex interaction of many factors that shape the nature of conversational and linguistic behaviors involving NNSs.

Selinker and Douglas (1985) argued that second language research must take into account the notion of context as an internal construct. One aspect of context is variation as a function of elicitation task, which we dealt with earlier in this chapter. Another has to do with the concept of *discourse domain*, which the authors define as "internally-created contexts, within which . . . IL structures are created differentially" (p. 190). That is, learners create discourse domains that relate to various parts of their lives and are important to them. IL forms are created within particular contexts or particular discourse domains. The evidence adduced comes from a learner who produces different IL structures within different discourse domains. Selinker and Douglas's argument rested on their belief that various aspects of SLA (e.g., transfer, fossilization, avoidance) occur differentially within discourse domains. To illustrate this, consider the two excerpts 9-16 and 9-17. In the former, the interviewer is discussing with Luis the contents of a technical article on engineering. In 9-17, the topic of discussion is food. In both episodes, Luis forgets a crucial word.

> (9-16) L = Luis (NNS); I = interviewer (NS)
>
>   L: . . . and then this is eff-eh-referring that the contractor maybe didn't adjust the equipment to the co-site conditions-maybe this you know the equipment can be effected by the-what is that the-I lost the word-I mean-because no-for-you have one equipment here in for example one estate and you want to move that equipment to for example you are working Michigan

and you want to move that equipment to Arizona or a
higher estate-you have to adjust your equipment
because the productivity of the equipment eh gets
down-eh because of the different eh height of the
(project) place

I: oh   I   see the a the ah altitude

L: yeah the altitude—that is ⌈the word =

I: ⌊that's the word

L: =I was looking for

I: yea the altitude-the altitude makes a difference

L: makes   a
difference in the productivity of the equipment

(9-17) L: I don't know if you know what machaca is

I: tell me-I
think I've had it once before

L: No-you you get some meat and you put that meat eh
to the sun an after that you-I don't know what is I-I
learned that name because I went to the sss-farmer
jack I saw that-you make like a little then-oh my god-
then you = you = forget it (laugh)

I: (laugh) make it into strips?

L: OK like a-you you have a steak no?   you first

I: uh huh

L: in the sun-you have

I: then it gets rotten and you throw it away

L: ummm-no no no no no only one day or two days

I: hmmm

L: after that with a stone you like escramble that like ah-

I: you grind it up?

L: Yes that psss you you start to what is that word oh my
god

I: mash?

L: exactly you have to you start making mash that meat

In the nontechnical domain, Luis appears willing to use a strategy of
abandonment (note his *forget it* in his second turn). In the technical
domain, the same communication breakdown does not occur because
Luis is able to continue without the necessary word. This he does by
describing the process presumably in the hopes of either getting his idea
across or of eliciting the word from the native-speaking interviewer. In
the conversation about food, Luis enters into a negotiated interaction
with the interviewer, resulting in a mutual word search. That is, both

conversational participants have as their goal the search for the appropriate lexical item. Thus, in these two examples, the NNS uses two distinct communication strategies in his attempt to explain a concept to a native speaker.

We have seen that there is considerable variation in second language learner data. The variation can be of two sorts, free and systematic, although systematic variation is far more prevalent. When forms vary systematically, there are a number of determining factors, some of which are linguistic, others of which are sociolinguistic or situational. R. Ellis (1987a, p. 183) proposed a role for both free and systematic variation in L2 development. Free variation occurs as an initial stage when two (or more) forms are involved. The next stage (systematic variation) involves consistency of form/meaning relationships with overlapping forms and meanings. The final stage, categorical use stage (assuming that a learner reaches that point) is the correct form/meaning assignment. This is diagramed in Figure 9.6.

To take the data presented in chapter 8 (Table 8.3) regarding the use of *no* and *don't*, we can match the data up with the model presented (see Table 9.10). What is interesting to note is that the categorical use stage for this learner is not the correct TL one.

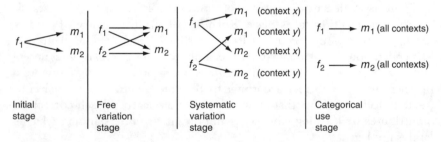

f = form
m = meaning
'context' refers to both situational and linguistic contexts

Figure 9.6 The role of free and systematic variation.

Source: From *Second Language Acquisition in Context*, by R. Ellis, 1987a, Prentice Hall. Reprinted by permission.

Table 9.10 Stages of IL Variation

Initial stage	*no* for all forms
Free variation stage	*no/don't* interchangeably
Systematic variation stage	*don't*/imperatives
	no and *don't*/indicatives
Categorical use stage	*don't*/imperatives
	no/indicatives

That learners vary in their production of TL forms is not in dispute. What is a matter of dispute, however, is the appropriate way of representing linguistic knowledge. Those whose major interest is in Chomskyan linguistics (see arguments in Gregg, 1990; Jordan, 2005) take as the domain of SLA research the determination of linguistic competence. Competence, being a representation of abstractions, is not variable. Variability in this view is part of performance, that is, part of putting language knowledge to use at a given point in time. On the other hand, SLA researchers such as R. Ellis (1990b) and Tarone (1990) view L2 knowledge itself as variable. That is, it is not a matter of performance, but variability is part of what learners know about their second language. Eckman (1994b) argued that the resolution of this issue lies not in theoretical argumentation over what is and what is not in the domain of a theory of SLA, as Gregg (1990) argued, but lies rather in empirical argumentation. On the side of those who argue that the appropriate domain for the study of SLA is linguistic competence, one would want to see evidence that such a theory could indeed account for the well-established phenomenon of variation. On the other hand, those who argue that variation data are crucial to a theory of SLA would want to show that there are data crucial to an understanding of second language development that cannot be accounted for in a competence model of SLA.

There is evidence to suggest that context is essential to understanding how acquisition takes place. Kormos (1999), in a review of studies dealing with monitoring and self-repair, showed that error detection is dependent on social context. For example, some contexts will necessitate a much greater level of accuracy than others. In other words, learners will self-correct according to the interlocutor and social context. It follows, then, that if we assume that learners' self-correction contributes to learning, context is important in understanding what is and is not learned.

Another study relevant to the issue of context is that of Tarone and Liu (1995). They argued, on the basis of interactional data in three settings, that a learner's involvement "in different kinds of interaction can differentially affect the rate and route of the acquisition process" (p. 108). The data come from a Chinese native speaker learning English in Australia. At the onset of data collection, the child was almost 5, and at the end, he was almost 7 years old. Data were collected in three situations: (a) in interactions with teachers, (b) in interactions with peers, and (c) in interactions with the researcher (in English, although the researcher was a native speaker of Chinese). Tarone and Liu considered the rate and route of the acquisition of interrogatives. With regard to rate, they argued that new forms nearly always emerge in one context (interaction with the researcher), then spread to the context with peers, and then to interactions with teachers. What is important, however, is the fact that new forms emerge from interactions themselves, and the differential demands of each interaction differentially allow for the emergence of new forms. In other words, different contexts push the learner to produce new forms to a greater extent than other contexts (see Tarone, 2000; Young, 1999).

The issue has come to the fore in articles by Firth and Wagner (1997, 1998), Gass (1998), Kasper (1997), Long (1997), and Poulisse (1997). The arguments revert back to earlier arguments of what the domain of a theory of second language acquisition is. The difference in opposing views can be reduced in simple terms to a difference in acquisition and use. Acquisition is fundamentally a psycholinguistic process (see Tarone, 2000), and the question is: To what extent is that psycholinguistic process affected by social context? The difference can be better understood by an understanding of the difference between acquisition and use. Figure 9.7 refers to the general field of research as second language studies, eliminating the misleading term *acquisition*. Acquisition is used: (1) in the true sense of acquisition (the process of obtaining new knowledge), (2) as a product, and (3) as language use.

The left part of Figure 9.7 refers to areas of acquisition studies, where there is little dispute about the contribution of those areas to knowledge. The solid lines connecting SLA and contributing areas of research (transfer and universals) represent an unquestionable connection. Similarly, the solid lines between second language use and its subareas represent unquestionable connections.[5] The dotted lines represent areas for which argumentation and empirical evidence must be brought to bear. In chapter 10, for example, we make the argument that interaction is a

Figure 9.7 A characterization of research in SLA.

Source: From "Apples and oranges: or, why apples are not orange and don't need to be: a response to Firth and Wagner," by S. Gass, 1998, *The Modern Language Journal*, 83–90. Reprinted by permission.

part of SLA. In this chapter, we saw areas in which variation may be considered to be important to an understanding of SLA.

Færch and Kasper (1987) similarly avoided the term *acquisition*. As they noted, "we have chosen to refer to the field of study as second language (SL) research, thus avoiding the bias towards developmental issues implicit in the more common term 'second language acquisition research'" (p. 5). Seliger (1983, p. 190) made a similar point about the importance of distinguishing between two major areas of concern. The first type of study is those

a   which are concerned with describing how the learner uses what he has acquired either by describing the external socio-linguistic or ecological conditions for such use or by describing the internalized system which he maintains which enables him to produce interlanguage performance. Such research, while obviously important and legitimate, begins with the assumption that the learner's output is the product of *a system in place*.

b   The second type of study is that concerned with explaining how interlanguage sources of knowledge are learned or acquired in the first place. That is, the second area of study is concerned with describing the process of the *acquisition of interlanguage systems*.

Seliger (1983) suggested the term *Second Language Studies* rather than *Second Language Acquisition* to cover the broad range of topics currently embraced by this disciplinary area. This exchange of articles has had an impact on the field of SLA, as argued in Gass, Lee, and Roots (2007), by opening up the door to a wide range of studies examining language in context in particular within a social-interactional framework. Within this framework, we focus on two areas as they have been conducted within SLA studies: Conversational Analysis and Sociocultural Theory.

9.4 Social interactional approaches

Common to the approaches to SLA discussed in this section is an understanding of language quite different than in other approaches dealt with in this book. Language is not an isolated phenomenon that can be understood out of its social context. Consequently, learning is not situated in an individual's cognition; that is, it is not an intrapsychological process. Rather it is linked to social and local ecology; it is adaptive to an emergent set of resources, resources that are embodied in social interaction. Learning is anchored in the social practices that a learner engages in. In this view linguistic utterances are sensitive to and reliant upon their interactional context. Unlike other approaches discussed in previous chapters, with a social interactive perspective on language, the linguistic code cannot be understood as an isolated phenomenon outside of its social context. Nor can one understand how learning takes place without the support of the social context. Isolated grammaticality judgments or experiments of psycholinguistic processing make little sense within this paradigm.

9.4.1 Conversation Analysis

Conversation Analysis (CA) is one manifestation of a social interactionist perspective. Evidence for learning is embedded in the changes in accomplishment of social activities, not necessarily in the linguistic code used to express those activities. In other words, the starting point for the study of language and, hence, for language learning, is a social activity and, thus, the focus is on a speaker's orientation toward language. One can view language in this framework as linked to social and local ecology and the linguistic encoding of utterances is sensitive to their interactional contexts.

Learning is seen as anchored in and through the social practices the learner engages in and, thus, is not an intrapsychological process. Thus, learning the linguistic code of a language is situated in social context.

What evidence is there that learning has taken place within this frame-work? One piece of evidence is the kinds of activities that learners engage in (e.g., social interactions) and are successful in. Thus, activities are the starting point for the study of human functioning and one can view the changes in activities as evidence that learning has taken place. Only language in its natural environment serves as data in this framework; hence, as noted above, grammaticality judgments or psycholinguistic experiments have no place in this area of study. Only the interactional configuration of a speaker's orientation toward language serves as useful data. This is not to say that certain learning conditions (e.g., attentional focus) are not relevant. Rather they are investigated through the course of activities.

Mori (2004) presents data from a Japanese classroom. Below (Table 9.11) is an excerpt from that study, along with the type of analysis that was given to the data. Kasper (2004) also presents data from learners of German (two excerpts) to show the contextual moorings necessary for interpretation (see Table 9.12).

A conversational analysis considers only what is observable, although this excerpt suggests that this is not always easy to avoid. We turn next to another social-interactionist perspective, that of socio-cultural theory.

Table 9.11 Analysis from a CA perspective (Mori)

Lines 39–49	Conversation analysis
David: °nan da?° 　　[°(wata-) .ss::° *What is it? [°(I-) .ss::°(39)* Alan:　　[ANO: 　　　watashi　　no uchi O::,　　aa:: abunaiku::　　naritai 　　　toKI::, (0.4) 　　　d[onna:: *Uhm when I want my hou::se to be:: ah: dangerous ((incorrect)), (0.4)　what ki::nd (40–41)*	Line 40—asks question about what David wants to say. Focus is on the lack of indication of appropriate ownership Lines 39→ use of Japanese suggests the importance of Japanese in classroom Lines 40–41—Alan formulates question that turns out to be basically a translation of English, but has the opposite meaning in Japanese
Teacher:　[abunaku 　　　naritai? *want to be dangerous? (42)* 　　　(0.4)　(43)*	
Alan:　aa[::: *aa::: (44)* David:　[uhe heh *uhe heh (45)*	Lines 44–46—Alan reacts to repair and reflects on what he said Line 45—David points out that what Alan has said is not correct
Alan:　abu-　aa[:::::: *dan- aa::::: (46)*	
David:[>°ie ie ie [a 　　ie°< 　　　　　*No no no oh* 　　no (47)*	Line 47—David points out that what Alan has said is not correct
Alan: [a! <u>yeah</u> abunaku 　　naritai toki:: *oh! yeah when we want to be dangerous (48)*	
	Summary: Focus is on the language used, who initiates the question and whose "original" language problem it was. Uses body language and gaze to support idea of ownership of language problem. Motivations are attributed to different participants a propos each one's desire to show the teacher how he is engaged in the task and engaged in learning.

Table 9.12 Analysis from a CA perspective (Kasper)

Interaction	Conversation analysis
NS: okay:, wie geht es dir? 　　　*how are you?* NNS:　es geht gut, 　　　*I'm okay,* NS:　ja?　　　(.) warum? 　　*are you! (.) why?* NNS:　u::mm (.) ts uh i- °er° am wochendende? It was lange? (　)= *at the weekend? it was long?*	The initial exchange is a routine adjacency pair. The NS questions the response by saying *warum* (why). This question shows the NS's "orientation to the event as a learning activity whose main purpose it is to 'get the learner to talk,' and to her interactional charge as provider of environments for learner talk." The NS responds as if this were a normal conversation. Therefore, the participants co-construct this "hybrid interactional form" that reflects "normal" conversation, as well as an event for language practice. Comment: This is clearly an emic perspective that attempts to get inside the head of the participants.

9.4.2 *Sociocultural theory*

As noted earlier, in recent years there has been an increased emphasis on language use. One consequence of this new emphasis is that the field has begun to incorporate approaches that go beyond the purely linguistic and psycholinguistic orientations that had focused on "in the head" phenomena of acquisition and that had been prevalent. Sociocultural theory is based on work by the Russian psychologist Vygotsky, and represents a fundamentally different way of looking at language and learning than has been discussed in other parts of this book. Sociocultural theory is grounded in the ontology of the social individual. This does not mean a divorce from psychological processes, for a sociocultural approach considers language and, by extension, second language acquisition as contextually situated and is concerned with situated language as it relates to internal processes.

There are a number of concepts that are different from more traditional approaches to SLA; namely, mediation and regulation, internalization, and the Zone of Proximal Development. Mediation is the most important of these, because sociocultural theory rests on the assumption that human activity (including cognitive activity) is mediated by what are known as symbolic artifacts (higher-level cultural tools) such as language and literacy and by material artifacts. These artifacts mediate the relationship between humans and the social and material world around us. To think of this in more concrete terms, one can consider how humans have developed tools to ease what might otherwise be an arduous process. If one wanted to put strands of wool together to create material, one could hold the strands taut and interweave other pieces of wool. But, over time, humans have developed tools to mediate the weaving process; namely, a loom with all of its component parts (e.g., the reed, the heddles) and a shuttle. Within sociocultural theory, humans use symbols as tools to mediate psychological activity and to control our psychological processes. This control is voluntary and allows us to attend to certain things, to plan, and to think rationally. The primary tool that humans have available is language and it is a tool that allows us to connect to our environment (both physical and social). Language gives humans the power to go beyond the immediate environment and to think about and talk about events and objects that are far removed both physically and temporally.

Regulation is a form of mediation. As children learn language, they also learn to regulate their activities linguistically. There are three stages of development on the way to self-regulation. The first stage involves the use of objects as a way of thinking (object-regulation). One can think of parents using objects (e.g., pieces of candy) to help children with the abstract concept of counting. A second stage is known as other-regulation whereby learning is regulated by others rather than objects. Finally, self-regulation, the final stage occurs when activities can be performed with little or no external support. This occurs through internalization of information (addition without the use of pieces of candy, although some external support is required in the case of more complex mathematical manipulations).

Another concept central to sociocultural theory is what is referred to as internalization. This is the process that allows us to move the relationship between an individual and his or her environment to later performance. One way internalization occurs is through imitation, which can be both immediate and intentional and delayed, as seen, for example, in early child language research by Weir (1962), in which imitation/practice was observed by children when they were alone in bed. This is also known as private speech and has been observed in L2 classrooms by Ohta (2001; see discussion in chapter 11) and by Lantolf and Yáñez (2003). The items focused on by learners in these imitation/private speech situations are controlled by the learner and not necessarily by the teacher's agenda.

Another concept that is associated with sociocultural theory is known as the Zone of Proximal Development, defined by Vygotsky (1978, p. 86) as: "the distance between the actual developmental level as determined by independent problem solving and the level of potential development as determined through problem solving under adult guidance or in collaboration with more capable peers." What this means is that learning results from interpersonal activity; it is interpersonal activity that forms the basis for individual functioning. This clearly embodies the social nature of learning and underscores the importance of collaborative learning as it shapes what is learned (see chapter 11).

Lantolf and Thorne (2006, 2007) show the applications to second language acquisition. For example, the concept of private speech as a means of regulating a task, that is, imposing order on a task (through meta-comments about the task itself), has been noted throughout the literature. In a study by McCafferty (1994), when describing a picture sequence, learners used regulatory language (e.g., *I see a man . . .* or *What do I see?*), a phenomenon absent in native speaker descriptions of the same language. This was argued to be an example of how learners use private speech to regulate task performance. In other words, private speech is proposed to be a way to regulate complex tasks and it is through self-regulation that researchers come to understand the processes used by learners.

In sum, in this view, human cognition results from the full context (historical, social, material, cultural) in which experiences take place. Thus, the experiences we have, and the interactions we engage in, are crucial in the development of cognition. Language is a tool (a symbolic artifact) that mediates between individuals and their environment.

9.5 Communication strategies

Many times learners are faced with a need to express a concept or an idea in the second language but find themselves without the linguistic resources to do so. A communication strategy must be employed. A communication strategy (to be differentiated from learning strategies, discussed in chapter 12, in section 12.9) is a deliberate attempt to express meaning when faced with difficulty in the second language.[6] Bialystok (1990a, p. 1) reports the following incident:

> While living in Colombia, a friend of mine wanted to buy some silk. The Spanish word for silk, *seda*, however, is apparently used for a variety of synthetic substitutes. Eager to have the genuine product, my friend went into the local shop and, roughly trans-lated from Spanish, said something like the following to the shopkeeper: "It's made by little animals, for their house, and then turned into material."

The person described in this episode did not know an unambiguous word for *silk*, nor the word for *silkworm* or *cocoon*, and thus had to resort to various descriptive devices to get the meaning across. The use of circum-locutions such as these is known as a communication strategy. Other examples of communication strategies include: approximation, literal translation, language switch, and avoidance. Examples are given in 9-18 to 9-21 (from Tarone, 1977).

(9-18) Approximation
      IL form = pipe
      TL form = waterpipe
(9-19) Literal translation
      IL form = He invite other person to drink
      TL form = They toasted each other
(9-20) Language switch
      IL form = balon
      TL form = balloon
(9-21) Avoidance
      IL form = the water (mumble)
      TL form = The water spills.

In dealing with the notion of communication strategies, most researchers have included three components in a definition of communication strategies: problematicity, consciousness, and intentionality (see Dörnyei and Scott, 1997, for an overview). Problematicity means that the learner, in using a communication strategy, must have first recognized that there is a problem of communication that must be overcome. Inherent in the notion of consciousness is the idea that learners must be aware that they have encountered a problem and be aware of the fact that they are, in fact, doing something to overcome that problem. Including intentionality as part of a definition of communication strategies implies that learners have control over various options and make choices about which option will have a particular effect (Bialystok, 1990a).

There are difficulties with all of these components of a definition of communication strategies. First, much of the language used when there is a problem is the same type of language used when there is no problem. If this is the case, it is difficult to include problematicity as part of the definition. For instance, suppose that someone finds a calculator (never having seen one before) and attempts to describe it to another person with the statement in 9-22 (Bialystok, 1990a):

(9-22) C'est une petite machine avec des nombres.
      "It's a small machine with numbers."

It is difficult to claim that in this case the speaker has recognized a problem, because the speaker is faced only with the task of describing an unknown object and has no idea that there is a name for the object. There are many instances of language use in which we are forced to describe objects; in these instances, there may be no sense of problematicity in the sense of being faced with a communication breakdown of any sort. If it is the case that nonproblematic language use makes use of the same type of strategy that is used in so-called problematic language use, it is difficult to use problematicity as a defining characteristic.

It is equally difficult to equate consciousness with communication strategies. As Bialystok noted, communication difficulties are solved with a small set of strategies, even in varied circumstances. Given the consistency of strategy use, it is not easy to make an argument about consciousness. That is, learners do not confront each new problematic situation with conscious choices, but rather pull from a small set of regularly used strategies. This is closely tied with the idea of intentionality. If choices are routinized, it is unlikely that there are conscious choices available.

In a review of the literature on communication strategies, Bialystok concluded that communication strategies do not have a privileged status. Rather, they are part of the same processes involved in nonstrategic language use. "They are the adjustments to the ongoing processes responsible for language acquisition and use that allow processing to be maintained. They are the means by which a system can perform beyond its formal limitations and communication can proceed from a limited linguistic system" (1990a, p. 147).

9.6 Interlanguage pragmatics

The final area we deal with in this chapter on language in context is pragmatics. Interlanguage pragmatics deals with both the acquisition and use of second language pragmatic knowledge. We noted in chapter 1 that in learning a second language one must learn more than just the pronunciation, the lexical items, and the appropriate word order; one must also learn the appropriate way to use those words and sentences in the second language. For example, we pointed out that one must learn that, within the context of a telephone conversation, *Is Josh there?* is not only a request for information but is also a request to speak with that person. In fact, children are known to respond to this question only on the basis of an information request such that a typical response from a child is *Yes*, with no further indication that he or she will call the person to the phone. Thus, a child in learning a first language must learn to go beyond the literal meaning of utterances to understand the pragmatic force. The same can be said for second language learning and use. Consider 9-23, an example a conversation between a British tourist and a native speaker of Finnish, provided by Maisa Martin (personal communication):

(9-23) Tourist: We're trying to find the railway station.
Could you help us?
NS of Finnish: Yes. (full stop)

In Finnish, the pragmatic force of a request for directions does not coincide with the pragmatic force in English. Thus, despite a native speaker of Finnish's perfectly grammatical English, one often finds what might be interpreted as abrupt responses.

Much of the work in interlanguage pragmatics has been conducted within the framework of *speech acts*. Speech acts can be thought of as functions of language, such as complaining, thanking, apologizing, refusing, requesting, and inviting. Within this view, the minimal unit of communication is the performance of a linguistic act. All languages have a means of performing speech acts, and presumably speech acts themselves are universal, yet the *form* used in specific speech acts varies from culture to culture. Thus, the study of second language speech acts is concerned with the linguistic possibilities available in languages for speech act realization and the effect of cross-cultural differences on both second language performance and the interpretation by native speakers of second language speech acts.

It is easy to imagine how miscommunication and misunderstandings occur if the form of a speech act differs from culture to culture. In 9-23, a native speaker of British English and a native speaker of Finnish were seen to differ in the ways they ask for directions and interpret requests for directions. When breakdowns occur, they are frequently disruptive because native speakers attribute not linguistic causes to the breakdown, but personality (individual or cultural) causes. Thus, in 9-23, the British tourist is likely to have interpreted the Finnish speaker's response as rude and/or uncooperative. Or, similarly, consider the response to the situation in 9-24, produced in English by a native speaker of Hebrew (Cohen and Olshtain, 1993, p. 54):

(9-24) *Context:*   You promised to return a textbook to your classmate within a day or two, after xeroxing a chapter. You held onto it for almost two weeks.

Classmate: I'm really upset about the book because I needed it to prepare for last week's class.

Response: I have nothing to say.

It is clear that this response sounds rude to an NS of English and suggests a lack of willingness to apologize. However, what was meant was the translation of something equivalent to *I have no excuse.*

In terms of language learning, the area of pragmatics is perhaps one of the most difficult areas for learners because they are generally unaware of this aspect of language and may be equally unaware of the negative perceptions that native speakers may have of them as a result of their pragmatic errors. Miscommunication resulting from NS perceptions of relatively proficient NNSs (as opposed to learners with low level comprehension and productive skills) is often serious in terms of interpersonal relations because the source of the difficulty is more likely to be attributed to a defect in a person (or a culture; e.g., Americans are insincere, Israelis are rude, Japanese are indirect) than to an NNS's inability to map the correct linguistic form onto pragmatic intentions. As Gumperz and Tannen (1979, p. 315) point out, because the interlocutors "assume that they understand each other, they are less likely to question interpretations." This is precisely the communicative situation that Varonis and Gass (1985a, 1985b) labeled the most dangerous: without a shared background, linguistic system, and specific beliefs, "when one interlocutor confidently [but inaccurately] interprets another's utterance, it is likely that participants will run into immediate problems because they do not share a common discourse space" (1985a, p. 341).

We take the speech act of refusal as a way of illustrating the speech act research paradigm. Refusals occur in all languages. However, not all languages/cultures refuse in the same way, nor do they feel comfortable refusing the same invitation or suggestion. That is, not all cultures view the same event as allowing a refusal. How does this affect second language use?

Refusals are a highly complex speech act primarily because they often involve lengthy negotiations as well as face-saving maneuvers to accommodate the noncompliant nature of the speech act. Because oral refusals are the result of an initial request (*Would you like to come to my house for dinner tonight?*), they preclude extensive planning on the part of the refuser.

A study by Beebe, Takahashi, and Uliss-Weltz (1990), in which the major concern was the existence of pragmatic transfer, deals specifically with second language refusals. Four groups of native speakers of Japanese and English (two NS controls and two second language groups) filled out a Discourse Completion Test involving 12 situations, including refusals of requests, refusals of invitations, refusals of suggestions, and refusals of offers. In describing the setting, it was made clear that the refuser was to take the role of a higher or lower status person. Each situation involved an initial segment of written speech followed by a blank and then followed by a rejoinder that forced the subjects to write a refusal in the preceding blank. In analyzing the results, the authors considered the order of semantic formulas. Semantic formulas consist of such factors as

289

expressions of regret, excuses, offers of alternatives, and promises. For example, a refusal to a dinner invitation at a friend's house might elicit the following response: *I'm sorry, I have theater tickets that night. Maybe I could come by later for a drink.* The order of formulas in this refusal is (a) expression of regret, *I'm sorry*; (b) excuse, *I have theater tickets that night*; and (c) offer of alternative, *Maybe I could come by later for a drink.*

The data from this research suggest evidence of pragmatic transfer. The range of formulas used is similar from language to language, but the *order* in which the formulas are used differs from language to language. For example, Table 9.13 shows Beebe, Takahashi, and Uliss-Weltz's data from refusals of requests.

Other work involving refusals, but using a different methodology for data elicitation, suggests that a complex and negotiated interaction takes place in second language refusal situations. Research by Houck and Gass (1996) and Gass and Houck (1999) on refusals, using roleplay as a source of data collection, showed that the refusals in these role-plays were often lengthy interactions in which the participants negotiated their way to a resolution. An example is given in 9-25:

(9-25) *Setting*: The NNS is a guest in a family's home. The family members have gone to a neighbor's home for a few minutes. The NNS has been instructed not to let anyone in. The NS in this role-play is playing the part of a cousin passing through town who would like to come in and wait for her cousin.

NS:	Oh hi how are you doing?
NNS:	oh fine thank you
NS:	is uh is uh Quentin in
NNS:	no uh no sh I'm not
NS:	no he's not in
NNS:	uh no no he's not in

Table 9.13 Order of semantic formulas in refusals of requests when refuser is of a higher status

Japanese native speakers	Positive opinion/empathy
	Excuse
English by native speakers of Japanese	Positive opinion/empathy
	Excuse
Native speakers of American English	Positive opinion
	Regret
	Excuse
	Can't

Source: Adapted from Beebe, Takahashi, and Uliss-Weltz (1990).

NS: ahh where'd he go

NNS: ahh he goes to neighbor house

NS: ah well do you mind if -I'm I'm his cousin and I'm just passing through Lansing tonight and I'm I'm on my way to Detroit. I'm on a on a business trip and and uh I'd like to see him. I've got about half an hour or so. Would you mind if I come in and wait for a minute or so until he comes back

NNS: ah no wait wait I'm a guest to uh this home the-I can't uh I don't uh uh um I can't I don't know what uh I do this situation then eh

NS: I'm sorry?

NNS: uh he he don't tell me uh

NS: ahh

NNS: if another person come in his home

NS: yeah yeah but I I I'm his cousin I'm sure it's going to be ok

NNS: but I don't know

NS: I I know it'll be all right

NNS: my first time to meet you I don't know you

NS: y'know actually this is the first time I've met you too how do you do

NNS: wait wait I think uh I think uh he came back uh not so late

NS: nice to meet you uh huh

NNS: yeh-uh please wait uh your car

In this example, the two speakers hemmed and hawed, cut each other off, self-corrected, modified and elaborated their positions, and generally became involved in negotiating semantic, pragmatic, and social meaning. The episodic nature of this example, with multiple refusals, requests, and rerequests, has not been documented in native speaker speech.

Acceptances are also difficult. Considering the following situation. A professor invites a number of students to lunch on the occasion of their graduation. A NNS replies to the invitation as follows:

(9-26) Thank you for the invitation. I would be willing to come.

To a native speaker of English, this response is strange, if not rude. Willingness suggests a possible reluctance and one wonders who is doing whom a favor.

In coming to an understanding of second language pragmatics, one must ultimately deal with the wide range of social variables that might determine how language is used. For example, what is the relationship between the two people involved in a particular speech event? Are they of equal status? Are they of equal age? Are they of the same sex? Are there other people witnessing the speech event? What is their relationship to those speaking?

Interlanguage pragmatics, in dealing with how people use language within a social context, must take into consideration not only how language is used (i.e., how grammatical forms are used to express semantic concepts), but also what it is being used for and who it is being used with.

The bulk of research on interlanguage pragmatics has focused on pragmatic use rather than on acquisition. In pointing this out, Bardovi-Harlig (1999a) and Kasper and Schmidt (1996) made the important point that there is a dearth of studies dealing with changes in or influences on pragmatic knowledge. Kasper and Schmidt also outlined a number of research questions that need to be addressed regarding the acquisition of second language pragmatic knowledge. We list some of those questions here. As can be seen, they share themes with many of the issues related to other parts of language discussed in this book.

1   Are there universals of pragmatics and how do these universals affect the acquisition of second language pragmatic knowledge?
2   What are the issues relating to methodology and measurement?
3   What is the role of the native language?
4   Is development of L2 pragmatic knowledge similar to the development of L1 pragmatic knowledge?
5   Is there a natural route of development?
6   What is the role of input? Instruction? Motivation? Attitude?
7   What are the mechanisms that drive development?

To this, Bardovi-Harlig (2004c) adds the question of native-like attainment: "the question of whether (or to what extent) adults can acquire the pragmatics of a second language is at the heart of interlanguage pragmatics research" (p. 6).

Bardovi-Harlig (1999a) made the important point that one cannot consider the development of pragmatic knowledge without a concomitant consideration of grammatical knowledge. Hence, for learners who do not have a variety of verbal forms as part of their linguistic repertoire, their use of verbal forms to express pragmatic functions will be limited. Scarcella (1979), for instance, found that low level learners relied on imperatives when making requests in every situation. As proficiency increased, imperatives were appropriately restricted to subordinates and intimates. Bardovi-Harlig (1999b, p. 694) gives the following example.

(9-27) *Context*:   Graduate students addressing a faculty advisor.
         Advisor: OK, let's talk about next semester.

NS: I *was thinking of* taking syntax.

NNS: I *will* take syntax.

According to Bardovi-Harlig, this example suggests that the NNS shows an understanding of the core meaning of *will* as an indicator of the future, but does not understand the subtlety of use of the progressive as a marker of the future. Thus, the pragmatic extension of progressives to refer to the future is a later developmental stage.

Bardovi-Harlig and Dörnyei (1998) conducted a study in which participants saw videoclips of events and were asked if they noticed pragmatic and/or grammatical infelicities and how serious these were. Interestingly, the learning environment played a role in interpretation of severity of error. Second language learners were more sensitive to pragmatic errors than foreign language learners, both in terms of noticing them and in terms of judging them as serious.

The range of issues in interlanguage pragmatics is broad. Bardovi-Harlig (2004c) conducted a thorough review of a range of studies including comprehension/judgment and production studies. She reports studies that show that learners can achieve native-like performance and others that show the opposite. Many issues remain, including the evaluation of success (e.g., does someone appear rude because they don't know the appropriate second language pragmatic norms or because he or she is a rude person?) as well as detailed descriptions of interactions with a range of learners and in a range of contexts.

9.7 Conclusion: SLA and other disciplines

In this chapter and the three preceding chapters, we have concerned ourselves with the relationship between second language acquisition and other disciplines, notably linguistics, psychology, and sociolinguistics. Of course, these are not the only areas that relate to second language acquisition. Others—such as neurolinguistics, sociology, anthropology, communication, artificial intelligence/natural language processing, cognitive science, and philosophy—are also potential contributors to an understanding of the nature of second language acquisition.

We have presented data to show how a linguist, a psycholinguist, and a sociolinguist would look at second language data. But what about the opposite direction? What is the significance of second language acquisition data to an understanding of these source disciplines? There are different perspectives one can take on this issue. Gass (1989) and Gass and Schachter (1989) argued, with regard to the fields of linguistics and second language acquisition, that there are important bidirectional implications to the relationship. We extend that argument to other fields as well. In other words, it is our belief that second language acquisition is not only dependent on other disciplines for models, theories, and ways of asking and answering questions, but also gives back to those fields a broader perspective on the nature of human language and the human mind.

The argument made in Gass and Schachter (1989) focused on the bidirectionality of second language acquisition and linguistics. With regard to the disciplines discussed in this chapter, it is clear that the disciplines form the starting point of second language acquisition research. However, there is another side to this story. If linguistics, psychology, and sociolinguistics (or whatever other disciplines might be involved) attempt to understand broader issues of the human mind, then any theory emanating from these disciplines must incorporate findings from second languages, for they too are systems produced by humans. Any theory that fails to account for second language data, in this view, would be invalidated.

A weaker view is one that attributes an "enhancing" position to second language acquisition. That is, second language data would not falsify linguistic theories, theories of psychology, or models of sociolinguistics but would enhance those theories or models. What is meant by enhancement? In chapter 5, we presented data from Kellerman (1979) on language transfer. One of the important notions he developed was what he referred to as *psychotypology*. By understanding what a learner transfers and does not transfer from the NL, we gain insight into the organizational structure that humans impose on their NL. Thus, knowledge of that structure is gained through the window of second language data. Using second language data provides researchers with the means of viewing humans in an active dynamic situation of language use.

Suggestions for additional reading

Second Language Acquisition and Linguistic Variation. Richard Bayley and Dennis Preston (Eds.). John Benjamins (1996).
Communication Strategies. Ellen Bialystok. Basil Blackwell (1990a).
Communication Strategies: Psycholinguistic and Sociolinguistic Perspectives. Gabriele Kasper and Eric Kellerman. Longman (1997).
Sociocultural Theory and Second Language Learning. James P. Lantolf (Ed.). Oxford: Oxford University Press (2000).
Sociocultural Theory and the Genesis of Second Language Development. James P. Lantolf and Steve Thorne. Oxford University Press (2006).
Variation in Interlanguage Morphology. Richard Young. Peter Lang (1991).
Pragmatics. George Yule. Oxford University Press (1996).

Points for discussion

1 Many English speakers have what is called an *r*-less dialect in which a word such as car is pronounced without the final *r*. In many of these

dialects, when the following word begins with a vowel the r is frequently added (My car is in the garage vs. My [ka] breaks down frequently). In addition, hypercorrection occurs. In words without r (in spelling or in any dialect), an r is inserted before words beginning with a vowel, as in Cuba(r) is a country to the south of Florida.

Consider now speakers of these dialects as ESL teachers. It is not uncommon to hear their students produce Californiar is a beautiful state.

However, not all students do this. What does this suggest about the importance of input and the interaction of a learner's knowledge and the input the learner receives?

2   In sentence 9-26 we saw an example of a nonnative speaker's lack of pragmatic competence when responding to a professor's invitation to lunch to celebrate graduation (Thank you for the invitation. I would be willing to come.) Why is this response inappropriate in this situation? What would you respond to your professor in this situation? Think about your second language, if you have one. Would you respond in the same way as in your first language? If possible, try to find a native speaker of your second language and ask them if they think your response is appropriate in the situation.

3   In a study by Maier (1992), written apologies were collected in a business context. The task that was given to both nonnative and native speakers of English follows:

> Yesterday was not your lucky day. On your way to a job interview in another city, your car broke down on the highway. By the time you reached a telephone it was after 5:00 and no one answered your call at the office. When you called this morning, the secretary in the personnel department told you that you were no longer being considered for the position because you had not only missed your interview, but you had also failed to call. You explained your situation and were told that the only possible way to get another interview would be to write a letter to the personnel manager. If your letter was convincing enough, you might get another chance. Write a letter to the personnel manager to explain why you missed your appointment yesterday. Persuade her to give you another interview.

Below are excerpts from the responses from the native and nonnative speakers (the grammatical errors from the nonnative speakers' responses have been edited out). Identify these responses according to whether you believe they were written by a native speaker or a nonnative speaker. What are the characteristics that led to your choice? Consider not only the style of what is said, but also the content of the responses. What do you think is the effect of the different responses on a reader?

a   Please accept this letter of apology for not being able to meet with you yesterday for our scheduled interview.
b   First, I want to say sorry for not attending the job interview.
c   I apologize for missing the interview.
d   I would like to take this opportunity to apologize for missing the scheduled meeting.
e   Due to circumstances beyond my control, I was unable to participate in the scheduled interview on Wednesday.
f   Last Thursday I missed your interview by accident.
g   I would like you to give me another chance.
h   I would very much appreciate your consideration once again and also be grateful to you to be able to reschedule our meeting.
i   Please consider me once again for the interview.
j   I would be very grateful if, under the circumstances, you would grant me another interview.
k   I hope you will give me a chance to interview again.
l   Would you please give me one more chance . . . Please, please give me one more interview.
m   I would like to be a part of your organization.
n   I am very interested in your company. Working in the ABC Corporation is my dream. I cannot give up my dream.
o   I really, really want to work in your company. It is for this reason that I graduated from my school. I really want to make good use of my studies.
p   I remain very interested in this position.
q   I'm sure I'll never let you down.
r   I believe that I can handle this job well enough. You already know what my background is.
s   I'll call again at 10 on Wednesday morning, February 20, hoping to hear your positive response.
t   I look forward to your reply.
u   I hope you give a good prompt response.

4   What do the bar graphs in Figure 9.4 in this chapter suggest about the role of the phonetic environment in phonetic learning?
5   There are many speech acts that could be studied as part of second language use. Take one of the following and gather data from second language speakers in their use of the particular speech act: complaining, insulting, thanking, apologizing, requesting, refusing, complimenting, suggesting. In gathering data, consider such factors as gender, status, and familiarity. How do they affect your results?

6   As a follow-up to problem 4, gather baseline NS data (from the L1 and the L2 of the speaker) and determine if possible the source of the NNS speech act behavior.

7   In this chapter we discussed the significance of the interlocutor in determining NNS speech patterns. Consider the data given in Figures 9a.1 and 9a.2. In this study, Young (1986) tape-recorded data from six intermediate ESL learners. Each NNS was recorded in two separate

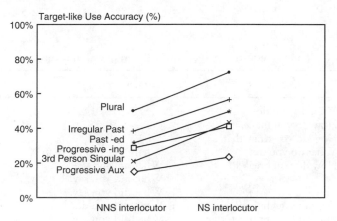

Figure 9a.1 Effect of interlocutor on TLU accuracy of bound morphemes and progressive auxiliary.

Source: From *Variation in Interlanguage Morphology* by R. Young, 1991, published by Peter Lang. Reprinted by permission.

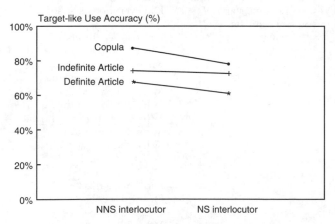

Figure 9a.2 Effect of interlocutor on TLU accuracy of free morphemes.

Source: From *Variation in Interlanguage Morphology* by R. Young, 1991, published by Peter Lang. Reprinted by permission.

297

interview situations, one with an English interviewer and one with an NNS interviewer.

How would you interpret these data? What conclusions can you draw regarding the effect of the interviewer on the speech patterns of these learners?

8 The data in Table 9a.1 are from a Japanese child learning English (Hakuta, 1974b). The data show her acquisition of questions in English.

Table 9a.1 Contexts requiring past auxiliary *did* in question form

Month	Present tense forms	Past tense forms
3	Why do you do?	
	How do you make?	
	How do you draw that?	
4	What do you do?	Where did you get that?
5	How do you break it?	What did she say?
		What did you say?
		What did you say?
6	Do you bought too?	What did you do?
	Do you bought this too?	What did you say?
	Do you put it?	
	Do you put it?	
	How do you put it?	
	How do you put it?	
7	How do you do it?	How did you get it?
8	Do you saw these peppermint?	Did you call?
	Do you saw some star eye?	Did everybody saw some blue hairs?
	Do you saw some star eye?	
9		Did you see the ghost?
		Did you know we locked the door when we come to here?
10		Did you use some blue?
		Why did you do that?
		Why did you get this?
		Why did you go to a hospital?
		Why did you draw?
11		What did you say?
		What did camel say?
		Did I made that?
		Did I make that?
		Did you see that?
		Did you see me?
		Why did you put this?
		I didn't correct this one, did I?
12		Did you what?

What can you determine from these data about this child's acquisition of past tense questions? Is the acquisition of the past auxiliary (*did*) in questions a case of all or nothing, or does acquisition appear to be gradual?

9   The graphs in Figure 9a.3 are the results for four IL forms from Japanese and Arabic learners of English. All learners were tested using three elicitation measures: (a) a grammaticality judgment test; (b) an oral interview, focusing on the learner's field of study; and (c) an oral narrative of events (video).

   Which of these three elicitation measures do you think requires the most attention to form? The least? Why?

Figure 9a.3 Style shifting on four IL forms by two NL groups on three tasks (TL—English).

Source: From "Variability in interlanguage use: a study of style-shifting in morphology and syntax" by E. Tarone, 1985, *Language Learning 35*, 373–404 by Research Club in Language Learning. Reprinted by permission.

Given your assessment of a progression from most attention to least attention to speech and the hypothesis that ILs would be most influenced by the TL on those tasks that required the most attention to form, how do these data bear on this issue? Are the results similar for all four IL forms? If not, what differences are there and how do you account for those differences?

10 The data in this problem reflect ways in which NSs and NNSs express agreement and disagreement (data from Porter, 1983). Part I deals with agreement and part II with disagreement. The NSs and NNSs were discussing three stories, all of which included the need to rank characters in the story in terms of which character is the most reprehensible, which character should be saved, and which is the most useful for surviving at sea.

PART I

NSs	NNSs
Initial responses	*Initial responses*
1. That's the same as mine.	1. Well, in the first, third we have the same.
2. Well, that's close.	2. It's agree, no? We're agree.
3. We're kind of agreed on some of them.	3. We are agree.
4. Well, I thought she was pretty bad too, but . . .	
After some discussion	*After some discussion*
5. I could go along with switching a little bit.	4. All right.
6. Well, I'm somewhat convinced by what you say.	5. I changed my mind.
7. That is somewhat good idea, I guess, in the extreme case.	6. It's OK. I think is OK.
8. I think basically you have a somewhat legitimate argument.	7. Yeah, I change to seven.

What similarities/differences are there between the way NSs and NNSs express agreement in these examples?

PART II

NSs	NNSs
1. (I ranked them—those two the worst.) Really, I ranked Abigail and Slug the worst.	
	1. No!
2. At this point, I was very arbitrary.	
	2. Well, I disagree with you.
3. But I don't know how it works.	
	3. I'm no agree with that.
4. I thought . . . but who would know for sure.	
	4. But that is not important.
5. Oh! It didn't even enter my head.	
	5. Is wrong.
6. I wouldn't necessarily agree with that.	
	6. No, no, forget it!
7. So I had him kind of towards the end of my list.	
	7. I'm not sure about.
	8. I didn't really pay attention of that part.
	9. Is very difficult.

What similarities/differences are there between NSs and NNSs in expressing disagreement? Considering both parts of this problem, do you think that the NNSs appear rude? If so, why? If not, why not? Do the NSs appear rude? Why or why not?

11 The following is a proposed taxonomy of communication strategies (modified from Tarone, 1977).

Avoidance (message abandonment)
Paraphrase
    Approximation
    Circumlocution
Conscious transfer
Literal translation
Language switch

Classify the following utterances (from Bialystok, 1990a, pp. 63–69) into one of the above categories. All are produced by English-speaking children learning French. What problems, if any, do you encounter in the classification? Evaluate the strategy used here in terms of the notions of problematicity, consciousness, and intentionality described in this chapter.

swing: C'est une sorte de, tu peux dire, chaise que quand tu "move." Des fois, c'est sur des arbres. [It's a kind of, you could say, chair for when you move. Sometimes it is in the trees.]

playpen: On peut mettre un bébé dedans. Il y a comme un trou. [You put a baby in it. It is like a hole.]

wooden spoon: On l'utilise pour prendre . . . si on mange . . . [You use it to make . . . if you eat . . .]

garden hose: Quelque chose qui est sur le mur et il y a un fausset avec un . . . [Something that is on the wall and there is a tap with a . . .]

spatula: Quelque chose que tu utilises souvent pour enlever quelque chose. [Something that you use often for picking up something.]

garden chair: De fois on le met dehors quand le soleil brille, ou sur la plage. [Sometimes you put it outside when the sun shines, or on the beach.]

can opener: C'est un object que tu . . . tu ouvres des "tins," des bôites en métal. [It's something that you . . . you open the tins, the metal boxes.]

can opener: C'est quand tu as une petite bouteille et il y a une machine et tu veux ouvrir la. [It's when you have a little bottle and there is a machine and you can (sic) open it.]

screwdriver: On utilise pour faire . . . il y a des gris, des rouges. Le rouge c'est comme on met tes mains au-dessus. L'autre part ça peut faire tu mettre les . . . [You use it to make . . . there are some grey and some red. The red is like you put your hands under it. The other part is so you can make the . . .]

wagon: Tu peux mettre des animaux ou des personnes dans et tu le tire. [You can put animals or people in it and you pull it.]

beater: C'est pour si on veut "mixer." [It's for if you want to mix.]

wrench: Quand tu as quelque chose qui est "stuck." Quand on a une bouteille du jus ou quelque chose et puis on veut ouvrir la petite chose que ist sur la bouteille. [When you have something that is stuck. When you have a bottle of juice or something and then you want to open the little thing that is on the bottle.]

garden hose: Quand tu as un jardin et tu veux que le jardin a de l'eau. [When you have a garden and you want the garden to have water.]

child's car seat: C'est une chaise pour bébé que tu mets dans la voiture pour tu sois "safe," sauf. [It's a chair for a baby that you put in a car to keep you safe.]

rubber stamp: Le part brun regarde comme c'est une tête. [The brown part looks like a head.]

See GSS, problems 5.1, 5.2, 6.7, and 7.2.

10

INPUT, INTERACTION, AND OUTPUT

10.1 Introduction

It is commonly believed that learning a second language involves learning the rules of grammar of the second language (often in the form of memorization), along with vocabulary items and correct rules of pronunciation. Putting those rules to use in the context of conversation is then construed as a natural extension of grammar acquisition. This view implicitly assumes that language use does not vary from first language situations to various second language situations, for all that would be needed to successfully converse in a second language would be to plug in the correct forms to say the same thing as one does in one's native language. In this chapter, we show how this view is an overly simplistic one (see also chapter 1). We first deal with the nature of the input to second language learners. We then focus on the interrelationship of second language use (especially conversation) and language learning.

10.2 Input

As we discussed in chapter 4, earlier conceptualizations of second language learning were based on a behaviorist view in which the major driving force of language learning (at least for children) was the language to which learners were exposed (the input). Because, in that view, learning a language involved imitation as its primary mechanism, the language that surrounded learners was of crucial importance. However, as behaviorist theories fell into disfavor, so did research interest in the input to the learner.

Interest shifted to the internal mechanisms that a learner (child or adult) brings to the language-learning situation, with research focusing on innateness and the nature of the innate system. As has been discussed elsewhere in this book, learners were viewed as creators of language systems; and, at least in the case of children, the input they received was of minor importance. If learners only need to discover which of a limited

304

number of possibilities are represented in their language, then it is possible that only a few instances of exposure are sufficient to trigger the appropriate language forms. As a consequence of this view, the significance of the input was minimized.

Corder, in 1967, made an important distinction between what he called *input* and *intake*. Input refers to what is available to the learner, whereas intake refers to what is actually internalized (or, in Corder's terms, "taken in") by the learner. Anyone who has been in a situation of learning a second/foreign language is familiar with the situation in which the language one hears is totally incomprehensible, to the extent that it may not even be possible to separate the stream of speech into words. Whereas this is input, because it is available to the learner, it is not intake, because it "goes in one ear and out the other"; it is not integrated into the current learner-language system. This sort of input appears to serve no greater purpose for the learner than does that language that is never heard. Conceptually, one can think of the input as that language (in both spoken and written forms) to which the learner is exposed.

What is the nature of the input to a language learner? Ferguson (1971), in a study designed to look at issues of linguistic simplicity, noted that in language directed toward linguistically deficient individuals (young children, NNSs of a language), NSs make adjustments to their speech in the areas of pronunciation, grammar, and lexicon. Speech directed toward young children he called *baby talk* (now known variably as *motherese, caretaker speech,* or *child-directed speech*); speech directed toward linguistically deficient NNSs he called *foreigner talk*. His goal was to explore the similarities between these two speech varieties. Here we focus on foreigner talk examples, taken from Ferguson's original work (see Table 10.1).

We can see that there are various means of altering the speech that would normally be expected in situations in which only NSs are conversing. For example, in the Spanish example from Table 10.1, the subject pronoun *yo* is changed to the direct object pronoun *mi*, the first person singular verb *veo* is expressed by the infinitival form *ver*, and the

Table 10.1 Examples of speech to NSs and NNSs

	Speech to NSs	Speech to NNSs
SPANISH	yo veo al soldado I I see DO soldier (DO = direct object marker)	mi ver soldado me to see soldier
ARABIC	ya'rif he knows	ya'rif used to mean: he/she/I/you know

Source: Ferguson (1971).

direct object marker *al* is omitted. In the Arabic example, the form that expresses third person singular in standard Arabic is used for all persons.

Table 10.2 presents examples from English, and Table 10.3, adapted from Hatch (1983), presents a partial listing of characteristics of foreigner talk speech. In general, foreigner talk adjustments reveal speech patterns that would not ordinarily be used in conversations with NSs. Foreigner talk shares features in common with caretaker speech, the language spoken to young children. Some of the most salient features of

Table 10.2 Examples of foreigner talk

NS speech	Foreigner talk
D'yu wanna go?	Do you want to go?
No, I can't.	No, I cannot.

Table 10.3 Summary of foreigner talk features

SLOW RATE = clearer articulation
    Final stops are released
    Fewer reduced vowels
    Fewer contractions
    Longer pauses
VOCABULARY
    High frequency vocabulary
        Less slang
        Fewer idioms
    Fewer pronoun forms
    Definitions
        Overtly marked (e.g., *This means* X)
        Semantic feature information (e.g., *a cathedral usually means a church, that's a very high ceiling*)
        Contextual information (e.g., *if you go for a job in a factory, they talk about a wage scale*)
    Gestures and pictures
SYNTAX
    Short and simple sentences
    Movement of topics to front of sentence
    Repetition and restatement
    New information at the end of the sentence
    NS grammatically repeats/modifies learners' incorrect utterances
    NS fills in the blank for learners' incomplete utterances
DISCOURSE
    NS gives reply within a question
    NS uses tag questions
    NS offers correction

Source: Adapted from Hatch (1983).

Table 10.4 A progression of foreigner talk

To an NS kindergarten class:
   These are babysitters taking care of babies. Draw a line from Q to q.
   From S to s and then trace.
To a single NS:
   Now, Johnny, you have to make a great big pointed hat.
To an intermediate level NS of Urdu:
   Now her hat is big. Pointed.
To a low intermediate level NS of Arabic:
   See hat? Hat is big. Big and tall.
To a beginning level NS of Japanese:
   Big, big, big hat.
To a beginning level NS of Korean:
   Baby sitter. Baby.

Source: Kleifgen (1985).

foreigner talk include: slow speech rate, loud speech, long pauses, simple vocabulary (e.g., few idioms, high frequency words), repetitions and elaborations, and paucity of slang. Additional examples are given in Table 10.4. In these examples, which come from a single kindergarten teacher's instructions to her students, there is a gradation from talk to NSs to nonproficient second language speakers. The teacher adjusts her speech as a function of the proficiency of her students.

Characteristics of foreigner talk are not always so obvious. Consider 10-1 and 10-2, which come from a survey on food and nutrition that NNSs conducted over the telephone (Gass and Varonis, 1985, p. 48):

(10-1) NNS: How have increasing food costs changed your eating habits?

NS: Well, we don't eat as much beef as we used to. We eat more chicken, and uh, pork, and uh, fish, things like that.

NNS: Pardon me?

NS: We don't eat as much beef as we used to. We eat more chicken and uh, uh pork and fish ... We don't eat beef very often. We don't have steak like we used to.

(10-2) NNS: There has been a lot of talk lately about additives and preservatives in food. In what ways has this changed your eating habits?

NS: I try to stay away from nitrites.

NNS: Pardon me?

NS: Uh, from nitrites in uh like lunch meats and that sort of thing. I don't eat those.

In these two examples, there was little indication of modified speech in the initial responses to the NNSs' questions. This is perhaps because the questions were scripted and rehearsed, and despite the obvious non-nativeness of the caller (Spanish in the first example and Arabic in the second), there was an appearance of fluency. However, once the NNS said *Pardon me?*, the NS in all likelihood realized the difficulty involved in the conversation and made modifications. In this case, the modification was not syntactic or phonological, as one typically expects with foreigner talk. Rather, the NS restated, repeated, and elaborated on the responses, the implication being that, given more information, the NNS would have an easier time understanding.

There are still other ways of modifying speech. From the same database come the following two examples:

> (10-3) NNS: How have increasing food costs changed your eat-
> ing habits?
> NS: Well, I don't know that it's changed THEM. I try to
> adjust.
> NNS: Pardon me?
> NS: I don't think it's changed MY EATING HABITS.

In 10-3, the NS specified the noun object more fully once the NNS indicated a lack of understanding.

In 10-4, implicit grammatical information is made more explicit by adding the subject and the auxiliary verb:

> (10-4) NNS: How have increasing food costs changed your eat-
> ing habits?
> NS: Oh, rising costs we've cut back on the more expen-
> sive things. GONE to cheaper foods.
> NNS: Pardon me?
> NS: WE'VE GONE to cheaper foods.

In looking at a composite picture of these data, one finds that modifi-cation of one's speech when addressing NNSs is a variable matter, with NSs reassessing an NNS's linguistic ability during the course of a conver-sational interaction. That is, one might engage in a conversation assuming either fluency on the one hand or lack of fluency on the other. However, as a result of a continuing conversation, one's assessment of the language ability, or language proficiency, of an NNS is likely to change. This will often result in a change in the speech patterns during the conversation.

What are the functions of foreigner talk in terms of language learning? Generally, one can claim that by hearing speech that has been simplified in the ways just described the second language learner will be better able to understand. It is a given that, without understanding the language, no learning can take place. Although understanding alone does not guarantee that learning will occur, it does set the scene for learning to take place. However, not all types of foreigner talk are created equal. In a review of the literature, Parker and Chaudron (1987) showed that simplifications resulting from discourse elaboration or modification of the conversational structure are more likely to aid comprehension than those simplifications which result from simplification at the linguistic level (i.e., foreigner talk).

We turn to the Input Hypothesis, developed by Krashen, as part of his overall Monitor Model and as part of his overall sketch of acquisition. It is a supplement to the Natural Order Hypothesis, which we discuss further in chapter 11. If there is a natural order of acquisition, how is it that learners move from one point to another? The Input Hypothesis provides the answer. Second languages are acquired "by understanding messages, or by receiving 'comprehensible input' " (Krashen, 1985, p. 2).

Krashen defined "comprehensible input" in a particular way. Essentially, comprehensible input is that bit of language that is heard/read and that is slightly ahead of a learner's current state of grammatical knowledge. Language containing structures a learner already knows essentially serves no purpose in acquisition. Similarly, language containing structures way ahead of a learner's current knowledge is not useful. A learner does not have the ability to "do" anything with those structures. Krashen defined a learner's current state of knowledge as i and the next stage as $i + 1$. Thus the input a learner is exposed to must be at the $i + 1$ level in order for it to be of use in terms of acquisition. "We move from i, our current level to $i + 1$, the next level along the natural order, by understanding input containing $i + 1$" (1985, p. 2).

Krashen assumed a Language Acquisition Device, that is, an innate mental structure capable of handling both first and second language acquisition. The input activates this innate structure. But only input of a very specific kind ($i + 1$) will be useful in altering a learner's grammar.

In Krashen's view, the Input Hypothesis is central to all of acquisition and also has implications for the classroom.

a   Speaking is a result of acquisition and not its cause. Speech cannot be taught directly but "emerges" on its own as a result of building competence via comprehensible input.

b   If input is understood, and there is enough of it, the necessary grammar is automatically provided. The language teacher need not attempt deliberately to teach the next structure along the natural order—it will be provided in just the right quantities and automatically reviewed if the student receives a sufficient amount of comprehensible input.

The teacher's main role, then, is to ensure that students receive comprehensible input. However, despite its attractiveness (and clearly no one would deny the importance and significance of input), there are numerous difficulties with the concept. First, the hypothesis itself is not specific as to how to define levels of knowledge. Thus, if we are to validate this hypothesis, we must know how to define a particular level (say, level 1904) so that we can know whether the input contains linguistic level 1905 and, if so, whether the learner, as a result, moves to level 1905. Krashen only stated that "We acquire by understanding language that contains structure a bit beyond our current level of competence ($i + 1$). This is done with the help of context or extralinguistic information" (1982, p. 21).

Second is the issue of quantity. Krashen states that there has to be sufficient quantity of the appropriate input. But what is sufficient quantity? How do we know whether the quantity is sufficient or not? One token, two tokens, 777 tokens? And, perhaps the quantity necessary for change depends on developmental level, or how ready the learner is to acquire a new form.

Third, how does extralinguistic information aid in actual acquisition, or internalization of a linguistic rule, if by "understanding" Krashen meant understanding at the level of meaning (see below and chapter 14 for a different interpretation of understanding)? We may be able to understand something that is beyond our grammatical knowledge, but how does that translate into grammatical acquisition? As Gregg (1984, p. 88) stated: "I find it difficult to imagine extra-linguistic information that would enable one to 'acquire' the third person singular -s, or yes/no questions, or indirect object placement, or passivization."

As mentioned in chapter 8, input also figures prominently in emergentist accounts of SLA where frequency of input is highly significant. Learners in this view are seen to extract regularities from the input as opposed to regularities being imposed by UG.

10.3 Comprehension

Crucial to the success of any conversation is the ability to understand and to be understood. Lack of comprehension is a characteristic of many conversations involving NNSs. What factors determine comprehensibility?

The first area of concern in a discussion of comprehension is the NS's ability to understand the NNS's pronunciation. However, this is clearly not the only factor; the NNS's ability to use the second language grammatically is yet another. In fact, in a study using a matched-guise format,[1] NS listeners were asked to judge sentences read by the same NNS (each of 14 NNSs read one pair of sentences, all of which were then randomized). The sentences varied according to whether or not they were grammatical. One version was grammatical and the other was not. Given that one speaker read both versions, pronunciation remained constant. Examples of grammatical and ungrammatical pairs are given in 10-5 (from Varonis and Gass, 1982, p. 135):

(10-5)	Grammatical	It is unusual for him to have a new car.
	Ungrammatical	He is unusual to have a new car.
	Grammatical	He always spends his holidays at home.
	Ungrammatical	He does spend his holidays always at home.

When asked to judge the NNSs' pronunciation on a two-pronged scale ("good" and "not good"), NSs for the most part judged the grammatical sentences as being spoken by a speaker with good pronunciation and the ungrammatical sentences spoken by a speaker with bad pronunciation. Although grammaticality had an influence on the majority of the responses, there were some speakers for whom grammaticality had little effect on NS judgments. These were the speakers who were judged, on an independent rating, to have very good or very bad pronunciation; that is, the two extremes. Thus, understanding an NNS's speech is dependent on at least the grammaticality of the NNS's speech as well as the pronunciation.

An additional factor determining comprehensibility is the NNS's ability to contextualize the language by using appropriate vocabulary and linking devices. To exemplify this, we reproduce a letter written by an NNS to an NS (one of the authors of this book). As can be seen, this letter is, at best, difficult to understand. Given the written mode, pronunciation is not a factor. What is particularly interesting is that the sentences for the most part are syntactically well-formed. Yet, as a whole, the letter is unclear. The letter was apparently written in response to an advertisement from the addressee's home institution.

Dear . . .

I'm very glad to receive your good request about expending for linguage. I looked it hardly and found that late.

I want to obtain publications which will help me to finish my formations in English or technological knowledge.

Many times I wrote over without best answer was obtained. With that discriminate area, I have disjointed several forms.

So, I ask a place to follow research learning, or, your useful publications.

I prefer to change my present job, so, all you'll do must be wellcome.

I'm interesting in world food program, or, in a field where research, campaigns are useful.

Thanks.

The first paragraph is interesting in that it is grammatically correct, but semantically anomalous. What makes it semantically anomalous? The choice of vocabulary items, namely *expending, linguage, hardly*, make the paragraph difficult to understand. It seems, then, that vocabulary choice is much more central to assigning meaning than is correct grammar.

The third paragraph supports the centrality of vocabulary and the secondary role of grammar. In the first sentence, *Many times I wrote over without best answer was obtained*, even though the second clause is grammatically ill-formed, it is not difficult to understand that the writer meant *without receiving a good answer*. However, in the second sentence, *With that discriminate area, I have disjointed several forms*, the sentence is grammatically well-formed, but the vocabulary is inappropriate (particularly *discriminate* and *disjointed*). The significance of inappropriate vocabulary is clear when we try to attach meaning to the sentence.

From these studies, we can conclude that in interpreting NNS utterances, grammar is less important than pronunciation and vocabulary.[2] Assuming that these results are borne out, we can ask: Why should this be the case? The main explanation has to do with range of choices. There is a more limited number of grammatical possibilities (or grammar rules) in language than there are vocabulary items or possible pronunciations. That is, if a learner fails to mark agreement or puts items in the wrong order, there is a greater likelihood that an NS can fall back on his or her grammatical knowledge to make sense of what a learner is saying. However, if a learner uses an inappropriate or nonexistent vocabulary item, the NS may be sent down a comprehension path from which there is little possibility of return.

The second area of concern in a discussion of comprehension is the NNS's ability to understand. In conversation, indications of understanding are given in a number of ways. Most common are what are called backchannel cues. These are generally verbal messages, such as *uh huh* or *yeah*, which are said during the time another person is talking.[3] When a conversation is face to face, as opposed to over the telephone, head nods can also serve the same function. To understand how important these backchannel cues are in conversation, consider a telephone conversation in which you are talking to someone who is not giving frequent indication that he or she is listening. In other words, consider a conversation in which there is complete silence on the other end. It does not take long before you begin to wonder if anyone is there. Nonnative speakers of a language quickly learn how to give appropriate backchanneling cues without the concomitant ability to actually understand the conversation.

In the following conversation (from Varonis and Gass, 1985a, pp. 332–333) we see how the major NNS contribution to this conversation is the provision of backchannel cues. As we can see during the course of the conversation, the NNS in all likelihood has little understanding of what the NS is saying but uses backchannel cues as a way of keeping the conversation going.

The context for this conversation is as follows: A native speaker of Spanish, studying English in the United States, called a store to inquire about the price of a TV set. However, he did not realize that when he looked up the telephone number in the telephone book he had looked up numbers for TV repair shops. Following is a transcription of that telephone conversation.

(10-6) NNS

    2. Hello could you tell me about the price and size of Sylvania color TV?

    4. Could you tell me about price and size of Sylvania TV color?

    6. Uh 17 inch huh?

    8. Yeah TV color.

10. OK.

12. Uh huh.

14. Ah Sony please.

16. Or Sylvania.

18. Uh huh.

20. OK.

22. Hm hm.

24. Hm hm.

NS

1. Hello.

3. Pardon?

PAUSE

    5. What did you want? A service call?

    7. What did you want a service call? Or how much to repair a TV?

    9. 17 inch.

SILENCE

11. Is it a portable?

13. What width is it? What is the brand name of the TV?

15. We don't work on Sonys.

17. Sylvania?

19. Oh, Sylvania OK. That's American made.

21. All right. Portables have to be brought in.

23. And there's no way I can tell you how much it'll cost until *he* looks at it.

25. And it's a $12.50 deposit.

26. OK.

27. And if he can fix it that applies to labor and if he can't he keeps the $12.50 for his time and effort.

28. Hm hm.

29. How old of a TV is it? Do you know off hand?

30. 19 inch.

31. How old of a TV is it? Is it a very old one or only a couple years old?

32. Oh, so so.

33. The only thing you can do is bring it in and let him look at it and go from there.

34. New television please.

35. Oh you want to know

SILENCE

how much a new television is?

36. Yeah I want buy one television.

37. Do we want to buy one?

38. Yeah.

39. Is it a Sylvania?

40. Sylvania TV color.

41. Well, you know even, even if we buy 'em, we don't give much more than $25 for 'em. By the time we fix 'em up and sell 'em, we can't get more than

42. Hm hm.

43. $100 out of 'em time we put our time and parts in it.

44. Is it 17 inch?

45. Well, I don't . . . the only thing I can tell you to do is you'd have to come to the shop. I'm on the extension at home. The shop's closed.

SILENCE

46. 19 inch? You don't have?

47. Do we have a 19 inch?

48. Yeah.

49. No, I've got a 17 inch new RCA.

50. OK. Thank you. Bye.

51. Bye.

If we look only at the NNS's speech, it is clear that it is dominated by *yeahs*, *uh huhs*, *hm hms*, and OKs. Yet, it is clear from the transcript that the NNS never realized that the NS was talking about repairing TVs. It is likely that this NNS's use of a large number of appropriately placed backchannel cues is what led the NS to continue the conversation

314

(see Hawkins, 1985, for a lengthier discussion of the role of signals of apparent understanding and actual understanding).

The more familiar NSs are with NNS speech, either through individual contact or through language background, the easier it is for NS comprehension to take place. In a study in which familiarity with NNS speech was the object of investigation (Gass and Varonis, 1984), it was found that the more experience NSs had in listening to NNS speech, the more they understood. In particular, comprehension appears to be facilitated by three factors: (a) familiarity with a particular NNS, (b) familiarity with nonnative speech in general, and (c) familiarity with the discourse topic. Experience with a particular NNS will result in ease of comprehension. This is not unlike what happens with child speech, as it is frequently the case that young children are only understood by their caregivers. General experience in conversations with NNSs also facilitates comprehension. A teacher of English to NNSs, for example, is more likely to understand other NNSs than someone who has had little or no interaction with NNSs. Finally, if the topic of the discourse is familiar, it is more likely that understanding is aided by an NS's ability to fill in with prior knowledge when individual words may not be understood. For example, now that you are familiar with the literature on SLA, if an NNS uttered sentence 10-7, you could probably fill in the words that you didn't understand just by what you know about SLA.

(10-7) An interlanguage is what is produced by
nonnat_____ _____of a language when learning a
second language.

Why does this happen? Listeners bring with them to the listening task a set of beliefs about the world. These beliefs allow easy interpretation of utterances that have a readily accessible real-world context. Thus sentences such as *Although he studies hard, he doesn't do well in school* are easily understandable because they fit in with our real-world expectations; on the other hand, a sentence such as *The chair sat down on the dog* is a more difficult sentence to understand (especially when spoken by a person with a nonnative accent) because there are few discourse hooks on which to hang the information contained in that sentence. In other words, we have no discourse context. As Labov and Fanshel (1977, p. 82) stated (based on NS conversations), "most of the information needed to interpret actions is already to be found in the structure of shared knowledge and not in the utterances themselves." In the situation regarding NNSs, shared knowledge can refer not only to actual real-world knowledge, but also to linguistic knowledge, such as pronunciation, grammar, and vocabulary.

We have seen that problems between an NS and an NNS can occur for a variety of reasons, ranging from an NNS's pronunciation to an NS's misreading of backchannel cues. However, in many instances when there is a lack of comprehension between speakers, they will stop the flow of conversation to question what is not understood. In other words, they will "negotiate the meaning" of an utterance. To better understand this and how it differs from what happens in NS speech, we next look at the nature of NS conversation.

It is commonly acknowledged that in most conversations the discourse progresses in a linear fashion. When participants in a conversation share a common background (social/cultural/language), the turn-taking sequence proceeds smoothly, with each speaker responding to what the previous speaker has said, while maintaining his or her own sense of direction in the discourse. In other words, barring loud noises, inattentiveness, and so forth, participants in a conversation have an understanding of what has been said, of what was intended, and of how their contribution to the conversation fits in with previous contributions (by them or by others).

The following example illustrates a typical NS conversation (Tannen, 1986, p. 119).

> (10-8) *Context*: Mike makes yogurt dressing, tastes it, and makes
> a face.
> Ken: Isn't it good?
> Mike: I don't know how to make yogurt dressing.
> Ken: Well, if you don't like it, throw it out.
> Mike: Never mind.
> Ken: What never mind? It's just a little yogurt.
> Mike: You're making a big deal about nothing.
> Ken: You are!

In the preceding example, each person takes a conversational turn understanding what has preceded. Both Ken and Mike know that they are talking about the yogurt dressing and that their comments refer first to its taste and second to whether or not the dressing should be retained. Had Mike not responded to Ken's first question by referring to the dressing but to a movie he had seen, Ken would perhaps have perceived this as somewhat out of place. This is not to say that all parts of NS conversation are grammatical, or complete, but it does suggest that the norm is for participants to be aware of where their contribution fits in to the emerging conversation.

In discourse where there is not shared background, or in which there is some acknowledged "incompetence" (e.g., incomplete knowledge of the language being spoken, or lack of knowledge of the topic), the conversational flow is marred by numerous interruptions, as in the following example from Gass and Varonis (1985, p. 41):

(10-9) NNS: There has been a lot of talk lately about additives and preservatives in food. How—

NS: —a a a lot, a lot of talk about what?

NNS: Uh. There has been a lot of talk lately about additives and preservatives in food.

NS: Now just a minute. I can hear you—everything except the important words. You say there's been a lot of talk lately about what [inaudible]

NNS: —additive, additive, and preservative, in food—

NS: Could you spell one of those words for me, please?

NNS: A D D I T I V E.

NS: Just a minute. This is strange to me.

NNS: H h.

NS: Uh—

NNS: 'n other word is P R E S E R V A

NS: —oh, preserves

NNS: Preservative and additive.

NS: —preservatives, yes, okay. And what was that— what was that first word I didn't understand?

NNS: OKAY in—

NS: —Additives?

NNS: OKAY.

NS: —Additives and preservatives

NNS: Yes.

NS: Ooh right . . .

10.4 Interaction

The interaction approach accounts for learning through input (exposure to language), production of language (output), and feedback that comes as a result of interaction (see summary by Gass and Mackey, 2006). Gass (2003) puts it this way: interaction research "takes as its starting point the assumption that language learning is stimulated by communicative pressure and examines the relationship between communication and acquisition and the mechanisms (e.g., noticing, attention) that mediate between them" (p. 224). Interaction involves a number of components including negotiation, recasts, and feedback. In what follows, we introduce the concept of negotiation of meaning. This is followed by a section on output within which we further discuss negotiation and focus on recasts, as parts of a broader concept of feedback.

When the flow of conversation is interrupted, as in 10-9, participants often compensate by questioning particular utterances (*You say there's been a lot of talk about what?*) and/or requesting conversational help (*could you spell one of those words for me?*). In other words, they negotiate what was not understood. Negotiation of this sort allows participants to maintain as well as possible equal footing in the conversation. Negotiation provides the means for participants to respond appropriately to one another's utterance and to regain their places in a conversation after one or both have "slipped."

Reference was made earlier to negotiation of meaning. This refers to those instances in conversation when participants need to interrupt the flow of the conversation in order for both parties to understand what the conversation is about, as in example 10-10 (see also 10-9). In conversations involving NNSs, negotiations are frequent, at times occupying a major portion of the conversation. An example is given in 10-10 (Varonis and Gass, 1985b, pp. 78–79).

> (10-10) J = NS of Japanese; S = NS of Spanish
> J: And your what is your mm father's job?
> S: My father now is retire.
> J: Retire?
> S: Yes.
> J: Oh yeah.
> S: But he work with uh uh institution.
> J: Institution.
> S: Do you know that? The name is . . . some thin like eh control of the state.
> J: Aaaaaaaah.
> S: Do you understand more or less?
> J: State is uh . . . what what kind of state?
> S: It is uhm.
> J: Michigan State?
> S: No, the all nation.
> J: No, government?
> S: All the nation, all the nation. Do you know for example is a the the institution mmm of the state mm of Venezuela.
> J: Ah ah.
> S: Had to declare declare? her ingress.
> J: English?
> S: No. English no (laugh) . . . ingress, her ingress.
> J: Ingress?
> S: Ingress. Yes. I N G R E S S more or less.
> J: Ingless.
> S: Yes. If for example, if you, when you work you had an ingress, you know?
> J: Uh huh an ingless?

S: Yes.

J: Uh huh OK.

S: Yes, if for example, your homna, husband works, when finish, when end the month his job, his boss pay—mm—him something.

J: Aaaah.

S: And your family have some ingress.

J: Yes ah, OK OK.

S: More or less OK? And in this in this institution take care of all ingress of the company and review the accounts.

J: OK I got, I see.

S: OK my father work there, but now he is old.

In the preceding conversation, the speakers spend the majority of their time involved in straightening out the meaning of words, specifically, *retire*, *institution*, *state*, and *ingress* ("income"). In conversations involving nonproficient NNSs, exchanges of the sort exemplified in 10-10 are frequent, with considerable effort going into resolving nonunderstandings as opposed to exchanging ideas or opinions (the typical material of conversation).

As we have seen, not only is the form of the speech produced by NSs modified in conversations with NNSs, but also the structure of the conversation itself. Long (1980) was the first to point out that conversations involving NNSs exhibited forms that did not appear to any significant degree when only NSs were involved. For example, confirmation checks (*Is this what you mean?*), comprehension checks (*Do you understand? Do you follow me?*) and clarification requests (*What? Huh?*) are peppered throughout conversations in which there is a nonproficient NNS participant. Examples of each are given in 10-11 to 10-14.

(10-11) Comprehension check
        NNS: I was born in Nagasaki. Do you know Nagasaki?

(10-12) Comprehension check
        NNS1: And your family have some ingress.
        NNS2: Yes ah, OK OK.
→   NNS1: More or less OK?

(10-13) Confirmation check
        NNS1: When can you go to visit me?
→   NNS2: Visit?

(10-14) Clarification request
        NNS1: . . . research.
        NNS2: Research, I don't know the meaning.

Furthermore, different kinds of questions are asked, often with the answer being suggested by the NS immediately after the question is asked. Example 10-15 comes from two NSs of English; example 10-16 is from an NS and an NNS (Long, 1983, p. 180).

(10-15) NS1: What do you think of Michigan?
NS2: It's nice, but I haven't gotten used to the cold weather yet.
(10-16) NS: Do you like California?
NNS: Huh?
NS: Do you like Los Angeles?
NNS: Uhm . . .
NS: Do you like California?
NNS: Yeah, I like it.

In 10-15, the conversation proceeds in step-wise fashion; in 10-16, there is an indication of nonunderstanding (*Huh?*), with the result being a narrowing down of the topic (*California* → Los Angeles), followed by a final repetition of the original question. These conversational tactics provide the NNS with as much information as possible as she attempts to ascribe meaning to the NS's stream of sounds.

In 10-17 the NS asks an "or-choice" question. That is, the NS not only asks a question but provides the NNS with a range of possible answers. The example is from a personal observation made in an ESL classroom during the first class back after a long holiday break. The teacher had asked a student what he did over the break. He responded that he had just relaxed.

(10-17) NS: Where did you relax?
Silence
NS: Did you relax out of town or in East Lansing?
NNS: East Lansing.

A similar example is given in 10-18, from the play *Fully Committed* by Becky Mode (1995), in which the NS gives multiple choices when the NNS does not understand. The setting is a restaurant reservations office.

(10-18) Sam: . . . How can I help you?
Watanabe: My name is Watanabe. "W" as in Wisconsin, "A" as—
S: Okay. How can I help you?
W: I want to take a table.
S: Okay, when would you like to come in?
W: We are four people.

320

S: All right. When would you like to come in?

W: Four people.

S: Okay . . . What day of the week would you like to come in?

W: Four.

S: I'll be right with you ma'am. (*Puts her on hold, takes a deep breath, then returns.*) Sorry about that.

W: No have four?

S: No, no. (*Trying a new tactic.*). Four people on Monday? Tuesday? Wednesday?

W: Ohhh! Tuesday.

S: Okay, Tuesday. Would you like to come in for lunch or dinner?

W: Lunch!

S: Okay! Lunch on Tuesday. What time?

W: Seven P.M.

S: Ma'am. That's dinner.

W: Dinner?

S: Yes seven P.M. is dinner and we are fully committed for dinner on Tuesday.

W: Ful-ly?

S: We don't have any tables.

W: Oh, I call you back.

In this excerpt, Sam, the native speaker, clearly understands that this is a difficult conversation and offers choices (Monday? Tuesday?) and rephrases *fully committed* (*we don't have any tables*), when it is apparent that the NNS does not know that word.

There are other, perhaps more subtle, differences between conversations involving only NSs and those involving at least one nonproficient NNS. For example, in conversations with NNSs, there is frequently a willingness on the part of everyone to change topics, often abruptly.

(10-19) Topic shift

NNS1: Are you going to attend today's party?

NNS2: I don't know yet, but probably I'll attend. (long pause, with intermittent "hm"s). So when will you go back to Japan?

(10-20) (from Gass and Varonis, 1986, p. 340). Talking about a book.

NNS1: Did you read it?

NNS2: Yes, of cou—

NNS1: Yes, I read it too.

NNS2: Oh really? I decided . . .

> NNS1: Well, you don't come from Kochi prefecture do
> you?

Topic shifts may also result from prolonged attempts to negotiate the meaning, as in 10-21 (from Hatch, 1978, pp. 420–421).

> (10-21) NS: Who is the best player in Colombia?
> NNS: Colombia?
> NS: Does uh . . . who is *the* Colombian player?
> NNS: Me?
> NS: No, in Colombia, who is *the* player?
> NNS: In Colombia plays. Yah.
> NS: No, on your team. On the Millionarios.
> NNS: Ah yah, Millionarios.
> NS: No, on the Millionarios team.
> NNS: Millionarios play in Colombia. In Sud America.
> In Europa.
> NS: Do, do they have someone like Pele in Colombia?
> NNS: Pele? In Colombia? Pele?
> NS: In Colombia? Who is, who is "Pele" in Colombia?
> Do you have someone?
> NNS: In Bogota?
> NS: Yeah, who is the best player?
> NNS: In Santo de Brazil?
> NS: OK (gives up) and are you center forward?

In all of the examples provided in this section, the effect of NS and NNS modifications (whether intentional or not) is to aid the NNS in understanding. This reduces the burden for the NNS in that he or she is assisted by others in understanding and in producing language appropriate to the situation. However, one could also argue that outward signs of negotiation and resolution of that negotiation are only strategies to show solidarity, rather than true indications of meaning negotiation (Aston, 1986; Hawkins, 1985).

One should not be misled, however, into thinking that comprehension is the same as acquisition. Comprehension, in the usual sense of the word, refers to a single event, whereas acquisition refers to a permanent state. (Other ways of viewing the notion of comprehension will be discussed in chapter 14.)

In chapter 9 we discussed conversation analysis (section 9.4.1). We presented data from Mori (2004) with her conversation analytic (CA) interpretation and data from Kasper (2004) with her conversation analytic interpretation. Below we present the same snippets of conversation with an interpretation that would be given by someone within an interactionist framework. We include the CA interpretation for purposes of comparison.

Lines 39–49	Conversation analysis	Input–Interaction

David: °nan da?°
  [°(wata-) .ss::°
 	
What is it? [°(I–) .ss::°(39)
Alan: [ANO:
  watashi
  no uchi O::,
  aa:: abunaiku::
  naritai
  toKI::, (0.4)
  d[onna::
 	
Uhm when I want my hou::se to be:: ah: dangerous ((incorrect)), (0.4) what ki::nd (40–41)
	Line 40—asks question about what David wants to say. Focus is on the lack of indication of appropriate ownership
	Lines 39→ use of Japanese suggests the importance of Japanese in classroom
	Lines 40–41—Alan formulates question that turns out to be basically a translation of English, but has the opposite meaning in Japanese
		Line 39—request for assistance—probably for a word
		Line 40—serves as a trigger for feedback for teacher

Teacher: [abunaku
  naritai?
want to be dangerous? (42)
 	
  (0.4) (43)
		Line 42—teacher provides feedback
		Line 43—pause possibly indicates "thinking" where Alan is attempting to process the feedback

Alan: aa[::: *aa::: (44)* David: [uhe heh *uhe heh (45)* Alan: abu- aa[:::::: *dan- aa::::: (46)*	Lines 44–46—Alan reacts to repair and reflects on what he said Line 45—David points out that what Alan has said is not correct	Line 44—Alan indicates an understanding of feedback Line 45—David also indicates an understanding of what was wrong with Alan's utterance (see Pica, 1992; Mackey, 1999; Ohta, 2001 about learning that can take place by nonparticipants)
David: [>°ie ie ie [a ie°< *No no no oh no (47)*	Line 47—David points out that what Alan has said is not correct	Line 47—David indicates an understanding of what was wrong with Alan's utterance

Lines 39–49	Conversation analysis	Input–Interaction
Alan: [a! *yeah* abunaku naritai toki:: *oh! yeah when we want to be dangerous* (48)		Line 48—Alan accepts feedback recognizing a problem with his utterance.
	Summary: Focus is on the language used, who initiates the question and whose "original" language problem it was. Uses body language and gaze to support idea of ownership of language problem. Motivations are attributed to different participants a propos each one's desire to show the teacher how he is engaged in the task and engaged in learning.	*Summary:* Focus is on feedback that student receives and the perception of that feedback by both participants resulting in an apparent recognition of the correct form. Uses pauses as an indication of "thinking" time that precedes verbal recognition. No social motivations are attributed. Researchers search for evidence of learning (e.g., pauses, repetitions, verbal recognition of learning).

Kasper (2004)'s data, presented below, comes from a German classroom. We present two excerpts and the analyses from an interactionist perspective and from a CA perspective to make it easier to see how the difference in orientation leads to different foci of the analysis.

Interaction	Conversation analysis	Input–Interaction
NS: okay:, wie geht es dir? *how are you?* NNS: es geht gut, *I'm okay,* NS: ja? (.) warum? *are you? (.) why?* NNS: u::mm (.) ts uh i- °er° am wochenende? It was lange? ( )= *at the weekend? it was long?*	The initial exchange is a routine adjacency pair. The NS questions the response by saying *warum* (why). This question (?)shows the NS's "orientation to the event as a learning activity whose main purpose it is to 'get the learner to talk,' and to her interactional charge as provider of environments for learner	An Input-Interaction analysis of this exchange would focus, if there were any comment at all on this exchange, on the learner and her reaction to the strange NS response. It would focus on the hesitation phenomena of the NNS and would "suggest" that this might be an indication of the fact that she was possibly

Interaction	Conversation analysis	Input–Interaction
	talk." The NS responds as if this were a normal conversation. Therefore, the participants co-construct this "hybrid interactional form" that reflects "normal" conversation' as well as an event for language practice. *Comment*: This is clearly an emic perspective that attempts to get inside the head of the participants.	thrown off by the unexpected response to a seemingly formulaic response. The Input–Interaction analysis would only look at surface facts and would not ascribe motivation to the NS as to why she responded in the way she did. Or, if such an interpretation were made, it would be bolstered by additional evidence, such as stimulated recall (Gass and Mackey, 2000). *Comment*: The need to bolster arguments from an interaction with the participants is, of course, antithetical to a CA analysis given the distance that the researcher keeps from the investigated parties and the need to interpret from "afar."

As can be seen from these two examples, the interactionist perspective does not include the same level of detail or elaboration as these aspects of conversation do not enter in to what might count as learning. Activities are not central to an interactionist framework and thus learning as increased accomplishment within an activity is not relevant (see also Gass, 2004).

10.5 Output

Up to this point we have dealt with the concept of input. We have also focused on conversational or interactional modifications that come as a result of an exchange in which a low proficiency NNS is involved. There is one final concept that needs to be mentioned, and that is comprehensible output (see Swain, 1985, 1995, 2005).

Input alone is not sufficient for acquisition, because when one hears language one can often interpret the meaning without the use of syntax.

For example, if one hears only the words *dog, bit, girl*, regardless of the order in which those words occur, it is likely that the meaning *The dog bit the girl* is the one that will be assumed rather than the more unusual *The girl bit the dog*. Similarly, if one hears a sentence such as *This is bad story*, one can easily fill in the missing article. Little knowledge, other than knowing the meanings of the words and knowing something about real-world events, is needed.

This is not the case with language production or output, because one is forced to put the words into some order. Production then "may force the learner to move from semantic processing to syntactic processing" (Swain, 1985, p. 249). In fact, the impetus for Swain's original study was the lack of second language development by immersion children even after years of academic study in that second language. Swain studied children learning French in an immersion context, suggesting that what was lacking in their development as native-like speakers of French was the opportunity to use language productively as opposed to using language merely for comprehension. She compared results on a number of different grammatical, discourse, and sociolinguistic measures of sixth grade children in a French immersion setting and sixth grade native French speaking children. The lack of proficiency on the part of the immersion children, coupled with their apparent lack of productive use of French, led Swain to suggest the crucial role for output in the development of a second language.

It is trivial to state that there is no better way to test the extent of one's knowledge (linguistic or otherwise) than to have to use that knowledge in some productive way—whether it be explaining a concept to someone (i.e., teaching) or writing a computer program, or, in the case of language learning, getting even a simple idea across. However, output has generally been seen not as a way of creating knowledge, but as a way of practicing already existing knowledge. In other words, output has traditionally been viewed as a way of practicing what has previously been learned. This was certainly the thrust behind early methods of language teaching in which the presentation-practice (i.e., drill and repetition) mode was in vogue. A second traditional role assigned to output was that it was the way in which additional (and perhaps richer) input could be elicited. The idea that output could be part of learning was not seriously contemplated prior to Swain's important paper in 1985, in which she introduced the notion of comprehensible output or "pushed" output. What is meant by this concept is that learners are "pushed" or "stretched" in their production as a necessary part of making themselves understood. In so doing, they might modify a previous utterance or they might try out forms that they had not used before.

Comprehensible output refers to the need for a learner to be "pushed toward the delivery of a message that is not only conveyed, but that is conveyed precisely, coherently, and appropriately" (Swain, 1985, p. 249). In a more recent explication of the concept, Swain claimed that "output may stimulate learners to move from the semantic, open-ended, non-deterministic, strategic processing prevalent in comprehension to the complete grammatical processing needed for accurate production. Output, thus, would seem to have a potentially significant role in the development of syntax and morphology" (Swain, 1995, p. 128).

Mackey (2002) empirically demonstrates this notion through the following example and the comments that followed this learner's struggle with the appropriate word.

(10-22) Example of pushed output
NNS: And in hand in hand have a bigger glass to see.
NS: It's err. You mean, something in his hand?
NNS: Like spectacle. For older person.
NS: Mmmm, sorry I don't follow, it's what?
NNS: In hand have he have has a glass for looking through for make the print bigger to see, to see the print, for magnify.
NS: He has some glasses?
NNS: Magnify glasses he has magnifying glass.
NS: Oh aha I see a magnifying glass, right that's a good one, ok.

Recall comments following this episode:

In this example I see I have to manage my err err expression because he does not understand me and I cannot think of exact word right then. I am thinking thinking it is nearly in my mind, thinking bigger and magnificate and eventually magnify. I know I see this word before but so I am sort of talking around around this word but he is forcing me to think harder, think harder for the correct word to give him so he can understand and so I was trying. I carry on talking until finally I get it, and when I say it, then he understand it, me.

The recall comments come immediately following the episode. As is clear from these comments, this learner understood that her language was not clear and struggled to come up with the appropriate expression. She was pushed through the negotiation sequences to make her language clearer.

The question becomes: In what ways can output play a central role in the learning process?[4] We consider four possible ways that output may provide learners with a forum for important language-learning functions:

(a) receiving crucial feedback for the verification of these hypotheses; (b) testing hypotheses about the structures and meanings of the target language; (c) developing automaticity in IL production; and (d) forcing a shift from more meaning-based processing of the second language to a more syntactic mode.

Izumi, Bigelow, Fujiwara, and Fearnow (1999) specifically investigated the noticing function of output, finding partial support for this hypothesis and pointing out the need to balance cognitive and linguistic demands. In particular, participants were exposed to written input and had to underline words that they felt would be essential to their subsequent reproduction of the same passage. The experimental group was then given a production task, whereas the control group was not. This was followed by a second exposure (again with underlining) and a second reproduction by the experimental group. Participants noticed the targeted feature (past hypothetical conditional, such as *If Kevin got up early in the morning, he would eat breakfast*) and incorporated the feature into their output, but this did not carry over into a posttest. In a second phase, both groups produced a written essay on a topic that called for the use of the target form. Despite the fact that the results after the first phase did not show retention on the posttest, there was greater improvement on this written essay by those who had produced output than by those in the control group, who had not been involved in a production task in phase 1, thereby suggesting that output may indeed be important for acquisition.

Izumi and Izumi (2004), in a study on the acquisition of relative clauses, had an experimental treatment that allowed for an "output" group and a "non-output" group, finding that the output group did not outperform the non-output group. Their output task was a production task which may not have allowed for the focus on form that they had intended. In another study, McDonough (2005) found evidence for language use (output), but her participants were engaged in an interactive task that forced attention to form, unlike the type of task in Izumi and Izumi's study.

McDonough (2005) tested the output hypothesis directly in her study of Thai learners of English. In a study investigating the acquisition of English questions, four groups carried out communicative tasks. The four groups focused on salience (enhancement) and opportunity to modify following feedback. Examples from each of the four groups are provided below:

> (10-23) Enhanced opportunity to modify
> NNS: what angel doing in this situation?
> NS: what angel doing? Huh?
> NNS: what is angel doing?

In this example, the response directs attention to the inaccurate form followed by a clarification request which gives the learner an opportunity to modify his or her output.

(10-24) Opportunity to modify
        NNS: what happen for the boat?
        NS: what?
        NNS: what's wrong with the boat?

Here, there is a request for clarification but no enhancement or drawing attention to the problematic part of the utterance.

(10-25) Feedback without opportunity to modify
        NNS: What we do with it?
        NS: What we do? Uh, let's see well we could talk about the purpose if you want.

The NS in this example points to the problem through the response—that is, makes the error salient—but continues without giving the learner an opportunity to modify her language.

(10-26) No feedback
        NNS: where you going the last holiday?
        NS: to Laos

Despite the error, there is no feedback, only a response. Her detailed study provides evidence that the best predictor of acquisition, in this case operationalized by the acquisition of more advanced questions, is the opportunity to modify one's speech.

In sum, output is generally considered to have a positive effect on learning, although results have been mixed. Some research (e.g., Izumi, Bigelow, Fujiwara and Fearnow [1999] and Izumi and Bigelow [2000]) found output to be beneficial, but Morgan-Short and Bowden (2006) did not. Two recent metaanalyses of the effect of output (Keck, Iberri-Shea, Tracy-Ventura and Wa-Mbalaka (2006) and Mackey and Goo (2007) yielded different results, although it must be kept in mind that the operationalization of pushed output differed in these studies. Output, then, as merely repetition may be less useful than output where learners are given opportunities to incorporate new forms into their production.

10.5.1 Feedback

Interactional feedback is an important source of information for learners. Most generally, it provides them with information about the success (or, more likely, lack of success) of their utterances and gives additional opportunities to focus on production or comprehension. There are numerous ways of providing feedback to learners from the explicit (stating that there is a problem) to the implicit (feedback during the course of an interaction). In this and the subsequent sections, we address the role of feedback and suggest ways that different types of feedback may impact learning. Figure 10.1 illustrates this concept with the mediating factor of attention.

Through interaction, learners' attention is drawn to some element(s) of language with the possible consequence that that element/those elements will be incorporated into a learner's developing system.

In chapter 6, where we discussed the role of negative evidence (information that a particular utterance is deviant vis-à-vis target language norms), it was pointed out that, at least with regard to children, it cannot be a necessary condition for acquisition. What, then, about second language learning? It is undoubtedly the case that adults (at least those in formal learning situations) do receive more correction than children, and it may further be the case that adults must have negative evidence (i.e., that it is a necessary condition) in order to accomplish the goal of learning a second language (Birdsong, 1989; Bley-Vroman, 1989; Gass, 1988a; Schachter, 1988). While this research has been based primarily on theoretical arguments, there is some empirical evidence that negative evidence is in some instances necessary for second language acquisition.

White (1991) considered the development of adverb placement by French children learning English. She was interested in the question of how learners learn not to do something in the L2 that is present in the native language. In particular, French learners of English have to learn that English allows subject–adverb–verb (SAV) order (*He always runs*) and that it does not allow subject–verb–adverb–object (SVAO) order (**He drinks always coffee*). White's study consisted of five classes of French NSs learning English as a second language (two classes at grade 5 and three classes at grade 6) and one control group of monolingual NSs of English. One of the grade 5 groups and two of the grade 6 groups were given explicit instruction on adverb placement as well as exercises and correction on adverb placement; the other groups were given instruction on questions using the same type of exercises but no explicit instruction on adverbs. The classroom treatment lasted two weeks. All children were given pretests, posttests immediately following the treatment sessions, a second posttest five weeks later, and a follow-up test a year later. The tests consisted of grammaticality judgment tasks (with correction), preference tasks, and a sentence-manipulation task. By comparing the groups' performance, White was able to show that negative evidence did indeed promote the learning of adverb placement. However, the effects of the treatment were not as long-lived as anticipated, as the two groups did not differ on their performance one year following the treatment.

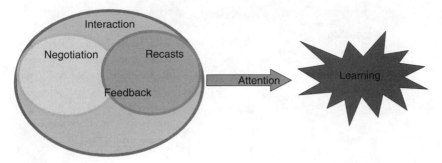

Figure 10.1 A model of interaction.

Source: From "Input, interaction and output: an overview" by S. Gass and A. Mackey, 2006. In K. Bardovi-Harlig and Z. Dörnyei (Eds.), *Themes in SLA Research*, *AILA Review*, 3–17. With kind permission by John Benjamins Publishing Company, Amsterdam/Philadelphia. *www.benjamins.com.*

10.5.1.1 *Negotiation*

Negotiation serves as a catalyst for change because of its focus on incorrect forms. By providing learners with information about incorrect forms, negotiation enables learners to search for additional confirmatory or nonconfirmatory evidence. If we accept that negotiation as a form of negative evidence and as a way of providing feedback serves the function of initiating change, we need to ask what factors determine whether the initiated change results in permanent restructuring of linguistic knowledge. As with any type of learning, there needs to be reinforcement of what is being learned. This is schematized in Figure 10.2. If additional input is not available, learners do not have the opportunity to obtain confirmatory/nonconfirmatory evidence. This, in fact, may explain the results of White's study. Without additional focused evidence, it is not surprising that the learners did not retain knowledge of English adverb placement. In other words, acquisition appears to be gradual and, to state the matter simplistically, takes time and often requires numerous "doses" of evidence. That is, there is an incubation period extending from the time of the initial input (negative or positive) to the final stage of restructuring and output.

Although White's study is important in showing that negative evidence may be necessary to trigger a permanent change in a learner's grammar, it does not show that positive evidence (i.e., input) alone is insufficient. (In fact, the question group of White's study received little information about adverbs from the naturalistic classroom data to which they were exposed.)

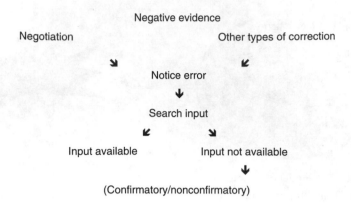

Figure 10.2 Function of negative evidence

Source: © 1997 from *Input, interaction and the second language learner* by S. Gass. Reproduced by permission of Lawrence Erlbaum Associates, a division of Taylor & Francis Group.

Trahey and White (1993) conducted a follow-up study to determine the effect of positive evidence. Their study consisted of two grade 5 classes of French students learning English. Both classes were given an input flood of English adverbs (positive evidence only) over a two-week period. The same timetable as that used in the earlier White studies was used with the exception of three-week rather than five-week follow-up testing and no testing one year later. What they found was that input was sufficient for learners to notice that SAV order is possible in English, but that it was not sufficient to detect the ungrammaticality of SVAO sentences. Thus, these two experiments showed that positive evidence can reveal to learners the presence of information in the second language that is different from their native language, but that negative evidence is necessary to show what is not possible in the second language when it is possible in the native language. Trahey (1996) showed that an abundance of positive evidence a year after exposure yielded knowledge of grammatical sentences, but did not succeed in eradicating the ungrammatical sentences. Thus, positive evidence alone is not sufficient.

Other studies of feedback have also suggested that feedback obtained through negotiation serves a corrective function (Gass and Varonis, 1989; Pica, Holliday, Lewis, and Morgenthaler, 1989). The latter study is interesting in that the authors provided the first systematic evidence that learners respond differentially to different types of feedback. In their study one important focus was on different types of NS signals to NNS errors. They found that the greatest amount of modification comes in response to clarification requests, as in the following example (Nobuyoshi and R. Ellis, 1993, p. 204):

(10-27) NNS: He pass his house.
          NS: Sorry?
          NNS: He passed, he passed, ah, his sign.

as opposed to seeking confirmation through modeling. What this suggests is that the fact that the NNS is "forced" to make the actual correction, as opposed to hearing and perhaps thinking about the correct form, is in itself a facilitator to acquisition. But again, we are left with the unknown factor of longer-term retention.

One study that suggested longer-term retention after focused attention is that of Nobuyoshi and R. Ellis (1993). Learners had to describe a series of pictures that depicted events that had happened the previous weekend and the previous day. The experimental group received feedback through clarification requests that focused on past tense forms. The control group did not receive such focused feedback. The results can only be considered suggestive given the very small sample size. However, in the experimental group, two of the three subjects were able to reformulate the correct forms after feedback and were able to maintain the correct forms at a subsequent administration one week later. In the control group, none of the subjects showed an accuracy gain.

Similarly, Lightbown (1992) compared corrective feedback provided by teachers immediately after the occurrence of an error in a communicative activity versus feedback on audiolingual drills or pure practice activities. She found that in both cases learners were able to self-correct, but only in the first case was the self-correction incorporated into their second language systems, as evidenced by use of the targeted form outside of the classroom.

An early study on the effect of corrective feedback on grammatical reorganization was carried out by Carroll, Roberge, and Swain (1992). The comparison was between groups with corrective feedback and groups with no corrective feedback. The linguistic focus was on regular noun formation in French. After receiving training on the relationship between verbs and nouns (e.g., *attelé-attelage*, "harnessed"/"harnessing"), learners were given new words to manipulate. Some participants were corrected and others were not. The results showed that corrective feedback was important in the learning of individual items, but that it had little effect on a learner's ability to generalize this information to new items.

Takashima (1995), in a study of Japanese learners of English, investigated the effects of feedback that was focused on particular morphological form (past tense and plural)[5] versus feedback that was communication-oriented. The focused feedback was in the form of clarification requests (*Sorry?*, *What did you say?*). Groups of students had to work together to make up a story based on a sequence of pictures, of which each student in the group had only one. One student was then nominated to tell the story to the class. This was the actual feedback session as the teacher provided either focused morphological feedback or content feedback. The accuracy rate for past tense increased at a faster rate during the time of the study (11 weeks) in the focused morphological correction group as opposed to the content correction group. Further, the magnitude of the difference increased as a function of time. Improved accuracy was noted for the particular student who was corrected (in front of the class) as well as for those students who were in the class observing the interaction. Interestingly, when considering the actual reformulations by individual students, there was no correlation between the reformulated utterances and improvement on the use of the structure on tests. This further suggests that the actual interaction does not constitute change itself, but is only a catalyst for later change. Illustrative of this is the following excerpt from Takashima (1995, p. 77), in which the first clarification request appears to fall short of the mark in that the student makes no change, but as the storytelling continues, the student seems to be more sensitive to the past tense forms, even self-correcting in the last turn.

(10-28) S = student; T = teacher
   S: One day, the fairy, sting the magic wand to Cinderalla.
   T: Sorry?
   S: One day, the fairy sting the magic wand to Cinderalla.
   T: OK.
   S: Cinde, ah, Cinderaella changed into, the beautiful girl. (Laugh) Ah, and, the, Cin, Cinderella wen Cinderella went to the palace by coach. The, the prince fall in love at a first glance.
   T: Sorry?
   S: Ah, the prince fall in, falled falled in love Cinderella at a first glance. And they dance, they danced . . . Ah, Cin, Cinderella have, Cinderella have to go home.

Here, the input has been enhanced through clarification requests and the output has similarly been enhanced (Takashima's term), apparently as a function of the input enhancement.

10.5.1.2 Recasts

Recasts are another form of feedback, though they are less direct and more subtle than other forms of feedback. A recast is a reformulation of an incorrect utterance that maintains the original meaning of the utterance, as in 10-29, where the NS reformulates the NNS's incorrect question (Philp, 1999).

    (10-29) NNS: Why he want this house?
→   NS: Why does he want this house?

Recasts are complex. For example, is it a partial recast? A full recast? A response to a single error or to multiple errors (how many changes are made)? We present two examples that illustrate forms that recasts can take. In 10-30, a recast with rising intonation, the auxiliary is added and the verbal morphology is corrected (Philp, 1999, p. 92). In 10-31 the verb form is corrected (from future to subjunctive, required after *avant que*) without rising intonation (Lyster, 1998, p. 58).

    (10-30) NNS: What doctor say?
             NS: What is the doctor saying?
    (10-31) S = student; T = teacher
             S: Avant que quelqu'un le prendra.
                 before   someone   it will take
                 "Before someone will take it."
             T: Avant que quelqu'un le prenne.
                 before   someone   it takes
                 "Before someone takes it."

There have been a number of recent reviews of recasts in the second language literature, focusing on experimental as well as theoretical concerns (Nicholas, Lightbown, and Spada, 2001; R. Ellis and Sheen, 2006; Long, 2007; Mackey and Goo, 2007). Because recasts are an indirect form of correction, it is not clear to what extent they are relevant to acquisition. There have been a number of empirical studies focused specifically on the effectiveness of recasts. The results from these studies are mixed.

Lyster and Ranta (1997) collected data from children in Grades 4–6 enrolled in French immersion programs. Their research considered recasts by teachers following errors and, importantly, the reaction by the student ("uptake," in their terminology) in the subsequent turn. They argued that uptake "reveals what the student attempts to do with the teacher's feedback" (p. 49). Even though there were numerous instances of recasts found in the data, they did not appear to be particularly effective. Rather, students were more prone to repair utterances following other types of feedback.

Unfortunately, an immediate response may not be revealing, in that learners may be "mimicking or repeating without true understanding" (Gass, 2003, p. 236). This makes recasts a somewhat elusive concept to deal with and research often produces mixed results. For example, Mackey and Philp (1998) found that an immediate response by a learner was not necessarily related to development, whereas Nabei and Swain

(2002) and Lyster (2004) found the reverse. As noted elsewhere in this chapter, it is not always possible to judge what the effects of learning are by immediate reactions.

Lyster (1998), using the same database as reported on in the Lyster and Ranta (1997) study, divided recasts into four types depending on two features: (a) declarative; (b) interrogative; (c) confirmation of the original utterance; or (d) additional information. Lyster found that there was some confusion between the corrective and approval functions of recasts. He argued that recasts may not be particularly useful in terms of corrective feedback, but they allow teachers to move a lesson forward by focusing attention on lesson content rather than on language form.

Lyster (2004), in a study that took place in immersion classrooms, compared the benefits of recasts and prompts. By prompts, he includes the following four types:

(10-32) Clarification requests
Student: Et le coccinelle . . . "And the (M) ladybug . . ."
Teacher: Pardon? "Sorry?"
Student: La coccinelle . . . "The (F) ladybug . . ."

(10-33) Repetitions
Student: La chocolat. "(F) Chocolate."
Teacher: La chocolat? "(F) Chocolate."
Student: Le chocolat. "(M) Chocolate."

(10-34) Metalinguistic clues
Student: Parce qu'elle cherche, euh, son, son carte. "Because she's looking for, um, her, her (M) card."
Teacher: Pas son carte. "Not her (M) card."
Student: Euh, sa carte? "Um, her (F) card?"

(10-35) Elicitation
Teacher: Il vit où un animal domestique? Où est-ce que ça vit? "Where does a pet live? Where does it live?"
Student: Dans un maison. "In a (M) house."
Teacher: Dans . . .? Attention. "In . . .? Careful."
Student: Dans une maison. "In a (F) house."

Data were collected within the context of a fifth-grade-content French immersion classroom. Teachers either provided no feedback, recasts, or prompts. The focus was on French grammatical gender. Determination of learning was made through both oral and written tasks following the five-week treatment sessions. He found that form-focused instruction with prompts was more successful than with recasts, based on the written measures. There was not a significant difference on the oral assessment measures. This study was conducted in a content-based classroom where there are numerous nonlinguistic demands made on the learner, possibly making it difficult to focus on the subtle corrective function of recasts.

The results of a study by Ammar and Spada (2006) are similar to those of Lyster (2004). Their study took place in intensive English classes (L1 French) in Montreal with Grade 6 pupils. The target grammatical area was possessive determiners (*his/her*), a structure notably difficult for French learners of English. Prompts turned out to be more effective than recasts. The effectiveness of recasts depended, in part, on proficiency level, with more advanced learners receiving more benefit than learners of lower proficiency.

Ellis, Loewen, and Erlam (2006) looked at metalinguistic explanation (explicit feedback) and recasts (implicit feedback), finding that on tests of both explicit and implicit knowledge the metalinguistic explanation group outperformed the recast group, most likely due to recognition of the overtly corrective nature of metalinguistic feedback. Explicit feedback benefited both implicit and explicit knowledge.

In general, a number of studies have suggested that there is a positive effect for recasts on later learning (see Nicholas, Lightbown, and Spada 2001 and Mackey and Goo, 2007 for reviews). Leeman (2003) looked at noun–adjective agreement in Spanish in attempting to determine the benefits of recasts, particularly because they serve to provide positive evidence in a salient way. She had three experimental groups: (1) recasts, which she proposed provided both negative evidence as well as enhanced salience of positive evidence; (2) negative evidence; and (3) enhanced salience of positive evidence. She found that the first and third groups (recast group and enhanced salience of positive evidence group) showed post-treatment benefits. In this way she was able to separate out the various parts of recasts (positive and negative evidence). Thus, it appears that recasts are useful due to the enhanced salience provided in recasts rather than negative evidence. Han (2002) investigated consistency of use of past tense morphology. She found that recasts were beneficial, but proposed four conditions for their usefulness: individualized attention, consistent focus, developmental readiness, and intensity.

McDonough (2007), in a study of the acquisition of past tense in an interactive context, compared clarification requests and recasts, finding that both positively influenced the acquisition of past tense. However, in a study on the acquisition of the comparative and past tense, R. Ellis (2007) considered the effect of recasts and metalinguistic feedback, not finding a positive effect for recasts. However, the treatment time in his study was much shorter than in other studies investigating the impact of recasts on the development of English past tense morphology.

Ishida (2004) considered Japanese morphology in her study of recasts.

In general, her results show a positive and lasting effect for recasts. As did Han (2002), she points to the need to consider developmental readiness in a full understanding of the utility of recasts. Iwashita (2003) considered the acquisition of Japanese word order and locative-initial constructions. She investigated more than just recasts, but in general found different effects for interaction moves (recasts, negotiation, models). Recasts were beneficial only for one of the verb forms. This further suggests the need to determine developmental readiness in order to fully understand the effect of recasts or any other interactional move. Mackey and Philp (1998) also found positive learning effects following recasts for the development of question formation.

McDonough and Mackey (2006) provide a detailed study on recasts looking at the relationship between: (1) recasts and learning and (2) learning and immediate responses to recasts. In an interaction-based study with Thai learners of English, they considered the acquisition of English questions. There were two experimental groups (recast and no feedback). Within the recast group, there were two recast types, as in 10-36, where there was an opportunity to respond, and 10-37, where there was no response opportunity.

> (10-36) Recast with opportunity to respond—from McDonough and Mackey (2006)
> Learner: Why he must say it like that?
> NS: Why did he say that?
> Learner: Yeah.
> (10-37) Recast with no opportunity to respond—from McDonough and Mackey (2006)
> Learner: How many sister you have?
> NS: How many sisters do I have? I have one sister.

They characterized responses to recasts in one of two ways: as a pure repetition or as what they termed a primed production, where there was some novel production. Examples of each are given in 10-38 and 10-39 below.

> (10-38) Repetition—from McDonough and Mackey (2006)
> Learner: When it happen?
> NS: When did it happen?
> Learner: When did it happen?
> (10-39) Primed production—from McDonough and Mackey (2006)
> Learner: Why he hit the deer?
> NS: Why did he hit the deer? He was driving home and the deer ran out in front of his car.
> Learner: What did he do after that?

Their study included three posttests and development was operational-ized as two questions with unique lexical items in different tasks. Both recasts and primed production were predictive of ESL question development. What was particularly interesting is that mere repetition of the recasted form (uptake in Lyster and Ranta's framework) was not correlated with development.

Other studies that show a positive effect for recasts point to two main problems with recast studies: the concept of uptake and the data to be included in analysis. Mackey and Philp (1998) pointed out that uptake (as defined by Lyster and Ranta, 1997) may be the wrong measure to use in determining effectiveness. Their data represented an attempt to go beyond the turn immediately following a recast. They make the point (cf. Gass, 1997; Gass and Varonis, 1994; Lightbown, 1998) that, if one is to consider effectiveness (i.e., development/acquisition), then one should more appropriately measure delayed effects. In particular, Mackey and Philp considered the effects of interaction with and without recasts on learners' knowledge of English questions. Their results showed that, for more advanced learners, recasts plus negotiation were more beneficial than negotiation alone. This was the case even though there was not always evidence for a reaction by the learner in the subsequent turn.

A study by Long, Inagaki, and Ortega (1998) also attempted to determine the role of recasts (in this case as opposed to models). They investigated (a) the acquisition of ordering of adjectives and a locative construction by English learners of Japanese, and (b) the acquisition of topicalization and adverb placement by English learners of Spanish. Their results were mixed inasmuch as only one of the learner groups (Spanish) showed greater learning following recasts as opposed to models. Furthermore, these findings were true for adverb placement only.

A problem having to do with the data used for analysis was noted by Oliver (1995). Frequently, after a recast, there is no opportunity for the original speaker to make a comment. This may be due to a topic shift, as in 10-40 (Oliver, 1995, p. 472), or the inappropriateness of making a comment because the recast had been in the form of a *yes/no* question and the appropriate response would not be a repetition, but a *yes/no* response.

(10-40) From Oliver (1995, p. 472)
      NNS: A [c]lower tree.
      NS: A flower tree. How tall is the trunk?

When the lack of opportunity/appropriacy is included, the percentage of "incorporated" recasts greatly increases. Lyster (1998) argued that the context of language use in these studies (child–child dyadic interactions in Oliver's research and teacher–student interactions in his own research) is different and that, in fact, in classrooms the teacher often keeps the floor, thereby (as mentioned earlier) drawing attention to content and not to language form. In his 2004 study, Lyster compares recasts with prompts (see examples 10-32 to 10-35 above) finding the superiority of prompts to recasts given the opportunity for some form of uptake.

There is one final issue to address before concluding this section on feedback. What do learners perceive? In a study by Mackey, Gass, and McDonough (2000), data were collected from 10 learners of English as a second language and 7 learners of Italian as a foreign language. The study explored learners' perceptions about feedback provided to them through task-based dyadic interaction. In the interactions, learners received feedback focused on a range of morphosyntactic, lexical, and phonological forms. After completing the tasks, learners watched videotapes of their previous interactions and were asked to introspect about their thoughts at the time the original interactions were in progress. Examples of the interactions and the recall comments of the learners follow.

(10-41) Morphosyntactic feedback (perceived as lexical feedback)
- NNS: C'è due tazzi.
  "There is two cups (m. pl.)."
- INT: Due tazz-come?
  "Two cup—what?"
- NNS: Tazzi, dove si può mettere té, come se dice questo?
  "Cups (m. pl.), where one can put tea, how do you say this?"
- INT: tazze?
  "Cups (f. pl.)?"
- NNS: ok, tazze.
  "Ok, cups (f. pl)."
- Recall: I wasn't sure if I learned the proper word at the beginning.

(10-42) Phonological feedback correctly perceived
- NNS: Vincino la tavolo è.
  "Near the table is (the correct form is *vicino*)."
- INT: Vicino?
  "Near?"
- NNS: La, lu tavolo.
  "The? table."
- Recall: I was thinking . . . when she said *vicino* I was thinking, OK, did I pronounce that right there?

(10-43) Lexical feedback correctly perceived
- NNS: There is a library.
- NS: A what?
- NNS: A place where you put books.
- NS: A bookshelf?

NNS: Bok?
NS: Shelf.
NNS: Bookshelf.
Recall: That's not a good word she was thinking about
        library like we have here on campus, yeah.

The results showed that learners were relatively accurate in their perceptions about lexical, semantic, and phonological feedback. However, morphosyntactic feedback was generally not perceived as such.

Consequently, it is not always clear that learners perceive feedback in the way it was intended (see also, Hawkins, 1985). Thus, there may be a differential role for feedback in different linguistic areas, as suggested by Pica (1994). For example, perhaps morphosyntactic feedback is not noticed because, as is typical in a conversational context, individuals are focused on meaning, not on language form. Phonological and lexical errors can interfere with basic meaning and hence need to be attended to on the spot if shared meaning is to result; the morphosyntactic examples in the Mackey, Gass, and McDonough (2000) study generally dealt with low-level nonmeaning-bearing elements.

10.5.2 Hypothesis testing

The notion of hypothesis testing has been central to research in second language acquisition for a number of years (see Schachter, 1983, 1992). Output, particularly when it occurs as part of a negotiation sequence, is a way of testing a hypothesis. This is not to say that hypotheses are being consciously tested every time a second language speaker produces an utterance. It is to say, however, that through negotiation and through feedback, learners can be made aware of the hypotheses that they are entertaining as they produce language. That is, the activity of using language helps create a degree of analyticity that allows learners to think about language (see section 10.5.3).

Swain (1995, pp. 133–134) suggested that learners are in fact involved in testing hypotheses and that they use the forum of interaction to work through those hypotheses. In support of this position, Swain presented the following example from two second language learners (age 13) in attendance at an immersion program in Canada. The teacher had just read aloud a text, and the students, having taken notes on the reading, worked in pairs to reconstruct the text as closely as possible in terms of both content and form. The sentence they were working on in this example is: *En ce qui concerne l'environment, il y a beaucoup de problemes qui nous tracassent* ("As far as the environment is concerned, there are many problems that face us") (Swain, 1995, pp. 133–134; translation, pp. 143–144).

(10-44) K = student; G = student; T = teacher

K: Wait a minute! No, I need a Bescherelle (verb reference book). Please open the Bescherelle at the page with, OK, at the last page (i.e., the index). OK look for *tracasse*, one page two pages.

G: *Tra, tra, tracer.*

K: *Tracasser* page six. Look for it please.

G: No problem.

K: It's on page . . .

G: Verb (on page) six. OK, it's the same as *aimer* (i.e., it is conjugated in the same way and *aimer* is given as the standard example for all verbs with this pattern of conjugation).

K: Let me see it please (reading from the page). The *passé simple* (K is trying to find a first person plural version of the verb which sounds like *tracasse*, the word he has written in his notes, but is unable to find one).

G: Perhaps it's here.

K: No, it's just *nous aime* (pause) ah, the present. *Tracasse.* Isn't it *aimons, tracasse* (to teacher who has just arrived)? You don't say *nous tracasse* (what he has written down in his notes). Shouldn't it be *nous tracassons?*

T: It's the *problems* that are worrying us (deliberately not directly giving the answer).

K: *Nous tracassons.*

G: <u>Oh</u> (beginning to realize what is happening).

K: Yeh? (So what?)

G: The problems which are worrying us. Like the (pause). It's the problems (pause) like, that concern us.

K: Yes, but *tracasse* shouldn't it be <u><o-n-s></u>?

G: <u>*Tracasse.*</u> It's not a, it's not a (pause), yeh, I dunno (unable to articulate what he has discovered).

K: OK, it says problems which worry us. Therefore, is *tracasse* a verb that you have to conjugate?

T: Uh huh.

K: So is it *tracassons?*

T: It's the **problems** which are worrying us.

G: Us, it's it's not, yeh, it's the problems, it's not, it's not us.

K: <u>Ah! E-n-t</u> (third person plural ending) OK. OK.

As Swain explains, the question here relates to the morphology of the French verb and the use of a relative clause. The difficulty lies in the fact that Student K had taken the French phrase *nous tracasse* without taking into consideration that the entire constituent was *qui nous tracasse* ("that we are faced with"). In the first instance, it appears that *nous* "we" is the subject and that the verb should therefore be *tracassons* to agree with the first person plural subject. In actuality *nous tracasse* is part of the relative clause *qui nous tracasse*, with *qui* "that" as the third person subject. The entire dialogue is one in which Student K is at first puzzled, then verbalizes the problem and then works to understand the syntax and hence the morphology. In sum, it is through this interaction that this child is able to come to a correct conclusion after an initial faulty hypothesis.

Another piece of evidence supporting the fact that learners test hypotheses through production is self-correction. Negotiation sequences produce many instances of corrective feedback to learners, from NSs and NNSs alike. And, importantly, these instances appear to have long-lasting effects on language development in some cases. In the following examples (Gass and Varonis, 1989, pp. 80–81), it appears that Hiroko is "ready" to accept a correction. Her quick and easy acceptance of Izumi's *at* suggests a tentativeness that bespeaks of hypothesis testing, rather than a conviction of the correctness of her own utterance.

(10-45) Hiroko: Ah, the dog is barking to—
Izumi: At
Hiroko: At the woman.
(10-46) Hiroko: A man is uh drinking c-coffee or tea uh with uh the saucer of the uh uh coffee set is uh in his uh knee.
Izumi: In him knee.
Hiroko: Uh on his knee.
Izumi: Yeah.
Hiroko: On his knee.
Izumi: So sorry. On his knee.

In this negotiation, it appears that both Hiroko and Izumi are tentative and are in a sense "fishing" for the right form. This is supported by the frequent hesitation on the part of Hiroko in her initial utterance and by the apology on Izumi's part at the end. Other examples suggest the longer-term retention that results from these negotiations. This can be seen in 10-47 (Gass and Varonis, 1989, p. 78).

(10-47) Atsuko: Uh holding the [kʌp].
Toshi: Holding the cup?
Atsuko: Hmm hmmm . . .
(seventeen turns later)

Toshi: Holding a cup.
Atsuko: Yes.
Toshi: Coffee cup?
Atsuko: Coffee? Oh yeah, tea, coffee cup, tea cup.
Toshi: Hm hm.

In this example, the initial clarification request by Toshi suggests to Atsuko that something is wrong with her pronunciation of the word *cup* [kʌp]. This indication caused her to notice something in her pronunciation that did not match the expectation of her partner. The remainder of the dialogue was one of hypothesis testing in which she matched her phonetic formulation against that of her partner's.

It should be noted, however, that Pica (1988, p. 68) did not find a large number of instances of self-corrections following feedback, leading her to suggest that "it was not evident from the data that the NNSs were *testing hypotheses* during negotiated interactions." In contrast, a later study by Pica, Holliday, Lewis, and Morgenthaler (1989) showed that clarification requests yielded modifications in learner output. The authors suggested that learners "test hypotheses about the second language, experiment with new structures and forms, and expand and exploit their interlanguage resources in creative ways" (1989, p. 64). The fact that in Pica's 1988 analysis of the effect of feedback she only considered immediate responses to feedback suggests only that the interaction did not result in immediate change, not that it did not *stimulate* change. There may be other variables in operation when determining whether or not there is an effect for feedback. Lin and Hedgcock (1996) analyzed data from classroom learners of Spanish (NSs of Chinese) versus well-educated (but not schooled) learners of Spanish (also NSs of Chinese). They found differences between these two populations in their ability to detect ungrammaticality and to incorporate negative feedback provided to them.

More direct evidence of hypothesis testing, however, comes from Mackey, Gass, and McDonough (2000), in which they used a stimulated recall procedure (see Gass and Mackey, 2000). They videotaped interactive tasks and immediately following replayed the video, asking learners what they were thinking about at the time of the interaction. Example 10-48 (from their study, but not published therein) below illustrates the notion of hypothesis testing.

   (10-48) Hypothesis testing (INT = interviewer)
        NNS: *poi un bicchiere*
             then a glass
        INT: *un che, come?*
             a what, what?

NNS: *bicchiere*
glass

Recall by NNS: "I was drawing a blank. Then I thought of a vase but then I thought that since there was no flowers, maybe it was just a big glass. So, then I thought I'll say it and see. Then, when she said '*come*' (what?), I knew that it was completely wrong."

I'll say it and see suggests that she was using the conversation as a way to see if a hypothesis was correct or incorrect.

10.5.3 Automaticity

A third function of output is the development of fluency and automaticity of processing (see chapter 8). As discussed earlier, the human mind is a limited processing system. Certain processes are deliberate, requiring a significant amount of time and working memory capacity. Others are routine and automatic, involving less time and capacity. McLaughlin (1987, p. 134) claimed that automatization involves "a learned response that has been built up through the consistent mapping of the same input to the same pattern of activation over many trials." Here we extend this notion to output, claiming that the consistent and successful mapping (practice) of grammar to output results in automatic processing (see also Loschky and Bley-Vroman, 1993).

10.5.4 Meaning-based to grammar-based processing

In some sense the study of output began with an understanding of the difference between meaning-based and grammar-based use of language. Swain's initial hypothesis stated that output "may force the learner to move from semantic processing to syntactic processing" (1985, p. 249). This notion has been dealt with throughout the book and is not re-elaborated on here. Suffice it to say that processing language only at the level of meaning will not and cannot serve the purpose of understanding the syntax of the language, a level of knowledge that is essential to the production of language.[6]

In sum, output provides learners the opportunity to produce language and gain feedback, which, through focusing learners' attention on certain local aspects of their speech, may lead them to notice either (a) a mismatch between their speech and that of an interlocutor (particularly if as part of the feedback a linguistic model is provided) or (b) a deficiency in their output. Noticing, then, leads to reassessment, which may be an on-the-spot reassessment or involve longer-term complex thinking about the issue. This latter process may be bolstered by the gathering of additional information through a variety of sources (e.g., input, direct questioning, and looking in grammar books and dictionaries). This, in essence, is the process of learning (see also Swain and Lapkin, 1995).

10.6 The role of input and interaction in language learning

What is the function of input and interaction? As a first step to learning, a learner must be aware of a need to learn. Negotiation of the sort that takes place in conversation is a means to focus a learner's attention on just those areas of language that do not "match" those of the language being learned.

The view of input and interaction that has been presented in this chapter appears to be in opposition to the view of language learning constrained by principles of Universal Grammar (see chapter 6). However, the goal of both perspectives is to come to an understanding of how second language grammars are formulated in light of the fact that the evidence learners have about the second language is so limited. In broad terms, as noted in chapter 6, learners have two kinds of linguistic information at their disposal. The first is known as positive evidence and refers to that limited set of (generally) well-formed utterances to which learners are exposed. The second, negative evidence, consists of information provided to a learner that her or his utterance is deviant in some way. Consider the following example:

(10-49) NS: Did you fly to Singapore yesterday?
NNS: Did I flied here yesterday?
NS: Pardon?
NNS: Did I flied here yesterday?
NS: Yes, did you fly here yesterday?

In 10-49, the first NS utterance provides positive evidence to this NNS about question formation. The second NS utterance provides feedback indicating that there is something incorrect/incomprehensible about the NNS utterance. The third NS utterance also provides indirect feedback to the learner (correct modeling) that the NNS utterance is incorrect. This is what we have been referring to in this chapter as negotiation.

When we look at the literature on child language acquisition, we find that claims have been made that negative evidence is neither frequent nor necessary for acquisition (e.g., Pinker, 1984; Wexler and Cullicover, 1980) (see also chapter 6). As children do not receive much correction, it cannot be a necessary condition for acquisition. In this view, how then does acquisition take place? What has been posited is a set of innate properties that limit the possibilities of grammar formation. The claim is that if

346

grammar formation is limited, the task of language learning is therefore reduced.

What about second language learning? With regard to the question of negative evidence, or correction, it is clear that adults (at least those in formal learning situations) do receive more than children. Furthermore, it may be the case that negative evidence is a necessary condition for adult second language learning (see section 10.5.1).

What function might negative evidence, or error correction, serve? One could argue that when errors are made and when, as a result, there is feedback, this feedback serves the purpose of providing the learner with information that an utterance is deviant. In an ideal situation, a learner's grammar is then modified. There are obvious limitations to this view. First, corrections cannot occur with all incorrect forms. Second, many so-called errors are errors of interpretation, in which case the learner may not even realize that an error has occurred (as seen in 10-50).

> (10-50) NS: When I get to Paris, I'm going to sleep for one
> whole day. I'm so tired.
> NNS: What?
> NS: I'm going to sleep for one whole day.
> NNS: One hour a day?
> NS: Yes.
> NNS: Why?
> NS: Because I'm so tired.

In 10-50, two women had just boarded a train in Calais after a long trip from London to Dover and a long delay in Dover before crossing the English Channel to Calais. They were both on their way to Paris. They had never met before and were sitting across from each other on the Paris-bound train. In this exchange, it is clear that the NNS had understood the NS to say *one hour a day* rather than *one whole day*. This error of interpretation was never realized. Each thought the other one somewhat peculiar and both lapsed into silence for the duration of the trip.

A third and perhaps most important limitation is that error acknowledgment, as in the case of expressions of nonunderstanding (e.g., *huh?*), does not provide sufficiently specific information to inform the learner where exactly an error has been made. That is, is the failure in communication the result of incorrect syntax, phonology, morphology, or vocabulary? Error acknowledgment also does not indicate what would have to be done in order to "correct" the error.

We now turn to another account of how second language grammars develop. This is an account that takes the linguistic input coupled with conversational interaction as the driving force of language development. Thus, understanding the learning environment (including the language information available to learners and the conversational interactions in which L2 learners engage) is central to an understanding of the nature of learning.

It is within this context that Krashen proposed his influential Input Hypothesis discussed earlier. His main claim is that the *sine qua non* of acquisition is input that is slightly beyond the learner's current level of grammatical knowledge. In his view, given the right kind of input, acquisition will be automatic. As we argued earlier, this account is inadequate. Minimally, one must also consider the role of negotiated interaction, as learning will be promoted in those instances when a conversational partner's assistance in expressing meaning can be relied on. Such assistance comes as a result of negotiation work, including such conversational features as comprehension checks, clarification requests, help with word searches, echoing, and so forth.

Wagner-Gough and Hatch (1975) argued that, with regard to SLA, conversational interaction forms the *basis* for the development of syntax rather than being only a forum for practice of grammatical structures. Syntax, they claimed, develops out of conversation rather than the reverse. The examples in 10-51 and 10-52 illustrate the ways learning can take place within a conversational setting, as the learners in these cases use the conversation to further their lexical development. In 10-51 (Mackey, 1999, pp. 558–559) we see recognition of a new lexical item as a result of negotiation of a new phrase. This example illustrates how the learner may have used the conversation as a resource to learn the new phrase *reading glasses*.

> (10-51) NS: There's there's a pair of reading glasses above the plant.
> NNS: A what?
> NS: Glasses reading glasses to see the newspaper?
> NNS: Glassi?
> NS: You wear them to see with, if you can't see. Reading glasses.
> → NNS: Ahh ahh glasses to read you say reading glasses.
> NS: Yeah.

In the penultimate line, the NNS acknowledges the fact that the new phrase *reading glasses* comes from the interaction and in particular as a consequence of the negotiation work.

Conversation is, of course, not limited to lexical learning. Example 10-52 is an excerpt from a conversation in which a teacher, an NS of English, is conversing with a native-speaking Punjabi child (from R. Ellis, 1985b, p. 79).

(10-52) NS: I want you to tell me what you can see in the pic-
ture or what's wrong with the picture.
NNS: A /paik/ (=bike)
NS: A cycle, yes. But what's wrong?
NNS: /ret/ (=red)
NS: It's red yes. What's wrong with it?
NNS: Black.
NS: Black. Good. Black what?
NNS: Black /tæs/ (=tires)

Prior to this point in time there were no examples of two-constituent utterances in this child's L2 discourse. As can be seen, the conversation itself provides the framework, or, as R. Ellis (1985b, p. 79) stated, "the breakthrough points," for a two-constituent utterance to develop. The teacher broke the task into parts and helped with the crucial vocabulary, which appears to have enabled the child to juxtapose *black* and *tires* as can be seen in her final utterance. From this time on there were frequent examples of two-constituent utterances in this child's speech.

According to R. Ellis (1984, p. 95):

> interaction contributes to development because it is the means by which the learner is able to crack the code. This takes place when the learner can infer what is said even though the message con-tains linguistic items that are not yet part of his competence and when the learner can use the discourse to help him/her modify or supplement the linguistic knowledge already used in production.

Thus, conversational interaction in a second language forms the basis for the development of language rather than being only a forum for practice of specific language features. This idea was expressed by Long (1996) as the Interaction Hypothesis:

> *negotiation for meaning*, and especially negotiation work that trig-gers *interactional* adjustments by the NS or more competent inter-locutor, facilitates acquisition because it connects input, internal learner capacities, particularly selective attention, and output in productive ways.
>
> (pp. 451–452)

It is proposed that environmental contributions to acquisition are mediated by selective attention and the learner's developing L2 processing capacity, and that these resources are brought together most usefully, although not exclusively, during *negoti-ation for meaning*. Negative feedback obtained during negotiation work or elsewhere may be facilitative of L2 development, at least for vocabulary, morphology, and language-specific syntax, and essential for learning certain specifiable L1–L2 contrasts.

(p. 414)

What this means is that, through focused negotiation work, the learner's attentional resources may be oriented to (a) a particular discrepancy between what he or she "knows" about the second language and what is reality vis-à-vis the target language or (b) an area of the second language about which the learner has little or no information. Learning may take place "during" the interaction, or negotiation may be an initial step in learning; it may serve as a priming device (Gass, 1997), thereby representing the setting of the stage for learning rather than being a forum for actual learning.

We have seen examples where learning appears to take place during the conversation. There is also evidence that conversation stimulates later learning, serving only as a catalyst. Example 10-47 repeated here as 10-53 illustrates delayed learning. Two NNSs are involved in a picture-description task. NNS1 is describing a part of the picture and initiates the description with an incorrectly pronounced word that NNS2 immediately questions. NNS1 most likely ponders the pronunciation problem, never again mispronouncing *cup*. To the contrary, after some time, she correctly pronounces *cup*. In other words, the negotiation itself made her aware of a problem; she was then able to listen for more input until she was able to figure out the correct pronunciation.

> (10-53) NNS1: Uh holding the [kʌp].
> NNS2: Holding the cup?
> NNS1: Hmm hmmm . . .
> (seventeen turns later)
> NNS2: Holding a cup.
> NNS1: Yes.
> NNS2: Coffee cup?
> NNS1: Coffee? Oh yeah, tea, coffee cup, tea cup.
> NNS2: Hm hm.

But what evidence is there that interaction indeed drives language development? Consider the conversations in 10-54 and 10-55, both of which involve two NNSs (Gass and Varonis, 1989, pp. 79, 81).

> (10-54) Hiroko: A man is uh drinking c-coffee or tea uh with the
> saucer of the uh uh coffee set is uh in his uh
> knee

Izumi: in *him* knee
Hiroko: uh on *his* knee
Izumi: yeah
Hiroko: on *his* knee.
Izumi: so sorry. On *his* knee
(10-55) Shizuka: When will you get married?
Akihito: When? I don't know. Maybe . . . uh . . . after thirty.
Shizuka: Thirty?
Akihito: Yeah, after thirty I'll get marriage—I'll get married . . .
           (3 turns)
Akihito: . . . then if I fall in lover with her, I'll get marriage with her.
           (11 turns)
Akihito: And . . . uh . . . when I saw her. I liked to get married with a Chinese girl because she's so beautiful.

In 10-54, Hiroko says *in his knee* with Izumi responding with an incorrect form, *in him knee*. Hiroko maintains the original form in terms of the pronominal case, although she changes the preposition from the original *in* to the correct *on*. As a result of the negotiation, both participants end up using the same correct form.

Similarly, in 10-55, Akihito hears the correct form *get married* at the beginning of the exchange. It is hypothesized that the form he initially provided (*get marriage*) was his learner-language form and that the correct modeling by Shizuka resulted in the confusion seen in Akihito's second utterance. It is only 16 turns later when we see the correct form "winning out."

In 10-56 is an exchange that involves not form, but lexical meaning. Three students were in a writing class negotiating how they were going to write a data commentary based on a graph depicting rental prices in China. In what is excerpted here, the participants are discussing the graph.

(10-56) (Data from Loewen and Basturkmen, 2005)

Episode 1
Jenny: <I just write the>
Doris: the charts
Jenny: th- the-
Doris: the figure?
(3.0)

351

Jenny: should I write the charts
Doris: okay

Episode 2
Jenny: the chart
Doris: shows
Jenny: shows or illustrates or
Doris: indicated (.) <strates>
Jong: actually it's about prime office rebel rental numbers comparison by location

Episode 3
Doris: what does prime office mean? Is that like head office for business?
Jenny: I think so.
Doris: the main office, right?
Jong: uh I'm not quite sure, but mm I think (.) good position, a better place for doing business,
Doris: mhm
Jong: when good facilities
Doris: oh okay
Jong: just like offices in Queen street
Doris: oh okay
Jong: prime
Doris: okay
Jong: it's actually the- prime means I think the good quality
Doris: good quality
Jong: yeah good quality
Doris: prime, prime
Jenny: I should write the chart compares,
Doris: um
Jenny: prime
Doris: do we need to write all the cities or we just choose one or two or three the most important ones to discuss

Episode 4
Jong: it's actually the- prime means I think the (.) good quality
Doris: good quality
Jong: yeah good quality

In this example, Doris starts off with a question about the meaning of *prime office.* Through the lengthy discussion, all three finally agree on the meaning of *prime,* as *good quality.*

More direct evidence of the importance of negotiated interaction comes from a number of studies. In one (Pica, Young, and Doughty, 1987), the researchers showed that there was better comprehension by a group of second language learners who were allowed interaction in the completion of a task versus those who were not allowed interaction but who were provided with modified input. A second study (Gass and Varonis, 1994) reported similar results, although in that study there was evidence that the effect of interaction was not only on immediate comprehension but was also noted in a follow-up activity that required productive language use. In that study, the learners were given modified input and were either allowed to negotiate or were not allowed to negotiate. In the first part of the task, NSs instructed NNSs as to where to place objects on a board. There were four conditions: (a) modified input, (b) nonmodified input, (c) negotiated interaction, and (d) nonnegotiated interaction. In the second part of the task, NNSs described to NSs where to place objects on a different board. In this part, there were two conditions: (a) negotiated interaction and (b) nonnegotiated interaction. The best performance (measured in terms of ability to give accurate instructions on the second part of the task as reflected in the NSs' ability to appropriately place objects) was obtained in that condition in which learners were allowed to negotiate on the first part of the task. What this suggests is that interaction is indeed beneficial and not just for the immediate present.

A third study (Loschky, 1989) was similar in that there were several experimental conditions, including modified input and negotiated interaction conditions. It differed in that the only effect negotiated interaction had was on online comprehension. There was no positive effect found for syntactic development or vocabulary retention.

A particularly compelling study by Mackey (1999) set out to establish the extent to which a relationship could be found between conversational interaction and second language development. She looked at the acquisition of question formation, building on the developmental model by Pienemann and Johnston (1987). In that model, originally developed to account for the acquisition of German word order by second language speakers, there were discernible and ordered stages of acquisition, each governed by processing mechanisms that constrained the movement from one stage to the next (see chapter 8). Although a detailed discussion of the model is not relevant to the present discussion (for details, see R. Ellis, 1994; Larsen-Freeman and Long, 1991), a brief explanation will help in putting Mackey's work in context.

The Pienemann and Johnston (1987) model makes a strong prediction of word order development such that a learner will start off (apart from single words and/or chunks) with a canonical order—for example, SVO (*I like Sydney, You are student?*). A second stage involves some movement, but movement that does not interrupt the canonical order (*In Vietnam, I am teacher, Do you have apartment, Why you no eat?*). In the next stage, canonical order is interrupted (*Have you job? I like to eat my friend's house*). In this stage, one can see the beginnings of syntactic development. In the fourth stage, movement entails the recognition that the moved elements are part of grammatical categories (*Why did you go?*—here the learner needs to know that the auxiliary must be in second position and that tense is marked on the auxiliary). Finally, learners recognize substrings and that grammatical operations can operate across the substrings (*He didn't leave, did he?*). Because this model makes a prediction about development and because conversational interaction within an input/ interaction framework is hypothesized to influence development, the Pienemann and Johnston model makes a fertile testing ground for both the model itself and for the Interaction Hypothesis.

Mackey (1999) conducted research in which learners of English were engaged in communicative tasks, with questions being the targeted structure and with opportunities for interaction between participants. She noted a positive relationship between interaction and development, in that learners who were involved in structure-focused interaction moved along a developmental path more rapidly than learners who were not. As she noted, interaction was able to "step up the pace" of development, but was not able to push learners beyond a developmental stage.[7] In other words, developmental stages could not be skipped. In conditions where learners received only premodified input but where no opportunities were allowed for interaction, little development was noted. Interesting was the fact that evidence for more developmentally advanced structures was noted in delayed posttests rather than taking place immediately. This supports the claim made throughout this book that interaction is a "priming device," allowing learners to focus attention on areas that they are "working on." In many instances, "thinking time" is needed before change takes place. It is further noteworthy that in Mackey's study the delayed effect is observed more often in more advanced structures, where it is reasonable to assume that more "thinking time" would be needed before a learner is able to figure out what changes to make and how to make them.

Recall from chapter 9 that Tarone and Liu (1995) found that different kinds of interaction differentially impacted the rate and route of acquisition. Whereas their findings were similar to those of Mackey with regard to the rate, they diverged from Mackey's with regard to the route. They found that the route could be altered depending on the context. For example, later-stage interrogatives occurred in interactions with the researcher before the appearance of earlier stages. As suggested by Liu

(1991), the explanation for this discrepancy may lie in the context of the interaction itself; in the interaction with the researcher, there were significant amounts of input of later-stage questions. An additional factor may be that the question forms that appeared to be absent from the child's speech were absent because they are ungrammatical in English and there is presumably no input (e.g., *Why you do that?*). Thus, it may be that later stages stemming from an input flood of grammatical utterances can be induced when earlier stages are ungrammatical and hence devoid of external input.

In this section we have discussed the relationship between interaction and learning, and presented evidence that the former may serve as a forum for or a facilitator of language development.

10.6.1 Attention

We now turn to the mechanism that may be at the heart of the Interaction Hypothesis (as Long, 1996 noted): selective attention (see also chapter 8). Negotiation and other types of corrective interaction focus learners' attention on parts of their language that diverge from NS language. In other words, negotiation requires attentiveness and involvement, both of which are necessary for successful communication. As reported, numerous studies suggest that interaction and learning are related. This observation is an important one, but is in need of an explanation in order to advance our understanding of how learning takes place. That is, what happens during a negotiation event that allows learners to utilize the content of the negotiation to advance their own knowledge? Long's (1996) statement, given earlier, suggests an important role for attention, as does Gass's (1997, p. 132) statement that "attention, accomplished in part through negotiation is one of the crucial mechanisms in this process."

In the recent history of SLA research, much emphasis has been placed on the concept of attention and the related notion of noticing (see Doughty, 2003, for an extended and related discussion of actual issues of processing during form-focused instruction). Schmidt (1990, 1993a, 1993b, 1993c, 1994) argued that attention is essential to learning; that is, that there can be no learning without attention. Although his strong claim is in dispute (see Schachter, Rounds, Wright, and Smith, 1998; Gass, 1997), it is widely accepted that selective attention plays a major role in learning.

It is through interaction (e.g., negotiation, recasts) that a learner's attention is focused on a specific part of the language, particularly on mismatches between TL forms and learner-language forms. There is both anecdotal and empirical evidence that learners are capable of noticing mismatches. Schmidt and Frota (1986) reported on the learning of Portuguese in which the learner documented the noticing and sub-sequent learning of new forms. This was exemplified earlier with specific examples that mismatches are recognized through interaction (see examples 10-53 and 10-54).

Doughty (2003) pointed out that this assumes that these mismatches are indeed noticeable (see Truscott, 1998, for a discussion of attention, awareness, and noticing) and that, if they are noticeable and if a learner is to use these mismatches as a source for grammar restructuring, he or she must have the capacity of holding a representation of the TL utterance in memory while executing a comparison. Doughty (2001, p. 229) provides three ways in which such a comparison could work:

1   Representations of the input and output utterances are held in STM and compared there.
2   Only a deeper (semantic) representation of the already-processed utterance is held in LTM, but it leaves useable traces in the STM against which new utterances may be compared.
3   The memory of the utterance passes to the LTM but readily can be reactivated if there is any suspicion by the language processor that there is a mismatch between stored knowledge and incoming linguistic evidence.

The role of memory in connection with attention has been noted by others. Williams (1999) found a strong relationship between individual differences in memory capacity and learning outcomes in an experiment involving a semiartificial form of Italian. He also recognized the impor-tance of the relationship between long-term memory and vocabulary learning.

10.6.2 Contrast theory

In this chapter, the issue of negative evidence has been raised (see also chapter 6). We have also pointed out that corrective feedback cannot be relied on in language learning (whether the language is first or second). In this section, we consider a broadened definition of negative evidence, one that relies heavily on conversational interaction. In so doing we are not making the argument that negative evidence can replace the need for an innate structure; rather, our point is simply that the concept of negative evidence in relation to learners' ability to attend to corrective feedback needs to be broadened. We take the following characterization from Saxton (1997, 2000), whose definition of negative evidence departed somewhat from the more general definition provided by Pinker (1989) and others: "Negative evidence occurs directly contingent on a child error, (syntactic or morphosyntactic), and is characterized by an immediate contrast between the child error and a correct alternative to the error, as supplied by the child's interlocutor" (Saxton, 1997, p. 145). According to this definition of negative evidence, researchers can determine the corrective potential of an utterance vis à vis two factors: (a) the linguistic content of the response and (b) the proximity of the response to an error. However, the definition is less clear on the question of whose perspective negative evidence is to be viewed from. It appears that it may be viewed from the point of view of the adult who supplies it. In fact, Saxton (1997, p. 145) stated that "there is ample evidence that negative evidence, as defined here, is supplied to the child." However, it is more important to view negative evidence from the perspective of the second language learner (child or adult) and to understand what learners are doing with the information provided.

Saxton (1997, 2000) proposed what he calls the Direct Contrast Hypothesis, which he defined within the context of child language acquisition as follows:

> When the child produces an utterance containing an erroneous form, which is responded to immediately with an utterance containing the correct adult alternative to the erroneous form (i.e. when negative evidence is supplied), the child may perceive the adult form as being in CONTRAST with the equivalent child form. Cognizance of a relevant contrast can then form the basis for perceiving the adult form as a correct alternative to the child form.
>
> (1997, p. 155; emphasis in original)

An example will make this clear.

(10-57) From Saxton, Houston-Price, and Dawson (2005)
Child: I thought they were all womans
Adult: They're not all women

Saxton, Houston-Price, and Dawson suggest that this exchange can provide two bits of information which are important as a child learns correct forms: the appropriate grammatical form and the potential ungrammaticality of his or her own form. There have been a number of studies that support this hypothesis (e.g., Saxton, Backley, and Gallaway, 2005; Saxton, Kulcsar, Marshall, and Rupra, 1998; Strapp, 1999; Strapp and Federico, 2000; Otomo, 2001; Chouinard and Clark, 2003).

The fact that a correct and an incorrect form are adjacent is important in creating a conflict for the learner. The mere fact of a contrast or a conflict draws a learner's attention to a deviant form, thereby highlighting the contrast through recasts or negotiation work. Saxton specifically tested two competing hypotheses, one based on nativism and one relying on contrast theory. The nativist hypothesis suggests that negative evidence, even when occurring adjacent to a child error, is no more effective than positive evidence in bringing about language change, whereas the contrast theory-based hypothesis suggests that the former is more effective than the latter. Saxton's research with children suggested that contrast theory was a more reliable predictor; that is, children reproduced correct forms more frequently when the correct form was embedded in negative evidence than in positive evidence.

Saxton and his colleagues (e.g., Saxton, 2005; Saxton, Houston-Price, and Dawson, 2005; Saxton, Backley, and Gallaway, 2005) have conducted a number of experiments in which they investigate corrective input, finding in general that the contrast that occurs in adjacent utterances (contingent models) has a facilitative function, for at least some grammatical functions. Saxton, Houston-Price, and Dawson (2005) specifically considered clarification questions finding support for Saxton's (2000) prompt hypothesis which assumes that clarification questions can be interpreted as a form of negative feedback, helping the child understand the ungrammaticality of his or her speech. Saxton, Houston-Price, and Dawson (2005) specifically investigated the role of clarification questions, finding support for the prompt hypothesis.

> This hypothesis is predicated on the assumption that specifically error-contingent CQs [clarification questions] can be interpreted by the child as a form of negative feedback for grammatical errors. The prompt hypothesis predicts that negative feedback can occasionally focus the child's attention on ungrammatical aspects of his or her speech, but only in cases where the child has prior knowledge of the correct grammatical form. The idea is that error-contingent CQs can function as a prompt, or reminder, to the child, cuing recall of a previously learned grammatical form. Prior knowledge of the correct form must be assumed, because there is nothing in a clarification request per se that conveys what the correct form is. For this reason, clarification requests are predicted to prompt, rather than teach, the child about preferred grammatical forms.
>
> (pp. 399–400)

The important point for SLA literature reported on earlier is to ensure that correct forms as a result or contrast not be limited to immediate responses. Long-term effectiveness must be ensured in order to claim that there is validity to this approach.

This is not unlike what has been dealt with in the SLA literature under the rubric of "noticing the gap"—that is, noticing where learner production differs from target language forms. Conversation provides the means for the contrasts to become apparent. The immediate juxta-position of correct and erroneous forms may lead learners to recognize that their form is in fact erroneous. However, as Doughty (2003) pointed out, many questions remain. What is the function of working memory? What happens when learners take the next step, which (at least in the case of syntax or morphosyntax) will undoubtedly involve some sort of analysis? Contrasts occurring within the context of conversation often do not have an immediate outcome. Research has not yet been successful at predicting when a single exposure—for example, through a negotiation sequence or a recast—will or will not suffice to effect immediate learning.

It is likely that there are limitations to what can and cannot be learned through the provision of negative evidence provided through conver-sation. One possibility is that surface level phenomena can be learned but abstractions cannot. This is consistent with Truscott's (1998) claim that competence is not affected by noticing. Negative evidence probably cannot apply to long stretches of speech given memory limitations (see Philp, 1999, 2003), but it may be effective with low level phenomena such as pronunciation or basic meanings of lexical items. Future research will need to determine the long-term effects of attention and, hence, inter-action on different parts of language (see Gass, Svetics, and Lemelin, 2003). Some differential effects of perception were noted by Mackey, Gass, and McDonough (2000).

10.6.3 Metalinguistic awareness

Another explanation for the importance of negotiated interaction con-cerns metalinguistic awareness, an important aspect of language learning. Metalinguistic awareness refers to one's ability to consider language not just as a means of expressing ideas or communicating with others, but also as an object of inquiry. Thus, making puns suggests an ability to think about language as opposed to only using it for expressive purposes. Similarly, judging whether a given sentence is grammatical in one's native language or translating from one language to another requires thinking about language as opposed to engaging in pure use of it.

NNSs in a classroom setting often spend more time on metalinguistic activities (e.g., studying rules of grammar or memorizing vocabulary words) than on activities of pure use. The ability to *think* about language is often associated with an increased ability to *learn* a language. In fact, bilingual children have been known to have greater metalinguistic aware-ness than monolingual children (Bialystok, 1988).

Much classroom activity in earlier language-teaching methodologies engaged learners in just this type of "consciousness raising," providing a direct means of making learners aware of the language at the expense of spending classroom time on practice activities. However, there are other ways of increasing metalinguistic awareness in learners in a classroom setting. To specifically relate this to the earlier discussion of negotiation, learners are made aware of errors in their speech (whether in grammar, pronunciation, content, or discourse) through the questioning and clarification that often go on in negotiation. In other words, negotiation is what makes NNSs aware of incongruities between the forms they are using and the forms used by NSs. In order to respond to an inquiry of nonunderstanding, NNSs must modify their output. For this to take place, learners must be aware of a problem and seek to resolve it. Hence, the more learners are made aware of unacceptable speech, the greater the opportunity is for them to make appropriate modifications. Although there is limited evidence as to the long-range effects of these modifications, one can presume that because negotiation leads to heightened awareness it ultimately leads to increased knowledge of the second language as well. For example, even though the NNS in the following exchange (from Pica, 1987, p. 6) does not produce the correct form, she is made aware of a pronunciation problem through the NS's indications of nonunderstanding.

(10-58) NNS: And they have the chwach there.
NS: The what?
NNS: The chwach—I know someone that—
NS: What does it mean?
NNS: Like um like American people they always go there every Sunday
NS: Yes?
NNS: You kn—every morning that there pr-that -the American people get dressed up to got to um chwach.
NS: Oh to church—I see.

10.7 Limitations of input

Sorace (1993a, 1993b, 1995; Bard, Robertson, and Sorace, 1996) argued that there are two kinds of changes which occur in learners' grammars: discontinuous and continuous. She considers in particular two kinds of verbs in Italian, verbs such as *andare* and *venire*, which mean "to go" and "to come" respectively and verbs such as *camminare*, which means "to walk." Both *andare* and *venire* are intransitive verbs which require *essere* ("to be") as an auxiliary, whereas *camminare*, also an intransitive verb, requires *avere* ("to have"). She was particularly interested in how learners of Italian learn the appropriate auxiliary to use with these two types of verbs. That is, do they use the auxiliary *essere* or the auxiliary *avere*?

Auxiliary choice is dependent on both syntactic and semantic factors. Some verbs are sensitive to both lexical-semantic distinctions as well as syntactic configurations. For example, there is a hierarchy such that verbs which take *essere* are most likely to be those which represent a change in location (i.e., "to come" or "to go"). Next on the hierarchy are those verbs which represent a change in condition (as, for example, the verb *crescere*, "to grow"). Even less likely to use *essere* are those which represent a continuation of a condition (as *durare* "to last" or *sopravvivere* "to survive"). Finally, and least likely to require *essere*, are those verbs which express existence of a condition (as *essere* "to be" or *esistere* "to exist") (see Table 10.5).

Other choices are dependent on syntactic configurations. That is, it is truly the syntactic structure which dictates the auxiliary to be used. As an example, consider the following.

> Obligatory AUX change with clitic-climbing.
> (10-59) Ho dovuto andare.
>   I had to go
> (10-60) Ci sono dovuto andare.
>   I had to go

In the preceding examples, once the clitic "*ci*" is part of the sentence, there is an obligatory change from *avere* to *essere* with no meaning difference. Hence, the choice of auxiliary is entirely dependent on the syntactic form.

What Sorace found in looking at data from learners of Italian was a differentiation in terms of input use with regard to auxiliary selection. They were sensitive to the input with regard to lexical-semantic properties of auxiliary selection (regardless of their L1), but they appeared to be impervious to the input with respect to some of the syntactic properties. Also lexical-semantic properties were acquired incrementally, whereas syntactic properties, if they were acquired at all, developed in a discontinuous fashion (personal communication, January 25, 1993).

Thus, in Sorace's work, it is possible for the input, or, in her terms, the

Table 10.5 Hierarchy of auxiliary choice

Most likely to take *essere*	
change in location	*andare* "to come"/*venire* "to go"
change in condition	*crescere* "to grow"
continuation of a condition	*durare* "to last"/*sopravvivere* "to survive"
existence of a condition	*essere* "to be"/*esistere* "to exist"
Least likely to take *essere*	

evidence available to learners, to have a varying effect depending on the part of the grammar to be affected—more so for lexical semantics and less so for syntax.

10.8 Conclusion

In this chapter, we have dealt with the nature and function of input in second language learning and with the role that output and interaction play in second language acquisition. In chapter 11, we extend these findings and focus attention on second language learning in a classroom context.

Suggestions for additional reading

Conversation in Second Language Acquisition: Talking to Learn. Richard Day (Ed.). Newbury House (1986).

Learning a Second Language Through Interaction. Rod Ellis. (Ed.) John Benjamins (2000).

Input and Interaction in Language Acquisition. Clare Gallaway and Brian J. Richards (Eds.). Cambridge University Press (1994).

Input, Interaction, and the Second Language Learner. Susan Gass. Lawrence Erlbaum Associates (1997).

Input in Second Language Acquisition. Susan Gass and Carolyn Madden (Eds.). Newbury House (1985).

Conversational Interaction in Second Language Acquisition: A Collection of Empirical Studies. Alison Mackey (Ed.). Oxford University Press (2007).

Input, Interaction and Corrective Feedback in L2 Learning. Alison Mackey. Oxford University Press (in press).

The Syntax of Conversation in Interlanguage Development. Charlene Sato. Gunter Narr Verlag (1990).

Points for discussion

1   Find an NNS of your language or pretend that you are speaking to an NNS. You need to convey the meanings of the following five sentences. Without letting your partner see the sentences, how would you get your meaning across (e.g., sentence by sentence)? Make careful note of exactly what you say and what you do.

   a   I don't know the person you're looking at.
   b   She's my cousin, not my friend.
   c   Were you listening to that woman?
   d   Come to my house on Friday. Don't forget!
   e   Yesterday I drove to the zoo and saw some monkeys.

Now reverse roles and do the same with the following five sentences:

  a   She's laughing at that man's accident. She's not nice.
  b   Who is that woman? Is she the president?
  c   He always travels with one suitcase.
  d   Where's the book I gave you yesterday?
  e   He will be leaving tomorrow.

2   Observe an NS and an NNS conversing, taking careful notes on how you think their speech differs from what you would expect in a conversation between NSs. Pay attention to all aspects of the NS's speech, including pronunciation, grammar, vocabulary, rate of speech, and so on. Do the features you note coincide with what is presented in Table 10.3? Are there features you noted that are not included in the table?

3   From Table 10.4, describe the differences in the speech of the kindergarten teacher in each of the instances given. What do you think the effect of the different modifications might be? Do you think that the teacher trained herself to speak like this? What evidence is there that using a modified form of speech is something that we begin doing at a young age? (Hint: Think of speech to NSs as well as to NNSs.)

4   Consider the summary data in Table 10a.1, taken from the teacher's speech referred to in problem 3 and in Table 10.4. Do these data support what you found in looking at the data from problem 3? What uniform explanation can you give to account for the data in this problem and those from problem 3?

Table 10a.1 Summary analysis of data from Table 10.4

Proficiency level	% teacher utterances (n = 269)	Mean length of utterance	Student NL
Beginning	40.5	3.18	Japanese
Low intermediate	27.9	3.37	Arabic
Intermediate	14.9	4.51	Urdu
Native speaker	16.0	5.27	English

WORD USAGE

Proficiency Level	% total Items (n = 933)	Type/token	Student NL
Beginning	37.62	0.33	Japanese
Low intermediate	24.75	0.41	Arabic
Intermediate	14.50	0.59	Urdu
Native speaker	23.47	0.48	English

5 The data that follow come from a telephone conversation in which an NNS was conducting an interview about food and nutrition (Gass and Varonis, 1985). Focus on the language following the NNS's *Pardon me?* How would you describe the difference between that response and the immediately preceding response? What functions do the modifications serve?

Example 1

NNS: There has been a lot of talk lately about additives and preservatives in food. In what ways has this changed your eating habits?

NS: Uh, I avoid them, I d-, I don't buy prepackaged foods uh, as much . . . Uh, I don't buy . . . say . . . potato chips that have a lot of flavoring on them . . . And uh, I eat better. I think.

NNS: Pardon me?

NS: Ummm, pardon me? I, I eat better, I think. I, I don't buy so much food that's prepackaged.

Example 2

NNS: How have increasing food costs changed your eating habits?

NS: Well, it doesn't, hasn't really.

NNS: Pardon me?

NS: It hasn't really changed them.

Example 3

NNS: How have increasing food costs changed your eating habits?

NS: Uh well that would I don't think they've change 'em much right now, but the pressure's on.

NNS: Pardon me?

NS: I don't think they've changed our eating habits much as of now . . .

6 In this chapter, we discussed the role of negotiation. We pointed out that negotiation aids the learner in understanding. What connection can be made between understanding at a particular point in time and actual acquisition (internalization of new linguistic information)? That is, because a learner is able to understand something in conversation, can we automatically say that he or she will internalize or even understand the same thing at a later point in time?

7 Swain (1985, p. 248) reported the following statement by an L2 learner in Grade 9: "I understand everything anyone says to me, and I can hear in my head how I should sound when I talk, but it never

comes out that way." Can you think of examples when this has happened to you in an L2? In your native language? What do you think the reason for this is?

8   Data from NSs engaged in conversations with NNSs follow (from Larsen-Freeman and Long, 1991, pp. 120–124). Describe the ways in which these NSs ask questions of the NNSs. What is the communicative effect of asking questions in these ways?

(10a-1)	Did you *like* San Diego?
(10a-2)	Do you *like* San Diego? San Diego, did you like it?
(10a-3)	Right. When do you take the break? At ten-thirty?
(10a-4) NS:	When do you go to the uh Santa Monica? You say you go fishing in Santa Monica, right?
NNS:	Yeah.
NS:	When?
(10a-5) NS:	Uh what does uh what does your father do in uh you're from Kyoto, right?
NNS:	Yeah.
NS:	What does your father do in Kyoto?
(10a-6) NS:	Are you going to visit San Francisco? Or Las Vegas?
NNS:	Yes I went to Disneyland and to Knottsberry Farm.
NS:	Oh yeah?
(10a-7) NS:	Do you like California?
NNS:	Huh?
NS:	Do you like Los Angeles?
NNS:	Uhm.
NS:	Do you like California?
NNS:	Oh! Yeah I like.

9   Find a picture that is relatively easy to describe. Make two recordings of an NS describing the picture to (a) another NS and (b) an NNS. Write down exactly what you hear. In what ways does the structure of the conversation differ? Are there examples of self-corrections, changes in grammar, confirmation checks, comprehension checks, or other interactional modifications? Is there evidence of co-operation? What are the participants doing to make communication easier?

10 The Input Hypothesis is crucially dependent on the notions of $i + 1$ and comprehensible input. How can one determine if there is sufficient comprehensible input? If a learner seems to have fossilized, does that mean there is insufficient input? If a learner has fossilized and one can show that the input is rich with a particular structure, what other explanation can be given for nonprogress?

11 Given the emphasis on input in Krashen's model, how would you

rate the possibility of success in a study-abroad situation? Suppose you discovered that in a study-abroad situation (let's say, in France) your fellow students were *not* members of the host community, but speakers of your native language. Consequently, the input you received was not standard French but what Wong-Fillmore (1976) called "junky data." Do you think practice with this type of input data would help, because "practice makes perfect"? Or do you think this type of input data would reinforce your interlanguage forms? If the situation were instead a foreign language classroom, would your answer be the same?

12 In chapter 9, we discussed conversational analysis (section 9.4.1) and in this chapter we discussed the Interaction Hypothesis. Both use conversational data as the basis for understanding learning. Consider the following transcript of a conversation from a French language class. Fill in the two columns with a conversation analysis interpretation and with an Input–Interaction interpretation.

Lines 17–29	CA interpretation	Input–Interaction interpretation

[cette chaîne,
This chain,

°chhhh:::::°
(·) Lorena une
phrase   avec
ce[tte
(trousse)
°chhhh:::::° (·)
Lorena a
phrase   with
thi[s   pencil
case

[cette trousse
est dans ma
valise
[this pencil
case is in my
bag

B   [(   )]
P: cette trousse
     est à moi
     this pencil
     case is mine
24 J: (cough))
25 K: cette trousse
     est   [(0.3)
     dans   ma:]
     (0.9) ma sac
     this pencil
     case   is

Lines 17–29   *CA interpretation*   *Input–Interaction interpretation*

    [(0.3) in my:
    (fem.)] (0.9)
    my (fem.) bag

    cette trousse
    est   [(0.3)
    dans   ma:]
    (0.9) ma sac
    this   pencil
    case is [(0.3)
    in my: (fem.)]
    (0.9)   my
    (fem.) bag

°mon:,°
°*my:,*° *(masc.)*

mon sac
my bag (28)
sac.
bag. (29)

                                  Summary: *Summary:*

See GSS, problems 1.3, 6.1–6.6, and 6.8.

11

INSTRUCTED SECOND LANGUAGE LEARNING

11.1 Introduction

This chapter is devoted to learning that takes place in the classroom. It is not a chapter intended to be a "how to" manual for teachers; rather, the focus is on learning that is specific to an instructed environment. In the other chapters in this book, we do not differentiate between different contexts of learning. In other words, even though some examples are taken from a classroom context and others from outside a classroom, we do not focus on the contextual difference in the conclusions we draw. This is mainly due to an assumption that processes involved in learning a second language can be thought of as independent of the context in which the language is being learned, though they may apply differentially by context. For example, whether or not some mechanism, such as UG, is responsible for the learning of core grammar is not to be thought of as dependent on the context of that learning. Whatever psycholinguistic processing takes place in a naturalistic situation presumably takes place in a classroom situation. Whatever starting point for learning turns out to be valid does not depend on where language learning takes place.

This is not to say that differences do not exist, for clearly they do, the most obvious being differences in the quantity and quality of input. For learners in a foreign language setting—that is, those learning another language in their home environment—there is not only limited input, but a large part of the input comes from classmates whose knowledge of the foreign language is restricted. Interactional opportunities are also severely restricted in a foreign language environment. In this chapter then, our concern is with those opportunities that can be and are shaped by the classroom context.

11.2 Classroom language

One of the main differentiating factors between classroom learning and so-called naturalistic learning is the language available from which learners can come to understand the workings of the L2 and formulate hypotheses. In language classrooms, the language addressed to learners may be somewhat modified, as we saw in chapter 10.

Gaies (1979) presented data from eight teacher trainees and their speech to (a) each other and (b) four groups of ESL students at four proficiency levels. Table 11.1 presents a portion of these data for each of these five groups. As can be seen, in all cases there is a progression from lesser to greater syntactic complexity as a function of proficiency level. In fact, the proficiency level is a statistically significant predictor of the syntactic complexity of these teachers' speech. In nearly all cases, there are statistically significant differences in proficiency level among these inexperienced ESL teachers.

In foreign language instruction, very often the only language that learners are exposed to is the one in the classroom. There are three sources of input: (a) teacher, (b) materials, and (c) other learners. We saw earlier that teacher talk can be limited. It is clear that learner talk to other learners is also limited and often filled with errors. To what extent these errors are picked up or ignored in the classroom is unclear. Perhaps surprisingly, there is evidence that learners do not pick up errors from one another. For example, Gass and Varonis (1989) reported data from two NNSs of English (different language backgrounds). The learners were performing a classroom task in which they had to go out onto the streets of Ann Arbor, Michigan (with a tape recorder) and ask people for directions to the train station. The tape recorder was left on during the entire time they were engaged in the task, including the time between stopping passersby for directions. They alternated stopping strangers to ask for directions. Following is a list of the questions they asked:

(11-1) NNS1: Can you tell me where is the train station?
NNS2: Can you tell me where the train station is?
NNS1: Can you tell me where is the train station?

Table 11.1 Complexity of teacher speech directed at different proficiency levels

Level	Words per T-unit	Ratio of clauses to T-units	Words per clause
Beginner	4.30	1.02	4.20
Upper beginner	5.75	1.14	5.04
Intermediate	6.45	1.24	5.18
Advanced	8.26	1.38	5.98
Baseline	10.97	1.60	6.84

T-Units are defined as "one main clause plus any subordinate clause or nonclausal structure that is attached to or embedded in it" (Hunt, 1970, p. 4).

Source: From "Linguistic input in first and second language learning" by S. Gaies, 1979. In F. Eckman and A. Hastings (Eds.), Studies in First and Second Language Acquisition (p. 190). Reprinted by permission.

NNS2: Can you tell me where the train station is?
NNS1: Can you tell me where is the train station?
NNS2: Can you tell me where the train station is?
NNS1: Can you tell me where the train station is?
NNS2: Can you tell me where the train station is?
NNS1: Can you tell me where the train station is?

To appreciate the significance of this example, it is important to note that nowhere in the conversation between requests for directions did the students discuss the discrepancy in their versions of indirect questions. Even so, NNS1 made an unprompted change in the form of her utterance from the incorrect *Can you tell me where is the train station?* to the correct *Can you tell me where the train station is?*, whereas NNS2 made no change. Importantly, the change was in the direction of the target language and not from a correct form to an incorrect form. Similarly, Bruton and Samuda (1980) listened to 10 hours of taped conversations and found only one example of a change from a correct form to an incorrect one. Thus, errors from classmates may not be incorporated into a learner's grammar. It may be that learners know when they are right and may also know when they are wrong or at least have a sense that they are not sure. When learners internalize a new form, they may use the positive evidence they hear/read to strengthen that knowledge. That is, they may receive confirmatory evidence for their correct hypotheses. When a hypothesis is not correct, there is no confirmatory evidence and the knowledge is loosely represented, resulting in uncertainty.

In chapter 10 we looked at interactions in which negotiation about a form leads to knowledge about the form. We present an example (from Swain and Lapkin, 1998, p. 329) of two classroom learners who are jointly writing an essay. They are grade 8 students who have been in a French immersion program since kindergarten. The vocabulary item *réveille-matin* "alarm clock" is in question. On a pretest, Kim knew the word, whereas Rick did not. On a posttest both students knew the word. What we see in this episode is the use of conversation as a tool for learning. Rick wavers between alternatives for alarm clock and, through questioning of Kim and responses from Kim, he comes to the correct French word *réveille-matin*.

TURN #
2 Kim: On peut pas déterminer qu'est-ce que c'est.
           "One can't figure out what it is."
3 Rick: Réveille-matin.
           "Alarm clock."
4 Kim: Et il y a un réveille-matin rouge . . . sur une table brune, et le
           réveille-matin dit six heures, et c'est tout.

"And there is a red alarm clock . . . on the brown table, and the alarm clock says six o'clock, and that's all."

9 Rick: Elle est en train de dormir après que . . . la rêve-matin est ancore sonné. Et le rêve-matin dit six heures un.
"She is sleeping after the alarm clock rang again. And the alarm clock says one minute after six o'clock."

55 Kim: Il y a un réveille-matin.
"There is an alarm clock."

56 Rick: Réveille-matin?
"Alarm clock?"

57 Kim: Réveille-matin.
"Alarm clock."

66 Rick: Se réveille à cause . . . du son . . .
"Wakes up because . . . of the sound . . ."

67 Kim: Réveille-matin.
"Alarm clock."

68 Rick: A cause du . . .
"Because of . . ."

69 Kim: Du réveille-matin qui sonne? Does that sound OK?
"Of the alarm clock that rings? Does that sound OK?"

70 Rick: Or what about . . . Jacqueline se lève à cause du . . . du réveille- . . . yeah, qui sonne
"Or what about . . . Jacqueline [the girl in their story] gets up because of the . . . of the alarm- . . . yeah, that rings."

71 Kim: Or you can say, du réveille-matin, or du sonnement du réveille-matin.
"OK. Or you can say, of the alarm clock, or the ring of the alarm clock."

72 Rick: No, réveille-matin qui sonne.
"No, alarm clock that rings."

92 Rick: Sur la rêv- . . . rêve-matin.
"On the alarm clock."

93 Kim: Sur le réveille-matin pour arrêter le sonnement.
"On the alarm clock to stop the ring."

94 Rick: Rêve-matin?
"Alarm clock?"

95 Kim: Réveille-matin.
"Alarm clock." (Stresses component meaning "wake.")

What we see in the example above is an exchange that includes hypothesis generation, hypothesis testing, and the extension of knowledge to new contexts. What is interesting is Rick's initial use of the correct word in turn 3, followed in turn 9 by two uses of the incorrect *rêve-matin* (once with the feminine article *la* and once with the masculine article *le*).

Clearly, this suggests his uncertainty, which is further seen in his pauses (turns 9, 66, and 70) and in turn 94 where he asks his partner if *rêve-matin* is acceptable. So, we see Rick's change to the correct form. The change is not a one-time affair, but shows a back and forth wavering between correct and incorrect forms. Rick is seen to generate hypotheses (his questions), and Kim's responses are either confirmatory or disconfirmatory. We note that Rick receives input and uses output as a means of learning the new word. In turn 56, Rick's attempt to write the word focuses his attention on his own uncertainty, forcing him to make a choice between the alternative hypotheses he has entertained. It is through collaborative dialogues as evidenced here that we return to the notion of the Zone of Proximal Development discussed in chapter 9. As noted in that chapter, potential development comes about through problem-solving in collaboration with more capable peers.

However, as mentioned earlier, it is not always the case that learner forms can serve as "good" input for other learners. In another excerpt from these same two learners (Swain and Lapkin, 1998, p. 333), it is clear that without teacher intervention these two participants will either walk away uncertain about the correct form or will learn something incorrect in French; that is, they will practice and automatize the interlanguage, perhaps far from target language norms.

> (11-2) Kim: [elle voit un] gars.
> "[She sees a] guy."
> Rick: . . . gars, qui s'en va à l'école.
> ". . . guy who is going to school."
> Kim: Qui marche vers l'école . . . marche.
> "Who is walking towards school, walking."

Both *marcher* ("walk") and *s'en aller* ("walk") exist in French, but in this context *marcher* is incorrect. The pair opts for the incorrect form probably because, as Swain and Lapkin suggested, *marcher* more closely resembles English usage and it is suggested by Kim, the one who in general is seen as having greater expertise in French. Thus, even though the classroom is a place where conversational interaction can often provide opportunities for learning, an important caveat is in order—teacher intervention is often essential.

11.3 Processing instruction

Processing instruction refers to a type of instruction that takes as its basis how learners process input (see chapter 8 for a discussion of input processing). In particular, it deals with the conversion of input to intake and specifically focuses on form–meaning relationships (VanPatten, 1995; VanPatten and Cadierno, 1993; VanPatten and Sanz, 1995). In a series of experiments, VanPatten and his colleagues presented a model for instructional intervention that relied heavily on the notion of attention to form and its crucial role in a learner's movement from input to intake and finally to output. They compared two instructional models, one in which input is practiced as a form of output manipulation (traditional grammar instruction in which information is presented to learners for practice) and the other in which an attempt is made to change the way input is perceived and processed (processing instruction) (see Figures 11.1 and 11.2).

Rather than allow an internalized system to (begin to) develop, the attempt is to influence the way that input is processed and hence the way the system develops.

Figure 11.1 Traditional instruction in foreign language learning.

Source: From "Explicit instruction and input processing" by B. VanPatten and T. Cadierno, 1993, *Studies in Second Language Acquisition, 15,* 227. Copyright 1993 by Studies in Second Language Acquisition. Reprinted with the permission of Cambridge University Press.

Figure 11.2 Processing instruction in foreign language teaching.

Source: From "Explicit instruction and input processing" by B. VanPatten and T. Cadierno, 1993, *Studies in Second Language Acquisition, 15,* 227. Copyright 1993 by Studies in Second Language Acquisition. Reprinted with the permission of Cambridge University Press.

VanPatten (2007a, 2007b; see also VanPatten, 2004) proposed principles of L2 input processing. VanPatten (2008) presents three premises that are the basis of processing instruction:

1   Learners need input for acquisition;
2   A major problem in acquisition might be the way in which learners process input;
3   If we can understand how learners process input, then we might be able to devise effective input enhancement or focus on form to aid acquisition of formal features of language.

VanPatten (2007b) outlines three basic features of processing instruction.

1   Give learners information about a structure or form.
2   Inform learners about a particular processing strategy that may get in the way of selecting the form/structure during comprehension.
3   Structure input so that learners must rely on form/structure to get meaning and not rely on natural processing tendencies.

He presents an example from the French causative, as in 11-3.

(11-3) Jean fait promener le chien à Marie.
        John makes to walk the dog to Mary
        "John makes Mary walk the dog."

The first step is to have learners answer the question *Who walks the dog?* Most English learners respond that John walks the dog because that is the first noun. This is part of the first stage in which information is provided to learners about the causative construction in French. This is followed by structured input activities in which other causative constructions might be read aloud and they have to respond by stating who is doing the action. VanPatten refers to these as referential activities because there is a right/wrong answer. These are followed by affective structured activities which are more open-ended and require learners to use information from the real world.

The results of experiments (both sentence-level and discourse-related) suggest a positive effect for processing instruction. Learners in the processing instruction group were better able to understand and produce the target structure (direct object pronouns in Spanish) than learners in the traditional instruction group (VanPatten and Cadierno, 1993; VanPatten and Sanz, 1995). These have been conducted with languages other than Spanish; for example, Wong (2004) and VanPatten and Wong (2004) in French, Benati (2004) in Italian. These have shown support for this approach. DeKeyser and Sokalski (1996), DeKeyser, Salaberry, Robinson, and Harrington (2002), and Salaberry (1997, 1998) have argued against this approach, although VanPatten (2007a) points out that the studies referred to in these papers have not dealt with the issue of why there is a processing issue.

In sum, this approach to processing instruction attempts to deal with not just a linguistic difficulty, but with a problematic processing strategy and attempts to interrupt that strategy with overt instruction and practice.

Another series of studies that considered the role of input processing, albeit in a slightly different manner, is known as the "garden path" studies by Tomasello and Herron (1988, 1989). Here input in the form of corrective feedback (the focus was on exceptions to a general rule) was provided either (a) before a faulty generalization was made (in the VanPatten framework, this is akin to the input-processing mode in which the focus is on processing input before the internalization of that input) or (b) after learners had been led down the "garden path" and induced into making an overgeneralization. Tomasello and Herron found that the corrective feedback was more meaningful after learners had been induced to produce an error as opposed to "preventing" an error.[1]

What is clear from these studies is that some sort of comprehension must take place before we can begin to talk about intake and acquisition. This, of course, begs the question of what is meant by comprehension. As noted earlier, comprehension can range from "an inferential process based on the perception of cues" (Rost, 1990, p. 33) to a detailed structural analysis. Thus, top–down processing relying on prior knowledge and contextual (visual, oral, etc.) cues, as well as bottom–up processing, in which attention to form is crucial, are both relevant to understanding comprehension. Clearly, however, comprehension and acquisition are not synonymous (see also Sharwood Smith, 1986). Some input will be utilized for meaning, whereas other input will be utilized for grammar development. It is argued here, however, that the former precedes the latter: Semantic comprehension is a prerequisite to syntactic comprehension and syntactic comprehension is a prerequisite to acquisition.[2] Neither guarantees the following step; in other words, semantic comprehension is necessary for syntactic comprehension but does not guarantee it.

Swain (1995) cited work by Clark and Clark (1977) that suggested a difference between these two types of comprehension:

> Listeners usually know a lot about what a speaker is going to say. They can make shrewd guesses from what has been said and from the situation being described. They can also be confident that the speaker will make sense, be relevant, provide given and new information appropriately, and in general be cooperative.

Listeners almost certainly use this sort of information to select among alternative parses of a sentence, to anticipate words and phrases, and sometimes even to circumvent syntactic analyses altogether.

(Clark and Clark, 1977, p. 72)

Assuming the validity of this notion, it follows that comprehension (in the usual sense of the word) may serve little purpose in helping learners understand the syntax of the language, which is an[3] ultimate goal of language learning. Similarly, Cook (1996, p. 76) noted that the ability to *decode* language for meaning—"processing language to get the 'message' "—is not the same as *code breaking*—the determination of the nature of the linguistic systems used for conveying meaning or the "processing [of] language to get the 'rules' " (p. 76).

11.4 Teachability/learnability

As early as the morpheme order studies, there has been an emphasis on acquisition orders; that is, the idea that acquisition takes place in some sort of natural order. In fact, Krashen stated this as part of the entire Monitor Model (see chapter 8) as the Natural Order Hypothesis, which claims that elements of language (or language rules) are acquired in a predictable order. The order is the same regardless of whether or not instruction is involved. The "natural order" was determined by a synthesis of the results of the morpheme order studies (see chapter 5) and is a result of the acquired system, without interference from the learned system. The source of the Natural Order Hypothesis stems from studies of English morpheme acquisition, which, as has been noted earlier in this book, are limited in scope and, hence, generalizability. Putting the parts of Krashen's model together, we can find difficulty in relating one part to another in a meaningful way. In general, the three hypotheses are dependent on one another and the arguments for one depend on the arguments for the others. For example, the Monitor is needed to account for discrepancies in the Natural Order; a Learning–Acquisition distinction is needed to justify the use of the Monitor. Thus, the argumentation is circular, rendering it vacuous.

Nonetheless, because Krashen's formulation as stated may not have theoretical validity, one cannot take this a step further and argue that an order of acquisition does not exist. The implication of acquisition order is that pedagogical intervention cannot alter (or can alter in only a trivial manner) natural acquisition orders (see Lightbown, 1983). The most explicit statement of this comes from work originally involving German as a second language. Recall from section 8.3.1 the discussion of the acquisition of English questions. Findings based on the natural progression within a classroom context are supported by a number of studies. Pienemann (1984, 1989) argued that stages in this developmental sequence cannot be skipped even as a result of instruction. He investigated German word-order development among 10 Italian children ranging in age from 7 to 9. They all had two weeks of instruction on a particular stage. Some were at the immediately preceding stage and others were at a much earlier stage. Only the former group learned the instructional target, suggesting that the other children could not learn because they were not developmentally ready.

As discussed in chapter 10, Mackey (1995, 1999) set out to determine the extent to which conversational interaction could alter the developmental progression of the acquisition of questions. In her research, there was a positive relationship between interaction and development in that learners who were involved in structure-focused interaction moved along a developmental path more rapidly than learners who did not. As she noted, interaction was able to "step up the pace" of development, but was not able to push learners beyond a developmental stage. In other words, developmental stages could not be skipped. There are constraints on learning such that even pedagogical intervention is likely to be unsuccessful in altering the order. In Chapter 8 we suggested that movement of elements in a sentence are constrained by three processing mechanisms: (a) canonical order strategy; (b) initialization/finalization strategy and (c) subordinate clauses strategy. These strategies constrain acquisition.

In chapter 7 we dealt with the acquisition of relative clauses showing that there is a predictable order of acquisition. Considering the Accessibility Hierarchy (AH) from the point of view of learnability, if difficulty is at the base of this universal, we would expect learners to learn to relativize according to the ordering of the AH positions. Yet another prediction comes in the form of learners' capacities to generalize. What would happen if, let's say, through instruction, a learner were to come to learn a more difficult relative clause position before learning an easier one. Would knowledge of that more difficult relative clause construction generalize to knowledge of the easier relative clause positions? This would not be unexpected because, in some sense, knowledge of a more difficult structure should incorporate knowledge of a related easier structure. In fact, two studies lend support to this prediction, one by Gass (1982) and the other by Eckman, Bell, and Nelson (1988). In the first study, two groups of second language learners were given specific instruction on relative clauses. One group was instructed on subject and direct object relatives, the second group on object of preposition relatives only. After the period of instruction, both groups were tested on relative clause types. The group that had received subject and direct object instruction only performed well on those two relative clause types, but not on others, whereas the second group performed well not only on their instructed relative clauses (object of preposition), but also on the relative clauses higher on the accessibility hierarchy—that is, subject and direct object relative clauses—but not lower.

The study by Eckman, Bell, and Nelson was similar. There were four groups of learners: a control group and three experimental groups. Each of the three experimental groups received instruction on one of three relative clause types: subject, direct object, or object of preposition. Their results are given in Figure 11.3.

The figure shows improvement rates for the three types of relative clauses. As can be seen, the greatest improvement on all three structures occurs in that group that was given instruction on the lowest position (the object of preposition group). The group with the next greatest improvement (i.e., improvement on two structures) was the direct object group, and then the subject group, although the subject group showed greater improvement than the direct object group on the relative clauses on which they had had instruction (subjects). The conclusions of both these

Figure 11.3 Interaction of group and relativized position.

Source: From "On the generalization of relative clause instruction in the acquisition of English as a second language" by F. Eckman, L. Bell, and D. Nelson, 1988, *Applied Linguistics*, 9, 1–20. Reprinted by permission.

studies suggest that learners' maximum generalization occurs from more marked (or difficult, in the terminology used here) structures to the less marked ones (see section 6.4.1). Generalization from less difficult to more difficult does not appear to occur. Hamilton (1994), also using ESL learners, found that learners generalized from the marked to the unmarked. Partial support of the generalization of the Accessibility Hierarchy comes from a study by Croteau (1995), who investigated relativization of foreign language learners of Italian (English as the L1). She found that when there was instruction on a higher position on the hierarchy, there was not generalization to a lower position. However, when there was instruction on a lower position, generalization did not occur in all instances. Specifically, those instructed on direct object relative clauses generalized to subject relative clauses, but those taught object of preposition relative clauses generalized to the direct object position, but not to the subject position. Not surprisingly, those taught genitive relative clauses did not generalize at all. This is not surprising because the genitive in previous studies did not behave according to the predictions of the hierarchy, possibly because the English genitive may behave as a unit that takes on another position of the hierarchy. For example, the genitive *whose brother* in the sentence *That's the man whose brother I saw* may be interpreted as a direct object of *I saw* and thus takes on the characteristics of the direct object position rather than a genitive.

More recently, a wider of range of languages has been the focus of study. In a study of Arabic learners studying English in Tunisia, Ammar and Lightbown (2003) found evidence of generalization to relative clause types less marked than the relative clause type on which they received instruction, as is generally predicted, but also found evidence of generalization in the other direction, suggesting bidirectional generalization does occur. This research dealt with learners of languages with postnominal relative clauses.

Yabuki-Soh (2007) considered pedagogical effects of relative clause acquisition by learners of Japanese, a language with prenominal relative clauses. Her study is primarily focused on different treatment types (form-based, meaning-based, and a combination of form/meaning-based) and the generalization possibilities from the instructed relative clause (oblique) to easier as well as more difficult relative clause types. Her instruction was on oblique relative clauses, which are generally equivalent to object of preposition relative clauses, although in Japanese there are postpositions (they occur after the noun) not prepositions. Her results showed that instruction type did affect the ability to generalize relative clauses. In particular, when there was a detailed analysis of the grammatical structure, comprehension and production was facilitated. With regard to generalization, her study suggests that generalization from more marked to less marked is possible and may indeed be an effective basis of syllabus design.

A final point to consider is that learning of relative clauses may not always be driven by language-related issues, but may also be mediated by an individual's capacities, working memory being a prime possibility.

11.5 Focus on form

Recall from Krashen's characterization of the Input Hypothesis, discussed in chapter 10, that what learners needed (at least at the early stages) was input and other forms of language modification or emphasis (for example explicit rule presentation, negative feedback) were not necessary. It soon became clear that more than input was needed, such as interaction and output, discussed in chapter 10. More explicitly, R. Ellis (2001) and Norris and Ortega (2000) among many others have argued that one needs an explicit focus on language to facilitate acquisition. This has led researchers to consider directly the effects of language focus in instruction.

Throughout this book we deal with the concept of attention. Implicit in this notion is the concept of focus on form.[4] Long (1991) distinguished between focus on *form* and focus on *formS*. The latter refers to earlier teaching methodologies in which the main organizing principle for language classrooms was the accumulation of individual language items (e.g., plural endings, passives). The former refers to a need for meaning-focused activity into which an attention to form is embedded. As Long (1991, pp. 45–46) stated, focus on form "overtly draws students' attention to linguistic elements as they arise incidentally in lessons whose overriding focus is on meaning or communication." This is similar to what Sharwood Smith (1991, 1993) referred to as enhanced input; that is, input that can be enhanced by an external source (e.g., a teacher) or an internal source (learners relying on their own resources).

Williams (1999) investigated eight classroom learners at different levels of proficiency. She found numerous examples of learner-generated attention to form, as well as considerable variation. The results suggest that learners at low levels of proficiency do not often spontaneously attend to language form. This is not surprising given the demands necessary just to maintain communication in an L2, particularly when knowledge of the L2 is scant. Williams also found that when there is learner-generated attention to form, the attention is generally given to words rather than to other linguistic features.

A study by Gass, Mackey, Alvarez-Torres, and Fernández-García (1999) supports the notion that freeing up the cognitive burden of focusing on both form and meaning allows greater opportunity to focus on form. In their study, participants performed an online telling of a short video clip. Participants who saw the same video multiple times (i.e., who did not have to focus on meaning during the latter viewings) showed improvement on overall measures of proficiency, morphosyntax, and lexical sophistication.

Learner-generated attention to form may not always come naturally and, clearly, may require some pedagogical training. Examples 11-4 and 11-5 come from a classroom context in which a teacher, as part of the curriculum, has assigned what she calls "interaction logs" to students. Interaction logs train students to think about their language use and particularly to notice the gap between their L2 language use and the language use of native or fluent speakers of the L2. They provide a means for learners to be detectives in the sense that they are responsible for gathering their own language data, analyzing evidence, and making and testing hypotheses. The logs are language diaries in which students write down what fluent speakers say, how they say it, in what situations and with whom, and how NSs react when a learner says something (Cohen, 1999). As the teacher says in her instructions to students, interaction logs are "to help you to notice how you are using language and how it may be different from how native speakers use language." She provides numerous examples of how students can interact, from the very simple task of asking for directions to making small talk with someone at the grocery store. An advantage of interaction logs is that they allow learners to analyze their own language in a format that goes beyond the ephemeral speech signal. Learners can record their own speech (in writing) and save it until a time when they can appropriately analyze it. Examples 11-4 and 11-5 show how two learners used interaction logs to learn how to analyze their own interaction (data from Cohen, 1999):

(11-4) I was talking about the bicycle with a secretary woman in the computer lab. When she said she bought her son Trumpet the day before and being a mother need to spend some money on the children's item, I wanted to "share the responsibility in communication." So I asked whether he liked it or not. She said "yes right now at least, but I'm not sure one month later," then she talked about other instrument she'd already bought for her son. Then I replied "Yes, really. I bought a bicycle for my son a week ago. The bike is expensive than I thought, partly because it has Star Wars decoration on." Then she asked me, "Did you? What kind of bike? The one with tri . . . neee . . . ll?" I couldn't catch her. It's a perfect time to use "manner of asking," because I understood rest of her talk except the last part. At that moment, I could guess it might be one part of bike, "I'm sorry, Deb, Did you say tranee . . . l? What's that?" I just imitated her sound. Then with some gesture she explained, training . . . eel! The wheels to train the for riding 2 big wheels." Actually I didn't catch her pronunciation at that point, because I have a difficult in listening "W" sound. However, I can understand what's it. "Oh, Training Wheel! O.K. . . . I didn't know the name. It's training wheel. I thought it might be "assisting wheels" or "supporting wheels."

(11-5) Last Friday, in the communication class, we talked about the interaction logs, one of the classmates mentioned when she went to the supermarket, the cashier asked her if she wanted to drive out or not. So I learned that phrase from her. Last Sunday, when I went to the supermarket, I was ready to hear that again and I was so excited about it. Because most of time, I was so nervous when the cashier asked me some questions and they all spoke quickly. But not this time, finally, after the cashier packed all my stuff into the plastic bag, he asked "Do you want to drive _____?" "No, thanks." I said. But I noticed he seemed to say some word instead of "out". The last word sounded like "off" or "up" or I was wrong. But I checked it up in the dictionary, "drive out" has a different meaning.

The carryover from the metalinguistic sensitization of the interaction logs into the classroom can be seen in the following example, observed by one of the authors of this book.

(11-6) T = Teacher; S = Student
    S: He finally success.
    T: What?
    S: He finally succeed.
    T: Succeeds.
    S: Yes.

Even though the student does not appreciate the full force of the teacher's indirect question, he understands that she is making a correction of form (rather than just indicating that she does not understand, which might yield merely a repetition of the early utterance), and he modifies his original utterance accordingly. Whether his *yes* indicates anything more than closure to the exchange is, of course, unclear. This example (as well as the examples from the interaction logs themselves) shows that metalinguistic training in focusing on form can result in sensitivity to grammatical form rather than just to lexical form, as occurs in most instances.

Ohta (2001) noted that students in a classroom context can assimilate corrective feedback even when it is not directed at them. In 11-7, one student (C) repeats recasts that are intended for a classmate:

(11-7) T = Teacher; K and C = students
        T: Kon shumatsu hima desu ka? Kylie-san.
            "This weekend are you free? Kylie."
        K: Um (. .) iie (.) um (.) uh∷ (.) hima- (.) hima: (.) hima nai.
            "Um, no, um, uh, not, not, not free. (Error: wrong negator)
        T: Hima ja arimasen?
            "You're not free?" (T corrects form.)
        K: Oh ja arim [asen
        C: [hima ja arimasen
            "Not free." (C repeats correct form.)

Student C gives a sotto voce rendition of the correct form, using the classroom as a venue for making a correction.

Mackey (2006) investigated learners' noticing of corrective feedback in a classroom context. Her linguistic focus was question formation and two morphological forms: English plurals and past tense. She found a relationship between noticing and learning for question formation, but not for the two morphological forms (plurals and past tense). One explanation might have to do with salience. Clearly, question formation, with syntactic movement and the addition of an auxiliary, is more salient than the addition of a plural or past tense marker. Another issue to be sorted out is the type of feedback provided. As Mackey reports, there were more instances of negotiation for questions than for the morphological forms. Morphological errors were more often recast rather than negotiated. Thus, it is not clear what the source of the lack of learning is—the type of feedback or the linguistic entity.

Clearly, instructed learning can offer a context for focus on form. This does not mean that all forms are "teachable" (see section 11.4). The English article system, for example, appears to be virtually impermeable to instruction (perhaps because the explanation for its use is, at least, partially semantic, bringing in a number of complex considerations (see chapter 2)). Furthermore, we saw in chapters 6 and 10 that different kinds of input might be necessary. In particular, we saw that there are limits to what positive evidence can do and that negative evidence appears to be necessary in some situations. Doughty and Williams (1998) outlined four areas to consider in the study of focus on form, two of which are relevant to our current discussion of instructed learning: timing and forms to focus on (see also Spada, 1997).

11.5.1 Timing

Harley (1998) investigated early focus-on-form intervention with young learners in order to determine the effect of early instructional focus on form. The learners in her study were Grade 2 students in an early French immersion program. The linguistic focus was acquisition of French gender, which in Harley's words is a "quintessentially formal aspect" of French (p. 156). There is little in the way of semantics incorporated into this feature. Gender assignment is a persistent problem for those schooled in an immersion program. Participants were pretested prior to the five-week experimental session and were post-tested following the session and again at six months following the treatment. The results indicate that focus-on-form instruction produces better results than no instructional focus, but learners do not extend their knowledge to other words. Harley suggested that "the experiment was more successful in inducing 'item learning' than 'system learning' " (p. 168). However, in post-experiment stimulated recalls (see Gass and Mackey, 2000, for an explanation of this technique), students tended to demonstrate metalinguistic knowledge of gender and of certain generalizations. This, in fact, may be a part of (or at least a precursor to) learning. In other words, one needs to learn what needs to be learned before being able to sort out the specific facts of what is to be learned.

Lightbown (1998) reviewed a number of studies that deal with timing issues. In particular, she cautioned researchers/teachers not to take too seriously the notion of developmental sequences within a pedagogical context. In other words, while it may be the case that input on stages that may be considerably beyond the learner's current level does not lead to learning, there is no harm done to the learner. What is relevant, however, is the need for teachers to have appropriate expectations of what learners will and will not be able to take from a lesson containing input on stages well beyond their levels.

Lightbown's own research (Spada and Lightbown, 1993) was conducted with learners who were essentially at the early stages of the Pienemann model discussed in section 11.4 and in Chapter 8. Following instruction with later staged questions, the learners were able to produce questions such as *Where is the dog?* and *Where is the shoe?* as well as even more complex questions such as *How do you say tâches in English?* However, as Spada and Lightbown pointed out, these may have been little more than substitutions with little understanding of the syntax underlying them. In other words, these were likely unanalyzed chunks. However, these forms were nonetheless present and may then have served as further input for learners' own developing systems. Thus, the fact that they were used in some form, even though not fully acquired, was certainly not detrimental. To the contrary, they served as an aid in future learning. In fact, even following instruction on questions, learners' knowledge increased (Spada and Lightbown, 1993).

Another way of looking at timing comes from a study by Gass and Alvarez Torres (2005). They looked at the ordering effects of classroom presentation of input and interaction. Their study consisted of four experimental conditions in which students were (1) only presented with input, (2) only presented with interaction, (3) presented first with input and then interaction, or (4) presented first with interaction and then with input. They considered these different types of information and the ordering of information with regard to vocabulary learning and mor-phosyntax. The students were English learners of Spanish and the morphosyntax structures were gender agreement (Spanish nouns and adjectives agree in number and gender) and the verb *to be*, which has two forms and is known to be problematic for English learners. Examples of gender agreement are given in 11-8 and 11-9 and examples of the use of the two verbs *to be* (*estar* and *ser*) are given in 11-10. Their study only concerned the use of *estar* to express location.

(11-8) Gender agreement (grammatical and ungrammatical)
Tengo una maleta amarilla.
I have a suitcase yellow (f).
"I have a yellow suitcase."

*Tengo una maleta amarillo.
I have a (f) suitcase (f) yellow (m).
"I have a yellow suitcase."

The second example in 11-8 is ungrammatical because the adjective has a masculine ending, but it modifies a feminine noun. Some nouns do not end in *a/o*, but still have grammatical gender, as in 11-9 below.

(11-9) Gender agreement with nouns not ending in *a/o*
a   El bigote pequeño (small mustache)
b   La llave rota (broken key)
c   El arból viejo (old tree)
d   La luz blanca (white light)
(11-10) Examples of *ser* (a) and *estar* (b) to express location
a   *La maleta es al lado de la puerta.
The suitcase is to the side of the door.
"The suitcase is next to the door."
b   La maleta está al lado de la puerta.
The suitcase is to the side of the door.
"The suitcase is next to the door."

Their results showed that there were significant gains for all conditions for vocabulary. The gains were not all-encompassing for either gender or *estar* learning. Recall from the discussion in chapter 10 that attention is the mechanism hypothesized to be at least partially responsible for learning through interaction. Recall also that interaction is what makes learners aware of some problem in their language, although it may not be the source of immediate learning. More input may be needed as a follow-up to the attention-drawing function of interaction. In fact, the only significant gains for gender and *estar* were with the interaction followed by input groups. Another finding of interest was that the groups that had two kinds of input (i.e., input and interaction), regardless of the order, did better than those with only input or only interaction.

Larsen-Freeman (2006) raises the question of variation as reflecting instability and suggests the relevance of pedagogical intervention at this juncture. She presents data from a learner who uses *at* and *in* seemingly in free variation at basically a single point in time and across modalities (oral and written) *I lived in Detroit* versus *I lived at Detroit*. She is cautious in her suggestion of the possibility of a pedagogical intervention given that there may be other sources of variation in the learner's grammar which might not be immediately apparent and which might suggest that this is not an area of instability and may in fact reflect "deeply entrenched rivals" (Sharwood Smith and Truscott, 2005).

11.5.2 Forms to focus on

It is clear that one cannot use focus on form instruction with all grammatical constructions. For example, some structures are so complex, involving movement, that it is not at all clear as to what could be focused on. Williams and Evans (1998) investigated the effect of focus on form on two structures: (a) participial adjectives of emotive verbs (*I am boring* vs. *I am bored*) and (b) passives (*The dog was chased by the cat*). Participial adjectives were used by the learners in this study incorrectly (e.g., *My trip to Niagara Falls was really excited*). Passives were used only rarely. Three groups of learners took part in this study: one group had explicit instruction and feedback, the second group received input only, and the third group served as the control. For the participial adjectives, the group that had explicit instruction and feedback outperformed the other two groups. For the passives, the results were more complex, showing only partial support for the hypothesis that the two experimental groups would outperform the control group and that there would be a difference between the two experimental groups. The overall results of this study suggest that learners' "readiness" contributes to their ability to focus on and take in new information. A second finding is that not all structures are created equal with regard to input type. For the participial adjectives, the learners had already noticed the form in the input, as is evidenced by their use of the form, albeit incorrectly. Here explicit instruction was more beneficial than providing input alone. For the passives, there was little difference between the two experimental groups. Any means of highlighting the form (input flood or instruction) serves equally to induce noticing.

In general, then, one needs to carefully consider what is being targeted to focus on and how best to relate that information to a learner's individual knowledge state and to the means by which a form is focused on.

11.5.3 Input manipulation and input enhancement

A significant function of language instruction is the manipulation of input. That is, teachers can provide varying degrees of explicitness in the input. A goal of SLA research is to determine the effectiveness of explicitness in terms of learners' developing grammars. The field has changed from a position in the 1970s and 1980s in which, following Krashen, what was needed to create implicit knowledge (more or less equivalent to linguistic competence) was comprehensible input. Explicit input led to explicit knowledge. In later years, the fusion of implicit/ explicit input and implicit/explicit knowledge became more apparent. For example, DeKeyser (2003) suggested that explicit learning (e.g., metalinguistic explanation) can result in implicit knowledge through practice.

The concept of practice is important in pedagogical contexts. Practice, as defined by the *American Heritage Dictionary*, is "to exercise or perform repeatedly in order to acquire or polish a skill." It is essential in understanding how explicit information might result in implicit knowledge or how declarative knowledge becomes procedural knowledge; it is essential in understanding how information might become automatized (see chapter 8). In earlier years, practice meant little more than rote repetition and/or substitution drills. In cognitive accounts of language learning, practice takes on a number of forms, but the common ingredient is that the learner interacts with the language in some meaningful (not solely rote) manner. This can include language use (some interactive-based task) or some response to an audio prompt (answering a comprehension question following a listening or reading passage). Loschky and Bley-Vroman (1993) proposed a scheme for determining language demands during language use, distinguishing whether a form is natural in the task, useful to the task, or essential to the task. They used this scheme to determine the proposed effectiveness of different kinds of tasks, in terms of automatization, control, and whether a task relates to comprehension or production.

The concept of input enhancement highlights ways in which input is made salient to learners (see Sharwood Smith, 1991). As Polio (2007) notes, Sharwood Smith's focus was not on what happened in the learner's mind, but rather on what was done to the input. Input enhancement can take place in a number of ways, through drawing attention to a form (e.g., by coloring or boldfacing in written input).

Underlying the importance of input enhancement is the concept of noticing discussed in chapter 10. Given that input enhancement is a means of drawing a learner's attention to something, an underlying assumption is that noticing is a prerequisite to processing of the input.

Salience, in Sharwood Smith's view, can come about by a learner's own internal devices (his or her own processing mechanisms) or by something that is externally created; this latter is input enhancement. Sharwood Smith refers to two variables involved in externally created salience: elaboration (e.g., repetition) and explicitness (e.g., metalinguistic information).

Input enhancement has not been treated in precisely the same way and the results have not always been consistent (cf. Polio, 2007, for an overview). For example, Jourdenais, Ota, Stauffer, Boyson, and Doughty (1995) found that noticing and learning resulted from textual enhancement; Izumi (2002) found noticing, but not learning; and Leow (1997) found neither noticing nor learning. Han (ms.), in her review of input enhancement studies, found numerous methodological differences among studies, making it difficult to state with certainty the extent to which visual input enhancement facilitates learning. She draws attention to 10 insights emanating from studies of input enhancement (pp. 29–30):

- Simple enhancement is capable of inducing learner noticing of externally enhanced forms in meaning-bearing input.
- Whether or not this then leads to acquisition depends largely on learner readiness.
- Learners can automatically notice forms that are meaningful.
- Simple enhancement of a longer term is more likely to incite learner noticing of the target form than simple enhancement of a short term.
- Simple enhancement is more likely to induce learner noticing of the target form when sequential to comprehension than when it is concurrent with comprehension.
- Simple enhancement of a non-meaningful form does not hurt comprehension.
- Simple enhancement of a meaningful form contributes to comprehension.
- Simple enhancement is more effective if it draws focal rather than peripheral attention.
- Simple enhancement, when combined with input flood, is likely to evoke aberrant noticing, resulting in overuse of the enhanced form.

- Compound enhancement [combining different types of enhancement, e.g., typographical enhancement with feedback] is more likely to induce deeper cognitive processing than simple enhancement, possibly to the extent of engendering "overlearning."

11.6 Uniqueness of instruction

Instruction can have its unique repercussions. In this section, we present two instances where the instruction (or lack thereof) may have produced unique results. Pavesi (1986) specifically compared naturalistic versus instructed learners in terms of their acquisition of relative clauses (see chapter 7 and section 11.4). All learners were Italian speakers learning English. There were 48 instructed learners and 38 naturalistic learners. The instructed learners were high-school students (aged 14–18) who had studied English for four years on average. They had had virtually no informal exposure to English. Their instruction had been grammar-based and they had had substantial written input. The second group was made up of 38 Italian workers living in Edinburgh with menial-type jobs (e.g., waiters); they ranged in age from 19 to 50 and had lived in the United Kingdom for an average of six years (ranging from three months to 25 years). Their exposure to English was almost entirely informal, with little, if any, formal instruction. The results from these learners support the findings already discussed elsewhere in this book that learning proceeds from the unmarked (e.g., subject relative clause) to the marked structure (e.g., object of comparative relative clause). The context of learning did not affect this acquisition order. However, a difference was noted in the number of marked relative clause types used, with the formal group using more. In addition, the informal groups used a greater number of noun copies (*Number five is the boy who the dog is biting the boy*) than the formal group, whereas the formal group used more pronoun copies (*Number five is the boy who the dog is biting him*). Therefore, it appears that the classroom context can provide a richness that an informal environment cannot. However, an important caveat in understanding these results is that the two groups differed in at least two important respects: (a) age differences may have contributed to the more sophisticated use of English by the formal group,[5] and (b) the socioeconomic level of the two groups was sufficiently different to call into question the findings based purely on learning context.

A second example of instructional uniqueness comes from work by Lightbown (1983). She noted that French learners of English tended to make a large number of overuse errors. In chapter 8 we discussed the concept of U-shaped learning. In that instance children exposed to *-ing* (progressive) associated that form with the present tense in French and thereby overextended its appropriate use. The overuse continued even when there was little exposure to the form in the input.

Kasper and Rose (2002), with regard to pragmatics, suggest that without instruction pragmatic knowledge will be difficult. Specifically, they claim that L2 pragmatics can be taught and that, in fact, instructional intervention is better than no instruction. In terms of explicitness, they claim that explicit instruction coupled with opportunities for practice provide the best chance for success. They report on pragmatic studies in a study-abroad context and find that appropriate pragmatic behaviour is not always acquired just by living abroad. This leads them to suggest that instruction coupled with a study-abroad experience provides the optimal condition for pragmatics learning.

Laufer (2005) makes the same point with regard to vocabulary. Input alone is insufficient for vocabulary learning. She takes this a step further and proposes that focus-on-form instruction is essential to instruction and does not need to be conducted with the context of a communicative task.

Thus, instructed learning may clearly result in inappropriate conclusions drawn by the learners precisely because the input is often impoverished and because emphasis on certain forms is selective.

11.7 Effectiveness of instruction

The effectiveness of instruction is often assumed, although not always accepted. For example, in approaches that assume that what is needed is large doses of (comprehensible) input, classroom effectiveness is limited. Similarly, in approaches that assume a natural immutable sequence of natural processes, classroom effectiveness is similarly limited. This was expressed succinctly by Felix (1981, p. 109):

> Foreign language learning under classroom conditions seems to partially follow the same set of natural processes that characterize other types of language acquisition . . . there seems to be a universal and common set of principles which are flexible enough and adaptable to the large number of conditions under which language learning may take place. These observations furthermore suggest that the possibility of manipulating and controlling the students' verbal behavior in the classroom is in fact quite limited.

Understanding the effectiveness of instruction entails an analysis of the type of instruction. For example, is it explicit, implicit? Is there a focus on meaning? A focus on form, or even a focus on forms? Norris and Ortega (2000), in their overview of instructed SLA, found that explicit focus is more effective than implicit focus and that a focus on form is more effective than a focus on forms. However, it is important to note, as the authors themselves point out, that these cumulative findings should be treated with caution given that (1) the measurements of learning outcomes in the studies they included usually favor explicit treatments, (2) implicit treatments may require a longer period of time for learning to take place and consequently may necessitate longer post-observation times than explicit treatments, and (3) there was often an inconsistent operationalization of each instructional approach. Finally, the linguistic forms targeted in most of the studies included are (relatively) easy and simple, which potentially favors explicit treatment. Truscott (2004), however, in his analysis of Norris and Ortega (2000), is led to different conclusions about the effectiveness of instruction.

As with many areas of SLA research, the results are not always clear cut. DeKeyser (1995) found positive effects for explicit rule presentation, as did de Graaf (1997). In this latter study, explicit rule presentation was beneficial when it was accompanied by two other important ingredients: input and practice. On the other hand, studies such as those by Rosa and O'Neill (1999) and VanPatten and Oikkenon (1996) did not show positive effects. In the case of the former study, the issue of task-demand came into play. Different tasks may elicit different types of output and different types of feedback. For example, in a study by Gass, Mackey, and Ross-Feldman (2005) concerned with a comparison of classroom versus laboratory interaction patterns, the authors used three tasks: a consensus task, a spot-the-difference task, and a one-way map task. Differences were found among task types, but not between different settings.

Explicitness cannot be considered in the abstract. Issues such as rule complexity, language area (e.g., morphosyntax, syntax, lexicon), and proficiency level are equally important variables (see de Graaf, 1997; Robinson, 2002). For example, Gass, Svetics, and Lemelin (2003) found that focused attention (manipulated through an experimental design) was more beneficial for syntactic learning than for morphosyntactic or lexical learning, probably due to the greater complexity of syntax and the ability of learners to self-focus their attention on the lexicon. Additionally, focused attention had a greater role in the early stages of acquisition, most likely due to the greater linguistic sophistication of more advanced learners, who have sufficient knowledge to focus on complex parts of language on their own without externally-focused attention. In addition, the question of feedback—when and if and, if so, how explicit—is relevant to understanding the role of explicitness of input. Here, too, there is not always agreement. Carroll and Swain (1993) in a well-known study of feedback found that metalinguistic feedback following treatment on dative alternation yielded better performance than other types of feedback (statement of correct/incorrect, recast). On the other hand, Sanz and Morgan-Short (2004), in a study of preverbal direct object pronouns in Spanish, found no difference between explicit feedback without explanation, feedback with no explanation, and no feedback. The latter study may indicate a difference in the moment of feedback.

Beyond mere focus on form or explicitness of input, there are numerous other variables that need to be considered when trying to understand the effectiveness of instruction, including, but not limited to, individual differences, such as learner aptitude and matches/mismatches between learning style and instructor approach. There are no easy answers. What is clear is that instruction does make a difference, but how precisely it makes a difference and what the contributing factors are to effectiveness continue to be issues that need to be resolved. Effectiveness of instruction is not a matter of *yes* or *no*, but a clearer understanding of what, how, and when (in terms of a learner's developmental readiness). These are all areas that must be dealt with empirically.

11.8 Conclusion

In this chapter, we have looked at instructed second language learning with an eye toward understanding how learning in and out of the classroom may or may not differ. In this final section, we briefly consider how an understanding of second language acquisition might inform classroom practices. Although many treatises exist on this topic (see Gass, 1997), we consider it from the slightly different perspective of Lightbown (1985). In an article titled "Great expectations," Lightbown made the important point that one way second language research can contribute to successful classroom practice is through the *expectations* that teachers have about what learners can and cannot achieve as a result of instruction. For example, we have discussed the role of interaction (chapter 10) as a priming device for learning. Even explicit instruction may serve as an introduction to information about a form rather than being the moment of learning. In sum, even though instruction is clearly an aid to learning (or, in some instances, a hindrance), it is essential to understand how second languages are acquired in general if we are to understand how they are acquired in a particular context. We next turn to a consideration of some of the influences on second language learning that are not dependent on language and which can affect the formation, restructuring, and fossilization of second language grammars.

Suggestions for additional reading

Focus on Form in Classroom Second Language Acquisition. Catherine Doughty and Jessica Williams. Cambridge University Press (1998).

Instructed Second Language Acquisition. Rod Ellis. Basil Blackwell (1990).

Second language Acquisition and Language Pedagogy. Rod Ellis. Multilingual Matters (1992).

Task-based Language Learning and Teaching. Rod Ellis. Oxford Applied Linguistics (2003).

Learning Languages, Learning Lifeskills: Autobiographical Reflexive Approach to Teaching and Learning a Foreign Language. Riita Jaatinen. Springer Verlag (2007).

Researching Second Language Classrooms. Sandra Lee McKay. Lawrence Erlbaum Associates (2006).

Input for Instructed L2 Learners: The Relevance of Relevance. Anna Nizegorodcew. Multilingual Matters (2007).

Cognition in Second Language Instruction. Peter Robinson (Ed.). Cambridge University Press (2001).

Individual Differences and Instructed Language Learning. Peter Robinson (Ed.), John Benjamins (2002).

Second Language Classroom Research: Issues and Opportunities. Jacquelyn Schachter and Susan Gass (Eds.). Lawrence Erlbaum Associates (1996).

From Input to Output: A Teacher's Guide to Second Language Acquisition. Bill VanPatten. McGraw Hill (2003).

Processing Instruction: Theory, Research, and Commentary. Bill VanPatten (Ed.). Lawrence Erlbaum Associates (2004).

Input Enhancement: From Theory and Research to the Classroom. Wynne Wong. McGraw-Hill (2005).

Points for discussion

1   What do you see as the relationship between second language acquisition and second language pedagogy? How are they different? How might they affect each other and how might the study of one influence the study or practices of the other? Relate your answers to a specific learning situation. In thinking about the relationship, consider whether or not all aspects of SLA relate (or should be able to relate) to classroom practice.

2   One reason people are interested in the field of SLA is because of their current or future interests in language pedagogy. In chapter 6 we dealt with the Subset Principle (section 6.3.3). What are some of the implications of this principle for language teaching? In groups, complete one of the following two sentences.

> If you are a language teacher, you had better know the Subset Principle because_____.
> If you are a language teacher, it makes no difference whether or not you know the Subset Principle because_____.

In your answer, you might want to consider the difference between being able to put a name on the phenomenon and understanding the effects of the Subset Principle.

3   In chapter 8 we described Krashen's view on the function of the Monitor and how it can "get in your way" with its focus on form. Does this mean that in language classes there should never be a focus on form and that, as a result, teachers should only provide well-organized input? When might grammar instruction (i.e., form-focused instruction) be appropriate or necessary?

4   Are all structures equally amenable to focus on form? Why or why not? Can you give examples from your own teaching/learning experience when you could not "figure out" what the correct generalization should be?

5   Consider the concept of negative evidence. When do you think negative evidence might be necessary for learning? (You might want to relate this question to your answer in problem 4.)

6   To English teachers' dismay, students often omit the third person singular -s even at fairly advanced proficiency levels. Given what you know about natural orders in L2 acquisition, how do you explain this phenomenon?

12

BEYOND THE DOMAIN
OF LANGUAGE

12.1 Introduction

One of the most widely recognized facts about second language learning is that some individuals are more successful in learning a second language than other individuals. In this chapter, we examine some of the factors that may be responsible for these differences, focusing in particular on nonlanguage factors, such as age, aptitude, motivation, attitude, and socio-psychological influences. In addition to some learners being more successful language learners, there is also the well-known phenomenon of fossilization, which has been part of the field of SLA since the middle part of the 20th century. It could even be argued that the field of second language acquisition was spurred into existence by this phenomenon. That is, the idea that no matter what learners do, they do not progress to the same extent as do children learning their first language. The phenomenon of "being stuck" in the L2 seems to occur to most if not all learners even at the most advanced stages (see Han, 2004).[1] There are many reasons for an apparent lack of success, many of which (but not all) are not related to language or psycholinguistic factors, but relate to the individual himself or herself. These are the subject of this chapter.

First of all, a word about the title of the chapter, "Beyond the domain of language." In much of the SLA literature, the subject matter of this chapter has been described as *individual differences* (see Dörnyei, 2005). The latter term, we maintain, is somewhat misleading. Even though all factors that influence second language learning can be observed only within an individual, the factors to be discussed here are not necessarily idiosyncratic. In fact, it may be social and societal backgrounds that are crucial, as we shall see. Even measures of aptitude, which would seem to be the most individualistic, often correlate with societal differences, in that individuals from more privileged backgrounds as a whole receive higher scores on aptitude measures. We have not included all aspects of what we included in the category of individual differences given space and limitations, and other topics have been dealt with in other chapters (for example, working memory) because they seemed to fit more appropriately there, even though they could be part of what one might consider an individual difference.

12.2 Research traditions

The question of the role of nonlanguage factors in second language learning has had less of an impact on SLA than has the research based on linguistics, psychology, and psycholinguistics. To understand how the research tradition that investigates such areas as aptitude, attitude, and motivation relates to the entire field of SLA, it is necessary to consider the general goals of those fields that have dominated SLA.

12.2.1 Linguistics

The research tradition in linguistics has tended to downplay a search for aptitude differences in learning a second language. This is not to say that there are explicit statements in theoretical linguistics to the effect that there are no aptitude differences in second language learning. The influence is more subtle than that.

Competence as a major concern of modern linguistics emphasizes what speakers *know*, rather than what they actually *do* on some particular occasion (*performance*). The first factor to recognize is that the emphasis on competence has resulted in a minimization of reports of differences in ability in native languages. However, it is not so clear whether the competence that linguists attempt to discover is common to all native speakers of a language. Chomsky, in various discussions (e.g., 1995), suggested a common, minimalist sense of competence. That is, the same competence would be shared by all native speakers. On the other hand, the methodology is based on the assumption of an ideal speaker-listener (sometimes called a speaker-hearer). The competence of an ideal person may differ from that of most speakers. This question about competence has largely been ignored. Early opponents of Chomsky pointed out that many ordinary speakers did not have the same grammaticality judgments reported in the linguistics literature (see Hill, 1961). (Recall from chapter 3 that judgments about the grammaticality of sentences have been the major source of data about linguistic knowledge/competence.) But these concerns were not seriously addressed by linguists at that time. Rather than saying that these individuals were less competent in language, the response was that they were less competent in making grammaticality judgments. Hence, the findings of Hill and others were deemed irrelevant for grammatical theory, because these results relate to performance and not to what an individual *knows* about his or her language.

For the purposes of this chapter, it is important to recognize that some individuals are better than others in certain language skills. For example, some are much better storytellers than others. The assumption in mainline linguistics is that these skills only represent what one can do with language, not what one knows about language. Because it is believed that all children without cognitive deficits learn language in roughly the same way and within the same time frame, and because there is equipotentiality in language (i.e., it is just as easy to learn Chinese as it is to learn Hausa as first languages), discussions of aptitude are not part of mainstream linguistics.

The immediate negative reaction linguists have toward differences in language abilities in a native language has also affected second language acquisition scholars trained in linguistics. On the one hand, they adhere to the orthodox opinion of linguistics that differences in language ability are not important in native languages. Thus, there has not been a tendency to look for such differences in second language learning. On the other hand, they are faced with the question: If there are differences in ability to learn a second language, how did these differences arise? If they are due to an individual's inherent language ability, then why did they not affect native language learning?

12.2.2 Psychology

In chapter 8 we dealt with some of the major influences on SLA from psychology. It is clear that issues of aptitude/motivation did not fit into that category, as they had earlier in the study of psychology. As Sorrentino and Higgins (1986, p. 4) noted: "Early in the history of North American psychology, motivation and cognition were both considered important factors. This can perhaps be traced back to the rise of behaviorism in North American psychology. Until that point, various views relating motivation and/or cognition to behavior were flourishing."

Behaviorism banished both cognition and motivation. Even though cognitive psychology has eventually come to occupy an important place within the field of psychology, it, too, had no role for affect and motivation, at least initially. The implication is that researchers trained in the tradition of cognitive psychology would not have tended to look for a significant role for motivation in the field of SLA.

12.2.3 Psycholinguistics

Psycholinguistics, with roots in both psychology and linguistics, is especially relevant for second language acquisition research. Sorrentino and Higgins, in the introduction to their anthology dealing with the importance of motivation, admit that "motivation had little place in [psycholinguistics]" (Sorrentino and Higgins, 1986, p. 5). They strongly implied that this is still the case for psycholinguistics.

To summarize to this point, the tradition of linguistics led to a downplaying of aptitude in the explanation of linguistic behavior. The tradition of cognitive psychology led to a downplaying of attitudes and motivation. Thus, it is not surprising that second language acquisition researchers, most influenced by these two research traditions, have tended to look for cognitive factors rather than aptitude or motivation in accounting for differential successes in second language learning. Dörnyei (2005) attributes the process-oriented approach of much SLA research and the conflicting product-oriented approach of most individual difference research, at least in the areas of attitude and motivation for the lack of full integration of these research areas into the mainstream of SLA research.

12.3 Affect

One of the dictionary definitions of *affect* is "a feeling or emotion as distinguished from cognition, thought, or action" (*American Heritage Dictionary*). In other words, it refers to feelings or emotions that individuals have about something. In the case of language learning, it can refer to feelings or emotional reactions about the language, about the people who speak that language, or about the culture where that language is spoken. In the next section, we discuss language shock and culture shock. Language shock refers to the realization that, as a learner, you must seem comical to speakers of the TL whereas culture shock refers to anxiety relating to disorientation from exposure to a new culture.

12.3.1 *Language shock and culture shock*

Diary studies suggest that both language shock and culture shock are important for second language learners, but whether they truly affect acquisition is yet another story. Jones (1977), in her own diary detailing her study of Indonesian in Indonesia, discussed language shock, culture shock, and general stress.

Language shock
June 19
Friday night there was a dinner reception in our honor at the auditorium at school. After we ate dinner, a few of the professors got up and told "funny" stories about their experiences in the U.S. Then they wanted all of us to get up and do the same about our experiences in Indonesia. I politely refused, but Walt and Glenn got up. The guests not only laughed at the stories, but also

at the awkward, nonfluent Indonesian used by them. I felt ter-
ribly embarrassed. The Indonesians did this because they hon-
estly thought it would be funny and thought we would laugh too.
I don't laugh when they try to speak English and I don't think it is
funny when I make a mistake. This is one time where I feel I
cannot get up and make a fool out of myself for others to laugh at
because I wouldn't think it was funny. I find that situations and
embarrassment like this inhibits my ability to speak.

July 15

It seems as if all the young people my age laugh at my Indonesian
pronunciation and lack of vocabulary. I don't enjoy being
laughed at, and I don't think it is funny!! I am unable to reply to
even simple sentences after incidents like these.

Culture shock and rejection

July 15

The young married couples sit around with nothing to do and
complain about how difficult life is or how tired they are. The
young unmarried people don't seem to carry on serious conversations with anyone and spend a lot of time in empty chatter.

July 18

I feel my language has deteriorated while I have been in
Yogyakarta because of the way part of the family has behaved
towards me. I have felt like an outsider and have rejected them.
I am tired of the attitude of some of the family, laughing at me or
being impatient with me in my attempt to learn their language.

Stress

June 14

One of the professors is arranging for a play to be given by the
participants. I have been cast in a play. I try to get myself out of it
but Pak Soesanto (the professor) doesn't seem to understand that
I just don't have enough time. I was advised to just not go to the
first rehearsal, so I didn't. The next day all the Indonesians connected with the play questioned me. I tried to explain that I had
already talked with Pak Soesanto and that I didn't have enough
time but I don't think they understand me. I just don't have the
vocabulary to adequately express myself and I feel so frustrated
and embarrassed in not really being able to make myself completely understood.

June 19

I have gone downtown by myself. The biggest problem is how to
ask for "thin" paper for airmail letters. I couldn't make myself

understood, so finally I just dropped the whole matter and went home without the paper. This really irritated me as I wanted to write some letters and finally had enough free time to do so.

Anxiety and stress are also prevalent in classroom learning as well as in individual learning contexts as shown in the examples above. Bailey (1983) conducted a diary study of her own language-learning experience when studying French at the university. She made frequent journal entries chronicling her own experiences and feelings (see also Mackey and Gass, 2005 and Gass and Mackey, 2007 for additional information regarding diary studies).

Bailey's (1983) entries illustrate such phenomena as the role of self-esteem, competitiveness, and anxiety, as in the following quotations:

"I feel very anxious about this class. I know I am (or can be) a good language learner, but I hate being lost in class. I feel like I'm behind the others and slowing down the pace . . ."

(pp. 75–76)

"Today I was panicked in the oral exercise where we had to fill in the blanks with either the past definite or the imperfect. Now I know what ESL students go through with the present perfect and the simple past. How frustrating it is to be looking for adverbial clues in the sentence when I don't even know what the words and phrases mean. I realized that the teacher was going around the room taking the sentences in order so I tried to stay one jump ahead of her by working ahead and using her feedback to the class to obtain confirmation or denial of my hypotheses. Today I felt a little scared. I'm so rusty!"

(p. 74)

In sum, anxiety, competitiveness as well as shock in a new, perhaps uncontrollable, situation can make the language-learning situation problematic and stressful.

12.3.2 Anxiety

Anxiety seems to represent a trait that falls within the broader scheme of factors affecting learning, but what is not clear is whether it is a matter of personality, an emotional reaction to a situation, or a combination.

Anxiety is not always a negative factor in learning. In general, anxiety, like many other factors (see Mizruchi, 1991, for a more general discussion), has a curvilinear effect on performance: low levels help, whereas high levels hurt. This makes sense. As noted earlier, if one doesn't care at all, there is little reason to try to do well. On the other hand, too much concern about failure can get in the way of success.

We provided examples earlier from Bailey's (1983) own diary study. One important point she makes is that anxiety depends on the situation in which learners find themselves. Too often, studies assume some uniform, global relationship between language-learning success and a motivating factor.

Although Bailey and others have catalogued the effects of anxiety on specific situations, there has been very little effort to determine whether general results about anxiety affect second language learning in what would seem to be the obvious manners. Consider two examples from Geen (1991) and Hoffman (1986). Geen noted that:

> Social anxiety essentially inhibits behavior. It may, for example, bring about disengagement—avoidance of social situations, withholding of communication ... or breaking of eye contact ... —or replacement of meaningful communication with innocuous sociability ... Leary et al. (1987) provide evidence that social anxiety is associated with a passive and self-defensive style of verbal behavior in two-person interaction.
>
> (1991, p. 392)

This would seem to have obvious implications for second language learning, especially for acquisition models or teaching methods that depend on successful interactions.

Hoffman (1986) noted that anxiety can direct attention away from meaning and toward pure form:

> In a [previous] review ... it was found that intense anxiety directs one's attention to physical features of words (acoustic properties, order of presentation, phonetic similarities) and that occurs to the relative neglect of semantic content. This suggests that affect can determine the extent to which semantic and nonsemantic modes of processing are brought into play.
>
> (p. 261)

This too has obvious implications for second language learning. To the extent that concentration on meaningful use of language is important in learning, anxiety could be a directly negative factor.

Dörnyei (2005) points out that there are two dimensions in the literature that are relevant to understanding anxiety: beneficial/facilitating vs. inhibitory/debilitating anxiety and trait vs. state anxiety. The first dichotomy refers to whether or not anxiety can be a positive or a negative force in learning and the second refers to whether anxiety is part of an

401

individual's makeup across many situations or whether it is a reaction in a particular situation (see also Scovel, 2001).

Horwitz (2001) in a review of the literature noted that there is something unique about L2 learning anxiety separate from other types of anxiety (see also MacIntyre, 1999, 2002). In a particularly interesting study, MacIntyre and Gardner (1994) in a study of learners of French attempted to induce anxiety by having a video recorder introduced during a vocabulary test. Correlations showed a relationship between anxiety and performance.

12.3.3 Affective Filter

The phenomenon of affect and its relationship to second language learning is well-known and has been experienced by most language learners. One of the main concepts that appeared early in the second language literature is what is known as the *Affective Filter*, which was intended to account in large part for why some people were able to learn second languages while others were not. As mentioned in chapter 10, one way of accounting for nonlearning in Krashen's (1985) view was to claim that learners had not received comprehensible input in sufficient quantities; another would be to claim that an inappropriate affect was to blame. Affect, from Krashen's perspective, is intended to include factors such as motivation, attitude, self-confidence, and anxiety. Krashen proposed an Affective Filter. If the Filter is up, input is prevented from passing through; if input is prevented from passing through, there can be no acquisition. If, on the other hand, the Filter is down, or low, and if the input is comprehensible, the input will reach the acquisition device and acquisition will take place. This is schematized in Figure 12.1.

According to Krashen, the Affective Filter is responsible for individual variation in second language acquisition and differentiates child language acquisition from second language acquisition because the Affective Filter is not something children have/use.

The Affective Filter hypothesis captures the relationship between affective variables and the process of second language acquisition

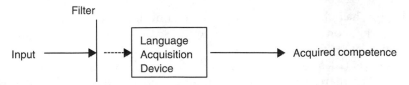

Figure 12.1 Operation of the Affective Filter.

Source: From *Principles and Practice in Second Language Acquisition* by S. Krashen, 1982, Pergamon. Reprinted by permission of the author.

by positing that acquirers vary with respect to the strength or level of their Affective Filters. Those whose attitudes are not optimal for second language acquisition will not only tend to seek less input, but they will also have a high or strong Affective Filter—even if they understand the message, the input will not reach that part of the brain responsible for language acquisition, or the Language Acquisition Device. Those with attitudes more conducive to second language acquisition will not only seek and obtain more input, they will also have a lower or weaker filter. They will be more open to the input, and it will strike "deeper."

(Krashen, 1982, p. 31)

To summarize, according to Krashen, two conditions are necessary for acquisition: comprehensible input (in Krashen's technical sense) and a low or weak Affective Filter.

The Affective Filter, which shields the Language Acquisition Device from input necessary for acquisition, is what differentiates one individual from another; it is intended to explain why some learners learn and others do not. It is also intended to explain child–adult differences. The Filter is not present (or, at least not operative) in children but is present in adults. But how does it work? Here we are left without explanation. How is the input filtered out by an unmotivated learner? One of the functions of the Filter noted by Dulay, Burt, and Krashen (1982) is that it will determine what parts of the language will be attended to and in what order. But, a question to ask is: How can affect be selective in terms of grammatical structures?

Gregg (1984) gave the example of a Chinese native speaker with near native-like knowledge of English. This speaker, however, had not acquired certain rules, such as third person singular -s. In Krashen's view, this incomplete knowledge of English would be due to the Affective Filter, but there is no explanation as to how the Filter could let most of the input pass through and filter out third person singular.

The relationship between affect and SLA is not in doubt, but, in and of itself, it cannot explain how acquisition takes place or does not take place. The picture is in actuality far too complex.

12.4 Social distance

A related concept to affect is social distance. There are many instances in which a second language learner does not feel an affinity with the target language community. In such instances learners create both a psychological distance and a social distance from speakers of the second language community. An immediate consequence is that this results in a diminished amount of input. The realization of the significance of social (group) distance and psychological (individual) distance formed the basis of Schumann's (1978a, 1978b) acculturation model. According to the precepts of this model, acculturation (made up of social and affective variables) is the causal variable of SLA. That is, if learners acculturate, they will learn; if learners do not acculturate, they will not learn. Thus, acculturation initiates a chain reaction including contact in the middle and acquisition as its outcome.

One of the social variables in the model that needs to be considered is the extent to which one group is dominant over another. One can think of situations in which an L2 group is dominant (e.g., colonization) or in which the L1 group is dominant (e.g., immigration). In the former case, learning is less likely to take place.[2] Another social situation to be considered is the extent to which a group integrates. In many immigrant communities, at least in the United States, there has been nearly total assimilation. In such situations, there is a high degree of learning. In others, there is emphasis on preserving one's own lifestyle and language. These situations result in language schooling for one's children in the home language. As a result of less contact, less learning would be predicted.

What kind of evidence might be adduced to support the Acculturation Model? Schumann based much of his original work on the language development (or lack thereof) of a 33-year-old Costa Rican man named Alberto (see Schumann, 1978b, for greater detail). Alberto graduated from a Costa Rican high school where he had studied English for six years. He moved to Cambridge, Massachusetts, at age 33, where he lived with another Costa Rican couple. At his workplace he was the only Spanish speaker in his department (although other nonnative speakers of English were also employed at the same location). Significantly, he socialized primarily with other Costa Ricans. Alberto's development was followed for a period of 10 months, at the end of which he exhibited little knowledge of English. For example, he continued to place the negative marker before the verb (with no subjects), he did not invert questions, and inflections were minimal. After 10 months of exposure to English in an English-speaking environment, one would expect greater development. However, despite Alberto's claims that he did want to learn English, his actions suggested that he didn't. He listened to Spanish music and he socialized and lived with Spanish speakers. Thus, he failed to acculturate in any significant way to the TL community and to speakers of the TL. According to the Acculturation Hypothesis, it is Alberto's lack of acculturation that resulted in his lack of linguistic development.

However, there is another learner, whose longitudinal development suggests that acculturation cannot be so closely linked to linguistic development. Wes (studied by Schmidt, 1983) is a 33-year-old Japanese artist who moved to Hawai'i. He had every reason to want to be integrated into the Hawaiian community. First and foremost was the need to make a living. But another important dimension of Wes is the fact that one of the reasons for moving to Hawai'i was "a general attraction to the people of Hawai'i." He had an American roommate and for all intents and purposes lived in an English-speaking world. Yet, his grammatical development was limited—although not to the same extent as Alberto's. The following is an example from Wes's speech (Schmidt, 1983, p. 168) (/ = pause breaks):

> I know I'm speaking funny English / because I'm never learning / I'm only just listen / then talk / but people understand / well / some people confuse / before OK / but now is little bit difficult / because many people I'm meeting only just one time / you know demonstrations everybody's first time / sometime so difficult / you know what I mean? / well / I really need English more / I really want speakmore polite English / before I'm always I hate school / but I need studying / maybe school / I don't have time / but maybe better / whaddya think? / I need it, right?

Given that Wes realized that his English was "not right" and given that he showed a desire to acculturate and that he appeared to have a desire to speak better English, it is difficult to justify the view that acculturation is the causal variable in SLA. Whereas there may be some personality variables that interact with the variable of acculturation, the data from Wes suggest that one cannot demonstrate a strong causal relationship between social and psychological distance and language learning. It is more accurate to consider distance and other variables discussed in this chapter as providing an impetus for learning, or perhaps even setting the stage for learning, but not as *causing* learning.

12.5 Age differences

It is commonly believed that children are better language learners than adults in the sense that young children typically can gain mastery of a second language, whereas adults cannot. This is reflected in what is known as the Critical Period Hypothesis (CPH). Birdsong (1999) defines the CPH as follows: "the CPH states that there is a limited developmental period during which it is possible to acquire a language be it L1 or L2, to normal, nativelike levels. Once this window of opportunity is passed, however, the ability to learn language declines" (p. 1). While many researchers use the term *CPH*, it is important to note that in actuality it is somewhat of a misnomer. Another term used is *sensitive* period, which is more gradual in its end point and allows for greater variation in attainment (Long, 1990).

The original formulation of the CPH came from Lennenberg (1967), who noted that "automatic acquisition from mere exposure to a given language seems to disappear [after puberty], and foreign languages have to be taught and learned through a conscious and labored effort. Foreign accents cannot be overcome easily after puberty" (p. 176). Early observations of this phenomenon come from Penfield and Roberts (1959), who had been concerned with the biological and neurological advantages that humans have for learning language as children rather than as adults. According to this hypothesis, there is an age-related point (generally puberty) beyond which it becomes difficult or impossible to learn a second language to the same degree as NSs of that language. However, not all researchers agree with this view. The Critical Period Hypothesis predicts a certain amount of discontinuity—that is, at a certain point, there should be a dramatic drop-off. The Sensitive Period Hypothesis predicts sensitivity, but not absolute drop-offs such that a learning decline might be gradual. The question of why adult second language acquisition is often difficult and incomplete intrigues researchers and laypeople alike because in most cognitive activities adults have an advantage.

One facet of the dispute is what it means to be a *more successful learner*. An initially attractive measure is speed of learning. In most studies in which measurements have been made of the speed of learning some aspect of a second language by learners of different ages, importantly, no advantages were found for young children. In fact, the advantage typically is in the other direction. College-aged, young adults do quite well on most tests measuring language learning speed. But as Larsen-Freeman and Long (1991, pp. 155ff.) pointed out, these studies typically involve the demonstration of mastery on morphological and/or syntactic rules, reflecting speed of learning, not ultimate attainment. The advantages for adults on even these tasks appear short-lived. Snow and Hoefnagle-Hohle (1978), in a study of naturalistic acquisition of Dutch by three groups of English speakers (children, adolescents, and adults), found that adults and adolescents outperformed children on tests given after three months of residence in the Netherlands, but after 10 months the children had caught up on most measures. This finding leaves many unanswered questions. Is this another example of the tortoise and the hare, with the results due to greater persistence by children even though they never had an absolute difference in speed? Did children or the older groups somehow change the way in which they went about learning Dutch?

Another set of relevant variables involves types of language-learning tasks. There are some language-learning tasks in which advantages have been shown for children even with regard to rate. For instance, Tahta, Wood, and Loewenthal (1981) found that American children's ability to replicate intonational patterns in French and Armenian diminished after the age of 8.

406

In general, results indicate that adults are able to achieve criterion scores on most tests of second language learning more rapidly than children, at least during the early stages of acquisition. The language skill involved also makes a difference, as the ability of older learners to quickly learn phonology, especially suprasegmental phonology, seems to atrophy rather quickly. This finding has been supported by a number of studies. Moyer (1999) examined highly proficient NNSs of German (English NSs) with an in-country experience as well as classroom instruction in German. They were graduate students in a U.S. university and were highly motivated. They had had no significant prepubescent exposure to German. The results showed that, despite all of these positive attributes, their accents were still nonnative-like. Moyer (1999) attributes this to motor skills. She argues that "late learners may face neurological or motor skill constraints, such as entrenched articulatory habits or restricted perceptual targets for phonetic categories, that render the possibility of nativelike attainment highly unlikely or impossible" (p. 82).

There is abundant evidence that individuals generally do not achieve a native-like accent in a second language unless they are exposed to it at an early age. Some researchers have argued that, although this is true, it is not necessarily true that adult learners cannot achieve native-like proficiency in phonology. For example, Neufeld (1979) argued that he was able to teach second language learners to perform like natives on certain tasks after specialized training. It is quite likely that improved teaching techniques can improve learners' proficiency quite dramatically, but performance on limited tasks is not equivalent to consistent performance in naturalistic situations. After all, it is much easier to mimic someone else's voice over the phone well enough to fool someone in a brief message than to fool them during a long conversation. The shorter and less demanding the task, the easier it is to feign. Neither Neufeld nor anyone else that we are aware of has demonstrated a teaching technique successful enough to guarantee that learners will "pass" for native speakers in everyday encounters. However, the issue, with regard to the Critical Period Hypothesis, is whether or not there is a gradual decline in abilities, as suggested by Flege (1999), or a precipitous drop-off, as would be expected if the Critical Period Hypothesis were in operation. Flege and others (Flege, Munro, and Mackay, 1995; Flege, Yeni-Komshian, and Liu, 1999; Patkowski, 1980; Yeni-Komshian, Flege, and Liu, 2000; Yeni-Komshian, Robbins, and Flege, 2001) have found that a foreign accent increases as one is exposed later and later to a second language and that a foreign accent can occur even when exposure begins at age 6 or earlier.

There is a general consensus that most older individuals cannot reasonably hope to ever achieve a native accent in a second language. There is no such consensus about other areas of language. Some studies indicate that second language learners cannot achieve complete mastery of syntax. Patkowski (1980) used experienced judges to evaluate transcripts of spoken passages by native and nonnative speakers of English. The judges rated the transcripts on the basis of syntactic proficiency. He found that learners who acquired English after the age of puberty received lower proficiency scores than did either the native speakers or the nonnative speakers who started learning English before puberty. One problem with this method is that it does not show that mastery cannot be achieved, merely that it was not for this group of learners. Another problem is that the method does not directly measure English competence. Perhaps those who learned English later made more errors (even in terms of what they themselves would consider correct), errors they could have caught if allowed to edit their transcripts. Because the transcripts were not provided in the study, we cannot say exactly what the differences were.

In a study carefully designed to assess differences in the acquisition of syntax by learners, Johnson and Newport (1989) investigated learners' proficiency based on different ages of arrival in the country of the second language. Their subjects ranged in age of arrival from 3 to 39. Johnson and Newport found that learners' performance on a test intended to measure second language syntactic knowledge was linearly related to age of arrival only up to puberty. Postpubescent learners generally performed poorly, but there was no correlation with age of arrival. These results can be seen in Figures 12.2 and 12.3. As can be seen in Figure 12.2, there is a linear relationship between the test score and the age of arrival (between the ages of 3 and 15). On the other hand, no such relationship exists for those arriving after the age of 16 (Figure 12.3).[3]

A further study (Slavoff and Johnson, 1995) examined children (NSs of Chinese, Japanese, Korean, and Vietnamese) learning English. The children had arrived in the United States between the ages of 7 and 12 and were tested on specific grammatical structures after various lengths of stay (ranging from six months to three years). Length of stay as opposed to age of arrival was an important variable in predicting knowledge of English syntax (as was gender—females performed better than males). It is important to keep in mind, however, that all of these children were below the age where the Critical Period Hypothesis is generally thought to take effect (roughly puberty).

Johnson and Newport (1991) investigated a property of language associated with Universal Grammar (and hence, supposedly innate) and found that there was a steady decrease in performance according to age of arrival, extending past puberty and with the steepest decline at ages 14–16. These studies and others suggest that there is a critical period for acquisition and that learners' capabilities for acquiring the syntax of a second language decline with age.

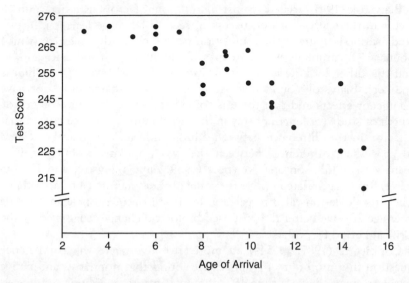

Figure 12.2 Learners arriving, ages 3–15.

Source: From "Critical period effects in second language learning: the influence of maturational state on the acquisition of English as a second language" by J. Johnson and E. Newport, 1989, *Cognitive Psychology*, *21*, 60–99. Reprinted by permission.

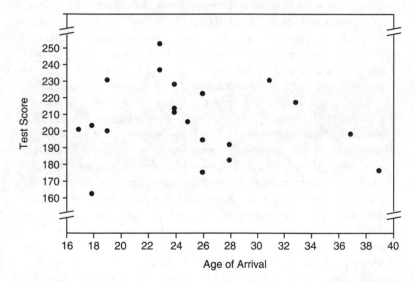

Figure 12.3 Learners arriving, ages 17–39.

Source: From "Critical period effects in second language learning: the influence of maturational state on the acquisition of English as a second language" by J. Johnson and E. Newport, 1989, *Cognitive Psychology*, *21*, 60–99. Reprinted by permission.

Bialystok (1997) argued against maturational factors as a determining factor in the success or nonsuccess of second language learning. In two studies, one looking at the acquisition of French gender marking (which nouns are feminine vs. which are masculine) by English and German NSs and the other looking at the acquisition of English syntax by Chinese speakers, Bialystok found that age of onset of learning does not have significant effects and that there is some support for the importance of length of study (or length of stay in the target culture). She suggested that a factor in the difference between adults and children may be related to processing differences between the two populations. Further, in a reanalysis of Johnson and Newport (1989) data, Bialystok and Hakuta (1994) found age-related effects for some of the structures, but not others. Their recalculations also revealed a deterioration in proficiency starting after age 20—well after the proposed biological changes suggested by the Critical Period Hypothesis.

Coppieters (1987, p. 544) attempted to investigate the competence question in a more direct manner.[4] He found that nonnative and native speakers may have strikingly different intuitions about sentences, although they produce essentially the same structures in actual use.

> Do native and native-like nonnative (i.e., near-native) speakers develop essentially identical underlying grammars of the same language? Results of extensive interviews indicate that native and near-native speakers of French have strikingly different intuitions on French sentences. In particular, the two groups have markedly divergent interpretations of sentences involving basic grammatical contrasts such as the two past tenses (imparfait and passé composé), the 3rd person pronouns il and ce, and the placement of the adjective before and after the noun. This is so in spite of the fact that the two groups appear to be equivalent at the level of language use and proficiency. These results provide a clear illustration of the relative independence of the two levels of language: on the one hand, language use, and on the other hand, underlying grammars as reflected by speakers' intuitions. It is suggested that the specific nature of the divergences between native and near-native speakers' underlying grammars also provides clues to the internal organization of language: in particular, the data indicate that near-native speakers diverge less from native speakers in formal features, such as those currently covered by studies in Universal Grammar, than in "functional" or "cognitive" aspects of grammar.

Birdsong (1992) also found differences in judgments of many grammatical structures between native speakers and very fluent nonnative speakers. However, Universal Grammar provided no basis for predicting on which structures they were like native speakers and on which they were not. And, importantly, unlike in previous studies, individual results indicated that some nonnative speakers performed within the native speaker range.

It would appear that there are several divergences between the syntax of native speakers and the syntax of even near-native speakers, but that these differences are often subtle and difficult to find. This raises a related issue. Does difference imply a lack of mastery? Consider the fact that rules based on Latin grammar had an influence on the views of English grammarians (e.g., do not split infinitives; this is a trivial rule of Latin grammar because Latin infinitives are single words, not two-word phrases, as in English). In this instance, knowledge of an L2 had an influence on intuitions about an L1. One would not say that these grammarians had failed to master English because they were susceptible to foreign influences.

Patkowski (1980, pp. 462ff.) discusses the "Conrad phenomenon," named after Joseph Conrad, the native Pole who learned English at the age of 18 and became one of the greatest English novelists. Patkowski (p. 463) cited the following remarks by Kurt Vonnegut:

> The writing style which is most natural for you is bound to echo the speech you heard when a child. English is the novelist Joseph Conrad's third language, and much that seems piquant in his use of English was no doubt colored by his first language, which was Polish.

Patkowski took this as an indication that Conrad's language was not native-like. It is certainly not like natives unexposed to other languages. But is it necessarily different from the writing style of someone who grew up around many nonnative speakers, as in many neighborhoods of New York? Nabokov's style in *Ada*, in which there are multilingual puns based on French, German, Russian, and English, is different from what one would expect in a typical English speaker, but does this imply lesser or greater mastery? We need to be more precise in describing the acquisition of syntax.

The question of morphosyntax is also at issue. DeKeyser (2000), in a study of Hungarian learners of English with differing ages of arrival in the U.S., categorized the structures that he investigated as easy or hard depending on their perceptual saliency, which he claims allows learners to notice an area where there is something to be learned. Examples of easy structures are word order in simple sentences and pronoun gender; examples of difficult structures are articles and subcategorization features. Easy structures did not show age-related effects, whereas difficult structures did. He ties this to explicit and implicit learning, claiming that younger learners have intact the ability for implicit and explicit learning whereas adults have lost their ability to learn implicitly (see also DeKeyser and Larson-Hall, 2005). In chapter 10 we discussed research that showed that learners do not interpret morphosyntactic feedback in the way that it is intended, whereas other areas (for example, phonological feedback) are interpreted appropriately. Thus, if we consider interaction to be an important part of learning due to the feedback received and if morpho-syntactic feedback is not useful, it becomes clear that morphosyntactic learning will be disadvantaged. In explaining the difference between adults and children vis-à-vis rate and ultimate attainment, DeKeyser and Larson-Hall (2005) invoke differences in implicit and explicit learning.

> Children necessarily learn implicitly; adults necessarily learn largely explicitly. As a result, adults show an initial advantage because of the shortcuts provided by the explicit structure, but falter in those areas in which explicit learning is ineffective, that is, where rules are too complex or probabilistic in nature to be apprehended fully with explicit rules. Children, on the other hand, cannot use shortcuts to the representation of structure, but eventually reach full native speaker competence through long-term implicit learning from massive input. This long-term effect of age of onset is most obvious to the casual observer in pro-nunciation, but on closer inspection appears to be no less robust in the domain of grammar.
>
> (p. 103)

In summarizing the results so far, the evidence indicates that young children are more likely to attain native-like proficiency in a second language than are teenagers or adults. Nevertheless, adults often learn certain parts of a new language more quickly (e.g., early morphological and syntactic development). The evidence is much more solid for an advantage for children in the acquisition of phonology, although there is some support for an advantage in other areas of language as well.

In a detailed review of the literature, Long (1990, p. 251) concluded:

1   Both the initial rate of acquisition and the ultimate level of attain-ment depend in part on the age at which learning begins.
2   There are sensitive periods governing language development, first or second, during which the acquisition of different linguistic abilities is successful and after which it is irregular and incomplete.
3   The age-related loss in ability is cumulative (not a catastrophic one-time event), affecting first one linguistic domain and then another, and is not limited to phonology.

4   The deterioration in some individuals begins as early as age 6—not at puberty as is often claimed.

The bulk of the evidence comes from the acquisition of English, and secondly the acquisition of other European languages. It is hoped that other languages will be the focus of investigation as the discipline of SLA further develops. Assuming that there is something like a critical period, or at least a sensitive period, the next question is: Why is this the case? Various explanations have been offered. Among them are the following:

- There are social psychological reasons for why adults learn languages less readily than children do. There are many different versions of this hypothesis. Some suggest that adults do not want to give up the sense of identity their accent provides. Some suggest that adults are un-willing to surrender their ego to the extent required to adopt a new language, which entails a new life-world.
- There are cognitive factors responsible for the inability of adults to learn successfully. Adults have greater cognitive abilities than children. Ironically, adopting the cognitive abilities in a language-learning task has been hypothesized to result in less successful learning than found in children, who, according to the hypothesis, rely to a greater extent on a specific Language Acquisition Device.
- There are neurological changes that prevent adults from using their brains in the same way children do on language-learning tasks. This is usually presented as a loss of plasticity, or flexibility, in the brain.
- Children are exposed to better input for language learning. The assumption here is that the type of modifications adults make for children provide better data about language.

None of these hypotheses is unchallenged. In fact, Long (1990, p. 251) argued that "affective, input, and current-cognitive explanations for the reduced ability are inadequate." If adults in some cultures do perform as well as children, then explanations based on cognitive or neurological factors are clearly wrong. There is no reason to assume any differences between cultures in these areas. Whereas there are social-psychological differences between children and adults, children are by no means immune to social-psychological factors. Input differences do not seem to be the major factor. The primary difference between children and adults is in the mastery of phonology, which can hardly be due to input dif-ferences. Moreover, adults are better at negotiating input, which should suggest better acquisition possibilities. Finally, there are indications that children do not receive input divergent from native speaker speech in certain cultures (i.e., there is no caretaker speech, as it is known in

Western cultures).[5] In these cultures, as in others, language learning appears to proceed normally.

If the neurological or cognitive hypotheses were correct, we would expect the process of language learning to be different in children and adults. We would further expect the patterns of acquisition to be different when adult and child learners are compared. Bley-Vroman, Felix, and Ioup (1988) investigated this question. In reviewing previous literature, they found that:

> in many crucial domains L2 learners' utterances do, in fact, show structural properties that are at least very similar to those characterizing the speech of first language learners . . . Furthermore, the types of interlanguage structures and the order in which certain features of the target language are mastered are close to identical in both L1 and L2 acquisition.
>
> (pp. 1–2)

The major differences noted between L2 and L1 were due to L1 influence, a factor that has nothing to do with age or maturation (with the obvious exception that very young children could not have mastery of a previous language). This indicates that the processes were not very different. Moreover, Bley-Vroman, Felix, and Ioup found evidence for UG influence on adult L2 learning, although the patterns are complicated. This demonstrates that access to UG is not simply lost at some maturational stage.

In a study of competence, White and Genesee (1996) tested high proficiency learners (NSs of French, described as "near-natives") on certain English structures known to be influenced by a critical period. The authors found no significant differences between these high proficiency speakers and native speakers of English. Therefore, they concluded that native competence is achievable even by postpubescent learners.

As noted earlier, there is no agreement as to whether there is a critical period or even whether native competence can be attained in a second language. In general, however, there is some evidence for an age-related decline in abilities. Various explanations have been put forward, such as age of first exposure, length of stay, and processing differences.

Hyltenstam and Abrahamsson (2003) claim that only children reach native-like proficiency. Some do appear to reach native-like proficiency, namely those who have age of arrival in a second language environment before puberty and most likely much earlier (even age 6). As they note, these individuals "reach proficiency levels above *the limit of perceivable non-nativeness*, thus making them *appear* to be nativelike" (p. 571; emphasis theirs). They go on to say that

Nevertheless, given the fact that there are no published accounts of a single adult starter who has reached nativelike overall L2 proficiency, and given the frequent observation of non-native features even in very early starters, we would suggest the *possibility* that absolute nativelike command of an L2 may in fact never be possible for any learner. According to such a view, the language learning mechanism would be designed in such a way that it requires immediate triggering from the environment in order for it to develop and work appropriately; that is, the learning mechanism inevitably and quickly deteriorates from birth if not continuously stimulated.

(p. 575)

Birdsong (1999) presented a number of possible explanations to account for the well-attested fact that most adults do not (or cannot) become fluent in a second language. Among them are the following:

- Loss of (access to) the language learning faculty. Successful language learning cannot take place after puberty because there is a loss of UG and possibly a loss of innate learning strategies. (See chapter 6.)
- Loss of neural plasticity in the brain. As a person ages, there is a progressive lateralization of cerebral functions. The consequence of this and other cerebral changes is that the neural substrate needed for language learning is no longer fully available later in life.
- Maladaptive gain of processing capacity. Processing and memory capacities change as a person matures.
- "Use it, then lose it." This is essentially an evolutionary argument. Once humans use whatever innate circuitry is available to them at birth, there is no longer any need for it and the circuitry is dismantled. According to Pinker (1994, pp. 294–295):

> Language-acquisition circuitry is not needed once it has been used; it should be dismantled if keeping it around incurs any costs. And it probably does incur costs. Metabolically, the brain is a pig. It consumes a fifth of the body's oxygen and similarly large portions of its calories and phospholipids. Greedy neural tissue lying around beyond its point of usefulness is a good candidate for the recycling bin.

A version of this is the "use it or lose it" explanation. If one doesn't use the innate faculty, it will atrophy with time. In other words, it is a slow loss rather than an all-at-once dismantling.

- Learning inhibits learning. In the connectionist models of learning, language learning involves accumulating and strengthening associations (see chapter 8). Thus, the strength of associations from the

415

native language (or other languages known) might interfere with the possibility of formulating and strengthening new associations.

Long (2007) proposes a neurophysiological explanation: exposure to more than one language before the close of the sensitive period ". . . and probably with no general cognitive correlate, conveys a lasting advantage on early L2 acquirers—an advantage that persists in adulthood" (p. 74). He further proposes that "early richer linguistic exposure leads to the creation of more, and more complex, neural networks before synaptic sheaths harden as part of the myelinization process, making new ones for new languages more difficult to create in older starters" (p. 74).

Future research will need to sort out these various explanations, if indeed there is a critical period. It may further be, as with many explanations of second language learning, that no single explanation can account for age-related differences. Finally, Marinova-Todd, Marshall, and Snow (2000) caution researchers and the lay public alike not to jump to conclusions about early learning. They propose that age differences may reflect more the situation of learning than a capacity for learning. In their words, "[t]he misconception that adults cannot master foreign languages is as widespread as it is erroneous" (p. 27). They argue that the prevailing view that there is a critical period and that the explanation resides in connections to the brain relies on three fallacies:

1   Misinterpretation
    a   Fallacy: Children are fast and efficient.
    b   Reality: Children learn languages slowly and effortfully.
2   Misattribution
    a   Fallacy: Language proficiency is tied to brain functioning.
    b   Reality: This may in fact turn out to be the case, but data currently in evidence cannot discern this.
3   Misemphasis
    a   Fallacy: Because there is frequent failure by adults to learn an L2 does not mean that it is impossible to do so.
    b   Reality: Most adults do end up short of native-like levels of proficiency, but there is often a lack of motivation, a lack of commitment of time or energy, and a lack of environmental support.

Marinova-Todd, Marshall, and Snow (2000) suggest that a greater emphasis on those "truly informative cases: successful adults who invest sufficient time and attention in SLA and who benefit from high motivation and from supportive, informative L2 environments" (p. 28) will move the field forward in understanding the role of the critical period and ultimate attainment.

12.6 Aptitude

The relationship between aptitude and second language learning success is a very important one, if only because opinions about aptitude can have enormous implications in our everyday lives. If aptitude measures are used to discourage individuals from studying foreign languages and if the measures are inaccurate, then certain students will be unfairly prevented from receiving whatever advantages may accrue from knowledge of other languages. Given the past history of aptitude measures in school, one could reasonably predict that it is disadvantaged students who are most likely to suffer. Some of the results found in the United Kingdom relating language aptitude to social background do nothing to allay these fears. On the other hand, if (a) an aptitude measure is accurate and (b) students are placed in an instructional program for which they have little aptitude and (c) it is possible to either increase their aptitude or place them in another instructional program for which they have greater aptitude, then failure to consider aptitude would penalize students unfairly. Aptitude, therefore, can have real-life consequences.

Aptitude, simply put, refers to one's potential for learning new knowledge or new skills. With regard to language aptitude, it refers to one's ability to learn another language; there is no talk of language aptitude for learning one's first language, at least not for children without cognitive deficits. When one breaks down the general construct of language aptitude, there are numerous components, such as verbal aptitude.

Even though aptitude is clearly of crucial importance, it has not always been a focus of investigation, in part for the same reasons illustrated above with regard to the general orientation of second language studies and, in part, because the construct is somewhat elusive and clearly multi-componential, so measuring it is not always clear cut. In studies where it has been included, aptitude has been shown to be an important differentiating factor. In fact, Skehan (1989, p. 38) stated that "aptitude is consistently the best predictor of language learning success." He counters arguments that attempt to diminish the role of aptitude by stressing the centrality of aptitude, which more recently is seen as part of working memory, discussed in chapter 8:

> It has been proposed that motivation . . . or cognitive style . . . or degree of acculturation . . . or personality and attitude are of greater significance than aptitude. This criticism is really an empirical question, and what is needed is evidence. In fact, such evidence as is available from quantification-based studies generally demonstrates that aptitude is *at least as important*, and usually more important, than any other variable investigated. Studies have reported multiple correlations between aptitude

battery totals and criterion scores as high as 0.70, and values of 0.50 are commonplace. Only motivation indices even approach such high figures. The values one obtains for personality measures and traits such as cognitive style are considerably lower, rarely going much above 0.30.

(p. 38)

J. B. Carroll is the name associated most with studies of second language learning aptitude. He is the originator of what Skehan called the "standard 'four component' view of language aptitude" (1989, p. 26):

1   Phonemic coding ability. This is an ability to discriminate among foreign sounds and to encode them in a manner such that they can be recalled later. This would certainly seem to be a skill involved in successful second language learning.
2   Grammatical sensitivity. This is the ability to recognize the functions of words in sentences. It does not measure an ability to name or describe the functions, but rather the ability to discern whether or not words in different sentences perform the same function. It appears logical that skill in being able to do this helps in learning another language.
3   Inductive language learning ability. This is the ability to infer, induce, or abduct rules or generalizations about language from samples of the language. A learner proficient in this ability is less reliant on well-presented rules or generalizations from a teacher or from materials.
4   Memory and learning. Originally this was phrased in terms of associations: the ability to make and recall associations between words and phrases in a native and a second language. It is not clear whether this type of association plays a major role in language learning, but memory for language material is clearly important. Some linguists (e.g., Becker, 1991) suggest that second language learning is much more an accomplishment of memory for text than of the analysis of text. That is, much more is memorized than is broken into parts and subjected to rule formation and/or generalizations.

Skehan (1989) questioned the appropriateness of separating grammatical sensitivity and inductive language-learning ability. He suggested that these be combined into one ability: language analytic ability.

These four (or three) abilities seem to be reasonable predictors of second language learning success in that a person who is excellent in one or more of these abilities would seem to be at an advantage in learning a second language. There is no *a priori* reason to believe that individuals will be equally skilled in all abilities. Indeed, Skehan (1989) suggested that all of the abilities (three in his scheme) are independent. If these three abilities are indeed independent, then there should be eight (2^3) learner types, because a person could be good on all three, good on the first but poor on the next two, and so forth.

It is one thing to agree that these abilities would be useful in learning a second language. It is another thing to say that one has a measure of these abilities. Various attempts have been made to measure them. Perhaps the best known is Carroll and Sapon's (1959) Modern Language Aptitude Test (MLAT). This test consists of five subtests:

Part One: Number Learning: The student is taught, on tape, the Kurdish number system from 1 to 4, plus the "tens" and "hundreds" forms of these numbers, then tested by hearing numbers which are combinations of these elements, e.g., 312, 122, 41, etc. The test aims at measuring associative memory.

Part Two: Phonetic Script: This sub-test measures phonemic coding ability. The student learns a system of phonetic notations for some English phonemes. He is then tested on this learning, e.g., "Underline the word you hear: Tik; Tiyk; Tis; Tiys."

Part Three: Spelling Clues: This is a high speed test that measures both native language vocabulary and phonemic coding ability. The student is given clues to the pronunciation of a word (e.g., "ernst" for "earnest") and is then asked to choose a synonym from a list of alternatives.

Part Four: Words in Sentences: This tests grammatical sensitivity. In a typical item, two sentences are presented, with one word in the first sentence underlined. In the second sentence five words are underlined. The student has to decide which of the under-lined words in the second sentence fulfils the same function as the underlined word in the first sentence.

Part Five: Paired Associates: The student studies a written Kurdish–English vocabulary list, practices the stimulus–response pairs seen, and is then tested by means of multiple-choice items. This is a test of associative memory.

(summary of tests by Skehan, 1989, p. 28)

It is important to remember that, although the skills themselves are listed, the only measurements used are those taken from tests, and one must assume that the tests are measuring what they purport to. The "words in sentences" subtest seems to have the best correspondence with the ability it seeks to measure (Skehan, 1989). The "paired associates" test relies on models of memory that are no longer generally accepted. The "spelling clues" test appears to depend heavily on social and regional dialects (because different dialects may have different pronunciations for the same spelling). In other words, what is a good clue for a speaker of one variety may be a poor clue for a speaker of another variety. In general, the abilities themselves are much more persuasive at first glance than the subtests used to measure them.

One might imagine that language aptitude is simply due to intelligence in general. This does not seem to be the case. First, it must be made clear that there are many approaches to intelligence (e.g., Gardner, 1983; Sternberg, 2002) and there is not agreement as to the components or hierarchical arrangement of the components of this construct. Many psychologists believe that there are multiple types of intelligence, although it must be recognized that many others claim that there is support for a notion of general intelligence (Carroll, 1992). Second, statistical investigations have demonstrated that language aptitude cannot be explained simply on the basis of the most common measurement of intelligence, IQ scores. There are clearly many overlapping traits, but there is not a one-to-one correspondence between measures on a general IQ test and measures of aptitude.

The particular tests devised by Carroll are not the only tests of language aptitude. Other tests have been developed for the U.S. military and for use in other countries. British research (summarized in Skehan, 1989), in particular, has delved into the question of the origins of language aptitude. One discovery is that there are significant differences in the rates of syntactic acquisition in a first language. There is a correlation between the rates (which may be viewed as an indication of native language aptitude, perhaps) and second language aptitude. Interestingly, the correlation is greater with second language aptitude than with achievement, which supports the idea that capability is being measured, even though various factors may lead children to perform below their capacity.

The British studies found that there is an even greater correlation between second language aptitude and social class and parental education. These two elements were found mixed in with vocabulary development in a factor termed *family background*. Not only does family background correlate with second language aptitude, but it also correlates quite highly with foreign language achievement.

These relationships should give us pause, because, at least on face value, they seem related to factors that lead to achievement that are not really based on inherent capabilities. As noted earlier, children from more privileged classes and with higher parental education are more likely to be rewarded with good grades in schools. Moreover, in the United Kingdom, as in North America, children with these backgrounds are more likely to be able to *use* foreign language skills abroad. Thus, they are good predictors of how likely a student is to get good grades or really use a foreign language, but it is harder to see how they can account for ability in the abstract.

More recent measures of aptitude have been devised by Grigorenko, Sternberg, and Ehrman (2000) and approach aptitude testing from a perspective of intelligence that takes as its base abilities that are necessary in daily life, as opposed to those needed for successful school learning. Their test, the CANAL-FT (Cognitive Ability for Novelty in Acquisition of Language), as is clear from the name, is grounded in cognitive theory, is dynamic, and is simulation-based. A major underlying idea of this test is that a central ability in foreign language learning requires the ability to cope with novelty and ambiguity (Ehrman, 1993, 1994, 1996; Ehrman and Oxford, 1995) and this ability is part of Sternberg's theory of human intelligence (1985, 1988, 1997).

There are five knowledge acquisition processes underlying their test.

- Selective encoding—distinguishing between more and less relevant information.
- Accidental encoding—understanding the background or secondary information.
- Selective comparison—determining the relevance of old information for a current task.
- Selective transfer—applying decoded or inferred rules in new contexts and/or tasks.
- Selective combination—synthesizing various bits of information gathered through selective and accidental encoding.

The test includes four areas of language (lexical, morphological, semantic, and syntactic) and two modes of input and output (visual and oral). The test is based on the gradual learning of an artificial language. A description of the sections is given below (taken from Dörnyei, 2005, pp. 52–53), followed by sample items taken from Grigorenko, Sternberg, and Ehrman, 2000, pp. 403–405. There were immediate and delayed recall tests; both immediate and delayed recall items are given here (see Grigorenko, Sternberg, and Ehrman, 2000, pp. 403–405 for a fuller example of recall items).

> The CANAL-FT comprises nine sections: Five involve immediate recall and the other four are identical to these five sections except that they are presented later and involve delayed recall (the last section does not have a delayed counterpart). A common element of the sections is that they all focus on the learning of an artificial language, Ursulu. This is presented gradually so that initially participants have no knowledge of the language: by the end of the test, however, they have mastered enough lexical, morphological, semantic, and syntactic knowledge to cope with a small story in Ursulu. The five sections are as follows:

1   **Learning meanings of neologisms from context:** Participants
    are presented with 24 brief paragraphs within a 2 × 3 factorial
    design (type of presentation: oral or visual × density of unknown
    words: low, medium, or high). Understanding is tested via a
    multiple-choice format, where students are asked to guess which
    of five alternatives is most likely to correspond to the meaning of
    an unknown neologism inserted into the text. Two multiple-
    choice items are presented immediately after receipt of every pas-
    sage and one item relevant to every passage is presented at least 30
    minutes after receipt of the passages in order to measure storage
    in long-term memory.

> **Example item (immediate recall) (partial text):** Rising
> tuition costs and increasingly large loans aren't the only
> financial issues facing *mukulu nafe-de*, the latest threat to
> *Yuve-Yuve ya-pama-de* pocketbooks comes from mandatory
> *twok-de*. One *laka* will require entering freshmen *fru hujuk* a
> *mukulu*-specified laptop *twok* at a cost of $3,000.
> **Questions:** *Fru hujuk* most likely means: (a) to arrange; (b)
>   having; (c) carrying; (d) to purchase; (e) to rent.
>   *Mukulu* in line (3) most likely means: (a) schools;
>   (b) student; (c) parent; (d) universities; (e) college.

2   **Understanding the meaning of passages:** The six test items in
    this part are identical in form to those in Section 1, but the
    assessment involves comprehension of whole passages rather
    than merely of lexical items. Again, half of the items are pre-
    sented visually, the other half orally, and the passages differ in
    terms of the density of unknown words. The test differs from
    standard reading and oral comprehension tests in the inclusion
    of unknown words in the passages. Such words render these
    passages more like those that would be encountered in the
    process of learning an L2.

> **Example item (immediate recall) (partial text):** The
> wealthy hunting *femo-de* of late glacial Europe might have
> maintained or even enriched culture, or *unta-u erto* to
> stagnate *ik* decline: *Yuve* could hardly have advanced *erto* to a
> higher form of civilization, for the environment *neunta-u erto*.
> But *Yuve-Yuve* future *cutta-u* not left in *Yuve-Yuve* own
> *sima-de*.
> **Question (delayed recall):** The author of the passage about
> the hunting society apparently believes that levels of civiliza-
> tion are determined by: (a) economic luck; (b) a balance of

solar energy; (c) the ambitions of the people; (d) a piece of magic; (e) climatic conditions.

3   **Continuous paired-associate learning**: In this test, participants are presented with 60 paired associates (word pairs), half of them visually, half of them orally. They are required to learn the successive pairings and during the process they are tested at irregular intervals on words learned more recently as well as less recently. The test differs from a straightforward paired-associates memory test in that there are certain rules that can facilitate learning, relating some of the terms to others.

> **Example pairs (immediate recall):**
> kiss   = lutik
> maki smelano = floweret
> to oppose   = fru prostoto
> threerish   = two
> to luxuriate   = fru shikta
> unteriapremu = fairytale
> to learn   = fruumbrad
> juk-de   = fingers
> yellow   = hukoi
> pjze_min-de   = workers
>
> **Questions:**
> In Ursulu,
>> *floweret* most likely means (a) *maki smelano*; (b) *ummake*; (c) *lutik*; (d) *pjze_min*; (e) *maki juk*.
>> *fru umbrad* most likely means: (a) to eat; (b) to go; (c) to learn, (d) to kiss; (e) to dream.

4   **Sentential inference**: Participants receive 20 sets of three to five sentences in the Ursulu language with their translations presented either visually or orally. They are then presented with a new sentence, either in English or in Ursulu, and are asked to indicate—based on inferences made from the previously presented sentence pairs—which of five multiple-choice answers best represents the translation.

> **Example item (immediate recall):**

Panlin-u Sumu Twah chuck	means I handed a stick to him.
Panlin-u Yut Twa dozz	means He handed an umbrella to me.
Panilcos-u Yut Twa flexta	means He handed a piece of paper to me.
Panleh-u Sumu Twah chuchu	means I handed a rope to him.

Question:
The sentence *Panilcos-u Sumu Twah otikum* most likely means:
(a) He handed a rod to me;
(b) I handed a cord to him;
(c) I handed a postcard to him;
(d) I handed a waterhose to him;
(e) I handed a tree-branch to her.

5 **Learning language rules**: Participants are given some vocabulary, some grammar, and some examples of how the Ursulu language works. From this type of information they are expected to learn some of the most evident rules of the language. To measure this learning, they are presented with 12 items (lexical, semantic, morphological, and syntactic) that test their understanding of the Ursulu language.

Example item (immediate recall):
In Ursulu, *ya-bum baqlo* means "the chief's mule," *ya* being the possessive and *ya-bum* the modifier of the noun *baqlo* "mule."

Match the corresponding pairs:
Question:
ya-fuama pokka
preumma chicca-de
ya-xori gazza
prebrutama tepla-de
ya-ayama xrosyo
preuntam rutuma
   (a) monkey's smile; (b) alligator gloves; (c) sheep wool; (d) cat's tail; (e) gigantic tiger; (f) wife's book.

The authors of this test report the results of a correlational study with the MLAT and with established intelligence measures. Thus, research in aptitude is making use of measurements that are able to tap into real-life capabilities. Regardless of the type of aptitude measure used, a question arises as to whether there can be any practical applications in terms of tailoring language classrooms to aptitude characteristics of students. Not many studies have investigated this in detail, probably due to the fact that it is difficult to isolate one factor in a complex learning environment as contributing to success or lack of success. Nonetheless, there are a few relevant studies.

Wesche (1981) and Skehan (1996) reported that students show greater satisfaction when instruction is matched to learner characteristics, as when more analytic methodologies are used with analytic learners and more memory-oriented learners did better with methodologies that involved exposure to longer chunks of language. Similarly, Harley and Hart (1997), in a study of immersion children, found positive relationships between (a) L2 success and analytical measures for immersion beginning in adolescence and (b) L2 success and memory ability for those students beginning immersion in grade 1.

Reves (1983) studied Arabic native speakers learning English in school in Israel and the same group learning Hebrew naturalistically. The aptitude measure was found to be a better predictor of success in the informal, naturalistic setting. Thus, it appears that aptitude is an important indicator of second language acquisition in both classroom and nonclassroom contexts.

Robinson (2001, 2002) has begun to look at aptitude complexes; that is, clusters of traits that lead to efficient learning. Aptitude, in his view, represents the totality of other abilities which he groups according to cognitive factors that can support learning in different contexts. This is supported by Segalowitz (1997), who places aptitude contextually. It is not a fixed trait "but rather a complex reflection of the whole learning situation" (p. 108).

The question arises as to where aptitude comes from. That is, is aptitude innate or does it develop? McLaughlin (1990b) suggested that prior language-learning experience has a positive effect on language learning. This positive effect can manifest itself as better learning (Nation and McLaughlin, 1986) or as better use of language-learning strategies (Nayak, Hansen, Krueger, and McLaughlin, 1990). In other words, aptitude develops. However, Harley and Hart (1997) did not find support for aptitude development. Their study compared two groups of students in grade 11, one that had been in early immersion programs and that had begun L2 (French) study (for the most part) in grade 1, and the other that had begun L2 (French) study in grade 7. The former group (early immersion experience) did not perform better than the latter group of students (late immersion experience). In other words, language-learning experience did not affect aptitude and, therefore, the claim cannot be made that aptitude develops as a function of language-learning experience.

Clearly, working memory is part of any discussion of aptitude and some believe that working memory is aptitude. In chapter 8, we reviewed the construct of working memory, which many believe is a component of aptitude. This is made clear by Miyake and Friedman (1998) when they say that working memory for language may be one (if not *the*) central component of language aptitude (p. 339). Models of aptitude have relied on issues of memory. Future research will undoubtedly investigate this relationship of two intertwined constructs.

As Dörnyei (2005) notes, current research views aptitude as a situated phenomenon, for example, in relation to motivation, a discussion of which we turn to next.

12.7 Motivation

A social-psychological factor frequently used to account for differential success in learning a second language is motivation. This has an intuitive appeal. It makes sense that individuals who are motivated will learn another language faster and to a greater degree. And, quite clearly, some degree of motivation is involved in initial decisions to learn another language and to maintain learning. Furthermore, numerous studies have provided statistical evidence that indicates motivation is a predictor of language-learning success. In recent years there has been a resurgence of interest in motivation research, with numerous reviews and book-length treatments of the topic (Dörnyei, 2001a, 2001b; Gardner, 2001; MacIntyre, 2002; Ushioda, 2003).

In general, motivation appears to be the second strongest predictor of success, trailing only aptitude (Skehan, 1989). Nevertheless, an investigation of the role of motivation in second language learning faces a hurdle just beyond the starting block: the exact nature of motivation is not so clear. Everyone agrees that it has something to do with drive, but when various definitions are compared, it becomes clear that these definitions differ in significant ways.

Gardner, through his early work with Lambert (1972) and in later work with colleagues at the University of Western Ontario, has become a primary figure in the field of motivation in second language learning. "Motivation involves four aspects, a goal, effortful behaviour, a desire to attain the goal and favourable attitudes toward the activity in question" (Gardner, 1985, p. 50).

Effort consists of a number of factors, including an inherent need to achieve, good study habits, and the desire to please a teacher or parent. This seems to be a mixed bag of components, as some pertain to what one has done and others to what one would like to do.

Central to this approach is the concept of integration, which refers to an individual's disposition toward the L2 group and the extent to which he or she desires to interact with and even become similar to that group. In Figure 12.4 is a representation of Gardner's basic model, showing the roles of both aptitude and motivation in language achievement. Integrativeness is "a complex of attitudes involving more than just the other language community. It is not simply a reason for studying the language" (Gardner, 2001, p. 5).

As can be seen, achievement comes from motivation, of which integrativeness is one component, and aptitude, discussed in the previous section. There are other factors that also contribute to achievement, of

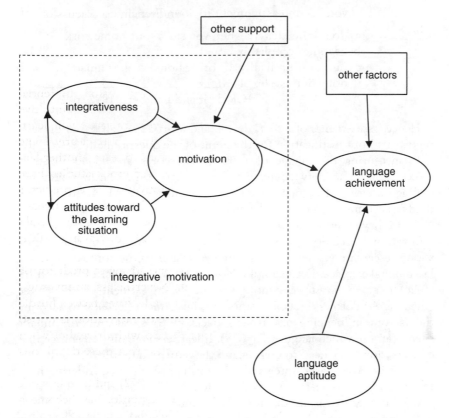

Figure 12.4 Basic model of the role of aptitude and motivation in second language learning.

Source: From "Integrative motivation and second language acquisition" by R. Gardner, 2001. In Z. Dörnyei and R. Schmidt (Eds.), *Motivation and Second Language Acquisition*, pp. 1–19. Honolulu: Second Language Teaching and Curriculum Center. Reprinted with permission.

which instrumental motivation, generally referring to a utilitarian goal such as obtaining a job, is one. But other sources of motivation are also possible, such as an inspiring teacher.

Gardner's basic method in early research was to administer questionnaires that call for self-report answers to questions (often based on a Likert scale), as in this example:

Place a check mark anywhere along the line below to indicate how much you like French compared to all your other courses.

French is my   French is my *most*
least preferred course   preferred course

_____ : _____ : _____ : _____ : _____ : _____ : __

When you have an assignment to do in French, do you:

_____a do it immediately when you start your homework.
_____b become completely bored.
_____c put it off until all your other homework is finished.
_____d none of these (explain)_____

(Gardner and Lambert, 1972, p. 153)

Hence, assessments of effort, desire, and attitude are all based on self-reports without justification for the items of the questionnaire.

In measuring the degree of motivation, scores are added together (except for an anxiety score, which is subtracted). Gardner and his colleagues grouped certain questions into categories, which are further used to account for success in language learning.

As we have seen in Gardner's model, motivation research has viewed motivation in relation to other constructs. But, more than that, motivation research considers motivation as it relates to the context in which learning takes place. For example, Norton (2000) and McKay and Wong (1996) refer to *investment*—more specifically, investment in the target language. As Potowski (2004) points out, investment "takes into account the factors influencing a learner's decision to speak—or to remain silent—and in which language" (p. 77). If learners are going to engage in a conversation, they need to understand the return on that investment.

What is particularly noteworthy in this approach is considering how motivation affects learning processes and overall disposition (Dörnyei, 2006). In other words, motivation is a dynamic construct.

12.7.1 *Motivations as a function of time and success*

Improving proficiency in a second language is a long-term project. Nevertheless, success in this long-term project depends on success in a series of short activities. A learner who is vigilant about instituting many encounters to gain comprehensible input is more likely to be successful in second language learning environments. A learner who expends the effort for memorization (even if unconsciously) is more likely to succeed in either foreign or second language environments. To obtain good school grades, students must perform many tasks successfully over a term or academic year. But, clearly, motivation is not static; it changes depending on the context and it changes over time.

A question regarding motivation and second language learning is whether it is better to say that motivation predicts success, in that the more successful one has been in language learning, the more motivated one will be to learn more. This can be broken down into at least two specific questions: (a) Can motivation change over time? and (b) What is the effect of success on performance?

12.7.2 Changes over time

Dörnyei and Ottó (1998; and detailed in Dörnyei, 2000, 2001a) proposed a model of motivation that allows for changes over time. Essentially, there are three components to this model which represent three temporal steps. The model chronicles how initial wishes are transformed into goals, how intentions are operationalized, then how they are enacted, and finally how a goal is accomplished and evaluated. The three phases are:

- *Preactional stage.* This is the stage during which motivation is generated. This leads to the selection of the goal that will be pursued.
- *Actional stage.* This is referred to as *executive motivation* and it relates to the sustaining of the activity even with distracting influences.
- *Postactional stage.* The third phase follows the completion of the action. This is referred to as *motivational retrospection.* This refers to the evaluation of how the activity went and feeds into future activities that might be pursued in the future.

These are schematized in Figure 12.5.

As Dörnyei (2005) points out, the division between stages is not as abrupt as would seem by this diagram on paper. Where one stage ends and another begins most likely includes some overlap. The model, however, is intended to show that different motives may be involved at different points in time. Further motives can be reassessed and modified during the process.

There have been some studies that have investigated how motivation changes over time (Gardner, Masgoret, Tennant, and Mihic, 2004; Williams, Burden, and Lanvers, 2002; Lim, 2002; Shedivy, 2004). Shoaib and Dörnyei (2005) found that specific episodes in people's lives had the consequence of restructuring their motivation.

12.7.3 Influence of success on motivation and demotivation

What should the effect of success on motivation be? Should it necessarily increase motivation? The argument earlier suggests that if learners realize that successful performance in some activity leads toward their goal (whether learning or getting good grades), then expectancies are likely to rise. This would appear to say that success will tend to increase motivation, but matters are not that simple. This argument considers potential motivation and ignores motivational arousal. Motivational arousal or initiation of motivation is likely based on a person's assumption of how much effort is needed to perform an activity correctly. Studies indicate that motivational arousal is greatest for tasks that are assumed to be of

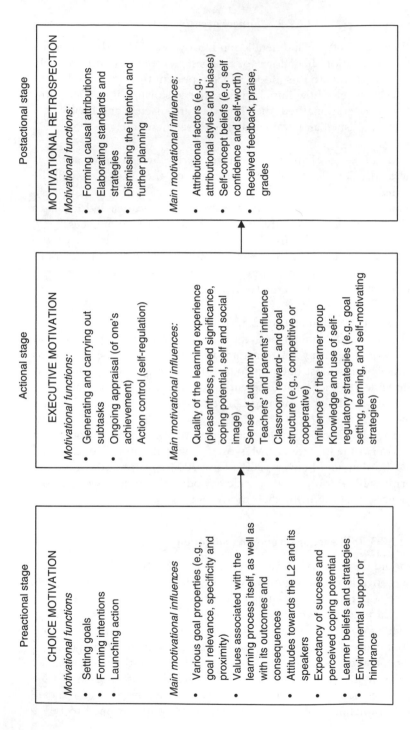

Preactional stage

Actional stage

Postactional stage

CHOICE MOTIVATION

Motivational functions:

- Setting goals
- Forming intentions
- Launching action

Main motivational influences

- Various goal properties (e.g., goal relevance, specificity and proximity)
- Values associated with the learning process itself, as well as with its outcomes and consequences
- Attitudes towards the L2 and its speakers
- Expectancy of success and perceived coping potential
- Learner beliefs and strategies
- Environmental support or hindrance

EXECUTIVE MOTIVATION

Motivational functions:

- Generating and carrying out subtasks
- Ongoing appraisal (of one's achievement)
- Action control (self-regulation)

Main motivational influences:

- Quality of the learning experience (pleasantness, need significance, coping potential, self and social image)
- Sense of autonomy
- Teachers' and parents' influence
- Classroom reward- and goal structure (e.g., competitive or cooperative)
- Influence of the learner group
- Knowledge and use of self-regulatory strategies (e.g., goal setting, learning, and self-motivating strategies)

MOTIVATIONAL RETROSPECTION

Motivational functions:

- Forming causal attributions
- Elaborating standards and strategies
- Dismissing the intention and further planning

Main motivational influences:

- Attributional factors (e.g., attributional styles and biases)
- Self-concept beliefs (e.g. self confidence and self-worth)
- Received feedback, praise, grades

Figure 12.5 A process model of L2 motivation.

Source: © 2005. From *The Psychology of the Language Learner: Individual Differences in Second Language Acquisition* by Z. Dörnyei. Reproduced by permission of Lawrence Erlbaum Associates, a division of Taylor & Francis Group.

moderate difficulty (see the discussion in Brehm and Self, 1989). If the success rate is considered very high or very low, motivational arousal is weakened. In other words, we try hardest for things we consider challenging but not nearly impossible.

If all of this is still true for language learning, then there is no reason to believe that good grades or good progress in language learning will lead to greater motivation. To the contrary, one may assume that the learners that do the best will find the tasks easy and as a result their motivational intensity should weaken.

Does success lead to better performance? There are different results presented in the literature. Moreover, a plausible argument can be made for either direction. Success can breed confidence, which results in greater success. On the other hand, success can breed overconfidence, which sets one up for a fall. Mizruchi (1991) provided interesting data on this question. Consider the following:

> The extent to which confidence and motivation affect task performance is a controversial issue among social psychologists. Although most participants believe that prior success breeds present success, many researchers have found no effect of prior performance on current performance. Contrary to the conventional view, I argue that in team competition, prior success breeds failure in current task performance because it decreases the necessity of success. Conversely, I suggest that prior failure breeds current success because it increases the urgency of success. I test this argument with data on playoff games between professional basketball teams from 1947 through 1982. Controlling for the advantage accruing to the home team as well as for the relative strength of the teams, I find that in back-to-back games at the same site, teams that won the previous game are more likely to lose the current game.
>
> (p. 181)

No one would suggest that competition between National Basketball Association teams is exactly analogous to second language learning situations, but this study provides further reason to doubt the automatic assumption that prior success leads to current or future success.

There is little research on what Dörnyei refers to as *demotivation*, which is "specific external forces that reduce or diminish the motivational basis of a behavioral intention or an ongoing action" (2001b, p. 143). What he means by this is that the positive motivations that were initially present when a choice was made to undertake some activity were diminished by some negative factor, very often some classroom experience, most

431

notably a teacher. Dörnyei (2005) cites Ushioda (2003, pp. 93–94) to illustrate this point.

> The inevitable problems in classroom motivation arise when there is not a happy fusion between internal and external forces but a negative tension, where the latter dominate at the expense of the former. In other words, individual motivation becomes controlled, suppressed or distorted by external forces . . . [t]his may happen through negative influences in the classroom social dynamic, or through regulating forces in the educational system . . . Collective motivation can all too easily become collective demotivation, boredom, or at the far end of the spectrum, collective dissatisfaction or rebellion, often in the form of class-room counter-cultures defined by rejection of educational aims and values.

As stated earlier, any discussion of attitude, aptitude, or motivation cannot be considered in the abstract; how they relate to individuals depends on that individual's makeup. This is where issues of learning style enter into the picture.

12.8 Personality and learning style

The term *learning style* refers in broad terms to the preferences that an individual has of obtaining, processing, and retaining information. In other words, how do individuals approach the task of learning? The term *learning style* is often used interchangeably with *personality*, although the former is undoubtedly more variable, whereas the latter refers to a stable trait of an individual (see review of learning style research in educational psychology research in Coffield, Moseley, Hall, and Ecclestone, 2004). Constructs that some refer to as a learning style, others refer to as part of personality. Unfortunately, there has not been much effort to separate these.

Personality research, which is related to learning styles, has a long tradition in psychology, with many of the common types being discussed by Jung. There are even discussions of personality in Aristotle. Certain types have been the focus of considerable research, such as types measured on the standard Myers-Briggs Type Indicator, based on research conducted in the 1950s and 1960s. Nevertheless, there is no theoretical limit to the number of personality types, as a psychologist could provide a new test to delineate new types at any time.

12.8.1 Extroversion and introversion

The stereotype of an introvert is someone who is much happier with a book than with other people. The stereotype of the extrovert is the opposite: someone happier with people than with a book. These stereotypes have implications for second language learning success, but the implications are somewhat contradictory. We might expect the introvert to do better in school. This has been borne out in research. For example, Skehan (1989) cited studies of British undergraduates showing a correlation of 0.25 between introversion and academic success. Nonetheless, the gregariousness associated with extroverts would suggest that they would engage in more talking and social activity in a second language and would thus learn the language better (see chapter 10). Hence, there are good reasons to think that both extroversion and introversion lead to success in second language learning, although in different ways.

Research data do not resolve this quandary. Evidence has been given in support of the advantages of both extroversion and introversion. It is probable that there is no correct global answer. The likely solution is that extroversion is beneficial for certain tasks and certain methods of language teaching, whereas introversion is beneficial for others. The task of researchers is to determine what the precise patterns are.

12.8.2 Risk taking

It has been suggested that a tendency to take risks is associated with success in second language learning. Risk taking has been defined as "a situation where an individual has to make a decision involving choice between alternatives of different desirability; the outcome of the choice is uncertain; there is a possibility of failure" (Beebe, 1983, p. 39). As we see later in the discussion of language-learning strategies, many of the strategies associated with good language learners involve a willingness to take risks.

Beebe (1983) presented data from Puerto Rican bilingual (Spanish–English) children. The children were interviewed on four occasions, once by a monolingual English interviewer, once by a bilingual (Spanish dominant) interviewer, once by a bilingual (English dominant) interviewer, and once by all three interviewers (in groups of three children). Beebe operationally defined risk taking in terms of a number of factors, among them, number of attempts to use particular grammatical structures, avoidance, amount of talk, and amount of information volunteering. The results showed that risk taking was greatest with the monolingual interviewer. This suggests that learners' willingness to take risks may depend on the situation, not just on their general type.

Ely (1986) found a correlation between risk-taking tendencies and classroom participation, but the relationship with actual success was relatively weak. This reinforces the idea that personality affects language learning in a much more local manner, helping on specific tasks but not necessarily affecting longer-term success.

To say that an individual is a risk taker is to say that she or he generally is more willing to take risks than the average person. Thus, risk taking should be based on a background of general behavior. For this reason, the important work of Kahneman, Slovic, and Tversky (1982) cannot be ignored. They found that individuals are generally risk-averse when contemplating a gain, but risk-seeking when contemplating a loss. To give common examples, if we have an opportunity to make a financial gain, we generally prefer conservative, but safer, investments. If we are threatened with a loss, we are much more willing to undertake risky actions that could ameliorate our losses if successful.

It is important to recognize that gain and loss are subjectively determined, not necessarily objective. Kahneman, Slovic, and Tversky (1982) determined that the same objective situation could be presented to subjects as either a gain or a loss. They described this as a framing problem. They found that when the situation was framed as a gain, subjects were generally risk-averse, but when it was framed as a loss, they were risk-seeking. Thus, a risk taker should undertake relatively riskier activities in either situation, but this personality trait is not necessarily more important than the framing. What we would need to know in studies of second language learning is whether the learners frame their situations in terms of gain or loss. For example, imagine that a student is called on in a language class. If the student believes that there is the chance of getting a poor grade (a loss), she may try almost anything. If she looks upon this as a chance of getting extra credit (a gain), he or she may be much more conservative. The student's evaluation of the situation (i.e., its potential outcome) may be much more important than the student's general personality trait for taking risks. It is important to consider that two learners faced with the same situation may frame the situation differently, one as a gain and the other as a loss.

12.8.3 Field independence/dependence

Field independence has its origins in visual perception. It distinguishes individuals dichotomously as to whether or not they are dependent on a prevailing visual field. If an individual is dependent on the prevailing visual, she or he cannot see something right in front of them. On the other hand, those who are field-independent are better able to notice details outside of the prevailing visual object and are not dependent on that object. Some individuals are better at finding objects in the middle

434

of clutter (field-independent), whereas others (field-dependent) cannot see things that may be obvious to those with a field-independent orientation. In other words, the "field" (surroundings) gets in the way of field-dependent individuals. In a review of the literature, Johnson, Prior, and Artuso (2000) report that field independents are, in general, better at performing cognitive tasks, but Chapelle (1995) pointed out that those who are field-dependent have an orientation that might be deemed more interpersonal and more sensitive to the social context. This would certainly have importance for their differential role in interaction studies. It would be predicted that field-dependent individuals would be more sensitive to implicit feedback than field-independent individuals and would, as a result, benefit more from interactions.

A common thread that runs through most of the senses of field independence is that the field-independent person tends to be highly analytic, ignoring potentially confusing information in the context (this is the inspiration for the term itself), and self-reliant. The field-dependent person, on the other hand, tends to pay great attention to context. These patterns are apparently robust over many different tasks and hence may be considered a personality trait.

Given this background, predictions can be made about the effects of this personality trait on second language learning. Logically, one might expect that field-independent individuals would be better at analytical tasks in second language learning. This would appear to be an advantage. On the other hand, field dependence would seem to help in social interactions. Linguists have often argued that the context provides much of the meaning that is missing in just the actual linguistic text itself. If field-dependent individuals pay more attention to the context, then this would seem to aid in context-dependent tasks.

Some studies reported correlations in the expected directions. Others found little support for a relationship at all. Skehan (1989, pp. 114–115) summarized:

> We have to conclude, therefore, that the studies that have been conducted into the relationship of field-independence and language learning success, which have between them covered a wide range of subject types and instructional conditions, have demonstrated, at best, a weak relationship, and often, no relationship at all. Worse, there are strong grounds for believing that field-independence only works when it is a disguised measure of intelligence, and it is the intelligence component of the test that accounts for the result. Interesting though the underlying hypothesis may be, the research results are not encouraging. Field-independence looks to be a seam which has been mined for all the value that is going to be found.

Chapelle and Green (1992) reopened the debate, suggesting that these earlier studies neither examined field independence in the right light nor looked at the most relevant aspects of second language learning. With regard to the first point, they reinterpreted the results of the most common test for field independence used in second language acquisition research, the Embedded Figures Test. In this test, participants are asked to find simple geometrical figures embedded within a more complex background. Those who do better are deemed field-independent. As Chapelle and Green rightly note, this measures ability as well as style. We cannot say for sure whether those who perform poorly did so because they used the wrong strategy or because they were not very good at using a reasonable strategy. Chapelle and Green argued that individuals who performed better on the test demonstrated fluid ability, which the authors described as abilities that are independent of any content area.

They further suggested that fluid ability is a significant factor in language aptitude. More precisely, they suggested that Skehan's (1989) language analytic ability (discussed in section 12.6) be divided into two: language analytic ability and general analytic ability. Language analytic ability is gained by linguistic experience in one's native language, in foreign languages, or in linguistics. General analytic ability is independent of experience. Chapelle and Green suggested that general analytic ability is correlated with fluid ability. This ability comes into play when learners are faced with a task for which they have no relevant linguistic experience. Chapelle and Green suggested that language analytic ability comes into play in learning related languages and general analytic ability comes into play in learning unrelated languages. This suggests empirical tests. Are those who are best at learning an unrelated language necessarily those who are best at learning related languages? If they are, then there is little empirical basis for stating that there are two fundamentally different analytic abilities involved.

There is another reasonable perspective that can be taken on the issue of field independence. If the measures, such as the Embedded Figures Test, do not really measure a style but an ability, then it might be best to dismiss the whole notion as theoretically flawed and unusable for second language acquisition research. This is the approach suggested by Griffiths and Sheen (1992).

One final point relates this construct to general intelligence. If field independents are better at performing cognitive tasks, then is this measure a disguised measure of intelligence, as Dörnyei and Skehan (2003) point out? In fact, in a report by Sternberg and Grigorenko (2001), it appears that field independence correlated with various aspects of intelligence, leading them to claim that " . . . the preponderance of evidence at this point suggests that field independence is tantamount to fluid intelligence" (p. 7).

To summarize, there is no evidence for any personality trait that predicts overall success in second language learning. Certain personality traits appear helpful in completing certain tasks that may play a role in second language learning. Thus, the value of the trait to the learner depends on how important the facilitated tasks may be. This depends on the teaching methods the student is subjected to (assuming formal instruction) and the particular way the student goes about learning another language. Personality is perhaps better investigated within the context of the contributions learners, teachers, methods, and materials make to the learning situation.

12.8.4 Visual/auditory/kinesthetic

We are all familiar with the commonly held belief that some individuals are visual learners and some are oral learners. How do learners best take information in? Through listening to a passage? Through a teacher writing on the blackboard?

Most successful learners use a variety of modalities in learning, as would be expected. In this way they can accommodate to the various modes in which incoming information is processed.

Visual learners are those who take in information visually. Thus, reading is preferred to listening. Blackboard use or PowerPoint presentations are preferred to straight lectures. They might rewrite lecture notes using color codings or other visual organizational schema. Auditory learners are those who prefer to take in information auditorily. They prefer listening to reading. Lectures are an effective means of absorbing information. They prefer to talk through material and even to have text read out loud. Kinesthetic (or even tactile) learners are better when the whole body is involved or when objects can be manipulated, such as in lab work. For kinesthetic learners, movement is a key issue and frequent breaks are necessary, as is moving while repeating/memorizing information important.

12.8.5 Obtaining learning style information

There are a number of extant surveys for assessment of learning styles (e.g., Ehrman and Leaver Learning Style, which has 10 subdimensions; Ehrman and Leaver, 2003; Ehrman, 2001; Leaver, Ehrman, and Shekhtman, 2005; Perceptual Learning Style Preference Questionnaire, Reid, 1995; Oxford's Style Analysis Survey, 1993; Cohen, Oxford, and Chi's Learning Style Survey, 2001). Below we take examples from these surveys to demonstrate some of the constructs that have been discussed above.

Extroversion and introversion

Wherever I go, I develop personal contacts. (Oxford, 1993)

In a large group, I tend to keep silent. (Oxford, 1993)

I learn better when I work or study with others than by myself. (Cohen, Oxford, and Chi, 2001)

I meet new people easily by jumping into the conversation. (Cohen, Oxford, and Chi, 2001)

Risk taking

I make lists of things I need to do. (Oxford, 1993)

I like to just let things happen, not plan them. (Oxford, 1993)

I like to be certain about what things mean in a target language. (Cohen, Oxford, and Chi, 2001)

I like to know how rules are applied and why. (Cohen, Oxford, and Chi, 2001)

Field independence/dependence

I not only attend to grammar but check for appropriate level of formality and politeness. (Cohen, Oxford, and Chi, 2001)

It is a challenge for me to both focus on communication in speech or writing while at the same time paying attention to grammatical agreement (e.g., person, number, tense, or gender). (Cohen, Oxford, and Chi, 2001)

When working with new material with additional subject matter around it, I comfortably find and use what is most important. I also like out-of-context material like grammar rules. You could say I make a lot of use of a spotlight to learn. (Ehrman and Leaver, 2003)

When there is a lot of information that comes with what I need to learn, it's hard to tell what's most important. It all seems to fall together sometimes, and it's hard work to sort things out. (Ehrman and Leaver, 2003)

Modality

I learn more by reading textbooks than by listening to others. (Reid, 1995)

I learn better in class when the teacher gives a lecture. (Reid, 1995)

When I do things in class, I learn better. (Reid, 1995)

I enjoy making something for a class project. (Reid, 1995)

12.9 Learning strategies[6]

A common observation is that not only are some language learners more successful than others, but also that good language learners sometimes do different things than poorer language learners. The term commonly used in the second language acquisition literature to refer to what learners do that underlies these differences is *learning strategies*. This is a difficult area, since, as with other approaches to second language acquisition, language learning and language use are intricately tied together. Selinker (1972) finds that the endorsement for the separation, in principle, of language-learning strategies and communication strategies is laid out, with both being postulated as basic processes leading to the formation of inter-language, though they are not always easy to disentangle.[7] The centrality of the intersection of structure and strategy use is still robust and can be used as a springboard to integrate the formation of second language knowledge with strategic use of structural information on the part of learners.

We begin with a definition. Cohen (1998, p. 4) defines language learning (and language use) strategies as:

> those processes which are consciously selected by learners and which may result in action taken to enhance the learning or use of a second or foreign language, through the storage, retention, recall, and application of information about that language.

Cohen went on to say that such strategies:

> include strategies for identifying the material that needs to be learned, distinguishing it from other material if need be, group-ing it for easier learning (e.g., grouping vocabulary by category into nouns, verbs, adjectives, adverbs, and so forth), having repeated contact with the material (e.g., through classroom tasks or the completion of homework assignments), and formally committing the material to memory when it does not seem to be acquired naturally (whether through rote memory techniques such as repetition, the use of mnemonics, or some other memory technique).
>
> (p. 5)

In a similar vein, Oxford (1999) refers to learning strategies as:

> Specific actions, behaviors, steps, or techniques that students use to improve their own progress in developing skills in a second or foreign language.
>
> (p. 518)

For example, in order to remember difficult vocabulary, you may consciously choose to associate a particular word with the situation in which you first seriously noticed that word. You would probably continue to do this if it turned out that this strategy of "first serious notice" did in fact consistently help you learn vocabulary. Another example comes from the area of interlanguage transfer (chapter 5). Suppose a native speaker of English has learned Spanish to a proficient degree and then started to learn Italian. While doing so, he or she substitutes Spanish words for his or her attempted Italian (e.g., *cómo* for the intended *come* "how, what," *por qué/porque* for the intended *perché*, "why, because," and, to take a common phonetic example, [s] for intended [z], [kasa] for intended [kaza]). It turns out to be difficult for her to eradicate these substitutions. Let's assume that this individual has a strong visual memory and during class exercises refers to a visual chart with the correct forms. The first learner is using a language-learning strategy and the second a language use strategy.[8] In this section, we concentrate on learning strategies.

Learning strategies clearly involve internal mental actions, but they may also involve physical actions as well. The claims made in the literature involve potential improvements in language learning related to the selection of information from the input and the organization and integration of it in terms of learner systems. The ways in which information is selected from the input are an important part of the concept.

Some characterizations of learning strategies include such notions as effortful, goal-directed, intentional (see Weinstein, Husman, and Dierking, 2000; Macaro, 2001). But perhaps the most useful way of thinking of strategic learning is in terms of a larger goal (learning a set of vocabulary items) and the steps that one might take to achieve that goal (tactical steps); for example, putting them on cards, coloring them, visualizing, etc. Thus, strategic learning involves an overall goal (become proficient in a second language), a plan to accomplish that goal (learn 10 vocabulary words a day), and the steps needed to achieve the goal (coloring, flashcards).

By now there are useful lists in the literature of learning strategies (summarized in O'Malley and Chamot, 1990). The categories include such phenomena as clarification, verification, analyzing, monitoring, memorizing, guessing, deductive versus inductive reasoning, emphasizing one thing over another, and practice and production "tricks." O'Malley and Chamot attempted to establish a foundation for placing the research on learning strategies in a cognitive context.

Recent research in this area is conducted under the auspices of an organization with the acronym IPOLLS (International Project on Language Learner Strategies). Current issues discussed by researchers in the area relate to:

- defining learning and other related strategies in terms of what actually constitutes a strategy and why it is so hard to define these
- relating such strategies to not only the short-term goals of learners but their long-term goals as well
- relating such strategies to individual differences versus what one might find out about group use in various situations. (cf. Cohen and Macaro, 2007 for discussion)

In the research agenda of this organization is an attempt to bridge the gap between psychological and sociocultural perspectives on L2 learner strategies and between the role of individual versus group differences. In the words of the editors, the goal is to produce interface work, with "cognitive and metacognitive processes involved in producing meaning within the limitations offered by the learner's interlanguage" (Cohen and Macaro, 2007, Introduction).

One recent proposal relates strategies to working memory, where strategies are conceived of as literally occurring in working memory (chapter 8) and are related, especially, to a broader framework of cognition, for example, strategic planning. An interesting proposal relates the results from using strategies in a chain or in a cluster to their success at given language tasks. Such strategies would form parts of clusters or combinations and the whole becomes greater than the sum of the parts through the role of metacognition, which orchestrates the parts and makes the combination effective.

Cohen and Macaro (2007) state that "there is general agreement that 'strategies' are environment-dependent . . . and/or task dependent . . ." This is a view of strategies that adds empirical support to the discourse domains view of interlanguage discussed earlier in chapter 9 (Selinker and Douglas, 1985; Douglas, 2000) that claims that important processes of learning work according to discourse domains.

Research in this area has considered strategic learning in terms of the pragmatics of speech acts, the practical goal being to provide "support" for learners who are acquiring pragmatic ability, "by providing them with strategies for enhancing how they learn and use speech acts" (Cohen, 2005, p. 296). In order to "support learners," one first has to understand them and their strategies from a research point of view and then assess whether what they have been taught in terms of learning strategies actually works. Here, L2 pragmatics is viewed from a learner perspective in terms of the learning and performance of pragmatics, focusing on learners approaching the norms of an L2 speech community in terms of a number of relationships concerning strategies and metacognition, aptitude, and motivation.

However, the field is not without its problems, for this is indeed a difficult area to be clear about;[9] in fact, Oxford and Cohen (1992, p. 3) stated "from the profusion of studies recently devoted to learning strategies . . . one might believe that this research area is fully coherent. However, this coherence is something of an illusion." They then went on to list and discuss "serious conceptual and classificatory problems" that exist in this area. Among them are the problems of the criteria used for classifying language-learning strategies, whether such strategies are conscious or unconscious, the relationship to learning styles, and the difficulty of showing what contributes to language learning. More recently, McDonough (1999) has echoed this concern. In listing six ways of conducting research on strategies, he stated that "none of these methods is without problems, and there is always a danger that method predetermines the kind of results obtained" (p. 3). However, McDonough is hopeful that the triangulation of various data sources is indeed a way out and can "provide stabilization of the data and interpretive clarity in particular studies" (p. 3).

Bialystok (1990a), in a detailed critique of this area, pointed out that it is difficult in practice to distinguish as strategic those learner behaviors that are clearly (a) concerned with problematic tasks, (b) conscious or unconscious, and (c) intentional or unintentional. Cohen (1998) took on such criticisms and claimed that strategies do not have to be directly associated with "problematic tasks" in that learners may very well be using their strategy preferences in all or most of their learning. Cohen is more positive about overcoming methodological difficulties, stating that one can devise "various kinds of verbal report tasks to determine the nature of the task for the learner (problematic or not), conscious or unconscious, intentional or unintentional" (Cohen, personal communication) (see Cohen, 1998; Gass and Mackey, 2000, for ways one can go about gathering verbal reports).

In this field, there has traditionally been a conceptual division between so-called good language learners and poor or poorer language learners, the idea being that if we can discover what the good language learner does, we can teach those strategies to poorer language learners so that they will improve (Rubin, 1975; Naiman, Fröhlich, Stern, and Todesco, 1978) (cf. Chamot, Barnhardt, El-Dinary, and Robbins, 1999; Cohen, 1998; Harris, 2003; Macaro, 2001; McDonough, 1999, for summaries of strategy training). Such a strict dichotomy is most likely too simplistic. It is more likely that language learners have personal "style preferences" as well as personal "strategy preferences" (e.g., Cohen, 1998; Lightbown and Spada, 2006; McDonough, 1999). Thus, we have to ask: Does the teaching of learning strategies[10] that appear to work for better language learners help the poorer ones? Or, if we do not accept this dichotomy, we can pose the question as to whether metacognitive awareness of the processes of strategizing and (self-reports thereof) and the increased use of strategies make a positive difference in language learning.

To delve into these questions deeper, one must consider and evaluate the researcher's sources of information about claimed learning strategies (cf. also Macaro, 2001). It turns out that the most common sources of information are observations, verbal self-reports, or online protocols (often referred to as think-aloud protocols). Self-reports have weaknesses (see Gass and Mackey, 2000). If learners in a study are asked to give examples of strategies they use, they are likely to mention things that (a) help with difficult tasks, (b) are conscious (at least in retrospect), and (c) seem intentional (again in retrospect), all of which may bias the information given. Also, concerning observation, there are weaknesses, given that it is difficult, though perhaps not impossible, to observe mental behavior of learners. In the end, a researcher may be forced to accept only reported behavior as strategic if it seems intentional, whereas the most important strategies may in fact not be so, and this is all the more reason that reported information must be presented in as accurate and detailed a way as possible.

One clear problem with some of the early examples of learning strategy research is that not all behavior can be accepted as strategic. For instance, Rubin (1975, p. 45) maintained that good language learners are "willing and accurate guesser[s]." This may accurately characterize the learners who were looked at, but it may not be strategic. First of all, a reasonable strategy might be "guess," but "be willing to guess" is problematic as a strategy. More problematic still is the attribution of accuracy. "Guess accurately" cannot be a strategy but a goal, although "willingness to guess" may be part of an individual's learning style preference and, if so, learners could be taught ways in which to maximize the use of that preference, such as how to guess better using context. Though, again, the learning success of such behavior is open to question and its relationship to improved interlanguage output must be researched given individual differences in interlanguage learner outcomes, as emphasized throughout this chapter.

Another problem area is that good or better language learners may self-report actions that all language learners in fact undertake, but only the good learners are somehow aware of. We can only say that these actions are differentiating if it can be shown that poor learners do not use them. Some studies neglect poor learners entirely. Those studies that do not include poor learners cannot then be used to say that poor learners do not do the same things that so-called good language learners do. It is to be noted, however, that sometimes it is difficult methodologically to compare good and poorer language learners. As Skehan (1989) argued, poor learners may be lacking the verbal skills to report what they do as readily as good learners can. If so, then differences in reporting skills may be misinterpreted by analysts as differences in strategies used.

Directionality is also a problem with learning strategies (cf. Skehan,

1989). Good learners may do certain things because they have the prerequisite abilities to do so. Even if poor learners tried to do these things, they may not be able to and might have to improve their second language skills before they could use these strategies. If so, then one could make the interesting claim that language-learning success causes the use of the strategy, in the sense that successful learning allows for the use of the strategy.

Finally, we return to the point made at the beginning of this section that some language learners seem better than others at learning languages and that the better ones sometimes do different things than poorer language learners. It is important to stress in understanding this area that, suppose we can show that better language learners do X, that this X is strategic, and that X in fact does contribute to their language learning. Logically, it does not follow that if X is then taught to a poor language learner, it will *necessarily* lead to language improvement. It is not impossible, of course, that the teaching of that X may in fact lead to language improvement. But the point is that it does not logically follow that it necessarily will and it must be shown empirically that it does. One way forward is to create procedures that would help individual learners find out (a) if they are better at some language learning tasks than others and, if so, in what contexts; (b) exactly what they do to help them succeed in these particular tasks; and (c) how such strategies relate to changes (and nonchanges) in their own interlanguages. This would then help to continue to shift the focus from an absolute emphasis on "good" versus "bad" for particular learners to both good *and* bad language learners, where the emphasis is on self-discovery to determine in which tasks and in which contexts using which strategies the individual learner is successful. In other words, a key is to create self-efficacy in learners.

McDonough (1999, p. 17) lists among his conclusions that the teaching of strategies "is not universally successful," though some success in some contexts has been reported. The serious claims to be further investigated are that the awareness of strategizing and the increased use of strategies through direct teaching improve language learning for particular learners in clear unambiguous ways. This must mean, at the least, an understanding of how specific strategies for specific individuals aid in the incorporation of specific target language linguistic features into the second language system—and not only incorporation of said linguistic features into the short-term system but, more importantly, incorporation of said linguistic features into one's long-term system. Unfortunately, there appears to be no longitudinal research of this sort. A next obvious step in the evolution of the research paradigm would be the undertaking of longitudinal studies that attempt to link learning strategies, which are thought to be helpful to an individual, to the L2 output these individuals produce. This could create a clear link to individual changes and non-changes in the underlying L2 system over time, becoming a key metric in which to judge the validity of strategy use.

In sum, recent efforts at organizing thought in this area of SLA research appear particularly promising in helping us understand the central question in SLA of how learners strategically use linguistic information to form and restructure their second language grammars. These various interfaces are in need of longitudinal studies.

12.10 Conclusion

Second language acquisition is complex, being influenced by many factors, both linguistic and nonlinguistic. This chapter has dealt with a number of areas that fall outside of the domain of language-related variables but that impact the acquisition of a second language. In the next chapter, we turn to a central part of the acquisition of a language—that of vocabulary acquisition.

Suggestions for additional reading

Communication Strategies. Ellen Bialystok. Basil Blackwell (1990).

Second Language Acquisition and the Critical Period Hypothesis. David Birdsong (Ed.). Lawrence Erlbaum Associates (1999).

Strategies in Learning and Using A Second Language. Andrew Cohen. Longman (1998).

Language Learner Strategies: Thirty Years of Research and Practice. Andrew Cohen and Ernesto Macaro (Eds.). Oxford University Press (2007).

The Psychology of the Language Learner: Individual Differences in Second Language Acquisition. Zoltán Dörnyei. Lawrence Erlbaum Associates (2005).

Motivation and Second Language Acquisition. Zoltán Dörnyei and Richard Schmidt (Eds.). University of Hawai'i Press (2001).

Fossilization in Adult Second Language Acquisition. ZhaoHong Han. Multilingual Matters (2004).

Communication Strategies: Psycholinguistic and Sociolinguistic Perspectives. Gabriele Kasper and Eric Kellerman. Longman (1997).

Ultimate Attainment in Second Language Acquisition: A Case Study. Donna Lardiere. Lawrence Erlbaum Associates (2007).

Learning Strategies in Second Language Acquisition. J. Michael O'Malley and Anna Chamot. Cambridge University Press (1990).

A Time to Speak: A Psycholinguistic Inquiry into the Critical Period for Human Speech. Tom Scovel. Newbury House (1988).

Learning New Languages: A Guide to Second Language Acquisition. Thomas Scovel. Heinle and Heinle (2001).

Individual Differences in Second-Language Learning. Peter Skehan. Edward Arnold (1989).

Points for discussion

1   It is a basic premise in SLA that some individuals are more successful at learning second languages than others. Specifically, how might differential language-learning success relate to child language acquisition of various kinds: monolingual, simultaneous bilingual, and consecutive bilingual?

2   From your own experience, do you agree that adults in learning a second language have differential success than children in learning a first language? In learning a second? How would you set up an experiment to deal with these questions?

3   Consider the term *individual differences*. What does this notion mean to you? Ask yourself in this light what it means to belong to a particular society or culture. Does everything that you see in an individual belong to that individual or do some things belong to one culture or another? How would you investigate this issue?

4   Consider *age* as a factor in language learning and our conclusion that there is no dispute that age may make a significant difference in language learning, but that the dispute, where it exists, is about the reasons. How would this point relate to other variables discussed, such as aptitude, motivation, personality, and cognitive strategies?

5   Now consider the notion *ability* in language learning. How does ability play a role in accounting for final SLA outcomes?

6   How would your answer differ if *aptitude* were substituted for ability in problem 5? In considering aptitude, how would we account for the uniform success of children in learning a first language?

7   How can we find valid measures of language aptitude, language ability, motivation, and personality characteristics? If there is always some difficulty and controversy over these measures, will we ever be able to put the entire picture of SLA into one coherent framework? If so, how?

8   In this chapter we discussed the concept of *differential success rates*. We can use a measure that is easy to obtain: course grades. What do you think of this measure, especially related to the statement that success in getting good grades in language learning is not necessarily equal to "really learning" a second language? What do you think of the conclusion that success in getting good grades in a foreign language classroom correlates well with getting good grades in any subject?

9   Is it possible that some people might be better able to learn a closely related second language, whereas others might be better able to learn an unrelated second language? If this is the case, why might this be so?

10   Do you believe that there is a difference between learning to use the syntax of a second language correctly and learning to pronounce a

second language correctly? What might the source of those differences be? Do you think that one or the other is easier to teach? Or easier to learn through instruction?

11 If personality types can affect one's ability to learn a second language, what implications might there be for teaching? That is, would learning be more successful if like learners were put in a classroom with a like teacher and a conducive methodology (e.g., one that requires significant analysis)? Why or why not?

12 If we know what the characteristics are of a good language learner, and if we know what strategies good language learners use, does it follow that teaching so-called poor language learners to use these same strategies will result in their successful language learning? Why or why not?

13 Look up the dictionary definition of the word *strategy*. Does the definition(s) you found seem appropriate to the discussion on learning strategies?

14 Concerning the difficulties of being clear about learning strategies, consider an analogy from basketball. Imagine a National Basketball Association player who always does the following when he goes to the free-throw line: pulls on his shorts, crosses himself, breathes deeply, flexes his knees, looks at the back of the rim, and shoots. Which of these behaviors are strategic and how would you decide? For example, is tugging at the shorts habitual behavior or strategic? Suppose that all coaches tell their players that breathing deeply, flexing one's knees, and looking at the back of the rim can aid in improving accuracy. Could it then be called strategic? Where does automatic behavior fit in? What about superstition? Does the notion of belief fit in? That is, what if the player believes that crossing himself increases his odds? Does it then become strategic? Now take this analogy and relate it to potential improvement in second language performance through the use of learning strategies.

15 a. Krashen accounted for incomplete knowledge of the second language by means of the Affective Filter. In chapters 4 and 5 we discussed the issue of transfer. How would transfer be dealt with in Krashen's model, or is there no room for it given the ability of the Affective Filter to "explain" incomplete knowledge? If you adopt this latter view, how can you account for the many documented cases of NL influence, particularly those of the more subtle variety that have been discussed in earlier chapters?

   b. Krashen suggested that the Affective Filter is not present or is not operative in young children. Do you agree with this claim? Can it be used to account for child–adult differences? Why or why not?

16 Do you agree that there exists an "affective filter" that prevents input

from getting through? What type of evidence might be used to justify its existence?

17 Consider Dörnyei's characterization of the stages of motivation. Think of an experience that you have had with language learning. Can you identify with the stages that he proposed? Be specific with your examples.

18 Take the Cohen, Oxford, and Chi (2001) Learning Style Survey (http://www.carla.umn.edu/about/profiles/CohenPapers/LearningStyles-Survey.pdf)—retrieved 3/9/07.

Before taking the survey, consider the categories of that survey:

> How I use my physical senses
> How I expose myself to learning situations
> How I handle possibilities
> How I deal with ambiguity and with deadlines
> How I receive information
> How I further process information
> How I commit material to memory
> How I deal with language rules
> How I deal with multiple inputs
> How I deal with response time
> How literally I take reality

How would you characterize yourself along these dimensions? Now take the survey. Do your results coincide with your predictions? Why or why not?

See GSS, problems 3.5 and 3.6.

13

THE LEXICON

13.1 The significance of the lexicon

In SLA research to date, there has been much less attention paid to the lexicon than to other parts of language, although this picture is quickly changing (see Nation, 2001; Singleton, 1999; Bogaards and Laufer, 2004). However, there are numerous reasons for believing that lexis is important in second language acquisition. In fact, the lexicon may be the most important language component for learners.

Of all error types, learners consider vocabulary errors the most serious (Politzer, 1978, as cited in Levenston, 1979, p. 147). Additionally, large corpora of errors consistently indicate that lexical errors are the most common among second language learners. Meara (1984, p. 229) cited Blaas (1982) as indicating that lexical errors outnumbered grammatical errors by 3:1 in one corpus. Moreover, native speakers find lexical errors to be more disruptive than grammatical errors (Johansson, 1978, as cited in Meara, 1984, p. 229). Gass (1988b) seconded this argument, noting that grammatical errors generally result in structures that are understood, whereas lexical errors may interfere with communication. As an example, consider 13-1. The listener may notice an error in 13-1 and may infer that the speaker is nonnative, but still would probably understand what was intended.

(13-1) Can you tell me where is the train station?

On the other hand, consider an error cited by Gairns and Redman (1986, p. 3):

(13-2) I feel sorry for people who live in the suburbs.

Presumably, the typical native speaker of English who heard this would wonder what the speaker felt was wrong with suburbs; perhaps they are too stilted and boring. Gairns and Redman argued that this utterance, made by a native speaker of Spanish, was presumably motivated by the Spanish "false friend" *suburbio* meaning "slum quarter, shantytown." The average English native speaker would misunderstand the sentence and never consider that the speaker had chosen the incorrect lexical item.

As pointed out in chapter 6, many linguistic theories place the lexicon in a central place, which also suggests its importance in language learning. Levelt (1989, p. 181) maintained that the lexicon is the driving force in sentence production (i.e., in encoding or sentence generation), which he described as a formulation process:

> . . . formulation processes are lexically driven. This means that grammatical and phonological encodings are mediated by lexical entries. The preverbal message triggers lexical items into activity. The syntactic, morphological, and phonological properties of an activated lexical item trigger, in turn, the grammatical, morphological and phonological encoding procedures underlying the generation of an utterance. The assumption that the lexicon is an essential mediator between conceptualization and grammatical and phonological encoding will be called the *lexical hypothesis*. The lexical hypothesis entails, in particular, that nothing in the speaker's message will *by itself* trigger a syntactic form, such as a passive or a dative construction. There must be mediating lexical items, triggered by the message, which by their grammatical properties and their order of activation cause the Grammatical Encoder to generate a particular syntactic structure.

Levelt was referring to production by competent, adult native speakers. In general, there is good reason to believe that the lexicon is an important factor, if not the most important factor, in accounting for the bulk of second language data, in that the lexicon drives language production.

The lexicon is also important in comprehension, especially oral comprehension, as Altmann (1990) showed in her overview of sentence comprehension. Lexical information is clearly used in helping to determine syntactic relationships. Comprehension is undoubtedly of great importance to second language acquisition. If words cannot be isolated from the speech stream and if lexical information cannot be used to interpret the utterances, the input will not be comprehended. Thus, comprehension of the input depends to a large extent on lexical skills (see section 13.5). The lexicon is also important in reading, but in the vast bulk of the world's orthographies the writing system itself, by virtue of having spaces between words, guides readers in the isolation of individual words.

In summary, there are various reasons for saying that the lexicon is important for second language learners. Both learners and native speakers recognize the importance of getting the words right and lexical errors are numerous and disruptive. In general, learners need good lexical skills to produce sentences and to understand them.

13.2 Categories of lexical knowledge: some dichotomies

The major task of second language lexical research is to discover what second language learners know about the lexicon of the second language, how they learn it, and why this particular path of development is followed.

13.2.1 Production and reception

An initial consideration is that learners appear to have differing degrees of knowledge of their second language lexicon. Nation (2001, p. 27) lists the following as word knowledge types necessary if one is to be considered to have complete knowledge of a word:

Form
- Spoken (what does it sound like? *eight* sounds like [eit])
- Written (spelling)

Meaning
- Form and meaning (what is the meaning of a particular form?)
- Concept and referents (what concepts are included?)
- Associations (what words do we think of when we hear this form?)

Use
- Grammatical functions (the patterns the word occurs in)
- Collocations (what words can occur with the word—for example, with *vacation*, one says *take*)
- Constraints on use (e.g., registers—in what contexts do we expect to hear this word?)

The above examples reflect receptive knowledge, but there is also productive knowledge to consider, which deals with aspects of pronunciation (knowing how to pronounce a word as opposed to recognizing it), spelling, nuances of meaning (as opposed to getting the general meaning), grammatical constraints (e.g., *impact* as a verb takes a direct object, but *impact* as a noun occurs in the phrase *has an impact on*).

If we take as an example the word *overextended*, there are many things we have to know, some of which are listed below.

Receptive knowledge includes:

- recognizing the word in writing or orally
- knowing the general meaning

- knowing the specific meaning in a specific context of use
- knowing that it is made up of the component parts—*over, extend, -ed*
- knowing that it has a possible negative connotation (as opposed to *overqualify*, which may or may not have a negative connotation)
- knowing that it generally occurs with *himself, herself, oneself, themselves, ourselves, yourself*
- knowing that the opposite is *underextended*.

On the other hand, productive knowledge involves greater specificity and includes, among others:

- knowing how to accurately pronounce a word or correctly spell it
- knowing the precise meaning in a variety of contexts
- knowing that *She overextended herself* is OK, but that *She overextended her chair* is probably not OK in the absence of a highly specific context
- knowing the precise context of use.

Learners generally have a wider range of receptive[1] vocabulary than productive vocabulary. However, as discussed in Teichroew (1982), the picture is really more complicated. Lexical knowledge cannot be captured by means of a simple dichotomy. Rather, Teichroew proposed that vocabulary knowledge can best be represented as a continuum with the initial stage being recognition and the final being production. In her view, production should not be viewed in a monolithic fashion, for productive knowledge includes producing both a range of meanings as well as appropriate collocations (i.e., what words go together), as has been described above. For example, in our discussion of the word *break* with regard to the work of Kellerman (chapter 5), we noted the many meanings of that word. Initially, learners may know the meaning of *break* as in *break a leg* or *break a pencil*, and only with time do they learn the full range of meanings and such collocations as *His voice broke at age 13*.

Another distinction to be made about the lexicon is one between *potential* and *real* vocabulary (Berman, Buchbinder, and Beznedeznych, 1968, as cited in Palmberg, 1987, p. 20). Potential vocabulary consists of words a learner will recognize even though she has not yet seen them in the second language. An example would be common scientific and technological terms. Much of this vocabulary spreads from language to language with little indication of whether the term was first coined by a Russian, English, German, or Danish speaker. Real vocabulary consists of words the learner is familiar with after (and because of) exposure.

Laufer and Paribakht (1998), based on research by Laufer (1998), investigated three types of vocabulary knowledge: passive, controlled active, and free active. Passive knowledge involves understanding the most frequent meaning of a word, controlled-active knowledge involves cued recall (e.g., a test item might include *The railway con_____the city with its suburbs*, where the first few letters of a word are included to eliminate other possibilities), and free-active knowledge involves spontaneous use of the word. Laufer and Paribakht found that these three knowledge types developed at different rates. Passive vocabulary knowledge was the fastest, whereas active (particularly free active) was the slowest. Furthermore, passive vocabulary was always larger than active vocabulary, although there was a difference between learners in a foreign language setting and those in a second language setting. The gap between knowledge types was smaller in the foreign language setting, suggesting a strong role for the environment in learning.

13.2.2 Knowledge and control

A different distinction was drawn by Bialystok and Sharwood Smith (1985)—one between *knowledge* and *control*. Knowledge was defined as "the way in which the language system is represented in the mind of the learner (the categories and relationships in long-term memory)," whereas control was defined as "the processing system for controlling that system during actual performance" (p. 104) The authors made an analogy to a library. The knowledge is in the books and in the way they are organized, and control is in the way the books are accessed. With regard to the latter, the library user/language user needs to know how to determine which books are in the library and how to locate the books. The first time one uses a library, it is difficult to find one's way around, but with repeated use, access gets easier and more efficient.

The distinction made between knowledge and control is particularly useful with regard to vocabulary because it is not bound to just reception or production. Rather, both production and reception include information regarding knowledge and control.

However, the analogy has its drawbacks. In considering the library analogy as it is applied to the lexicon, there are a number of questions to be addressed, among them: What is a representation? How exhaustive are the representations? In other words, do the representations capture everything we know about words?

The library analogy, while useful, does not capture the dynamic changing nature of the second language lexicon. Books in a library are static and unchanging. A book purchased 10 years ago does not change in any significant way on the owner's shelf. Unchanging, static, formalized, symbolic descriptions cannot account for all of lexical learning.

The library metaphor may work reasonably well for phonological knowledge of the lexicon. There is a need for some sort of phonological idealizations, or what may be called *representations*, if only as targets for pronunciation (see Linell, 1982; Ard, 1989). However, representations do not capture everything important about lexical pronunciations. For example, they do not capture special effects (including unusual patterns of stress or emphasis) a speaker may choose to place on a word. In certain situations, a speaker may address an interlocutor as *darling*, while imitating the pronunciation of a Gabor sister to show affectation.

Tyler (1989, p. 444) noted that "the representation of a word cannot contain all the various and subtle interpretations that the word could have in different real-world contexts." She noted that pragmatic inferencing is required along with real-world knowledge. The point of this for SLA is that learners have to know more than just the representation to be able to use a word and understand it in a way approximating native speakers.

In sum, finding meaning is not simply a matter of finding stored, fixed information. Rather, constructive processes are involved in finding meanings for words. Because processes are involved, we cannot rule out the possibility that there can be varying degrees of control over these processes. Similarly, we demonstrate later that processes in using words, such as in production and in comprehension, have to be learned. Thus, we can talk of varying degrees of knowledge of the processes. Knowledge and control are both important, but their relationship is more intertwined than sequential. One does not just have knowledge and then try to control it.

13.2.3 Breadth and depth

The distinction between breadth and depth is tantamount to a distinction between quantity and quality. Breadth of knowledge refers to the number of words learners know (Nation, 2001; Nassaji, 2004). On the other hand, depth of vocabulary knowledge is a quality measure (Meara, 1996; Read, 1993, 2000; Nassaji, 2004). Earlier we discussed what knowing a word entails and it is this complexity that is referred to as vocabulary knowledge depth. As mentioned earlier, this might include not only the meaning of the word, but also semantic relationships with other words, syntactic patterning, collocations, pronunciation, and so forth.

Research has shown that both breadth and depth of knowledge play a role in comprehension, although most studies have investigated reading comprehension. For example, numerous studies (e.g., Koda, 1989; Coady, Magoto, Hubbard, Graney, and Mokhtari, 1993; Haynes and Baker, 1993; Laufer, 1997a, 1997b; Qian, 1999) have shown that there is relationship between breadth of knowledge and reading comprehension; depth of knowledge was a better predictor of L2 reading comprehension than just breadth of knowledge. Similarly, Nassaji (2004) found that depth of knowledge could be tied to particular strategy use (e.g., identifying, evaluating, and monitoring), to more effective lexical inferencing strategies, and to the success of inferencing. The following excerpts illustrate the difference in lexically skilled and lexically less skilled participants in his study.

Lexically skilled	"Sewage in their nose . . ." "smell of their sewage in their nose . . ." "have dust between their toes and the smell of sewage in their nose . . ." I think, there a lot of dirty things around the city and that those things are making smells, and the smell goes to their noses, so sewage are things like dirty things, garbage, like, according to this . . . "and the smell of the sewage in their nose." Yes.
Lexically less skilled	". . . and the smell of sewage in their nose . . . in their nose . . . their toes . . ." "the toes and the smell of sewage in their nose," "their toes . . ." umm . . . because it is in their nose, I think . . . "between their toes . . ." I am not sure . . . because something in their nose their . . . mmm . . . is . . . mmm . . . maybe it's their . . . it's their . . . I'm not sure. "the smell of sewage . . ." it's the smell . . . the sewage it is something . . . there is some smell . . . may be sew . . . I'm not sure.

The differences between these two excerpts are striking. The first major difference is that the lexically less skilled participant is primarily repeating what is in the text peppered with *umms* and other hesitation phenomena. She or he never focuses on the actual meaning of the text. The first participant repeats a large chunk of relevant speech that includes *dust between their toes*. And, *dust* provides an important clue in unraveling the meaning of *sewage*.

Pulido (2003) looks at a range of issues (proficiency and topic familiarity) with regard to reading comprehension, but germane to this discussion is the finding that sight vocabulary knowledge (which measured breadth of knowledge of a limited set of vocabulary items; namely, the non-targeted words in the experimental reading passages) had an impact on incidental vocabulary gain. Laufer (1997a) goes a step further and claims that, at least for L2 readers, the "threshold for reading comprehension is, to a large extent, lexical" (p. 21).

Read (2004) discusses various ways of conceptualizing depth of knowledge, including precision of meaning, comprehensive word knowledge, and network knowledge. He notes that different researchers mean different things by depth of knowledge with some using meaning, others using comprehensiveness, and others using network associations. He further notes that any of these terms is problematic because the lexicon is "something that is inherently ill-defined, multidimensional, variable and thus resistant to neat classification" (p. 224).

As can be seen, knowing a second language word involves different ways of knowing, including receptive and productive knowledge. In the next section, we consider more specific details of what learners have to know about a word, including its meaning, subcategorization restrictions, associations, and collocations.

13.3 Lexical knowledge, development, and influences

Second language learners are known to have difficulty with vocabulary learning. This takes a number of forms which were mentioned earlier in this chapter; we turn to some of them now.

13.3.1 Subcategorization

As native speakers of our language, we know that some verbs require objects, some verbs require indirect and direct objects, some verbs require animate subjects, and so forth. Additionally, native speakers of English, for example, know how to interpret the role certain noun phrases play in the action described by the verb. For example, a native English speaker knows the relationships between 13-3 and 13-4:

(13-3) X rents Y to Z.
(13-4) Z rents Y from X.

or, a native speaker of Italian knows that

(13-5) mi   piacciono i   cani
        to me like (pl)   the dogs
        "I like dogs."

even though the subject is *the dogs*, the meaning is that I like dogs (the dogs are pleasing to me). This is an area of difficulty, as we saw in chapter 8 in the discussion of input processing. Thus, it is not enough to know the meanings of individual words. In 13-3 and 13-4, a speaker must know that when *rent* is accompanied by *to* the subject is the owner. On the other hand, when *rent* is accompanied by *from*, the subject is the person who takes possession of the property for a short time.

This type of information can differ from language to language. Adjemian (1983) found that second language learners tended to transfer lexical patterns from their L1 to their L2. The scope of his research was the lexical acquisition of French by native English speakers and of English by native French speakers. The following sentences were produced by the native French speakers learning English.

(13-6) At sixty-five years old they must *retire themselves* because this is a rule of society.
(13-7) They want to *fight themselves* against this (tuition increase).

Note that the reflexives in these sentences are not intended to indicate emphasis. In the translation equivalents of these sentences in French, the verbs require the reflexive morpheme *se* (*se retirer* and *se battre*).

English learners of French produced ungrammatical sentences such as 13-8.

(13-8) Elle marche les chats.
        She walks   the cats.

Sentence 13-8 is ungrammatical in French because the verb *marcher* "to walk" cannot take a direct object. Another verb (*se promener*) must be used. Learners in both cases assume that verbs in their second language take the same kinds of subjects and objects as they do in their native language.

13.3.2 Word associations and networks

As mentioned above, part of what is involved in knowing a word, and in particular in knowing a word in a manner similar to native speakers, is the association that is made to other words. Meara (1978) investigated the lexical associations made by learners of French. Modern theories of lexical semantics are concerned with the relationships between words. Word associations would appear to be a reasonable means of determining how individuals relate words. Meara found that learners tended to produce rather different associations from those made by native speakers of French. Native speakers primarily gave paradigmatic or syntagmatic associations, based on semantic factors:

Paradigmatic
Stimulus   *Response*
man   woman
                 dog
                 boy
                 child

Syntagmatic

Stimulus	*Response*
brush	teeth
hold	hands
black	mark
bank	robber

Learners tended to give responses based on phonological similarity, such as *plafond* "ceiling" or *professeur* "professor" to the stimulus *profond* "deep." A possible interpretation is that the learners had not constructed the network of relationships necessary for fluent word associations in their L2. A later study by Schmitt and Meara (1997) investigated word associations by Japanese learners of English, specifically word associations and their relationship with verbal suffixes. The authors found that the ability to produce native-like word associations, not surprisingly, is related to suffix knowledge as well as to vocabulary size and general proficiency.

In both our L1 and our L2, we establish networks which may be semantic networks, syntactic networks (words behave in similar/same ways syntactically), phonological networks, and so forth. Essentially, a lexical network involves the linking of words in some way. Henriksen (1999) uses exactly this approach in her discussion of depth of vocabulary knowledge. Various forms of word association measures have been used in second language research (e.g., Söderman, 1993; Schmitt, 1998a; Singleton, 1999; Meara and Fitzpatrick, 2000), with considerable discussion on development in terms of a movement from phonological to semantic associations.

13.3.3 Word formation

Knowledge of the lexicon also involves knowing how to combine elements to create novel lexical items. The importance of word formation varies from language to language. Word formation is much less important in English than in many other languages. Hankamer (1989) noted that Turkish contains much more productive derivational morphology than does English, allowing it to form more words through morphology. The situation is even more extreme in a language such as Eskimo or in a language with both verbal and nominal incorporation, such as Chukchee. For example, in Chukchee verbs meaning "to whale hunt," "to walrus hunt," and "to reindeer hunt" are formed from the words meaning "hunt," "whale," "walrus," and "reindeer."

Another factor that should be pointed out for English word formation is that many of the complicated words in English are taken from Latin and Greek. The average English speaker is not aware of how these words are formed. The situation is different in German. The German word *Wasserstoff* means "hydrogen" and is a part-by-part translation (*hydro* means "water," which is *Wasser* in German, and *gen* means "substance," or *Stoff* in German). A German speaker is thus more likely to recognize the word-formation process in *Wasserstoff* than is an English speaker in *hydrogen*. We might expect German speakers to be more sensitive to word-formation processes in general in learning a second language as well.

Olshtain (1987) investigated the development of word-formation processes by learners of Hebrew. She considered the use of new words from the perspective of production and interpretation. In the case of production tasks, learners showed a progression toward target language patterns. For example, native speakers tended to provide innovative words to tasks 74% of the time, advanced learners 67%, and intermediate learners only 19%. Additionally, when intermediate learners did innovate, the mechanisms they used differed from those of both advanced learners and native speakers. Only the intermediate students relied predominantly on suffixes, emphasized in their language classes as the major means of forming new words. Both the advanced learners and native speakers used a greater variety of means of forming new words. They were much more likely to use compounding, blending, and root changing than were the intermediate learners. However, on an interpretation task, a task that required learners to assign meaning to new words, neither group of learners performed like native speakers. On this task, learners were asked to interpret words out of context. The inability to interpret words in a native-like fashion, even by those who *produced* words like native speakers, suggests that even advanced speakers are highly context-bound in their use of the L2.

13.3.4 *Word combinations, collocations, and phraseology*

Individual words often appear together on a regular basis. For example, native speakers of English when confronted with an economics article and see the word *underdeveloped* might predict that the next word will be *nation* or *country*. In other words, the choice of the next word is quite narrow. Other collocations, such as *broad daylight*, *green with envy*, and *deep sigh* are common in language and are often processed as single units. These are different from idioms such as *kick the bucket* and multiword structures that signify a particular meaning and are represented by single words in many languages, such as *yellow jacket*. Unfortunately, in English, orthography is not always a good indicator of the status of words. *Matchbox*, *match-box*, and *match box* are all attested spellings. Learners have to learn these multiword units as wholes. Of course, in a perceptual situation a learner may err and interpret bound phrases like these word by word. The interpretation gained in this manner will generally not make any sense in its context.

An important factor about these combinations is that they are not totally free. In fact, there are strong statistical constraints on possible co-occurrences, as is shown in gap-filling tests. Consider what words could be chosen in the following frames:

I'm afraid I have some _____ news.
She looked out the window and breathed a _____ sigh.
I wonder what's wrong. She's been in there a _____ time.
He's very stubborn. He's had a _____ will ever since he was a baby.
I know that's true as a _____ rule, but this may be an exception.

Akhmatova (1974, p. 24) suggested that:

It follows that word-combination becomes "free" in the sense of not having any constraints imposed upon it only when words are combined by *creative* or "imaginative" speakers who are not content with merely reproducing the already existing complexes. Words are combined "freely" only by people who strive for novelty and originality. It is mainly in fiction or other types of imaginative speaking and writing that we find word-combinations that are really "free."

Until recently, relatively little attention had been paid to these problems in second language learning. Meara (1983, 1987) gave only four sources for collocations in his bibliographies for vocabulary in a second language: Alexander (1982), Binon and Cornu (1985), Brown (1974), and Cowie (1978). All of these studies dealt only with the pedagogical problem. None discussed how learners acquire competence in word combinations and collocations.

In recent years, research has looked at collocations as one form of language chunk. Nation (2001) characterizes the position of N. Ellis (2001) as follows:

language knowledge and language use can be accounted for by the storage of chunks of language in long-term memory and by experience of how likely particular chunks are to occur with other particular chunks, without the need to refer to underlying rules. Language knowledge and use is based on associations between sequentially observed language items. This viewpoint sees collocational knowledge as the essence of language knowledge.

(p. 318)

An interesting experiment regarding idiom learning was conducted by Bogaards (2001), in which Dutch learners of French were presented with

French idioms. He presented new words and idioms with similar meanings to the learners and found that multiword expressions that contained known words (e.g., *homme à femmes* versus *dragueur*—both meaning "womanizer") were easier to learn than words that are completely new. He suggests that initial knowledge of form helps learners as they learn new meanings attached to those forms.

We discussed chunking[2] and prefabricated patterns in chapter 8. Essentially, we can think of chunks as prefabricated patterns where the learner may not know how to "unpackage" the component parts, as was seen with the Japanese child Uguisu's use of *doyou* as a single unanalysed unit. Or, one can think of chunks as a form of collocation where with repeated exposure we learn that *take a bath* or *take a shower* go together as opposed to *do a bath* or *do a shower*. One can further see that this reduces the learning burden, in that storage (see chapter 8) is often limited to a limited number of items and, if some of them are multiword, less processing time may be involved.

As an example, one might think of learning a language with a different script. At first we have difficulty in determining the different parts of letters. Let us consider the following examples from Hebrew, Arabic, and Korean.

Hebrew:	ו	ל	ז
Arabic:	ك	ش	ق
Korean:	언	어	

When learning a language with a different script, it is often difficult to recognize individual letters (and even more difficult to produce the letter) or to determine one letter from another. With repeated exposure, learners can see each letter as a unified whole much as those familiar with a Latin script can see the letters *a*, *b*, *c*, etc. as unified wholes without seeing the individual strokes and can identify the letter quickly and effortlessly. At a later stage, we chunk larger items together, such as individual words, and can understand them without "seeing" the component parts. For example, very frequent words, such as *the* or *and*, are recognized without decomposing them into each letter.

Learners are often forced to be innovative in their word combinations. The result is that misunderstandings abound. Consider the following example. Normal synonyms for *local* include *parochial* and *provincial*. Consider the differences among the following statements:

(13-9) The *Detroit Free Press* is a local paper.
(13-10) The *Detroit Free Press* is a parochial paper.
(13-11) The *Detroit Free Press* is a provincial paper.

461

The first of these descriptions is just a matter-of-fact account. The second two ascribe pejorative evaluations about the quality of the newspaper. A learner who said one of the latter two might be surprised to hear an interlocutor object that she thinks the paper is pretty good. When we hear something unusual, we assume that the speaker had a good reason to say things in this unusual manner. The problem for the learner is to learn how not to be innovative and stick to the standard combinations.

13.4 L1 influence

In all aspects of language learning, the L1 (or other languages known; see chapters 2 and 5) undoubtedly play an important role. The lexicon is no exception. Singleton (1999) reviews a number of studies and comes to the conclusion that there is connectivity between the L1 and the L2 lexicon. Note that he uses the term *connectivity* to rule out a disconnect between the two lexica as well as to rule out total integration. ". . . L1 and L2 lexis are separately stored, but that the two systems are in communication with each other—whether via direct connections between individual L1 and L2 lexical nodes, or via a common conceptual store (or both)" (pp. 189–190). He also raises the question of individual differences and notes "that the relationship between a given L2 word and a given L1 word in the mental lexicon will vary from individual to individual" (p. 190). What is particularly interesting is that he attributes this to factors of acquisition and on the extent to which formal and/or semantic connections are made by the learner of the L1 and L2 word.

There is evidence to suggest that both languages remain activated even with advanced proficiency in a second language (Jared and Kroll, 2001; Marian and Spivey, 2003). This, it is claimed, is the case even though automaticity increases with proficiency (see Segalowitz and Hulstijn, 2005). Sunderman and Kroll (2006) report that in words that have close forms (neighbors) in the L1 and L2, there is influence from both languages even when performing a task in only one of the languages. They cite the example in English of the word *gate*, which has neighbors in English (*game*) and in Spanish (*gato*, "cat"). Regardless of what language a task is being conducted in, both languages show influence of neighbors in both languages. Sunderman and Kroll (2006) investigated English-speaking learners of Spanish at two levels of proficiency and found that there was L1 activation for both groups, but that the sensitivity to the L1 translation decreased with increasing proficiency.

Jiang (2000, 2002, 2004) proposes and presents evidence to support a three-stage model of adult second language vocabulary learning. The first stage is a lexical association stage in which learners recognize some form as a word. They understand the meaning of the word because they

462

associate it with their L1—hence the association phase of learning. This phase of lexical representation only contains the form of the word (phonology, orthography) and something that points it to a comparable word in the L1. All processing is done through the L1 translations. With continued exposure and use, the semantic/syntactic information from the L1 is transferred to the L2 word. At this point the lexical representation contains L2 form information and the transferred syntactic and semantic information that has been transferred from the L1, and there is a direct link between the L2 word (weak or strong) and the conceptual representation. He calls this the L1 lemma mediation stage since processing still involves L1 information. The third stage is one in which L1 information is discarded, but Jiang (2000) suggests that, for many words, the second stage remains the steady-state stage. His various empirical studies verify these claims with Korean learners of English (Jiang, 2004) and Chinese learners of English (Jiang, 2002).

Lee (2007) argues against Jiang's semantic transfer hypothesis, pointing out that L2 proficiency, but not L1 influence, is a key factor in explaining semantic overgeneralization, at least within the conceptual domains that Jiang explored. Specifically, Lee added a NNS comparison group, pointing out that in any L1 transfer research, there have to be two groups of NNSs. Otherwise, one is left not knowing whether transfer or developmental factors are involved. In Lee's study, high-advanced Korean ESL learners were compared with advanced Korean ESL learners, high-advanced Chinese ESL learners, and NSs of English, with respect to semantic overgeneralization in contextualized environments. The findings revealed the comparable overgeneralization behaviors of high-advanced Korean ESL and high-advanced Chinese ESL groups, indicating that the semantic overgeneralization may be an indicator of L2 development but not that of crosslinguistic influence.

In the next sections, we focus on learning, both incidental and incremental learning.

13.4.1 Incidental vocabulary learning

A great deal of attention has been paid to what is known as *incidental vocabulary learning* (see Gass, 1999, for a discussion of the controversial nature of this term). Wesche and Paribakht (1999b, p. 176) defined incidental learning as what takes place when "learners are focused on comprehending meaning rather than on the explicit goal of learning new words." In other words, learning is a by-product of something else (e.g., reading a passage).

A number of studies have shown that incidental learning is indeed possible. Rott (1999) examined exposure through reading and its effect on acquisition and retention of vocabulary. Her study of the acquisition of

German by NSs of English investigated the effects of differential exposure to lexical items: exposure two, four, or six times. The results showed that only two exposures were sufficient to affect vocabulary growth and that six exposures resulted in the greatest amount of knowledge growth. Retention, following exposure, was greater for receptive knowledge than for productive knowledge.

Paribakht and Wesche (1997) divided learners of English into two instructional conditions. In one group, learners read passages and answered comprehension questions. In the other group, learners read passages and then did vocabulary activities. The same words were targeted for both groups. Although both groups made gains on vocabulary knowledge, the first group's knowledge was limited to recognition, whereas the second group acquired productive knowledge as well.

In a follow-up study, Paribakht and Wesche (1999), using think-aloud and retrospective methodology, focused on the strategies that learners used in the process of learning a new word. Inferencing was one of the most common strategies that learners appealed to. Surprisingly, dictionary use did not predominate (see also Fraser, 1999). Learners used morphological and grammatical information as aids in the inferencing process.

Gu and Johnson (1996) investigated the lexical strategy use by Chinese university students learning English. Strategies such as guessing from context, dictionary use (for learning purposes as opposed to comprehension only), and relying on word formation were noted. Oral repetition correlated with general proficiency, but visual repetition (writing words over and over, memorizing the spelling letter by letter, writing new words and translation equivalents repeatedly) negatively predicted vocabulary size and general proficiency. The least successful group of students used memorization and visual repetition of word lists. There was more than one way to achieve vocabulary growth: through extensive reading as well as by employing a wide range of strategies.

Hulstijn, Hollander, and Greidanus (1996), in their study of advanced learners of French (Dutch NSs), found that for this group the availability of a bilingual dictionary or marginal glosses fostered acquisition of word meanings. They claimed that when there is access to external information (e.g., dictionaries or glosses), the formation of a form–meaning relationship is fostered upon repeated exposure. In other words, if a learner looks up the meaning of an unknown word the first time that word is encountered, each subsequent encounter reinforces the meaning of the word. On the other hand, when no such external information is available, learners often ignore an unknown word (see also Paribakht and Wesche, 1999), or infer incorrect meanings. Thus, repeated exposure has little effect.

R. Ellis and He (1999), in an investigation of the role of negotiation in incidental vocabulary learning, found that when learners have the opportunity to use new lexical items in a communicative context (including negotiation), those words are retained (in the short and long term) to a greater extent than when they are only exposed to input. However, Newton (1995) found that negotiation was not always a precursor to learning a new vocabulary word. Other factors such as task type played a role in whether or not a word was learned. Gass (1999) proposed that incidental learning is most likely to occur when the words in the two languages are cognates, when there is significant exposure, and when related L2 words are known. In other cases, greater intentionality (e.g., through attention) is required.

Hulstijn and Laufer (2001) and Laufer and Hulstijn (2001) relate retention of vocabulary learning to the concept of *depth of processing* (Craik and Lockhart, 1972), which in its simple form predicts that memory retention is due to whether something is shallowly or deeply processed. We have discussed earlier that knowing a word involves many possibilities, including understanding the phonological form, the meaning, collocations, etc. It is predicted that processing a vocabulary word at the level of meaning is more deeply processed than processing at the level of phonological form and, presumably, knowing meaning and collocations suggests even deeper processing. A related concept is Craik and Tulving's (1975) richness of encoding. Hulstijn and Laufer and Laufer and Hulstijn take these concepts a step further by introducing the concept of *involvement*. Involvement in their model consists of need, search, and evaluation. Need refers to motivation and the need can be either moderate or strong. Need is strong when it is motivated by the internal needs of the learner and it is moderate when it is motivated by an external source (e.g., a teacher). Search and evaluation are both cognitive constructs. The former refers to the attempt to determine the meaning of a word (e.g., looking it up in a dictionary). Evaluation represents an attempt to determine whether the word is the correct one given the context. Evaluation involves a decision, for example, following a comparison of one meaning of a word with other meanings. This would be moderate involvement, but if a decision involves combination of the new word with other words, this is strong involvement.

Laufer and Hulstijn (2001) analyzed a number of studies and their effect on vocabulary retention, showing that in general the tasks that were effective were those that had high involvement. Hulstijn and Laufer (2001) conducted an experiment to determine if greater involvement would lead to greater retention of receptive knowledge. They constructed three tasks with different levels of involvement (reading comprehension with glosses in the margins, reading comprehension plus fill in the blank, and writing a composition using the target words). It was predicted that writing the composition entailed the greatest involvement, and reading with glosses involved the least. Their participants were learners of

English from the Netherlands and Israel. The Israeli participants fully supported the order, but the Dutch students performed better on the reading with glosses in the margins than on the reading with the fill in the blank. In general, the greater use that learners make of vocabulary items, the greater the likelihood that they will retain these items both in form and in meaning. This is not unlike what we saw in the discussion of the Output Hypothesis in chapter 10. Using language promotes acquisition. It also suggests that breadth of vocabulary knowledge is only relevant when accompanied by depth of knowledge.

13.4.2 Incremental vocabulary learning

Learning vocabulary is not a one-time affair. In other words, it is unrealistic to believe that a learner hears a word or, in the case of some pedagogical methods, memorizes a word with the consequence being full knowledge of the word. It is perhaps sufficient to think about what happens when we encounter words in our native language that we don't know. One interesting fact is that, once that happens, we seem to encounter that word quite frequently, making us wonder how we could have missed it for so long. Learning the meaning and use of the word requires us to listen to how it is used in different contexts and perhaps even to consult a dictionary before being brave enough to attempt to use it ourselves. Thus, a first encounter with a word may draw a learner's attention to that item. Subsequent encounters provide learners with opportunities to determine relevant semantic and syntactic information. The important point is that learning words is a recursive process and does not occur instantaneously (see also Schmitt, 1998b). In fact, Paribakht and Wesche (1993) developed a Vocabulary Knowledge Scale with five stages: (a) the word is unfamiliar, (b) the word is familiar but the meaning is not known, (c) a translation into the NL can be given, (d) the word can be used appropriately in a sentence, and (e) the word is used accurately both semantically and grammatically.

Schmitt (1998b) conducted a longitudinal study investigating the acquisition of 11 words by three adult learners during a one-year period of time. His focus was on four kinds of knowledge: spelling, associations, grammatical information, and meaning. All were advanced learners of English. The results were not conclusive. Spelling was not a problem for any of the learners. For association knowledge, two of the learners developed, but one did not. With regard to meaning knowledge, none of the learners had anything more than partial mastery of all the meaning senses. Two of the learners made progress in meaning knowledge; one did not. The one that did not was not the same as the one who did not make progress in association knowledge. For grammatical knowledge, only one student made steady progress; the other two were somewhat erratic across the time period. What was not found, however, was any sort of developmental hierarchy of knowledge types.

13.5 Using lexical skills

Thus far in this chapter we have primarily dealt with lexical knowledge. We now turn our attention more toward things learners do or try to do with words. We look at lexical skills involved in using language. A particular goal of this discussion is to relate second language research findings to psycholinguistic research. We compare certain findings about how learners use words with descriptions of psycholinguistic processes to determine what relationships, if any, exist.

13.5.1 Production

The primary evidence about second language lexical use comes from production. Production processes and strategies may have a strong effect on what learners produce. In ordinary conversation, learners generally rely on sentence production processes, except in unusual situations where they repeat something that has been memorized as a whole. Even many experimental and/or standardized tests, such as gap-filling exercises or tests in which learners select from a list of words to fit in a context, may encourage learners to run through an analogue of sentence production to complete the task. For example, if asked to fill in the blank in:

Credit card payment is _____ to lock-in any instant purchase fares.

either a learner or a native speaker may use skills normally used in sentence production to fulfill the task by generating a word that would be meaningful and would make sense in the syntactic environment.

As mentioned earlier, there is good reason to believe that lexical information is crucial in the sentence production strategies of competent native speakers. Hence, it at first seems paradoxical that little evidence of this is found in the early stages of second language acquisition. Klein and Perdue (1989) provided a thorough discussion of principles that might determine word order arrangements by second language learners in naturalistic (untutored) settings. In their conclusion they wrote:

The objective . . . was to analyze whether there are any principles according to which learners with a limited repertoire put their words together. It was shown—with some exceptions and some degree of uncertainty—that there are basically three rules which determine the arrangement of words in early learner varieties (plus one rule for the type of NP [noun phrase] which may occur in a specific position): a phrasal, a semantic, and a pragmatic rule.

(p. 326)

In this article, there was no specific discussion of the role of particular words. Nevertheless, the particular words in a sentence are major factors in determining the semantics and/or pragmatics. Even so, there is no indication from the data in that study that learners are yet attending to particularities of lexical items that go beyond general semantic and pragmatic factors. It may be that the stage described by Klein and Perdue is one in which this degree of analysis is not yet available for the learners. Until they control the vocabulary better, specific lexical factors are ignored in sentence production in favor of more global factors.

Ard and Gass (1987) presented further evidence of the fact that lexical information plays little role in early stages. They found that in earlier stages of second language acquisition, grammaticality judgments were relatively uniform, with particular lexical items making little difference. As acquisition progressed, there was much more difference among responses to the same structure with different words. They looked at learner judgments about such sentences as the following:

1   The teacher demonstrated the new machine to the students.
2   The teacher showed the new machine to the students.
3   The teacher demonstrated the students the new machine.
4   The teacher showed the students the new machine.
5   The judge told the lawyer his decision.
6   The judge informed the lawyer his decision.
7   The judge told his decision to the lawyer.
8   The judge informed his decision to the lawyer.
9   The judge told the lawyer of his decision.
10 The judge informed the lawyer of his decision.

Ard and Gass found that learners at relatively low levels of proficiency were more likely to judge sentences with *demonstrate* and *show* (and with *tell* and *inform*) more uniformly (i.e., all correct or all incorrect) than were learners at higher stages of proficiency. They interpreted this to mean that the learners, as they progress, learn additional lexical information, namely which structures are possible for particular words.

Both of the studies by Klein and Perdue and by Ard and Gass suggested that, in early stages, learners tend to ignore specific lexical information and rely on other information—namely syntax, semantics, or pragmatics. As noted earlier, Adjemian (1983) found that learners may utilize L1 lexical rules in their L2.

468

In summary, learners have to, and do, learn the lexical constraints on sentence production. However, we still do not know much about the details of how this sort of learning takes place. The evidence indicates that learners initially make little use of lexical information (Ard and Gass, 1987; Klein and Perdue, 1989) or that learners use lexical information appropriate for the L1 (Adjemian, 1983).

Sentence production strategies may also play a part in explaining some of the findings of Blum-Kulka and Levenston (1987) about the acquisition of what they call lexical-grammatical pragmatic indicators. For example, the Hebrew construction *efšar* + infinitive ("possible" + infinitive) is limited to situations that express a speaker's perspective. Thus, 13-12 is acceptable, 13-13 is not:

(13-12) Efšar leqabel et hamaxberet selax leqama yamim?
         "Is it possible to have/receive your notebook for a few days?"
(13-13) Efšar latet li et hamaxberet?
         "Is it possible to give me the notebook?"

Blum-Kulka and Levenston found that learners of Hebrew fail to make this distinction and, from the perspective of standard Hebrew, often overgeneralize *efšar* to all requests. They did not present any additional evidence about the knowledge these learners have of *efšar*. It is certainly possible that this word with a following infinitive has been learned with the meaning "possible" and, thus, these learners have no awareness of additional connotations. On the other hand, these learners may know this additional information and be unable to use it in free speech. There are many situations in second language learning when learners are unable to do everything in real-time production that they may show knowledge of. For example, Russian learners of English will generally learn about the use of articles before they can use them well in production. It can be concluded that the nature of sentence production processes contributes to learner difficulties in lexical use.

Levelt (1989) presented a detailed model of sentence production. A blueprint of the basics is given in Figure 13.1.

Levelt argued that formulation processes are primarily lexically driven. He did not discuss second language acquisition data but did provide information on child first language acquisition and cross-linguistic differences in language production. From these discussions, one can infer implications for second language acquisition with the proviso that they must be tested in the second language domain.

First of all, we should note that Levelt divided the production process into two stages. The speaker initially conceives of a preverbal message. This in itself is a complex activity. Levelt mentioned that, as a part of

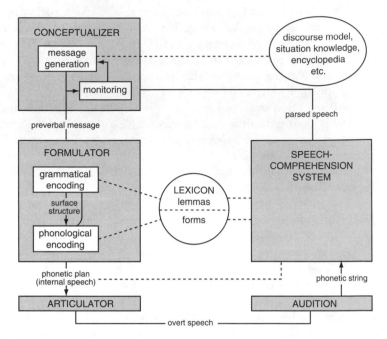

Figure 13.1 A blueprint for the speaker. Boxes represent processing components; circle and ellipse represent knowledge stores.

Source: From *Speaking: From Intention to Articulation* by W. J. M. Levelt. Reprinted by permission. © 1989 Massachusetts Institute of Technology Press.

conceiving of a preverbal message, a speaker must establish a purpose. A speaker must "order information for expression, keep track of what was said before . . . attend to his own productions, monitoring what he is saying and how" (1989, p. 9). The cover term that Levelt used for all of this is *conceptualizing* and the name for the processing system that does this is the Conceptualizer. The Conceptualizer determines the notions that will be expressed in the actual verbal message. The preverbal plan, the output of the Conceptualizer, must be converted into actual words (and ultimately speech). The processing system that does this is called the Formulator.

Levelt noted that languages differ in their requirements about what must be specified by the Conceptualizer. Spanish has a three-way distinction for spatial deixis (*aquí* "here," *allí/ahí* "there," *aquel* "(way over) there").[3] Levelt gave the additional example of classifiers based on concepts such as shape. For example, in several languages, including some in Australia, Africa, and the Americas, adjectives must agree with nouns in *class*. Class is partially determined by such things as whether the noun is long and thin, or a liquid, or round. In some instances, English codes information that other languages do not. For example, as Levelt noted, tense is an obligatory category in English, but is not in many other languages, the example he gave being Malay.

Levelt argued that there is no reason to believe that speakers of different languages think differently or view the world differently. Rather, the Conceptualizers must present different information to be coded in different languages. He suggested that in language acquisition there needs to be feedback between the Formulator and the Conceptualizer.[4] As we learn our native language, we learn what information is needed. Once this state is reached, "it is no longer necessary for the Conceptualizer to ask the Formulator at each occasion what it likes as input. In short, the systems have become autonomous" (Levelt, 1989, p. 105).

Let us now consider second language acquisition. In Levelt's terms, learners realize that they have to acquire a new Conceptualizer. The Formulator is a different matter. Whether or not they are consciously aware that they have to plan differently in producing sentences in a second language, the natural tendency would seem to be to rely on the Formulator developed in acquiring the first language.

Let us now reconsider the examples of *efšar* in Hebrew and articles in Russian for learners of English. It is not enough for learners to know the complexities of these elements. They must also modify their Conceptualizer to add the relevant information to the plans for productions and learn how to formulate the correct structures. If English speakers learning Hebrew ignore the issue of speaker's perspective in generating the conceptual plan for the sentence, then the Formulator will not have access to the distinction and the overgeneralization found by Blum-Kulka and Levenston (1987) would be expected. Similarly, if Russian learners of English do not consider specificity in constructing conceptual plans, there is little reason to believe that correct article use would be formulated.

The distinction between the Conceptualizer and Formulator may also play a role in explaining the common use of what one might call lexical decompositions by learners. Learners frequently use circumlocutions such as *go up* for monomorphemic words such as *climb*. If the Conceptualizer produces a plan that provides semantic notions, as Levelt suggested, then it may be easier for learners to produce the utterance by using higher frequency words that are less specific. We would expect that learners will have more difficulty finding lower frequency words than do native speakers.

We need to make it plain that these are only hypotheses. We suggest that the model developed by Levelt may be useful in explaining facts of second language production (see also de Bot, Paribakht, and Wesche, 1997). This is an empirical issue.

13.5.2 Perception

Different languages utilize different distinctions in their phonological systems. For example, many of the world's languages utilize tone as a distinctive feature in separating words. English, of course, does not. On the other hand, English utilizes distinctions between tense and lax vowels (as in *sheep* vs. *ship*) that are not used to distinguish words in other languages, such as Spanish. Given these differences in phonological inventories, it is not surprising to find that speakers of different languages tend to use different strategies in word perception, as has been noted in a series of studies by Cutler (e.g., 1990).

Cutler (1990) found that English speakers use a strategy of focusing on strong syllables (i.e., those containing an unreduced vowel) in word recognition. There are various sorts of data for this proposal. One type comes from studies in which participants are asked to respond whenever they hear a particular target word. They were more likely to erroneously respond to *trombone* when the target was *bone* than to *trumpet* when the target was *pet*. The second syllable in *trombone* is strong, whereas it is weak in *trumpet*. A second type of evidence comes from tasks in which participants are asked to determine which word is a part of a nonsense word. They were able to find *mint* with greater speed and accuracy in the nonsense word *mintef* (where the second vowel is a schwa) than in the nonsense word *mintayf* (where the second vowel is strong).

Cutler (1990) suggested that this strategy of focusing on strong syllables is not found in French, where there is no phonological motivation for it. French speakers tend to pay equal attention to all syllables. Spanish phonology and Chinese phonology are similar to French in their treatment of syllables. In other words, they pay equal attention to stressed and unstressed syllables. This makes the following finding of Meara (1984, pp. 234–235 added) particularly intriguing:

> We have also carried out studies on Spanish speakers, and these suggest that there may be some *unexpected* and interesting differences between the way native speakers of English and Spanish handle words. At the moment we are working on the idea that syllables play a much more important role in the representation of words for Spanish speakers than is the case for English.

Meara also claims that Chinese speakers "pay more attention to the ends of words than English speakers do" (p. 234). This does not mean that Chinese speakers pay less attention to other syllables than they do to final syllables. If English speakers are focusing on the strong syllables, which tend not to be final in polysyllabic words, and if Chinese and Spanish speakers tend to attend to all syllables more equally than English speakers do, then these patterns are just what we would expect. It seems likely that a major reason that Spanish and Chinese learners perform differently with English words is that they are utilizing the processing strategies they learned in their native languages.

Word perception is generally the primary problem in understanding ongoing speech, as mentioned earlier. If the words are not perceived correctly, then the listener is unlikely to be able to determine the meaning of the discourse. Being able to understand enough words in real time to follow a conversation is a difficult task in a second language, one that usually requires considerable work with the language.

Even among competent speakers of a language, lexical considerations are often paramount in explaining the flow of a conversation. Typically, investigators looking at a conversation analyze transcripts of the conversation. However, as Linell (1985) noted, this often gives an unrealistic picture of what the participants in the conversation have to do. We can read a transcript in any order; in particular, referring back when it is helpful. This gives much more of an impression of semantic wholeness than is usual in actual ongoing speech. Participants in a conversation cannot retain everything in memory. They often attend only to limited features in the conversation. For example, responses are often based on a particular word or group of words that a conversational partner said. Especially because speech is planned before another interlocutor finishes, words early in the interlocutor's utterance are likely to be very important. Consider the following segment of an interview. This example was taken from a textbook designed for ESL learners.

Interviewer: On the matter of careers, a lot of the jobs that people go into are sort of lifetime careers. What about baseball? Is it a full lifetime career?

Cornutt: It's been—uh . . . I mean, it's been . . . Baseball's been my life so far, . . . you know. I mean, I know someday—could be tomorrow—that I'm going to be out of it.

Interviewer: But how long can you expect to . . . to play, let's say actively?

Cornutt: Well, I think that—of course, me—I've set goals, and I made my first goal, which was to make it to the big leagues. And now, my next goal is to make it through four years . . . and get my pension. And after that, everything is.

Interviewer: But how many years can you expect to play professional ball . . .?

Cornutt: It's . . . it's diff—I'm a pitcher, and it's difficult, as a pitcher, to really say how many years . . . because you never know whether you're going to have a sore arm, whether it's going to go on you or wh . . . what the problem may be. But uh . . . as a pitcher, I guess the prime—I'm 24 years old now, and this is my sixth year—and the prime time for a pitcher is 27 to 30.

(Cornelius, 1981, p. 124)

In classes, both native and nonnative speakers felt that Cornutt was either rude and uncooperative or misunderstood the questions. The fact that the interviewer was more fluent and kept asking questions that in retrospect appear to be different phrasing of the same question reinforces the belief that the canonical interpretation of each question was something like, *How long will your baseball career last?*

Even if Cornutt was uncooperative or misunderstood, the question remains of what motivated his responses. We suggest that these responses were well motivated by certain words in the interviewer's question. The first question asks about a lifetime career. Normally, when a 20-year-old is asked about a career we assume he or she will look forward, but when a 70-year-old is asked, we assume that the look will be backward. Cornutt is clearly looking backward and informs his interviewer that baseball has indeed been a lifetime career. He probably started playing when he was 5 or 6 years old. This response ignores some of the information in the question but directly addresses the words *lifetime career*.

In the second response, Cornutt responds primarily to the word *expect* as in *expect to play*. Cornutt's expectations are hardly based on disinterested prognostication. He has goals, wants to meet them, and has certain expectations of how successful he will likely be. He tells the interviewer what his goals are but is wary about saying how fully he expects to reach the goals he has not yet attained.

In the third response, Cornutt finally gives the answer the interviewer wants. Perhaps he realizes that that was the intent all along or perhaps he views this more explicit question as really different from the first two. Our purpose has been to see that each response in this apparently anomalous conversation is in fact well motivated by key lexical items in the preceding question.

Cornutt and the interviewer are both native speakers of English. The conversation can be even more divergent if a nonnative listener misinterprets a word and uses that misinterpreted word as the key word around which to base a response. Unfortunately, not enough is known about how lexical perceptions affect discourse by nonnative speakers.

13.6 Conclusion

In this chapter we have shown the complexities and importance of the lexicon. Because of these complexities, there has been less research on the lexicon in SLA than its importance might warrant. It is one of the most difficult areas for learners to acquire with any large degree of success. In the final chapter we interrelate the findings presented throughout this book and discuss ways in which the various views we have presented on SLA can be integrated.

Suggestions for additional reading

Vocabulary in a Second Language: Selection, Acquisition and Testing. Paul Bogaards and Batia Laufer (Eds.). John Benjamins (2004).

Vocabulary and Language Teaching. Ronald Carter and Michael McCarthy (Eds.). Longman (1988).

Second Language Vocabulary Acquisition. James Coady and Thomas Huckin (Eds.). Cambridge University Press (1997).

Learning Vocabulary in Another Language. I. S. P. Nation. Cambridge University Press (2001).

Vocabulary in Language Teaching. Norbert Schmitt. Cambridge University Press (2000).

Vocabulary: Description Acquisition and Pedagogy. Norbert Schmitt and Michael McCarthy. Cambridge University Press (1997).

Exploring the Second Language Mental Lexicon. David Singleton. Cambridge University Press (1999).

Incidental L2 Vocabulary Acquisition: Theory, Current Research, and Instructional Implications. Marjorie Wesche and Sima Paribakht (Eds.). Special issue of *Studies in Second Language Acquisition*, 21, (1999a).

Points for discussion

1   In this chapter, we noted that Levelt's model of speech production in Figure 13.1 was intended for first language cross-linguistic data. What implications might the model have for second language speech production? What aspects of L2 use might the model not be able to account for? For example, can it accommodate NL transfer?

2   In discussing the conversation between Cornutt and the interviewer, we noted that the answers Cornutt gave were motivated by key words in the interviewer's questions. Consider again the conversation given in chapter 10 between a native speaker and a nonnative speaker discussing the purchase of a TV set (see example 10-6). Analyze this conversation from the perspective of key-word understanding on the part of both the native speaker and the nonnative speaker.

3   Sentences such as the following are frequently uttered by nonnative

speakers of English: *I need one ride home from the party.* What is strange about this sentence? Why do you think this type of error occurs?

4   Provide examples of lexical complexities from English or from another language you know and speculate what sort of learning difficulties might arise.

5   The following data are from intermediate level ESL students in an intensive course program. The students are from a variety of native languages. Part I is from oral data and Parts II and III are from written compositions.

Part I
(1)   I had one *discuss* with my brother.
(2)   You have a business *relation* (relationship).
(3)   You get happy very *easy.*
(4)   There will be two *child.*
(5)   You say he's a *science.*
(6)   We have to think about Franklin, the *science.*
(7)   She has a good chance to *life.*
(8)   Maybe they don't finish their *educated.*

a   How do the forms in italics differ from standard English usage?
b   Is there a consistent predictable relationship between these learner forms and standard usage?

Part II
(1)   Actually such *behaves* lead mostly to misunderstanding.
(2)   The people give presents to *they* friend and their family.
(3)   Some people didn't *belief* this was a better way.
(4)   No matter how *differ* in age between us.
(5)   *Differ* from other parents in my country, they never told us what we must study.
(6)   Taught me how to choose the more *advantages* values.
(7)   This is a strange but *interest* continent.
(8)   The most *advantage* way.

c   Focus on the words in italics in each sentence. Work out a generalization and explanation for the patterns you find.
d   Is the generalization you have come up consistent with the generalization you found in Part I?

Part III
(1)   Soccer is the most common *sporting.*
(2)   America refused continual *supported our military request.*

(3) When he was 7 years old, he went *schooling*.

(4) About two hours driving *eastern* from Chicago.

(5) After finished my college *studied*, I went to my country.

(6) Doctors have the right to *removed* it from him.

(7) There is a night for *asleep*.

(8) Moreover it may lead to *conflicting*.

(9) I am not going to get married when I will *graduation* the school.

> e Work out an IL generalization that might account for the forms in italics. How can you explain it?
>
> f Does this generalization change the one(s) you came up with for Parts I and II? If so, how?
>
> g Given the data presented in all three parts of this problem, what strategy/strategies have these learners come up with regarding lexical use?

6 The data in this problem are from both written and oral sources. The native language is Arabic.

Part I

(1) You eat a cabbage roll *one time*.

(2) I need my hair to be *tall*.

(3) I hope to become *bigger* than this age.

(4) *Close* the television.

(5) And imagine that kind of people *graduate* every night from the bars.

(6) You have hard time *to collecting* your money.

(7) So, when I like to park my car, there is no place to *put it*, and *how many ticket I took*.

(8) I did not *find my money in the street*.

(9) This "sambousa" is not sweet or *pastry*. It's main course.

(10) If I will not follow from *first*, I will not understand.

(11) If you *appreciate* your money, you won't buy American car.

(12) If you appreciate your money, you won't buy American car. You'll pay *expensive*.

> a Describe (sentence by sentence) what these students are doing in terms of word meaning.
>
> b Provide sentence-by-sentence interpretations of these utterances.
>
> c What IL generalizations might account for these data? Provide a justification for your conclusions. What general strategy has been adopted in the acquisition of English word meaning by these learners?

Part II

The following are the intended meanings of the sentences from Part I. These are the meanings that were discerned from playback sessions in the native language.

(1)   You ate a cabbage roll once.
(2)   I want my hair to be long.
(3)   I am looking forward to the day when my children will be older.
(4)   Turn off the television.
(5)   And imagine the kind of people who will leave the bar every night.
(6)   You have a hard time earning your money.
(7)   Because there are not enough parking spaces, I get a lot of tickets.
(8)   Money doesn't grow on trees.
(9)   The "sambousa" is not a dessert. It's a main course.
(10) If I don't follow the lectures from the beginning, I won't understand.
(11–12) If you value your money, you won't buy an American car. You will pay a lot of money if you do.

    d   Compare your interpretations from Part I with those given in Part II. What differences do you find? What do these differences suggest about NS biases in interpretation?
    e   Do the results of your comparison affect or change your previous IL generalizations? If so, how and why?

7   After learning a new word that we believe to have never heard before, it seems to appear frequently in both written and oral contexts. How would you explain this phenomenon? Is it just that the word has become more frequently used or is it a learner's perception? Is it unique to a second language context or does this happen in one's native language as well?

See GSS, problems 2.1–2.3.

14

AN INTEGRATED VIEW OF SECOND LANGUAGE ACQUISITION

14.1 An integration of subareas

As has become clear throughout this book, the learning of a second language is a multifaceted endeavor. In order to fully understand this phenomenon, one must consider what is learned and what is not learned, as well as the contexts in which that learning and nonlearning take place. The latter includes the various influences on the learning process that are the focus of the majority of this book. In chapters 4 and 5, we explained how the native language plays an important role in learning. In chapter 6, we presented some of the tenets associated with Universal Grammar and showed its centrality in an understanding of SLA. We also noted, however, that it accounts for only a portion of the complex phenomenon of second language acquisition. In chapter 7, we discussed the role of language universals on the acquisition of a second language and also discussed the acquisition of phonology as well as the tense/aspect system. In chapter 8, we discussed psycholinguistic approaches to SLA. In chapter 9, we considered the role of social and discoursal context in SLA. In chapter 10, the concepts of input, interaction, and output were presented and we explained how these ideas are relevant to acquisition itself. Chapter 11 examined how instruction can (or cannot) affect L2 learning. Chapter 12 dealt with nonlinguistic factors involved in SLA, and chapter 13 focused on the importance of the lexicon.

All of these approaches to acquisition are crucial in dealing with *a part of* what happens in learning a second language. However, none of them alone is able to account for the total picture. In this chapter, a model is presented that will explain where the various pieces discussed throughout this book fit and how each relates to a larger picture of acquisition. The focus of this chapter is a consideration of what a learner must do to convert input to output. There are five stages in this process: (a) apperceived input, (b) comprehended input, (c) intake, (d) integration, and (e) output. We deal with each of these levels and elaborate on the factors that mediate between one level and another.[1]

As will be recalled from chapter 6, a major controversy in language acquisition research (both first and second) is whether or not acquisition can best be characterized by means of innateness. One view holds that a child comes to the learning task with a UG that allows the child to construct a grammar of a language on the basis of limited data. Another view maintains that language acquisition is a form of (and results from) social interaction (chapter 10).

Within the first approach, research focuses on the nature of UG (see chapter 6). Those working within this paradigm take as the scope of investigation linguistic descriptions of grammars. In so doing, an idealized speaker-hearer is assumed, with the claim being made that in order to understand formal constraints on language, one needs to isolate that linguistic system and investigate it in and of itself without external (e.g. social) influences. With regard to second language acquisition, the question most often asked is: What is the role of UG in adult second language acquisition? Is UG (which is assumed to be available to children acquiring a first language) available to adults learning a second language?

In the social interactionist view, it has been argued that language and social interaction cannot be separated without resulting in a distorted picture of the development of linguistic and interactive skills (chapters 9 and 10). From this point of view, language and cognitive development are deeply embedded in context; thus, an understanding of the development of syntax, for example, can only come about as one investigates how syntax interacts with other relevant aspects of the learning situation.

These conflicting positions have resulted in the development of different research traditions as a result of the different questions being asked. This has at times created conflicting views about the "best" way to gather data and/or the "correct" questions to be asked (see chapter 3). When data-gathering methods and research questions are tied to research paradigms, it is far less useful to compare the value of each than it is to question how the various research questions and research findings relate to one another.

Figure 14.1 presents a schematic view of the model of SLA being discussed in this chapter. We begin by referring to the top of the diagram. It is clear that input of some sort is necessary in order for acquisition to take place. What sort of input is necessary is less clear. For example, does it have to be modified (chapter 10)? If not, are there other ways in which input can be controlled or limited? If so, what are those ways? Can input come from fellow learners or do learners pay attention only to the input from so-called authority figures such as teachers or native speakers?[2] Once a learner filters out some of the input, what happens

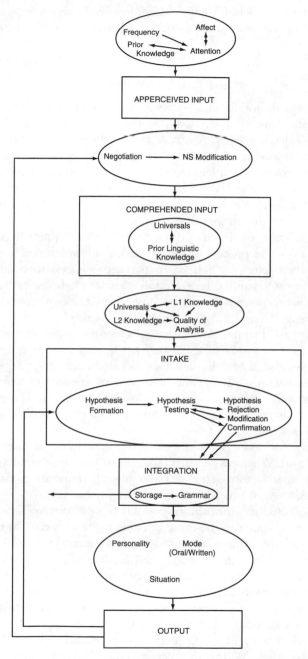

Figure 14.1 A model of second language acquisition.

Source: From "Integrating research areas: a framework for second language studies" by S. Gass, 1988, *Applied Linguistics*, 9, 198–217. Reprinted by permission of Oxford University Press.

next? We consider each of the five stages involved in conversion of input to output: apperceived input, comprehended input, intake, integration, and output.

14.1.1 Apperceived input

The first point to note is that learners are exposed to a body of second language data. This is known as input, the characteristics of which were discussed in detail in chapter 10. A well-established fact about second language acquisition is that not everything that learners hear/read is used as they form their second language grammars. Some language data filter through to learners and some do not. A concern in second language acquisition research has been with the limits on what filters through to learners and what determines those limits.

The first stage of input utilization is called apperceived input. Apperception is the process of understanding by which newly observed qualities of an object are related to past experiences. In other words, past experiences relate to the selection of what might be called *noticed* material. Apperception is an internal cognitive act, identifying a linguistic form as being related to some prior knowledge. We can think of apperception as a priming device that tells us which parameters to attend to in analyzing second language data. That is, it is a priming device that prepares the input for further analysis. What is noticed, or apperceived, then interacts with a parsing mechanism that attempts to segment the stream of speech into meaningful units for the learner. Thus, apperceived input is that bit of language that is noticed in some way by the learner because of some particular features.

Why are some aspects of language noticed by a learner, whereas others are not? What are the mediating factors at this initial stage? Put differently, what factors serve as input filters? There are a number of possibilities, a few of which are discussed in this chapter.

An obvious factor is *frequency*—possibly at both extremes. Something which is very frequent in the input is likely to be noticed. On the other hand, particularly at more advanced stages of learning, stages at which expectations of language data are well established, something that is unusual because of its *infrequency* may stand out for a learner. For example, given a particular context, one that is familiar to the learner, a new word or phrase may appear. This then may be noticed by the learner, and is thus available for eventual integration into the learner's system.[3]

A second factor that influences apperception is what has been described as *affect*. Within this category are included such factors as social distance, status, motivation, and attitude. This is exemplified by work of Krashen, who proposed that individuals have what he called an Affective Filter (see section 12.3.3). Another explanation has been put forth by Schumann, who argued that social distance is important in preventing a learner from obtaining input data. If a learner feels psychologically or socially distant from the target language community, the language input will not be available to that learner. This may be the case because a learner physically removes herself or himself from speakers of the target language. These nonlinguistic influences were discussed in detail in chapter 12.

A third factor that may determine whether language data are apperceived has to do with the broad category of associations and *prior knowledge*. Learning involves integration of new knowledge with prior knowledge. Importantly, one needs some sort of anchor on which to ground new knowledge. Prior knowledge is one of the factors that determine whether the input is meaningful. Prior knowledge is to be interpreted broadly and can include knowledge of the native language, knowledge of other languages, existing knowledge of the second language, world knowledge, language universals, and so forth. All of these play a role in a learner's success or lack of success in interpreting language data, in that they ultimately determine whether a learner understands and what level of understanding takes place. Precisely how these factors ultimately determine acquisition has been a question central to acquisition research over the past decade (see chapters 4 and 5).

A final factor to mention is that of *attention*. At a given point in time, does a learner attend to the input? One can think of many reasons why the input is not attended to. Many of these are trivial and don't concern second language acquisition (e.g., falling asleep in class); others are not trivial (e.g., an *a priori* realization that the input is not manageable, or task demands that make multiple foci of attention difficult or impossible).[4] Why is attention important? It is important because it allows a learner to notice a mismatch between what he or she knows about the second language and what is produced by speakers of the second language. If one is going to make modifications in one's grammar, one must first recognize that changes need to be made. Thus, readjustment of one's grammar is triggered by the perception of a mismatch.

These categories (i.e., frequency, affect, prior knowledge, and attention) are not intended to be necessarily independent. For example, attention may be related to, or influenced by, affective variables. If a learner has little desire to deal with the target language community, he or she may block out all the input, attending only to that which is necessary to conduct business or to get through the day. Similarly, affective variables may be influenced by prior knowledge. Whether a learner is positively or negatively disposed toward the target language (community) is presumably determined by prior linguistic knowledge (perhaps the learner does or does not like the sound of the language or does or does not find the language difficult to learn) and even by prior experience with speakers of the target language. Thus, a significant role is assigned to prior know-ledge and experience as activators of selective attention.

The preceding discussion has dealt with some issues that may deter-mine why or why not some input is noticed by the learner. There are also factors specific to conversational interactions that are relevant to how the input can be shaped so that it can be comprehended. Here are included the concepts of negotiation and foreigner talk, as discussed in chapter 10. Negotiation and modification differ from the previously mentioned factors in that they involve production and feedback. They are not neces-sary conditions, but rather serve to increase the possibility of a greater amount of input becoming available for further use.

14.1.2 Comprehended input

The factors mentioned thus far in this chapter contribute to the poten-tiality of comprehension of the input. But there is another point to con-sider: the concept of comprehended input. There are two differences between the notion of comprehended input and that of comprehensible input, as detailed in chapter 10. One is that comprehensible input is con-trolled by the person providing input, generally (but not necessarily) a native speaker of the second language, whereas comprehended input is learner-controlled; that is, it is the learner who is or who is not doing the "work" to understand. This distinction is crucial in the eventual relation-ship to intake, because it is the learner who ultimately controls that intake. A second difference is that comprehensible input, in Krashen's sense, is treated as a dichotomous variable; that is, it is either compre-hensible or it is not. But there are different levels of comprehension that can take place. The most typical meaning of *comprehension* is at the level of semantics.

However, there is a broader sense of the word, one that includes com-prehension of structure as well as meaning. Comprehension represents a continuum of possibilities ranging from semantics to detailed structural analyses. In other words, comprehended input is potentially multistaged. For example, one can comprehend something at the level of meaning; that is, one can have an understanding of the general message. On the other hand, one can imagine a more analytic understanding taking place, with learners performing a mini-linguistic analysis. They might under-stand what the component parts of an utterance are and thus gain an understanding of the syntactic or phonological pattern represented. This recognition of different levels of analysis is important in relation to the subsequent level of intake.

In dealing with comprehension, one must further remember from chapter 1 that there are many aspects of language that second language learners must learn. These include not only the more common areas of syntax and phonology (including knowledge about segments, syllable structure, and prosody), but also less commonly thought of areas such as discourse (chapter 10), pragmatics (chapter 9), and vocabulary (chapter 13).

There are a number of means by which one can reach a particular analysis. For example, the most common way of getting at a syntactic analysis is by first having an understanding of the meaning. However, one can also imagine having an understanding of the syntax yet not being able to arrive at a meaning. This would be so in the case of idioms, for example, or a proverb.

What is the difference between apperceived and comprehended input? Apperception is conceptualized as a priming device. It prepares the learner for the possibility of subsequent analysis. For example, in learning a language with contrastive vowel length, a learner might apperceive that vowel length is an important feature of the language. In comprehending, however, the task facing the learner is to analyze the input in order to determine what the vowel length is in some particular context and then to relate the particular vowel length to a specific meaning. To take a specific example, Japanese uses vowel length for the purpose of differentiating the meanings of words: /biru/ "building" versus /biːru/ "beer." A learner of Japanese has to first recognize that Japanese differentiates between words on this basis (apperception), then recognize the difference between /biru/ and /biːru/ (comprehension), and then match /biru/ with the concept of 'building' and/or /biːru/ with the concept of 'beer' (another level of comprehension).

There is another necessary separation of components—that of comprehended input from intake (see chapter 10). This separation is important because not all input that is comprehended becomes intake. For example, input may be comprehended only for the immediate purpose of a conversational interaction, or it may be used for purposes of learning. Færch and Kasper (1980) proposed something similar when they differentiated between intake as communication and intake as learning, where the first is language intake only for the purpose of immediate meaning in the course of a conversational interaction, and the second is intake incorporated into a learner's grammar. Intake in the approach being discussed in this chapter only includes the second of these possibilities, because intake refers to the *process* of attempted integration of linguistic information. Thus, input that is only used in a conversation and for the sake of that conversation is not regarded as intake.

One factor that determines whether a particular instance of comprehended input will result in intake is the level of analysis of the input a learner achieves. For example, an analysis at the level of meaning is not as useful for intake as an analysis made at the level of syntax. This proposal is supported by Færch and Kasper (1986), who, in the context of foreign language teaching, argued that one way of improving formal correctness is to provide learners with tasks designed to promote recognition of formal features rather than overall comprehension of meaning. Support is also found from Call (1985), who argued for the importance of syntax and structural awareness in listening comprehension. A second factor is the time factor. Pressures of conversational interaction may preclude sufficient analysis for the purposes of intake. In this case, the input (even though comprehended) may have no further role in acquisition.

What will determine whether the second language is comprehended? Prior linguistic knowledge (e.g., knowledge of the NL, of the TL, language universals, knowledge of other languages) is an important aspect (chapters 4 and 5). These same factors are important in the determination of apperception as well. This is not surprising because linguistic knowledge is in some ways cumulative. One needs a place to attach new information and one needs some basis for the analysis (i.e., comprehension) of new information. Comprehension cannot take place in a vacuum. Prior knowledge forms the basis for comprehension (in either a narrow or broad sense).

14.1.3 Intake

Intake is the process of assimilating linguistic material (see chapter 10). Intake refers to the mental activity that mediates between input and grammars and is different from apperception or comprehension, as the latter two do not necessarily lead to grammar formation. This, of course, suggests that intake is not merely a subset of input. Rather, input and intake refer to two fundamentally different phenomena.

What mediates between what has been comprehended and what is eventually important for intake? We have already mentioned that the quality of analysis (i.e., comprehended input) is an important factor. Clearly, knowledge of the L1 and the L2 is also significant (see chapters 4 and 5). Additionally, whether a particular feature is part of UG (representing something innate) or is part of a universal typological feature will also bear upon eventual intake. These factors are not to be understood as being necessarily independent. Features that are part of universal knowledge and/or present in the native language (or other languages known) are most likely to be candidates for a deeper analysis and hence candidates for intake.

How can we describe the intake component? It is that component where psycholinguistic processing takes place (chapter 8). That is, it is where incoming information is matched up against prior knowledge and where, in general, processing takes place against the backdrop of the existing internalized grammatical rules. It is where generalizations and so-called overgeneralizations are likely to occur; it is where memory traces are formed; and finally, it is the component from which fossilization stems. Fossilization results when new (correct) input fails to have an impact on the learner's nontarget-like grammar. That is, the correct input is not apperceived or is not comprehended, and thus it is not further processed.

Some of the major processes that take place in the intake component are hypothesis formation, hypothesis testing, hypothesis rejection, hypothesis modification, and hypothesis confirmation.

Hypothesis formation takes place with the addition of new information. A beginning learner (let's assume an NS of Spanish) hears the English sentence *It's pretty* and forms the hypothesis that English sentences can be of the form verb + adjective. The learner arrives at this conclusion by (a) attending to the form, (b) apperceiving it in terms of the Spanish sentence like *Es bonito*, and (c) understanding the sentence in terms of both its meaning and its syntactic structure. The error in the learner's analysis comes from the fact that *it's* is heard as being similar to *es* and the learner assumes a similar syntactic structure. Thus, knowledge of the L1 facilitates that conclusion. Prior knowledge led (a) to apperception, (b) to actual syntactic and semantic comprehension, and (c) to intake because the analysis matched up with something the learner already knew (*es bonito*).

The hypothesis of verb + adjective is tested against a reasonable assumption, that of native–target language similarity. The hypothesis is confirmed. At a later point in time, the learner might see the printed version of *it's* and question the single-word analysis originally given to this form. This would cause the learner to modify this hypothesis and possibly further test it against new data. If the hypothesis is modified in such a way as to eliminate the first hypothesis, that first hypothesis is rejected and is no longer relevant for grammar formation.

14.1.4 Integration

After there is language intake, there are at least two possible outcomes, both of which are a form of *integration*: the development *per se* of one's second language grammar and storage. The distinction made here is between integration and nonintegration of new linguistic information.

Let's consider how this relates to input. There are essentially four possibilities for dealing with input. The first two take place in the intake component and result in integration, the third takes place in the integration component, and the fourth represents input that exits the system early on in the process.

1   *Hypothesis confirmation/rejection (intake)*. This first possibility for input is useful as part of the confirmation or rejection of a current hypothesis. This results in integration.

2   *Apparent nonuse.* Apparent nonuse stems from the fact that the information contained in the input is already incorporated into a learner's grammar. However, the fact that the information is already incorporated into a grammar does not necessarily exclude it from being utilized—but in a different way than what one normally thinks of. When the information contained in the input is already a part of one's knowledge base, the additional input might be used for *rule strengthening* or hypothesis reconfirmation. Part of becoming a fluent speaker of a second language involves the automatic retrieval of information from one's knowledge base. The knowledge base is developed through practice or repeated exposures to exemplars. Thus, information that may appear to be redundant may in fact be serving an important purpose in terms of the access a learner has to that information.

3   *Storage.* The third possibility is that input is put into storage, perhaps because some level of understanding has taken place, yet it is not clear how integration into a learner's grammar can or should take place. An example will help to make this clear. A Spanish-speaking ESL student had heard the word *so* in the following sentence: *So, what did you do yesterday?* The student could neither figure out what it meant nor how to use it and asked a direct question in an ESL class as to the meaning. From this, one can infer that the learner had stored this information and was waiting for it to be available for integration.

4   *Nonuse.* In this final possibility, learners make no use of the input at all. This may be because they have not succeeded in comprehending it at a useful level.

Integration is not necessarily a one-time affair. Rather, there are different levels of analysis and reanalysis from storage into the grammar, and within the grammar itself, as part of integration.

Importantly, the integration component does not function as an independent unit. This is particularly significant in the model we are discussing (and SLA in general) because SLA is dynamic and interactive, with knowledge itself being cumulative and interactive.

Language information that is processed and deemed appropriate for language development, yet that is not put into storage, becomes part of a learner's knowledge system, or grammar. A significant amount of work has been done in this area; indeed, it represents the bulk of the work in second language acquisition over the past few decades. This includes most of the work on linguistic (see chapters 6 and 7) and psycholinguistic (chapter 8) aspects of acquisition.

What are some factors that mediate among comprehended input, intake, and integration? Some are similar to those that are also available at the level of apperception. For example, the organizational structure of the native language may shape the way the learner's grammar is structured. Existing knowledge of the second language will also shape the way integration takes place. Universal principles of language may also play a role in second language grammar formation (see chapters 6 and 7). Given a particular element in the input, there are universal factors that interact with it, resulting in a generalization of the initial input to other related domains.

A factor that provides the impetus or motivation for changes in one's knowledge base is the recognition of a mismatch between what is present in the input and the learner's grammar. For learners to modify their speech, they must first recognize that there is something in need of modification—that there is a perceived mismatch between native speaker speech and their own learner grammars.

Evidence for integrated knowledge can be seen in one of two ways. First, there can be changes in the rule system that surface in the output. This is in fact what is typically thought of when one considers developmental changes.

Second, there may be changes in the underlying system although there is no output change. Changes in underlying systems with no surface manifestation are typically subsumed under the category of reanalysis or restructuring (see section 8.3.2).

Within a second language context, we can think of reanalysis in two ways. First, a reanalysis of the underlying system may affect the *potential* for output. For example, one can imagine a learner having learned the lexical item *orange juice* as a single lexical item *orangejuice* and only at a later point in time reanalyzing it as *orange + juice*. This reanalysis sets the stage for the potential forms *apple juice, grapefruit juice*, and so forth.[5] Thus, reanalysis allows for the potential creation of novel forms. Second, on a syntactic level, prefabricated patterns may be analyzed (initially) with little output change. As discussed in Chapter 5, Hakuta (1974a) cited the speech of Uguisu, a 5-year-old child learning English. In the first month of data collection, the following were typical utterances:

(14-1) Do you know?
(14-2) Do you want this one?

In later periods, it became obvious that *do you* was a (possibly monomorphemic) question marker. When reanalysis did finally take place and *do you* was analyzed into its component parts, with the result being a productive rule of question formation, there was no output difference. Sentences 14-3 and 14-4 are taken from the fifth month and sixth month, respectively, of data collection:

(14-3) How do you break it?
(14-4) Do you put it?

Thus, whereas there was no output difference as a function of reanalysis, the underlying systems were different, as evidenced by other forms in this learner's grammar (see section 8.3.2 on restructuring).

14.1.5 Output

The final stage that needs to be examined is that of output. In chapter 10, we discussed the concept and importance of comprehensible output. There are two points to emphasize. First, there is the role of comprehensible output in testing hypotheses. Thus, there can be a feedback loop back into the intake component. Second, there is the role output plays in forcing a syntactic rather than a solely semantic analysis on language. This conceptualization of output necessitates a feedback loop to comprehended input.

Learners' output is often equated with their grammar. For example, it is frequently inferred that changes in the output represent changes in a learner's grammar. However, as can be seen in Figure 14.1, the two should not be equated. That the output is not identical to one's grammar is suggested by a number of factors. Among these is the recognition that there are individual differences in what learners are willing to say. Personality factors such as confidence in one's ability to produce correct target language sentences may influence whether or not a learner produces target language material. Additionally, learners produce different linguistic forms that have varying amounts of accuracy depending on the context and the task performed (see chapter 9). For example, what learners can produce in writing is not what they can produce in speaking; what they can understand from a printed page is not equivalent to what they can understand from an oral stimulus. Finally, different grammatical information may be used in different genres. Undoubtedly, this has to do with the ability to use different channels to express linguistic information. It is also a matter of limitations of access that one has to one's knowledge base.

Not only is confidence in one's ability a determining factor in output, but we can also consider how strongly represented the knowledge is. There may be different degrees of strength of knowledge representation (perhaps related to the automaticity of language processing) that will in part determine what output will take place and how it will take place. An example is provided by Swain (1985, p. 248), who quoted from an eighth grade immersion student who said, "I can hear in my head how I should sound when I talk, but it never comes out that way." Thus, there appear to be limitations on the translation of knowledge into output.

In sum, the output component represents more than the product of language knowledge; it is an active part of the entire learning process.

14.2 Conclusion

This chapter has presented a conceptualization of the ways in which the pieces of acquisition fit together, integrating aspects of language acquisition that have been discussed in greater detail in the preceding chapters of this book.

The model in Figure 14.1 is intended to reflect the dynamic and inter-active nature of acquisition. It also shows the multiple roles of language transfer and universals. Their roles can only be understood in relation to a specific part of the process. For example, language transfer, as part of prior knowledge, can have a filtering role, as was seen in going from input to apperceived input; a facilitating role when aiding comprehension; and a processing role, as was seen at the level of intake.

Furthermore, such aspects as personality and affect, factors that are under the learner's control to the greatest extent, are important at the initial stages of apperception. Their role is less significant at the levels of intake and integration, areas that are affected by pure linguistic factors (e.g., universals of either a formal or functional type) devoid of cultural and social context and psycholinguistic factors. Finally, personality and affect once again emerge as important factors at the level of output. In other words, those factors that are under the learner's control to the greatest extent have the greatest effect only at the peripheries; that is, at the levels of initial apperceived input and output.

Psycholinguistic processing and linguistic phenomena in the middle are more influenced by mental constraints that are less accessible to direct manipulation. What one would thus expect is: (a) a correlation between affective variables and what is apperceived, on the one hand, and what is produced, on the other; and (b) a *lack* of correlation between affective variables and aspects of, for example, Universal Grammar.

In sum, there is a major role for apperceived input, determined to a large extent by selective attention. Without selective attention, grammar development does not take place. In other words, a first step in grammar change is the learner's noticing (at some level) a mismatch between the input and his or her own organization of the target language.

When there is a nonoccurrence of a linguistic phenomenon in the input, change is less likely to come about than in those instances in which forms are overtly present in the target language. It is the areas of the grammar that result from nonoccurrence that are most likely to remain fossilized. Recall the discussion in chapter 10 (section 10.5.1 on feedback) regarding adverb placement. French speakers learning English frequently produce utterances such as 14-5:

(14-5) John drinks slowly his coffee.

Because the input does not provide a forum for the learner to readily detect a discrepancy between his or her learner language and the target language, fossilization is likely to occur.

Another area that must be dealt with has to do with variation in learner languages. Variation (both nonrandom and free) (see chapter 9) in second language acquisition has been well documented. It can be seen diachronically as well as synchronically. Diachronic variation is that variation that represents a change in a learner's knowledge over time; synchronic variation is variation dependent on demands of task type, situation, and language. The important questions are: How do variation and acquisition interact, and what are the constraints on possible variable parts of one's grammar? The concept of automaticity/strength of knowledge discussed in this book is a major factor in the determination of what can and cannot vary. For example, knowledge that is "strongly" represented is least likely to vary; knowledge that is "weakly" represented is most likely to vary.

But what contributes to the degree of strength of knowledge? If we think of strength of knowledge as being related to memory and prior knowledge, we can understand that the native language and/or language universals as well as memory capacity are central to this consideration.

Within the present framework, we have pointed to the fact that there is much mileage that needs to be traveled between the input the learner receives and what the learner produces. We cannot assume that with mere presentation of language information, whether implicitly or explicitly, learners will necessarily convert it to output or to an internal representation. It is an arduous task for the learner to (a) extract information from the input, (b) utilize it in forming a grammar, and (c) produce target language forms. Some parts of the process are more accessible to direct learner intervention; others (e.g., psycholinguistic and linguistic phenomena) are less so. It is up to research in future decades to work this process out in all its rich detail.

This book has attempted to integrate components of second language acquisition by presenting a view of acquisition that is dynamic and interactive in nature. It is only by considering second language acquisition in its many and diverse aspects that we can begin to understand the complexities and the interrelationships of this process.

Suggestions for additional reading

The Handbook of Second Language Acquisition. Catherine Doughty and Michael Long (Eds.). Blackwell Publishing (2003).
Second Language Acquisition. Rod Ellis. Oxford University Press (1997).
Theory Construction in Second Language Acquisition. Geoff Jordan. John Benjamins (2004).

An Introduction to Second Language Acquisition Research. Diane Larsen-Freeman and Michael Long. Longman (1991).

How Languages are Learned. Patsy Lightbown and Nina Spada. Oxford University Press (2006).

Second Language Learning Theories. Rosamond Mitchell and Florence Myles. Edward Arnold (2004).

Mind and Context in Adult Second Language Acquisition: Methods, Theory, and Practice. Cristina Sanz (Ed.). Georgetown University Press (2005).

Theories in Second Language Acquisition: An Introduction. Bill VanPatten and Jessica Williams (Eds.). Lawrence Erlbaum Associates (2007).

Points for discussion

1   Choose two or three topics dealt with in this book and discuss them in the context of the model of SLA presented in this chapter.

2   In terms of this model, how can one justify the fact that concepts such as transfer and language universals have multiple roles in the acquisition process?

3   Are there parts of SLA that are not accounted for in the model presented in this chapter?

4   What is your view on the question of whether interlanguages are "natural languages"? Be sure to support your view. In your answer, consider the question of linguistic complexity and language learning. That is, in principle can ILs be as complex as natural (primary) languages? How would this issue differ depending on the level of language learning (i.e., beginning learners vs. more advanced learners)?

5   Consider standard Spanish, where one has double negatives:

> No sabe   nada.
> not know nothing
> "S/he doesn't know anything."

> No tiene nada   de dinero
> not have nothing of money
> "S/he doesn't have any money."

And standard English, where one does not:

> He knows nothing.
> She doesn't know anything.
> He has no money.
> She doesn't have any money.

What would you predict would be the forms a native speaker of Spanish would use in learning English? Consider also the effects of time and environment—that is, the length of time of exposure to

English and the location of exposure (classroom vs. naturalistic). What if the Spanish speaker were exposed to a dialect of English in which double negatives were common?

What would you predict would be the forms a native speaker of English would use in learning Spanish? Would the factors of time and environment have the same effects?

Which of these two groups of learners would have the easier time learning the standard L2 form? Justify your answer.

6 Imagine a particular structure that might be present in the input to a learner. What might and might not happen to that structure as far as the learner is concerned? Trace the path of that structure according to the principles of the model presented in this chapter.

7 The following statements were given in problem 9 in chapter 1, where you were asked to determine whether each was true or false. Do so again. Working with a partner, determine whether your answers and your partner's answers are the same or different. Discuss the statements for which your answers differ.

a Any child without cognitive disabilities can learn any language with equal ease.

b Learning a second language is a matter of learning a new set of habits.

c The only reason that some people cannot learn a second or foreign language is that they are insufficiently motivated.

d All children can learn a second language accent-free.

e No adult can learn a second language accent-free.

f All human beings have an innate capacity to learn language.

g Vocabulary is the most important part of learning a second language.

h Vocabulary is the most difficult part of learning a second language.

i Language instruction is a waste of time.

j Learning a second language takes no more time than learning a first language.

8 The following metaphors were created to represent SLA for a class project. How well do you think these do or do not express the concepts presented in this book?

Metaphor: Building a house (Margaret Johnson)

Contrastive Analysis Hypothesis

Premise: The distances between languages influence second language acquisition.

Metaphor: When building a second house, the builder refers to strategies he used in the past and applies them to the construction.

Behaviorism
Premise: Learning by imitation, mimicry, and memorization.
Metaphor: Builder looks to other houses in the neighborhood and uses them as a model to go off of when constructing his/her own house.

Innatist perspective
Premise: Proposes that at least some aspects of language are innate and hardwired.
Metaphor: Before a house is constructed, there is usually a blueprint, or a plan that guides the builder in creating the house.

Connectionism
Premise: Emphasizes environment influence and exposure to language towards a gradual buildup of language.
Metaphor: The builder needs the assistance of others to help construct the house; he cannot do it entirely on his own.

Processability theory
Premise: The sequence of second language acquisition is consistent in order, but not necessarily consistent in rate.
Metaphor: There is an undeniable order to building a house, beginning with the base, then a lower level, followed by (possibly) more levels, and then a roof. This is true despite the kind of house or where it is built.

Riding a bicycle (Karen Cheung)

Overview
When learning to ride a bicycle, many children first start off with training wheels. With training wheels, children don't have to think of balancing the bike; they just have to focus on pedaling and steering the wheel. Some children may not even focus on pedaling; they may just put their feet on the pedals and just pedal. When a child has gotten used to the training wheels, the training wheels are taken off so that all is left is two wheels. Someone usually helps the child when the child first rides a two wheeler. A person may hold the back of the seat to help the child

balance on the bicycle. At one point, the person will release their hand to let the child ride by themselves. The child may be able to balance by themselves or fall down, but eventually, the child would get used to riding the two wheeled bike by themselves. With more and more practice, the child would be more comfortable riding by themselves. Once a person is able to ride the bicycle independently, there may be factors that may affect their ability to ride. The environment can affect the ability for people to ride their bikes. It is easier to ride a bike on a smooth pavement than a rocky pavement or grass. It is easier to ride downhill than uphill. It is easier to ride a bike on a nice sunny/cloudy day than in a raining/snowing/sleeting day. All these factors may make it hard for some to ride their bicycle, but with motivation and determination, a person can get through anything.

Specifics
Training wheels
A two wheeled bike represents a person learning a second language. Like an adult guiding the child to ride on a two wheeled bike, there is usually guidance from a teacher when learning a second language. The teacher guides the learner in learning the second language and eventually, the learner will be able to communicate in that second language. This concept is similar to the Zone of Proximal Development in that what a child can do with assistance is different than what a child can do independently. The guidance of an adult helping a child during the first day(s) of riding a two wheeled bike is helpful in that a child may have fewer accidents. The child can feel how the bike is supposed to be balanced so that they can try to balance on their own. So in second language learning, assistance can help a learner so that they will be able to complete their work independently. Once a learner can understand that concept/idea that they are working on, then that concept/idea becomes internalized just like how a child can then ride their by bike by themselves without assistance.

Similar to learning to ride a bicycle, it may be hard at first when riding a two wheeled bike but then it begins to get easier. With more and more practice, a learner can get better at learning a second language. There are factors, though, that may affect the way learners learn a second language and that is the environment.

Two wheeled bike
Learning to ride a bicycle is just like learning a second language.

When a learner first learns a language (first language acquisition), they are like the first stage—training wheels—of riding a bicycle. It starts off pretty easy for the learners because they are born into a language. Everybody around them is speaking the same language. The first language is innate to the child. When children are on the bike, they just begin to pedal the bike; it is innate for them to pedal the bike. From the innatist perspective, "Chomsky argued that children are biologically programmed for language and that language develops in the child in just the same way that other biological functions develop" (Lightbown and Spada, 2006, p. 15). So it is innate to ride a bicycle just like it is innate for people to learn languages. Once the child gets used to pedaling the bike, they move on to a two wheeled bike.

The environment

When riding a bicycle one type of pavement may be easier than another. The weather may make it easier or harder for a person to ride in. Hills can make it easier or harder for riders. In socio-cultural theory, environment plays a vital role in second language learning. From conversing with others to reading a book, the environment is important in second language learning. A learner may learn better if they are in an environment where everyone is speaking that second language or where they have to speak in that second language. Also, if a learner is receiving positive reinforcement when they did something correct, learners are encouraged to continue doing it correctly. Positive reinforcement is part of the behaviorists' perspective, where they believed that "when children imitated the language produced by those around them, their attempts to reproduce what they heard received 'positive reinforcement.' Thus, encouraged by their environment, children would continue to imitate and practice these sounds and patterns until they formed 'habits' of correct language use" (Lightbown and Spada, 2006, p. 10). So a child may receive positive reinforcement when riding their bicycle when they are doing something correctly. This will help the child to know that they are doing it correctly, and should continue to do it that way.

Mathematics (Jennifer Grima)

The basics

The laws

There are laws in math, but like the rules of grammar, there are always exceptions.

When dealing with radicals, there can never be a negative number under the radical, except when dealing with imaginary numbers.

Only humans are able to comprehend math.

No other animals can grasp mathematical concepts.

Developmental sequences

A person must first learn the basics of math in order to eventually comprehend the other components of math.

Basic algebra (1 + 2) is the basics of all other levels of math (calculus, trigonometry, geometry).

Regardless of the country it's learned in, math is learned in the same basic order.

Addition and subtraction

Multiplication and division

Pre-algebra

Algebra

Pre-calculus

Calculus I, II, III

Acquisition

Behaviorist/Interactionist

The more you are exposed to math concepts, the more you will learn and the better you will get.

Taking a couple math classes in college will result in better math skills.

If a person's math skills aren't used for a while, some aspects will be forgotten, while other aspects will never be forgotten.

Once a person learns how to add, he/she will never lose that ability. However, other math skills, such as derivatives, can be easily forgotten.

Some people comprehend math faster, while others take longer to acquire the knowledge.

Critical Period Hypothesis

The older you get, the harder it is to learn math. You have previous experiences and knowledge that may interfere with the laws or rules of math.

Pythagorean Theorem—How did they get this? Older people will analyze it.

Imaginary numbers—There is no such thing.

Previous knowledge of different types of math may interfere with learning another type.

In trigonometry the sin and cos laws interfere with Calculus laws of sin and cos.

Painting a picture (Amanda Craik)

In order to illustrate second language acquisition, I first need to illustrate first language acquisition. First language acquisition is like painting a picture of your immediate surroundings—painting a picture of a place you grew up in and are familiar with. All of your experiences and thoughts are defined by this place you grew up in. This is like first language acquisition; the first language is surrounding you all the time, most of your life experiences deal with this first language, and the input of language is always in this first language.

Second language acquisition is like painting a picture of a place you have maybe seen in a picture and have heard about from other people. You are given the same paintbrushes and paints to paint this picture as you were given to paint the picture of your immediate surroundings. In some ways this picture is easy to paint, because you have already used and practiced certain cognitive processes in painting your first picture and understanding the world around you. For example, you already know what a tree is, so when someone tells you to paint a tree you understand what this means. However, this can also hinder you—if someone tells you to paint a tree you may paint a pine tree like in your first painting, because this is what you are familiar with, when in fact you were supposed to paint a palm tree. Even after you learn what a palm tree is, you may continue to accidentally paint pine trees. Also, even if lots of people tell you what this new place is like or if you get a glimpse of this new place from a postcard, you don't have the same experience of living in that place and having memories of that place. Another factor is that it will be easier to paint the second place if it is similar to the first place, but the more different it is, the harder it will be to paint. Also, while you are trying to paint this new place your original familiar surroundings are still all around you, continuing to influence you as you paint. It will be hard to complete the picture; it will probably be an ongoing process that will never look exactly like the place you are trying to paint.

The paintbrushes in this metaphor are like Universal Grammar. In both first and second language acquisition, we start out with the same basic tools for understanding the grammatical structure of a language. In the first language, though it may be hard to produce (paint) the language perfectly at the beginning because you are not experienced with the language (or with the place you are painting), eventually the user of the language becomes proficient. There is a constant input of the first language (the immediate surroundings) and the person catches on. With the second language, there is input from others (pictures and people) in the second language, but there continues to be input in the first language. This makes it more difficult to learn, because the input is not as constant. Another reason it is harder to learn the second language is because the learner simply does not have background experience with the language. The learner does not have certain connotations or memories that go with certain words. This means, as the sociocultural theory states, the learner will continue to rely on the first language for internal thinking, because it is comfortable and what he or she is used to. Also, it will be easier to paint the second place if it is more similar to the first place—like the Contrastive Analysis Hypothesis states, it will be easier to acquire a language that is more similar to your first language than one that is much different.

One main thing my metaphor doesn't address is if a person is immersed into a language (such as if you were to move to another country), or if they acquire a second language very close to the time they acquire the first (such as when a child is still very young). Rather, it is a metaphor that shows how a second language is acquired when a person with a lot of experience in their first language learns from a classroom setting or a setting that is not immersion-based.

Baking a cake (Megan Sutton)

General overview

Every culture has food, but not everyone eats sweet masses of dough baked in pans. Similarly, every culture has language, but not everyone speaks the same language. Language and food are universal; specific languages and cake are not.

When learning to make cake after growing up with a diet that does not include it, learners are likely to acquire different taste preferences and baking styles. They may put their own spin on recipes, adding different spices or substituting applesauce for oil. Parallel to this is the fact that most second language learners never acquire completely native-like production. They may retain an accent and occasionally use forms that indicate they are using their second language, but as long as this does not interfere with communication, they are considered proficient. We would not consider a scrumptious cake a failure just because it was slightly different from what we were used to, and we do not consider language acquisition a failure just because it is not completely native-like.

Recipes and grammar

The rules for combining the ingredients for cake are often written down in recipes. Recipes are helpful, but not sufficient, for learning to make cakes. Handing a person who has never made a cake, seen a cake being made, heard of cake, or eaten a cake will not be enough for them to be able to make a cake. Being given written instructions for making cake is no substitute for having background knowledge about cake. On the other hand, observing someone make a cake, if repeated enough times, would probably be enough for a learner to figure out how to make a reasonably tasty dessert. Having a recipe to refer to might be helpful, as it would provide them with a framework of understanding, but watching a demonstration or interacting directly with a baker would be optimal.

In this metaphor, direct instruction in the grammar of a language is the recipe that explains how the ingredients of sounds, words, and phrases are combined. The grammar exists even without the recipe, as is clearly shown by the numerous cooks who can make a cake without referring to instructions. An astute learner could learn these rules by observing a cook, just as motivated learners often pick up a second language if given enough meaningful input to it. Still, direct instruction may increase the pace of acquisition because the learner does not have to figure out the rules entirely for themselves.

Theories

Sociocultural theory

Vygotsky states that learners acquire skills faster if they are supported by a more skilled individual whose goal is to help them reach independence. By this metaphor, a child or adult who wants to learn to make cake will benefit the most from working with a mother, grandmother, or other experienced baker who will take into account their current culinary experience (actual development level) and what they are able to accomplish with help (Zone of Proximal Development).

For example, maybe a learner is familiar with breaking eggs and softening butter. Those two skills are within their actual development level. Perhaps pouring the cake batter into the pan is difficult for them, as they must manage lifting a bowl and holding a spatula simultaneously. The experienced individual might hold the bowl the first time, still requiring the novice to do as much of the work as possible, but allowing them to master one skill before moving on to the next. Similarly with language acquisition, sociocultural theory assumes that learners benefit most from working with more advanced interlocutors who can move them toward self regulation on an individualized path that takes into account language features they have mastered and others with which they struggle.

Universal Grammar

According to this perspective, all humans possess an innate knowledge of language that allows them to acquire language. This almost instinctive ability is so fundamental it can be compared to the sense of taste by which we analyze food.

The multitude of possible taste sensations we experience stem from a vast array of combinations of just a few flavors: sweet, sour, bitter, and salty. Similarly, there is a limit to the number of possible phonemes, grammar rules, morphological rules, and other "ingredients" of language. These interact in different ways to create the vast array of human languages.

The taste buds of the tongue are specialized to provide information about the type of food we eat. They tell us if the food we eat contains sugar or salt, bases or acids, and in what proportions they are combined. The Language Acquisition Device functions in a comparable manner. It analyzes the incoming language data, determining what elements are present in the data and how they are combined. Of course, the comparison is not exactly that simple, since the taste buds themselves can't tell us how to make a cake; we need more overt instruction for that. The language capacity of the human mind is truly remarkable in that it both analyzes incoming data and provides the basis for production.

Input processing

VanPatten proposes that learners' processing capacity is limited, and therefore when they cannot hold all the information about both form and meaning, they pay attention first to meaning. Therefore, grammar words like *at* and *that* are overlooked in favor of content words like *girl* or *house*. This process is analogous to learning to make a cake in that a learner would be more likely to pay more attention to adding the main ingredients than to smaller matters like what mixer speed to use or sifting the flour.

Imagine someone who has never made a cake. An experienced baker takes them through the entire process. What are they most likely to remember? The order in which everything is placed into the mixing bowl? Or the fact that cake contains eggs, milk, and flour? If they forget the latter ingredients, the cake is likely to be inedible, so after they've had a bit of experience they'll probably at least remember the main ingredients. The cake might have a strange consistency without the leavening agent, just as sentences sound strange without proper word order, but the end product would probably be suitable for eating. Eventually, we would expect a novice baker to remember to add all the necessary ingredients in the right amounts and order. Similarly, learners first process the aspects of language that they perceive to be most important, and gradually move to a more native-like comprehension of their second language.

Contrastive Analysis Hypothesis
This school of thought surmises that learners pair their second language with their first, making it easier for a learner to acquire a language that is more similar to their first, and more difficult to acquire forms that are very different from their native language. Translating this into baking terms, learners should have acquired the ability to bake a cake if they come from a culture that has a similar food, like brownies. If their cooking background consists of only barbecuing, they may struggle more as they learn about mixers, ovens, and baking ingredients.

The flaw in this theory, in either a language or a baking model, is that learners may have interference if their experience is too similar to what they are learning. For example, the most significant difference between brownies and cake is the presence of leavening. Forgetting to put in baking soda could have considerable consequences for the cake, just as omitting word endings can have disastrous consequences in communication. Additionally, not every mistake learners make can be related to their previous experience; some are equally likely to occur in people with brownie and barbecue backgrounds.

Ode to SLA by Erich Ziroll

SLA is like Coin-Star type of machine,
Based on proto-types and frequency,
Separating and connecting different ideas,
Developing a language system oh so fancy.

SLA is like a labyrinth of constraining walls to be navigated,
Figuring out which direction you must go at each turn,
Using principles of language as your guide,
Whilst a second language you begin to learn.

SLA is like a game of throw and catch,
Participating in negotiation of meaning and correction,

Receiving a constant supply of feedback,
Making adjustments for every little detection.

SLA is like a caterpillar "internalized" in a cocoon,
With the intention of becoming a butterfly,
Along with the assistance of others,
To emerge anew, floating toward the sky.

SLA is like a spider in the process of building its web,
Expanding by matching functions to forms and forms to
    functions,
Following the certain paths to get to the next language stage,
Until the web of language has adequate conjunctions.

SLA is like a switch pad waiting for a code to activate it,
Gaining access to all principles of language through input,
At last the door opens revealing the treasure of language,
With every possible combination given to you afoot.

9   As a class project, reflect upon the ideas presented in this book and
    come up with a metaphor that synthesizes your view of SLA. Create
    a poster that symbolizes your view of second language acquisition.
    (Thanks to Ben White [via Jerri Willet] for this idea.)

NOTES

1 INTRODUCTION

1 The distinction made between second and foreign language learning is blurred in this book given our belief that a theory of learning a language beyond the first must be all-encompassing and must include instances of learning where the target language is spoken natively and where it is not.

2 In reality, the picture is more complex because there are language-learning situations where a variety of the language being learned is spoken widely although for the most part it is not natively spoken (e.g., English in India).

3 An * is used to indicate a form that does not or cannot exist in a language.

4 Since the early 1970s, a number of terms have been used to describe basically the same concept: *approximative system* (Nemser, 1971b), *transitional competence* (Corder, 1967), *idiosyncratic dialect* (Corder, 1971), *learner language* (Færch, Haastrup, and Phillipson, 1984). Each of these terms has a slightly different focus. However, interlanguage is the most commonly used one.

2 RELATED DISCIPLINES

1 Valdés (2001b) points out that, up until 1996, heritage speakers of Spanish had been primarily referred to as native speakers of Spanish.

2 This may be an oversimplification, because there is also variation from individual to individual within each of these disciplines.

3 There are many interesting issues that surround the acquisition of sign language. They are, however, beyond the scope of this book.

4 Foster-Cohen (1999) stated that, although smiling may occur as early as the third week of life, it may not have the precise meaning it has in later life.

3 SECOND AND FOREIGN LANGUAGE DATA

1 We thank the many students and teachers who have provided insights into these data sets, most especially Walid Abu Halaweb of Ibrahimieh College in Jerusalem. None of them is responsible for the particular interpretations finally presented here. Many of the examples in this chapter originally appeared in Selinker and Gass (1984). We thank Sandra Deline, Patricia Jensen, and Asma Omari for their assistance in gathering these data.

2 Within the second language literature the idea of "spontaneous utterance" is generally opposed to forced elicitation. The latter refers to language samples gathered in an experimental context.

3 Transitive verbs are verbs that take a direct object, as in *I saw the dog*; whereas intransitive verbs do not take direct objects, as in *The baby is sleeping*.

4 This could be a simplification strategy of a common kind: the one to many principle, where one form is used for several functions (see Rutherford, 1987).

5 The concept "covert error" was established by Corder (1967) to describe the situation in which the learner has a grammatically correct target-like form, but the form is semantically or pragmatically inappropriate. Corder provided an example in which an NS of German said, "You mustn't take off your hat," when he intended to say, "You don't have to take off your hat."

6 Although not precisely an analogous situation, one can think of the example of Latin categories being imposed on English standards. Most of us can remember our high-school English teachers and earlier telling us not to split infinitives. Yet, we also know that this is common in spoken English (*I want to explicitly state* . . .). The origin of this rule of English is from Latin, where infinitives are one word (as in Romance languages today) and can therefore not be split. The rule, as applied to English, is inappropriate in that it results from the imposition of the category of one language onto another.

7 There is a theoretical distinction to be made between grammaticality judgments and acceptability judgments, despite the fact that the two terms are often used interchangeably. The former, in strict linguistic terms, refers to those sentences that are generated by the grammar, whereas the latter refers to those sentences about which speakers have a feel of well-formedness. As a theoretical construct, grammaticality judgments are not directly accessible but are inferred through acceptability judgments.

8 VSO order is somewhat limited in Italian. It can be used for stress (as in 3-73). With a noun rather than a pronoun, there is often a pause after the subject.

9 The growing significance of replication can be seen by the emergence of a section in *Language Teaching*, beginning in 2008, dedicated to replication studies.

10 Although more detail is presented concerning the acquisition of relative clauses in chapter 7, we give some preliminary information here in order to make it easier to interpret the table. Both tables list six kinds of relative clauses. These reflect the syntactic role of the noun that is being modified in the relative clause. The first sentence exemplifies the relative clause type and the second sentence exemplifies a sentence with a resumptive pronoun.

Subject relative clause:
That's the man [*who* ran away] (*who* is the subject of the clause).
*That's the man who *he* ran away.

Direct object relative clause:
That's the man [*whom* I saw yesterday] (*whom* is the object of its clause).
*That's the man who I saw *him* yesterday.

Indirect object relative clause:
That's the man [to *whom* I gave the letter].
*That's the man to whom I gave *him* the letter.

Object of preposition relative clause:
That's the man [*whom* I told you about].
*That's the man whom I told you about *him*.

Genitive relative clause:
That's the man [*whose sister* I know].
*That's the man who *his sister* I know.

Object of comparative:
  That's the man [*whom* I am taller than].
  *That's the man whom I am taller than *him*.

4 THE ROLE OF THE NATIVE LANGUAGE: AN HISTORICAL OVERVIEW

1 During the 1960s there were entire books devoted to contrasting the structures of two languages (see Agard and Di Pietro, 1965a, 1965b; Stockwell, Bowen, and Martin, 1965a, 1965b).

2 Those working on linguistic analysis during this period of time (e.g., Bloomfield, Sapir) were primarily involved with languages for which there was no writing system. This may have influenced their views on the primacy of speech over writing. Writing in this earlier view was seen as a means of transcribing oral language. "Writing is not language, but merely a way of recording language by means of visible marks" (Bloomfield, 1933, p. 21).

3 Zobl (1980) hypothesized that this discrepancy occurs due to other factors of the L2. For French speakers learning English, the fact that English always has verb–object order (with both noun and pronominal objects) does not allow the French speaker to find any similarity between the native language and the TL with regard to pronominal placement. Thus, the native speaker of French is thwarted in his or her efforts to find congruence. However, the native speaker of English does find congruence between the NL and the TL. Word order of the type verb–object does occur in French (although only with noun objects). Furthermore, the object–verb order seems to be a more complex construction than the verb–object one, with French children showing a bias toward the latter. Hence, one can still employ the concept of native language influence, although clearly not in a simple way, as was predicted by a behaviorist theory.

4 Intralingual errors are also known as developmental errors. The claim here is that they are common to all language learners, thereby being part of language development.

5 This is codified in the "Multiple Effects Principle" (Selinker and Lakshmanan, 1992). The view is critiqued in the recent case study of a fossilized learner (Lardiere, 2007).

5 RECENT PERSPECTIVES ON THE ROLE OF PREVIOUSLY KNOWN LANGUAGES

1 This assumes that the *I'm* is part of the progressive.

2 This is not unlike what happens in other reduced language systems (see Valdman, 1977; Valdman and Phillips, 1975).

3 Some studies (e.g., Papadopoulu and Clahsen, 2003; Felser, Roberts, Gross, and Marinis, 2003) have shown different results using a different methodology (eye-tracking in some studies versus self-paced reading in others). Frenck-Mestre, however, argues that this may be due to the proficiency level or the mixed results within a group which could have nullified the transfer effect.

6 FORMAL APPROACHES TO SLA

1 A notable exception comes from one of the authors of this book who, during a recent trip to New Zealand, had a difficult time resetting her driving parameter from right (United States) to left (New Zealand). She frequently found herself straddling the middle and was thankful for the paucity of cars on many of the

roads in New Zealand. The second author who comes from a right-driving culture (United States), at one point in his life lived in a left-driving culture (United Kingdom). He had no difficulty returning to the right, but did have trouble resetting his second culture street-crossing parameter from left (United Kingdom) to right (rest of Europe). Unfortunately, there is no paucity of cars in Europe.

2 In actuality, there is a third type of evidence: *indirect negative evidence*. As Chomsky (1981, p. 9) stated:

> a not unreasonable acquisition system can be devised with the operative principle that if certain structures or rules fail to be exemplified in relative simple expressions, where they would be expected to be found, then a (possibly marked) option is selected excluding them in the grammar, so that a kind of "negative evidence" can be available even without corrections, adverse reactions, etc.

Plough (1994) claimed that the term *indirect negative evidence* is a misnomer because it is not a form of indirect correction, or any sort of correction. Rather, she claimed the term is an "indirect means of letting the learner know that a feature is not possible because it is never present in the *expected environment*" (p. 30). It may be easier to understand this concept in second language acquisition than in first because a crucial part of the notion rests on the concept *expected environment*. Essentially, there are two choices for these expectations: (a) from the innately specified principles and parameters of Universal Grammar or (b) from the first language (or other languages known).

An example can be provided from the animal world. In certain types of primates, babies must learn the difference between predatory birds and nonpredatory birds. In the case of the former, the entire community screeches loudly when these birds approach. However, in the case of nonpredatory birds, the absence of screeches (in the context that screeches are to be expected) provides information to the babies that allows them to distinguish between predatory and nonpredatory birds.

3 This is, of course, a performance-level phenomenon and does not directly relate to learners' underlying knowledge of a language system. It only relates to the ways in which that knowledge system is put to use.

4 Even though this new lexical item has permeated the English lexicon, the spelling is not yet codified; *Time* uses *dotcom*, *Newsweek* uses *dot-com*.

5 For those familiar with the theory on which this is based, this violation occurs because elements cannot jump over more than one bounding node. In English, IP and NP are bounding nodes. The underlying structure of the sentence is as follows:

$$[_{CP}\text{Who}_i \text{ do } [_{IP} \text{ you agree with } [_{NP} \text{ the idea } [_{CP} \text{ that } [_{IP} \text{ David loves } t_i]]]]]$$

Hence, the movement of the question word to the front of the sentence involves jumping over three nodes and, therefore, is a violation of subjacency.

6 See White (1989) for a theoretical discussion of alternative explanations for Schachter's data.

7 White (2003) presents data from Kellerman, van Ijzendoorn, and Takashima (1999) that purport to refute the claims of Kanno, arguing that Kellerman *et al.*'s data do not truly reflect the conclusions that they came to.

8 Arabic is similar to Spanish in that it allows optional pronouns in subject position. Japanese allows zero topics that can be either subjects or objects. As far as word order is concerned, Arabic has verb–subject word order as basic; Japanese is rigidly verb-final and hence does not allow verb–subject order.

Japanese does not allow *that*-trace; Arabic is more complex in that extraction of a subject is dependent on the main verb.

9 Ildikó Svetics (personal communication) pointed out that sentence 6-20 could possibly be acceptable, but with a very different reading. For example, it could mean something like "Harvey broke under continuous questioning."

10 The analogy is of course limited as, in a kaleidoscope, the elements in the system are fixed. No new elements can enter or leave. This is not the same with SLA, where new elements/patterns are added, as is the case when a new grammatical structure is learned.

11 Voicing contrasts (i.e., the difference between voiced and voiceless sounds) have to do with whether or not the vocal cords are vibrating during speech. They distinguish between a number of sounds that are made with the same tongue and lip position. Examples are sounds such as [b] and [p] and [s] and [z].

7 TYPOLOGICAL AND FUNCTIONAL APPROACHES

1 See chapter 3, note 10 for an explanation of these relative clause types.

2 The interested reader is referred to Keenan and Comrie (1977) and Comrie and Keenan (1979) for further elaboration on their claim and on possible exceptions.

3 See Fox (1987) and Keenan (1975) for further elaboration.

4 For an explanation of the unpredicted findings of the genitive, refer to Gass (1979a, 1979b).

5 As with the results of the Gass study, the genitive results in Hyltenstam's study were out of hierarchical order.

6 There are exceptions to this generalization in these data that are accounted for by assuming that these learners have an optional rule of devoicing rather than an obligatory one. Obstruents are those sounds in which the airstream is obstructed. They are represented by /p/, /t/, /k/, /f/, /s/, /θ/ (*th* as in *forth*), /ʃ/ (as in *shin*), /tʃ/ (as in *church*), /b/, /d/, /g/, /v/, /z/ /ð/ (as in *then*), /dʒ/ (as in *judge*).

7 NP refers to noun phrase. T-units are defined as "one main clause plus any subordinate clause or nonclausal structure that is attached to or embedded in it" (Hunt, 1970, p. 4).

8 See Gass and Ard (1980) for an explanation based on prototypicality and core meanings.

8 LOOKING AT INTERLANGUAGE PROCESSING

1 Some successful network simulations of L2 learner data were reviewed by Broeder and Plunkett (1994).

2 As might be predicted, the picture is more complex. L1/L2 cue similarities/ differences, cue type (grammatical vs. semantic), and L2 proficiency all interact to produce the observed patterns. For example, Japanese ESL learners actually continue to use case-marking cues as their dominant strategy in the L2, but they do rely on animacy more heavily than in their NL (see Sasaki, 1994). In Heilenman and McDonald (1993) and McDonald and Heilenman (1992), English learners of French quickly lost their L1 word order strategy yet did not show stronger animacy cue use. Dutch learners of English and English learners of Dutch, similarly, transferred inappropriate L1 grammatical strategies but showed no animacy effect (McDonald, 1987).

3 Thanks go to Caroline Latham for bringing this example to our attention.

4 U-shaped learning is documented in the child language literature, as well as in other areas of cognition (see Carlucci, Jain, Kimber, and Stephan, 2005).

5   Numerous commentaries can be found in *Applied Psycholinguistics* (2006), 27, 1.
6   Van Valin (1991) has shown that in languages where aspect is expressed through morphology, it is acquired before or at the same time as tense, but never after.
7   This is similar to the case in French immersion brought up earlier (Harley and Swain, 1984), where the learner equates one word in the interlanguage (e.g., *j'ai*), with two words in the target, producing forms like *j'ai as* in the context of a three-place construction *j'ai as oublié*.
8   Krashen (1985, p. 2) hypothesized that only two conditions need to be met: focus on form and knowledge of rule. The condition of time was dropped after research by Hulstijn and Hulstijn (1984) showed that, when there was no focus on form, the time condition was no longer valid. In other words, focus on form did make a difference; but without it, learners did not perform differently as a function of time limits.

9 INTERLANGUAGE IN CONTEXT

1   It should be noted that interlanguage, as an integral part of historical language change primarily resulting from language contact, is now recognized and embedded in historical linguistic accounts (e.g., Chambers, Trudgill, and Schilling-Estes (2002, pp. 639ff., passim).
2   The probability weights are based on VARBRUL, a statistical package (Pintzuk, 1988; Rand and Sankoff, 1990) designed for analyzing variation data. Probability weights allow researchers to determine what the possible influence might be that would predict when something will occur.
3   There were two acceptable TL variants in this study, given that these speakers were living in New York City, where there is great variation as to the acceptable form.
4   Major (1987) argued against Beebe's interpretation of the source of the variants. He pointed out that in Thai the trilled /r/ characterizes formal speech, but in running speech (reading of sentences in Thai), a variant similar to an American /r/ occurs. Major claimed that in the English of these speakers, the prevalence of the trilled /r/ in formal speech and the American /r/ in casual conversation are both due to transfer.
5   Clearly, these are not the only areas of L2 study. Rather, they are taken as examples of what legitimately is part of SLA and what needs to be argued to be a part of SLA.
6   Interestingly, the term *learning strategy* seems to be rooted in a neighboring field (psychology), while the term *communication strategy* seems indigenous to early SLA. Selinker (1972) attributes the term to Coulter (1968). The data from his study are described in Selinker (1992, chapter 5).

10 INPUT, INTERACTION, AND OUTPUT

1   In a matched-guise format, the same speaker is used for two different sets of tape-recorded utterances or passages. Listeners are then asked to characterize the speakers according to a variety of possible attributes, which vary depending on the purpose of the study in question.
2   We should treat this conclusion cautiously given the few studies involved to date. However, this conclusion is interesting in light of those language-teaching practices where the emphasis falls on grammar instruction as a way toward intelligibility.

3   Within the field of conversational analysis, these are often seen as continuers whose function it is to keep the conversation going. As Varonis and Gass (1985b) pointed out in their discussion of "conversational continuants," these utterances are often ambiguous; it is not always possible to determine whether their function is to keep the conversation going or to indicate understanding.

4   As with other kinds of learning, one must put one's knowledge to use. One cannot imagine learning how to play tennis by watching, observing, and understanding the motions involved. Parts of the game of tennis can be learned that way (e.g., knowledge of the rules of the game, strategies, etc.), but actual implementation cannot.

5   In actuality, only the past tense part of the study could be analyzed, due to the paucity of examples of plural markers that could be corrected in the experimental group.

6   We are not including here so-called "reading knowledge" of a language, necessary for many graduate degree programs. In those instances, it may indeed be possible to know little of the syntax (perhaps other than basic word order phenomena) and to rely on lexical knowledge and knowledge of the subject matter as the sole decoding cues. It is often the case that individuals who have "reading knowledge" are incapable of encoding that language or of decoding the language in anything but a written format.

7   This is in some sense reminiscent of early work by Zobl (1982), who, in discussions of the role of the native language, noted that native language background affects the speed at which certain developmental stages are transversed.

11 INSTRUCTED SECOND LANGUAGE LEARNING

1   It should be noted that criticisms have been allayed against the Tomasello and Herron studies regarding both the methodology and the analysis (e.g., see Beck and Eubank, 1991, as well as the response by Tomasello and Herron, 1991).

2   Whether this is the case for all parts of language is questionable. For example, Gass (1984) and Sheldon and Strange (1982) noted that accurate speech production of particular sounds often precedes the perception of those sounds.

3   An rather than the is used because it is clear that there are important aspects of language to be learned beyond syntax (e.g., pragmatics, phonology). However, the focus on these aspects at a detailed level of analysis is also a prerequisite to their acquisition. For example, within the realm of pragmatics, it is not sufficient to understand that someone is being polite (akin to understanding at the level of meaning); it is also necessary to understand the means by which politeness takes place (akin to understanding at the level of syntax).

4   In this discussion of focus on form, we do not intend to imply that language is the only aspect focused on. McNeill, Cassell, and McCullough (1994) suggested that we also pay attention to communication through gesture and integrate gestural information with verbal information. We are grateful to Elizabeth Hauge for pointing this reference out to us.

5   Keenan (1975) reported that, in a comparison between a sophisticated writer (in this case, a philosopher) and tabloid newspaper writers, there was a greater amount of lower position use of relative clauses among the former.

12 BEYOND THE DOMAIN OF LANGUAGE

1   The phenomenon of fossilization seemed to force early SLA researchers, working within a contrastive analysis framework (e.g., Brière, 1966, 1968; Nemser, 1961; and Selinker, 1966), into independently positing intermediate

linguistic systems that in some sense did not always exhibit perceptible change. These systems were thought to be "intermediate" between and different from the native language and from the target language, an "approximative" system in Nemser's terms. Fossilization is a much discussed, yet little understood, second language acquisition concept.

2 This situation often sees the rise of pidgin varieties of language.

3 Note that Figures 12.2 and 12.3 do not have the same scale.

4 Coppietiers' data are based on elicitations of grammaticality judgments. This elicitation methodology focuses on a determination of a learner's knowledge (see also chapter 3). It is important to note that, whereas grammaticality judgment tasks are frequently used as an indirect *reflection* of competence, they in no way *directly* reflect competence.

5 In cultures where modified input, as it is known in Western cultures, does not exist, speech to children nonetheless differs from that addressed to adults. Schieffelin (1986) reported on the acquisition of Kaluli, pointing out that when small children are addressed, it is often a "language instruction" format. Speech will be preceded by *a:la:ma*, which translates "Say like that." This serves the function of "framing" the speech and may serve a similar function to the modifications used in Western cultures.

6 We thank Andrew Cohen and Rebecca Oxford for discussing the matters presented in this section on learning strategies, though, of course, neither is responsible for our conclusions.

7 Cohen and Macaro (2007) acknowledge this difficulty and suggest the cover term *language learner strategies*.

8 Strategizing is not confined to language learning and appears to be basic to human cognition. An example of nonlanguage learning strategizing would be in the area of the learning of hatha yoga. To learn to get "deeply" into some postures, it is usually thought necessary to "warm up" with simpler yoga postures. Suppose you are a runner and instead of doing your yoga stretching first, you realize that you can learn to get deeper into difficult yoga practice *after* you do your running, then you will probably tend to continue with this strategy. The interested reader may wish to turn to Riding and Rayner (1998) or Riding (2002, 2003), where many of the general problems of strategy learning and identification are discussed in more general cognitive terms.

9 Dörnyei (2005, 2006) introduces the conundrum of what exactly a learning strategy is. He provides the following example:

> If someone memorises vocabulary by simply looking at a bilingual vocabulary list, most people would say that this is an example of learning. But if the person applies some colour marking code to highlight the words in the list which he or she still does not know, suddenly we can start talking about strategic learning. But what is the difference? The colour code? (2006, p. 57)

See Grenfell and Macaro (in press) for a counterargument.

10 The terminology is difficult here. McDonough (1999, p. 2), in a useful review of the literature, pointed out that "strategies have been isolated and described" in a wide area (e.g., learning an L2, learning to learn, learning to use the L2, learning to communicate, learning to compensate for communication breakdowns, and in macro-skill areas, such as reading, writing, and so forth). Given this range, he pointed to a change in some parts of the literature away from the term *learning strategies* to use of the term *learner strategies*, where the emphasis shifts to the learner as "a problem-solver and reflective organizer" (p. 2) of the knowledge and skills necessary for "effective language use" (p. 2).

13 THE LEXICON

1 Receptive vocabulary is often referred to as passive vocabulary. This term is inappropriate in that receptive knowledge of vocabulary is not passive at all. Learners are actively involved in the use of receptive knowledge.

2 Chunking is a concept associated with working memory capacity. In general 7 (+/-2) is the average amount of information that we can hold in active memory, as determined by looking at responses to a digit span task (see chapter 8). To understand this concept, consider the following sequence of numbers: 5821647856231548. If you were to hear the numbers, you would be hard-pressed to remember them in order. If, on the other hand, you were to hear the following sequence of numbers, 1111222233334444, you could probably remember them more easily, even though there is the same number of numbers. That is because we can chunk the numbers into units (presumably 1111, 2222, 3333, 4444), thereby reducing the memory burden.

3 Interestingly, although Levelt did not note this fact, English used to have a three-way distinction, with the additional term *yon*, with *yonder* and *hither and yon*, being relics of that distinction.

4 See also Hatch and Hawkins (1985), Kempen (1977, 1978), and Kempen and Hoenkamp (1981, 1987).

14 AN INTEGRATED VIEW OF
SECOND LANGUAGE ACQUISITION

1 Much of this chapter is based on an article entitled "Integrating research areas: a framework for second language studies," originally published as Gass (1988a).

2 See Beebe (1985) for an extensive discussion of the role of different types and sources of input.

3 This issue is related to the general notion of salience and to what is noticed. For example, phonological salience due to syllable stress may result in a form being noticed to a greater extent than unstressed syllables.

4 In many cases learners will find themselves engaged in a conversation with a native speaker and know beforehand that they will understand very little. The learners may do nothing more than provide minimal feedback to the native speaker so as not to appear rude, while at the same time tune out completely to the conversation. This is likely the case of the nonnative speaker in chapter 10 who called about the price of TV sets.

5 One could also imagine the reanalysis coming from the other direction. A learner might encounter *apple juice*. Once the learner realizes *apple juice* is made up of two words, that knowledge could serve as a trigger for reanalysis of the original *orangejuice*.

GLOSSARY

access to UG Hypothesis   The claim that the innate language facility is operative in second language acquisition and constrains the grammars of second language learners.

Accessibility Hierarchy   A continuum of relative clause types such that the presence of one type implies the presence of other types higher on the hierarchy.

Acculturation Model   A model consisting of social and affective variables. It is based on the notion that learners need to adapt to the target language culture in order for successful acquisition to take place.

Affective Filter   Part of the Monitor Model. The claim is that affect is an important part of the learning process and that one has a "raised" or "lowered" affective filter. The latter leads to better learning.

apperceived input   That part of the language that a learner is exposed to and that is noticed by the learner.

aspect   A verbal category that marks the way a situation takes place in time (e.g., continuous, repetitive). (*See also* tense.)

aspect hypothesis   The claim that first and second language learners will initially be influenced by the inherent semantic aspect of verbs or predicates in the acquisition of tense and aspect markers associated with or affixed to these verbs.

attention   The concentration of mental powers.

automaticity   The degree of routinized control that one has over linguistic knowledge.

Autonomous Induction Theory   A theory that attributes difficulties in learning a second language to parsing problems.

babbling   The sounds infants make that often sound like words to adults.

baby talk   The language addressed to a young child. (*See also* caretaker speech; child-directed speech; motherese.)

backchannel cues   Generally, verbal messages such as *uh huh* and *yeah* that are said during the time another person is talking.

behaviorism A school of psychology that bases learning on a stimulus—response paradigm.

Bilingual Syntax Measure (BSM) A testing instrument that measures the morphological knowledge children have in a second language.

bilingualism The ability to use more than one language.

caretaker speech The language addressed to a young child. (*See also* baby talk; child-directed speech; motherese.)

child-directed speech The language addressed to a young child. (*See also* baby talk; caretaker speech.)

clarification request A device used in conversation to ask for more information when something has not been understood.

coalescing A term used in the Stockwell and Bowen (1965) Hierarchy of Difficulty to refer to the collapsing of two native language categories into one target language category. (*See also* Hierarchy of Difficulty.)

collocation Words that belong together, such as *to make a case*.

communication strategies An approach used by learners when they need to express a concept or an idea in the second language, but do not have or cannot access the linguistic resources to do so.

Competition Model One model of language processing based on how people interpret sentences.

comprehended input The language that a learner understands.

comprehensible input Originally formulated as part of the Monitor Model, this concept refers to the understandable input that learners need for learning. Input that is slightly more advanced than the learner's current level of grammatical knowledge.

comprehensible output The language produced by the learner.

comprehension check A device used in conversation to ensure that one's interlocutor has understood.

concept-oriented approach An approach that maps language functions that a learner wants to express to the form that she or he needs to express it.

conceptualizer Part of the production process that has to do with the determination of the message that will be communicated. (*See also* formulator.)

confirmation check A device used in conversation to determine whether one has been understood correctly.

connectionism An approach that assumes that learning takes place based on the extraction of regularities from the input. (*See also* emergentism.)

contrastive analysis A way of comparing two languages to determine similarities and dissimilarities.

Contrastive Analysis Hypothesis The prediction that similarities between two languages do not require learning and that the differences are what need to be learned.

conversation analysis Uses conversation as a resource for showing how micro-moments of socially distributed cognition are seen in conversation and reflect changes in participants' knowledge.

corrective feedback An intervention that provides information to a learner that a prior utterance is incorrect. (*See also* feedback.)

correspondence A term used in the Stockwell and Bowen (1965) Hierarchy of Difficulty to refer to the situation in which there exists a one-to-one relationship between a native language and target language form. (*See also* Hierarchy of Difficulty.)

Creative Construction Hypothesis The proposal that child second language learners construct rules of the second language on the basis of innate mechanisms.

critical period A time after which successful language learning cannot take place. (*See also* sensitive period.)

cross-linguistic influence Any language influence from the L1 to the L2, from one IL to another or from the L2 back to the L1. (*See also* language transfer.)

cross-sectional data A data-gathering procedure in which data are gathered from groups of learners in order to view particular behaviors at a single point in time. One often gathers cross-sectional data from learners at different proficiency levels and infers that the differences represent change over time. (*See also* pseudolongitudinal.)

declarative knowledge Knowledge that learners have about something. This information is relatively accessible to conscious awareness. (*See also* procedural knowledge.)

differentiation A term used in the Stockwell and Bowen (1965) Hierarchy of Difficulty to refer to the situation in which a single form in the native language corresponds to two different forms in the target language. (*See also* Hierarchy of Difficulty.)

Direct Contrast Hypothesis When a child produces an utterance containing an erroneous form, which is responded to immediately with an utterance containing the correct adult alternative to the erroneous form (i.e., when negative evidence is supplied), the child may perceive the adult form as being in contrast with the equivalent child form. Cognizance of a relevant contrast can then form the basis for perceiving the adult form as a correct alternative to the child form.

discourse-completion test A procedure commonly used in gathering data about interlanguage pragmatics and speech acts. Generally, a situation is described and learners have to write/say what they would typically say in that particular situation.

emergentism An approach that assumes that learning takes place based on the extraction of regularities from the input. (*See also* connectionism.)

error analysis   A procedure for analyzing second language data that begins with the errors learners make and then attempts to explain them.

errors   The incorrect forms (vis-à-vis the language being learned) that learners produce.

explicit knowledge   Knowledge about language that involves awareness. (*See also* declarative knowledge, explicit learning, implicit knowledge, implicit learning, procedural knowledge.)

explicit learning   Acquisition of language that involves deliberate hypothesis testing as learners search for structure. (*See also* declarative knowledge; explicit knowledge; implicit knowledge; implicit learning; procedural knowledge.)

extroversion   Refers to where an individual's attention is focused; namely, the world and people outside of the individual. (*See also* introversion.)

facilitation   The use of the first language (or other languages known) in a second language context resulting in a target-like second language form. (*See also* language transfer; positive transfer.)

feedback   An intervention in which information is provided to a learner that a prior utterance is correct or incorrect. (*See also* corrective feedback.)

field-dependent   A personality style in which an individual uses the context for interpretation. (*See also* field-independent.)

field-independent   A personality style in which an individual does not use the context for interpretation. (*See also* field-dependent.)

focus on form   Drawing learners' attention to form within a context of meaning.

foreign language learning   The learning of a second language in a formal classroom situation that takes place in a country where the NL is spoken (e.g., learning French in the United States; learning Hebrew in Japan).

foreigner talk   The modified language used when addressing a nonnative speaker.

formulator   Part of the production process that has to do with putting into words the conceptual notions to be communicated. (*See also* conceptualizer.)

fossilization   The cessation of learning. Permanent plateaus that learners reach resulting from no change in some or all of their interlanguage forms. (*See also* interlanguage; stabilization.)

free variation   An alternation of possible forms, perhaps randomly.

functional categories   Categories that carry primarily grammatical meaning, such as morphemes for tense and determiners.

Fundamental Difference Hypothesis The claim that child first language and adult second language acquisition are different.

general nativism A position that maintains that there is no specific mechanism designed for language learning. (*See also* special nativism.)

heritage learner A learner who is learning the language of his or her ancestors. Usually, the learner has had exposure through the home environment to that language.

Hierarchy of Difficulty A proposed ordering of more-to-less difficult learning situations.

implicational universals Common hierarchies across the world's languages in which particular language elements are predicted by the existence of other language elements. (*See also* typological universals.)

implicit knowledge Knowledge about language that does not involve awareness of that knowledge. (*See also* declarative knowledge; explicit learning; explicit knowledge; implicit learning; procedural knowledge.)

implicit learning Acquisition of knowledge about the underlying structure of a complex stimulus environment without doing so consciously. (*See also* explicit knowledge; explicit learning; implicit knowledge.)

incidental vocabulary learning Learning that takes place with an explicit focus on meaning as opposed to having an explicit goal being the learning of new words.

indeterminacy The incomplete or lack of knowledge that a language learner has of the target language.

indirect negative evidence Evidence based on the lack of occurrence of forms. (*See also* negative evidence; positive evidence.)

initial state The beginning point of learning.

input The language that is available to learners; that is, exposure.

input enhancement A technique that attempts to make parts of the input salient.

instrumental motivation Motivation that comes from the rewards gained from knowing another language. (*See also* integrative motivation.)

intake That part of the language input that is internalized by the learner.

integrative motivation Motivation that comes from the desire to acculturate and become part of a target language community. (*See also* instrumental motivation.)

interactionist approaches Approaches that consider conversational interaction as a locus of learning.

interference The use of the first language (or other languages known) in a second language context when the resulting second language form is incorrect. (*See also* language transfer; negative transfer.)

interlanguage The language produced by a nonnative speaker of a language (i.e., a learner's output). Refers to the systematic knowledge underlying learners' production.

interlanguage transfer The influence of one L2 over another in instances where there are multiple languages acquired after the L1.

interlocutor The person with whom one is speaking.

introversion Refers to where an individual's attention is focused, namely, towards the individual's own inner world. (*See also* extroversion.)

L1 A person's first language. (*See also* L2.)

L1 = L2 Hypothesis The claim that a second language is acquired in the same manner as a first language.

L2 A person's second language. To be more specific, one could refer to a person's L3, L4, and so on. However, the general term *L2* is frequently used to refer to any language learning or use after the first language has been learned. (*See also* L1.)

Language Acquisition Device (LAD) A language faculty that constrains and guides the acquisition process.

language aptitude A natural ability to learn non-primary languages.

language neutral Part of language that learners perceive to be common to (at least) the native and the target language.

language specific Parts of language that learners perceive to be unique to a specific language.

language transfer The use of the first language (or other languages known) in a second language context. (*See also* cross-linguistic influence; facilitation; interference; negative transfer; positive transfer.)

learning strategy A strategic plan undertaken by a learner in learning.

learning style The preferred way of taking in and processing new information and/or skills.

longitudinal A data-gathering procedure in which data are gathered from one or more learners over a prolonged period of time in order to gather information about change over time.

Markedness Differential Hypothesis A proposal based on the markedness values of different forms. Unmarked forms are learned before marked forms.

mean length of utterance (MLU) A measure used in child language research to determine a child's linguistic development.

metalinguistic knowledge What one knows (or thinks one knows) about the language. It is to be differentiated from what one does in using language.

mistakes Nonsystematic errors that learners produce. These are "correctable" by the learner.

Monitor Model A model of second language acquisition based on the concept that learners have two systems (acquisition and learning) and that the learned system monitors the acquired system.

morpheme The minimal unit of meaning in language. Elements of meaning may be smaller than words (e.g., the word *unclear* contains two units, *un* + *clear*).

morpheme order studies A series of studies carried out to determine the order in which certain English morphemes are acquired.

morphology The study of how morphemes form words and function in language.

motherese The language addressed to a young child. (*See also* baby talk; caretaker speech; child-directed speech.)

motivation The characteristic that provides the incentive for learning.

native language (NL) A person's first language.

negative evidence Information provided to a learner concerning the incorrectness of a form. (*See also* indirect negative evidence; positive evidence.)

negative transfer The use of the first language (or other languages known) in a second language context resulting in a nontarget-like second language form. (*See also* interference; language transfer; positive transfer.)

negotiation of meaning The attempt made in conversation to clarify a lack of understanding.

Ontogeny Phylogeny Model A model that shows the relationship between transfer and developmental processes over time.

overextension Using a word with a wider referential range than is correct in standard adult language (e.g., when a child uses *doggie* to refer to dogs as well as other animals, such as cows). (*See also* underextension.)

personality A set of traits that characterize an individual.

phonology The sound patterns of language.

positive evidence Evidence based on forms that actually occur. (*See also* indirect negative evidence; negative evidence.)

positive transfer The use of the first language (or other languages known) in a second language context when the resulting second language form is correct. (*See also* cross-linguistic influence; facilitation; interference; language transfer; negative transfer.)

Poverty of the Stimulus A proposal made within the confines of Universal Grammar that input alone is not sufficiently specific to allow a child to attain the complexities of the adult grammar. (*See also* Universal Grammar.)

pragmatics The ways in which language is used in context.

prefabricated patterns Parts of language that are learned as a whole without knowledge of the component parts.

private speech A part of sociocultural theory. It refers to language we use when we talk to ourselves.

procedural knowledge Knowledge that relates to cognitive skills that involve sequencing information. This information is relatively inaccessible. (*See also* declarative knowledge.)

Processability Theory A theory that proposes that production and comprehension of second language forms only takes place to the extent that they can be handled by the linguistic processor. Understanding how the processor functions allows one to understand developmental paths.

pronominal reflex A pronoun used (almost) immediately after a noun to refer to that noun (e.g., *The man he went home* or *The man who he went home was ill*. (*See also* resumptive pronoun.)

pseudolongitudinal The use of cross-sectional data to gather information about change over time. This is frequently done by using groups of learners at different proficiency levels. (*See also* cross-sectional data.)

psychotypology The organizational structure that learners impose on their native language.

recasts Reformulations of an incorrect utterance that maintain the original's meaning.

restructuring Changes or reorganization of one's grammatical knowledge.

resumptive pronoun A pronoun used (almost) immediately after a noun to refer to that noun (e.g., *The man he went home* or *The man who he went home was ill*. (*See also* pronominal reflex.)

risk taking The extent to which people are willing to do something without being certain of the outcome.

second language acquisition (SLA) The learning of another language after the first language has been learned. The use of this term does not differentiate among learning situations. (*See also* L2.)

semantics The phenomena relating to the meaning of words and sentences.

sensitive period A time during which most successful learning is likely to take place. (*See also* critical period.)

Sociocultural Theory A theory based on work by the Russian psychologist Vygotsky that considers knowledge/learning arises from a social context. Learning, being socially mediated, comes from face-to-face interaction. Knowledge is internalized from learners jointly constructing knowledge in dyadic interactions.

special nativism A proposal that there exist special principles for language learning. These principles are unique to language (learning) and are not used in other cognitive endeavors. (*See also* general nativism.)

speech act What one does with language (i.e., the functions for which language is used). Examples include complaining, complimenting, and refusing.

stabilization The plateaus that learners reach when there is little change in some or all of their interlanguage forms (*See also* fossilization; interlanguage.)

Structural Conformity Hypothesis The notion that all universals that are true for primary languages are also true for interlanguages.

suppliance in obligatory context A method used to determine a second language learner's knowledge of a given structure by measuring how many times a particular form is used when it is required in the target language.

syntax Generally known as grammar, syntax deals with the order of elements in sentences and sentence structure.

target language (TL) The language being learned.

telegraphic A typical stage of speech in child language acquisition in which only content words are present (e.g., *Mommy go work*).

tense The time of an event or action, often indicated by an inflectional category. (*See also* aspect.)

T-unit One main clause plus any subordinate clause or nonclausal structure that is attached to or embedded in it.

typological universals Universals derived from an investigation of the commonalities of the world's languages. The goal is to determine similarities in types of languages, including implicational universals. (*See also* implicational universals.)

underextension Using a word with a narrower referential range than is correct in standard adult language (e.g., a child may not use *tree* to refer to a tree in the dead of winter with no leaves). (*See also* overextension.)

Universal Grammar A set of innate principles common to all languages.

UG parameters A principle of UG that is not invariant. They allow for cross-language variation.

UG principles A constraint that governs all languages.

U-shaped learning Learning whereby early forms appear to be correct, followed by a period of incorrect forms, with a final stage of correct forms.

verbal reports Based on verbal reporting, it is a type of introspection that consists of gathering information by asking individuals to say what is going through their minds as they are solving a problem or doing a task.

Voice Contrast Hierarchy The claim that a voicing contrast in initial position is the least marked, whereas a voicing contrast in final position is the most marked.

working memory Memory that involves storage capacity and processing capacity.

REFERENCES

Abunuwara, E. (1992). The structure of the trilingual lexicon. *European Journal of Cognitive Psychology, 4*, 311–313.

Adamson, H. D. (1988). *Variation Theory and Second Language Acquisition.* Washington, DC: Georgetown University Press.

Adjemian, C. (1976). On the nature of interlanguage systems. *Language Learning, 26*, 297–320.

Adjemian, C. (1983). The transferability of lexical properties. In S. Gass and L. Selinker (Eds.), *Language Transfer in Language Learning* (pp. 250–268). Rowley, MA: Newbury House.

Agard, F. and Di Pietro, R. (1965a). *The Grammatical Structures of English and Italian.* Chicago: University of Chicago Press.

Agard, F. and Di Pietro, R. (1965b). *The Sounds of English and Italian.* Chicago: University of Chicago Press.

Akhmatova, O. (1974). *Word-Combination: Theory and Method.* Moscow: Izdatel'stvo Moskovskogo Universiteta.

Akmajian, A., Demers, R., Farmer, A., and Harnish, R. (1995). *Linguistics: An Introduction to Language and Communication.* Cambridge, MA: MIT Press.

Alexander, R. (1982). Vocabulary acquisition and the "advanced learner of English": a brief survey of the issues. *Arbeiten aus Anglistik und Amerikanistik, 7*, 59–75.

Altmann, G. (1990). Cognitive models of speech processing: an introduction. In G. Altmann (Ed.), *Cognitive Models of Speech Processing: Psycholinguistic and Computational Perspectives* (pp. 1–23). Cambridge, MA: MIT Press.

American Psychological Association (1994). *Publication Manual of the American Psychological Association*, 4th ed. Washington, DC: American Psychological Association.

Ammar, A., and Lightbown, P. M. (2003). Teaching marked linguistic structures—more about the acquisition of relative clauses by Arab learners of English. In A. Housen and M. Pierrard (Eds.), *Investigations in Instructed Second Language Learning* (pp. 167–198). Berlin: Mouton de Gruyter.

Ammar, A., and Spada, N. (2006). One size fits all? Recasts, prompts and L2 learning. *Studies in Second Language Acquisition, 28*, 543–574.

Andersen, R. (1976). A functor acquisition study in Puerto Rico. Paper presented at the 10th annual meeting of the Teachers of English to Speakers of Other Languages, New York, March.

Andersen, R. (1977). The impoverished state of cross-sectional morpheme acqui-sition accuracy methodology. In C. Henning (Ed.), *Proceedings of the Second Language Research Forum* (pp. 308–319). Los Angeles: University of California, Department of Applied Linguistics.

Andersen, R. (1983). Transfer to somewhere. In S. Gass and L. Selinker (Eds.), *Language Transfer in Language Learning* (pp. 177–201). Rowley, MA: Newbury House.

Andersen, R. (1984). The one-to-one principle of interlanguage construction. *Language Learning, 34*, 77–95.

Andersen, R. (1986). El desarrollo de la morfologia verbal en el español como segundo idioma [The development of verbal morphology in Spanish as a second language]. In J. Meisel (Ed.), *Adquisición de lenguaje/Aquisição da linguagem* [*Acquisition of Language*] (pp. 115–138). Frankfurt: Vervuert.

Andersen, R. (1990). Models, processes, principles and strategies: second language acquisition inside and outside the classroom. In B. VanPatten and J. F. Lee (Eds.), *Second Language Acquisition–Foreign Language Learning* (pp. 45–78). Clevedon, UK: Multilingual Matters.

Andersen, R. (1991). Developmental sequences: the emergence of aspect marking in second language acquisition. In T. Huebner and C. Ferguson (Eds.), *Cross-currents in Second Language Acquisition and Linguistic Theories* (pp. 305–324). Amsterdam: John Benjamins.

Andersen, R., and Shirai, Y. (1994). Discourse motivations for some cognitive acquisition principles. *Studies in Second Language Acquisition, 16*, 133–156.

Andersen, R., and Shirai, Y. (1996). The primacy of aspect in first and second language acquisition: the pidgin–creole connection. In W. Ritchie and T. Bhatia (Eds.), *Handbook of Second Language Acquisition* (pp. 527–570). San Diego, CA: Academic Press.

Anderson, J. (1987). The markedness differential hypothesis and syllable structure difficulty. In G. Ioup and S. Weinberger (Eds.), *Interlanguage Phonology* (pp. 279–291). Rowley, MA: Newbury House.

Antinucci, F., and Miller, R. (1976). How children talk about what happened. *Journal of Child Language, 3*, 167–189.

Aoyama, K., Flege, J., Guion, S., Yamada, T., and Akahane-Yamada, R. (2004). Perceived phonetic dissimilarity and L2 speech learning: the case of Japanese /r/ and English /l/ and /r/. *Journal of Phonetics, 23*, 233–250.

Ard, J. (1989). A constructivist perspective on non-native phonology. In S. Gass and J. Schachter (Eds.), *Linguistic Perspectives on Second Language Acquisition* (pp. 243–259). Cambridge: Cambridge University Press.

Ard, J., and Gass, S. (1987). Lexical constraints on syntactic acquisition. *Studies in Second Language Acquisition, 9*, 235–255.

Ard, J., and Homburg, T. (1983). Verification of language transfer. In S. Gass and L. Selinker (Eds.), *Language Transfer in Language Learning* (pp. 157–176). Rowley, MA: Newbury House.

Ard, J., and Homburg, T. (1992). Verification of language transfer. In S. Gass and L. Selinker (Eds.), *Language transfer in language learning*, 2nd ed. (pp. 47–70). Amsterdam: John Benjamins.

Ardilla, A. (2003). Language representation and working memory with bilinguals. *Journal of Communication Disorders, 36*, 233–240.

REFERENCES

Ardilla, A., Roselli, M., Ostrosky-Sois, F., Marcos, J., Granda, G., and Soto, M. (2000). Syntactic comprehension, verbal memory, and calculation abilities in Spanish–English bilinguals. *Applied Neuropsychology, 7,* 3–16.

Aston, G. (1986). Trouble-shooting in interaction with learners: the more the merrier? *Applied Linguistics, 7,* 128–143.

Baddeley, A. D. (2000). The episodic buffer: a new component of working memory? *Trends in Cognitive Sciences, 4,* 417–423.

Baddeley, A. D. (2003a). Working memory and language: an overview. *Journal of Communication Disorders, 36,* 189–208.

Baddeley, A. D. (2003b). Working memory: looking back and looking forward. *Neuroscience, 4,* 29–839.

Baddeley, A. D., and Hitch, G. (1974). Working memory. In G. H. Bower (Ed.), *The Psychology of Learning and Motivation* (pp. 47–90). New York: Academic Press.

Bailey, K. M. (1983). Competitiveness and anxiety in adult second language learning: looking at and through the diary studies. In H. W. Seliger and M. H. Long (Eds.), *Classroom Oriented Research in Second Language Acquisition* (pp. 67–103). Rowley, MA: Newbury House.

Bailey, N., Madden, C., and Krashen, S. (1974). Is there a "natural sequence" in adult second language learning? *Language Learning, 24,* 235–243.

Baker, C., and Prys Jones, S. (Eds.) (1998). *Encyclopedia of Bilingualism and Bilingual Education.* Clevedon, UK: Multilingual Matters.

Baker, C. L. (1979). Syntactic theory and the projection problem. *Linguistic Inquiry, 10,* 533–581.

Bard, E., Robertson, D., and Sorace, A. (1996). Magnitude estimation of linguistic acceptability. *Language, 72,* 32–68.

Bardovi-Harlig, K. (1987). Markedness and salience in second-language acquisition. *Language Learning, 37,* 385–407.

Bardovi-Harlig, K. (1992a). The relationship of form and meaning: a cross-sectional study of tense and aspect in the interlanguage of learners of English as a second language. *Applied Psycholinguistics, 13,* 253–278.

Bardovi-Harlig, K. (1992b). The use of adverbials and natural order in the development of temporal expression. *International Review of Applied Linguistics, 30,* 299–320.

Bardovi-Harlig, K. (1994). Anecdote or evidence? Evaluating support for hypotheses concerning the development of tense and aspect. In E. Tarone, A. Cohen, and S. Gass (Eds.), *Research Methodology in Second Language Acquisition* (pp. 41–60). Hillsdale, NJ: Lawrence Erlbaum Associates.

Bardovi-Harlig, K. (1998). Narrative structure and lexical aspect: conspiring factors in second language acquisition of tense–aspect morphology. *Studies in Second Language Acquisition, 20,* 471–508.

Bardovi-Harlig, K. (1999a). Exploring the interlanguage of interlanguage pragmatics: a research agenda for acquisitional pragmatics. *Language Learning, 49,* 677–713.

Bardovi-Harlig, K. (1999b). From morpheme studies to temporal semantics: tense–aspect research in SLA. *Studies in Second Language Acquisition, 21,* 341–382.

Bardovi-Harlig, K. (2000). *Tense and Aspect in Second Language Acquisition: Form, Meaning, and Use.* Language Learning Supplement. Malden, MA: Blackwell.

Bardovi-Harlig, K. (2004a). The emergence of grammaticalized future expression in longitudinal production data. In B. VanPatten, J. Williams, S. Rott, and M. Overstreet (Eds.), *Form–meaning Connections in Second Language Acquisition* (pp. 115–137). Mahwah, NJ: Erlbaum.

Bardovi-Harlig, K. (2004b). Monopolizing the future or How the *go*-future breaks into *will*'s territory and what it tells us about SLA. In S. Foster-Cohen (Ed.), *EuroSLA Yearbook* (pp. 177–201). Amsterdam: John Benjamins.

Bardovi-Harlig, K. (2004c). Pragmatic competence of the advanced learner. Indiana University manuscript.

Bardovi-Harlig, K. (2005). The future of desire: lexical futures and modality in L2 English future expression. In L. Dekydtspotter, R. A. Sprouse, and A. Liljestrand (Eds.), *Proceedings of the Seventh Generative Approaches to Second Language Acquisition Conference (GASLA 2004)* (pp. 1–12). Somerville, MA: Cascadilla Press.

Bardovi-Harlig, K. (2006). Interlanguage development: main routes and individual paths. In K. Bardovi-Harlig and Z. Dörnyei (Eds.), *Themes in SLA Research*, *AILA Review*, 19 (pp. 69–82). Amsterdam: John Benjamins.

Bardovi-Harlig, K. (2007). One functional approach to second language acquisition: the concept-oriented approach. In B. VanPatten and J. Williams (Eds.), *Theories in Second Language Acquisition: An Introduction* (pp. 57–75). Mahwah, NJ: Lawrence Erlbaum Associates.

Bardovi-Harlig, K., and Bergström, A. (1996). The acquisition of tense and aspect in SLA and FLL: a study of learner narratives in English (SL) and French (FL). *Canadian Modern Language Review*, 52, 308–330.

Bardovi-Harlig, K., and Dörnyei, Z. (1998). Do language learners recognize pragmatic violations? Pragmatic versus grammatical awareness in instructed L2 learning. *TESOL Quarterly*, 32, 233–262.

Bardovi-Harlig, K. and Hartford, B. (1996). Input in an institutional setting. *Studies in Second Language*, 18, 171–188.

Bardovi-Harlig, K., and Reynolds, D. W. (1995). The role of lexical aspect in the acquisition of tense and aspect. *TESOL Quarterly*, 29, 107–131.

Bartlett, F. (1964). *Remembering: A Study in Experimental and Social Psychology.* Cambridge: Cambridge University Press. (Original work published 1932.)

Bates, E., and MacWhinney, B. (1981). Second language acquisition from a functionalist perspective: pragmatics, semantics and perceptual strategies. In H. Winitz (Ed.), *Annals of the New York Academy of Sciences Conference on Native Language and Foreign Language Acquisition* (pp. 190–214). New York: New York Academy of Sciences.

Bates, E., and MacWhinney, B. (1982). Functionalist approach to grammar. In E. Wanner and L. Gleitman (Eds.), *Language Acquisition: The State of the Art* (pp. 173–218). New York: Cambridge University Press.

Bayley, R., and Preston, D. (Eds.). (1996). *Second Language Acquisition and Linguistic Variation.* Amsterdam: John Benjamins.

Beck, M.-L., and Eubank, L. (1991). Acquisition theory and experimental design: a critique of Tomasello and Herron. *Studies in Second Language Acquisition*, 13, 73–76.

Becker, A. L. (1991). Language and languaging. *Language and Communication*, 11, 33–35.

Beebe, L. (1980). Sociolinguistic variation and style shifting in second language acquisition. *Language Learning, 30,* 433–447.

Beebe, L. (1983). Risk-taking and the language learner. In H. W. Seliger and M. Long (Eds.), *Classroom Oriented Research in Second Language Acquisition* (pp. 39–65). Rowley, MA: Newbury House.

Beebe, L. (1985). Input: choosing the right stuff. In S. Gass and C. Madden (Eds.), *Input in Second Language Acquisition* (pp. 404–430). Rowley, MA: Newbury House.

Beebe, L., and Takahashi, T. (1989). Do you have a bag?: social status and patterned variation in second language acquisition. In S. Gass, C. Madden, D. Preston, and L. Selinker (Eds.), *Variation in Second Language Acquisition: Discourse and Pragmatics* (pp. 103–125). Clevedon, UK: Multilingual Matters.

Beebe, L., Takahashi, T., and Uliss-Weltz, R. (1990). Pragmatic transfer in ESL refusals. In R. C. Scarcella, E. S. Andersen, and S. D. Krashen (Eds.), *Developing Communicative Competence in a Second Language* (pp. 55–73). New York: Newbury House.

Beebe, L., and Zuengler, J. (1983). Accommodation theory: an explanation for style shifting in second language dialects. In N. Wolfson and E. Judd (Eds.), *Sociolinguistics and Second Language Acquisition* (pp. 195–213). Rowley, MA: Newbury House.

Benati, A. (2004). The effects of structured input activities and explicit information on the acquisition of the Italian future tense. In B. VanPatten (Ed.), *Processing Instruction: Theory, Research, and Commentary* (pp. 207–225). Mahwah, NJ: Lawrence Erlbaum Associates.

Berko, J. (1958). The child's learning of English morphology. *Word, 14,* 150–177.

Berman, I. M., Buchbinder, V. A., and Beznedeznych, M. L. (1968). Formirovanie potentialnogo slovarnogo pri obuchenii russkomu jazyku kak inostrannomu [Forming a potential vocabulary in teaching Russian as a foreign language]. *Russkij jazyk za rubežom, 4,* 57–60.

Bhatia, T. (2006). Introduction to part I. In T. Bhatia and W. Ritchie (Eds.), *The Handbook of Bilingualism* (pp. 5–6). Malden, MA: Blackwell.

Bhatia, T. and Ritchie, W. (Eds.). (2006). *The Handbook of Bilingualism.* Malden, MA: Blackwell.

Bialystok, E. (1978). A theoretical model of second language learning. *Language Learning, 28,* 69–84.

Bialystok, E. (1987). Words as things: development of word concept by bilingual children. *Studies in Second Language Acquisition 9,* 133–140.

Bialystok, E. (1988). Levels of bilingualism and levels of linguistic awareness. *Developmental Psychology, 24,* 560–567.

Bialystok, E. (1990a). *Communication Strategies.* Oxford: Basil Blackwell.

Bialystok, E. (1990b). The competence of processing: classifying theories of second language acquisition. *TESOL Quarterly, 24,* 635–648.

Bialystok, E. (1997). The structure of age: in search of barriers to second language acquisition. *Second Language Research, 13,* 116–137.

Bialystok, E. (2001a). *Bilingualism in Development: Language, Literacy and Cognition.* Cambridge, UK: Cambridge University Press.

Bialystok, E. (2001b). Metalinguistic aspects of bilingual processing. *Annual Review of Applied Linguistics, 21,* 169–181.

Bialystok, E., and Hakuta, K. (1994). *In Other Words: The Science and Psychology of Second-Language Acquisition*. New York: Basic Books.

Bialystok, E., and Sharwood Smith, M. (1985). Interlanguage is not a state of mind: an evaluation of the construct for second-language acquisition. *Applied Linguistics*, 6, 101–117.

Binon, J., and Cornu, A. M. (1985). A semantic approach to collocations: a means to reduce the random character of the co-occurrence of lexical items. *ABLA Papers*, 9, 37–61.

Birdsong, D. (1989). *Metalinguistic Performance and Interlinguistic Competence*. New York: Springer.

Birdsong, D. (1992). Ultimate attainment in second language acquisition. *Language*, 68, 706–755.

Birdsong, D. (1999). Introduction: whys and why nots of the Critical Period Hypothesis for second language acquisition. In D. Birdsong (Ed.), *Second Language Acquisition and the Critical Period Hypothesis* (pp. 1–22). Mahwah, NJ: Lawrence Erlbaum Associates.

Blaas, L. (1982). Fossilization in the advanced learner's lexicon. Unpublished manuscript, University of Utrecht, Department of English, The Netherlands.

Bley-Vroman, R. (1983). The comparative fallacy in interlanguage studies: the case of systematicity. *Language Learning*, 33, 1–17.

Bley-Vroman, R. (1989). What is the logical problem of foreign language learning? In S. Gass and J. Schachter (Eds.), *Linguistic Perspectives on Second Language Acquisition* (pp. 41–68). Cambridge: Cambridge University Press.

Bley-Vroman, R., Felix, S., and Ioup, G. (1988). The accessibility of Universal Grammar in adult language learning. *Second Language Research*, 4, 1–32.

Bloomfield, L. (1933). *Language*. New York: Holt, Rinehart and Winston.

Blum-Kulka, S., and Levenston, E. (1987). Lexical-grammatical pragmatic indicators. *Studies in Second Language Acquisition*, 9, 155–170.

Bogaards, P. (2001). Lexical units and the learning of foreign language vocabulary. *Studies in Second Language Acquisition*, 23, 321–343.

Bogaards, P. and Laufer, B. (Eds.). (2004). *Vocabulary in a Second Language: Selection, Acquisition and Testing*. Amsterdam: John Benjamins.

Brehm, J., and Self, E. A. (1989). The intensity of motivation. *Annual Review of Psychology*, 40, 109–131.

Brière, E. (1966). An investigation of phonological interference. *Language*, 42, 768–796.

Brière, E. (1968). *A Psycholinguistic Study of Phonological Interference*. The Hague: Mouton.

Broeder, P., and Plunkett, K. (1994). Connectionism and second language acquisition. In N. Ellis (Ed.), *Implicit and Explicit Learning of Languages* (pp. 421–453). San Diego, CA: Academic Press.

Broselow, E. (1987). An investigation of transfer in second language phonology. In G. Ioup and S. Weinberger (Eds.), *Interlanguage Phonology* (pp. 261–278). Cambridge, MA: Newbury House.

Broselow, E., Chen, S.-I., and Wang, C. (1998). The emergence of the unmarked in second language phonology. *Studies in Second Language Acquisition*, 20, 261–280.

Broselow, E., and Finer, D. (1991). Parameter setting in second language phonology and syntax. *Second Language Research*, 7, 35–59.

Brown, D. F. (1974). Advanced vocabulary teaching: the problems of collocation. *RELC Journal*, 5, 1–11.

Brown, R. (1973). *A First Language*. Cambridge, MA: Harvard University Press.

Brown, R., and Hanlon, C. (1970). Derivational complexity and the order of acquisition in child speech. In J. Hayes (Ed.), *Cognition and the Development of Language* (pp. 155–207). New York: Wiley.

Bruton, A., and Samuda, V. (1980). Learner and teacher roles in the treatment of error in group work. *RELC Journal*, 11, 49–63.

Burt, M. K., Dulay, H. C., and Hernandez Chavez, E. (1973). *Bilingual Syntax Measure*. Harcourt Brace Jovanovich.

Call, M. (1985). Auditory short-term memory, listening comprehension, and the input hypothesis. *TESOL Quarterly*, 19, 765–781.

Campbell, R. N., and Rosenthal, J. W. (2000). Heritage languages. In J. W. Rosenthal (Ed.), *Handbook of Undergraduate Second Language Education* (pp. 165–184). Mahwah, NJ: Lawrence Erlbaum Associates.

Carlisle, R. (1998). The acquisition of onsets in a markedness relationship: a longitudinal study. *Studies in Second Language Acquisition*, 20, 245–260.

Carlucci, L., Jain, S., Kimber, E., and Stephan, F. (2005). Variations on U-shaped learning. In Peter Auer, Ron Meir (Eds.), *Learning Theory, Proceedings of the 18th Annual Conference on Learning Theory, COLT 2005. Lecture Notes in Computer Science* n. 3559 (pp. 382–397), Berlin/Heidelberg: Springer.

Carreira, M. (2002). A Connectionist approach to enhancing the phonological competence of heritage language speakers of Spanish. In J. Sullivan (Ed.), *Literacy and the Second Language Learner* (pp. 239–259). Greenwich, CT: Information Age Publishing.

Carroll, J. B. (1992). Cognitive abilities: the state of the art. *Psychological Science*, 3, 266–270.

Carroll, J. B., and Sapon, S. (1959). *Modern Language Aptitude Test—Form A*. New York: The Psychological Corporation.

Carroll, S. (2001). *Input and evidence: The Raw Material of Second Language Acquisition*. Amsterdam: John Benjamins.

Carroll, S. (2007). Autonomous induction theory. In B. VanPatten and J. Williams (Eds.), *Theories in Second Language Acquisition: An Introduction*. Mahwah, NJ: Lawrence Erlbaum Associates.

Carroll, S., Roberge, Y., and Swain, M. (1992). The role of feedback in adult second language acquisition, error correction, and morphological generalizations. *Applied Psycholinguistics*, 13, 173–198.

Carroll, S., and Swain, M. (1993). Explicit and implicit negative feedback: an empirical study of the learning of linguistic generalizations. *Studies in Second Language Acquisition*, 15, 357–386.

Carter, R., and McCarthy, M. (Eds.). (1988). *Vocabulary and Language Teaching*. London: Longman.

Cazden, C. (1972). *Child Language and Education*. New York: Holt, Rinehart and Winston.

Cazden, C. (1976). Play with language and metalinguistic awareness: One dimension of language experience. In J. S. Bruner, A. Jolly, and K. Silva (Eds.), *Play: Its Role in Development and Evolution* (pp. 603–618). New York: Basic.

Cenoz, J. (2001). The effect of linguistic distance, L2 status and age on cross-linguistic influence in third language acquisition. In J. Cenoz, B. Hufeisen, and U. Jessner (Eds.), *Cross-Linguistic Influence in Third Language Acquisition: Psycholinguistic Perspectives* (pp. 8–20). Clevedon, UK: Multilingual Matters.

Cenoz, J. (2005). Review of T. Bhatia and W. Ritchie (Eds.), *Handbook of Bilingualism, Studies in Second Language Acquisition, 27,* 638–639.

Cenoz, J., and Genesee, F. (1998). Psycholinguistic perspectives on multilingualism and multilingual education. In J. Cenoz and F. Genesee (Eds.), *Beyond Bilingualism: Multilingualism and Multilingual Education* (pp. 16–32). Clevedon, UK: Multilingual Matters.

Chamot, A., Barnhardt, S., El-Dinary, P. B., and Robbins, J. (1999). *The Learning Strategies Handbook.* New York: Longman.

Chambers, J. K., Trudgill, P. and Schilling-Estes, N. (Eds.). (2002). *The Handbook of Language Variation and Change.* Malden, MA and Oxford: Blackwell.

Chao, W. (1981). Pro-drop languages and nonobligatory control. *Occasional Papers in Linguistics, 7,* 46–74. Amherst: University of Massachusetts.

Chapelle, C. (1995). Field-dependence/field-independence in the L2 classroom. In J. M. Reid (Ed.), *Learning Styles in the ESL/EFL Classroom* (pp. 158–168). Boston: Heinle and Heinle.

Chapelle, C., and Green, P. (1992). Field independence/dependence in second language acquisition research. *Language Learning, 42,* 47–83.

Chaudron, C. (1983). Research in metalinguistic judgments: a review of theory, methods and results. *Language Learning, 33,* 343–377.

Chaudron, C. (2003). Data collection in SLA research. In C. J. Doughty and M. H. Long (Eds.), *The Handbook of Second Language Acquisition* (pp. 762–828). Malden, MA: Blackwell.

Cho, S. (1999). The acquisition of relative clauses: experimental studies on Korean. Unpublished doctoral dissertation, University of Hawai'i at Manoa.

Chomsky, N. (1959). Review of B. F. Skinner, *Verbal Behavior. Language, 35,* 26–58.

Chomsky, N. (1968). *Language and Mind.* New York: Harcourt Brace Jovanovich.

Chomsky, N. (1975). *Reflections on Language.* New York: Pantheon.

Chomsky, N. (1981). *Lectures on Government and Binding.* Dordrecht, The Netherlands: Foris.

Chomsky, N. (1986). *Barriers.* Cambridge, MA: MIT Press.

Chomsky, N. (1995). *The Minimalist Program.* Cambridge, MA: MIT Press.

Chomsky, N. (2000). *New Horizons in the Study of Language and Mind.* Cambridge: Cambridge University Press.

Chomsky, N. (2002). *On Nature and Language.* Cambridge: Cambridge University Press.

Chouinard, M. M., and Clark, E. V. (2003). Adult reformulations of child errors as negative evidence. *Journal of Child Language, 30,* 637–669.

Clahsen, H. (1984). The acquisition of German word order: a test case for cognitive approaches to L2 development. In R. Andersen (Ed.), *Second Languages: A Crosslinguistic Perspective* (pp. 219–242). Rowley, MA: Newbury House.

Clahsen, H., and Felser, C. (2006). Grammatical processing in language learners. *Applied Psycholinguistics, 27,* 3–42.

Clark, H., and Clark, E. (1977). *Psychology and Language: An Introduction to Psycholinguistics.* New York: Harcourt Brace.

Coady, J., and Huckin, T. (Eds.). (1997). *Second Language Vocabulary Acquisition.* Cambridge: Cambridge University Press.

Coady, J., Magoto, J., Hubbard, P., Graney, J., and Mokhtari, K. (1993). High frequency vocabulary and reading proficiency in ESL readers. In T. Huckin, M. Haynes, and J. Coady (Eds.), *Second Language Reading and Vocabulary Learning* (pp. 217–228). Norwood, NJ: Ablex.

Coffield, F., Moseley, D., Hall, E., and Ecclestone, K. (2004). *Learning styles and pedagogy in Post-16 Learning: A systematic and critical review.* London: Learning and Skills Research Centre. Retrieved March 8, 2007, from *www.lsrc.ac.uk*

Cohen, Al. (1999). Helping students to help themselves. Paper presented at MITESOL Conference, Ann Arbor, MI, October.

Cohen, A. (1998). *Strategies in Learning and Using a Second Language.* London: Longman.

Cohen, A. (2005). Strategies for learning and performing L2 speech acts. *Intercultural Pragmatics. 2,* 275–301.

Cohen, A. and Macaro, E. (2007). *Language Learner Strategies: Thirty Years of Research and Practice.* Oxford: Oxford University Press.

Cohen, A., and Olshtain, E. (1993). The production of speech acts by EFL learners. *TESOL Quarterly, 27,* 33–56.

Cohen, A., Oxford, R., and Chi, J. C. (2001). *Learning Style Survey for Young Learners.* Retrieved March 9, 2007, from *http://www.carla.umn.edu/about/profiles/CohenPapers/LearningStylesSurvey.pdf*

Comrie, B. (1981). *Language Universals and Language Typology.* Chicago: University of Chicago Press.

Comrie, B. (2003). Typology and language acquisition: the case of relative clauses. In A. Ramat (Ed.). *Typology and Second Language Acquisition* (pp. 19–37). Berlin: de Grutyer.

Comrie, B., and Keenan, E. (1979). Noun phrase accessibility revisited. *Language, 55,* 649–664.

Conway, A., Kane, M., Bunting, M., Hambrick, D. Z., Wilhelm, O., and Engle, R. W. (2005). Working memory span tasks: a methodological review and user's guide. *Psychonomic Bulletin and Review, 12,* 769–786.

Cook, V. (1988). *Chomsky's Universal Grammar.* Oxford: Basil Blackwell.

Cook, V. (1991). The poverty of stimulus argument and multi-competence. *Second Language Research, 7,* 103–117.

Cook, V. (1992). Evidence for multi-competence. *Language Learning, 42,* 557–591.

Cook, V. (1996). *Second Language Learning and Language Teaching,* 2nd ed. London: Edward Arnold.

Cook, V. (1997). *Inside Language.* London: Edward Arnold.

Cook, V. (Ed.). (2003). *Effects of the Second Language on the First.* Clevedon, UK: Multilingual Matters.

Cook, V. (2005). Multi-competence: black-hole or worm-hole? Paper presented at the Second Language Research Forum, Teachers College, Columbia University, New York, October.

Coppieters, R. (1987). Competence differences between native and non-native speakers. *Language, 63,* 544–573.

Corder, S. P. (1967). The significance of learners' errors. *International Review of Applied Linguistics, 5,* 161–170.

Corder, S. P. (1971). Idiosyncratic dialects and error analysis. *International Review of Applied Linguistics, 9,* 147–159.

Corder, S. P. (1981). *Error Analysis in Interlanguage.* Oxford: Oxford University Press.

Corder, S. P. (1983). A role for the mother tongue in language learning. In S. Gass and L. Selinker (Eds.), *Language Transfer in Language Learning* (pp. 85–97). Rowley, MA: Newbury House.

Corder, S. P. (1992). A role for the mother tongue. In S. Gass and L. Selinker (Eds.), *Language Transfer in Language Learning,* 2nd ed. (pp. 18–31). Amsterdam: John Benjamins.

Cornelius, E. T. (1981). *Interviews.* New York: Longman.

Coulter, K. (1968) Linguistic error analysis of the spoken English of two native Russians. Unpublished thesis. University of Washington.

Cowan, R., and Hatasa, Y. (1994). Investigating the validity and reliability of native speaker and second-language learner judgments about sentences. In E. Tarone, S. Gass, and A. Cohen (Eds.), *Research Methodology in Second-Language Acquisition* (pp. 287–302). Hillsdale, NJ: Lawrence Erlbaum Associates.

Cowie, A. P. (1978). Vocabulary exercises within an individualized study programme. *ELT Documents, 103,* 37–44.

Craik, F. I. M., and Lockhart, R. S. (1972). Levels of processing: a framework for memory research. *Journal of Verbal Learning and Verbal Behavior, 11,* 671–684.

Craik, F. I. M., and Tulving, E. (1975). Depth of processing and the retention of words in episodic memory. *Journal of Experimental Psychology: General, 104,* 268–294.

Crookes, G. (1989). Planning and interlanguage variation. *Studies in Second Language Acquisition, 11,* 367–383.

Crookes, G. (1991). Second language speech production research: a methodologically oriented review. *Studies in Second Language Acquisition, 13,* 113–132.

Croteau, K. (1995). Second language acquisition of relative clause structures by learners of Italian. In F. Eckman, D. Highland, P. Lee, J. Mileham, and R. Rutkowski Weber (Eds.), *Second Language Acquisition Theory and Pedagogy* (pp. 115–128). Mahwah, NJ: Lawrence Erlbaum Associates.

Cutler, A. (1990). Exploiting prosodic probabilities in speech segmentation. In G. Altmann (Ed.), *Cognitive Models of Speech Processing: Psycholinguistics and Computational Perspectives* (pp. 105–121). Cambridge, MA: MIT Press.

Dagut, M., and Laufer, B. (1985). Avoidance of phrasal verbs—a case for contrastive analysis. *Studies in Second Language Acquisition, 7,* 73–79.

Dahl, Ö. (1985). *Tense and Aspect Systems.* Oxford: Blackwell.

Dahl, Ö. (2000). *Tense and Aspect in the Languages of Europe.* Berlin: de Gruyter.

Daneman, M., and Capenter, P. A. (1980). Individual differences in working memory and reading. *Journal of Verbal Learning and Verbal Behavior, 19,* 450–466.

Day, R. (Ed.). (1986). *Conversation in Second Language Acquisition: Talking to Learn.* Rowley, MA: Newbury House.

De Angelis, G. (1999, March). Interlanguage transfer and multiple language acquisition: a case study. Paper presented at the annual TESOL conference, New York.

de Bot, K., Paribakht, S., and Wesche, M. (1997). Toward a lexical processing model for the study of second language vocabulary acquisition: evidence from ESL reading. *Studies in Second Language Acquisition, 19*, 309–329.

de Graaf, R. (1997). The eXperanto experiment: effects of explicit instruction on second language acquisition. *Studies in Second Language Acquisition, 19*, 249–276.

de Groot, A. M. B., and Hoeks, J. (1995). The development of bilingual memory: evidence from word translation by trilinguals. *Language Learning, 45*, 683–724.

De Houwer, A. (1995). Bilingual language acquisition. In P. Fletcher and B. MacWhinney (Eds.), *The Handbook of Child Language* (pp. 219–250). Oxford: Blackwell.

de Jong, N. (2005). Can second language grammar be learned through listening? An experimental study. *Studies in Second Language Acquisition, 27*, 205–234.

DeKeyser, R. (1995). Learning second language grammar rules: an experiment with a miniature linguistic system. *Studies in Second Language Acquisition, 17*, 379–410.

DeKeyser, R. (1997). Beyond explicit rule learning: automatizing second language morphosyntax. *Studies in Second Language Acquisition, 19*, 195–221.

DeKeyser, R. (2000). The robustness of critical period effects in second language acquisition. *Studies in Second Language Acquisition, 22*, 499–533.

DeKeyser, R. (2001). Automaticity and automatization. In P. Robinson (Ed.), *Cognition and Second Language Instruction* (pp. 125–151). Cambridge: Cambridge University Press.

DeKeyser, R. (2003). Implicit and explicit learning. In C. Doughty and M. H. Long (Eds.), *The Handbook of Second Language Acquisition* (pp. 313–347). Oxford: Blackwell.

DeKeyser, R., and Larson-Hall, J. (2005). What does the critical period really mean? In J. F. Kroll and A. M. B. De Groot (Eds.), *Handbook of Bilingualism: Psycholinguistic Approaches* (pp. 88–108). Oxford: Oxford University Press.

DeKeyser, R., Salaberry, R., Robinson, P., and Harrington, M. (2002). What gets processed in processing instruction? A commentary on Bill VanPatten's "Processing instruction: an update." *Language Learning, 52*, 805–823.

DeKeyser, R., and Sokalski, K. (1996). The differential role of comprehension and production practice. *Language Learning, 35*, 613–642.

de Villiers, J., and de Villiers, P. (1973). A cross-sectional study of the acquisition of grammatical morphemes in child speech. *Journal of Psycholinguistic Research, 2*, 267–278.

Deuchar, M., and Quay, S. (2000). *Bilingual Acquisition: Theoretical Implications of a Case Study*. Oxford: Oxford University Press.

Dewaele, J.-M. (1998). Lexical inventions: French interlanguage as L2 versus L3. *Applied Linguistics, 19*, 471–490.

Dickerson, L. (1975). The learner's interlanguage as a system of variable rules. *TESOL Quarterly, 9*, 401–407.

Dickerson, L., and Dickerson, W. (1977). Interlanguage phonology: current research and future directions. In S. P. Corder and E. Roulet (Eds.), *The Notions of Simplification, Interlanguages and Pidgins and Their Relation to Second Language Learning* (Actes du 5ème Colloque de Linguistique Appliquée de Neuchâtel, pp. 18–29). Paris: AIMAV/Didier.

Dietrich, R., Klein, W., and Noyau, C. (1995). *The Acquisition of Temporality in a Second Language.* Amsterdam: John Benjamins.

Dinnsen, D., and Eckman, F. (1975). A functional explanation of some phonological typologies. In R. E. Grossman, L. J. San, and T. J. Vance (Eds.), *Functionalism* (pp. 126–134). Chicago: Chicago Linguistic Society.

Dörnyei, Z. (2000). Motivation in action: towards a process-oriented conceptualization of student motivation. *British Journal of Educational Psychology, 70,* 519–538.

Dörnyei, Z. (2001a) *Motivational Strategies in the Language Classroom.* Cambridge: Cambridge University Press.

Dörnyei, Z. (2001b). *Teaching and Researching Motivation.* Harlow: Longman.

Dörnyei, Z. (2003). *Questionnaires in Second Language Research: Construction, Administration, and Processing.* Mahwah, NJ: Lawrence Erlbaum Associates.

Dörnyei, Z. (2005). *The Psychology of the Language Learner: Individual Differences in Second Language Acquisition.* Mahwah, NJ: Lawrence Erlbaum Associates.

Dörnyei, Z. (2006). Individual differences in second language acquisition. In K. Bardovi-Harlig and Z. Dörnyei (Eds.), *Themes in SLA Research. AILA Review, 19* (pp. 42–68). Amsterdam: John Benjamins.

Dörnyei, Z., and Ottó, I. (1998). *Motivation in Action: A Process Model of L2 Motivation.* In *Working Papers in Applied Linguistics,* vol. 4 (pp. 43–69). London: Thames Valley University.

Dörnyei, Z., and Scott, M. (1997). Communication strategies in a second language: definitions and taxonomies. *Language Learning, 47,* 173–210.

Dörnyei, Z., and Skehan, P. (2003). Individual differences in second language learning. In C. Doughty and M. H. Long (Eds.), *The Handbook of Second Language Acquisition* (pp. 589–630). Oxford: Blackwell.

Doughty. C. (1991). Second language instruction does make a difference: evidence from an empirical study of SL relativization. *Studies in Second Language Acquisition, 13,* 431–469.

Doughty, C. (2001). Cognitive underpinnings of focus on form. In P. Robinson (Ed.), *Cognition and Second Language Instruction* (pp. 206–257). Cambridge: Cambridge University Press.

Doughty, C. (2003). Instructed SLA: constraints, compensation, and enhancement. In C. Doughty and M. H. Long (Eds.), *The Handbook of Second Language Acquisition* (pp. 256–310). Oxford: Blackwell.

Doughty, C., and Williams, J. (1998). *Focus on Form in Classroom Second Language Acquisition.* Cambridge, UK: Cambridge University Press.

Douglas, D. (2000). *Assessing Languages for Specific Purposes.* Cambridge: Cambridge University Press.

Duff, P. (2008). *Case Study Research in Applied Linguistics.* New York: Taylor & Francis.

Dulay, H., and Burt, M. (1973). Should we teach children syntax? *Language Learning, 23,* 245–258.

Dulay, H., and Burt, M. (1974a). Natural sequences in child second language acquisition. *Language Learning, 24,* 37–53.

Dulay, H., and Burt, M. (1974b). You can't learn without goofing. In J. Richards (Ed.), *Error Analysis: Perspectives on Second Language Acquisition* (pp. 95–123). London: Longman.

Dulay, H., and Burt, M. (1975). Creative construction in second language learning and teaching. In M. Burt and H. Dulay (Eds.), *On TESOL '75: New Directions in Second Language Learning, Teaching and Bilingual Education* (pp. 21–32). Washington, DC: Teachers of English to Speakers of Other Languages.

Dulay, H., Burt, M., and Krashen, S. (1982). *Language Two.* New York: Oxford University Press.

Dušková, L. (1983). On sources of errors in foreign language learning. In B. Robinett and J. Schachter (Eds.), *Second Language Learning: Contrastive Analysis, Error Analysis, and Related Aspects* (pp. 215–233). Ann Arbor: University of Michigan Press.

Dušková, L. (1984). Similarity—an aid or hindrance in foreign language learning? *Folia Linguistica, 18,* 103–115.

Eckman, F. (1977). Markedness and the Contrastive Analysis Hypothesis. *Language Learning, 27,* 315–330.

Eckman, F. (1981a). On predicting phonological difficulty in second language acquisition. *Studies in Second Language Acquisition, 4,* 18–30.

Eckman, F. (1981b). On the naturalness of interlanguage phonological rules. *Language Learning, 31,* 195–216.

Eckman, F. (1992). Secondary languages or second-language acquisition? A linguistic approach. Plenary address at the Second Language Research Forum, East Lansing, MI, April.

Eckman, F. (1994a). Local and long distance anaphora in second-language acquisition. In E. Tarone, S. Gass, and A. Cohen (Eds.), *Research Methodology in Second-Language Acquisition* (pp. 207–225). Hillsdale, NJ: Lawrence Erlbaum Associates.

Eckman, F. (1994b). The competence–performance issue in second-language acquisition theory: a debate. In E. Tarone, S. Gass, and A. Cohen (Eds.), *Research Methodology in Second-Language Acquisition* (pp. 3–15). Hillsdale, NJ: Lawrence Erlbaum Associates.

Eckman, F. (1996). On evaluating arguments for special nativism in second language acquisition theory. *Second Language Research, 12,* 398–419.

Eckman, F. (2007). Hypotheses and methods in second language acquisition: testing the noun phrase accessibility hierarchy on relative clauses. *Studies in Second Language Acquisition, 29,* 321–327.

Eckman, F., Bell, L., and Nelson, D. (1988). On the generalization of relative clause instruction in the acquisition of English as a second language. *Applied Linguistics, 9,* 1–20.

Eckman, F., Elreyes, A., and Iverson, G. (2003). Some principles of second language phonology. *Second Language Research, 19,* 169–208.

Eckman, F., Moravcsik, E., and Wirth, J. (1989). Implicational universals and interrogative structures in the interlanguage of ESL learners. *Language Learning, 39,* 173–205.

Edwards, J. (1994). *Multilingualism.* London: Routledge.

Edwards, J. (2006). Foundations of bilingualism. In T. Bhatia and W. Ritchie (Eds.), *The Handbook of Bilingualism* (pp. 5–29). Oxford: Blackwell.

Ehrman, M. (1993). Ego boundaries revisited: toward a model of personality and learning. In J. A. Alatis (Ed.), *Georgetown University Roundtable on Languages and Linguistics* (pp. 330–362). Washington, DC: Georgetown University Press.

Ehrman, M. E. (1994). The type differentiation indictor and adult foreign language learning success. *Journal of Psychological Type, 30,* 10–29.

Ehrman, M. E. (1996). *Understanding Second Language Learning Difficulties.* Thousand Oaks, CA: Sage Publications.

Ehrman, M. (2001). Bringing learning strategies to the learner: the FSI language learning consultation service. In J. E. Alatis and A. Tan (Eds.), *Language in Our Time: Bilingual Education and Official English, Ebonics, Standard English, Immigration and the Unz Initiative* (pp. 41–58). Washington, DC: Georgetown University Press.

Ehrman, M., and Leaver, B. L. (2003). Cognitive styles in the service of language learning. *System, 31,* 391–415.

Ehrman, M., and Oxford, R. (1995). Cognition plus: correlates of language learning success. *Modern Language Journal, 79,* 67–89.

Eisenstein, M., and Starbuck, R. (1989). The effect of emotional investment on L2 production. In S. Gass, C. Madden, D. Preston, and L. Selinker (Eds.), *Variation in Second Language Acquisition: Psycholinguistic Issues* (pp. 125–137). Clevedon, UK: Multilingual Matters.

Ellis, N. (1994). Implicit and explicit language learning—an overview. In N. Ellis (Ed.), *Implicit and Explicit Learning of Languages* (pp. 1–31). London: Academic Press.

Ellis, N. (2001). Memory for language. In P. Robinson (Ed.), *Cognition and Second Language Instruction.* Cambridge, UK: Cambridge University Press.

Ellis, N. (2002). Frequency effects in language processing: a review with implications for theories of implicit and explicit language acquisition. *Studies in Second Language Acquisition, 24,* 143–188.

Ellis, N. C. (2005). At the interface: dynamic interactions of explicit and implicit language knowledge. *Studies in Second Language Acquisition, 27,* 305–352.

Ellis, N. (2007). The associate-cognitive CREED. In B. VanPatten and J. Williams (Eds.), *Theories in Second Language Acquisition: An Introduction.* Mahwah, NJ: Lawrence Erlbaum Associates.

Ellis, N., and Schmidt, R. (1997). Morphology and longer distance dependencies: laboratory research illuminating the A in SLA. *Studies in Second Language Acquisition, 19,* 145–171.

Ellis, R. (1984). *Classroom Second Language Development: A Study of Classroom Interaction and Language Acquisition.* Oxford, UK: Pergamon.

Ellis, R. (1985a). *Understanding Second Language Acquisition.* Oxford: Oxford University Press.

Ellis, R. (1985b). Teacher–pupil interaction in second language development. In S. Gass and C. Madden (Eds.), *Input in Second Language Acquisition* (pp. 69–86). Rowley, MA: Newbury House.

Ellis, R. (Ed.). (1987a). *Second Language Acquisition in Context.* London: Prentice-Hall.

Ellis, R. (1987b). Interlanguage variability in narrative discourse: style shifting in the use of the past tense. *Studies in Second Language Acquisition, 9*, 1–20.

Ellis, R. (1990a). *Instructed Second Language Acquisition.* Oxford, UK: Basil Blackwell.

Ellis, R. (1990b). A response to Gregg. *Applied Linguistics, 11*, 118–131.

Ellis, R. (1990c). Grammaticality judgments and learner variability. In H. Burmeiser and P. Rounds (Eds.), *Variability in Second Language Acquisition: Proceedings of the 10th Meeting of the Second Language Research Forum* (pp. 25–60). Eugene: University of Oregon, Department of Linguistics.

Ellis, R. (1991). Grammaticality judgments and second language acquisition. *Studies in Second Language Acquisition, 13*, 161–186.

Ellis, R. (1992). *Second Language Acquisition and Language Pedagogy.* Clevedon, UK: Multilingual Matters.

Ellis, R. (1994). *The Study of Second Language Acquisition.* Oxford: Oxford University Press.

Ellis, R. (1997). *Second Language Acquisition.* Oxford: Oxford University Press.

Ellis, R. (Ed.). (2000). *Learning a Second Language through Interaction.* Amsterdam: John Benjamins.

Ellis, R. (2001). Methodological options in grammar teaching materials. In Hinkel and S. Fotos (Eds.), *New Perspectives on Grammar Teaching in Second Language Classrooms.* Mahwah, NJ: Lawrence Erlbaum.

Ellis, R. (2004). The definition and measurement of L2 explicit knowledge. *Language Learning 54*, 227–275.

Ellis, R. (2005). Measuring implicit and explicit knowledge of a second language: a psychometric study. *Studies in Second Language Acquisition, 27*, 141–172.

Ellis, R. (2007). The differential effect of corrective feedback on two grammatical structures. In A. Mackey (Ed.). *Conversational Interaction and Second Language Acquisition: A Series of Empirical Studies* (pp. 339–360). Oxford: Oxford University Press.

Ellis, R., and Barkhuizen, G. (2005). *Analysing Learner Language.* Oxford: Oxford University Press.

Ellis, R., and He, X. (1999). The roles of modified input and output in the incidental acquisition of word meanings. *Studies in Second Language Acquisition, 21*, 285–301.

Ellis, R. and Loewen, S. (2007). Confirming the operational definitions of explicit and implicit knowledge in Ellis (2005): responding to Isemonger. *Studies in Second Language Acquisition, 29*, 119–126.

Ellis, R., Loewen, S., and Erlam, R. (2006). Implicit and explicit corrective feedback and the acquisition of L2 grammar. *Studies in Second Language Acquisition, 28*, 339–368.

Ellis, R., and Sheen, Y. (2006). Re-examining the role of recasts in L2 acquisition. *Studies in Second Language Acquisition, 28*, 575–600.

Elman, J., Bates, E., Johnson, M., Karmiloff-Smith, A., Parisi, D., and Plunkett, K. (1996). *Rethinking Innateness: A Connectionist Perspective on Development.* Cambridge, MA: MIT Press.

Ely, C. M. (1986). An analysis of discomfort, risktaking, sociability, and motivation in the L2 classroom. *Language Learning, 36*, 1–25.

Epstein, S., Flynn, S., and Martohardjono, G. (1996). Second language acquisition: theoretical and experimental issues in contemporary research. *Brain and Behavioral Sciences*, 19, 677–714.

Epstein, S., Flynn, S., and Martohardjono, G. (1998). The strong continuity hypothesis in adult L2 acquisition of functional categories. In S. Flynn, G. Martohardjono, and W. O'Neil (Eds.), *The Generative Study of Second Language Acquisition* (pp. 61–77). Mahwah, NJ: Lawrence Erlbaum Associates.

Ervin-Tripp, S. (1974). Is second language learning like the first? *TESOL Quarterly*, 8, 111–127.

Eubank, L. (1993). Sentence matching and processing in L2 development. *Second Language Research*, 9, 253–280.

Eubank, L. (1993/1994). On the transfer of parametric values in L2 development. *Language Acquisition*, 4, 183–208.

Eubank, L. (1996). Negation in early German–English interlanguage: more value-less features in the L2 initial state. *Second Language Research*, 12, 73–106.

Færch, C., Haastrup, K., and Phillipson, R. (1984). *Learner Language and Language Learning*. Clevedon, UK: Multilingual Matters.

Færch, C., and Kasper, G. (1980). Processes in foreign language learning and communication. *Interlanguage Studies Bulletin*, 5, 47–118.

Færch, C., and Kasper, G. (1986). The role of comprehension in second language learning. *Applied Linguistics*, 7, 257–274.

Færch, C., and Kasper, G. (1987). From product to process—introspective methods in second language research. In C. Færch and G. Kasper (Eds.), *Introspection in Second Language Research* (pp. 5–23). Clevedon, UK: Multilingual Matters.

Felix, S. (1981). The effect of formal instruction on second language acquisition. *Language Learning*, 31, 87–112.

Felser, C., Roberts, L., Gross, R., and Marinis, T. (2003). The processing of ambiguous sentences by first and second language learners of English. *Applied Psycholinguistics*, 24, 453–489.

Ferguson, C. (1971). Absence of copula and the notion of simplicity: a study of normal speech, baby talk, foreigner talk and pidgins. In D. Hymes (Ed.), *Pidginization and Creolization of Languages* (pp. 141–150). Cambridge: Cambridge University Press.

Firth, A., and Wagner, J. (1997). On discourse, communication and (some) fundamental concepts in SLA research. *Modern Language Journal*, 81, 285–300.

Firth, A., and Wagner, J. (1998). SLA property: no trespassing! *Modern Language Journal*, 82, 91–94.

Fishman, J. (2001). 300-plus years of heritage language education in the United States. In J. K. Peyton, D. A. Ranard, and S. McGinnis (Eds.), *Heritage Languages in America: Preserving a National Resource* (pp. 81–97). McHenry, IL: Center for Applied Linguistics/Delta Systems.

Fisiak, J. (1991, April). Contrastive linguistics and language acquisition. Paper presented at the Regional English Language Center (RELC) Conference, Singapore.

Flashner, V. E. (1989). Transfer of aspect in the English oral narratives of native Russian speakers. In H. Dechert and M. Raupach (Eds.), *Transfer in Language Production* (pp. 71–97). Norwood, NJ: Ablex.

Flege, J. E. (1987a). Effects of equivalence classification on the production of foreign language speech sounds. In A. James and J. Leather (Eds.), *Sound Patterns in Second Language Acquisition* (pp. 9–39). Dordrecht, The Netherlands: Foris.

Flege, J. E. (1987b). The production of "new" and "similar" phones in a foreign language: evidence for the effect of equivalence classification. *Journal of Phonetics, 15*, 47–65.

Flege, J. E. (1990). English vowel production by Dutch talkers: more evidence for the "similar" vs. "new" distinction. In J. Leather and A. James (Eds.), *New Sounds 90: Proceedings of the Amsterdam Symposium on the Acquisition of Second-Language Speech* (pp. 255–293). Amsterdam: University of Amsterdam.

Flege, J. E. (1992). The intelligibility of English vowels spoken by British and Dutch talkers. In R. D. Kent (Ed.), *Intelligibility in Speech Disorders: Theory, Measurement, and Management*, vol. 1 (pp. 157–232). Amsterdam: John Benjamins.

Flege, J. E. (1993). Production and perception of a novel, second language phonetic contrast. *Journal of the Acoustical Society of America, 93*, 1589–1608.

Flege, J. E. (1995). Second language speech learning: theory, findings, and problems. In W. Strange (Ed.), *Speech Perception and Linguistic Experience: Issues in Cross-Linguistic Research* (pp. 233–277). Timonium, MD: York Press.

Flege, J. E. (1999). Age of learning and second language speech. In D. Birdsong (Ed.), *Second Language Acquisition and the Critical Period Hypothesis* (pp. 101–131). Mahwah, NJ: Lawrence Erlbaum Associates.

Flege, J. E. (2007). Language contact in bilingualism: phonetic system interactions. In J. Cole and J. I. Hualde (Eds.), *Laboratory Phonology 9* (pp. 353–382). Berlin: Mouton de Gruyter.

Flege, J. E., Birdsong, D., Bialystok, E., Mack, M., Sung, H., and Tsukada, K. (2006). Degree of foreign accent in English sentences produced by Korean children and adults. *Journal of Phonetics, 34*, 153–175.

Flege, J. E., Munro, M., and Mackay, I. (1995). Factors affecting degree of perceived foreign accent in a second language. *Journal of the Acoustical Society of America, 97*, 3125–3134.

Flege, J. E., Yeni-Komshian, G. E., and Liu, S. (1999). Age constraints on second language acquisition. *Journal of Memory and Language, 41*, 78–104.

Flexner, S. B., and Hauck, L. C. (Eds.). (1988). *Random House Dictionary of the English Language*, 2nd ed. New York: Random House.

Flynn, S. (1987). *A Parameter-Setting Model of L2 Acquisition*. Dordrecht, The Netherlands: Reidel.

Flynn, S. (1996). A parameter-setting approach to second language acquisition. In W. Ritchie and T. Bhatia (Eds.), *Handbook of Second Language Acquisition* (pp. 121–158). San Diego, CA: Academic Press.

Flynn, S., and Martohardjono, G. (1994). Mapping from the initial state to the final state: the separation of universal principles and language-specific principles. In B. Lust, M. Suner, and J. Whiteman (Eds.), *Syntactic Theory and First Language Acquisition: Cross-Linguistic Perspectives*, vol. 1, *Heads, Projections and Learnability* (pp. 319–335). Hillsdale, NJ: Lawrence Erlbaum Associates.

Foss, D., and Hakes, D. (1978). *Psycholinguistics*. Englewood Cliffs, NJ: Prentice-Hall.

Foster-Cohen, S. (1999). *An Introduction to Child Language Development*. London: Longman.

Fox, B. (1987). The noun phrase accessibility hierarchy revisited. *Language, 63*, 856–870.

Fraser, C. (1999). Lexical processing strategy use and vocabulary through reading. *Studies in Second Language Acquisition, 21*, 225–241.

Frenck-Mestre, C. (2005). Eye-movement recording as a tool for studying syntactic processing in a second language: a review of methodologies and experimental findings. *Second Language Research, 21*, 175–198.

Fries, C. (1945). *Teaching and Learning English as a Foreign Language*. Ann Arbor: University of Michigan Press.

Fries, C. (1957). Foreword. In R. Lado, *Linguistics Across Cultures*. Ann Arbor: University of Michigan Press.

Fromkin, V., Rodman, R., and Hyams, N. (2007). *An Introduction to Language*, 8th ed. Boston, MA: Heinle.

Gaies, S. (1979). Linguistic input in first and second language learning. In F. Eckman and A. Hastings (Eds.), *Studies in First and Second Language Acquisition* (pp. 185–193). Rowley, MA: Newbury House.

Gairns, R., and Redman, S. (1986). *Working with Words: A Guide to Teaching and Learning Vocabulary*. New York: Cambridge University Press.

Gallaway, C., and Richards, B. J. (Eds.). (1994). *Input and Interaction in Language Acquisition*. Cambridge: Cambridge University Press.

Gardner, R. C. (1983). *Frames of Mind: The Theory of Multiple Intelligences*. New York: Basic Books.

Gardner, R. C. (1985). *Social Psychology and Second Language Learning: The Role of Attitudes and Motivation*. London: Edward Arnold.

Gardner, R. C. (2001). Integrative motivation and second language acquisition. In Z. Dornyei and R. Schmidt (Eds.), *Motivation and Second Language Acquisition* (pp. 1–19). Honolulu, HI: University of Hawai'i, Second Language Teaching and Curriculum Center.

Gardner, R. C., and Lambert, W. (1972). *Attitudes and Motivation in Second Language Learning*. Rowley, MA: Newbury House.

Gardner, R. C., Masgoret, A.-M., Tennant, J., and Mihic, L. (2004). Integrative motivation: changes during a year-long intermediate-level language course. *Language Learning, 54*, 1–34.

Gass, S. (1979a). An investigation of syntactic transfer in adult second language acquisition. Unpublished doctoral dissertation, Indiana University, Bloomington.

Gass, S. (1979b). Language transfer and universal grammatical relations. *Language Learning, 29*, 327–344.

Gass, S. (1980). An investigation of syntactic transfer in adult L2 learners. In R. Scarcella and S. Krashen (Eds.), *Research in Second Language Acquisition* (pp. 132–141). Rowley, MA: Newbury House.

Gass, S. (1982). From theory to practice. In M. Hines and W. Rutherford (Eds.), *On TESOL '81* (pp. 129–139). Washington, DC: Teachers of English to Speakers of Other Languages.

Gass, S. (1984). A review of interlanguage syntax: language transfer and language universals. *Language Learning, 34*, 115–132.

REFERENCES

Gass, S. (1986). An interactionist approach to L2 sentence interpretation. *Studies in Second Language Acquisition*, 8, 19–37.

Gass, S. (1987). The resolution of conflicts among competing systems: a bidirectional perspective. *Applied Psycholinguistics*, 8, 329–350.

Gass, S. (1988a). Integrating research areas: a framework for second language studies. *Applied Linguistics*, 9, 198–217.

Gass, S. (1988b). Second language vocabulary acquisition. *Annual Review of Applied Linguistics*, 9, 92–106.

Gass, S. (1989). Language universals and second language learning. *Language Learning*, 39, 497–534.

Gass, S. (1994). The reliability of second-language grammaticality judgments. In E. Tarone, S. Gass, and A. Cohen (Eds.), *Research Methodology in Second-Language Acquisition* (pp. 303–322). Hillsdale, NJ: Lawrence Erlbaum Associates.

Gass, S. (1997). *Input, Interaction, and the Second Language Learner*. Mahwah, NJ: Lawrence Erlbaum Associates.

Gass, S. (1998). Apples and oranges: or, why apples are not orange and don't need to be: a response to Firth and Wagner. *Modern Language Journal*, 81, 83–90.

Gass, S. (1999). Discussion: incidental vocabulary learning. *Studies in Second Language Acquisition*, 21, 319–333.

Gass, S. (2003). Input and interaction. In C. Doughty and M. H. Long (Eds.), *The Handbook of Second Language Acquisition* (pp. 224–255). Oxford: Basil Blackwell.

Gass, S. (2004). Conversation and input-interaction. *Modern Language Journal*, 88, 597–616.

Gass, S., and Alvarez-Torres, M. (2005). Attention when? An investigation of the ordering effect of input and interaction. *Studies in Second Language Acquisition*, 27, 1–31.

Gass, S. and Ard, J. (1980). L2 data: their relevance for language universals. *TESOL Quarterly*. 14, 443–452.

Gass, S., and Ard, J. (1984). L2 acquisition and the ontology of language universals. In W. Rutherford (Ed.), *Second Language Acquisition and Language Universals* (pp. 33–68). Amsterdam: John Benjamins.

Gass, S., and Houck, N. (1999). *Interlanguage Refusals: A Cross-Cultural Study of Japanese-English*. Berlin: Mouton de Gruyter.

Gass, S. Lee, J., and Roots, R. (2007). Firth and Wagner: new ideas or a new articulation? *Modern Language Journal*, 91, 786–797.

Gass, S. and Lewis, K. (2007). Perceptions of interactional feedback: differences between heritage language learners and non-heritage language learners. In A. Mackey (Ed.), *Conversational Interaction in Second Language Acquisition: A Series of Empirical Studies* (pp. 173–196). Oxford: Oxford University Press.

Gass, S., and Mackey, A. (2000). *Stimulated Recall Methodology in Second Language Research*. Mahwah, NJ: Lawrence Erlbaum Associates.

Gass, S., and Mackey, A. (2006). Input, interaction and output: an overview. In K. Bardovi-Harlig and Z. Dörnyei (Eds.), *AILA Review* (pp. 3–17). Amsterdam: John Benjamins.

Gass, S., and Mackey, A. (2007). *Data Elicitation for Second and Foreign Language Research*. Mahwah, NJ: Lawrence Erlbaum Associates.

Gass, S., Mackey, A., Alvarez-Torres, M., and Fernández-García, M. (1999). The effects of task repetition on linguistic output. *Language Learning, 49,* 549–581.

Gass, S., Mackey, A., and Ross-Feldman, L. (2005). Task-based interactions in classroom and laboratory settings. *Language Learning, 55,* 575–611.

Gass, S., and Madden, C. (Eds.). (1985). *Input in Second Language Acquisition.* Rowley, MA: Newbury House.

Gass, S., Madden, C., Preston, D., and Selinker, L. (Eds.). (1988a). *Variation in Second Language Acquisition: Discourse and Pragmatics.* Clevedon, UK: Multilingual Matters.

Gass, S., Madden, C., Preston, D., and Selinker, L. (Eds.). (1988b). *Variation in Second Language Acquisition: Psycholinguistic Issues.* Clevedon, UK: Multilingual Matters.

Gass, S., Roots, R., and Lee, J. (2006). Inhibition and working memory capacity in a second language. Paper presented at the 16th European Second Language Association Conference, Antalya, Turkey, September.

Gass, S., and Schachter, J. (Eds.) (1989). *Linguistic Perspectives on Second Language Acquisition.* Cambridge: Cambridge University Press.

Gass, S., and Selinker, L. (Eds.) (1992). *Language Transfer in Language Learning.* Amsterdam: John Benjamins.

Gass, S., Sorace, A., and Selinker, S. (1999). *Second Language Learning: Data Analysis.* Mahwah, NJ: Lawrence Erlbaum Associates.

Gass, S., Svetics, I., and Lemelin, S. (2003). Differential effects of attention. *Language Learning, 53,* 497–545.

Gass, S., and Varonis, E. (1984). The effect of familiarity on the comprehension of nonnative speech. *Language Learning, 34,* 65–89.

Gass, S., and Varonis, E. (1985). Variation in native speaker speech modification to non-native speakers. *Studies in Second Language Acquisition, 7,* 37–57.

Gass, S., and Varonis, E. (1986). Sex differences in NNS/NNS interactions. In R. Day (Ed.), *Talking to Learn: Conversation in Second Language Acquisition* (pp. 327–351). Rowley, MA: Newbury House.

Gass, S., and Varonis, E. (1989). Incorporated repairs in NNS discourse. In M. Eisenstein (Ed.), *Variation and Second Language Acquisition* (pp. 71–86). New York: Plenum.

Gass, S., and Varonis, E. (1994). Input, interaction and second language production. *Studies in Second Language Acquisition, 16,* 283–302.

Gatbonton, E. (1978). Patterned phonetic variability in second language speech: a gradual diffusion model. *Canadian Modern Language Review, 34,* 335–347.

Geen, R. G. (1991). Social motivation. *Annual Review of Psychology, 42,* 377–399.

Genesee, F., Boivin, I., and Nicoladis, E. (1996). Talking with strangers: a study of bilingual children's communicative competence. *Applied Psycholinguistics, 17,* 427–442.

George, H. (1972). *Common Errors in Language Learning.* Rowley, MA: Newbury House.

Giacalone Ramat, A., and Banfi, E. (1990). The acquisition of temporality: a second language perspective. *Folia Linguistica 25* (3–4), 405–428.

Giles, H., and St. Clair, R. N. (Eds.). (1979). *Language and Social Psychology.* Oxford: Basil Blackwell.

Giles, H., and Smith, P. M. (1979). Accommodation theory: optional levels of convergence. In H. Giles and R. N. St. Clair (Eds.), *Language and Social Psychology* (pp. 45–65). Oxford: Basil Blackwell.

Girden, E. (1996). *Evaluating Research Articles: From Start to Finish*. Thousand Oaks, CA: Sage Publications.

Glew, M. (1998). The acquisition of reflexive pronouns among adult learners of English. Unpublished doctoral dissertation, Michigan State University, East Lansing.

Goldschmidt, M. (1996). From the addressee's perspective: imposition in favor-asking. In S. Gass and J. Neu (Eds.), *Speech Acts Across Cultures* (pp. 241–256). Berlin: Mouton de Gruyter.

Goldschneider, J. and DeKeyser, R. (2005). Explaining the "Natural order of L2 morpheme acquisition" in English: a meta-analysis of multiple determinants. *Language Learning, 55*, Supplement 1, 27–77.

Goss, N., Ying-Hua, Z., and Lantolf, J. (1994). Two heads may be better than one: mental activity in second-language grammaticality judgments. In E. Tarone, S. Gass, and A. Cohen (Eds.), *Research Methodology in Second-Language Acquisition* (pp. 263–286). Hillsdale, NJ: Lawrence Erlbaum Associates.

Greenberg, J. H. (1963). Some universals of grammar with particular reference to the order of meaningful elements. In J. H. Greenberg (Ed.), *Universals of Language* (pp. 73–113). Cambridge, MA: MIT Press.

Gregg, K. (1984). Krashen's monitor and Occam's razor. *Applied Linguistics, 5*, 79–100.

Gregg, K. (1990). The variable competence model of second language acquisition and why it isn't. *Applied Linguistics, 11*, 364–383.

Grenfell, M. and Macaro, E. (in press). Claims and critiques. In A. Cohen and E. Macaro (Eds.), *Language Learner Strategies: Thirty Years of Research and Practice*. Oxford: Oxford University Press.

Griffiths, R., and Sheen, R. (1992). Disembedded figures in the landscape: a reappraisal of L2 research on field dependence/independence. *Applied Linguistics, 13*, 133–148.

Grigorenko, E., Sternberg, R., and Ehrman, M.E. (2000). A theory based approach to the measurement of foreign language learning ability: the CANAL-F theory and test. *Modern Language Journal, 84*, 390–405.

Grosjean, F. (2001). The bilingual's language modes. In J. Nicol (Ed.), *One Mind, Two Languages: Bilingual Language Processing*. Malden, MA: Blackwell.

Gu, Y., and Johnson, R. (1996). Vocabulary learning strategies and language learning outcomes. *Language Learning, 46*, 643–679.

Guiora, A., Brannon, R. C., and Dull, C. (1972). Empathy and second language learning. *Language Learning, 22*, 111–130.

Gumperz, J., and Tannen, D. (1979). Individual and social differences in language use. In C. Fillmore, D. Kempler, and W. S.-Y. Wang (Eds.), *Individual Differences in Language Ability and Language Behavior* (pp. 305–325). New York: Academic.

Hakuta, K. (1974a). A preliminary report on the development of grammatical morphemes in a Japanese girl learning English as a second language. *Working Papers in Bilingualism, 3*, 18–43.

Hakuta, K. (1974b). Prefabricated patterns and the emergence of structure in second language learning. *Language Learning, 24*, 287–297.

Hakuta, K. (1976a). A report on the development of grammatical morphemes in a Japanese girl learning English as a second language. In E. Hatch (Ed.), *Second Language Acquisition: A Book of Readings* (pp. 132–147). Rowley, MA: Newbury House.

Hakuta, K. (1976b). Becoming bilingual: a case study of a Japanese child learning English. *Language Learning, 26*, 321–351.

Hamilton, R. (1994). Is implicational generalization unidirectional and maximal? Evidence from relativization instruction in a second language. *Language Learning, 44*, 123–157.

Hamilton, R. (1996). Against underdetermined reflexive binding. *Second Language Research, 12*, 420–446.

Han, Z.-H. (2000). Persistence of the implicit influence of L1: the case of the pseudo-passive. *Applied Linguistics, 21*, 78–105.

Han, Z.-H. (2002). A study of the impact of recasts on tense consistency in L2 output. *TESOL Quarterly, 36*, 543–572.

Han, Z.-H. (2004). *Fossilization in Adult Second Language Acquisition*. Clevedon, UK: Multilingual Matters.

Han, Z.-H. (ms.). Does visual input enhancement enhance learning? A review of the research.

Hanania, E. (1974). Acquisition of English Structures: a case study of an adult native speaker of Arabic in an English-speaking environment. Unpublished doctoral dissertation, Indiana University, Bloomington.

Hancin-Bhatt, B. (2000). Optimality in second language phonology: codas in Thai ESL. *Second Language Research, 16*, 201–232.

Hancin-Bhatt, B., and Bhatt, R. (1997). Optimal L2 syllables: interactions of transfer and developmental effects. *Studies in Second Language Acquisition, 19*, 379–400.

Hankamer, J. (1989). Morphological parsing in the lexicon. In W. Marslen-Wilson (Ed.), *Lexical Representation and Process* (pp. 392–408). Cambridge, MA: MIT Press.

Harley, B. (1998). The role of focus-on-form tasks in promoting child L2 acquisition. In C. Doughty and J. Williams (Eds.), *Focus on Form in Classroom Second Language Acquisition* (pp. 156–174). Cambridge: Cambridge University Press.

Harley, B., and Hart, D. (1997). Language aptitude and second language proficiency in classroom learners of different starting ages. *Studies in Second Language Acquisition, 19*, 379–400.

Harley, B., and Swain, M. (1984). The interlanguage of immersion students and its implications for second language teaching. In A. Davies, C. Criper, and A. Howatt (Eds.), *Interlanguage* (pp. 291–311). Edinburgh: Edinburgh University Press.

Harrington, M. (1987). Processing transfer: language-specific strategies as a source of interlanguage variation. *Applied Psycholinguistics, 8*, 351–378.

Harrington, M. and Sawyer, M. (1992). L2 working memory capacity and L2 reading skill. *Studies in Second Language Acquisition, 14*, 25–38.

Harris, V. (2003). Adapting classroom-based strategy instruction to a distance learning context. *TESL-EJ, 7*, 1–19.

Hasbún, L. (1995). The role of lexical aspect in the acquisition of tense and grammatical aspect in Spanish as a foreign language. Unpublished doctoral dissertation, Indiana University, Bloomington.

Hatch, E. (1978). Discourse and second language acquisition. In E. Hatch (Ed.), *Second Language Acquisition: A Book of Readings* (pp. 401–435). Rowley, MA: Newbury House.

Hatch, E. (1983). *Psycholinguistics: A Second Language Perspective*. Rowley, MA: Newbury House.

Hatch, E., and Hawkins, B. (1985). Second-language acquisition: an experiential approach. In S. Rosenberg (Ed.), *Advances in Applied Psycholinguistics*, vol. 2 (pp. 241–283). New York: Cambridge University Press.

Hawkins, B. (1985). Is an "appropriate response" always so appropriate? In S. Gass and C. Madden (Eds.), *Input in Second Language Acquisition* (pp. 162–178). Rowley, MA: Newbury House.

Haynes, M., and Baker, I. (1993). American and Chinese readers learning from lexical familiarizations in English text. In T. Huckin, M. Haynes, and J. Coady (Eds.), *Second Language Reading and Vocabulary Learning* (pp. 130–150). Norwood, NJ: Ablex.

Heilenman, K., and McDonald, J. (1993). Processing strategies in L2 learners of French: the role of transfer. *Language Learning, 43*, 507–557.

Henkes, T. (1974). Early stages in the non-native acquisition of English syntax: a study of three children from Zaire, Venezuela, and Saudi Arabia. Unpublished doctoral dissertation, Indiana University, Bloomington.

Henriksen, B. (1999). Three dimensions of vocabulary development. *Studies in Second Language Acquisition, 21*, 303–317.

Herwig, A. (2001). Plurilingual lexical organization: evidence from lexical processing in L1–L2–L3–L4 translation. In J. Cenoz, B. Hufeisen, and U. Jessner (Eds.), *Cross-Linguistic Influences in Third Language Acquisition: Psycholinguistic Perspectives* (pp. 115–137). Clevedon, UK: Multilingual Matters.

Hill, A. (1961). Grammaticality. *Word, 17*, 1–10.

Hilles, S. (1986). Interlanguage in the pro-drop parameter. *Second Language Research, 2*, 33–52.

Hoek, D., Ingram, D., and Gibson, D. (1986). Some possible causes of children's early word extensions. *Journal of Child Language, 13*, 477–494.

Hoffman, M. L. (1986). Affect, cognition and motivation. In R. M. Sorrentino and E. T. Higgins (Eds.), *Handbook of Motivation and Cognition* (pp. 244–280). New York: Guilford.

Horwitz, E. K. (2001). Language anxiety and achievement. *Annual Review of Applied Linguistics, 21*, 112–126.

Houck, N., and Gass, S. (1996). Non-native refusals: a methodological perspective. In S. Gass and J. Neu (Eds.), *Speech Acts Across Cultures* (pp. 45–64). Berlin: Mouton de Gruyter.

Housen, A. (1995). It's about time. Unpublished doctoral dissertation, Vrije Universiteit, Brussels, Belgium.

Hudson, G. (1999). *Essential Introductory Linguistics*. Oxford, UK: Basil Blackwell.

Huebner, T. (1979). Order-of-acquisition vs. dynamic paradigm: a comparison of method in interlanguage research. *TESOL Quarterly, 13*, 21–28.

Huebner, T. (1983). *A Longitudinal Analysis of the Acquisition of English*. Ann Arbor, MI: Karoma.

Hulstijn, J. (2005). Theoretical and empirical issues in the study of implicit and explicit second-language learning: introduction. *Studies in Second Language Acquisition, 27,* 129–140.

Hulstijn, J., Hollander, M., and Greidanus, T. (1996). Incidental vocabulary learning by advanced foreign language students: the influence of marginal glosses, dictionary use, and reoccurrence of unknown words. *Modern Language Journal, 80,* 327–339.

Hulstijn, J., and Hulstijn, W. (1984). Grammatical errors as a function of processing constraints and explicit knowledge. *Language Learning, 34,* 23–43.

Hulstijn, J., and Laufer, B. (2001). Some empirical evidence for the involvement load hypothesis in vocabulary acquisition. *Language Learning, 51,* 539–558.

Hulstijn, J., and Marchena, E. (1989). Avoidance: grammatical or semantic causes? *Studies in Second Language Acquisition, 11,* 241–255.

Hunt, K. W. (1965). *Grammatical Structures Written at Three Grade Levels* (NCTE Research Report no. 3). Champaign, IL: National Council of Teachers of English.

Hunt, K. W. (1970). Syntactic maturity in school-children and adults. *Monographs for the Society for Research in Child Development, 35* (1, serial no. 134).

Hyams, N. (1983). The acquisition of parameterized grammars. Unpublished doctoral dissertation, City University of New York.

Hyltenstam, K. (1977). Implicational patterns in interlanguage syntax variation. *Language Learning, 27,* 383–411.

Hyltenstam, K. (1984). The use of typological markedness conditions as predictors in second language acquisition: the case of pronominal copies in relative clauses. In R. Andersen (Ed.), *Second Languages: A Crosslinguistic Perspective* (pp. 39–58). Rowley, MA: Newbury House.

Hyltenstam, K., and Abrahamsson, N. (2003). Maturational constraints in SLA. In C. Doughty and M. H. Long (Eds.), *The Handbook of Second Language Acquisition* (pp. 539–588). Oxford: Blackwell.

Ingram, D. (1986). Phonological development: production. In P. Fletcher and P. Garman (Eds.), *Language Acquisition,* 2nd ed. (pp. 223–239). Cambridge: Cambridge University Press.

Ioup, G. (1984). Is there a structural foreign accent? A comparison of syntactic and phonological errors in second language acquisition. *Language Learning, 34,* 1–17.

Isemonger, I. (2007). Operational definitions of explicit and implicit knowledge: a response to R. Ellis (2005) and some recommendations for future research in this area. *Studies in Second Language Acquisition, 29,* 101–118.

Ishida, M. (2004). Effects of recasts on the acquisition of the aspectual form *te i(ru)* by learners of Japanese as a foreign language. *Language Learning, 54,* 311–394.

Iwashita, N. (2003). Negative feedback and positive evidence in task-based interaction: differential effects on L2 development. *Studies in Second Language Acquisition, 25,* 1–36.

Izumi, S. (2002). Output, input enhancement and the noticing hypothesis: an experimental study on ESL relativization. *Studies in Second Language Acquisition, 24,* 541–577.

REFERENCES

Izumi, S. and Bigelow, M. (2000) Does output promote noticing and second language acquisition? *TESOL Quarterly*, *34*, 239–278.

Izumi, S., Bigelow, M., Fujiwara, M., and Fearnow, S. (1999). Testing the output hypothesis: effects of output on noticing and second language acquisition. *Studies in Second Language Acquisition*, *21*, 421–452.

Izumi, Y., and Izumi, S. (2004). Investigating the effects of oral output on the learning of relative clauses in English: issues in the psycholinguistic requirements for effective output tasks. *Canadian Modern Language Review*, *60*, 587–609.

Jannedy, S., Poletto, R., and Weldon, T. (Eds.). (1994). *Language Files*, 6th ed., Columbus: Ohio State University Press.

Jared, D., and Kroll, J. F. (2001). Do bilinguals activate phonological representations in one or both of their languages when naming words? *Journal of Memory and Language*, *44*, 2–31.

Jarvis, S. (2002). Topic continuity in L2 English article use. *Studies in Second Language Acquisition*, *24*, 387–418.

Jeon, K.S. and Kim, H-Y. (2007). Development of relativization in Korean as a foreign language: Noun Phrase Accessibility Hierarchy in head-internal and head-external relative clauses. *Studies in Second Language Acquisition*, *29*, 253–276.

Jiang, N. (2000). Lexical representation and development in a second language. *Applied Linguistics*, *21*, 47–77.

Jiang, N. (2002). Form–meaning mapping in vocabulary acquisition in a second language. *Studies in Second Language Acquisition*, *24*, 617–637.

Jiang, N. (2004). Semantic transfer and its implications for vocabulary teaching in a second language. *Modern Language Journal*, *88*, 416–432.

Johansson, S. (1978). *Studies in Error Gravity: Native Reactions to Errors Produced by Swedish Learners of English*. Göteberg, Sweden: Acta Universitatis Gothoburgensis.

Johnson, J., and Newport, E. (1989). Critical period effects in second language learning: the influence of maturational state on the acquisition of ESL. *Cognitive Psychology*, *21*, 60–99.

Johnson, J., and Newport, E. (1991). Critical period effects on universal properties of language: the status of subjacency in the acquisition of a second language. *Cognition*, *39*, 215–258.

Johnson, J., Prior, S., and Artuso, M. (2000). Field dependence as a factor in second language communicative production. *Language Learning*, *50*, 529–567.

Jones, R. (1977). Social and psychological factors in second language acquisition: a study of an individual. In C. Henning (Ed.), *Proceedings of the Second Language Research Forum* (pp. 331–341). Los Angeles: University of California, Department of Applied Linguistics.

Jordan, G. (2005). *Theory Construction in Second Language Acquisition*. Amsterdam: John Benjamins.

Jourdenais, R., Ota, M., Stauffer, S., Boyson, B., and Doughty, C. (1995). Does textual enhancement promote noticing: a think-aloud protocol analysis. In R. Schmidt (Ed.), *Attention and Awareness in Foreign Language Learning* (pp. 183–216). Honolulu: University of Hawai'i Press.

Kahneman, D., Slovic, P., and Tversky, A. (Eds.). (1982). *Judgment under Uncertainty: Heuristics and Biases.* Cambridge: Cambridge University Press.

Kanno, K. (1996). The status of a nonparameterized principle in the L2 initial state. *Language Acquisition, 5,* 317–332.

Kanno, K. (2007). The role of an innate acquisition device in second language acquisition. In M. Nakayama, R. Mazuka, and Y. Shirai (Eds.), *Handbook of East Asian Psycholinguistics.* Cambridge: Cambridge University Press.

Kaplan, M. A. (1987). Developmental patterns of past tense acquisition among foreign language learners of French. In B. VanPatten, T. R. Dvorak, and J. F. Lee (Eds.), *Foreign Language Learning: A Research Perspective* (pp. 52–60). Rowley, MA: Newbury House.

Kasper, G. (1997). "A" stands for acquisition. *Modern Language Journal, 81,* 307–312.

Kasper, G. (2004). Participant orientations in German conversation-for-learning. *Modern Language Journal, 88,* 551–567.

Kasper, G., and Kellerman, E. (1997). *Communication Strategies: Psycholinguistic and Sociolinguistic Perspectives.* London: Longman.

Kasper, G., and Rose, K. R. (2002). *Pragmatic Development in a Second Language.* Oxford: Blackwell.

Kasper, G., and Schmidt, D. (1996). Developmental issues in interlanguage pragmatics. *Studies in Second Language Acquisition, 18,* 149–169.

Kawaguchi, S. (2005). Argument structure and syntactic development in Japanese as a second language. In M. Pienemann (Ed.), *Cross-Linguistic Aspects of Processability Theory* (pp. 253–298). Amsterdam: John Benjamins.

Ke, C. (1998). Effects of language background on the learning of Chinese characters among foreign language students. *Foreign Language Annals 31,* 91–100.

Keck, C., Iberri-Shea, G., Tracy-Ventura, N., and Wa-Mbalaka, S. (2006). Investigating the empirical link between interaction and acquisition: A quantitative metaanalysis. In J. M. Norris & L. Ortega (Eds.). *Synthesizing research on language learning and teaching* (pp. 91–131). Philadelphia, PA: John Benjamins.

Keenan, E. (1975). Variation in Universal Grammar. In R. Fasold and R. Shuy (Eds.), *Analyzing Variation in Language* (pp. 136–148). Washington, DC: Georgetown University Press.

Keenan, E., and Comrie, B. (1977). Noun phrase accessibility and Universal Grammar. *Linguistic Inquiry, 8,* 63–99.

Kellerman, E. (1979). Transfer and non-transfer: where we are now. *Studies in Second Language Acquisition, 2,* 37–57.

Kellerman, E. (1985). Dative alternation and the analysis of data: a reply to Mazurkewich. *Language Learning, 35,* 91–101.

Kellerman, E. (1987). Aspects of transferability in second language acquisition. Unpublished doctoral dissertation, Katholieke Universiteit te Nijmegen.

Kellerman, E., and Sharwood Smith, M. (Eds.). (1986). *Cross-Linguistic Influence in Second Language Acquisition.* Elmsford, NY: Pergamon.

Kellerman, E., van Ijzendoorn. J. and Takashima, H. 1999. Retesting a universal: the Empty Category Principle and learners of (pseudo)Japanese as a second language. In K. Kanno (Ed.), *Studies on the Acquisition of Japanese as a Second Language* (pp. 71–87). Amsterdam: John Benjamins.

Kempen, G. (1977). Conceptualizing and formulating in sentence production. In

S. Rosenberg (Ed.), *Sentence Production: Developments in Research and Theory* (pp. 259–274). Hillsdale, NJ: Lawrence Erlbaum Associates.

Kempen, G. (1978). Sentence construction by a psychologically plausible formulator. In R. N. Campbell and P. T. Smith (Eds.), *Recent Advances in the Psychology of Language: Formal and Experimental Approaches* (pp. 103–123). New York: Plenum.

Kempen, G., and Hoenkamp, E. (1981). *A Procedural Grammar for Sentence Production* (Internal Report no. 81). Nijmegen, The Netherlands: Katholieke Universiteit, Vakgroep psychologische functieleer, Psychologisch taboratorium.

Kempen, G., and Hoenkamp, E. (1987). An incremental procedural grammar for sentence formulation. *Cognitive Science, 11*, 201–258.

Kilborn, K., and Ito, T. (1989). Sentence processing strategies in adult bilinguals. In B. MacWhinney and E. Bates (Eds.), *The Crosslinguistic Study of Sentence Processing* (pp. 257–291). Cambridge: Cambridge University Press.

Kleifgen, J. A. (1985). Skilled variation in a kindergarten teacher's use of foreigner talk. In S. Gass and C. Madden (Eds.), *Input in Second Language Acquisition* (pp. 59–85). Cambridge, MA: Newbury House.

Klein, E. (1995). Evidence for a "wild" L2 grammar: when PP's rear their empty heads. *Applied Linguistics, 16*, 87–117.

Klein, W., and Perdue, C. (1989). The learner's problem of arranging words. In B. MacWhinney and E. Bates (Eds.), *The Crosslinguistic Study of Sentence Processing* (pp. 292–327). Cambridge: Cambridge University Press.

Kleinmann, H. (1977). Avoidance behavior in adult second language acquisition. *Language Learning, 27*, 93–107.

Klima, E., and Bellugi, U. (1966). Syntactic regularities in the speech of children. In J. Lyons and R. J. Wales (Eds.), *Psycholinguistics Papers* (pp. 183–219). Edinburgh: Edinburgh University Press.

Koda, K. (1989). The effects of transferred vocabulary knowledge on the development of L2 reading proficiency. *Foreign Language Annals, 22*, 529–540.

Kormos, J. (1999). The timing of self-repairs in second language speech production. *Studies in Second Language Acquisition, 22*, 145–167.

Krashen, S. (1977). Some issues relating to the monitor model. In H. Brown, C. Yorio, and R. Crymes (Eds.), *On TESOL '77: Teaching and Learning English as a Second Language: Trends in Research and Practice* (pp. 144–158). Washington, DC: Teachers of English to Speakers of Other Languages.

Krashen, S. (1982). *Principles and Practice in Second Language Acquisition*. London: Pergamon.

Krashen, S. (1985). *The Input Hypothesis: Issues and Implications*. New York: Longman.

Krashen, S., Butler, J., Birnbaum, R., and Robertson, J. (1978). Two studies in language acquisition and language learning. *ITL: Review of Applied Linguistics, 39–40*, 73–92.

Krashen, S., Houck, N., Giunchi, P., Bode, S., Birnbaum, R., and Strei, G. (1977). Difficulty order for grammatical morphemes for adult second language performers using free speech. *TESOL Quarterly, 11*, 338–341.

Kroll, J. F., and Sunderman, G. (2003). Cognitive processes in second language learners and bilinguals: the development of lexical and conceptual representations. In C. Doughty and M. H. Long (Eds.), *The Handbook of Second Language Acquisition* (pp. 104–129). Cambridge, MA: Blackwell.

Kumpf, L. (1984). Temporal systems and universality in interlanguage: a case study. In F. Eckman, L. Bell, and D. Nelson (Eds.), *Universals of Second Language Acquisition* (pp. 132–143). Rowley, MA: Newbury House.

Labov, W. (1969). Contraction, deletion, and inherent variability of the English copula. *Language, 45*, 715–762.

Labov, W. (1970). The study of language in its social context. *Studium Generale, 23*, 30–87.

Labov, W., and Fanshel, D. (1977). *Therapeutic Discourse*. New York: Academic.

Lado, R. (1957). *Linguistics Across Cultures*. Ann Arbor: University of Michigan Press.

Lakshmanan, U. (1986). The role of parametric variation in adult second language acquisition: a study of the "pro-drop" parameter. *Papers in Applied Linguistics–Michigan, 2*, 97–118.

Lakshmanan, U. (1995). Child second language acquisition of syntax. *Studies in Second Language Acquisition, 17*, 301–329.

Lakshmanan, U., and Teranishi, K. (1994). Preferences versus grammaticality judgments: some methodological issues concerning the governing category parameter in second language acquisition. In E. Tarone, S. Gass, and A. Cohen (Eds.), *Research Methodology in Second Language Acquisition* (pp. 185–206). Hillsdale, NJ: Lawrence Erlbaum Associates.

Lantolf, J.P., and Thorne, S. (2006). *Sociocultural Theory and the Genesis of Second Language Development*. Oxford: Oxford University Press.

Lantolf, J. P. and Thorne, S. (2007). Sociocultural theory and second language learning. In B. VanPatten and J. Williams (Eds.), *Theories in Second Language Acquisition: An Introduction* (pp. 201–224). Mahwah, NJ: Lawrence Erlbaum Associates.

Lantolf, J. P. and Yáñez, M. C. (2003). Talking yourself into Spanish: the role of private speech in second language learning. *Hispania, 86*, 98–110.

Lardiere, D. (1998). Case and tense in the "fossilized" steady state. *Second Language Research, 14*, 1–26.

Lardiere, D. (2007). *Ultimate Attainment in Second Language Acquisition: A Case Study*. Mahway, NJ: Lawrence Erlbaum Associates.

Larsen-Freeman, D. (1975a). The acquisition of grammatical morphemes by adult ESL students. *TESOL Quarterly, 9*, 409–430.

Larsen-Freeman, D. (1975b). The acquisition of grammatical morphemes by adult learners of English as a second language. Unpublished doctoral dissertation, University of Michigan, Ann Arbor.

Larsen-Freeman, D. (1976). An explanation for the morpheme acquisition order of second language learners. *Language Learning, 26*, 125–134.

Larsen-Freeman, D. (1978). An explanation for the morpheme accuracy order of learners of English as a second language. In E. Hatch (Ed.), *Second Language Acquisition: A Book of Readings* (pp. 371–379). Rowley, MA: Newbury House.

Larsen-Freeman, D. (2006). The emergence of complexity, fluency, and accuracy in the oral and written production of five Chinese learners of English. *Applied Linguistics, 27*, 590–619.

Larsen-Freeman, D., and Long, M. (1991). *An Introduction to Second Language Acquisition Research*. London: Longman.

Laufer, B. (1997a). The lexical plight in second language reading: Words you don't know, words you think you know, and words you can't guess. In J. Coady and T. Huckin (Eds.), *Second Language Vocabulary Acquisition: A Rationale for Pedagogy* (pp. 20–33). Cambridge: Cambridge University Press.

Laufer, B. (1997b). What's in a word that makes it hard or easy: some intralexical factors that affect the learning of words. In N. Schmitt and M. McCarthy (Eds.), *Vocabulary: Description, Acquisition and Pedagogy* (pp. 140–180). Cambridge: Cambridge University Press.

Laufer, B. (1998). The development of passive and active vocabulary in a second language: same or different? *Applied Linguistics, 19*, 255–271.

Laufer, B. (2005). Focus on form in second language vocabulary learning. In S. Foster-Cohen, M. del Pilar García Mayo, and J. Cenoz (Eds.), *EuroSLA Yearbook* (pp. 223–150). Amsterdam: John Benjamins.

Laufer, B., and Eliasson, S. (1993). What causes avoidance in L2 learning: L1–L2 difference, L1–L2 similarity, or L2 complexity? *Studies in Second Language Acquisition, 15*, 33–48.

Laufer, B., and Hulstijn, J. (2001). Incidental vocabulary acquisition in a second language: the construct of task-induced involvement. *Applied Linguistics, 23*, 1–26.

Laufer, B., and Paribakht, S. (1998). The relationship between passive and active vocabularies: effects of language learning context. *Language Learning, 48*, 365–391.

Leary, M. R., Knight, P. D., and Johnson, K. A. (1987). Social anxiety and dyadic conversation: a verbal response analysis. *Journal of Social and Clinical Psychology, 5*, 34–50.

Leaver, B. L., Ehrman, M., and Shekhtman, B. (2005). *Achieving Success in Second Language Acquisition*. Cambridge: Cambridge University Press.

Lee, J. (2007). The inside of the L2 lexicon and semantic overgeneralization. Ms. Michigan State University.

Leeman, J. (2003). Recasts and second language development: beyond negative evidence. *Studies in Second Language Acquisition, 25*, 37–63.

Lennenberg, E. (1967). *Biological foundations of language*. New York: John Wiley.

Leow, R. (1997). Attention, awareness, and foreign language behavior. *Language Learning, 47*, 467–505.

Leow, R. (1998). Toward operationalizing the process of attention in SLA: evidence for Tomlin and Villa's (1994) fine-grained analysis of attention. *Applied Psycholinguistics, 19*, 133–159.

Leow, R. (2000). A study of the role of awareness in foreign language behavior: aware versus unaware learners. *Studies in Second Language Acquisition, 22*, 557–584.

Leow, R. (2001). Attention, awareness, and foreign language behavior. *Language Learning, 51* (supplement 1), 113–155.

Levelt, C., Schiller, N., and Levelt, W. J. M. (1999). A developmental grammar for syllable structure in the production of child language. *Brain and Language, 68*, 291–299.

REFERENCES

Levelt, W. J. M. (1989). *Speaking: From Intention to Articulation*. Cambridge, MA: MIT Press.

Levenston, E. (1979). Second language acquisition: Issues and problems. *Interlanguage Studies Bulletin*, 4, 147–160.

Lightbown, P. (1983). Exploring relationships between developmental and instructional sequences in L2 acquisition. In H. Seliger and M. H. Long (Eds.), *Classroom Oriented Research in Second Language Acquisition* (pp. 217–243). Rowley, MA: Newbury House.

Lightbown, P. (1985). Great expectations: second language acquisition research and classroom teaching. *Applied Linguistics*, 6, 173–189.

Lightbown, P. (1992). Can they do it themselves? A comprehension-based ESL course for young children. In R. Courchêne, J. Glidden, J. St. John, and C. Thérien (Eds.), *Comprehension-Based Second Language Teaching* (pp. 353–370). Ottawa: University of Ottawa Press.

Lightbown, P. (1998). The importance of timing in focus on form. In C. Doughty and J. Williams (Eds.), *Focus on Form in Classroom Second Language Acquisition* (pp. 177–196). Cambridge: Cambridge University Press.

Lightbown, P., and Spada, N. (2006). *How Languages are Learned*. Oxford: Oxford University Press.

Lim, H. Y. (2002). The interaction of motivation, perception, and environment: one EFL learner's experience. *Hong Kong Journal of Applied Linguistics*, 7, 91–106.

Lin, Y.-H., and Hedgcock, J. (1996). Negative feedback incorporation among high-proficiency and low-proficiency Chinese-speaking learners of Spanish. *Language Learning*, 46, 567–611.

Linell, P. (1982). The concept of phonological form and the activities of speech production and speech perception. *Journal of Phonetics*, 10, 37–72.

Linell, P. (1985). Problems and perspective in the study of spoken interaction. In L. S. Evensen (Ed.), *Nordic Research in Text Linguistics and Discourse Analysis* (pp. 103–136). Trondheim, Norway: TAPIR.

Liu, G. (1991). Interaction and second language acquisition: a case study of a Chinese child's acquisition of English as a second language. Unpublished doctoral dissertation, La Trobe University, Australia.

Loewen, S. (2003). Grammaticality judgment tests: what do they really measure? Paper presented at the Second Language Research Forum, Tucson, AZ.

Loewen, S., and Basturkmen, H., (2005). Interaction in group writing tasks in genre-based instruction in an EAP classroom. *Journal of Asian Pacific Communication*, 15, 171–189.

Lombardi, L. (2003). Second language data and constraints on Manner: explaining substitutions for the English interdentals. *Second Language Research*, 19, 225–250.

Long, M. H. (1980). Input, interaction and second language acquisition. Unpublished doctoral dissertation, University of California, Los Angeles.

Long, M. H. (1983). Linguistic and conversational adjustments to non-native speakers. *Studies in Second Language Acquisition*, 5, 177–193.

Long, M. H. (1990). Maturational constraints on language development. *Studies in Second Language Acquisition*, 12, 251–285.

Long, M. H. (1991). Focus on form: a design feature in language teaching methodology. In K. de Bot, R. Ginsberg, and C. Kramsch (Eds.), *Foreign Language Research in Cross-cultural Perspective* (pp. 39–52). Amsterdam: John Benjamins.

Long, M. H. (1996). The role of the linguistic environment in second language acquisition. In W. Ritchie and T. Bhatia (Eds.), *Handbook of Second Language Acquisition* (pp. 413–468). San Diego, CA: Academic Press.

Long, M. H. (1997). Construct validity in SLA research. *Modern Language Journal*, 81, 318–323.

Long, M. H. (2003). Stabilization and fossilization in interlanguage development. In C. Doughty and M. H. Long (Eds.), *The Handbook of Second Language Acquisition* (pp. 487–535). Malden, MA: Blackwell.

Long, M. H. (2007). *Problems in SLA*. Mahwah, NJ: Lawrence Erlbaum Associates.

Long, M., Inagaki, S., and Ortega, L. (1998). The role of implicit negative feedback in SLA: models and recasts in Japanese and Spanish. *Modern Language Journal*, 82, 357–371.

Long, M. H., and Sato, C. (1983). Classroom foreigner talk discourse: forms and functions of teachers' questions. In H. Seliger and M. H. Long (Eds.), *Classroom Oriented Research in Second Language Acquisition* (pp. 268–285). Rowley, MA: Newbury House.

Loschky, L. C. (1989). *The Effects of Negotiated Interaction and Premodified Input on Second Language Comprehension and Retention* (Occasional Papers no. 16). University of Hawai'i at Manoa.

Loschky, L., and Bley-Vroman, R. (1993). Grammar and task-based methodology. In G. Crookes and S. Gass (Eds.), *Tasks and Language Learning: Integrating Theory and Practice* (pp. 122–167). Clevedon, UK: Multilingual Matters.

Lust, B., Chien, Y-C., and Flynn, S. (1987). What children know: methods for the study of first language acquisition. In B. Lust (Ed.), *Studies in the Acquisition of Anaphora*, vol. 2, *Defining the Constraints*. Dordrecht: Reidel.

Lust, B., Flynn, S., and Foley, C. (1996). What children know about what they say: elicited imitation as a research method for assessing children's syntax. In D. McDaniel, C. McKee, and H. S. Cairns (Eds), *Methods for Assessing Children's Syntax* (pp. 55–76). Cambridge, MA: MIT Press.

Lyster, R. (1998). Recasts, repetition, and ambiguity in L2 classroom discourse. *Studies in Second Language Acquisition*, 20, 51–81.

Lyster, R. (2004). Differential effects of prompts and recasts in form-focused instruction. *Studies in Second Language Acquisition*, 26, 399–432.

Lyster, R., and Ranta, L. (1997). Corrective feedback and learner uptake: negotiation of form in communicative classrooms. *Studies in Second Language Acquisition*, 20, 37–66.

Macaro, E. (2001). *Learning Strategies in Foreign and Second Language Classrooms*. London: Continuum Press.

MacIntyre, P. D. (1999). Language anxiety: a review of the research for language teachers. In D. J. Young (Ed.), *Affect in Foreign Language and Second Language Learning* (pp. 24–45). Boston, MA: McGraw-Hill.

MacIntyre, P. D. (2002). Motivation, anxiety and emotion in second language acquisition. In P. Robinson (Ed.), *Individual Differences and Instructed Language Learning* (pp. 45–68). Amsterdam: John Benjamins.

MacIntyre, P. D. and Gardner, R. C. (1994). The subtle effects of language anxiety on cognitive processing in the second language. *Language Learning*, 44, 283–305.

Mackey, A. (1995). Stepping up the pace—input, interaction and interlanguage development: an empirical study of questions in ESL. Unpublished doctoral dissertation, University of Sydney, Australia.

Mackey, A. (1999). Input, interaction and second language development. *Studies in Second Language Acquisition*, 21, 557–587.

Mackey, A. (2002). Beyond production: learners' perceptions about interactional processes. *International Journal of Educational Research*, 37, 379–394.

Mackey, A. (2006). Feedback, noticing and instructed second language learning. *Applied Linguistics*, 27, 405–430.

Mackey, A., and Gass, S. (2005). *Second Language Research: Methodology and Design*. Mahwah, NJ: Lawrence Erlbaum Associates.

Mackey, A., Gass, S., and McDonough, K. (2000). Learners' perceptions about feedback. *Studies in Second Language Acquisition*, 22, 471–497.

Mackey, A. and Goo, J. (2007). Interaction research in SLA: a meta-analysis and research synthesis. In A. Mackey (Ed.), *Conversational Interaction in Second Language Acquisition: A Series of Empirical Studies* (pp. 407–452). Oxford: Oxford University Press.

Mackey, A., and Oliver, R. (2002). Interactional feedback and children's L2 development. *System 30*, 459–477.

Mackey, A., and Philp, J. (1998). Conversational interaction and second language development: Recasts, responses, and red herrings. *Modern Language Journal*, 82, 338–356.

Mackey, A., Philp, J., Egi, T., Fujii, A., and Tatsumi, T. (2002). Individual differences in working memory, noticing of interactional feedback, and L2 development. In P. Robinson (Ed.), *Individual Differences and Instructed Language Learning* (pp. 181–209). Philadelphia: John Benjamins.

MacWhinney, B. (2002). The Competition Model: the input, the context, and the brain. In P. Robinson (Ed.), *Cognition and Second Language Instruction*. New York: Cambridge University Press.

MacWhinney, B. (2004). A unified model of language acquisition. In J. F. Kroll and A. M. B. de Groot (Eds.), *Handbook of Bilingualism: Psycholinguistic Approaches*. Oxford: Oxford University Press.

MacWhinney, B., Bates, E., and Kliegl, R. (1984). Cue validity and sentence interpretation in English, German, and Italian. *Journal of Verbal Learning and Behavior*, 23, 127–150.

Maier, P. (1992). Politeness strategies in business letters by native and non-native English speakers. *ESP Journal*, 11, 189–205.

Major, R. (1987). Foreign accent: recent research and theory. *International Review of Applied Linguistics*, 25, 185–202.

Major, R. (2001). *Foreign accent: The Ontogeny and Phylogeny of Second Language Phonology*. Mahwah, NJ: Lawrence Erlbaum Associates.

Major, R., and Kim, E. (1999). The similarity differential rate hypothesis. *Language Learning*, 49, 151–183.

Makino, T. (1979). Acquisition order of English morphemes by Japanese secondary school students. *Journal of Hokkaido University of Education, 30*, 101–148.

REFERENCES

Mandell, P. (1999). On the reliability of grammaticality judgment tests in second language acquisition research. *Second Language Research, 15*, 73–99.

Maneva, B., and Genesee, F. (2002). Bilingual babbling: evidence for language differentiation in dual language acquisition. In B. Skarabela, S. Fish, and A. Do (Eds.), *BUCLD 26: Proceedings of the 16th Annual Boston University Conference on Language Development*, vol. 1 (pp. 383–392). Somerville, MA: Cascadilla Press.

Marian V., and Spivey, M. (2003). Bilingual and monolingual processing of competing lexical items. *Applied Psycholinguistics, 24*, 173–193.

Marinova-Todd, S., Marshall, D. B., and Snow, C. E. (2000). Three misconceptions about age and second-language learning. *TESOL Quarterly, 34*, 9–34.

Markee, N. (2000). *Conversation Analysis*. Mahwah, NJ: Lawrence Erlbaum Associates.

Mazurkewich, I. (1984). The acquisition of dative alternation by second language learners and linguistic theory. *Language Learning, 34*, 91–109.

McCafferty, S. (1994). Adult second language learners' use of private speech: a review of studies. *Modern Language Journal, 78*, 421–436.

McDonald, J. (1987). Sentence interpretation in bilingual speakers of English and Dutch. *Applied Psycholinguistics, 8*, 379–413.

McDonald, J., and Heilenman, K. (1992). Changes in sentence processing as second language proficiency increases. In R. J. Harris (Ed.), *Cognitive Processing in Bilinguals* (pp. 375–396). Amsterdam: North-Holland.

McDonough, K. (1999). Learner Strategies. *Language Teaching Research, 32*, 1–18.

McDonough, K. (2005). Identifying the impact of negative feedback and learners' responses on ESL question development. *Studies in Second Language Acquisition, 27*, 79–103.

McDonough, K. (2007). Interactional feedback and the emergence of simple past activity verbs in L2 English. In A. Mackey (Ed.), *Conversational Interaction and Second Language Acquisition: A series of Empirical Studies* (pp. 323–338). Oxford: Oxford University Press.

McDonough, K., and Mackey, A. (2006). Responses to recasts: repetitions, primed production, and linguistic development. *Language Learning, 56*, 693–720.

McDonough, S. H. (1999). Learner strategies: state of the art article. *Language Teaching, 32*, 1–18.

McKay, S. L., and Wong, S. C. (1996). Multiple discourses, multiple identities: investment and agency in second-language learning among Chinese adolescent immigrant students. *Harvard Educational Review, 66*, 577–608.

McLaughlin, B. (1978a). *Second-Language Acquisition in Childhood*. Hillsdale, NJ: Lawrence Erlbaum Associates.

McLaughlin, B. (1978b). The monitor model: some methodological considerations. *Language Learning, 28*, 309–332.

McLaughlin, B. (1987). *Theories of Second Language Learning*. London: Edward Arnold.

McLaughlin, B. (1990a). Restructuring. *Applied Linguistics, 11*, 113–128.

McLaughlin, B. (1990b). The relationship between first and second languages: Language proficiency and language aptitude. In B. Harley, P. Allen, J. Cummins, and M. Swain (Eds.), *The Development of Second Language Proficiency* (pp. 158–178). Cambridge: Cambridge University Press.

REFERENCES

McLaughlin, B., and Heredia, R. (1996). Information-processing approaches to research on second language acquisition and use. In W. Ritchie and T. Bhatia (Eds.), *Handbook of Second Language Acquisition* (pp. 213–228). San Diego: Academic Press.

McLaughlin, B., Rossman, T., and McLeod, B. (1983). Second language learning: an information processing perspective. *Language Learning, 33,* 135–158.

McNeill, D. (1966). Developmental psycholinguistics. In F. Smith and G. Miller (Eds.), *The Genesis of Language* (pp. 15–84). Cambridge, MA: MIT Press.

McNeill, D., Cassell, J., and McCullough, K.-E. (1994). Communicative effects of speech mismatched gesture. *Research on Language and Social Interaction, 27,* 223–237.

Meara, P. (1978). Learners' word associations in French. *Interlanguage Studies Bulletin, 43,* 192–211.

Meara, P. (Ed.). (1983). *Vocabulary in Second Language,* vol. 1. London: Centre for Language Teaching and Research.

Meara, P. (1984). The study of lexis in interlanguage. In A. Davies, C. Criper, and A. Howatt (Eds.), *Interlanguage* (pp. 225–235). Edinburgh: University of Edinburgh Press.

Meara, P. (Ed.). (1987). *Vocabulary in Second Language,* vol. 2. London: Centre for Language Teaching and Research.

Meara, P. (1996). The dimensions of lexical competence. In G. Brown, K. Malmkjaer, and J. Williams (Eds.), *Performance and Competence in Second Language Acquisition* (pp. 35–53). Cambridge: Cambridge University Press.

Meara, P. and Fitzpatrick, T. (2000). Lex-30: An improved method of assessing productive vocabulary in an L2. *System, 28,* 19–30.

Mel'čuk, I. (1985). Lexicography and verbal government: On a dictionary by Ju. Apreszjan and E. Páll. *Folia Linguistica, 19,* 253–266.

Milon, J. (1974). The development of negation in English by a second language learner. *TESOL Quarterly, 8,* 137–143.

Mitchell, R., and Myles, R. (1998). *Second Language Learning Theories.* London: Edward Arnold.

Miyake, A., and Friedman, N. (1998). Individual differences in second language proficiency: working memory as language aptitude. In A. F. Healy and L. E. Bourne, Jr. (Eds.), *Foreign Language Learning: Psycholinguistic Studies on Training and Retention* (pp. 339–364). Mahwah, NJ: Lawrence Erlbaum Associates.

Miyake, A., and Shah, P. (Eds.). (1999). *Models of Working Memory: Mechanisms of Active Maintenance and Executive Control.* Cambridge, UK: Cambridge University Press.

Mizruchi, M. S. (1991). Urgency, motivation, and group performance: the effect of prior success on current success among professional basketball teams. *Social Psychology Quarterly, 52,* 181–189.

Mode, B. (1995). *Fully Committed.* New York: Dramatists Play Service.

Montrul, S. (2002). Incomplete acquisition and attrition of Spanish tense/aspect distinctions in adult bilinguals. *Bilingualism: Language and Cognition, 5,* 39–68.

Montrul, S. (2004). Subject and object expression in Spanish heritage speakers: a case of morphosyntactic convergence. *Bilingualism: Language and Cognition, 7,* 125–142.

Mori, J. (2004). Negotiating sequential boundaries and learning opportunities: a case from a Japanese language classroom. *Modern Language Journal*, 88, 536–550.

Morgan-Short, K. and Bowden, H. (2006). Processing instruction and meaningful output-based instruction. *Studies in Second Language Acquisition*, 28, 31–65.

Mourelatos, A. (1981). Events, processes, states. In P. Tedeschi and A. Zaenen (Eds.), *Tense and Aspect*, Syntax and Semantics 14 (pp. 191–212). New York: Academic Press.

Moyer, A. (1999). Ultimate attainment in L2 phonology: the critical factors of age, motivation, and instruction. *Studies in Second Language Acquisition*, 21, 81–108.

Nabei, T. and Swain, M. (2002). Learner awareness of recasts in classroom interaction: a case study of an adult EFL student's second language learning. *Language Awareness*, 11, 43–63.

Nagasawa, F. (1995). L1, L2, bairingaru no nihongo bunpoo nooryoku [Comparative grammatical competence among L1, L2, and bilingual speakers of Japanese]. *Nohongo kyooiku*, 86, 173–189.

Naiman, N., Fröhlich, M., Stern, H. H., and Todesco, A. (1978). *The Good Language Learner*. Research in Education Series 7. Toronto, Ontario: Ontario Institute for Studies in Education.

Nassaji, H. (2004). The relationship between depth of vocabulary knowledge and L2 learners' lexical inferencing strategy use and success. *Canadian Modern Language Review*, 61, 107–134.

Nation, I. S. P. (2001). *Learning Vocabulary in Another Language*. Cambridge: Cambridge University Press.

Nation, R., and McLaughlin, B. (1986). Experts and novices: an information-processing approach to the "good language learner" problem. *Applied Psycholinguistics*, 7, 41–56.

Nayak, N., Hansen, N., Krueger, N., and McLaughlin, B. (1990). Language learning strategies in monolingual and multilingual adults. *Language Learning*, 40, 221–240.

Nemser, W. (1961). The interpretation of English stops and interdental fricatives by native speakers of Hungarian. Unpublished doctoral dissertation, Columbia University.

Nemser, W. (1971a). *An Experimental Study of Phonological Interference in the English of Hungarians*. The Hague: Mouton.

Nemser, W. (1971b). Approximative systems of foreign learners. *International Review of Applied Linguistics*, 9, 115–124.

Neufeld, G. (1979). Towards a theory of language learning ability. *Language Learning*, 29, 227–241.

Newton, J. (1995). Task-based interaction and incidental vocabulary learning: a case study. *Second Language Research*, 11, 159–177.

Nicholas, H., Lightbown, P. M. and Spada, N. (2001). Recasts as feedback to language learners. *Language Learning*, 51(4), 719–758.

Nobuyoshi, J., and Ellis, R. (1993). Focused communication tasks and second language acquisition. *English Language Teaching*, 47, 203–210.

Norris, J., and Ortega, L. (2000). Effectiveness of L2 instruction: a research synthesis and quantitative meta-analysis. *Language Learning*, 50, 417–528.

Norris, J., and Ortega, L. (2003). Defining and measuring SLA. In C. Doughty and

557

M. H. Long (Eds.), *The Handbook of Second Language Acquisition* (pp. 717–761). Oxford: Blackwell.

Norton, B. (2000). *Identity and Language Learning: Gender, Ethnicity and Educational Change.* Essex: Pearson Education Limited.

Odlin, T. (1989). *Language Transfer.* Cambridge: Cambridge University Press.

Odlin, T. (2005). Cross-linguistic influence and conceptual transfer: what are the concepts? *Annual Review of Applied Linguistics, 25,* 3–25.

Odlin, T. (2008). Conceptual transfer and meaning extensions. In P. Robinson and N. Ellis (Eds.), *Handbook of Cognitive Linguistics and Second Language Acquisition.* London: Routledge.

Odlin, T., and Alonso-Vázquez, C. (2006). Meanings in search of the perfect form: a look at interlanguage verb phrases. *Rivista di psicolinguistica applicata, 6,* 53–63.

O'Grady, W. (1996). Language acquisition without Universal Grammar: a general nativist proposal for L2 learning. *Second Language Research, 12,* 374–397.

O'Grady, W. (2003). The radical middle: nativism without universal grammar. In C. Doughty and M. H. Long (Eds.), *The Handbook of Second Language Acquisition* (pp. 43–62). Malden, MA: Blackwell.

O'Grady, W. (2005). *Syntactic Carpentry: An Emergentist Approach to Syntax.* Mahwah, NJ: Lawrence Erlbaum Associates.

O'Grady, W. (2006). The problem of verbal inflection in second language acquisition. Paper presented at the 11th PAAL Conference, Chuncheon, Korea, July.

O'Grady, W., Lee, M., and Choo, M. (2003). A subject–object asymmetry in the acquisition of relative clauses in Korean as a second language. *Studies in Second Language Acquisition, 25,* 433–448.

Ohta, A. (2001). *Second Language Acquisition Processes in the Classroom: Learning Japanese.* Mahwah, NJ: Lawrence Erlbaum Associates.

Oliver, R. (1995). Negative feedback in child NS–NNS conversation. *Studies in Second Language Acquisition, 17,* 459–481.

Oliver, R. (1998). Negotiation of meaning in child interactions. *Modern Language Journal 82,* 372–386.

Oliver, R. (2002). The patterns of negotiation of meaning in child interactions. *Modern Language Journal, 86,* 97–111.

Oliver, R., and Mackey, A. (2003). Interactional context and feedback in child ESL classrooms. *Modern Language Journal, 87,* 519–533.

Oller, J., and Ziahosseiny, S. (1970). The Contrastive Analysis Hypothesis and spelling errors. *Language Learning, 20,* 183–189.

Olshtain, E. (1987). The acquisition of new word formation processes in second language acquisition. *Studies in Second Language Acquisition, 9,* 223–234.

O'Malley, J. M., and Chamot, A. (1990). *Learning Strategies in Second Language Acquisition.* Cambridge: Cambridge University Press.

Osaka, M., and Osaka, N. (1992). Language-independent working memory as measured by Japanese and English reading span tests. *Bulletin of the Psychonomic Society, 30,* 287–289.

Otomo, K. (2001). Aternal responses to word approximations in Japanese children's transition to language. *Journal of Child Language, 28,* 29–57.

Otsu, Y., and Naoi, K. (1986). Structure dependence in L2 acquisition. Paper presented at the meeting of the Japan Association of College English Teachers (JACET), Keio University, Tokyo, September.

Oxford, R. (1993). *Style Analysis Survey (SAS)*. University of Alabama.

Oxford, R. (1999). Learning strategies. In B. Spolsky (Ed.), *Concise Encyclopedia of Educational Linguistics* (pp. 518–522). Oxford: Elsevier.

Oxford, R., and Cohen, A. (1992). Language learning strategies: crucial issues of concept and classification. *Applied Language Learning, 3*, 1–35.

Ozeki, H. and Shirai, Y. (in press). The consequences of variation in the acquisition of relative clauses: an analysis of longitudinal production data from five Japanese children. In Y. Matsumoto, D. Oshima, O. Robinson, and P. Sells (Eds.), *Diversity in Language: Perspectives and Implications*. Stanford, CA: CSLI Publications.

Palmberg, R. (1987). Patterns of vocabulary development in foreign-language learners. *Studies in Second Language Acquisition, 9*, 201–219.

Papadopoulou, D., and Clahsen, H. (2003). Parsing strategies in L1 and L2 sentence processing: a study of relative clause attachment in Greek. *Studies in Second Language Acquisition, 25*, 501–528.

Papagno, C., and Vallar, G. (1992). Phonological short-term memory and the learning of novel words: the effect of phonological similarity and item length. *Quarterly Journal of Experimental Psychology, 44A*, 47–67.

Paribakht, T., and Wesche, M. (1993). Reading comprehension and second language development in a comprehension-based ESL program. *TESL Canada Journal, 11*, 9–29.

Paribakht, T., and Wesche, M. (1997). Vocabulary enhancement activities and reading for meaning in second language vocabulary development. In J. Coady and T. Huckin (Eds.), *Second Language Vocabulary Acquisition: A Rationale for Pedagogy* (pp. 174–200). New York: Cambridge University Press.

Paribakht, T., and Wesche, M. (1999). Reading and "incidental" L2 vocabulary acquisition: an introspective study of lexical inferencing. *Studies in Second Language Acquisition, 21*, 195–223.

Park, H. (2004). A minimalist approach to null subjects and objects in second language acquisition. *Second Language Research, 20*, 1–32.

Parker, K., and Chaudron, C. (1987). The effects of linguistic simplifications and elaborative modifications on L2 comprehension. *University of Hawai'i Working Papers in English as a Second Language, 6*, 107–133.

Patkowski, M. (1980). The sensitive period for the acquisition of syntax in a second language. *Language Learning, 30*, 449–472.

Pavesi, M. (1986). Markedness, discoursal modes, and relative clause formation in a formal and informal context. *Studies in Second Language Acquisition, 8*, 38–55.

Penfield, W., and Roberts, L. (1959). *Speech and Brain Mechanisms*. New York: Athenaeum.

Philp, J. (1999). Interaction, noticing and second language acquisition: an examination of learners' noticing of recasts in task-based interaction. Unpublished doctoral dissertation, University of Tasmania, Australia.

Philp, J. (2003). Constraints on noticing the gap: nonnative speakers' noticing of recasts in NS–NNS interaction. *Studies in Second Language Acquisition, 25,* 99–126.

Philp, J., and Duchesne, S. (in press). When the gate opens: the interaction between social and linguistics goals in child second language development. In J. Philp, R. Oliver, and A. Mackey (Eds.), *Child's play? Second Language Acquisition and the Younger Learner.* LL and LT monograph series. Amsterdam: John Benjamins.

Pica, T. (1983). Methods of morpheme quantification: their effect on the interpretation of second language data. *Studies in Second Language Acquisition, 6,* 69–78.

Pica, T. (1987). Second-language acquisition, social interaction, and the classroom. *Applied Linguistics, 8,* 3–21.

Pica, T. (1988). Interlanguage adjustments as an outcome of NS–NNS negotiated interaction. *Language Learning, 38,* 45–73.

Pica, T. (1992). The textual outcomes of native speaker–nonnative speaker negotiation: what do they reveal about second language learning? In C. Kramsch and S. McConnell-Ginet (Eds.), *Text and Context: Cross-Disciplinary Perspectives on Language Study* (pp. 198–237). Lexington, MA: D. C. Heath and Co.

Pica, T. (1994). Research on negotiation: what does it reveal about second-language learning conditions, processes, and outcomes? *Language Learning, 44,* 493–527.

Pica, T., Holliday, L., Lewis, N., and Morgenthaler, L. (1989). Comprehensible output as an outcome of linguistic demands on the learner. *Studies in Second Language Acquisition, 11,* 63–90.

Pica, T., Young, R., and Doughty, C. (1987). The impact of interaction on comprehension. *TESOL Quarterly, 21,* 737–758.

Pienemann, M. (1984). Psychological constraints on the teachability of languages. *Studies in Second Language Acquisition, 6,* 186–214.

Pienemann, M. (1989). Is language teachable? *Applied Linguistics, 10,* 52–79.

Pienemann, M. (1999). *Language Processing and Second Language Development: Processability Theory.* Amsterdam: John Benjamins.

Pienemann, M. (2007). Processability theory. In B. VanPatten and J. Williams (Eds.), *Theories in Second Language Acquisition: An Introduction* (pp. 137–154). Mahwah, NJ: Lawrence Erlbaum Associates.

Pienemann, M., and Johnston, M. (1987). Factors influencing the development of language proficiency. In D. Nunan (Ed.), *Applying Second Language Acquisition Research* (pp. 45–141). Adelaide, Australia: National Curriculum Resource Centre, AMEP.

Pinker, S. (1984). *Language Learnability and Language Development.* Cambridge, MA: Harvard University Press.

Pinker, S. (1987). The bootstrapping problem in language acquisition. In B. MacWhinney (Ed.), *Mechanisms of Language Acquisition* (pp. 399–441). Hillsdale, NJ: Lawrence Erlbaum Associates.

Pinker, S. (1989). *Learnability and Cognition.* Cambridge, MA: MIT Press.

Pinker, S. (1994). *The Language Instinct: How the Mind Creates Language.* New York: Morrow.

Pintzuk, S. (1988). *VARBRUL Programs.* Philadelphia: University of Pennsylvania, Department of Linguistics.

Platzack, C. (1996). The initial hypothesis of syntax. In H. Clahsen (Ed.), *Generative Perspectives on Language Acquisition* (pp. 369–414), Amsterdam: John Benjamins.

Plough, I. (1994). A role for indirect negative evidence in second language acquisition. Unpublished doctoral dissertation, Michigan State University, East Lansing.

Polinsky, M. (1995). Cross-linguistic parallels in language loss. *Southwestern Journal of Linguistics, 14*, 87–125.

Polinsky, M. (2000). A composite linguistic profile of a speaker of Russian in the USA. In O. Kagan and B. Rifkin (Eds.), *The Learning and Teaching of Slavic Languages and Cultures* (pp. 437–466). Bloomington, IN: Slavica.

Polinsky, M. (in press). Heritage language narratives. In D. Brinton and O. Kagan (Eds.), *Heritage Languages: A New Field Emerging*. Hillsdale, NJ: Lawrence Erlbaum.

Polio, C. (2007). A history of input enhancement: defining an evolving concept. In C. Gascoigne (Ed.), *Assessing the Impact of Input Enhancement in Second Language Education*. Stillwater, OK: New Forums Press.

Polio, C., and Gass S. (1997). Replication and reporting: a commentary. *Studies in Second Language Acquisition, 19*, 499–508.

Polio, C., Gass, S., and Chapin, L. (2006). Using stimulated recall to investigate native speaker perceptions in native–nonnative speaker interaction. *Studies in Second Language Acquisition, 28*, 237–267.

Politzer, R. (1978). Errors of English speakers of German as perceived and evaluated by German natives. *Modern Language Journal, 62*, 253–261.

Porter, J. (1977). A cross-sectional study of morpheme acquisition in first language learners. *Language Learning, 27*, 47–62.

Porter, P. (1983). Variations in the conversations of adult learners of English as a function of the proficiency level of the participants. Unpublished doctoral dissertation, Stanford University, California.

Postman, L. (1971). Transfer, interference and forgetting. In J. W. Kling and L. A. Riggs (Eds.), *Woodworth and Schlosberg's Experimental Psychology* (pp. 1019–1132). New York: Holt, Rinehart and Winston.

Potowski, K. (2004). Student Spanish use and investment in a dual immersion classroom: implications for second language acquisition and heritage language maintenance. *Modern Language Journal, 88*, 75–101.

Poulisse, N. (1997). Some words in defense of the psycholinguistic approach. *Modern Language Journal, 81*, 324–328.

Preston, D. (1989). *Sociolinguistics and Second Language Acquisition*. Oxford: Basil Blackwell.

Preston, D. (2000). Three kinds of sociolinguistics and SLA: a psycholinguistic perspective. In B. Swierzbin, F. Morris, M.E. Anderson, C.A. Klee, and E. Tarone (Eds.), *Social and Cognitive Factors in Second Language Acquisition: Selected Proceedings of the 1999 Second Language Research Forum* (pp. 3–30). Sommerville, MA: Cascadilla Press.

Preston, D. (2002). A variationist perspective on second language acquisition: psycholinguistic concerns. In R. Kaplan (Ed.), *The Oxford Handbook of Applied Linguistics* (pp. 141–159). Oxford: Oxford University Press.

Prince, A. and Smolensky, P. (1997). Optimality: from neural networks to Universal Grammar. *Science, 275,* 1604–1610.

Pulido, D. (2003). Modeling the role of second language proficiency and topic familiarity in second language incidental vocabulary acquisition through reading. *Language Learning, 53,* 233–284.

Qian, D. (1999). Assessing the roles of depth and breadth of vocabulary knowledge in reading comprehension. *Canadian Modern Language Review, 56,* 282–308.

Radford, A. (1997). *Syntactic Theory and the Structure of English: A Minimalist Approach.* Cambridge: Cambridge University Press.

Ramsay, R. (1980). Language-learning approach styles of adult multilinguals and successful language learners. *Annals of the New York Academy of Sciences, 75,* 73–96.

Rand, D., and Sankoff, D. (1990). GoldVarb: a variable rule application for the Macintosh (version 2.0). Montreal: Centre de Recherche Mathématiques, Université de Montréal.

Ravem, R. (1968). Language acquisition in a second language environment. *International Review of Applied Linguistics, 6,* 175–186.

Ravem, R. (1974). The development of *Wh-* questions in first and second language learners. In J. Richards (Ed.), *Error Analysis: Perspectives on Second Language Acquisition* (pp. 134–155). London: Longman.

Read, J. (1993). The development of a new measure of L2 vocabulary knowledge. *Language Testing, 10,* 355–371.

Read, J. (2000). *Assessing vocabulary.* Cambridge: Cambridge University Press.

Read, J. (2004). Plumbing the depths: how should the construct of vocabulary knowledge be defined? In P. Bogaards and B. Laufer (Eds.), *Vocabulary in a Second Language* (pp. 209–227). Amsterdam: John Benjamins.

Reid, J. (1995). *Learning Styles in the ESL/EFL Classroom.* Boston: Heinle and Heinle.

Rendell, R. (1983). *Speaker of Mandarin.* New York: Ballantine Books.

Reves, T. (1983). What makes a good language learner? Unpublished doctoral dissertation, Hebrew University of Jerusalem.

Richards, J. C., and Sampson, G. (1974). The study of learner English. In J. C. Richards (Ed.), *Error Analysis: Perspectives on Second Language Acquisition* (pp. 3–18). London: Longman.

Riding, R. (2002). *School Learning and Cognitive Style.* London: David Fulton.

Riding, R. (2003). On the assessment of cognitive style: a commentary on Peterson, Deary, and Austin. *Personality and Individual Differences, 34,* 893–897.

Riding, R., and S. Rayner. (1998). *Cognitive Styles and Learning Strategies: Understanding Style Differences in Learning and Behaviour.* London: David Fulton Publishers.

Ringbom, H. (1987). *The Role of the First Language in Foreign Language Learning.* Clevedon, UK: Multilingual Matters.

Robinson, P. (1995). Attention, memory, and the "noticing" hypothesis. *Language Learning, 45,* 283–331.

Robinson, P. (1996). *Consciousness, Rules, and Instructed Second Language Acquisition.* New York: Peter Lang.

Robinson, P. (2001). Individual differences, cognitive abilities, aptitude complexes and learning conditions in second language acquisition. *Second Language Research, 17,* 368–392.

Robinson, P. (2002). Learning conditions, aptitude complexes and SLA: a framework for research and pedagogy. In P. Robinson (Ed.), *Individual Differences and Instructed Language Learning* (pp. 113–133). Amsterdam: John Benjamins.

Robison, R. (1990). The primacy of aspect: aspectual marking in English interlanguage. *Studies in Second Language Acquisition, 12,* 315–330.

Robison, R. (1995). The Aspect Hypothesis revisited: a cross-sectional study of tense and aspect marking in interlanguage. *Applied Linguistics, 16,* 344–370.

Rocca, S. (2002). Lexical aspect in child second language acquisition of temporality: a bidirectional study. In R. Salaberry and Y. Shirai (Eds.), *Tense–Aspect Morphology in L2 Acquisition.* Amsterdam: John Benjamins.

Rocca, S. (2007). *Child Second Language Acquisition: A Bi-Directional Study of English and Italian Tense–Aspect Morphology.* Amsterdam: John Benjamins.

Rohde, A. (1996). The Aspect Hypothesis and emergence of tense distinction in naturalistic L2 acquisition. *Linguistics, 34,* 1115–1138.

Rohde, A. (2002). The aspect hypothesis in naturalistic L2 acquisition—what uninflected verb forms in early interlanguage tell us. In R. Salaberry and Y. Shirai (Eds.), *Tense and Aspect Morphology in L2 Acquisition.* Amsterdam: John Benjamins.

Rosa, E., and Leow, R. (2004). Awareness, different learning conditions, and L2 development. *Applied Psycholinguistics, 25,* 269–292.

Rosa E., and O'Neill, M. D. (1999). Explicitness, intake, and the issue of awareness. *Studies in Second Language Acquisition, 21,* 511–556.

Rosansky, E. (1976). Method and morphemes in second language acquisition research. *Language Learning, 26,* 405–425.

Rost, M. (1990). *Listening in Language Learning.* London: Longman.

Rott, S. (1999). The effect of exposure frequency on intermediate language learners' incidental vocabulary acquisition and retention through reading. *Studies in Second Language Acquisition, 21* 589–619.

Rounds, P., and Kanagy, R. (1998). Acquiring linguistic cues to identify AGENT: evidence from children learning Japanese as a second language. *Studies in Second Language Acquisition, 20,* 509–542.

Rubin, J. (1975). What the good language learner can teach us. *TESOL Quarterly, 9,* 41–51.

Rutherford, W. (Ed.). (1984). *Language Universals and Second Language Acquisition.* Amsterdam: John Benjamins.

Rutherford, W. (1987). *Second Language Grammar: Learning and Teaching.* New York: Longman.

Safir, K. (1982). Syntactic chains and the definiteness effect. Unpublished doctoral dissertation, MIT, Cambridge, MA.

Safire, W. (1999). *New York Times Magazine,* On language; McCawley, May 9.

Salaberry, R. (1997). The role of input and output practice in second language acquisition. *Canadian Modern Language Review, 53,* 422–451.

Salaberry, R. (1998). On input processing, true language competence, and pedagogical bandwagons: a reply to Sanz and VanPatten. *Canadian Modern Language Review, 54,* 274–285.

Sanz, C., and Morgan-Short, K. (2004). Positive evidence versus explicit rule presentation and explicit negative feedback: a computer-assisted study. *Language Learning*, 54, 35–78.

Sasaki, Y. (1991). English and Japanese comprehension strategies: an analysis based on the competition model. *Applied Psycholinguistics*, 12, 47–73.

Sasaki, Y. (1994). Paths of processing strategy transfers in learning Japanese and English as foreign languages: a competition model approach. *Studies in Second Language Acquisition*, 16, 43–72.

Sasaki, Y. (1997a). Individual variation in a Japanese sentence comprehension task: form, functions, and strategies. *Applied Linguistics*, 18, 508–537.

Sasaki, Y. (1997b). Material and presentation condition effects on sentence interpretation task performance: methodological examinations of the competition experiment. *Second Language Research*, 13, 66–91.

Sato, C. (1984). Phonological processes in second language acquisition: another look at interlanguage syllable structure. *Language Learning*, 34, 43–57.

Sato, C. (1985). Task variation in interlanguage phonology. In S. Gass and C. Madden (Eds.), *Input in Second Language Acquisition* (pp. 181–196). Rowley, MA: Newbury House.

Sato, C. (1990). *The Syntax of Conversation in Interlanguage Development*. Tübingen: Gunter Narr Verlag.

Saxton, M. (1997). The contrast theory of negative input. *Journal of Child Language*, 24, 139–161.

Saxton, M. (2000). Negative evidence and negative feedback: immediate effects on the grammaticality of child speech. *First Language*, 20, 221–252.

Saxton, M. (2005). "Recast" in a new light: insights for practice from typical language studies. *Child Language Teaching and Therapy*, 21, 23–38.

Saxton, M., Backley, P., and Gallaway, C. (2005). Negative input for grammatical errors: effects after a lag of 12 weeks. *Journal of Child Language*, 32, 643–672.

Saxton, M., Houston-Price, C., and Dawson, N. (2005). The prompt hypothesis: clarification requests as corrective input for grammatical errors. *Applied Psycholinguistics*, 26, 393–413.

Saxton, M., Kulcsar, B., Marshall, G., and Rupra, M. (1998). The longer term effects of corrective input: an experimental approach. *Journal of Child Language*, 25, 701–721.

Scarcella, R. (1979). On speaking politely in a second language. In C. A. Yorio, K. Perkins, and J. Schachter (Eds.), *On TESOL '79* (pp. 275–287). Washington, DC: TESOL.

Schachter, J. (1974). An error in error analysis. *Language Learning*, 24, 205–214.

Schachter, J. (1983). A new account of language transfer. In S. Gass and L. Selinker (Eds.), *Language Transfer in Language Learning* (pp. 98–111). Rowley, MA: Newbury House.

Schachter, J. (1988). Second language acquisition and its relationship to Universal Grammar. *Applied Linguistics*, 9, 219–235.

Schachter, J. (1989). Testing a proposed universal. In S. Gass and J. Schachter (Eds.), *Linguistic Perspectives on Second Language Acquisition* (pp. 73–88). New York: Cambridge University Press.

Schachter, J. (1990). On the issue of completeness in second language acquisition. *Second Language Research*, 6, 93–124.

Schachter, J. (1992). A new account of language transfer. In S. Gass and L. Selinker (Eds.), *Language Transfer in Language Learning* (pp. 32–46). Amsterdam: John Benjamins.

Schachter, J., and Celce-Murcia, M. (1971). Some reservations concerning error analysis. *TESOL Quarterly*, 11, 441–451.

Schachter, J., and Gass, S. (Eds.). (1996). *Second Language Classroom Research: Issues and Opportunities*. Mahwah, NJ: Lawrence Erlbaum Associates.

Schachter, J., Rounds, P. L., Wright, S., and Smith, T. (1998). Comparing conditions for learning syntactic patterns: attention and awareness. Unpublished manuscript.

Schachter, J., and Rutherford, W. (1979). Discourse function and language transfer. *Working Papers in Bilingualism*, 19, 3–12.

Schachter, J., Tyson, A., and Diffley, F. (1976). Learner intuitions of grammaticality. *Language Learning*, 26 67–76.

Schieffelin, B. (1986). Teasing and shaming in Kaluli children's interactions. In B. Schieffelin and E. Ochs (Eds.), *Language Socialization Across Cultures* (pp. 165–181). Cambridge: Cambridge University Press.

Schmidt, R. (1977). Sociolinguistic variation and language transfer in phonology. *Working Papers on Bilingualism*, 12, 79–95.

Schmidt, R. (1983). Interaction, acculturation, and the acquisition of communicative competence: a case study of an adult. In N. Wolfson and E. Judd (Eds.), *Sociolinguistics and Language Acquisition* (pp. 137–174). Rowley, MA: Newbury House.

Schmidt, R. (1990). The role of consciousness in second language learning. *Applied Linguistics*, 11, 129–158.

Schmidt, R. (1993a). Awareness and second language acquisition. *Annual Review of Applied Linguistics*, 13, 206–226.

Schmidt, R. (1993b). Consciousness in second language learning: introduction. Paper presented at the meeting of AILA 10th World Congress of Applied Linguistics, Amsterdam.

Schmidt, R. (1993c). Consciousness, learning and interlanguage pragmatics. In G. Kasper and S. Blum-Kulka (Eds.), *Interlanguage Pragmatics* (pp. 21–42). New York: Oxford University Press.

Schmidt, R. (1994). Implicit learning and the cognitive unconscious: of artificial grammars and SLA. In N. Ellis (Ed.), *Implicit and Explicit Learning of Languages* (pp. 165–209). London: Academic Press.

Schmidt, R. (1995). Consciousness and foreign language learning: a tutorial on the role of attention and awareness in learning. In R. Schmidt (Ed.), *Attention and Awareness in Foreign Language Learning* (Technical Report 9, pp. 1–64). Honolulu: University of Hawai'i at Manoa, Second Language Teaching and Curriculum Center.

Schmidt, R. (2001). Attention. In P. Robinson (Ed.), *Cognition and Second Language Instruction* (pp. 3–32). Cambridge: Cambridge University Press.

Schmidt, R., and Frota, S. (1986). Developing basic conversational ability in a second language: A case study of an adult learner of Portuguese. In R. Day

(Ed.), *Talking to Learn: Conversation in Second Language Acquisition* (pp. 237–326). Rowley, MA: Newbury House.

Schmitt, N. (1998a). Quantifying word association responses: what is native-like? *System, 26,* 389–401.

Schmitt, N. (1998b). Tracking the incremental acquisition of second language vocabulary: a longitudinal study. *Language Learning, 48,* 281–317.

Schmitt, N. (2000). *Vocabulary in Language Teaching.* Cambridge: Cambridge University Press.

Schmitt, N., and McCarthy, M. (1997). *Vocabulary: Description, Acquisition and Pedagogy.* Cambridge: Cambridge University Press.

Schmitt, N., and Meara, P. (1997). Researching vocabulary through a word knowledge framework: word associations and verbal suffixes. *Studies in Second Language Acquisition, 19,* 17–36.

Schumann, J. (1978a). *The Pidginization Process: A Model for Second Language Acquisition.* Rowley, MA: Newbury House.

Schumann, J. (1978b). The acculturation model for second language acquisition. In R. Gingras (Ed.), *Second Language Acquisition and Foreign Language Teaching* (pp. 27–50). Arlington, VA: Center for Applied Linguistics.

Schumann, J. (1979). The acquisition of English negation by speakers of Spanish: a review of the literature. In R. Andersen (Ed.), *The Acquisition and Use of Spanish and English as First and Second Languages* (pp. 3–32). Washington, DC: Teachers of English to Speakers of Other Languages.

Schumann, F. E., and Schumann, J. H. (1977). Diary of a language learner: an introspective study of second language learning. In H. D. Brown, C. A. Yorio, and R. H. Crymes (Eds.), *On TESOL '77, Teaching and Learning English as a Second Language: Trends in Research and Practice.* Washington, DC: TESOL.

Schwartz, B. (1998). On two hypotheses of "transfer" in L2A: minimal trees and absolute influence. In S. Flynn, G. Martohardjono, and W. O'Neil (Eds.), *The Generative Study of Second Language Acquisition* (pp. 35–59). Mahwah, NJ: Lawrence Erlbaum Associates.

Schwartz, B., and Sprouse, R. (1994). Word order and nominative case in non-native language acquisition: a longitudinal study of (L1 Turkish) German interlanguage. In T. Hoekstra and B. Schwartz (Eds.), *Language Acquisition Studies in Generative Grammar: Papers in Honor of Kenneth Wexler from the 1991 GLOW Workshops* (pp. 317–368). Amsterdam: John Benjamins.

Schwartz, B., and Sprouse, R. (1996). L2 cognitive states and the full transfer/full access model. *Second Language Research, 12,* 40–72.

Schwartz, B., and Sprouse, R. (2000). When syntactic theories evolve: consequences for L2 acquisition research. In J. Archibald (Ed.), *Second Language Acquisition and Linguistic Theory* (pp. 156–186). Oxford: Basil Blackwell.

Scovel, T. (1988). *A Time to Speak: A Psycholinguistic Inquiry into the Critical Period for Human Speech.* Cambridge: Newbury House.

Scovel, T. (2001). *Learning New Languages: A Guide to Second Language Acquisition.* Boston: Heinle and Heinle.

Segalowitz, N. (1997). Individual differences in second language acquisition. In A. M. B. de Groot, and J. F. Kroll (Eds.), *Tutorials in Bilingualism: Psycholinguistic Perspectives* (pp. 85–112). Mahwah, NJ: Lawrence Erlbaum Associates.

Segalowitz, N. (2003). Automaticity and second languages. In C. Doughty and

M. H. Long (Eds.), *The Handbook of Second Language Acquisition* (pp. 382–408). Malden, MA: Blackwell.

Segalowitz, N., and Hulstijn, J. (2005). Automaticity in bilingualism and second language learning. In J. F. Kroll and A. M. B. de Groot (Eds.), *Handbook of Bilingualism: Psycholinguistic Approaches* (pp. 371–388). Oxford: Oxford University Press.

Seliger, H. (1983). The language learner as linguist: of metaphors and realities. *Applied Linguistics, 4,* 179–191.

Selinker, L. (1966). A psycholinguistic study of language transfer. Unpublished doctoral dissertation, Georgetown University.

Selinker, L. (1972). Interlanguage. *International Review of Applied Linguistics, 10,* 209–231.

Selinker, L. (1992). *Rediscovering Interlanguage.* London: Longman.

Selinker, L., and Baumgartner-Cohen, B. (1995). Multiple language acquisition: "Damn it, why can't I keep these two languages apart?" In M. Ben-Soussan and I. Berman (Eds.), *Language Culture and Curriculum* (special issue), 8, 1–7.

Selinker, L., and Douglas, D. (1985). Wrestling with "context" in interlanguage theory. *Applied Linguistics, 6,* 190–204.

Selinker, L., and Gass, S. (1984). *Workbook in Second Language Acquisition.* Rowley, MA: Newbury House.

Selinker, L. and Lakshmanan, U. (1992). Language transfer and fossilization: the "multiple effects principle"+. In S. Gass and L. Selinker (Eds.), *Language Transfer in language Learning,* 2nd ed. (pp. 47–70). Amsterdam: John Benjamins.

Selinker, L., Swain, M., and Dumas, E. (1975). The interlanguage hypothesis extended to children. *Language Learning, 25,* 139–152.

Service, E., and Craik, F. (1993). Differences between young and older adults in learning a foreign vocabulary. *Journal of Memory and Language, 32,* 608–623.

Service, E., and Kohonen, V. (1995). Is the relation between phonological memory and foreign language learning accounted for by vocabulary acquisition? *Applied Psycholinguistics, 16,* 155–172.

Service, E., Simola, M., Metsaenheimo, O., and Maury, S. (2002). Bilingual working memory span is affected by language skill. *European Journal of Cognitive Psychology, 13* 383–407.

Sharwood Smith, M. (1978). Strategies, language transfer and the simulation of the second language learner's mental operations. Unpublished manuscript.

Sharwood Smith, M. (1986). Comprehension versus acquisition: two ways of processing input. *Applied Linguistics, 7,* 239–256.

Sharwood Smith, M. (1988). L2 acquisition: logical problems and empirical solutions. In J. Pankhurst, M. Sharwood Smith, and P. Van Buren (Eds.), *Learnability and Second Languages: A Book of Readings* (pp. 9–35). Dordrecht, The Netherlands: Foris.

Sharwood Smith, M. (1991). Speaking to many minds: on the relevance of different types of language information for the L2 learner. *Second Language Research, 7,* 118–132.

Sharwood Smith, M. (1993). Input enhancement in instructed SLA: theoretical bases. *Studies in Second Language Acquisition, 15,* 165–179.

Sharwood Smith, M. and Truscott, J. (2005). Stages or continua in second language acquisition: A MOGUL solution. *Applied Linguistics, 26,* 219–240.

Shedivy, S. L. (2004). Factors that lead some students to continue the study of foreign language past the usual 2 years in high school. *System, 32,* 103–119.

Sheldon, A., and Strange, W. (1982). The acquisition of /r/ and /l/ by Japanese learners of English: evidence that speech production can precede speech perception. *Applied Psycholinguistics, 3,* 243–261.

Shirai, Y. (1995). Tense–aspect marking by L2 learners of Japanese. In D. MacLaughlin and S. McEwen (Eds.), *Proceedings of the 19th Annual Boston University Conference on Language Development,* vol. 2 (pp. 575–586). Somerville, MA: Cascadilla Press.

Shirai, Y., and Kurono, A. (1998). The acquisition of tense–aspect marking in Japanese as a second language. *Language Learning, 48,* 245–279.

Shoaib, A., and Dörnyei, Z. (2005). Affect in life-long learning: exploring L2 motivation as a dynamic process. In P. Benson and D. Nun (Eds.), *Learners' Stories: Difference and Diversity in Language Learning* (pp. 22–41). Cambridge: Cambridge University Press.

Singleton, D. (1999). *Vocabulary Learning in Another Language.* Cambridge: Cambridge University Press.

Sjoholm, K. (1976). A comparison of the test results in grammar and vocabulary between Finnish and Swedish-speaking applicants for English, 1974. In H. Ringbom and R. Palmberg (Eds.), *Errors Made by Finns and Swedish-Speaking Finns in the Learning of English,* AFRIL, vol. 5 (pp. 54–137). Åbo: Åbo Åkademi, English Department Publications.

Skehan, P. (1989). *Individual Differences in Second-Language Learning.* London: Edward Arnold.

Skehan, P. (1996). A framework for implementation of task-based instruction. *Applied Linguistics, 17,* 38–62.

Slabakova, R. (2003). Semantic evidence for functional categories in interlanguage grammars. *Second Language Research, 19,* 42–75.

Slavoff, G., and Johnson, J. (1995). The effects of age on the rate of learning a second language. *Studies in Second Language Acquisition, 17,* 1–16.

Sleight, W. G. (1911). Memory and formal training. *British Journal of Psychology, 4,* 386–457.

Smith, N. (1973). *The Acquisition of Phonology: A Case Study.* Cambridge: Cambridge University Press.

Snow, C., and Hoefnagle-Hohle, M. (1978). The critical age for second language acquisition: evidence from second language learning. *Child Development, 49,* 1114–1128.

Söderman, T. (1993). Word associations of foreign language learners and native speakers: the phenomenon of a shift in response type and its relevance for lexical development. In H. Ringbom (Ed.), *Near-Native Proficiency in English* (pp. 91–182). Åbo: Åbo Akademi, English Department Publications.

Sokolik, M. (1990). Learning without rules: PDP and a resolution of the adult language learning paradox. *TESOL Quarterly, 24,* 685–696.

Sokolik, M., and Smith, M. (1992). Assignment of gender to French nouns in primary and secondary language: a connectionist model. *Second Language Research, 8,* 39–58.

Sorace, A. (1993a). Incomplete vs. divergent representations of unaccusativity in non-native grammars of Italian. *Second Language Research, 9,* 22–47.

Sorace, A. (1993b). Unaccusativity and auxiliary choice in non-native grammars of Italian and French: asymmetries and predictable indeterminancy. *Journal of French Language Studies, 3*, 71–93.

Sorace, A. (1995). Acquiring linking rules and argument structures in a second language: the unaccusative/unergative distinction. In L. Eubank, L. Selinker, and M. Sharwood Smith (Eds.), *The Current State of Interlanguage: Studies in Honor of William E. Rutherford* (pp. 153–175). Amsterdam: John Benjamins.

Sorrentino, R. M., and Higgins, E. T. (1986). Motivation and cognition: warming up to synergism. In R. M. Sorrentino and E. T. Higgins (Eds.), *Handbook of Motivation and Cognition* (pp. 3–19). New York: Guilford.

Spada, N. (1997). Form-focussed instruction and second language acquisition: a review of classroom and laboratory research. [State of the Art Article] *Language Teaching, 30*(2), 73–87.

Spada, N., and Lightbown, P. (1993). Instruction and the development of questions in the L2 classroom. *Studies in Second Language Acquisition, 15*, 205–221.

Stedje, A. (1977). Tredjerspråksinterferens i fritt tal—en jämförande studie. In R. Palmberg and H. Ringbom (Eds.), *Papers from the Conference on Contrastive Linguistics and Error Analysis*. Åbo: Åbo Åkademi.

Sternberg, R. J. (1985). *Beyond IQ: A Triarchic Theory of Human Intelligence*. New York: Cambridge University Press.

Sternberg, R. J. (1988). *The Triarchic Mind: A New Theory of Human Intelligence*. New York: Viking.

Sternberg, R. J. (1997). *Thinking styles*. New York: Cambridge University Press.

Sternberg, R. J. (2002). The theory of successful intelligence and its implications for language-aptitude testing. In P. Robinson (Ed.), *Individual Differences and Instructed Language Learning* (pp. 13–43). Amsterdam: John Benjamins.

Sternberg, R. J., and Grigorenko, E. (2001). A capsule history of theory and research on styles. In R. J. Sternberg and L.-F. Zhang (Eds.), *Perspectives on Thinking, Learning, and Cognitive styles* (pp. 1–21). Mahwah, NJ: Lawrence Erlbaum Associates.

Stockwell, R., and Bowen, J. (1965). *The Sounds of English and Spanish*. Chicago: University of Chicago Press.

Stockwell, R., Bowen, J., and Martin, J. (1965a). *The Grammatical Structures of English and Italian*. Chicago: University of Chicago Press.

Stockwell, R., Bowen, J., and Martin, J. (1965b). *The Grammatical Structures of English and Spanish*. Chicago: University of Chicago Press.

Strapp, C. M. (1999). Mothers', fathers', and siblings' responses to children's language errors: comparing sources of negative evidence. *Journal of Child Language, 26*, 373–391.

Strapp, C. M., and Federico, A. (2000). Imitations and repetitions: what do children say following recasts? *First Language, 20*, 273–290.

Sunderman, G., and Kroll, J. F., (2006). First language activation during second language lexical processing: an investigation of lexical form, meaning and grammatical class. *Studies in Second Language Acquisition, 28*, 387–422.

Swain, M. (1985). Communicative competence: some roles of comprehensible input and comprehensible output in its development. In S. Gass and C. Madden (Eds.), *Input in Second Language Acquisition* (pp. 235–253). Rowley, MA: Newbury House.

Swain, M. (1995). Three functions of output in second language learning. In G. Cook and B. Seidlhofer (Eds.), *Principle and Practice in Applied Linguistics* (pp. 125–144). Oxford: Oxford University Press.

Swain, M. (2005). The output hypothesis: theory and research. In E. Hinkel (Ed.), *Handbook of Research in Second Language Teaching and Learning* (pp. 471–483). Mahwah, NJ: Lawrence Erlbaum Associates.

Swain, M., and Lapkin, S. (1995). Problems in output and the cognitive processes they generate: a step towards second language learning. *Applied Linguistics, 16,* 371–391.

Swain, M., and Lapkin, S. (1998). Interaction and second language learning: two adolescent French immersion students working together. *Modern Language Journal, 82,* 320–337.

Tahta, S., Wood, M., and Loewenthal, K. (1981). Foreign accents: factors relating to transfer of accent from the first language to the second language. *Language and Speech, 24,* 265–272.

Takashima, H. (1995). A study of focused feedback, or output enhancement, in promoting accuracy in communicative activities. Unpublished doctoral dissertation, Temple University, Japan.

Tannen, D. (1986). *That's Not What I Meant! How Conversational Style Makes or Breaks Relationships.* New York: Ballantine.

Tarone, E. (1977). Conscious communication strategies in interlanguage. In H. D. Brown, C. A. Yorio, and R. C. Crymes (Eds.), *On TESOL '77: Teaching and Learning English as a Second Language: Trends in Research and Practice* (pp. 194–203). Washington, DC: Teachers of English to Speakers of Other Languages.

Tarone, E. (1979). Interlanguage as chameleon. *Language Learning, 29,* 181–191.

Tarone, E. (1980). Some influences on the syllable structure on interlanguage phonology. *International Review of Applied Linguistics, 18,* 139–152.

Tarone, E. (1983). On the variability of interlanguage systems. *Applied Linguistics, 4,* 142–163.

Tarone, E. (1985). Variability in interlanguage use: a study of style-shifting in morphology and syntax. *Language Learning, 35,* 373–404.

Tarone, E. (1988). *Variation in Interlanguage.* London: Edward Arnold.

Tarone, E. (1990). On variation in interlanguage: a response to Gregg. *Applied Linguistics, 11,* 392–399.

Tarone, E. (2000). Still wrestling with "context" in interlanguage theory. In W. Grabe (Ed.), *Annual Review of Applied Linguistics: Applied Linguistics as an Emerging Discipline* (pp. 182–198). New York: Cambridge University Press.

Tarone, E., Frauenfelder, U., and Selinker, L. (1976). Systematicity/variability and stability/instability in interlanguage systems. *Language Learning,* special issue no. 4, 93–134.

Tarone, E., and Liu, G. (1995). Situational context, variation, and second language acquisition theory. In G. Cook and B. Seidlhofer (Eds.), *Principle and Practice in Applied Linguistics: Studies in Honour of H. G. Widdowson* (pp. 107–124). Oxford: Oxford University Press.

Teichroew, F. M. (1982). A study of receptive versus productive vocabulary. *Interlanguage Studies Bulletin, 6,* 3–33.

Tesar, B., and Smolensky, P. (1996). *Learnability in Optimality Theory*. (Technical Report JHU-CogSci–96–3). Baltimore, MD: Johns Hopkins University.

Tesar, B., and Smolensky, P. (1998). Learnability in optimality theory. *Linguistic Inquiry*, 29, 229–268.

Thakerar, J. N., Giles, H., and Cheshire, J. (1982). Psychological and linguistic parameters of speech accommodation theory. In C. Fraser and K. R. Scherer (Eds.), *Advances in the Social Psychology of Language* (pp. 205–255). New York: Cambridge University Press.

Thomas, J. (1988). The role played by metalinguistic awareness in second and third language learning. *Journal of Multilingual and Multicultural Development*, 9, 235–246.

Thomas, M. (1989). The interpretation of English reflexive pronouns by non-native speakers. *Studies in Second Language Acquisition*, 11, 281–303.

Thomas, M. (1991). Universal Grammar and the interpretation of reflexives in a second language. *Language*, 67, 211–239.

Thomas, M. (1993). *Knowledge of reflexives in a second language*. Amsterdam/Philadelphia: John Benjamins.

Thomas, M. (1994). Assessment of L2 proficiency in second language acquisition research. *Language Learning*, 44, 307–336.

Thomas, M. (1995). Acquisition of the Japanese reflexive zibun and movement of anaphors in logical form. *Second Language Research*, 11, 206–234.

Tomasello, M., and Herron, C. (1988). Down the garden path: inducing and correcting overgeneralization errors in the foreign language classroom. *Applied Psycholinguistics*, 9, 237–246.

Tomasello, M., and Herron, C. (1989). Feedback for language transfer errors: the garden path technique. *Studies in Second Language Acquisition*, 11, 385–395.

Tomasello, M., and Herron, C. (1991). Experiments in the real world: a reply to Beck and Eubank. *Studies in Second Language Acquisition*, 13, 513–517.

Tomlin, R. S., and Villa, V. (1994). Attention in cognitive science and second language acquisition. *Studies in Second Language Acquisition*, 16, 183–203.

Trahey, M. (1996). Positive evidence in second language acquisition: some long-term effects. *Second Language Research*, 12, 111–139.

Trahey, M., and White, L. (1993). Positive evidence and preemption in the second language classroom. *Studies in Second Language Acquisition*, 15, 181–204.

Tremblay, P., and Gardner, R. (1995). Expanding the motivation construct in language learning. *Modern Language Journal*, 79, 505–518.

Truscott, J. (1998). Noticing in second language acquisition: a critical review. *Second Language Research*, 14, 103–135.

Truscott, J. (2004). The effectiveness of grammar instruction: analysis of a meta-analysis. *English Teaching and Learning*, 28, 17–29.

Tyler, L. (1989). The role of lexical representations in language comprehension. In W. Marslen-Wilson (Ed.), *Lexical Representation and Process* (pp. 439–462). Cambridge, MA: MIT Press.

Ushioda, E. (2003). Engaging with the curriculum through the European Language Portfolio. *Neusprachliche Mitteilungen*, 3, 147–153.

Vainikka, M., and Young-Scholten, M. (1994). Direct access to X-theory: evidence from Korean and Turkish adults learning German. In T. Hoekstra and B. Schwartz (Eds.), *Language Acquisition Studies in Generative Grammar* (pp. 265–316). Amsterdam: John Benjamins.

Vainikka, M., and Young-Scholten, M. (1996a). Gradual development of L2 phrase structure. *Second Language Research, 12*, 7–39.

Vainikka, M., and Young-Scholten, M. (1996b). The early stages of adult L2 syntax: additional evidence from Romance speakers. *Second Language Research, 12*, 140–176.

Valdés, G. (1995). The teaching of minority languages as "foreign" languages: pedagogical and theoretical challenges. *Modern Language Journal, 79*, 299–328.

Valdés, G. (2001a). *Learning and Not Learning English: Latino Students in American Schools.* New York: Teachers College Press.

Valdés, G. (2001b). Heritage language students: Profiles and possibilities. In J. Peyton, D. Ranard, and S. McGinnis (Eds.), *Heritage Languages in America: Preserving a National Resource.* Washington, DC: Center for Applied Linguistics.

Valdman, A. (1977). On the relevance of the pidginization–creolization model for second language learning. *Studies in Second Language Acquisition, 1*, 55–75.

Valdman, A., and Phillips, J. (1975). Pidginization, creolization and the elaboration of learner systems. *Studies in Second Language Acquisition, 1*, 21–40.

van den Noort, M., Bosch, P., and Hugdahl, K. (2006). Foreign language proficiency and working memory capacity. *European Psychologist, 11*, 289–296.

VanPatten, B. (1995). Input processing and second language acquisition: on the relationship between form and meaning. In P. Hashemipour, R. Maldonado, and M. van Naerssen (Eds.), *Festschrift in Honor of Tracy D. Terrell* (pp. 170–183). New York: McGraw-Hill.

VanPatten, B. (2004). Input processing in SLA. In B. VanPatten (Ed.), *Processing Instruction: Theory, Research, and Commentary* (pp. 5–31). Mahwah, NJ: Lawrence Erlbaum Associates.

VanPatten, B. (2007a) Input processing in adult second language acquisition. In B. VanPatten and J. Williams (Eds.), *Theories in Second Language Acquisition: An Introduction* (pp. 115–135). Mahwah, NJ: Lawrence Erlbaum Associates.

VanPatten, B. (2007b). Processing instruction. In C. Sanz (Ed.), *Mind and Context in Adult Second Language Acquisition* (pp. 267–281). Washington DC: Georgetown University Press.

VanPatten, B. (2008). Processing matters in input enhancement. In T. Piske and M. Young-Scholten (Eds.), *Input Matters.* Clevedon: Multilingual Matters.

VanPatten, B., and Cadierno, T. (1993). Explicit instruction and input processing. *Studies in Second Language Acquisition, 15*, 225–243.

VanPatten, B., and Keating, G. (2007). *Getting Tense: Lexical Preference, L1 Transfer and Native and Non-Native Processing of Temporal Reference.* Paper presented at AAAL, Costa Mesa, CA.

VanPatten, B. and Oikkenon, S. (1996). The causative variables in processing instruction: explicit information versus structured input activities. *Studies in Second Language Acquisition, 18*, 495–510.

VanPatten, B., and Sanz, C. (1995). From input to output: processing instruction and communicative tasks. In F. Eckman, D. Highland, P. Lee, J. Mileham, and R. Weber (Eds.), *Second Language Acquisition Theory and Pedagogy* (pp. 169–186). Hillsdale, NJ: Lawrence Erlbaum Associates.

VanPatten, B., and Wong, W. (2004). Processing instruction and the French causative: another replication. In B. VanPatten (Ed.), *Processing Instruction: Theory, Research, and Commentary* (pp. 97–118). Mahwah, NJ: Lawrence Erlbaum Associates.

Van Valin, R. (1991). Functionalist linguistic theory and language acquisition. *First Language, 11*, 7–40.

Varonis, E., and Gass, S. (1982). The comprehensibility of non-native speech. *Studies in Second Language Acquisition, 4*, 114–136.

Varonis, E., and Gass, S. (1985a). Miscommunication in native/non-native conversation. *Language in Society, 14*, 327–343.

Varonis, E., and Gass, S. (1985b). Non-native/non-native conversations: a model for negotiation of meaning. *Applied Linguistics, 6*, 71–90.

Vihman, M. (1996). *Phonological Development: The Origins of Language in the Child*. Oxford: Basil Blackwell.

Vildomec, V. (1963). *Multilingualism*. Leyden, The Netherlands: A. W. Sythoff.

Vygotsky, L. S. (1978). *Mind in Society: The Development of Higher Psychological Processes*. Cambridge, MA: Harvard University Press.

Wagner-Gough, K., and Hatch, E. (1975). The importance of input in second language acquisition studies. *Language Learning, 25*, 297–308.

Wakabayashi, S. (1996). The nature of interlanguage: SLA of reflexives. *Second Language Research, 12*, 266–303.

Wei, L. (2000). *The Bilingual Reader*. London: Routledge. Revised 2006 as *The Bilingualism Reader*.

Weinreich, U. (1953). *Languages in Contact*. New York: Linguistic Circle of New York.

Weinstein, C. E., Husman, J., and Dierking, D. R. (2000). Self-regulation interventions with a focus on learning strategies. In M. Boekaerts, P. R. Pintrich, and M. Zeldner (Eds.), *Handbook of Self-Regulation* (pp. 727–747). San Diego: Academic Press.

Weir, R. (1962). *Language in the Crib*. The Hague: Mouton.

Weist, R., Wysocka, H., Witkowska-Stadnik, K., Buczowska, E., and Konieczna, E. (1984). The defective tense hypothesis: on the emergence of tense and aspect in child Polish. *Journal of Child Language, 11*, 347–374.

Wesche, M. (1981). Language aptitude measures in streaming, matching students with methods, and diagnosis of learning problems. In K. C. Diller (Ed.), *Individual Differences and Universals in Language learning Aptitude*. Rowley, MA: Newbury House.

Wesche, M., and Paribakht, S. (Eds.). (1999a). Incidental L2 vocabulary acquisition: theory, current research, and instructional implications. Special issue of *Studies in Second Language Acquisition, 21*.

Wesche, M., and Paribakht, S. (1999b). Introduction. *Studies in Second Language Acquisition, 21*, 175–180.

Wexler, K., and Cullicover, P. (1980). *Formal Principles of Language Acquisition*. Cambridge, MA: MIT Press.

White, L. (1985). The "pro-drop" parameter in adult second language acquisition. *Language Learning, 35*, 47–62.

573

White, L. (1989). *Universal Grammar and Second Language Acquisition*. Amsterdam: John Benjamins.

White, L. (1991). Adverb placement in second language acquisition: some effects of positive and negative evidence in the classroom. *Second Language Research*, 7, 133–161.

White, L. (1992). Universal Grammar: is it just a new name for old problems? In S. Gass and L. Selinker (Eds.), *Language Transfer in Language Learning* (pp. 219–234). Amsterdam: John Benjamins.

White, L. (2003). *Second Language Acquisition and Universal Grammar*. Cambridge: Cambridge University Press.

White, L., Bruhn-Garavito, J., Kawasaki, T., Pater, J., and Prevost, P. (1997). The researcher gave the subject a test about himself: problems of ambiguity and preference in the investigation of reflexive binding. *Language Learning*, 47, 145–172.

White, L., and Genesee, F. (1996). How native is near-native? The issue of ultimate attainment in adult second language acquisition. *Second Language Research*, 12, 233–265.

Whitman, R., and Jackson, K. (1972). The unpredictability of contrastive analysis. *Language Learning*, 22, 29–41.

Whong-Barr, M. (2005). Transfer of argument structure and morphology. In L. Dekydtspotter, R. Sprouse, and A. Liljestrand (Eds.), *Proceedings of the Seventh Generative Approaches to Second Language Conference (GASLA 2004)* (pp. 269–282). Somerville, MA: Cascadilla Press.

Williams, J. (1990). Discourse marking and elaboration and the comprehensibility of second language speakers. Paper presented at the Second Language Research Forum, Eugene, OR, March.

Williams, J. (1999). Memory, attention, and inductive learning. *Studies in Second Language Acquisition*, 21, 1–48.

Williams, J. (2004). Implicit learning of form–meaning connections. In J. Williams, B. VanPatten, S. Rott, and M. Overstreet (Eds.), *Form–Meaning Connections in Second Language Acquisition* (pp. 203–218). Mahwah, NJ: Lawrence Erlbaum Associates.

Williams, J., and Evans, J. (1998). What kind of focus and on which forms? In C. Doughty and J. Williams (Eds.), *Focus on Form in Classroom Second Language Acquisition* (pp. 139–155). Cambridge: Cambridge University Press.

Williams, J., and Lovatt, P. (2003). Phonological memory and rule learning. *Language Learning*, 53, 67–121.

Williams, M., Burden, R., and Lanvers, U. (2002). "French is the language of love and stuff": student perceptions of issues related to motivation in learning a foreign language. *British Educational Research Journal*, 28, 503–528.

Williams, S., and Hammarberg, B. (1998). Language switches in L3 production: implications for a polyglot speaking model. *Applied Linguistics*, 19, 295–333.

Wode, H. (1976). Developmental principles in naturalistic L1 acquisition. *Arbeitspapiere zum Spracherwerb*, 16. Kiel: Department of English, Kiel University.

Wode, H. (1977). On the systematicity of L1 transfer in L2 acquisition. *Proceedings from 1977 Second Language Research Forum (SLRF)* (pp. 160–169). Los Angeles: University of California, Department of Applied Linguistics.

REFERENCES

Woken, M., and Swales, J. (1989). Expertise and authority in native–non-native conversations: the need for a variable account. In S. Gass, C. Madden, D. Preston, and L. Selinker (Eds.), *Variation in Second Language Acquisition: Discourse and Pragmatics* (pp. 211–227). Clevedon, UK: Multilingual Matters.

Wolfe-Quintero, K. (1996). Nativism does not equal Universal Grammar. *Second Language Research, 12,* 335–373.

Wong, W. (2004). Processing instruction in French: the roles of explicit information and structured input. In B. VanPatten (Ed.), *Processing Instruction: Theory, Research, and Commentary* (pp. 187–205). Mahwah, NJ: Lawrence Erlbaum Associates.

Wong-Fillmore, L. (1976). The second time around: cognitive and social strategies in second language acquisition. Unpublished doctoral dissertation, Stanford University, Palo Alto, California.

Yabuki-Soh, N. (2007). Teaching relative clauses in Japanese: exploring the explicitness of instruction and the projection effect. *Studies in Second Language Acquisition, 29,* 219–252.

Yeni-Komshian, G. H., Flege, J. E., and Liu, S. (2000). Pronunciation proficiency in the first and second languages of Korean–English bilinguals. *Bilingualism, Language and Cognition, 3,* 131–149.

Yeni-Komshian, G. H., Robbins, M., and Flege, J. E. (2001). Effects of word class differences on L2 pronunciation accuracy. *Applied Psycholinguistics, 22,* 283–299.

Young, R. (1986). The acquisition of a verbal repertoire in a second language. *Penn Working Papers in Educational Linguistics, 2,* 85–119.

Young, R. (1991). *Variation in Interlanguage Morphology.* New York: Peter Lang.

Young, R. (1999). Sociolinguistic approaches to SLA. In W. Grabe (Ed.), *Annual Review of Applied Linguistics, 19, Survey of Applied Linguistics* (pp. 105–132). New York: Cambridge University Press.

Young-Scholten, M. (1995). The negative effects of "positive" evidence in phonology. In L. Eubank, L. Selinker, and M. Sharwood Smith (Eds.), *The Current State of Interlanguage* (pp. 107–121). Amsterdam: John Benjamins.

Young-Scholten, M. (1997). Second language syllable simplification: Deviant development or deviant input? In J. Leather and A. James (Eds.), *New Sounds 97.* Klagenfurt, Austria: University of Klagenfurt.

Young-Scholten, M., Akita, M., and Cross, N. (1999). Focus on form in phonology: orthographic exposure as a promoter of epenthesis. In P. Robinson and J. O. Jungheim (Eds.), *Pragmatics and Pedagogy: Proceedings of the Third PacSLRF,* vol. 2. Tokyo: Aoyama Gakuin University.

Young-Scholten, M., and Archibald, J. (2000). Second language syllable structure. In J. Archibald (Ed.), *Second Language Acquisition and Linguistic Theory* (pp. 64–101). Oxford: Basil Blackwell.

Zobl, H. (1980). The formal and developmental selectivity of L1 influence on L2 acquisition. *Language Learning, 30,* 43–57.

Zobl, H. (1982). A direction for contrastive analysis: the comparative study of developmental sequences. *TESOL Quarterly, 16,* 169–183.

Zobl, H. (1992). Prior linguistic knowledge and the conservatism of the learning procedure: grammaticality judgments of unilingual and multilingual learners.

In S. Gass and L. Selinker (Eds.), *Language Transfer in Language Learning* (pp. 176–196). Amsterdam: John Benjamins.

Zuengler, J. (1989). Performance variation in NS–NNS interactions: ethnolinguistic difference, or discourse domain? In S. Gass, C. Madden, D. Preston, and L. Selinker (Eds.), *Variation in Second Language Acquisition: Discourse and Pragmatics* (pp. 228–244). Clevedon, UK: Multilingual Matters.

AUTHOR INDEX

References to notes, tables and figures are indexed as, e.g. 513n, 27t, 116f.

SUBJECT INDEX

References to notes, tables and figures are indexed as, e.g. 513n, 27t, 116f. Headings for specific interlanguages are constructed with languages in the order of acquisition, ie the interlanguage of an Arabic-speaking learner of English would be entered as Arabic-English interlanguages.